Oahu

Hawaii

H A W A I I

Mexico City

Clipperton

Kiritimati

Line Islands

I

C O O K   I S L A N D S

RICAN
AMOA

Soc

Rarotonga

Austral Is

uth Pacific Ocean

Easter

DATE DUE

THE PACIFIC ISLANDS

Prepared for the Center for Pacific Islands Studies
University of Hawaii at Manoa
by Manoa Mapworks, 1987.
Revised 1991.

W—E

155°W

140°W

125°W

110°W

Tides of History

TIDES OF HISTORY

THE PACIFIC ISLANDS IN THE TWENTIETH CENTURY

K. R. Howe, Robert C. Kiste, Brij V. Lal, editors

UNIVERSITY OF HAWAII PRESS
HONOLULU

Published in North America by
University of Hawaii Press
2840 Kolowalu Street
Honolulu, Hawaii 96822

Published in Australia by
Allen & Unwin Pty Ltd
P.O. Box 8500
9 Atchison Street
St Leonards, NSW 2065

Printed in Singapore

Library of Congress Cataloging-in-Publication Data

Tides of history : the Pacific Islands in the twentieth century / K. R.
  Howe, Robert C. Kiste, Brij V. Lal, editors.
      p.   cm.
  Includes bibliographical references and index.
  ISBN 0–8248–1597–1
  1. Ocean—History.   I. Howe, K. R.   II. Kiste, Robert C., 1936– .
III. Lal, Brij V.
DU28.3.T53   1994
995—dc20   93–34015
                                                      CIP

The general editors of this volume gratefully acknowledge the valuable contribution of Linley Chapman in editing these essays. Without her labour and efforts, the book could not have been published.

Contents

Maps

Preface

This book contributes to and extends developments in the academic study of Pacific Island history. As a 'modern' discipline, Pacific Island history has its origins in the decolonising *mentalité* following World War Two, when historians moved from studying colonisers in their imperial context to examining colonised peoples in their cultural context. In particular, indigenous communities were now seen to have an identity and past worthy of serious academic study. Much modern Pacific Island history has taken the form of island-centred culture-contact studies. In general terms, these studies investigated cultural interaction between indigenous societies and the increasing Western presence and influence, and the social, economic, political, and intellectual consequences for island communities. The significance and dominance of this agenda was largely unquestioned and fruitfully occupied a generation of scholarship, particularly from the 1960s well into the 1980s.

The limitations of this scholarship have always been acknowledged by its practitioners but it is perhaps only now, in retrospect, that some of its underlying characteristics can be seen in a broader perspective. Scholars involved in that generation of culture-contact studies were enthused by its apparent relevance in a post-colonial era. Yet ironically many, if not most of their studies were not really informed by the Pacific Island present. Or rather, the nature of that present, as it was perceived, did not offer any obvious contemporary political agenda or conscious ideology that historians could impose on their studies of the Pacific past. By contrast, historians of countries in Africa, South and South-East Asia, or Latin America, who were at the same time also decolonising their subjects, were greatly influenced by contemporary events in those countries, particularly bloody struggles for national liberation. The international scholarly discourse on such events, often neo-Marxist and anticolonial, gave a particular ideological edge and a set of related analytical structures to the historical investigation of such regions.

The contemporary Pacific Islands, seemingly characterised by an essentially untroubled, co-operative transition from colonial rule to constitutional independence, did little to influence historians' views of the Pacific past. The apparent uniqueness of the Pacific, widely encapsulated in cultural catch-phrases like 'the Pacific way', was for most Pacific historians paralleled in what many imagined was the quiet empiricism of their scholarship.

The basic attraction of such study remained consciously or subconsciously antiquarian and romantic. Budding historians were drawn to the discipline far more by ingrained images of sunny tropical isles than by any historical dialectics. Much as this scholarship tried to deconstruct romantic myths about Oceanic history, the 'new' interpretations were still fundamentally tinted by the concept of Paradise, regardless of whether found or lost.

One of the more obvious consequences of this approach was that Pacific Island historical scholarship focused overwhelmingly on pre-colonial events and issues. The year 1900 persistently marked the terminal date for its articles and monographs. However, this emphasis on pre-colonial times by Pacific historians had an additional cause. The discipline's post-war rejection of the imperial historical approach was all too zealous in that the study of colonial government itself, even if divorced from older imperial values, simply became unfashionable. With few exceptions Pacific historians left the twentieth century to geographers, anthropologists, and others.

If there was a symbolic moment when the community of Pacific historians was jolted by the Pacific present, it came with the Fiji coup of May 1987. But it was not brought about by an isolated event. Seen in the wider context of certain emerging tensions in the Pacific Islands, the heady optimism that earlier accompanied the peaceful transition of many islands from colonial rule to self-government and independence now seemed somewhat misplaced. Among the more contentious issues were conflicts between Western constitutional traditions and indigenous values; tensions between regions and the superimposed nation states; ever more apparent contradictions between constitutional independence and economic dependence; growing demands for self-government or independence where that still had not been achieved; and the often-related strategic and nuclear implications. By the later 1980s many Pacific islands seemed considerably less placid places than they had been in previous decades.

Recent Pacific historical study has reflected these concerns insofar as historians are more conscious of their present. The historical agenda of earlier decades is now more informed by current events. One symbolic institutional reflection of this concern is the launching of a new interdisciplinary journal in 1989—*The Contemporary Pacific: A Journal of Island Affairs*. Whereas this volume chronologically follows on from an earlier general history of the Pacific Islands to 1900—*Where the Waves Fall*—its concerns are in some respects rather different. All history is a product of its time. This book is a product of a particular moment, perhaps milestone, in the evolution of Pacific historical scholarship. It is a moment when a concern for the Pacific present has refocused that scholarship on this century, now itself coming to an end. In the process, some of the assumptions and characteristics of the previous island-centred culture-contact studies are being modified. For example, Pacific history is seen less in narrow terms of European–Islander culture contact and the moral issues implicit in that contact, but with a greater appreciation of more complex interactions, especially between and among indigenous peoples themselves. The 'history' is less exclusively the preserve of historians and reflects a more multi- and inter-disciplinary approach.

Most significantly the perception of 'islands' is altering. The long-standing island-centred perspectives are becoming modified as the islands are viewed increasingly as part of both Pacific rim and world-wide systems of investment, trade, and defence. In an ironic way, perhaps, this shift in perspective represents something of a return to some of the concerns of the older, imperial Pacific history so thoroughly rejected by the post-war, island-centred generation of scholars. Pacific historiography is ultimately determined by changing notions of centres and peripheries. For the imperial historians there was no question where the peripheries were; the post-war, island-centred historians reversed that perception. Now historians are moving back towards the concept of islands as someone else's periphery. Pacific historians still physically and perceptually locate themselves in or on the islands, but they are increasingly less able to accept the islands as unique centres in themselves. This book attempts to capture something of this historiographic transition.

When the editors planned this volume, it soon became apparent that there were innumerable ways to structure an account of the Pacific Islands in the twentieth century. This book offers merely one possibility, one that best suited our particular requirements. The main organisational problem was to balance geographic coverage, chronology, and thematic investigation. The terms *Polynesia*, *Melanesia*, and *Micronesia* are used in a loose geographic rather than cultural sense, and where it has suited our purposes the boundaries of these regions are somewhat flexible. Moreover, we have permitted a minor degree of content overlap between some chapters in order to enhance their internal coherence within the overall context of the book.

In part 1 the indigenous and imperial framework at the opening of this century is established and then the interplay of colonial rule and indigenous life from the high noon of colonial empire through to the outbreak of World War Two is examined. Within this section chapters are variously organised on a geographic and 'political' basis. The reason for what might initially appear a rather complex division has nothing to do with any unconscious imposition of any 'European' construct, but rather a quite conscious one: we have attempted to highlight fundamental political realities for island communities—realities determined by certain geographic and environmental factors and by the nature of colonial overlordship in any particular locality. In chapters 3 and 4 respectively, the geographic regions of Melanesia and Polynesia are considered, and in chapters 5 and 6 those localities in Melanesia, Micronesia, and Polynesia variously controlled by France, Japan, and the United States are covered. By not having a consistency of focus on either a geographic region or particular colonial rulers in part 1, we foreshadow the respective experiences of island communities in the post-war world. In particular, the island countries covered in chapters 3 and 4 generally achieved constitutional independence, whereas those considered in chapters 5 and 6 have not moved, or are only now moving in that direction.

In part 2 the impact of World War Two, which marks a major turning point for colonial systems and indigenous aspirations, is examined. Following are investigations of the processes and effects of decolonisation where it occurred, and the consequences where it did not. As with part 1, the specific chapter divisions are intended to reflect the predominant determinants, which now have less to do with geography and environment and relate to the actions of the respective post-war colonial rulers. The evolving chapter organisation between parts 1 and 2 reflects the transition of communities from the pre- and early colonial period, when they were products of local and regional influences and characteristics, to the late twentieth century, when sociopolitical and economic status were determining factors.

Part 3 contains wide ranging thematic chapters that examine crucial aspects of modern life in the islands. The perspective is both from 'above', investigating major political, economic, and strategic infrastructures, and from 'below', considering local and regional sociocultural adaptations and implications. Part 3 concludes with a retrospective and prospective overview of the islands and their historiography.

Though writing to a broad structural brief, authors were free to develop their own interpretations. No attempt has been made to try to impose any standardised methodology or values or even styles on any of the chapters. In this regard, this book has an interdisciplinary character encompassing history from a variety of perspectives—economics, political science, anthropology, sociology, literature. The diversity of opinion and approaches within the broad framework of this book both reflects the state of the art of modern Pacific scholarship and enhances an understanding of the complexity of the past.

Every attempt has been made to include the broadest possible range of contributors. In the final analysis, however, editors get what they inspect, not always what they expect. On behalf of Bob Kiste and Brij Lal, I thank the contributing authors for their co-operation and productivity.

K. R. Howe

Contributors

Judith A. Bennett teaches Pacific history at the University of Otago, Dunedin, New Zealand. She is the author of *Wealth of the Solomons: A History of a Pacific Archipelago, 1800–1978* (1987), the third title in the Pacific Islands Monograph Series. She is currently working on a forest history of Solomon Islands and conservation policies of colonial governments in the western Pacific.

Paul de Deckker is a Professor of Social Anthropology at the *Université Française du Pacifique* in Noumea, New Caledonia, and Professor at the Centre for International and Strategic Studies at the University of Brussels. He has edited and published several books on the Pacific Islands, and is currently working on a book on the Pacific Islands from the cultural viewpoint.

Stewart Firth teaches at Macquarie University in Sydney, Australia. He is the author of *New Guinea under the Germans* (1982) and *Nuclear Playground* (1987) and has recently co-edited *Nauru, 1888–1900* (1992), a collection of documents dealing with early German administration on that island. His research in recent years has focused on strategic issues in the Pacific Islands, Australian policy in particular.

David Hanlon teaches history at the University of Hawai'i at Mānoa. He is the author of *Upon a Stone Altar: A History of the Island of Pohnpei to 1890* (1988), and the editor of *The Contemporary Pacific: A Journal of Island Affairs*.

Peter Hempenstall is a historian of the Pacific and Australia based at the University of Newcastle, Australia. His major published work on the Pacific has been on the German colonial empire, colonial resistance movements, and cargo cults. He is working on a book about the relationship between the Samoan people and Wilhelm Solf, governor of German Samoa before World War One.

STEPHEN HENNINGHAM is a Senior Research Fellow in the Division of Pacific and Asian History, Australian National University. His publications include *France and the South Pacific: A Contemporary History* (1992), and the collection, co-edited with R. J. May, *Resources, Development, and Politics in the Pacific Islands* (1992).

VILSONI HERENIKO is Assistant Professor in Pacific Literature at the Center for Pacific Islands Studies, University of Hawai'i at Mānoa, Honolulu. Prior to joining the University of Hawai'i, he wrote and directed numerous plays for the University of the South Pacific and the wider community in Suva, Fiji. His latest book, *Woven Gods: Ritual Clowning in Rotuma*, is scheduled for publication by University of Hawai'i Press in 1994.

RICHARD HERR teaches international relations at the University of Tasmania in Hobart, where he is currently Head of the Department of Political Science. He edited *The Forum Fisheries Agency: Achievements, Challenges and Prospects* (1990). His current research into the influence of non-state actors in the Pacific Islands continues earlier work on microstate diplomacy and regional organisations.

K. R. HOWE has a Personal Chair in History at Massey University, New Zealand. He has written extensively on Pacific history and historiography. Among his main publications are *Where the Waves Fall: A New South Sea Islands History from First Settlement to Colonial Rule* (1984) and *Singer in a Songless Land: A Life of Edward Tregear* (1991).

ROBERT C. KISTE is an anthropologist and Director of the Center for Pacific Islands Studies at the University of Hawai'i. He is the author of *The Bikinians: A Study in Forced Migration* (1974) and of numerous journal articles and book chapters. He is the general editor of the Pacific Islands Monograph Series and South Sea Books, both published by University of Hawai'i Press; chair of the editorial board of *The Contemporary Pacific: A Journal of Island Affairs*; and a member of the editorial board, University of Hawai'i Press. Dr Kiste has held a number of consultancy and advisory positions with, for example, the Asia Foundation; the Fulbright Board for Australia, New Zealand, and Pacific Islands; the US Agency for International Development; the US Information Agency; and the US Department of State.

BRUCE KNAPMAN is a Senior Lecturer in Economics and Associate of the Centre for Applied Economic Research and Analysis at James Cook

University of North Queensland. He is the author of *Fiji's Economic History, 1874–1939* (1987) and co-author of *Tourism and Gold in Kakadu* (1991). His current research interest is environmental economics.

BRIJ V. LAL is currently a Senior Fellow in the Institute of Advanced Studies and Lecturer in Pacific history in the Faculties at the Australian National University, which he joined after a decade of teaching at the University of Hawai'i. Among his many publications are *Girmitiyas: The Origins of the Fiji Indians* (1983), *Power and Prejudice: The Making of the Fiji Crisis* (1988) and *Broken Waves: A History of the Fiji Islands in the Twentieth Century* (1992).

HUGH LARACY is Associate Professor of History at the University of Auckland, New Zealand. His interest in World War Two has grown out of his extensive research on the history of the Solomon Islands, for which he was awarded the Solomon Islands Medal in 1992. Among his publications are *Marists and Melanesians: A History of Catholic Missions in the Solomon Islands* (1976); *Tuvalu: A History* (1983); *Pacific Protest: Maasina Rule, Solomon Islands, 1944–52* (1987); and *Ples Blong Iumi: Solomon Islands, the Past Four Thousand Years* (1989).

PETER LARMOUR is a senior lecturer in the Department of Political Science at the University of Tasmania. He has worked at the University of Papua New Guinea and the University of the South Pacific, where he edited a number of books on land tenure and politics in the region. He is currently working on a comparative study of states and societies in the Pacific Islands.

BARRIE MACDONALD is Professor of History at Massey University, Palmerston North, New Zealand. His research interests cover colonialism, decolonisation and development issues in the Pacific Islands, the politics of small states, and the geopolitics of the wider Pacific region. He is the author of *Cinderellas of the Empire: Towards a History of Kiribati and Tuvalu* (1982) and, with Maslyn Williams, *The Phosphateers: A History of the British Phosphate Commissioners and the Christmas Island Phosphate Commission* (1985).

PENELOPE SCHOEFFEL is an anthropologist specialising in the study of social change and development and a senior researcher with the New Zealand Institute of Social Research and Development. She is co-editor and a co-author of *Lagaga: A Short History of Western Samoa* (1987) with Mālama Meleiseā, and has published papers on the history of gender relations in Samoa, as well as many papers on social aspects of development. She is currently working on a book about sociological variables influencing the outcome of development aid projects in the Pacific Islands.

ROGER C. THOMPSON is a senior lecturer in history of the University of New South Wales at the Australian Defence Force Academy, Canberra. His main research interest is Australia and the Pacific Islands. He is the author of *Australian Imperialism in the Pacific: The Expansionist Era, 1820–1920* (1980).

TERENCE WESLEY-SMITH is a political scientist and an associate professor in the Center for Pacific Islands Studies of the University of Hawai'i. He edits the political review section of *The Contemporary Pacific: A Journal of Island Affairs* and was guest editor of the special issue *A Legacy of Development: Three Years of Crisis in Bougainville* (1992).

Part 1

Colonisation

Pre-colonial times

Robert C. Kiste

The Pacific as it is generally thought of today is an invention of the West.[1]
When Europeans first came upon the vast ocean, they had to create a conceptual framework in order to record, ponder, and analyse their discoveries.
The first attempt to define and label it went wrong. As far as is known, the
Spanish explorer Vasco Nuñez de Balboa was the first European to discover
the Pacific Ocean, and he named it the great South Sea. Balboa's vantage
point was not a ship but the isthmus of Panama. As A. J. Furnas noted in
Anatomy of Paradise, the isthmus 'so twists that Balboa first saw the Pacific
south of him, whereas two-fifths of it actually lay to the north'.[2] Nonetheless,
from that time in 1513 and for the next two hundred years or so, the *South
Sea* meant the Pacific Ocean for most of the Western world. The term *South
Seas* with all of its romantic connotations would come later.

The Portuguese navigator Ferdinand Magellan provided the name that
eventually stuck, but it is something of a misnomer. Magellan was the first
European to cross the Pacific and to sight an inhabited island there. His
crossing was from east to west, the year was 1521, and the island was Guam,
the southernmost of what would become known as the Mariana Islands
in the western Pacific. Magellan enjoyed favourable sailing conditions, his
voyage was relatively uneventful, and he was misled. He was spared the
typhoons (cyclones), tsunamis (tidal waves), earthquakes, volcanic eruptions, and other natural calamities that frequently occur in the region. Further,
he could not have known about the intra- and inter-island warfare that was
common among the indigenous peoples. Magellan thought the area was
peaceful and named it the Pacific Ocean.[3]

Magellan and those who followed were impressed by the size of the
Pacific. It spans thirteen time zones and the international date line. Magellan's
crossing took three and a half months. In contrast, travel by jet aircraft
tends to obscure distances, but even today, flights from San Francisco to
Honolulu and on to Sydney require a combined flying time of more than
fourteen hours.

More tangibly, the Pacific is the largest and deepest of all oceans. Covering about one-third of the surface of the globe, it is the world's largest geographical feature with an area into which all of the land masses of the earth would fit. At the equator, the Pacific has a width of more than sixteen thousand kilometres, and the distance from the Bering Strait to Antarctica is over fourteen thousand kilometres. The average depth of the ocean is around four thousand metres, but west of Guam depths reach more than ten thousand metres.

Within the Pacific, there are about twenty-five thousand islands, more than those of the rest of the world's oceans combined. The discrepancy between the areas of land and sea is great, and one of the ocean's most striking features is its emptiness of land. Diversity also marks the region and is reflected in the large differences in the sizes of the islands (see endpaper map). New Guinea is the world's second largest island, with more than twice the area of Japan (Greenland is the largest; Borneo is third in size). New Guinea, with a land area of 872 350 square kilometres, is more than two thousand kilometres long and has a span of 800 kilometres at its widest. At the other end of the continuum, the tiny single island nation of Niue is approximately 17 by 15 kilometres, with an area of 258 square kilometres.

Culture areas

In their first attempts at mapping the islands, Europeans often tried to determine indigenous place names. Unfamiliar with the local languages, they frequently erred, and even when they did get them right, their renditions of vernacular place names were sometimes difficult to recognize by those who followed. Not infrequently, they named islands after their fellow explorers or patrons at home—the Marshalls, the Gilberts, the Sandwich Islands—or gave them European place names—New Caledonia, New Ireland, New Britain. The very mapping of the Pacific imposed a European template on the island world.

In the same context, the major divisions within the Pacific were also the creations of the outsiders as they sought to make sense of the Pacific. The three culture areas of Polynesia, Micronesia, and Melanesia have provided convenient points of reference for Europeans, but once they were labelled and incorporated into the larger construct of a Pacific region, they took on a reality of their own (see map page 5). It is easily forgotten that originally and in the final analysis, the culture areas are no more than abstractions with boundaries that are arbitrary at best. Writing in 1945, the anthropologist Felix M. Keesing noted: 'The names given here are obviously scientific labels. They have as yet little if any meaning to the peoples concerned. Most of the islanders, still living within very local horizons, speak of themselves by their district, tribal, or village names.'[4]

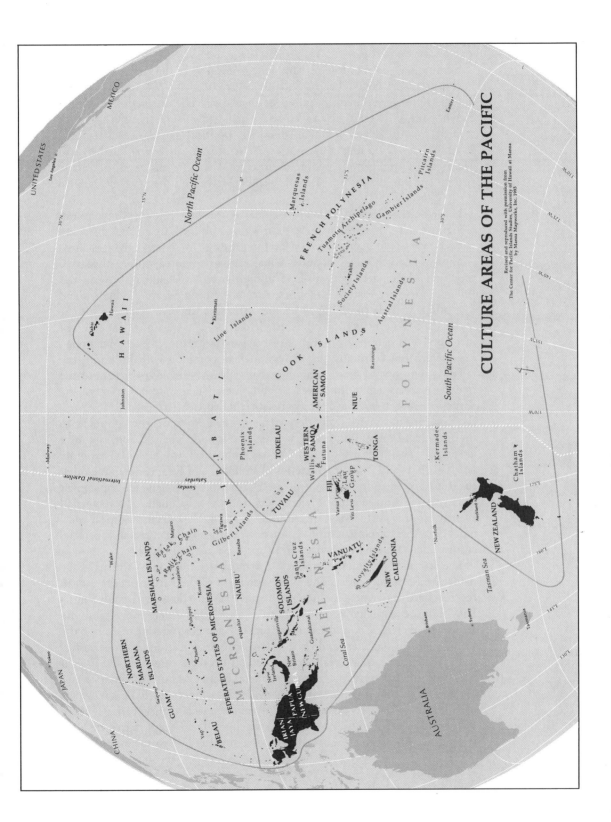

CULTURE AREAS OF THE PACIFIC

Revised and reproduced with permission from
The Center for Pacific Islands Studies, University of Hawai'i at Mānoa
by Manoa Mapworks, Inc. 1993

Keesing was correct for his time but, ironically, in the last four decades Pacific Islanders have taken notions that were once the purview of anthropologists and given them meanings of their own. The distinctions between Polynesians, Micronesians, and Melanesians now have significance with regard to cultural and national identities, political agendas, and regional affairs. They are no longer categories of use only to outsiders. Further, and again for the indigenous people themselves, the very notion of a 'Pacific region' and the identity of 'Pacific Islander' have only become meaningful since World War Two.

Nonetheless, Polynesia (many islands) is the best known to the West. Geographically, it is the largest of the three culture areas, and distances between its island groups are by far the greatest. Micronesia (tiny islands) is appropriately labelled because a majority of the area's more than two thousand islands are coral atolls. The high volcanic islands of Kosrae and Pohnpei form the eastern Carolines, and in the far west are the high island formations of Belau and Yap. Melanesia (black islands) was named for the dark skin of its inhabitants. Fiji is usually included as part of Melanesia, but in reality it is a transition area. Most Fijians are primarily of Melanesian racial stock but culturally they have much in common with Polynesians.

Fiji is only one of many examples that reflect the arbitrary nature of the boundaries between culture areas. The Gilbert Islands are now part of the nation of Kiribati and have always been classified as Micronesian. However, their culture has many traits derived from their Polynesian neighbours to the south, and many Polynesian words have found their way into the local language, which is clearly Micronesian in grammatical structure. The elaborate chieftainships and stratified societies of Pohnpei and Kosrae have traits that suggest Polynesian influences. In western Micronesia, Belau and Yap appear to have been influenced by Melanesians, and the inhabitants of a few small islands off the north coast of extreme western New Guinea appear very much like the Carolinian atoll dwellers in both physical type and material culture; they have even been referred to as para-Micronesians.[5]

The so-called Polynesian outliers are another reflection of the arbitrary nature of the culture areas. The main settlement of the Pacific occurred with the eastward movement of peoples from Asia (particularly island South-East Asia), eventually as far as Easter Island. However, the region has always been dynamic, and islanders did not remain fixed in place for the convenience of outsiders and their schemes of classification. After centuries of movement east, some restless Polynesians reversed direction and moved back towards the west to occupy peripheral islands in both Micronesia and Melanesia. The atoll communities of Kapingamarangi and Nukuoro south of Pohnpei are the two examples of Polynesian outliers in Micronesia. More than a dozen are found in Melanesia stretching from Nuguria east of New Ireland via Anuta and Tikopia to Bellona and Rennell to the south.

Geographical setting

The geographer William Thomas has distinguished four major types of islands, two of which are high islands—continental and volcanic—and two of which are low—atolls and raised atolls.[6] All of the Melanesian islands are continental high islands composed of mixed rock structures similar to those of continents. They are larger, older, and geologically more complex than the other islands. With its extremely rugged interior mountain ranges that reach heights of over five thousand metres, New Guinea is the best example. The interior is sliced by divided plateaus, sharp ridges, and precipitous valleys. Although villages on neighbouring ridges frequently appear within easy distance, strenuous hours of descending and climbing are required to get from one to another. Soils on the steep slopes are often unstable and mud slides are common. Lower and coastal areas are divided by twisting rivers, alternating coastal plains and swamps with narrow coastal shelves. Travel and transport are always difficult. The topography of Melanesia has created barriers that have kept human populations separated and divided into small political and linguistic communities. Except in New Caledonia, malaria and a host of other diseases are endemic to Melanesia, making it the least healthy region of the Pacific.

As their name implies, the high volcanic islands are volcanic peaks thrust upwards from the ocean floor. Most have mountain ranges divided by deep valleys that open up to flat coastal zones. Erosion of older islands, especially on their windward sides, has produced gentle slopes. Hawai'i, Tahiti, and many other islands in the Society and Marquesas groups as well as Rarotonga in the Cook Islands are examples of high volcanic islands in Polynesia, as are Pohnpei and Kosrae in Micronesia. Like continental islands, the high volcanic formations have freshwater rivers and streams. Most volcanic islands are surrounded by fringing reefs. Good fishing grounds are often found between shore and reef but, importantly, such reefs provide the foundations for low-lying coral atolls.

The most common type of low island is the coral atoll, composed of a number of islands, *motu*, resting on a coral reef that typically encloses a lagoon. Some atolls have passages that allow entrance to the lagoon; others do not and are closed atolls. Atolls originated as fringing reefs around volcanic peaks that sank beneath the sea millions of years ago. As the peaks gradually submerged, coral growth continued to build upward, and reefs remained close to the ocean's surface. The islands themselves are a mixture of coral debris, sand, and humus. Being flat, of low elevation, and seldom reaching more than three to ten metres above sea level, they are extremely vulnerable to tropical storms.

Except for Easter Island, Pitcairn, and New Zealand in the southern temperate zones, the Pacific Islands lie within the tropics. Temperatures and humidities are relatively high and uniform throughout the year. In contrast, however, the highlands of the Melanesian islands can be quite cool. New Guinea is the extreme example where frosts occur in irregular and unpredictable cycles every few years. For the most part, however, there are no abrupt seasonal changes, and for most of the region, years are divided into rainy and dry seasons. While most of the Pacific is well watered, some areas are drier than others and suffer occasional droughts. Without rivers or streams and with little or no ground water, the atolls are the most precarious for human habitation.

In pre-European times, the flora and fauna of the islands were almost entirely derived from Asia, and the number of species rapidly declines from west to east across the Pacific, the farther they are from their Asian origins. Birds and their droppings deposited some seeds on the islands, and others were carried by winds and ocean currents. The ancestors of today's island peoples speeded up the process when they migrated to the region, carrying with them the inventory of most plants needed for subsistence. Coconuts, breadfruit, pandanus, bananas, papayas, and tubers such as taro and yams, were the mainstays. Of the subsistence crops, only the sweet potato originated outside Asia; it was imported from South America. The full inventory of subsistence crops was found only on some high islands, and only coconuts, pandanus, and arrowroot survived on some dry coral atolls. Such islands could not have supported human habitation were it not for the abundant fish and other marine life found in lagoons and surrounding seas. Marine fauna was the main source of protein for most islanders, but many of the inhabitants of the interiors and highlands of the largest Melanesian islands seldom if ever saw the ocean and subsisted mainly on vegetable crops.

Prior to European times, terrestrial fauna was extremely limited. Bats, rats, and in New Guinea, a variety of marsupials, were the only land mammals to precede humans into the Pacific. Early migrations helped carry the rat eastward (presumably not by design but as stowaways on sailing canoes) as well as pigs, dogs, and chickens, although the three were not found everywhere. Small lizards were ubiquitous. Snakes were primarily a Melanesian phenomenon, and crocodiles were limited to New Guinea, the Solomons, and Belau in the west. Seabirds provided a minor part of the diet.

Although it is little appreciated, the first settlers of the area began the human transformation of the region, with their baggage of Asian flora and fauna. Agriculture and hunting radically altered island landscapes and ecologies. Many flightless birds were hunted to extinction, the most striking example being the giant moa of New Zealand.

Prehistory and linguistics

The origins of Pacific Islanders have fascinated and challenged the imaginations of Europeans ever since first contact. A vast body of literature has accumulated, much of it speculative in nature. Despite the absence of written languages among the islanders themselves, their oral histories were abundant with accounts of far distant homelands, heroic voyages of exploration, and the settlement of new landfalls.[7]

Because of similarities in their languages, the early European explorers realised that there must be connections among Polynesians. Their ultimate origins were obscure, however, and there were other puzzles. At first glance, the Polynesians did not appear to have many affinities with the peoples of Melanesia. Early in the nineteenth century, one of the first missionaries in Hawai'i suggested American Indians were ancestral to ancient Polynesians. In more recent times, a similar argument has been kept alive by those who see the sweet potato as evidence of South American origins. India has also been nominated as the ancestral homeland of the Polynesians, and on the outer fringes of speculation, a submerged and lost continent of Mu has been posited as the source of Pacific peoples.

Scientific inquiries into prehistory came late to the Pacific. With the exception of New Zealand, no controlled archaeological excavations were undertaken until after World War Two, and Pacific prehistory remained in its infancy until the 1960s. Since then, however, research from a very wide variety of disciplines has accumulated, and an outline of the early movements of people in the Pacific can be constructed with a greater degree of confidence.

By 40 000 years ago, and perhaps 10 000 years earlier, populations of hunters and gatherers had reached Australia and New Guinea from regions in what is now insular south-east Asia.[8] During the Ice Ages of the Pleistocene era, sea levels were lower. A land bridge connected Australia and New Guinea, and Indonesia was part of the south-east Asian mainland. The earliest settlements in New Guinea were inundated and lost when glaciers retreated and sea levels rose, but stone tools dating from 26 000 BP have been found inland in the southern highlands of New Guinea. Excavations in the highlands also indicate that a fairly complex system of irrigated agriculture had been developed by no later than 9000 BP, a time when Europeans were still hunters and gatherers. Sites in the highlands near Mt Hagen reveal that pigs were part of the domestic economy by 6000 BP.

Migrations from New Guinea eastward into the rest of Melanesia may have begun before 12 000 BP. An archaeological deposit in New Ireland has been dated at between 6000 and 7000 BP. New Britain and perhaps the Solomons were probably reached at about the same time, and by 4000 BP, it appears that migrants had arrived in New Caledonia and Vanuatu.

Somewhere around five thousand years ago, another flow of people out of south-east Asia began.[9] These migrants were probably ancestral to the Polynesians and Micronesians of today and were speakers of related languages that belong to the Austronesian language family. Reconstructions of proto-Austronesian suggest that ancient speakers of its languages made pottery, had seagoing outrigger canoes, and practised a variety of fishing techniques.

The first settlements of Austronesians appear to have occurred along the northern coast of New Guinea. Later, it is likely that they moved directly from insular south-east Asia into the three westernmost archipelagoes of Micronesia: Belau, Yap, and the Marianas. Between 3000 and 3500 BP, Lapita, a culture named after a site in New Caledonia, appeared in the archaeological record all across Melanesia and parts of western Polynesia. Distinct forms of pottery were part of the culture, and evidence shows that its people had the seagoing skills to move back and forth across great distances. Obsidian from New Britain has been found at Lapita sites in New Caledonia almost two thousand kilometres to the south-east and in Fiji more than twenty-five hundred kilometres distant. Other material remains suggest an economy that included reef fishing, domesticated pigs and chickens, and an agricultural system based on tubers and fruits (taro, yams, breadfruit, bananas, coconuts, and sago).

Linguistic evidence suggests that eastern Micronesia was settled by a movement northward from eastern Melanesia in the vicinity of Vanuatu. By about 3000 BP, Fiji, Tonga, and Samoa had been settled by Lapita people. Over the next thousand years, the early forms of Polynesian culture evolved in Tonga and Samoa. Sometime around the birth of Christ, the early Polynesians began their voyages in large double-hulled canoes to the rest of the Polynesian triangle. The Marquesas Islands in eastern Polynesia were reached by about AD 300. Easter Island, one of the most isolated spots on earth, was probably settled within the next one hundred years. Over the next five hundred years, most of Polynesia was inhabited, with New Zealand the last, around AD 900.

The vast body of archaeological, ethnological, linguistic, botanical, zoological, and other evidence all points to south-east Asian origins for the ancestors of Pacific Islanders. The descendants of the Lapita seafarers appear to have possessed the requisite technology and navigational skills and may have sailed to South America and returned to Polynesia with the sweet potato.

All languages of the Pacific are classified either as belonging to the Austronesian language family or as one of the Papuan languages, a somewhat catch-all category that groups together all non-Austronesian languages (which do not constitute a language family). With its distribution from Madagascar to Easter Island, encompassing all of insular south-east Asia and parts of mainland south-east Asia, the Austronesian language family is the most widespread in the world. Reflecting the ancient migrations into the region, all Micronesian languages, all Polynesian languages, and some of the languages of Melanesia belong to the Austronesian family.

Linguistic diversity in the Pacific is directly related to the duration of human settlement in the different island groups. Polynesia, the last to be occupied, is linguistically the most homogeneous. The languages of each major archipelago and those of some isolated small islands, such as Niue and Easter, are mutually unintelligible. However, the languages are closely related, and islanders are quick to learn languages other than their own. There are about eighteen languages within the Polynesian triangle and another twelve or so among the outliers.

Micronesia is linguistically more complex. The languages of the three westernmost groups (Belau, Yap, and the Marianas), which were settled first and directly from insular south-east Asia, form a subgroup. They have a greater antiquity in the area and differ substantially from each other. Except for the two Polynesian outliers, all other Micronesian languages are classified as 'nuclear Micronesian'. They share many lexical and grammatical features that appear to reflect a common origin in eastern Melanesia. Linguists do not agree about the number of separate and mutually unintelligible languages in Micronesia, but there are at least twelve.

With its mixture of Austronesian and Papuan languages and greater time depth for human settlement, Melanesia is the most complex linguistically. The number of languages has been conservatively estimated at no less than twelve hundred. Many of the languages are spoken by only a few hundred people at best, and each major archipelago has dozens of languages. The island of New Guinea alone has at least nine hundred. Variations of Pidgin English, also known as Neo-Melanesian, are spoken in Papua New Guinea, the Solomons, and Vanuatu, where it is known as Bislama. Pidgin serves as a lingua franca and provides a common bond for the inhabitants of today's Melanesian nations.

Traditional societies

The cultures that evolved over many centuries in the Pacific represented adaptions to a wide range of ecological niches and exhibited considerable variability. Nonetheless, many of the societies in Polynesia and Micronesia had features that distinguished them from the majority of those in Melanesia. In both Polynesia and Micronesia a high degree of social stratification existed, and social status and rank were associated with control over land, a resource that is never abundant on volcanic islands and atolls. In the larger continental islands of Melanesia, the same ruggedness of terrain that divided people into many linguistic groups also promoted cultural differentiation and tended to foster small social groupings. Land played a less important role in determining social position.

Polynesia

For much of the outside world, Polynesia has always been the most familiar of the region's culture areas. The accounts of such early explorers as James Cook, William Bligh, and Louis Antoine de Bougainville inflamed the imaginations of Westerners. The domains of the greatest of the Polynesian chiefs and the trappings of their courts were not only impressive but often equated with the kingdoms well known to Europeans. The apparent relative ease of life, the seemingly endless bounty of tropical islands, and the accounts of casual sexuality had a tremendous impact on Victorian Europe.

Most Polynesian societies were organised around the two principles of bilateral descent and primogeniture. Denoting their branching characteristics, the basic units of society were descent groups commonly referred to as ramages. Descent in a ramage was traced to a founding ancestor with a number of children. The firstborn, regardless of sex, had the highest rank. Subsequent offspring were ranked according to birth order, and they in turn became the founders of branches within the larger ramages, which themselves were ranked according to the birth order of their founders. The process tended to repeat itself with each new generation, and new branches came into being in a continuous process of expansion. In recalling genealogies, descent was usually traced through the ancestor, male or female, of highest rank in each generation. Thus, descent was neither matrilineal nor patrilineal but bilateral. The system allowed for flexibility, an adaptive advantage in an environment where some balance had to be maintained between the relative size of kin groups and limited land resources.

Although the ramage organisation was bilateral in structure, there was a preference for descent connections through males and a rule of primogeniture. The firstborn, particularly a male, was innately superior. Ideally, succession to chieftaincy was from a man to his eldest son, and a line of senior-ranking males was traced to the founding ancestor.

The ramage was a category of people connected in a complicated variety of ways through their fathers, their mothers, and, more usually, both. Each ramage member was ranked according to relative position within the genealogy. The senior male of the senior line had the highest rank. He occupied the status of chief, known as *ariki, ali'i,* or variants thereof. Males of lesser seniority were chiefs of a lower order with perhaps authority over subdivisions of the ramage. The most junior lines of descent were commoners, but the distinction between chiefs and commoners was graded and often vague; everyone could claim some relationship to persons of chiefly rank. Chiefly genealogies were of the greatest importance and were recalled for scores of generations.

Chiefs, especially the most senior in rank, possessed *mana* (power to accomplish), which could reside in people, places, or inanimate objects. By definition, any person or object capable of extraordinary performance had *mana*. A chief skilled in leadership, diplomacy, oratory, and warfare, or a fish-hook that caught exceptional quantities of fish, had *mana*, which was self-evident by performance. *Mana* commanded respect and was both sacred and dangerous. Charged with such invisible power, a chief was always separated from others by rites of avoidance or *tabu*. Chiefs could declare sections of land or sea off-limits or *tabu*, and the collection of resources was forbidden until the *tabu* was lifted.

Chiefs had authority and commanded respect and deference. They exercised political and economic leadership, but with the exception of a few of the most socially stratified societies, they were not despots, and those of lesser rank were in no way their serfs. Although chiefs had much control over decisions regarding the use of land, lagoons, and reef areas, and received tribute during first-fruit ceremonies, they did not live off the labour of others. Rather, they cultivated their own crops and earned their own livelihood as did their followers.

In his monumental work *Ancient Polynesian Society*, anthropologist Irving Goldman classified the kind of Polynesian society described here as 'traditional', and most were of this type.[10] They included the Maori, who settled New Zealand relatively late, and smaller-scale societies of the coral atolls and the smaller volcanic islands such as Tikopia. In traditional societies, seniority of descent provided *mana* and sanctity, defined rank, and allocated authority and power in an orderly fashion. A traditional society was essentially a religous system headed by a sacred chief and given stability by a religiously sanctioned gradation of worth.

Goldman distinguished two other kinds of Polynesian societies: open and stratified. The open societies may have been transitional between the traditional and the stratified. In the open system, the importance of seniority was downplayed to allow political and military effectiveness to determine status and political control. Society was more strongly political and military than religious, and stability was maintained more directly by secular power. Status differences were not graded but tended to be sharply defined, as for example in Easter Island, the Marquesas, Samoa, and Niue.

The Marquesas Islands may have been the most fully evolved example of an open society. Although genealogical and achieved statuses were of about equal importance, genealogical status was not adequate by itself; the ultimate test of political power was a chief's ability to attract followers. For a chief who could not build a following, could not control both kin and allies, the title was of little value. A chief was either a political chief or none at all. In Samoa, descent and seniority of line were even less important. Chiefs known as *matai* were selected by their kin to head extended families by reason of their abilities and accomplishments.

Stratified societies were found where populations and resources were the largest and most abundant. In Hawai'i, Tahiti, and Tonga clearly defined and hierarchically ordered social classes were highly developed. Because chiefs ruled thousands of people, genealogical connections could not be traced between all segments of society. Because of the magnitude of their *mana*, the most powerful chiefs could not come into direct contact with commoners, and objects they touched were avoided. The chiefs formed a class unto themselves and married among themselves. The highest-ranking chiefs controlled all land, and their administrations were impersonal and authoritarian.

Hawai'i had the most highly stratified society of all, with eleven grades of *ali'i*. Entire islands or major divisions of the larger islands were held by a single *ali'i nui*, who was often a despot. The domain of such a chief was subdivided among lesser chiefs in return for tribute and service. Lesser chiefs served at the pleasure of the *ali'i nui*. The chiefs had great sanctity and were thought to be descended from gods.

Shortly after European contact, the Hawaiian Islands were unified under one chief who came to be known as King Kamehameha I. Although he used Europeans to consolidate his rule over all the islands, the process was well under way and might have occurred without the assistance of foreigners. Similar developments occurred in Tahiti, and Tonga, which remains a monarchy to this day.

Throughout most of Polynesia the pantheon of powerful gods varied only slightly from one archipelago to another and was supported by a variety of nature deities as well as ancestral gods. The proper worship of major gods was conducted by priests, often drawn from the lesser chiefly lines. Among commoners, the heads of extended families looked after the ancestors. An exception to the more general Polynesian pattern was Samoa, where society was more secular, less attention was paid to the supernatural, and the notion of *mana* was weak.

Warfare was almost universal. The power and reputation of rival chiefs were at stake, and, as Goldman stressed, status rivalry was particularly acute in Polynesian societies and made much of Polynesian behaviour intelligible.

Polynesia has undergone radical transformations since European contact, but vestiges of the past remain. Samoans have proven remarkably resilient, and the organisation of their society, particularly in Western Samoa, has retained much of its traditional form. On many islands, particularly remote ones, the ramage organisation still defines relations among kin and rights to land. Chiefly powers have been greatly diminished almost everywhere, and they no longer exist in highly Westernised Hawai'i.

Micronesia

With few exceptions, matrilineal institutions prevailed throughout Micronesia. At birth, both females and males became members of their mother's matrilineage. Lineages were relatively shallow, with a genealogical depth of three to five generations, and were the corporate groups that held land. As in Polynesia, siblings were ranked by the order of their birth, and sublineages within a lineage were ranked by the birth order of their founding sisters. The head of each lineage was its senior-ranking male, and succession to lineage headship was matrilineal, that is, a male was succeeded by his younger brothers according to relative age, and they in turn were succeeded by their eldest sister's eldest son and his brothers.

In most cases aggregations of lineages shared a common name and formed a social category or matriclan. The lineages of the same clan were scattered over several islands and usually were not linked by remembered genealogical connections. Nonetheless, clan members had a sense of common kinship, and the clan was exogamous, that is, spouses were acquired from outside the clan. The exogamous and dispersed clans functioned as large security nets. Islanders were obliged to protect and provide for their clan members, whether strangers or friends.

Paramount chiefdoms and distinct social classes were characteristic of the social organisation of most of the high islands and the Marshallese atolls. On the high islands of the Marianas, Pohnpei, and Kosrae, and the low-lying Marshalls, certain clans or lineages were of paramount chiefly status, and their members constituted a privileged ruling class. The islands were divided among the paramount chiefs who had ultimate authority over the land within their domains. Their powers were substantial and sometimes included the ability to render judgments of life or death on members of the commoner class. Between the ranks of the paramount chiefs and the commoners were layers of lesser chiefs and nobles.

The centralised political regimes of Pohnpei and Kosrae were reminiscent of the most highly stratified of Polynesia. In both cases, a single chiefly line ruled the entire island. On Pohnpei, the ruling dynasty left behind a vast complex of monumental architectural structures, artificial islands, and canals that now constitute the largest archaeological site in the entire Pacific. For reasons that are unclear, the Pohnpei dynasty collapsed shortly before the arrival of Europeans, leaving only Kosrae with a centralised political structure at the time of contact.

In contrast, the social organisation of the Carolinian atolls, which stretch from Chuuk in the east to Ulithi and neighbouring atolls in the west, was quite egalitarian. Within the large Chuuk Lagoon, each island was divided into two or more districts, and each was occupied by a relatively small and politically autonomous community. Landholding lineages were ranked not by seniority of descent lines but according to the order in which they had originally settled in the district. According to oral histories, the highest ranking lineage was the first to have settled in the district, and its head was the community's chief. Most of the Carolinian atolls were similarly organised.

Exceptions to matrilineal organisation were found in Yap, the Gilberts, and the two Polynesian outliers south of Pohnpei. Yap was unique and had the most complex stratified social organisation in the entire Pacific. Exogamous matriclans were similar to those elsewhere in Micronesia, but villages were organised around patrilineal landholding corporations. Villages belonged to and were divided between high and low castes. In turn, the two castes were divided into nine ranked social classes. Located in the transition zone between Micronesia and Polynesia, the Gilbert Islands exhibited Polynesian influences in both language and culture. Gilbertese social organisation was bilateral, and paramount chiefs headed communities in part of the archipelago. The outliers of Kapingamarangi and Nukuoro fit the pattern of Goldman's traditional Polynesian society.

With few exceptions, the religious systems of Micronesia were not as complex as those of Polynesia. Absent was a widespread pantheon of deities, and cosmologies tended to be relatively simple. Ancestral spirits were important everywhere, and supernatural beings that resided in objects of nature were common in some areas. As in Polynesia, warfare was endemic. Among the egalitarian communities of Chuuk, small political entities were engaged in almost continuous conflict. Elsewhere, paramount chiefs fought among themselves in attempts to extend their respective domains.

The social organisation and culture of the people of the Marianas were virtually destroyed soon after European contact, and Kosrae lost its centralised chiefly system. Yap and the Carolinian atolls have maintained much of their traditional forms of culture and social organisation. Although their powers have been greatly reduced, the paramount chiefs of Belau, Pohnpei, and the Marshalls remain important figures of influence. The paramount chiefs of the Gilberts have been eclipsed, but the bilateral organisation of society has changed little.

Melanesia

Except for New Caledonia, most Melanesian societies have retained much of their traditional cultures. In the Solomon Islands, Vanuatu (formerly the New Hebrides), and Papua New Guinea, well over 80 per cent of the populations remain subsistence agriculturalists. Ann Chowning has provided a useful summary of Melanesian cultures.[11] She and other scholars have emphasised the great diversity within this largest culture area of the Pacific.

Europeans frequently perceive Melanesians as industrious agriculturalists, preoccupied with trade, the accumulation of wealth, the ramifications of kinship, ancestor worship, and, in some places, secret societies. In contrast to the rest of the Pacific, there is a general absence of large and complex political structures. Groups no larger than a few hundred people are common in the lowlands, the main exceptions being in the Sepik River region of New Guinea where groups may have a thousand or more people. The largest groups are found in the highlands of New Guinea and may number several thousand.

Political units are commonly headed by a man or several men, each of whom is known as a big man. The status is largely achieved, and though it is not hereditary, the sons of big men do have an advantage over others. A big man must be ambitious and energetic, have the ability to manipulate others and manoeuvre them into his debt, organise large-scale activities, be successful in the accumulation of wealth (pigs, garden produce, and a large variety of indigenous valuables), and be generous in the distribution of that wealth. In the past, and in some areas yet today, a big man had to prove himself as a warrior. Polygyny was considered useful insofar as multiple wives provide a workforce to cultivate gardens and nurture pigs.

Exceptions to the big-man type of polity are found, for example in the Trobriand Islands off the east coast of New Guinea. Trobriand society has ranked matriclans and paramount chiefs with extensive authority. In New Caledonia, paramount chiefs were similar to those of Polynesia, and a hereditary two-class system with chiefly statuses exists in a number of Melanesian societies.

Settlement patterns range from the elaborately laid out villages of the Trobriands to the much more common dispersed hamlets found throughout most of the area. Land tenure systems vary greatly and are linked to descent groups of which almost every possible variation is found somewhere. In the broadest of terms, matrilineal systems are mostly found in eastern Melanesia. Many of the societies of the New Guinea highlands are patrilineal in ideology, but in practice they exhibit great flexibility, with numerous exceptions.

Two forms of wealth are ubiquitous: pigs and small portable valuables. Pig exchanges are an integral part of ceremonial life, usually involved in the payment of bride-price, a practice common in Melanesia. The small valuables take a variety of forms and include dogs' teeth, curved boars' tusks, porpoise teeth, pierced stone disks, shell ornaments, red feather belts, and packets of salt, a scarce commodity in the New Guinea highlands.

Trade and exchange networks were common in Melanesia. In many instances food and utilitarian items continue to be exchanged along well-established networks of great antiquity. Fish and shells are traded inland from coastal areas. Some islanders specialise in the manufacture of pottery and exchange their products for food and other items. Other networks exchanged traditional valuables, the most well known being the great ceremonial trading expeditions known as the *kula* ring in the Trobriands.

Nowhere in the Pacific are the differences between the sexes as marked as in Melanesia. Women suffer an inferior status, yet are often quite feared by men. Women are viewed as sexually, physically, and spiritually draining. An excess of sex and contact with women is avoided. Especially during menstruation and after childbirth, women are thought to be dangerous and contaminating, not just to men but to everything they come in contact with. In many places, men and women sleep apart in separate houses, and men, as if to emphasise their separateness, and perhaps fear, may belong to secret societies with huge and elaborately decorated clubhouses.

More than anywhere else in the Pacific, there is a concern, if not a downright preoccupation, with magic and sorcery. Practically every facet of life is associated with ritual. Magical spells ensure the growth of crops, bring success in fishing, guarantee victory in war, and cure sickness. The writings of Malinowski on Trobriand magic and Reo Fortune on sorcery on Dobu in the D'Entrecasteaux Islands reflect the Melanesian preoccupation with these concerns and the attention they have received in the anthropological literature.[12] The supernatural permeates almost every facet of life. A host of spiritual beings are part of the ordinary physical world and are not transcendental. Ancestor worship is almost universal, and roughly the same sorts of spiritual beings are parts of the belief systems of many different peoples.

In the past, warfare was a constant feature of Melanesian life, and it still is in the highlands of New Guinea. Every community continually warred with at least some of its neighbours. Revenge or 'pay back' was the most frequent cause. Each killing or injury had to be repaid, and the process was endless. Head-hunting and cannibalism were common in many areas.

Melanesian creativity reached its zenith in its elaborate art forms, particularly in the lowlands. Painting, wood carving, and inlay work are lavish and are found in such ceremonial objects as masks, human and animal figures, drums, canoes, and innumerable other items. In some areas of the Solomons and New Guinea, almost every object, no matter how utilitarian, is decorated. Elsewhere, particularly in the New Guinea highlands, decoration is focused on the human body, taking the form of facial and body paint, elaborate head-dresses, and costumes. In many respects Melanesian societies tend to represent the extremes. Indeed, anthropologist Ronald Berndt used the title *Excess and Restraint* for his study of four linguistic groups in the eastern New Guinea highlands.[13]

The European period

Magellan's landing on Guam in 1521 opened a radically new era in Pacific history. His voyage demonstrated the immense size of the Pacific, but the European discovery of other islands was left to those who followed. During the rest of the sixteenth century, the Spanish and Portuguese dominated exploration in the region. Expeditions from both nations sighted and claimed New Guinea. The Solomon Islands were discovered by the Spaniard Alvaro de Mendaña in 1568, and, near the very end of the century, he also came upon the Marquesas, the first inhabited Polynesian islands seen by Europeans.

While charting the south coast of New Guinea in the early 1600s, Dutch navigators discovered Australia, which they unimaginatively called New Holland, and the Netherlands launched the major voyages of exploration in the seventeenth century. In 1642, Abel Tasman encountered the island that now bears his name, along with New Zealand, Tonga, and parts of Fiji. After Tasman, no major discoveries were made in the Pacific for eight decades, until 1722, when another Dutchman, Jacob Roggeveen, put Easter Island, the Tuamotus, and Samoa on the map.

Four decades later, the British and the French became the major players in the region. The Englishman Samuel Wallis discovered Tahiti in 1776. Louis Antoine de Bougainville, the most well known of the French navigators, followed Wallis to Tahiti and made a number of landfalls throughout Melanesia. Although his accomplishments were considerable, the eighteenth-century voyages of exploration were dominated by the British, and Captain James Cook was the most formidable navigator of them all. Between 1768 and 1779, he made three voyages, further exploring the Society Islands, surveying the coasts of New Zealand and the east coast of Australia, discovering Niue, New Caledonia, and Norfolk Island, and charting new islands in the Tuamotus, the Cooks, and the Marquesas. His final voyage took him to Hawai'i where he met his death at the hands of the Hawaiians in 1779.

The era of major exploration and new discoveries essentially ended after Cook's voyages. By the end of his time, the major archipelagoes had been located and mapped, and Cook's observations and charts would prove remarkably accurate. The first contacts between Europeans and islanders were often as not marked with misunderstandings and violence. Violence accompanied both the beginning and the end of the era. During his call at Guam in 1521, when the local Chamorros made off with a skiff, Magellan retaliated by burning houses and canoes and killing several men. Likewise, a stolen cutter was the immediate cause of Captain Cook's death.

On the heels of the explorers, and beginning sometime in the late eighteenth century, the first interlopers to take up residence in the islands began to appear. The earliest settled in Polynesia and Micronesia, and, for a time, Melanesia was avoided because of the hostility of the inhabitants and the inhospitable environment. In addition, the general absence of chiefs made it more difficult to deal with the Melanesians. The outsiders have been variously referred to as beachcombers, sealers, whalers, and traders. First to arrive were the beachcombers, men who had jumped ship or survived shipwrecks. They were later joined by escapees from the British and French penal colonies in Australia, Norfolk Island, and New Caledonia. Many were adventurers fascinated by tales of the South Seas, or malcontents at home. As a group, they have commonly been described as overly fond of alcohol and generally of unsavory character. Most came from Europe and America, but many nations of the earth were represented.

Although many were rogues of one sort or another, these men played an important part in island history. The beachcombers were the first foreigners to establish residence in the islands and learn the indigenous languages. Many married or formed long-term liaisons with local women and left numerous offspring. A few became attached to chiefs and served as advisers or intermediaries in relations with Europeans. Many became traders and facilitated the early involvement of the islands in the larger world economy. Beachcombers of all sorts gained considerable prominence and influence and finished out their lives in the islands; others left or died with little trace.

In the late 1790s, Western economic ventures began to affect the region. Commercial ships began to carry sealers and fur traders between the American north-west and China. They exchanged trade goods for supplies of food and fresh water, and for them, as well as for the whalers who followed, the islands were welcome recreation spots.

Long valued in China, sandalwood caused great excitement when it was discovered in Polynesia and Melanesia. The resource was quickly exhausted and the trade did not last long, but it wrought havoc and violence virtually everywhere it touched. Generally, the sandalwooders were after easy money and earned a poor reputation; they often attempted to short-change islanders or bullied them into participating in the trade. Chiefs, especially those in Hawai'i, used the trade to enhance their own welfare at the expense of commoners. During the first three decades of the nineteenth century, Fiji, Hawai'i, and the Marquesas were the first to be affected. The trade came to Melanesia in the 1820s, primarily Vanuatu, the Loyalty Islands, and New Caledonia, and lasted until about 1865. In many respects, it was fortunate that the trade ran its course in relatively short order. Other Pacific products that found markets in China were bêche-de-mer, mother-of-pearl, and tortoiseshell.

More important, following the discovery of rich whaling grounds in the Pacific, a whaling industry grew rapidly, and by the 1820s whalers were operating all over the region. For most of its duration, the industry was dominated by New England interests. The crews, however, were a mixed bag composed not only of New Englanders but also American Indians, runaway slaves, renegade British sailors, other Europeans of diverse nationalities and backgrounds, and Pacific Islanders, especially Hawaiians. At its peak during the 1850s, more than seven hundred American whaling vessels plied the Pacific. Over the next two decades, the industry declined as whaling grounds were depleted and whale oil for lamps was replaced by kerosene.

Ports of call sprang up, partly in response to the whaling industry. Whalers put ashore to repair and resupply their vessels and for rest and recreation. The nineteenth-century seafarers demanded relief from the rigours of the sea—fresh food, new faces, alcohol, and sex. Hawai'i, Tahiti, and the Marquesas were among the first to feel the impact in Polynesia, and eventually New Zealand was involved. Pohnpei and Kosrae were the favourite spots in Micronesia. Honolulu in Hawai'i, Pape'ete in Tahiti, and Kororareka in New Zealand were especially popular. The first two survived and continued to thrive after the decline of whaling; Kororareka gave way to the sleepy town of Russell.

Everywhere, contact with Europeans had deleterious consequences for Pacific Islanders, and in describing those consequences, Alan Moorehead titled his account *The Fatal Impact*.[14] The sailors aboard the voyages of exploration introduced venereal diseases to the islands, and as their incidence increased, European residents arrived and brought other novel afflictions such as measles and influenza, to which the islanders had no natural immunity. Violence was common. Alcohol ravaged people unaccustomed to strong drink, and firearms heightened the seriousness of indigenous conflicts. Depopulation became a serious problem throughout the region, and by the end of the nineteenth century, most Westerners believed Pacific Islanders doomed to extinction.

In the economic sphere, the copra trade touched the lives of Pacific Islanders more than any other economic activity. By the mid-nineteenth century, a German trading firm had established large coconut plantations in Samoa. Similar large-scale operations followed elsewhere, and islanders were attracted to producing copra on their own lands. Coconut palms thrive almost everywhere and are suited to even the poorest and most remote of the coral atolls. Copra was a natural product for the islands; production is simple, requiring little or no capital investment for the small producer. It became the major income earner for island peoples, and furthered their integration into the world economy. The vessels of small traders as well as large trading firms collected copra throughout the islands and exchanged cash and goods in return. As the planting of coconut palms increased, the copra trade altered the landscapes of entire islands, especially the atolls.

The missions

In most places, missionaries arrived shortly after the first beachcombers. Their impact has been immeasurable, and Christian missionisation has been at least as successful in the Pacific as in any other area of the world. It all began with Catholicism on Guam. The Spanish sailing route between the New World and the Philippines made Guam a convenient port of call. In 1668, Catholic missionaries and a small contingent of soldiers were landed on the island, and the Spanish established the first successful European colony in the Pacific Islands. Although it would later suffer reverses, the mission effort experienced some initial success, and a strategy was set in motion that would become commonplace in the nineteenth century. The priests first sought to convert chiefs, whose example was soon followed by the common people.

A century elapsed before the next round of missionisation. In 1797, the Protestants entered Polynesia when the London Missionary Society began work in Tahiti. The paramount chiefs were again the first converted, and within twenty years the Tahitian mission was enjoying considerable success.

The Spanish Catholic Church at Kolonia, Pohnpei, near the end of the nineteenth century. (US Trust Territory Department of Education Library, Saipan, Northern Mariana Islands)

By the 1830s, the London Missionary Society had extended its effort through the Society Islands, the Cooks, and Samoa.

Other Protestant missions from England soon entered the fray, and in 1814 a mission station was established in New Zealand to spread the gospel among the Maori. Within a few years, the Protestants had reached Tonga, Fiji, and the Loyalty Islands, which represented their first intrusion into insular Melanesia. What came to be called the Melanesian Mission was started in New Zealand, and more outposts were opened in Melanesia. In 1866, a mission school was established on Norfolk Island, and Melanesians were brought there for instruction.

In 1820, the Americans joined the cause when the Boston-based American Board of Commissioners for Foreign Missions landed its first missionaries in Hawai'i. Also known as the Boston Mission, it too followed the strategy of working through the highest-ranking chiefs and enjoyed relatively quick success. By the early 1850s, its missionaries, including some Hawaiian converts, were laboring in eastern Micronesia.

The Catholics launched their first serious effort in the eastern Pacific with the arrival of a band of priests in Hawai'i in 1827. In a manoeuvre that foreshadowed future relations between the two branches of Christianity, the Protestants had the unwanted competition expelled. After several years in retreat, the Catholics re-entered Polynesia with an adroit move in 1834, landing priests in the remote Mangareva Islands south-east of Tahiti where they were unwatched and unopposed. Within two years, they had moved on to Tahiti, and in 1838 a mission was opened in the Marquesas. In 1843, the Catholics were the first missionaries to reach New Caledonia. Fiji and Samoa saw their first Catholic missions in 1844.

By the 1850s and 1860s missionaries were established in all major island groups. As usual, Melanesia came last and was the most difficult to penetrate. The absence of chiefs, the small and fragmented polities, and the diversity of languages made it a true proselyter's nightmare. Indeed, the American and English missionaries were reluctant to take up the challenge and sent their recent Polynesian converts instead.

The Protestants and the Catholics had different strategies of mission-isation. The Protestants wanted acceptance of not only their religion but also their lifestyle and work ethic. They attempted to suppress sexuality, insisted on clothing women from head to foot, urged islanders to adopt Western-style houses, stressed the virtues of hard work, and railed against the evils of rum and tobacco. Their message had more hell-fire and brim-stone than compassion and neighbourly love.

Another element shaped the style of missionisation. The Protestants re-ceived much encouragement but less financial generosity from home. In the field, they emphasised training indigenous pastors and other church leaders and making congregations economically self-sufficient. The missionaries themselves often engaged in agriculture and commerce, and in some in-stances their offspring would later become kingpins in local politics and economies. The ultimate goal for the missions, however, was to indigenise the local churches. Through their involvement in local politics Protestant missionaries or their offspring were influential in shaping the monarchies of Hawai'i, Tahiti, and Tonga.

In contrast, and with the exception of Micronesia, the Catholics were French. For geopolitical reasons of its own at the time, France supported the mission effort and, with some exceptions, the Catholics were generally better off. As a whole, the Catholics were more tolerant of traditional cul-tures and behaviours and did not attempt to impose the strict regimes of the Protestants. Nonetheless, they did promote the French language and culture as well as the tenets of their faith. There was no attempt to create an indi-genous church organisation, and the French fathers remained very much in control.

Eventually, the Protestant and Catholic missions overlapped almost everywhere, but in most island groups, one or the other enjoyed more influence. Both sides exhibited considerable intolerance and bigotry. Each claimed to have the only true faith and portrayed the other's message as that of false prophets if not Satan himself. Not infrequently, antagonisms be-tween the denominations erupted into acts of violence and destruction. The missions began the process of formal education in the islands. In keeping with their own objectives, Protestants and Catholics alike developed orthographies for some of the more widely used Pacific languages. To read the Scriptures it was necessary to be literate, and the art of reading was taught with great vigour.

By the middle of the nineteenth century, the initial stage of pioneering in the Pacific by outsiders was over, and the stage was set for two major developments with long-term consequences for all parties involved in the region. First, the expansion of commercial development would benefit the interlopers. Second, the partitioning of the Pacific that had begun on Guam in the seventeenth century would be completed.

Expanded commercial development

Douglas L. Oliver has identified the three categories of people that shaped economic trends as planters, labour recruiters, and merchants.[15] Planters had arrived in Samoa as early as the 1850s; their numbers dramatically increased during the late 1800s, and most of the newcomers were from Australia and New Zealand. As Oliver has pointed out, the planters were a new kind of outsider. They did not come for refreshment or in search of souls, but they came to stay, to make a commitment, and to acquire land. Although other commercial crops were tried, the ones with real potential were relatively few: the ubiquitous copra, sugar, coffee, cacao, vanilla, some fruits, cotton, and rubber. The last was mainly limited to New Guinea, and cotton enjoyed a boom only in Fiji during the American Civil War.

Planters required cheap labour, but found the Polynesians and Micronesians unwilling. Neither would tolerate the monotony of plantation life and chores, and the solution was to find labourers elsewhere. For the sugar plantations of Hawai'i and Fiji, labourers from outside the region were imported. In Hawai'i, Japanese, Chinese, and eventually Filipinos were brought in, and they stayed to become an integral part of island society. In Fiji, Indians were imported as indentured labourers, and many of them stayed to make a new home in the islands. The importation of foreign labour brought revolutionary changes to both Hawai'i and Fiji.

For plantations elsewhere in the Pacific and for the sugar fields of Queensland, labourers were recruited in Melanesia, mainly from the Solomons and the New Hebrides. The recruiters, known in the early days as blackbirders, introduced a system of indenture whereby islanders obligated their labour for a few years in exchange for subsistence, a small wage, and a bonus of cash or goods on their return home. In practice, islanders were often tricked or kidnapped. Some of them were reasonably well treated, but many were not, and their rewards were not always as promised. Sometimes by choice, a minority never saw their homelands again. At its worst, the labour trade—blackbirding—was akin to slavery, and towards the end of the nineteenth century public outcry forced the colonial powers to end the practice and institute controls over the recruiting and return of labourers.

Along with the planters and indentured labourers, several large mercantile firms came into existence, supplying imported items for settlers and missionaries and catering to the growing indigenous demand for tools, calico, and other Western goods. German merchants were active for a time, but Australian and New Zealand interests prevailed. Sydney and Auckland became the financial capitals of the South Pacific.

Partition established

Prior to the mid-nineteenth century, only two colonial powers had made territorial claims in the region. The Spanish administered Guam and the rest of the Marianas, and Spain had laid claim to much of the remainder of Micronesia but had made no effort to establish any real control. The Dutch, as a consequence of their own voyages of exploration and their involvement in the East Indies, had been familiar with New Guinea since the seventeenth century. In 1828, they claimed the western half of the island, but seventy years would elapse before they established an administration.

Britain had founded a penal colony in Australia in 1788, and convicts who had served their time, or escaped, and free settlers from there soon spilled over into New Zealand. With the Treaty of Waitangi in 1840, Britain took possession, and New Zealand became a colony separate from those in Australia. Subsequently, fearing encroachment by a non-English-speaking power, Australia and New Zealand strongly urged Britain to annex almost every island and reef in the Pacific. Not wanting further expansion in the area, the British initially refused. The Dutch had no further colonial ambitions in the region. The United States, although involved in whaling and the North-west fur trade, had neither possessions nor ambitions for expansion in the islands.

France did have such ambitions. A proposal to build the Panama Canal was current at the time, and it appeared that the Marquesas and Tahiti might become valuable ports of call on a route between Panama and Australia or New Zealand. France made its move in 1842 by declaring sovereignty over the Marquesas and a protectorate over Tahiti. New Caledonia, a major prize, came under the tricolor in 1853. With control of these territories, France had established itself as a major power in the Pacific. Later, between 1881 and 1887, France annexed other islands near Tahiti to become dominant in eastern Polynesia and consolidate what is now French Polynesia.

After New Caledonia, the next major territorial acquisition was made by Britain. In 1874, Fiji's chiefs ceded their land to the British in what was essentially a salvage operation. On this occasion and later, Britain acquired territories to satisfy Australia and New Zealand, to establish law and order, and to halt blackbirding.

Australia and New Zealand had also been disturbed, if not alarmed, by Germany's entry into the Pacific. The German firm that had begun its operations in Samoa in the 1850s had spread its agents across the ocean within a few years. Near the end of the century, Samoa itself was in turmoil. The Americans were interested in the excellent harbour at Pago Pago; the Germans were set on protecting their own interests; and the Samoans were engaged in a civil war among themselves. Britain was involved, but had much less direct interest at stake. As with Fiji, some stability was needed, but rivalry among the three external powers precluded an easy solution.

Meanwhile, Germany continued to expand its commercial interests and made its first territorial acquisition in 1884, when it annexed the north-eastern portion of New Guinea and the adjacent Bismarck Archipelago. In the following year, Germany declared a protectorate over the Marshall Islands in eastern Micronesia. As later events would prove, Germany was far from finished, and in 1886, it added Nauru to its empire.

Events in New Guinea caused considerable anxiety in Australia. The last thing the Australians wanted was another non-English-speaking power in their vicinity; having the French in New Caledonia was quite enough. They were relieved when the still-reluctant British moved at last to claim Papua—the south-eastern portion of New Guinea. Over the next few years, Britain began to exercise what Australia and New Zealand viewed as its proper role in the area. Its next acquisitions were not impressive, however, as they were mostly atolls. By 1892, British protectorates had been declared over the Cook Islands, the Phoenix Islands, Tokelau, and the Gilbert and Ellice Islands. In 1883, the Australians were especially pleased when Britain declared a protectorate over most of the Solomon Islands on their north-eastern flank. The New Hebrides remained the only group in Melanesia not under colonial rule.

The years 1898 and 1899 witnessed the demise of Spain in the Pacific, the entry of the United States, further German expansion, and a resolution of the problems in Samoa. In 1898, the United States defeated Spain in the Spanish–American War and acquired the Philippines and Guam. For a mere pittance, Germany purchased the rest of Spanish Micronesia. American business interests in Hawai'i were instrumental in the overthrow of the Hawaiian monarch in 1893. Under their guidance, a republic was established, and in 1898 Hawai'i was annexed by the United States. America had acquired its second Pacific colony.

In the following year, Britain, Germany, and the United States resolved the Samoan problem. Britain renounced any claims it might have had, and in 1899, Germany and the United States divided the archipelago. Germany took the lion's share in what was to become Western Samoa; the United States acquired the smaller eastern portion with its coveted Pago Pago

Harbor, and American Samoa was born. Britain did not come away empty-handed. Germany renounced any rights or claims to Tonga and Niue in favour of Britain and gave the British undisputed claim to all of the Solomon Islands east and south-east of Bougainville.

Some tidying up of the colonial order was required. In 1900 Niue was made a British protectorate, and in the following year, Britain turned both Niue and the Cook Islands over to New Zealand for annexation. In 1900 Tonga and Britain signed a treaty of friendship that gave Britain control over Tonga's foreign affairs. Tonga never became a colony in any official sense, but its affairs, both internal and external, were extensively guided and influenced by the British.

Only the New Hebrides remained. After two decades of administration by a joint naval commission, Britain and France, wary of further German ambitions, established a condominium government in 1906. The arrangement was without parallel, always awkward, and never satisfactory to anyone, but it closed the islands to others. In the same year, Australia assumed the administration of Papua. What had begun on Guam in 1668 had been completed. The Pacific had been partitioned among eight colonial powers. Spain had been forced out, leaving seven at the beginning of the twentieth century: Australia, Britain, France, Germany, the Netherlands, New Zealand, and the United States.

Notes

1 For this chapter I have drawn on three main sources: an earlier overview of the Pacific prepared for another volume: Robert C. Kiste, 'Overview', in *Oceania: A Regional Study*, ed. Frederica M. Bunge and Melinda W. Cook, Foreign Area Studies, American University, and Department of the Army, US Government Printing Office, Washington, DC, 1984, 1–53; K. R. Howe, *Where the Waves Fall: A New South Sea Islands History from First Settlement to Colonial Rule*, Allen & Unwin, Sydney, and University of Hawai'i Press, Honolulu, 1984; Douglas L. Oliver, *The Pacific Islands*, 3rd edn, University of Hawai'i Press, Honolulu, 1989.
2 A. J. Furnas, *Anatomy of Paradise*, William Sloane, New York, 1948, 14.
3 John Dunmore, *Who's Who in Pacific Navigation*, University of Hawai'i Press, Honolulu, 1991, 167–168.
4 Felix M. Keesing, *Native Peoples of the Pacific World*, Macmillan, New York, 1945, 9.
5 Stewart Firth, *New Guinea under the Germans*, Melbourne University Press, Carlton, VIC, 1983, photographs opposite p. 82.
6 William L. Thomas, Jr, 'The Pacific Basin: An Introduction', in *Peoples and Cultures of the Pacific*, ed. Andrew P. Vayda, National History Press, Garden City, NY, 1968, 12–18.
7 Sir Peter H. Buck (Te Rangi Hiroa), *Vikings of the Sunrise*, Stokes Press, New York, 1938.

8 Pamela Swadling, *Papua New Guinea's Prehistory: An Introduction*, National Museum and Art Gallery, Boroko, Papua New Guinea, 1986, 1.

9 Douglas L. Oliver, *Oceania: The Native Cultures of Australia and the Pacific Islands*, vol. 1, University of Hawai'i Press, Honolulu, 1989, 67–72.

10 Irving Goldman, *Ancient Polynesian Society*, University of Chicago Press, Chicago and London, 1970.

11 Ann Chowning, *An Introduction to the Peoples and Cultures of Melanesia*, Cummings, Menlo Park, CA, 1977.

12 Bronislaw Malinowski, *Argonauts of the Western Pacific*, E. P. Dutton, New York, 1961; R. F. Fortune, *Sorcerers of Dobu*, E. P. Dutton, New York, 1963.

13 R. M. Berndt, *Excess and Restraint: Social Control Among a New Guinea Mountain People*, University of Chicago Press, 1962.

14 Alan Moorehead, *The Fatal Impact: An Account of the Invasion of the South Pacific, 1767–1840*, Harper & Row, New York, 1966.

15 Oliver, 1989, 62.

Imperial manoeuvres

Peter Hempenstall

As the twentieth century opened, the Pacific was no longer a hidden vastness of isolated cultures following their separate paths of economic subsistence, exchange, and ritual renewal. Two centuries and more of encounters with European traders, sailors, missionaries, and settlers had transformed the region into fragments of empires annexed or 'protected' by powerful European nation-states.

How the empires came about has been one of the richest areas of debate among historians of both Europe and the colonised lands over the last hundred years. The multiplicity of arguments—which tend to concentrate on the nature of European imperialism at the end of the nineteenth century—is too voluminous and complex to deal with in any detail. Nonetheless, the briefest of outlines will set the Pacific Islands in the context of the world history of which they have become a part.

Arguments about the nature of late nineteenth-century imperialism focused initially on the post-Industrial-Revolution phenomenon of the British economy: Britain had become the workshop of the world, exporting vast amounts of capital to foreign places and to its colonial offshoots, opening up new continents, controlling the world's sea lanes through the Royal Navy, creating a network of empire the like of which the world had never seen. The historian Sir John Seeley claimed that, despite this, Britain was not imperialist, but had acquired empire 'in a fit of absence of mind'.[1] Later historians refined that to stress the pressures on Britain to annex even when it did not wish to. Britain's aspiration in the nineteenth century was 'trade with informal control if possible; trade with rule when necessary'.[2] A tougher set of economic determinists drew on the industrial history of Europe to argue for the transformation of capitalism during the nineteenth century and its lust for expansion. Lenin, drawing on Marx and Hobson, wrote 'imperialism is the monopoly stage of capitalism.... The division of the world is the transition from a colonial policy which has extended without hindrance to territories unoccupied by any capitalist power, to a colonial policy of monopolistic possession of the territory of the world which has been completely divided up'.[3] More recent historians have combined analysis of all these forces with a consideration of the interaction between the major European power players and unstable societies in the less developed world where the Europeans were active in the late nineteenth century. Imperialist rule was the result of a set of 'unequal contracts' between European interest groups on the periphery and local indigenous elites who had little chance of resisting imperial penetration because of the imbalance in economic and military power.[4]

From the perspective of the Pacific region, a number of intersecting forces in Europe and the Pacific best explain the intensifying—and permanent— imperial relationship between the Western industrialised world and the Pacific Islands that took place in the nineteenth century. These include, first, the geopolitical changes that occurred globally as British domination of trade and industry began to decline and other countries began to catch up. Germany particularly was becoming the ascendant power on the Continent while, outside Europe, the United States was already well on the way to international economic hegemony and was casting around to extend its sphere of influence. Second, internal economic and political developments within metropolitan powers themselves generated a drive for colonies. Again, Germany provides the most telling example, as Bismarck's 'social imperialism' strategy—the acquisition of colonies as an instrument to distract attention from domestic class and political crises—began to bite, to be replaced after his fall by a new aggressive foreign-policy drive to achieve political and diplomatic pre-eminence world-wide. Third, relations between Europeans and Pacific Islanders led to a series of crises that could no longer be contained locally but spilled over to affect the perceptions of European powers about their security needs. The results of this chain reaction, in virtually every case, were decisions to annex and incorporate more and more land into the mosaic of European empires. The Pacific is a particularly good example of what was happening world-wide.

The earliest European colonial forays, however, were perhaps motivated by different concerns, notably the establishment by Britain of the penal colony of New South Wales in 1788, and the British annexation of New Zealand in 1840, an act largely occasioned by humanitarian pressure for the protection of Maori against alleged incursions by lawless British nationals and others.[5]

Early commercial activity did not necessarily provide a direct impetus for the establishment of political empires over most Pacific islands. North of the equator, Spanish galleons had been transporting Chinese products and bullion between South-East Asia and Mexico since the early seventeenth century. British and American traders from the 1790s developed a thriving trade in furs to China in return for tea, silk, and other goods. From the early nineteenth century economic enterprise in the South Pacific was based on sealing and whaling, timber and flax, and the collection of island products like sandalwood, marine delicacies, and coconut oil. These were carried in small boats working for larger merchant firms to Sydney where they were transshipped to European or Asian ports.

An economic revolution after 1860, stemming from Europe's resource needs, tied the Pacific Islands much more tightly to the world economy. A large rise in the demand for cotton stimulated by the American Civil War, and better prices for vegetable oils encouraged European trading companies to invest in plantations. Gradually more complex economies evolved, based on land management and the large-scale and long-term transfer of islander labour from one group to another. The Germans were the first to develop such a system, establishing coconut and cotton plantations in Samoa, organising labour from the Gilbert and Ellice Islands, New Britain, and the Marshalls (for the Samoans would not work for them), and linking a network of trading stations throughout the central Pacific to encourage islanders to grow coconuts, make copra, and sell it to company traders.

This revolution had direct political consequences for island societies. The alienation of land from village communities became a source of continuing conflicts between Islanders and the new municipalities of Europeans created out of the economic expansion. The introduction into homogeneous island societies of foreign labour from other islands and from Asia also created new tensions. Combined with the rivalry between various national groups of Europeans, these factors intensified relationships among the varied peoples inhabiting the Pacific, putting an increasing strain on the 'unequal bargains' between the elites of all groups.

Fiji's fate was settled in the 1870s by such pressures. Chief Seru Cakobau, from the small island of Bau off the coast of Viti Levu, had in the 1850s established an uneasy pre-eminence in Fijian political struggles with the help, first, of beachcombers' firepower, and then the direct assistance of King Taufa'ahau of Tonga. But he was opposed by the restive Tongan chief, Henele Ma'afu, in the Lau group, and burdened by enormous financial debts to European settlers. When an American warship in 1855 tried to pry money loose for an American citizen, Cakobau offered the Fijian Islands to Britain in the hope of extricating himself from alliances that had left him cornered.

Britain was reluctant to accept new colonial responsibilities. A mixture of official ennui, hostile Treasury sentiments and occasional, if momentary, public enthusiasm set the varied hues of Britain's policy towards overseas expansion in mid-century. Territory only hindered the free play of commerce that brought civilisation and peace and made people (or at least the merchants of Britain) happier. Cakobau's initial offer was refused. The strain on his attempts to rule amid European penetration increased in the next twenty years as white planters flooded into Fiji.

The historian David Fieldhouse has argued that from this point on Fiji was an example of a peripheral society unable to provide a stable and neutral political basis for European activity.[6] But the problem lay less with Cakobau, who several times was able to bring the settlers into line and prevent coups d'état by the use of judiciously applied armed force, than with complicating internal and external forces. The war with the *Kai Colo*, the hill tribes of Fiji, diverted Cakobau's energies and, despite its containment, conveyed to outside observers the impression that the government could not control its subjects. Added was the collapse of the cotton boom, which put great pressure on the European community and its economy. Much of the damage was done by two British commissioners sent out to investigate after Cakobau in 1873 made another offer of cession to Britain. 'Rampant Anglo Saxons'[7] and died-in-the-wool imperialists, they exceeded their instructions by bullying and threatening the Fijian chiefs into signing a deed of cession, though the chiefs made it clear they were prepared to cede the administration of Fiji but not sovereignty over the land or people. Fiji was annexed in October 1874.

The partition of the Samoan Islands between Germany and the United States twenty-five years later provides a variation on the theme of interwoven forces from the centre and the periphery. Samoa was ripe for imperialist intervention by the 1880s because of the substantial economic interests in land and planting held by competing European national groups, together with the seeming inability of the Samoans to create an ordered political system across the group, and the changing European balance of power in favour of annexation. A large-scale plantation economy had developed after 1850, with German firms holding the largest share of trade and British, Australian, New Zealand, and American interests competing for commercial, missionary, and territorial influence. Planters, traders, and consuls all wanted 'native stability' to enable them to prosecute their ambitions unhindered. They viewed Samoan political life as a nationally disastrous series of fierce contests over petty titles that rendered centralised order and the mobilisation of Samoans for the European economy impossible. European settlers and their governments' consuls spent much of the period after 1850 intriguing to link villages into a pyramid of district administrations capped by the paramount authority of one Samoan 'king'.

K. R. Howe has argued that because the Samoans were not like the Tongans and Tahitians, who chose to order their political system along preferred European lines of central authority, the powers had little choice but to solve in their way the problem of anarchy and disorder on this part of the periphery.[8] As European power tied the Samoan economy into world markets, the settlers, even in conflict with one another, would never be satisfied with whatever measures Samoans took to develop a stable form of central government. The Samoans made several attempts before 1899 to create more integrated structures that would control factionalism, but each was either overthrown by Europeans or tinkered with till useless.[9]

Major changes in the relations between Britain, Germany, and the United States also determined the fate of Samoa. During the civil wars of the 1880s which consistently led to international complications, America's anti-imperialist stand prevented Germany and Britain from agreeing to partition the islands, but by 1899 America had redefined its 'manifest destiny' to include colonial ambitions of its own in the Pacific. Germany, not willing to force the issue under the reluctant colonial policies of Bismarck, had adopted a more militant posture by the turn of the century as the Kaiser strove to achieve 'a place in the sun' for the German empire; Samoa by then was the test case of a new aggressive colonial policy. Britain was never committed to owning Samoa. Only pressure from its colonies in Australia and New Zealand kept it engaged in the competition for influence. By 1899 the prospect of an international agreement with Germany that would tidy up several ends of empire, as well as a naval assessment that placed Tonga ahead of Samoa for harbour facilities, induced Britain to withdraw from the fray.

It was ultimately impossible for the Samoan Islands to remain outside the imperialist scramble of the Europeans. Superior force and indomitable ambition were at the heart of imperialism. Along with the warship and the Maxim gun, Europeans possessed the moral belief in their superiority and mission to civilise, and the will to dominate, which would not recognise an equal partnership in power with 'primitive' peoples. However, Samoa's decentralised politics and dispersed centres of power did stave off the European drive for control for several decades.

Fiji and Samoa were just two of the more intensively colonised island groups. Their fates were influenced significantly by imperialist pressures from white settler communities, which were themselves the external arms of larger white immigrant societies on the south-western rim of the Pacific. The colonists of Australia and New Zealand held visions of Oceania as a powerful and wealthy dominion for the British empire. And as the trade and plantations of French, German, and American interests grew, they argued the strategic danger of allowing foreign powers to prey on territories close to their own.

New Zealand had grandiose aspirations for a Pacific Islands empire throughout the latter half of the nineteenth century, but had to be content, finally, with annexing the Cook Islands, a British protectorate since 1888, in 1901.[10] The Australians lobbied hard in London to have the New Guinea mainland and islands annexed by the English rather than the Germans, who had been building up plantations in New Britain and recruiting labour for Samoa since the 1870s. A German presence in New Guinea would not only disrupt Australian investments in trade, labour recruitment, and missions, but would represent a serious threat to the security of northern Australia. In 1883, in response to the rumour that a German chartered company would begin colonising the mainland of eastern New Guinea, the government of Queensland promised to subsidise a British administration and sent a magistrate to declare sovereignty there. Britain repudiated such presumption, but the Australian colonies continued to press for action, agreeing to finance the cost of a British protectorate. In late 1884 both Britain and Germany finally moved to establish their spheres of influence by annexation; by negotiated agreement in 1886 Britain retained the south-eastern New Guinea mainland (later renamed Papua) and adjacent islands, the southern Solomon Islands, and the Gilbert and Ellice Islands in the central Pacific, over which a protectorate was declared in 1892 to counter the trading and recruiting activities of German companies. Germany acquired the north-eastern corner of New Guinea, the islands of the Bismarck Archipelago and the northern Solomons (Bougainville); the Micronesian islands of Palau, the Carolines, and the Marshalls were acknowledged part of its sphere. Ironically this extensive partitioning of interests proceeded from no lust for empire on the part of the chancelleries of Europe, but from that chain reaction of fear that annexation by the other power would disrupt commercial interests, along with the pressure to annex or be annexed from insecure settler groups in the Pacific.

Only one island group in the south-west Pacific escaped such pressure, if only just. Tonga, long the scene of rival German and British mercantile activities, was brought into the orbit of the British empire by a treaty of friendship in 1878, followed by the proclamation of a protectorate in 1900 after Germany and Britain had resolved their Samoan differences. Tonga avoided outright annexation thanks to Britain's distaste for extra territory if other alternatives were available. In Tonga's case these amounted to a constitution cast by the Tongans on Western lines, which welded the Tongan monarchy to a semblance of a system of Western laws and parliamentary procedures. Though British consuls and commissioners tried over the years to tighten the noose of dependence around Tonga, astute appeals to British courts by its king left Tonga an intact state within the empire in the twentieth century, though with circumscribed authority.

The northern Pacific had been largely ignored in the international competition for empire that consumed the south. Spain had an imperial history there dating back to Magellan in the sixteenth century, but by the late nineteenth century the oldest area of contact, the Mariana Islands, had been reduced to a threadbare fortress designed merely to deny territory to foreign nations that might raid the shipping lanes to the Americas.[11] Two hundred years of alternating oppression and neglect had reduced the Chamorro population and allowed corrupt administrations to prosper.

Farther south, the Micronesian island chains of the Carolines and Marshalls shared more intensively in the waves of European contact brought by whalers, traders, and gunboats of various nations in the eighteenth and nineteenth centuries. While the Spanish took little notice of the islands, German traders were building up a commanding presence in the copra trade. By 1880 Jaluit in the Marshalls was the busiest port in Micronesia, and a treaty with the local high chief, Kabua, established most-favoured-nation status for Germany. A round of secret negotiations between Germany and Britain in the 1870s, designed to divide the western Pacific into spheres of influence and block possible expansionist plans of the United States, heralded an accelerated drive for empire in the northern Pacific. Treaties made between German gunboats and local chiefs delivered an early form of imperial power into the hands of German trading firms, especially the Jaluit Gesellschaft in the Marshalls, and the beginning of the German Pacific empire was formalised with the annexation of the Marshall Islands in 1885. This was an empire founded on naked commerce, not a civilising mission; Bismarck was keen to spare Berlin the cost of governing these pinpricks of empire. Legal control of the entire administration of the area was awarded to the Jaluit Gesellschaft as a chartered company, a method Bismarck tried again in New Guinea, with less success.

When German traders moved more forcefully into the Carolines to the west, Spain finally woke from its torpor and contested possession of the islands. They were awarded to Spain in an arbitrated settlement by Pope Leo XIII. Though Spain reactivated its presence in the Carolines in 1887 by planting governors and garrisons, its colonial flame flickered only briefly, coming to an ignominious end in war with America in 1899 and in a series of violent clashes with Carolinian communities (especially Pohnpei). Spain sold the Carolines to Germany.[12]

Americans had always been engaged in most phases of the contact process, in the whaling industry, as traders and planters, and as missionaries. Their most energetic efforts to profit and to convert were focused on the Hawaiian Islands, where foreign settlement had been going on since the late eighteenth century. One hundred years later Hawai'i had become a society composed of American capitalists on the make and an alienated indigenous population reduced by disease, their *kapu* (taboos) abolished and their land holdings individualised in a series of revolutions that transferred most of the land to foreign control. Immigration from the United States, Japan, and China had created a polyglot society whose white business leaders plotted for the overthrow of the Hawaiian monarchy and for American annexation. America remained cautious till caught up in its own manifest destiny by the war against Spain in 1898. Though the United States government had over the years signed treaties with island chiefs all around the Pacific, not until the Spanish–American War was it truly projected beyond its continental base. Strategic objectives and hopes for larger export markets led to the holding of the Philippines and the taking of Guam. The annexation of Hawai'i followed as a simple consequence in the minds of many Americans, along with the partitioning of Samoa after decades of opposing it. Only briefly did America share with other nations the ideological commitment to imperial rule as the shared burden of Western superiority over backward peoples.

The guarded entrance to the Spanish colony on Pohnpei, circa 1895. (US Trust Territory Department of Education Library, Saipan, Northern Mariana Islands)

An older American tradition of republicanism encouraged an air of uncertainty about its imperial image until, with the election of Woodrow Wilson in 1912, the government returned to an official anti-imperialist platform (without abandoning the spoils of empire in the Philippines, Hawai'i, Samoa, or Guam).[13]

A similar inconsistency between the 'official mind' on the worth or otherwise of colonies and the actual taking of territory characterized France's imperialism in the Pacific. Nineteenth-century French governments rarely pursued a consistent imperial design. The rise and fall of post-revolutionary regimes kept official metropolitan attention focused on internal reconstruction and the problems of domestic stability. This left them vulnerable to the pressure of unofficial pro-colonial groups at home and the dubious initiatives of naval and consular adventurers in the Pacific or Africa or Asia. The diplomatic imperatives of continuing rivalry with the British added to the forces impelling the French to secure the second largest colonial empire in the world by the end of the nineteenth century.[14]

The annexation of the Marquesas in 1842, and of Tahiti in 1880, resulted from scientific, commercial, and strategic convictions held by powerful players on the periphery and in Paris, and from the problems of 'competitive coexistence'[15] with other European nations seeking elbow-room for their nationals in the islands. Admiral Dupetit Thouars singled out the Marquesas as the group with potential as a penal colony, a reprovisioning centre for whalers and other commercial agents, and a base for outward expansion to keep pace with the British. His official orders in Tahiti in 1842 were to investigate complaints by French settlers and Catholic missionaries about the conduct both of consular officials and Tahitians. The wish to assert French pre-eminence in Tahiti led him to inaugurate an experimental protectorate on his first visit, but the pace at which peripheral crises developed after his departure, with the Tahitians seeking British help to roll back increasingly irksome French pressures and the British consul and navy refusing to co-operate with the provisional government, drove Dupetit Thouars further. On his return in 1843 he proclaimed French sovereignty. Paris repudiated this ultimate step at the time, but approved it in 1880 after the complete erosion of Tahitian chiefly authority and with the expectation that the opening of the Panama Canal would bring new wealth to the islands. Support for such measures from naval and colonial departments in Paris, when it came, flowed from the momentary coalescence of political interests at home and abroad and did not demonstrate a coherent imperialist ideology.

The same was true of New Caledonia. The strength and success of the French presence lay with missionaries and some traders, though the islands were viewed more widely by British interests as virtually part of the colony of New South Wales. A French naval commander in 1844 did obtain a deed of cession from several local chiefs, but it was repudiated by the French government under British pressure. Colonial aspirations were resurrected under Napoleon III, and the island, along with the Isle of Pines, was formally annexed in 1853 by naval authorities. French motives ran the gamut from plans to establish a penal colony, through public pressure for reasons of national prestige, to competition with the British and their Australian colonies. Part of the equation leading to annexation was the imperialism of New South Wales settlers, who saw New Caledonia as a natural British domain, but after a flurry of agitation they settled down to wait for the islands to fall into Australian hands as part of its own manifest destiny. Though unable to stop French moves in New Caledonia, Australian fears did sway France to hold off annexing the New Hebrides and to enter into a joint governing arrangement with Britain.[16]

This curious, ambiguous concept of a shared obligation to rule, yet not to rule alone, symbolises the continuing shapelessness of imperialist ambitions on the part of European nations. Except for the brief period of the 'scramble' in the last quarter of the nineteenth century, European imperialism in the Pacific was made up of politicians in European capitals oscillating between enthusiasm and hostility, similar but unsynchronised waves of public fervour and indifference, a consistent resistance by state treasuries, and an irregular pattern of crises between islanders and European settlers. By the beginning of the twentieth century, no part of the island world was untouched by the spheres of power controlled by Europe and the United States. Most were firmly installed within an international legal framework as fragments of empire. A few, like Tonga, were held in looser forms of oversight. All were subject to that blend of force, or the threat of force, by European rulers and consent to foreign power on the part of local inhabitants, that held colonial empires in uneasy suspension at the beginning of the twentieth century. Yet while Europeans dominated the heights of the struggle that created the colonial empires in the Pacific—and the boundaries of the new states that eventuated—the terrain of those fragments continued to be largely controlled by the people whose homes they were and who, through their contribution to the colonial process, gave real shape to European imperialism in the twentieth century.

Notes

1 Sir John Seeley, *The Expansion of England*, 1883, quoted in *British Imperialism in the Nineteenth Century*, ed. C. C. Eldridge, Macmillan, London, 1984, 4.

2 R. Robinson and J. Gallagher, 'The Imperialism of Free Trade', *Economic History Review 6* (1,1953): 13. This article galvanised a fresh debate on the causes of imperialism in the nineteenth century.

3 V. I. Lenin, *Imperialism: The Highest Stage of Capitalism*, 1916, quoted in *The Theory of Capitalist Imperialism*, ed. D. K. Fieldhouse, Longmans, London, 1967, 108–109. This is a good anthology of classical readings on imperialism, with Fieldhouse's arguments attached.

4 R. Robinson, 'The Excentric Idea of Imperialism, With or Without Empire', in *Imperialism and After: Continuities and Discontinuities*, ed. W. J. Mommsen and J. Osterhammel, Allen & Unwin, London, 1986, 284. This book has an excellent last chapter summary by Mommsen, and fresh perspectives from Robinson, Schwabe, and others.

5 Peter Adams, *Fatal Necessity: British Intervention in New Zealand 1830–1847*, Auckland University Press and Oxford University Press, Auckland, 1977.

6 D. K. Fieldhouse, *Economics and Empire 1830–1914*. Macmillan, London, 1973, 242–244. This is the best general survey of imperial annexations, though it uses out-of-date sources for the Pacific.

7 D. Scarr, 'John Bates Thurston, Commodore J. G. Goodenough and Rampant Anglo-Saxons in Fiji', *Historical Studies Australia and New Zealand* 11 (1964): 361–382. See also his *Fiji: A Short History*, Allen & Unwin, Sydney, 1984, which is the best summary of the developing relations of Fijians and Europeans.

8 K. R. Howe, *Where the Waves Fall: A New South Sea Islands History from First Settlement to Colonial Rule*, Allen & Unwin, Sydney, and University of Hawai'i Press, Honolulu, 1984, 230–254.

9 Peter Hempenstall and Noel Rutherford, *Protest and Dissent in the Colonial Pacific*, Institute of Pacific Studies, Suva, 1984, 18–23 (has short introductory summaries of protest themes, with extended case studies); Mālama Meleiseā, *The Making of Modern Samoa: Traditional Authority and Colonial Administration in the History of Western Samoa*, Institute of Pacific Studies, Suva, 1987 (the best modern history of imperialism on the ground for any island).

10 Angus Ross, *New Zealand Aspirations in the Pacific in the Nineteenth Century*, Clarendon Press, Oxford, 1964.

11 This section is based on: Francis X. Hezel and Marjorie M. Driver, 'From Conquest to Colonization: Spain in the Mariana Islands 1690–1740', *Journal of Pacific History* 23 (1988): 137–155; Hempenstall and Rutherford, 98–118; Michael Kohler, *Akkulturation in der Sudsee: Die Kolonialgeschichte der Karolinen-Inseln im pazifischen Ozean und der Wandel ihrer sozialen Organisation*, Peter Lang, Frankfurt, 1982, 201–264.

12 Francis X. Hezel, *The First Taint of Civilization: A History of the Caroline and Marshall Islands in Pre-colonial Days 1521–1885*, Pacific Islands Monograph Series no. 1, University of Hawai'i Press, Honolulu, 1983, 290–318 (should be read in conjunction with Hezel's articles in the *Journal of Pacific History*); David Hanlon, *Upon a Stone Altar: A History of the Island of Pohnpei to 1890*, Pacific Islands Monograph Series no. 5, University of Hawai'i Press, Honolulu, 1988; Hempenstall and Rutherford, 106–118.

13 Klaus Schwabe, 'The Global Role of the United States and Its Imperial Consequences 1898–1973', in Mommsen and Osterhammel, 17–18.

14 C. M. Andrew and A. S. Kanya-Forstner, 'Centre and Periphery in the Making of the Second French Colonial Empire 1815–1920', *Journal of Imperial and Commonwealth History* 16 (May 1988): 9–28.

15 Colin Newbury, *Tahiti Nui: Change and Survival in French Polynesia 1767–1945*, University Press of Hawai'i, Honolulu, 1980, 102. Newbury's chapter 4 is a sound and comprehensive coverage of the processes of imperialist expansion.

16 John Connell, *New Caledonia or Kanaky? The Political History of a French Colony*, National Centre for Developing Studies, Australian National University, Canberra, 1987, 33–38. This is probably the best English-language update on the fractured history of New Caledonia under French influence.

3

Holland, Britain, and Germany in Melanesia

Judith A. Bennett

Empire was holding operation without a terminal date.

D. K. Fieldhouse

Colonialism in Melanesia touched thousands of lives and reordered destinies. Until World War Two, which was to engender further and more dramatic change, colonialism under one flag or another, and in more than one guise, had its most extensive effects on indigenous societies in the east in Fiji and New Caledonia and its least in Dutch New Guinea. That this gradient mirrored proximity to the equator is not a geographical coincidence. For Europeans, malaria was Melanesia's Cerberus. Buxton's line did not simply mark the border of the distribution of the malarial vector, the anopheles mosquito; it also represented the boundary of intensive settlement by Europeans in much of the pre-war period. Another barrier was size—the larger the island, the slower European penetration. Even as late as World War Two, large tracts of the interior of New Guinea were known only to the indigenous inhabitants, who had been there for millennia.

Formal government was not the only agent of colonialism. Christian missionaries, brown and white, were a potent force, having greater long-term effects than administrations because, in time, they spoke the language of the spirit and touched the world of the Melanesian. Often, as in the kingdoms of Polynesia, missionaries facilitated development of new law codes for many Melanesian societies. At times they co-operated with colonial governments; at others they opposed them. Some missionaries shared the racial prejudices of their contemporaries in government and business, but most tried to protect their converts from the excessive demands of these parties. To Melanesians at first, they were a puzzling people, for no Melanesians preached their particular cosmology to their neighbours, let alone devoted their lives to it.

Less puzzling were the European commercial interests. Early entre-preneurs traded in goods and men; later ones came to stay and take up land. They needed a colonial government to guarantee their possession and facilitate the procurement of labour; the government needed them to create revenues. Business and missionary interests occasionally coincided, sometimes clashed. Few missionaries criticised the fundamental premise that peace, ordered living, obedience to authority, and work itself (and, in many cases, working for the white man) were good things—and thus the activities of business and government had mission-given ideological underpinnings. But as gov-ernment, business, and mission were to discover, no people had a monopoly on Christianity; Melanesians took Christianity, scraped off its European patina, and acculturated it, as its hearers had been doing for over a millen-nium around the world.

For all the nineteenth-century diplomatic manoeuvring over Melanesia, its initial value for the colonial powers was not high. It had three uses—strategic in a pre-emptive sense; as a labour reserve for areas outside Melan-esia (except Fiji and New Caledonia); and as a source of tropical crops. Except for some minerals—mainly nickel, chromite, and gold—most of Melanesia had little but the potential for plantations to offer the European investor.

To make the plantation economies work and so underwrite the finances of a colonial administration, three basic needs of investors had to be met before anything else—abundant accessible land, a reliable source of cheap labour, and a peaceful population in areas of economic activity. In attempting to satisfy the first two needs, there was a strong likelihood of upsetting the last, as was the case in pre-cession Fiji. Because no colonial administration in a peripheral area like Melanesia wanted to expend huge sums of money on military 'pacification', wise administrators tried to maintain traditional societies—with some modifications to meet the demands of the capitalist mode of production. Capitalism, by its nature, disrupted subsistence-based societies where redistributive mechanisms plus the lack of storable valuables prevented the accumulation of wealth and its transmission over time.

Since there was no glittering prize in Melanesia, capitalism's effects had to be tempered.[1] One way was to give the Melanesians a place in the new order, to encourage a 'permanent economic alliance'.[2] At the minimum this meant lands for subsistence and providing the means to address Melanesian grievances in their relationships with the foreigners and, to some extent, with each other. Commercial interests then, as now, were rarely capable of the foresight to restrain their demands, so the colonial government's role was one of mediator between business and Melanesians. If it failed it would have to deal with any disruption caused by excesses. Part of this role was to prevent the development of new groupings based on a common interest that could be antagonistic to the capitalists and ultimately to the administration. Such groupings could evolve because of opposition to loss of leadership privilege among a chiefly class in some areas, to land alienation, to exploitation of labour, to excessive taxation, or, something more subtle, the loss of self-respect in the face of an oppressive and incomprehensible array of colonial power. To mobilise these transformations new ideologies developed, based occasionally on a secular synthesis of political accommodation, or more commonly on a reinterpretation of indigenous cosmologies, adaptations of Christianity, or a combination of both. In the Melanesian situation, the colonised also experimented with new ways of dealing with the colonisers by using Western colonial institutions and ideological arbiters such as the church and the legal system. As Melanesians perforce had to redefine themselves, the colonisers found that sometimes their own weapons could be used against them.[3]

Fiji

Unlike most of Melanesia, Fijian society was characterised by large tribal organisations that were potentially formidable in opposition. The signatures of Cakobau and the other coastal chiefs on the Deed of Cession of 1874 did not indicate universal consent to British rule. Many Fijians were disturbed by the new order, especially after a measles epidemic in 1875 carried off more than 20 per cent of the population. The inland tribes of west and central Viti Levu resisted the colonial government and its allies, the Bau-Lau clique of chiefdoms, in 1876. These 'friendly' tribes were instrumental in an inexpensive British victory in the 'little war' with the hill peoples.[4]

The government of Fiji, under Sir Arthur Gordon, then set about a plan that would make further Fijian resistance less likely and prevent the excesses seen in the Anglo-Maori wars in New Zealand in the 1860s. Fijian lands would be protected, although some earlier land sales to Europeans were recognised. Gordon and his successor, James B. Thurston, put in place 'native regulations' and labour laws designed to preserve the viability of the subsistence economy and the labour supply at no cost to employers.[5] Gordon also instituted a 'native administration' with a hierarchy of councils. Its apex, the Great Council of Chiefs, acquiesced and then supported Gordon's policy because it gave the chiefly class a definite role in the new order. Gordon persuaded himself that all this was a reflection of old Fiji, but in fact it was a new orthodoxy with an acceptable veneer of tradition.

The colonial apparatus still had to be funded. Fijians were to pay taxes-in-kind. The government acted as a central marketing system, selling the results by tender. It gave good returns: the government got its tax, which helped to pay Fijian chiefly functionaries; the districts and villages reaped a cash income when sales exceeded taxation due; and small traders, soon replaced by large concerns such as Burns, Philp of Australia in the 1890s, had a regular supply of produce to sell overseas at excellent profits. Fijians received some benefits from the cash economy, but stayed mainly in their villages, subject to chiefly disposition. Gordon's system of 'indirect rule' was an inexpensive and satisfying form of administration for most. Unique in Melanesia, its success in part rested with a common language and basic literacy, a legacy of missionary education from the mid-1830s on.[6]

To boost revenue further, Gordon and Thurston extended plantation agriculture, seeking labour outside Fiji so that what they saw as traditional Fijian society (and chiefly compliance) would be preserved. In pre-cession Fiji, the New Hebrides (now Vanuatu), the Solomons, and the Gilbert and Ellice Islands (now Kiribati and Tuvalu) had been the first reserves of labour for Fiji. To Gordon, however, the attendant abuses gave the labour trade a moral taint, while competition from higher-paying Queensland threatened the supply.[7]

Gordon began bringing Indians to Fiji in 1879. The British Indian government insisted on a four-to-ten ratio of female to male migrants, which allowed families to form. This was the flaw in Gordon's plan, for it provided the potential for a new class of landless proletarians within Fiji society.[8] The Indians supplied labour for planters and for the New South Wales–based Colonial Sugar Refining Company (CSR) which entered the colony in 1880 and, within twenty-six years, dominated the economy.

Early in the twentieth century, British policy shifted. The Fijian population, as with most indigenous peoples in the Pacific Islands, was declining rapidly, from 114 748 in 1881 to a nadir of 84 475 in 1901. Administrators saw a falling population making little use of land and felt that economic competition might stimulate the long-sheltered Fijians into a demographic resurgence. Governor Everard im Thurn encouraged a money tax and a cash substitute for communal services to force Fijians into the cash economy. The most significant change, in land policy in 1905, allowed limited freehold purchase and rental of unused Fijian land. Im Thurn made the mistake of criticising Gordon, then a revered member of England's House of Lords. Gordon's lobbying saw the law regarding alienation rescinded in 1908 after the sale of 104 412 acres. Even so, these changes were involving the Fijians more directly in capitalism and gradually undermining the control their chiefs had over them.[9]

At this unsettling time, about 1913, two figures emerged in Fiji who represented antithetical ways of dealing with the demands of capitalism and the declining importance of Fijians: Apolosi Nawai and Ratu Lala Sukuna. Nawai was a commoner from Ra who had a charismatic appeal as an orator and as a vessel of the spirits of old Fiji. He perceived that the European and Chinese traders were draining off profits that once accrued indirectly to Fijians under the old taxation-in-kind system. Nawai's solution was not based on district loyalties orchestrated by chiefs. He started the Viti Company to collect, market, and eventually transport the produce of the Fijian villagers. He attracted thousands. Tolerated at first by the administrators because he displayed commercial enterprise, his activities challenged not only European economic dominance, but also chiefly and colonial control, because the company had the potential of mobilising vast numbers of ordinary Fijians. Fortunately for the colonial government, Nawai's ignorance of financial recording and his misappropriation of funds provided an excuse to exile him in 1917, in 1930, and again in 1940.[10]

One of Nawai's sternest critics was Ratu Sukuna, who was connected to the Bau and Lau elites. Well educated in Fiji, New Zealand, and at Oxford, war hero decorated by the French, steeped in Fijian history and lore, Sukuna was both chief and competent second-generation colonial bureaucrat. His solution to the problems of Fiji society was not revolutionary, but reactionary. He sought a return to the rural idyll of the Gordon–Thurston era. He wanted the restoration of taxation-in-kind and of obligatory communal duties, the shoring-up of village social organisation, and the maintenance of the colonial order. This would certainly provide a better social-welfare system for Fijians and a good cash income for the community, not the individual. It would also provide the same for the chiefs, as their privileges would be reinstated.[11] And, although the idea was never enunciated, the Indians, as before, would provide the human subsidy not only for the colony's essential sugar industry, but also for the felicity of Fijian village life.

No longer could the Indians be taken for granted. In 1916, because of nationalist agitation in India over the degradation of those under indenture, migration of labour ceased, and all indentures in Fiji were to be cancelled in 1920. As the bulk of labour for the industry had to be obtained from the resident Indians—many of whom had the right to a free passage home—this gave the Indians a strong bargaining position.

By 1921 there were 60 634 Indians in Fiji. Disunited by cultural and religious disputes, neglected by the government and the Christian missions, the Indians had been exploited by the Colonial Sugar Refining Company. Profiteering merchants took advantage of them in the post-war years by holding the prices of basic commodities artificially high. Workers in Suva, Rewa, and Navua struck over this issue in 1920. By their numbers, the Indians were now revealed as a threat to the colonial order. The government forcibly put the strike down. The following year the sugar workers in rural areas began a strike for better wages and conditions that brought the sugar industry to a halt for almost six months. But without income, they could not hold out indefinitely. The strike ended with CSR reducing the Indians' cost of living, but refusing a wage increase.

Disillusioned with Fiji, many Indian workers decided on repatriation. This threat to the sugar industry was removed when the parlous state of repatriates in India became known. Meanwhile the Europeans had found allies in the Fijians, some of whom were employed as special constables against the strikers. During 1921, with chiefly support, the company employed Fijians to keep the plantations viable.[12]

The strikes represented an assertion of Indian rights as British subjects that strengthened in the 1930s as the Indians pushed for democratic representation in the Legislative Council. Representation would have given the increasing population of Indians near equality with the Fijians and a basis for ownership of the land they had been permitted only to lease from Fijians. Sukuna successfully opposed the move. Fijian interests were still dominant, but under challenge from the growth of unionism among Indians, when World War Two broke out.[13]

In part, though initially a clever solution to the colonial dilemma of balancing the demands of the capitalist state with maintaining the traditional order, British policy created long-term problems for the government of Fiji, whether colonial or independent. The policy's Achilles heel was the creation of a major group, partly based on class, and certainly on race, that was beginning to question the colonial government and European economic dominance. To counter this challenge and the unlikely marriage of Fijian and Indian interests, the political alliance between the Fijian chiefly elite and the colonial government was strengthened. In turn, chiefly control over ordinary Fijians and Fijian ownership of land were largely maintained.

New Hebrides

In French eyes, the New Hebrides was to be an extension of New Caledonia; instead it became a sphere of joint interest with Britain because of pressure by Australia, spurred by mission and business interests. For Australia, the New Hebrides was an imperial goal from the 1880s, much to Britain's consternation. These varying attitudes carried directly into policies concerning land, labour, and 'native administration'. France, although its settlers were to need labour for their plantations, had little regard for the fate of the Melanesians. As in New Caledonia, getting the land into the hands of settlers outweighed considerations of preserving the labour reserve. The British presence, critical but inactive, was a light brake on French ambitions, although its rigorous labour regulations could not be extended beyond its own subjects.

Conventions signed in 1887 and 1906 by France and Britain defined the responsibilities of each. Very little was done to administer the indigenous population, with France and Britain each remaining focused on their respective nationals. So skeletal was the dual administration that a head tax was never imposed.[14]

In regard to land, the French company, Société Français des Nouvelles Hébrides (SFNH) and planters claimed over 776 000 hectares (1 917 496 acres), mostly through paper purchases unknown to the inhabitants. Despite British discomfort, both governments in 1906 deemed these claims valid and legally questionable only on very limited grounds. Conflicts between settlers and inhabitants occurred as the newcomers moved onto the land. However, wholesale displacement did not eventuate because of the impossibility of occupying claims without settlers and, more significant, of the unavailability of labour to work them. Because demand exceeded supply, labour became increasingly expensive to the planters—wages, for example, trebled between 1902 and 1922 as Melanesians opted for short-term employment and earning cash by increasing their own copra production.[15]

France assisted its nationals by importing labour mainly from French Indo-China. By 1940, 21 915 Asians had come under five-year indentures. When bankruptcy threatened French planters during the Great Depression, the government absorbed most of the debts and the control of the leading company (SFNH). British planters could not employ French subjects and received no other help in the 1930s. Their numbers declined to 190, while the French remained around 760, a tiny reef of white settlers in a sea of 65 000 Melanesians who had already found ways to protest the massive alienation of their lands.[16]

In some islands where the Presbyterian missionaries had been active since the mid-nineteenth century, they had encouraged a form of local government, as had the Church of Christ. This consisted of courts made up of male elders, with punishments in the form of fines or labour on roads. Most Christians, forming roughly two-thirds of the population by 1914, lived on small islands or on the coasts of larger ones.[17] Because these people had access to copra groves, the missionaries encouraged them to work at home and not on the plantations, which the missionaries considered morally degrading to the Melanesians. These communities sometimes became over-enthusiastic in encouraging conformity to the mission. The inland bush people and their pagan customs were the objects of zealous attention, with Christianity very conveniently used to harass these old enemies of the coastal peoples. However, just as Christianity became a new weapon, backed by the resources of an influential mission, so too did the colonisers and their law, in a complex combination.

The Presbyterians, mainly Australians, disliked the French authorities because of their traditional Catholic sympathies and opposed French acquisition of land on these grounds and in natural justice. The French in turn saw them as agitators against their land and labour recruitment policies. Although too timid to push matters far, most of the British authorities supported the local governments under mission auspices, because they created a semblance of law and order which the Condominium had not.

Encouraged by their missionaries, New Hebrideans sought independent legal advice when the French prevented the Joint Naval Court's Native Advocate (established in 1906) from moving around the islands to investigate land problems. The lawyer, Edward Jacomb, in 1911 had already represented labourers who had come to him to complain of ill-treatment on plantations. The New Hebrideans contributed funds to pay Jacomb, who advised his clients to resist occupancy of the land claims. Resistance usually meant physical conflict and intervention by the Joint Naval Court, not disestablished despite the 1906 convention. As the French ship was the only one in the area, the French, representing the Joint Naval Court, arrested these objectors and others associated with the Presbyterians accused of 'extortion with threats' who had collected Jacomb's fee.

The bush people, on the other hand, allied themselves to the French because this was a way they could humiliate their coastal persecutors. When the French warship arrested the resisters, the French acknowledged the rights of the bush people to follow their customs and instructed the coastal people to disband their courts. French motives were transparent—without any help from missionaries or lawyers, the bush people would have only violence to fall back on when their own lands came to be absorbed; then a punitive expedition would be justified to quell them. In the meantime they provided much of the Melanesian labour force, and it was expedient to conciliate them.[18]

Through Protestant Christianity, large numbers of New Hebrideans found a new unity within a regime that sometimes seemed harsh to critical outsiders who did not always realise that the pre-Christian mores were equally if not more demanding. To the bush people, loyalty to old customs was a way of rejecting the foreign influence that had contaminated the coastal peoples. 'Custom' was becoming more self-conscious and more political.[19] Although it weakened some barriers between coastal neighbours, the advent of capitalism, colonialism, and Christianity had exacerbated ancient divisions between inland and coastal peoples based on varying environments and contact histories.

The conflicts generated by resistance to the French occupation of the lands, running from about 1911 to 1914, brought some respite for the New Hebrideans. Those arrested had been detained illegally for long periods. On behalf of an Epi man, Harry Wenham, Jacomb brought a writ of habeas corpus in the British National Court against the Joint Naval Commission, which Jacomb contended had no jurisdiction in the case. The legal furore that resulted, the deaths of some New Hebrideans in a French prison, plus Jacomb's highly critical book, *France and England in the New Hebrides*, forced British Colonial Office officials to examine the conditions in the Condominium and caused embarrassment to the French. Meetings in Europe in 1914 resulted in a protocol that set up a complex but workable legal system and a 'native administration' that gave wider protection to New Hebrideans in matters such as labour recruitment. Britain's concern was subsumed to its need for an ally in Europe in World War One, so the old position that gave the French almost incontestable rights over their land claims remained undisturbed. The rate of implementation of these changes is best reflected by the fact that the protocol signed in 1914 did not even begin to come into effect until 1922.[20] For all its chaotic if not farcical

nature, the imposition of the dual regime was never hurried in the archipelago because neither home government thought the islands of significance
beyond mere possession. France held on mainly because it hoped Britain
would let go; Britain held on because Australia forced it to, and none had
much concern for the islanders.

Papua   (British New Guinea)

During the period when Papua was under British control (1884–1906) and
subsidised by the Australian colonies, the administration concentrated on
acquainting the Papuans with its existence by means of extensive patrolling.
Sir William MacGregor, adminstrator from 1888 to 1898, was the moving
force for this policy, sometimes made more testing for both sides by the
discovery of gold, particularly in the northern district (1896) where the people
did not have a long experience of Western contact.[21]

Beside the discovery of gold there was virtually no economic development in Papua until the Australians assumed control in 1906. MacGregor's
philosophy, largely followed by Hubert Murray, was that administration
must precede 'civilisation'. Little land was taken up by investors who, during
the depression of the 1890s in Australia, had little excess capital.[22]

The push for investment in plantations in Papua came too late. Prices of
tropical products peaked from 1906 to 1913, with World War One inflating
prices but often interfering with access to markets. By 1920 world prices
began to fall and often fluctuated markedly. From 1906 to 1914 Australian
and British concerns showed interest in Papua, but the government's system
of ninety-nine-year leases was not attractive to planters who wanted freehold. The investing companies were undercapitalised. Although they took
up 59 693 hectares (147 500 acres) by 1911, only 9713 hectares (24 000 acres)
were cultivated by 1918, a situation that persisted until World War Two. As
Lieutenant-Governor Murray considered the labour supply limited, he
introduced stringent controls on the indenture system established by
MacGregor.[23]

Although most of the fifteen hundred white people in Papua thought
otherwise, these were not the fundamental reasons for the failure of the
plantation economy to expand. Australia's domestic preoccupations were
more important than its annexe, Papua. Australian protectionism denied
market access to Papuan produce until the late 1920s. The federal government applied the Navigation Act to Papua in 1921, driving up costs by forcing
all imports and exports to go via Australia until the act was repealed in
1925.[24]

Murray had been committed to the extension of white settlement and
also believed in the protection of the Papuans. This 'dual mandate' had
inherent contradictions, which, along with economic realities, altered

Murray's policies by 1918. World War One and the creation of the League of Nations had directed Western attention to the fate of dependent peoples. By then the Papuan population appeared to have stabilised, and white settlement and development were stagnating. Murray now emphasised the gradual encouragement of development by the Papuans—to force them to work as peasant proprietors and prevent them becoming a proletariat, the eventual slaves of the settlers. In 1918 he introduced the Native Plantation Ordinance, designed to get Papuans growing crops on their own land. An added incentive to the coercion within the ordinance was the introduction of an adult male head tax in 1919. Men could work on village plantations instead of paying the tax. As only half of the profits from these compulsorily worked plantations went back to the producers, these well-intentioned policies failed to stimulate viable production of cash crops.[25]

As elsewhere in Melanesia, settlers were vastly outnumbered by the estimated four hundred thousand Papuans.[26] Fear and racism often made the settlers nervous, and they demanded laws to protect themselves from the Papuans. In the towns of Port Moresby and Samarai, regulations governed native dress, native use of public facilities, the native curfew, and the beating of drums. Village regulations governed such matters as the growing of sufficient subsistence crops, the disposal and inheritance of property, movement from place to place, and village 'public works'. These regulations made it clear that the government not only controlled the Papuans in town but also dictated to them 'better' ways of looking after themselves in the subsistence sector. The indenture system was premised on the same principles. This constant interference in the minutiae of village life sapped traditional leadership.[27]

Settler unease was demonstrated in 1926. Following several sexual assaults on white females by Papuan males, none of which was a rape case, Port Moresby's white population was in uproar. For years, Murray had been the target of settler criticism for his refusal to allow an elected white legislative council and for his 'pro-native' policies. Murray bent under the pressure and consented to a new ordinance that established a mandatory death penalty for any male convicted of rape or *attempted* rape of a European female. Although in theory white men could be charged (but not under this ordinance) with similar offences against *native* females, none ever was. The law was aimed at Papuan men and was widely promulgated in the villages. Discriminatory about the race of the victim, it was also a Draconic law: only New South Wales and Victoria hanged rapists, and in all Australian states except Queensland attempted rape was only a misdemeanour. Before World War Two, two men, Miaro and Stephen Gorumbaru, were sentenced to death under this law, and the latter was hanged.[28]

All these laws reflect the deep-seated fears of the colonisers and the means by which the government sought to control the behaviour of the colonised, to keep them apart from the whites and each other and 'in their place'.

Large-scale Papuan resistance was impossible because of the indigenous polity and the introduced laws. One of the ways the Papuans 'managed' the Europeans and their impact was by incorporating them into the indigenous world-view. As Albert Maori Kiki from the Gulf district explained, the years before World War Two in the Pacific thrust great revelations on the Melanesians:

> *Our people had strange notions about Europeans in those days. They were supposed to be our dead relatives who had to change their appearance when they returned to live with us. Seeing us, their former brothers and children, they would often open their houses, but could never show their emotion in the open . . . for there was always a big man watching them. The slightest mistake they made, or any attempt on their part to betray their secret, and they were sent back to the island of the dead by the big man. We further believed that whenever one of our people died he would walk under the ground until he got to the home of a white man. There his body would be washed, and the 'bad' black skin would be taken off. Once he was all white, he would be put on the next ship sailing to the island of the dead.*[29]

Even this explanation of the European betrays a sense of superiority of white over black, indicating that the self-image of the Papuans suffered under the barrage of mild colonial policies in terms of material demands on Papuans. However, they were policies that dispossessed Papuans of their rights, and thus their confidence, to make often simple decisions about how to conduct their lives. In many ways, this colonisation of the consciousness was the worst feature of the colonial experience, in Papua and elsewhere.

Dutch New Guinea

British criticism, voiced by MacGregor of British New Guinea, awakened Dutch concern for West New Guinea in the 1890s, but as in the 1820s and 1840s it aimed at a token presence in the area. MacGregor had complained that the Dutch were not controlling the head-hunters in the Marind area on the south coast, who yearly would sweep across a border they knew nothing of and take heads to ensure their spiritual strength. Negotiations between the Hague and London ground on, resulting in an agreement for a Dutch military post in the area. For the first time, in 1898 the Netherlands government made a grant to administer West New Guinea. That year, the Dutch opened bases at Manokwari and Fak Fak in the north, to be followed after a long search for a southern site by one at Merauke in 1902. The start at Merauke was inauspicious. Despite barbed-wire fences and blockhouses, the head-hunters picked off the unfortunate Javanese convicts brought in as labourers to build the settlement, while the survivors succumbed to beriberi.[30]

It was no wonder that West New Guinea was seen as 'the Devil's own country' for government officials in the twentieth century. The Dutch sent their least trained and least competent officials, including Indonesians, to the outpost. Although the Dutch encouraged exploration of the interior, the administration clung to the coast. As in the New Hebrides, the missions often became the unofficial government of some regions. Until the 1930s the Dutch had little use for West New Guinea. They wanted neither labour nor land on a large scale, concentrating their attention on the rich East Indies. Even by the 1930s fewer than ten thousand acres (four thousand hectares) were alienated, let alone developed. Oil exploration gathered momentum in the 1930s under a consortium of Dutch, British, and American interests. By 1938 eleven hundred Papuans were employed in the industry and fewer than a thousand on Japanese and Dutch plantations.

Measured against the huge area of West New Guinea and the population of around seven hundred thousand, these operations were minor. Nonetheless, the Dutch presence changed the lives of the coastal people. Near their bases the Dutch acquired land for lease and forced the people into compact villages with a house for each nuclear family. As elsewhere in Melanesia, officials as well as missionaries wanted the people in places easy of access, but they frequently achieved this at the cost of ecological, agricultural, and pig-husbandry efficiency, so creating village tensions. When villagers tried to continue old practices, the Dutch destroyed garden houses. The people soon learned to use them as 'occasional places of rendez-vous rather than community centers'.[31] In societies that had no communal leaders other than heads of descent groups, the Dutch created 'chiefs' to direct the people.[32]

The Dutch found that without a demand for labour, taxation was difficult in the controlled areas in the early 1900s. They offered the alternative of taxation-in-kind in the hope that this would stimulate output of produce. In West New Guinea, unlike early Fiji, any excess over the tax often went into the pocket of the collector and not to the producer. Demands on controlled villages increased when in 1906 the Dutch, like the Germans, introduced forced labour for village work and roading around administrative centres.

Until 1941 the only medical work by the Dutch focused on large epidemics of venereal disease and smallpox on the coast. Education remained the province of the missionaries, although the Dutch government subsidised schools. By 1937 there were 15 200 pupils in mission schools. As in much of Melanesia, the missions did not develop the human secular intellect of their followers, nor, given the minimal impact of the West, did they see it as necessary. They concentrated more on Christianising than on teaching technical knowledge and skills.[33]

Melanesians had cosmologies based on religious epistemological systems. When faced with new, inexplicable forms of technology and power, the Papuans connected Christianity with material culture. The Christian message, devoid of Western technical culture and systems of knowledge, was not the response they required. Moreover, the experience of Papuans on plantations and later in oil exploration provided few models for acquiring the secret of the material wealth of the foreigners. With limited information available, Papuans melded bits of Western (and Asian) technology, the varied behaviour of the foreigners, and the new religions to both their existing cosmological conceptions and their perception of relative deprivation.

The resultant mix was 'cargo cult'. There were many cults, varying enormously with time, place, and the needs of the Papuans. Several of the cults of the north-west coast and the adjacent islands, including Biak, have the longest recorded pedigrees in Melanesia, dating back to the 1850s and 1860s and centring on the Mansren myth. Mansren, an old man, obtained creative power and youth by capturing the morning star, Kumeseri. Mansren married a beautiful young woman who bore him a son. In his voyages around the north-west, Mansren created features of the landscape and social groups. While his people believed in him, he took care of all their needs. However, when a woman doubted he could save her son, Mansren abandoned his followers and the people suffered and died. They held to the hope that one day Mansren would return and bring again the Golden Age, without sickness, death, and deprivation. From 1867 on, each decade saw the rise of various *konor* (heralds) or manifestations of Mansren. Once the Dutch established posts on the islands they exiled or imprisoned the *konor*. By 1911 leading *konor* were preaching passive resistance to the payment of tax and compulsory labour after the Dutch had forcibly put down Papuan protest in 1906, at Mankuker and Arwan.[34]

Each phase of the movement incorporated altered strategies, as well as new aspects of introduced technology and eventually Christianity. For example, small steamships with trade goods called at the Geelvinck Bay area in the second half of the nineteenth century; by 1886 a prophet predicted the coming of a ship full of goods for the people—a recurring theme strengthened by the inclusion of New Guinea on a major shipping network after 1892.[35] These cults were centred on the Biak–Geelvinck Bay area, where mission-based education had been concentrated from the 1850s, and where by 1940 there were thirty thousand converts on Biak and Supiore alone. Christian elements were used to explain why the Dutch, including the missionaries, had failed to give the Papuans the true knowledge—the whites had torn out pages of the Bible to hide that Christ was a Papuan. In continuing to suppress the movements and by imprisoning the *konor*, the Dutch in a sense confirmed Papuan suspicion that the whites were hiding much: they had stolen the cargo that Mansren and the ancestors had meant for the Papuans.

In 1939 a sick old woman, Angganita, miraculously regained her health and became a *konor*. She openly preached resistance against the Dutch, foretelling the coming of ships with cargo from the ancestors. The Dutch put her in gaol, resulting in riots on Biak. About this time, events of World

War Two became part of the Mansren movement ideology. Holland was defeated, and Mansren was now able to leave there and come back via Germany or Japan (i.e., the enemies of the Dutch). Cultural reassertion strengthened, and the movement spread. As the Japanese advanced south, Angganita's successor, Stephanus Simiopiaref spoke of a Papuan empire ranging from Gebe to Hollandia. Following the internment of the Dutch, all the good things that had been appropriated by them would be delivered by the Japanese. However, the Japanese failed to realise the Papuans' hopes. Recognising the political threat inherent in the movement, the Japanese suppressed it—to the point of machine-gunning Mansren followers in July 1942 near Rani. The aim of the movement then became the overthrow of the Japanese, who in turn stepped up their cruelties. A new saviour was at hand in the form of the American troops who defeated the Japanese, but they too left Dutch New Guinea. During and after the war in some areas, cults such as the Mansren complex on Biak became more and more political in a secular sense, yet elsewhere, such as Muji near Merauke where Western contact was later and less intense, the 'cargo' element predominated.[36]

German New Guinea (Company rule)

In German New Guinea there was no disguising of the foundation of policy: the colony had to make money. The German Reich gave a charter to the New Guinea Company in 1885 to set up an administration. Except for a brief period from 1889 to 1892 when the Reich assumed responsibility, the company was the government in New Guinea until 1899, when administration passed entirely to the Reich.

The company concentrated on the north-east coast of the New Guinea mainland (Kaiser Wilhelmsland) around Astrolabe Bay, an area with practically no experience of Europeans, unlike the Bismarck Archipelago. There, coastal people had been involved in trading since the early nineteenth century, when whalers visited for supplies, followed in time by traders, and, later, planters. The people of the Astrolabe Bay region, resentful of the company's spurious claims which diminished lands available for subsistence, soon reacted violently and continued to do so at various times from 1886 to 1899. They refused to work for the Germans. Without local workers and with none of the anticipated German settlers who were to buy the land it claimed, the company concentrated on plantations, working them with labourers from Asia as well as from the New Guinea islands.

Astrolabe Bay proved a charnel-house for the newcomers. Endemic malaria affected them all, as did dysentery and exotic diseases such as smallpox and influenza. The harsh German labour regime added further to the insalubrity of the place for labourers, of whom about half died by 1899. These losses paralleled the company's finances—by 1899, nine million marks had been buried, like the dead, in the soil of Kaiser Wilhelmsland.

Company rule failed to produce profits because, in a sense, profit was its obsession. It did not try to bring to the immediate coast and hinterland a settled administration that would have facilitated a regular labour supply acclimatised to the area. It failed to incorporate the local peoples into the new economic order. To protect its officials and workers it relied on raids to retaliate for 'offences' by the local people. Its history is a case study of how not to run a colony. Yet the Reich, because of political pressure at home, saved the New Guinea Company propping it up after it relinquished control of the colony in 1899. With the colonial government paying it four hundred thousand marks annually for ten years, plus rights to take up fifty thousand hectares of land in Kaiser Wilhelmsland, it continued to be the dominant company in the area until 1916.[37]

German New Guinea (Reich)

In terms of administration, the New Guinea Company's impact on the Bismarck Archipelago had been minimal, as Imperial Judge Albert Hahl found (1896–1898). As governor (1902–1914), Hahl tried to establish a systematic administration in both the islands and the mainland, where the still largely unknown population numbered about two million. Yet always the needs of commerce and the demands of the settlers dominated. Where the people retaliated against Europeans because of often-forced recruiting of labour, where new plantations were attacked, or where abundant labour was available, the flag followed trade. Because the flag followed and did not precede trade, the violence typical of Company rule continued. To punish quickly, Hahl raised a local police force of six hundred men, the largest in Melanesia (excluding New Caledonia).[38]

Hahl wanted to get the Melanesians involved in the new economy as producers of labour, copra, and taxes, and as consumers of trade goods, all of which suited the commercial interests in the colony. In 1903 he introduced forced labour to build roads around the Gazelle Peninsula, facilitating the traffic of food and labour to plantations. By delaying until 1906 the introduction of a head-tax to substitute, if required, for forced labour, he lessened the likelihood of resistance. The delay also meant that if men did not want to do compulsory government labour they would have to seek work on plantations to find the tax money. What annoyed the planters was that some people extended their production of village copra. To carry out his policies at village level, Hahl established the *luluai* system of appointed village officials to help with labour recruitment, organization of road gangs, and collection of taxes. Beyond this the Melanesians were left to themselves.[39]

However, Hahl's labour policies had no support from the planters. Hahl wanted restrictions on the recruitment of women and a 'closed season' approach in areas where depopulation had occurred. The subsistence society had to be preserved because it determined the health of the plantation economy. Hahl, like Murray in his early years, believed that the New Guineans had more than enough land, but seeing the problems on the Gazelle Peninsula in the 1890s, he introduced a system of reserves for the local Tolai people, to ensure they had land for subsistence.[40]

Commercial interests with metropolitan political clout bedevilled Hahl. He was forced to allow the New Guinea Company 5500 hectares around Madang in Astrolabe Bay. As the company cleared land between 1900 and 1904, the original inhabitants were dispossessed. In 1904 the people of Astrolabe Bay organised to rid themselves of about a hundred whites, both planters and missionaries. The plan, centered on the use of ex-policemen from the villages concerned, was betrayed by Nalon of Bilia. The police met the eighty armed men, killing one of them; six were later hanged.

By this time the Madang people no longer believed the Germans to be kindly deities as they had at first, but their material superiority had still to be explained. The belief developed that local deities, Kilibob and Manup, had created the advanced technology, but that the New Guineans in mythical times had rejected it. Their own stupidity had got them into the impasse with the Germans. But one version of the Madang myth held out hope: when the two deities returned they would bring the goods of the whites to the New Guineans, including their weapons. Meanwhile, the Madang people remained sullen and unco-operative. Eventually there was talk of another plot to kill the Europeans in Madang in 1912. The government acted quickly, rounding up suspects and banishing villagers to outer areas, effectively breaking resistance for the rest of the German period.[41]

The experience of the Madang people contrasted with that of the Tolai, who lost less land. There had been several conflicts between the Tolai and the foreigners in company times, and the last, in 1902, focused on Tolai assertion of sovereignty over the land. Hahl did not solve the problems of plantations encroaching on 40 per cent of all Tolai land, but he eased it for the time with the concept of reserves. Tolai prospered during the German regime because of the fertility of the Gazelle area. First, as traders and copra growers they had forced up the traders' prices. Second, the Tolai leader, To Bobo of the Vunamami district confederation, persuaded Hahl of the wisdom of the Tolai keeping land planted in coconuts as well as in subsistence crops. These reserves of alienated land had to be planted and populated with Tolai or else 'revert' to the foreigners. To Bobo lowered the bride-price, so early marriage and population increased. Throughout the Gazelle area planting went ahead, and by 1914 some 80 per cent of all native copra in the archipelago came from there, about 15 per cent of German New Guinea's total exports. The Tolai traded along the German roads. With the help of the Catholic and Methodist missions they obtained some formal education and health services, gaining, with economic prosperity, the edge over their neighbours in the new society created by colonialism.[42]

The Madang and the Tolai are contrasting examples that, with variations, could be multiplied across the frontier along the coasts of the colonial state from the Admiralties to Bougainville, from Aitape to Morobe. Overall, in terms of capitalist development, the German government was successful, despite its inauspicious start under Company rule. Copra exports alone in 1913 were 14 526 tonnes, eleven times those of Papua and almost three times those of the Solomons.[43] That the labour force was only double that of Papua demonstrates the extent of local copra production, the fertility of the islands, and the efficacy of Hahl's approach. It created an infrastructure for development, particularly in building roads, which were virtually non-existent in the rest of western Melanesia, but the human cost was higher.

New Guineans were probably the lowest-paid workers in Melanesia. Apart from the alienation of land—often, as in Astrolobe Bay, accompanied by impoverishment of the local people—about one quarter of some one hundred thousand labourers, Hahl estimated, died under the indentures so often forced on men and some women before 1914. The overall death rate for Melanesians in New Guinea was higher than in, say, Queensland or the Solomons, or for Indians in Fiji. The conditions of indenture, with the possible exception of the French in the New Hebrides, were the harshest, with flogging a standard punishment. The Germans were tough colonists and killed more Melanesians than either the Dutch, the British, or the Australians.[44] Hahl's ideas of fostering the labour force were received sympathetically by a concerned colonial department just before the war, but it seems that, had planters had their way, their New Guinea might have become another New Caledonia.

The Mandate of New Guinea

When World War One broke out in 1914, Australian troops occupied the German colony. The military controlled German New Guinea until 1921, when it became a mandate of Australia, which had to submit reports of its guardianship to the League of Nations. In practice, the mandate was treated as an Australian territory, like Papua. The military regime was often inept, but tried to maintain the status quo. Administrative control shrank, although the military continued to aid the recruitment of labour and to collect taxes (ten shillings a year) with greater severity than the Germans. Copra production and the number of labourers increased. When the Australian government expropriated all German property, selling it off to Australian companies like Burns, Philp and W. R. Carpenter and to Australian soldier settlers, its value as a capital asset had improved. Commercial concerns influenced Australian policy. Burns, Philp's island manager, Walter Henry Lucas, was one of three commissioners to conduct an inquiry into the future of New Guinea in 1919 and later the head of the Expropriation Board. Atlee Hunt, secretary of the Department of Home and Territories (Australia), and Murray were the other two. Lucas and Hunt opted for continued economic development of New Guinea, separate from Papua. Murray's attempt to extend his policies to New Guinea failed.

For the colonial economy, the 1920s were buoyant enough, despite the Navigation Acts that limited New Guinea as much as they had Papua. The New Guinea plantation economy was more mature and able to sustain early losses; the Australian ex-servicemen were not, and, with the Great Depression, their mortgages fell into the hands of Burns, Philp and Carpenter's. New Guinea's economy was largely carried by gold, discovered in 1928. By 1938 it provided a third of the mandate's export earnings. As early as 1926 New Guinea's administration was locally financed, and policies aimed at keeping the economy functioning dominated. Both mines and plantations needed workers. By 1938, 7000 workers were indentured to mining concerns, and 21 000 to plantations. Despite the depression the total indentured labour force was the largest in Melanesia, at 41 000 in 1939, a huge increase from 17 500 in 1914.[45]

In one sense Australian policy followed German: new country, such as Sepik and Morobe, was opened to administration when new labour reserves or mineral resources were discovered. However, in 1925 the Uncontrolled Areas Ordinance forbade any European from entering areas beyond government control. Consequently the frontier, extended through government patrols, was less violent in terms of loss of life than in early German times or even in MacGregor's Papua, but the new administration introduced the same kinds of 'native regulations' as in Papua; in this Papua and New Guinea were alike, as were their white settlers. Racist attitudes reflecting both fear and arrogance set up barriers between the races, especially where both lived in proximity in the town.

Rabaul in 1929 had the nearest thing to an urban proletariat in western Melanesia. About three thousand New Guinean workers were living in the vicinity—plantation labourers, mission and government employees, stevedores, boat crew, police, cooks, and domestic servants. Yet this was not a landless proletariat because there was always enough land for subsistence at home and because of the moving labour frontier, reflecting the distaste of Melanesians for indentured labour when they had a choice.[46]

The Rabaul workforce consisted of transients who depended on wage labour and their employers for shelter. New Guineans had little access to information except by word of mouth aided by the spread of New Guinea Pidgin and by direct observation. These sources were sufficient to teach some in Rabaul that the white men had a higher living standard than New Guineans, that New Guineans worked hard for low wages, and that although the country was exporting copra and gold, little wealth came to the people. Violent protest was futile, as decades of punitive raids had proved. A small group of New Guineans decided to strike for higher wages. One of the leaders, Sumsuma from the Tanga Islands, was captain of a schooner owned by the Expropriation Board and had travelled around the islands and recruited labour. Sometimes, with bonuses, he earned £7 on top of his wage of £5 a month, while ordinary workers got about five shillings, a disparity that began to concern him. During 1928, through various conversations with other men off coastal vessels, Sumsuma learned about strikes. He sought an ally, the senior sergeant major of the New Guinean division of the police force of about two hundred, N'Dramei from Manus Island. They planned to ask for a wage of £12 a month for all workers. They decided to assemble all workers outside Rabaul at the Catholic and Methodist missions, which they thought would be safe places for negotiations with the Europeans. In late December 1928, the word spread. Although some refused to take part and even told their employers (who disbelieved them), on the evening of 2 January 1929 more than three thousand men stopped work and walked to the mission stations. At dawn the next day the surprised missionaries urged the men to disperse. The strikers had no recourse, because they had not anticipated the missionaries' refusal to assist. Eventually workers drifted back to work. European reaction was swift. The planters and other whites blamed the soft policies of the administration; some blamed 'Bolsheviks' or a white mastermind.

The significance of the strike was twofold. First, it showed that given the means of communication and interaction, men from different areas could co-operate in a common cause. Second, it revealed the depth of European insecurity. This community did not want to see the New Guineans as more than a mindless labour force. A few months after the strike, when the administration planned to send seven young men to Queensland for further education, the Citizens' Association of Rabaul successfully protested. The strike had shown that New Guineans could organise across local and district barriers; educate them and they might revolt entirely against the colonial order.

Settler pressure resulted in harsh punishment of those involved in the strike. By twisting a vague clause in the Queensland Criminal Code, the administration charged the leaders with conspiracy to commit an offence. Of them, twenty-one were sentenced to three years' confinement, twelve to terms varying from twelve to thirty months. Most served their sentences as labourers on the goldfields, carrying fifty-pound loads in the mountainous jungle between Salamaua and Wau, where several died.[47]

Not far from the Wau region in inland New Guinea, village life proceeded untouched by the Rabaul strike, or for that matter, the colonial administration. For example, the Foraba speakers of the Tehera region saw their first government patrol and white people in 1929 and exchanged a stone axe for a steel knife. During the 1930s, government patrols and miners came into central New Guinea from the south and east. Although steel goods were soon appreciated, the New Guineans demanded various shells that were prized by people who had never seen the sea and thought they grew on trees. The miners, missionaries, and patrols in the Wahgi Valley and adjacent areas introduced, in exchange for food and portage, new shells by the ton. Their helpers from the coast also took part in the trade, bartering empty tins for fresh food, for example. This influx had a huge inflationary effect on exchanges such as marriage. The newcomers tried to control prices, but the people's demand soon set the pace of exchange. In one sense their 'strikes' for higher returns were far more successful than that of their sophisticated contemporaries in Rabaul, for they could still dictate conditions to the vulnerable newcomers. Although World War Two ended patrols for years, and the economic and ceremonial aspects of societies in central New Guinea had been modified by a handful of white men distributing new or superior goods, lives were still lived very much on New Guinean terms. Inland people continued to trade not simply new goods, but also the usual items, such as salt, pigs, feathers, and seeds. Many thousands of these people would not encounter the Australian colonial government until after the war. New Guinea, more than other places in Melanesia, did not invite easy colonisation.[48]

British Solomon Islands Protectorate

In line with British policy, the first administrator, C. M. Woodford, who arrived in 1896, immediately set about encouraging investment, because the protectorate needed revenue. Along with Papua, the Solomons did not have a substantial planter-settler community at annexation. Woodford made land available on long lease (999 years) by simply declaring some seemingly unoccupied land in the Western Solomons 'waste'. He permitted freehold sale until 1912, when the government became the sole buyer and lessor of land to prevent speculation. Britain's Lever Brothers was a major investor, along with Burns, Philp subsidiaries and other Australian-based companies.

Land had to be secured, a task that was not easy given Woodford's scant resources. His first assistant, Arthur Mahaffy, arrived in 1898 and was posted to the New Georgia group, home of raiding head-hunters. Using an armed militia from Santa Isabel, Mahaffy 'pacified' the Roviana, Simbo, and Mbilua head-hunters by wrecking their canoes and destroying coastal settlements. Such raids typified the extremes of government activity in the west until 1909 and in the east until about 1916, although Malaita and inland Guadalcanal took little cognizance of the government until the late 1920s and early 1930s. Compared to, say, German New Guinea, the number of punitive raids and killings was small, reflecting the relative accessibility of the Solomons archipelago, and, more important, the size of the population, which in 1893 was probably not greater than one hundred thousand. However, the Christian missions, especially their indigenous teachers such as Jone Hopa, Emosi Tozaka, and Stephen and Molu Gadepeta (Methodists), and David Sango (SSEM), can take much of the credit for preaching and bringing peace to large areas of the Solomons.[49]

Labour was just as essential to plantation development as were settled conditions. Since the late 1860s the Solomons had been a labour reserve for Queensland, Fiji, and Samoa. When Queensland closed in 1906, Woodford and the planters were anxious to see the flow to Fiji diverted locally. Even when this happened in 1911, there was still a labour shortage. By 1914, 463 425 acres (187 548 hectares) or about 5 per cent of the land in the Solomons had been alienated. This would need a labour force of at least forty-six thousand. Both the planters and the colonial administrators tried to persuade the British government to permit the entry of Asian labourers, but the costs were too high and the likely reaction from Australia too risky. When it seemed that the Asian solution was beyond reach, the administration from 1921 to 1923 introduced an adult male tax that was designed to 'encourage' recruiting. However, the maximum number of recruits offering, sixty-five hundred, remained about the same and came from Malaita, south Guadalcanal, and parts of San Cristobal.

By the early 1920s the government had enforced a reasonable set of regulations for the supervision of indentured workers and their employers, but plantation life was very demanding of labourers.[50]

As in the mandate, the Great Depression saw the merchant and shipping companies of Burns, Philp and W. R. Carpenter foreclose on the many white planters in their debt. Levers' and Burns, Philp's subsidiaries economized by cutting management, amalgamating plantations, and producing better quality copra. However, the Solomon Islanders bore the brunt of the greatest economies—their wage was cut by half in 1934. More significant, the number of those employed was also reduced by half, yet still produced the same amount of copra as before 1930. In some cases the price for this was the abuse of labour regulations that had characterised the plantation system prior to World War One. Labourers, especially Malaitans, who made up two-thirds of the work force, responded with active and passive resistance to ill-treatment, ranging from beating of overseers to go-slow tactics and boycotts of specific plantations. However, partly because of the nature of plantation society—scattered plantations and regular turn-over of the male workforce—and because of the limited political organisation of Malaitan and Guadalcanal societies operating on the big-man system, resistance, though continual, was not large scale or co-ordinated.[51]

Other Solomon Islanders in the western and central Solomons developed strategies to both manage and exploit the colonial forces in the western Solomons. For example, the Methodist mission began evangelisation in 1902, just when government pacification was reducing political and economic opportunities in the traditional order and the population had declined as a result of European contact. Gradually, conversion spread as the mission offered new life in its health services and new learning in its schools. It intervened to prevent killing in punitive raids at Marovo and Mbilua in 1909. Whatever their specific motivation, by the 1920s many of the western people participated in mission activities. Because older chiefs had often allowed their children to be educated by the mission, by then the younger chiefs were mostly Christians.

To see Christianity as something imposed on Solomon Islanders would be misleading . They chose it for their own purposes. In the main, it served them well, providing an institutional framework through which they could both address and seek redress from the government. In the early 1930s, the leading chiefs of the eastern New Georgia Islands objected to the rate of tax in times of depression. In September 1933 they met with the Methodist chairman, J. F. Goldie. Goldie then communicated their views to the government, stating that the annual tax of £1 was inequitable because copra earnings had fallen by four-fifths. The chief of Roviana, Boaz Sunga, wrote letters to chiefs of the district to organise a meeting at Gizo to petition for a reduced tax. Soon after, Sunga and a candidate for the ministry, Belshazzar Gina, led six hundred people to present their case to the district officer at Gizo, using Goldie as interpreter and adviser. The Methodist Synod had already protested to the government, and after the district officer imprisoned tax defaulters, Goldie threatened to involve the Colonial Office in Britain. Some of the leading chiefs continued the line of passive resistance. A rise in the price of copra gave some respite, but when copra prices fell again in 1937, the concerted, articulate protests of people and mission had persuaded the government to apply the tax with five- to six-hundred exemptions, compared to only two in 1933.

A few years later an Anglican priest, Richard Fallowes, accepted a similar role from his co-religionists in the central Solomons; for leading the movement and presenting petitions for political representation for islanders as well as mild reforms, he was deported.

Government and missions in the Solomons were allies in wider questions, but it was an uneasy alliance because the missions, with their spiritual dimension and universal aspect, always had far more potential to provide a new unity: such a unity among its subjects was something a numerically weak and financially strained Solomons administration feared. In the 1930s throughout the western and central Solomons, people were organising themselves on a regional basis backed by Christianity; elsewhere the plantation experience was teaching former enemies about each other and often providing them with a common history of oppression and resistance for future association.[52]

Conclusion

Imperial concern in Melanesia stemmed from the politics of the periphery, much of which was pre-emptive: get one's own dog into the manger first.

In Melanesia and elsewhere, the loose threads of colonial interest in places distant from Europe had to be sewn up and neatened lest they pulled and unravelled vaster imperial patterns of real significance to the Europeans.

Policies and processes of annexation were one thing, the practices of administration another. All worked under budgetary constraints, although France was willing to underwrite loans to its citizens to uphold its presence in the New Hebrides. Britain kept tighter control on spending, persuading the Australian colonies to contribute to British New Guinea and making Fiji and the Solomons self-financing within a few years. Only the British administration in the New Hebrides ran on a grant for decades, but expenditure was always minimal. From 1907 the German colonial government, burdened with compensatory repayment to the company, was tightening its budget in the face of reduced grants from Germany and ordering its policies along more British lines. Australia kept Murray out of the mandate to continue economic development after the German model because Murray's Papua cost Australia money.

Where revenue had to be found primarily from within a colony, administrative policies treated the indigenous people as an asset to economic development. 'Protective' measures were taken to preserve their reproduction in the subsistence sectors of Fiji, the Solomons, Papua, and the mandate. Although New Guinea was the most heavily subsidized of all Germany's colonies until 1908, Hahl recognised the necessity of preserving the indigenous population in the face of settler demands. He and Murray had much in common, though Murray was under less pressure because of Papua's insignificance to Australia. France had no Hahl and certainly no Murray in the New Hebrides, so the only protection for the people was somewhat impotent British scrutiny and their own increasing unwillingness to sign indentures.

This did not mean that Melanesians were disenchanted with the cash economy; it signalled participation, but on Melanesian terms. Certainly by the 1920s this could not be an entirely free choice, because all colonial powers, except in the Condominium, imposed taxes. In early Fiji and Dutch New Guinea this policy was moderated by the alternative of taxation-in-kind. In German New Guinea it benefitted from the backlash of the unpopular alternative of compulsory labour. Although the most protectionist of administrators, Murray eschewed forced labour, but in reality he forced Papuans to work on village plantations that produced scant return to them. If he, like the British in the Solomons, had levied only a cash tax, it is probable that the Papuans, like Melanesians everywhere, would have expanded the alternative of producing crops to sell for cash. Instead, village production in Papua languished because there was little surplus labour left for individual production after the needs of subsistence, government plantations, and commercial plantations were met. Of course, not every Melanesian could produce cash crops or collect, say, reef products for sale. In some areas, usually away from the seaboard in places of dense population, life was harder; the people had only their labour to sell.

Inland, little land was alienated or, if alienated, little was occupied. Where alienation was under way on the coast, administrators who wished to safeguard the labour reserve set aside land for subsistence needs. Although slow to be adopted in German New Guinea, this was British and Australian policy from the start, except in the Condominium, where French claims on land were outrageous. Outside Fiji, what often seemed empty or 'waste' land to administrators was frequently insufficiently examined for native ownership, resulting in extensive disputes. Administrators had no understanding of the large areas of land needed for Melanesian slash-and-burn horticulture. Much freehold transfer was misunderstood by the Melanesians, most of whose societies had no equivalent.

Some administrations, such as the Dutch, the British in the Solomons (by 1912), and the Australians, favored government purchase and long leases of land. This was not to provide for the future of the indigenous population, but to prevent speculation and underdevelopment of land (which occurred in the New Hebrides) as well as to create rents for the government. Lack of capital often retarded progress, as in Papua, while shortage of labour was a problem in the Solomons and the New Hebrides; by comparison, the Germans were less troubled by such difficulties before the end of their regime. None of these problems concerned the Dutch, as the Indies was their investment area. West New Guinea was little more than a buffer zone, a relic of their seventeenth-century economic strategy, until oil and mineral discoveries seemed likely in the 1930s. However, throughout the 1920s the fall in prices for tropical products, especially vegetable oils, that culminated in the Great Depression, was in much of Melanesia the most significant factor to limit the expansion of European holdings, whether under lease or freehold.

If the depression stymied settler ambitions, World War Two and the massive shift in the locus of world power from Europe to America completed their demise. Because of the settlers' incessant demands for cheap land and labour, their interests were diametrically opposed to those of the indigenous people. Administrators, even those with good intentions, found it difficult to combine the welfare of both groups unless an expedient like the Fiji 'solution' could be introduced. Elsewhere, as long as administrators could control the legislative apparatus, the indigenous people had a better chance of life beyond mere existence. Yet the goal of the administrators in preserving much of traditional society in the face of settler demands was, given limited capitalist penetration, to underwrite existing commercial enterprise and prevent the growth of a wider group identity among the indigenous peoples. It was an impossible balancing act that weighed eventually on the Melanesians' side (except in New Caledonia)—far more by the accidents of climate, disease, the weak colonial economies of Australia and New

Zealand, distance from markets, and the Great Depression, than by any widespread resistance by the people themselves.

In terms of the place and future of the Melanesians and their lands, the colonial 'development' goals during this era were 'pacification' for areas of economic potential, and marginal but controlled involvement in the cash economy. With limited budgets, colonial governments saw these goals as central to the sustaining of the bases of the capitalist economy—plantations and, in some places, mining. In many areas, by the 1920s, Melanesians on their own initiative were increasingly selling produce for cash, which annoyed planters, who preferred surplus labour to be channelled to their plantations. Governments were less alarmed because cash paid taxes and this involvement kept Melanesians content with the status quo.

Except for Britain in pre-cession Fiji, no imperial power saw in the fragmented polities and traditional technologies of Melanesia the faintest harbingers of a nation-state. Progress, even purely economic or of a welfare nature in education and health, would necessarily be slow. Any political development, beyond the micro-politics of local groups, was so far in the future as to be beyond contemplation. And no one was in a hurry. In the late nineteenth and early twentieth centuries, the establishment of administrative control largely rested on the old 'divide and rule' tactics of any coloniser. In much of Melanesia, divisions were already so embedded that there was no need to manufacture them.

Following World War One, the League of Nations highlighted the need for the promotion of social progress among colonial peoples, Melanesia was the last carriage on everyone's imperial train: a huge, economically unpromising region with an almost infinite number of socio-linguistic groups in difficult terrain, touched by a small expatriate population on its fringes. Before anything else, Melanesia had to start to pay for itself and its administration. Whether this was achieved or not, commercial interests supported by clamorous racist settlers were to be fostered before any indigenous development. Colonial policies reflected such attitudes—some, like the French, the New Guinea Company, and the British in Fiji, with little forethought to long-term outcomes for the people and the land. In western Melanesia particularly, any grand ideas of indigenous social progress and education, such as were prefigured by the early Murray and discussed by the British Colonial Office in the 1930s, were frozen as the Great Depression reduced the colonial establishment to mere survival mode just when the apparent indigenous population decline was turning around. The depression reinforced the colonial notion that time was a near-infinite factor: retrenchment and holding on remained practice until World War Two changed everything. Especially in western Melanesia, just as some of the colonised began to develop more effective strategies for dealing with the colonisers, Melanesian gains and new aspirations were eroded by this economic catastrophe beyond the control of both. The depression's onset also saw the first questionings of the incoming economic system by Melanesians, who found wages and returns from produce suddenly and inexplicably reduced and greater output forced from them on plantations. The Fiji Indians, far more dependent on wages for their livelihood, had questioned this policy earlier, in 1920. Such reactions were to feed the discontent that crystallised in some areas under the catalyst of the Pacific War.

Until the war, most of the comings and goings of colonial rulers, the redrawing of colonial borders, to say nothing of the reasoning behind such actions, eluded practically all Melanesians. Although their political nous was equal to that of the European, it seldom extended beyond village or region, and the colonisers tried to keep it that way. Melanesian comprehension—retarded by language, illiteracy, and lack of information—was as limited as the Australian military's conversance with New Guinea Pidgin when the demise of the German regime was proclaimed in 1914: 'No more 'um Kaiser, God save 'um King.'[53]

What mattered to the Melanesians was what happened to them and the meaning they took from those events. The very first contacts with Europeans, whether enemies or ancestors, were traumatic enough. For three generations in some coastal areas the foreigners came and went. When they came to stay, to demand not only labour for a few years, but also to take land and sovereignty, the multitudinous Melanesian worlds were shaken and transformed. Adjustment of this magnitude, the rapid 'expansion of their cosmos' was outside all prior experience.[54] Many Melanesians knew something of colonisers, but little of imperialists. The 'fawny invaders', the Tongans,[55] had fought and married their way into Fiji via Lau long before cession. In New Guinea, the Tolai, who originated in New Ireland, had colonised the Gazelle area of New Britain, driving the Baining people further into the bush and enslaving some of them. Melanesian colonists, not unlike the Australians in Papua, sometimes institutionalised their own notions of power and sexuality. Among the Buin of south Bougainville, the chiefly descendants of invaders ruled over the original people, who as bondsmen were not permitted to look at the wife or daughter of a chief; hamlets had to be scattered to avoid this offence.[56]

On the micro level the Tongans were very different from the Fijians, and the Tolai from the Baining, but their differences fade to near insignificance when compared with the colonising Europeans, of whatever nationality. Their world view and scale of organisation, be it political, economic, or religious, were of so great an order as to make them seem like demigods, as many Melanesians first believed. What made the Europeans powerful was that they believed in their own culture's superiority, so amply demonstrated in its technology. What made the Melanesians vulnerable—beside the givens of small-scale societies, simple technologies, and so on—was the time it was taking them, on the periphery of the Western empires, to understand the incoming European ideas, unhelped as they were by most Europeans other than the missionaries. Although politically or militarily vanquished, the colonised Melanesians did not surrender everything to the colonisers. All over Melanesia they sought to explain the unknown in terms of the known— why the white men came and why they had technological superiority were all to do with the provisions of the ancestors, as the people of Astrolabe Bay and the Gulf region found. Even when their descendants failed in ritual, the ancestors promised hope, which sustained their spirits though their bodies suffered. When the old order was shaken, the missions found hearers of the Word. Hope continued to be provided by the Christian message with its awesome potential to create new social and thus political groupings. The growth of the later Mansren movement in Dutch New Guinea and the Fallowes movement in the Solomons, very different in character and organisation, used Christianity in this way. The new religion bonded coastal people in parts of the New Hebrides, but reinforced divisions between them and the bush people attached to 'custom'.

Not all aggression in Melanesia focused on the colonisers—much of it, under new guises, was still directed at ancient enemies. Melanesian 'cargo' cults and Christianity apart, the colonial economic geography provided a new milieu for some Melanesians to explore their common humanity— which was, to them, a very new concept. 'Pacification' extended mobility and allowed new charismatic leaders, like Apolosi Nawai in Fiji and Angganita and Simiopiaref in Dutch New Guinea, to draw together followers from disparate tribal groups when they felt a common need. Colonial towns, though few, created neutral places where old responses to former enemies could be set aside. There, the colonisers provided reasons for seeking community, as with the Melanesians around Rabaul in 1929 as well as with the Indians near Suva in 1920. The ubiquitous plantations of Melanesia, in providing a common experience, opened the way for strangers to learn about each other and provided a basis for new ties.

Even the more esoteric introduced legal codes, given a key man with a knowledge of their practice and protocol, could turn tools of control to weapons of resistance, as with the New Hebrideans who fought for their land rights through Jacomb in the court, and the western Solomon Islanders who won an equitable tax structure through Goldie, petitions, and peaceful protest meetings. Indigenous leaders, like Goldie's friends, Boaz Sunga and Gina, who were both valued by their own society and respected by a section of the colonial apparatus, were rare, but a man like Sukuna was exceptional. Because Fijian societies were larger, and Christian conversion and literacy came two or three generations earlier, Sukuna's base was greater than that of perhaps any other single Melanesian leader. Through an extensive Western education, Sukuna became not a rebel, but a go-between for two worlds. Although seen as a patriot for his defence of Fijian interests, he also protected indigenous power structures that he judged integral to the continuance of Fijian culture, which was under challenge by capitalism and the presence of the Indians, a necessary adjunct to the functioning of that system. Sukuna, like To Bobo of the Gazelle Peninsula, was a realist and wanted his people to survive.

Prior to World War Two, throughout the territories of Melanesia, colonialism in all its forms was causing many Melanesians to examine more of what they held in common and less of what divided them. Yet in one sense, all these were minority developments. No more than half the Melanesian population came under colonial control before World War Two, and that control was often tenuous.[57] The majority of Melanesians, mostly in New Guinea, were colonised in a more benign era, characterised by notions of trusteeship and development policies with the goal of self-government and even eventual independence. The experience of the colonised differed enormously with time and place, and probably more than with any particular colonial power. For example, the Tolai involvement in capitalism, though not without pain, was a more materially rewarding experience than that of the Astrolabe Bay people in the German era. Under the British, the western Solomon Islanders, after the trauma of 'pacification', retained more dignity and self-respect in the face of colonial capitalists than did their poorer neighbours from Malaita.

On the periphery of the European empires, much of Melanesia incurred only minimal penetration of indigenous structures, which perhaps has meant less human suffering than in colonies elsewhere, but has also permitted the endemic Melanesian disunity and localism to survive, with a questionable legacy for modern states. Even before World War Two, when group redefinition occurred, it rarely coincided with the perimeter of the colonial state, but was often simply island or language based—the old uniting factors of residence and kinship writ large. Not even Fiji's Gordon-imposed 'traditional' order, endorsed by most chiefs, eliminated the 'commoner' demands that Nawai voiced, nor has it bridged the gap between western and eastern Fiji. The variety of colonial experience has provided little common foundation for modern nationalism, which more recently has been, and continues to be, manufactured by the new rulers, the educated indigenous elite. That recent ideological concepts like 'the Melanesian way' and *Kastom* (Custom) are founded on communalities—respect for 'traditional' ways, the virtues of the extended family, sharing, and reciprocity—reveals a potentially divisive paradox. Each society has different ideas on customs, while sharing and reciprocity are for one's own group, and not necessarily extended to the modern state.[58] This frail ideology of communality may well collapse, not because colonialism before or after World War Two was too harsh, but because it was not harsh enough, and, for the independent states, has disappeared.

In a real sense the colonial powers, given the insignificance of Melanesia, did their job well—they prevented the development of new groupings that would have threatened their tenuous hegemony. When empire became unfashionable and too expensive, political control ceased in the 1970s and 1980s, but economic influence continued, along with extensive aid-giving by important metropolitan powers, such as Australia, Japan, New Zealand, Britain, and the European Community. There seems little doubt that if aid givers were to refuse to underwrite the patronage-ridden modern nations, localism and regionalism would re-emerge, recreating in essence the very problem European powers had to solve by annexation in the nineteenth century. Whereas colonialism once ensured a balance for Europe in the region, aid now subsidises stability, perhaps yet another holding operation, if for a different array of 'powers' mainly on the Pacific rim.

Notes

1 Peter Fitzpatrick, *Law and State in Papua New Guinea*, Academic Press, London, 1980, 50–53, 56–57.

2 Peter J. Hempenstall, *Pacific Islanders under German Rule: A Study in the Meaning of Colonial Resistance*, Australian National University, Canberra, 1978, 174.

3 Fitzpatrick, 56–59, 71–90.

4 W. P. Morrell, *Britain in the Pacific Islands*, Oxford University Press, London, 1960, 364–369; Deryck Scarr, *Fiji: A Short History*, Institute for Polynesian Studies, Laie, Hawai'i, 1984, 75–76.

5 'Atu Bain, 'A Protective Labour Policy? An Alternative Interpretation of Early Colonial Labour Policies in Fiji', *Journal of Pacific History* 23 (2, 1988): 123–124.

6 Peter France, *The Charter of the Land: Custom and Colonisation in Fiji*, Oxford University Press, Melbourne, 1969, 103–128; T. J. Macnaught, *The Fijian Colonial Experience: A Study of Neotraditional Order under British Colonial Rule Prior to World War Two*, Australian National University, Canberra, 1982, 4–11, 49–63; Scarr, 13; Morrell, 379–382; Michael Moynagh, *Brown or White? A History of the Fiji Sugar Industry, 1873–1973*, Australian National University, Canberra, 1981, 19–20.

8 Morrell, 381–383; K. L. Gillion, *The Fiji Indians: Challenge to European Dominance, 1920–1946*, Australian National University Press, Canberra, 1977, 1–17.

9 Moynagh, 2; Scarr, 107–113; France, 149–164; Macnaught, 25–48.

10 Macnaught, 75–92.

11 Macnaught, 134–137.

12 Macnaught, 64–74; Bain, 134–136; Moynagh, 92–112; Gillion, 18–65.

13 Gillion, 130–172.

14 Roger C. Thompson, *Australian Imperialism in the Pacific: The Expansionist Era, 1820–1920*, Melbourne University Press, Melbourne, 1980; Deryck Scarr, *Fragments of Empire: A History of the Western Pacific High Commission, 1877–1914*, Australian National University Press, Canberra, 1967, 218–251.

15 Howard Van Trease, The *Politics of Land in Vanuatu: From Colony to Independence*, Institute of Pacific Studies, University of the South Pacific, 1987, 46–47; Ron Adams, 'Indentured Labour in Vanuatu, 1867–1922', *Journal de la Société des Océanistes* 42, (1986): 41–63.

16 Ralph Shlomowitz and Richard Bedford, 'The Internal Labour Trade in the New

Hebrides and the Solomon Islands, 1890–1941', *Journal de la Société des Océanistes* 86 (1988): 69. Joël Bonnemaison, 'Passions et misères d'une société coloniale: Les plantations au Vanuatu entre 1920 et 1980', *Journal de la Société des Océanistes* 42 (1986): 65–84. Jeremy V. MacClancy, *To Kill a Bird with Two Stones*, Vila, 1980, 91.

17 Edward Jacomb, *France and England in the New Hebrides: The Anglo-French Condominium*, Melbourne, n.d. [1914], 28.

18 Scarr 1967, 234–248.

19 Bonnemaison, 80–83.

20 Scarr, 1967, 248, 251; Adams, 57; Jacomb.

21 Hank Nelson, *Black, White and Gold: Goldmining in Papua New Guinea, 1878–1930*, Australian National University, Canberra, 1976, 91–120.

22 R. B. Joyce, *Sir William Macgregor*, Oxford University Press, Melbourne, 1971, 122–126, 141–143, 208–213; C. D. Rowley, *The Australians in German New Guinea, 1914–1921*, Melbourne University Press, Melbourne, 1958, 293.

23 P. Biskup, B. Jinks and H. Nelson, *A Short History of New Guinea*, Angus & Robertson, Sydney, 1968, 76, 162; James Griffin, Hank Nelson, and Stewart Firth, *Papua New Guinea: A Political History*, Heinemann, Richmond, VIC, 1979, 23; Frances West, *Hubert Murray: The Australian Pro-Consul*, Oxford University Press, Melbourne, 1968, 122; G. T. Harris, 'Papuan Village Agriculture', in *A History of Agriculture in Papua New Guinea: A Time to Plant and a Time to Uproot*, ed. Donald Denoon and Catherine Snowden, Institute of Papua New Guinea Studies, n.p. [Port Moresby], n.d. [c. 1980], 132; Joyce, 199–205.

24 Griffin, Nelson and Firth, 70; K. Buckley and K. Klugman, *The Australian Presence in the Pacific: Burns Philp 1914–1946*, Allen & Unwin, Sydney, 1983, 106–107, 235; Harris, 136.

25 West, 64–65, 136–137, 143, 185–186, 207; Harris, 133, 135, 136; Rowley, 181–182.

26 Griffin, Nelson, and Firth, 70.

27 West, 70, 212, 225–228; Griffin, Nelson, and Firth, 31; Fitzpatrick, 78–90.

28 Amirah Inglis, *'Not a White Woman Safe': Sexual Anxiety and Politics in Port Moresby 1920–1934*, Australian National University, Canberra, 1976.

29 Albert Maori Kiki, *Kiki: Ten Thousand Years in a Lifetime*, F. W. Cheshire, Melbourne, 1968, 55–56.

30 Paul W. van der Veur, *Search for New Guinea's Boundaries: From Torres Strait to the Pacific*, Australian National University, Canberra, 1966, 10–13, 62–74; Paul W. van der Veur, 'Dutch New Guinea' in *Encyclopaedia of Papua New Guinea*, ed. Peter Ryan, Melbourne University Press in association with University of Papua New Guinea, Melbourne, 1972, 1:277; A. E. Pratt, *Two Years among New Guinea Cannibals: A Naturalist's Sojourn among the Aborigines of Unexplored New Guinea*, Seeley, London, 1906, 43–57.

31 Van der Veur, 279.

32 Justus M. van der Kroef, 'Culture Contact and Culture Conflict in Western New Guinea' in *Anthropological Quarterly* 32 (3, July 1959): 138.

33 Van der Veur, 277–283.

34 Peter Worsley, *The Trumpet Shall Sound: A Study of 'Cargo' Cults in Melanesia*, MacGibbon & Kee, London, 1957, 26–135.

35 Van der Veur, 280.

36 Worsley, 126–145; van der Kroef, 142–146.

37 Stewart Firth, *New Guinea under the Germans*, Melbourne University Press, 1983, 4, 23, 27–28, 35–43, 44–65; Hempenstall, 19, 119–139.

38 Firth, 86, 91–92, 110.

39 Firth, 62–64, 73–75, 85; Edward P. Wolfers, *Race Relations and Colonial Rule in Papua New Guinea*, Australia and New Zealand Book Company, Sydney, 1975, 67–68.

40 Firth, 25, 118–119; West, 129–130.

41 Firth, 34, 89–90, 112–135; Hempenstall, 180–182. Peter Lawrence, *Road Belong Cargo: A Study of the Cargo Movement in the Southern Madang District, New Guinea*, Melbourne University Press, Melbourne, 1964, 71.

42 Firth, 78–80; Hempenstall, 134–135.

43 Firth, 165, 167; Judith A. Bennett, *Wealth of the Solomons: A History of a Pacific Archipelago, 1800–1978*, Pacific Islands Monograph Series no. 3, University of Hawai‘i Press, Honolulu, 1987, 199.

44 Firth, 134, 165–174; Bennett, 176.

45 Rowley; Buckley and Klugman, 96–97, 106–107, 156–159; Biskup, Jinks and Nelson, 98–99; Griffin, Nelson and Firth, 54.

46 Fitzpatrick, 57–58, 82.

47 Bill Gammage, 'The Rabaul Strike, 1929', *Journal of Pacific History* 10 (3–4, 1975): 3–29.

48 Ian Hughes, *New Guinea Stone Age Trade: The Geography and Ecology of Traffic in the Interior*, Department of Prehistory, Australian National University, Canberra, 1977, 48–59.

49 Bennett, 100–124, 195; George G. Carter, *Tiè Varanè: Stories about People of Courage from Solomon Islands*, Unichurch, Auckland, 1981, 15–29.

50 Bennett, 150–166; Hubert Murray, Report on BSK Labour Supply, 29 April 1916, Western Pacific High Commission, Inwards Correspondence, Western Pacific Archives, Microfilm, Turnbull Library, Wellington, 1779/16 (estimates 1 man to 10 acres); Michael Panoff, 'Travailleurs, recruteurs et planteurs dans l'Archipel Bismarck de 1885 à 1914', Journal de la Société des Océanistes 35, 64 (1979): 159–173 (estimates 1 man for 2 hectares [5 acres]). These numbers are for *maintenance* of established plantations.

51 Judith A. Bennett, '"We Do Not Come Here to be Beaten": Resistance and the Plantation System in the Solomon Islands to World War II', in *Resistance and Accommodation on Plantations*, ed. Brij Lal, Edward Beechert, and Douglas Munro, University of Hawai‘i Press, Honolulu, in press.

52 Bennett, 241–259.

53 Wolfers, 74.

54 C. L. Sentinella, trans. and ed., *Miklouho-Maclay: New Guinea Diaries, 1871–1883*, Kristen Pris, Madang, Papua New Guinea, 1975, 335.

55 Seri, 'The Cooked-Prawn Men in Long Canoes', *Seaweeds and Constructions* 7 (1984): 62. Mana Publications.

56 Griffin, Nelson and Firth, 59.

57 Harold Brookfield, *Colonialism, Development and Independence: The Case of the Melanesian Islands in the South Pacific*, Cambridge University Press, 1972, 84–87.

58 Roger M. Keesing and Robert Tonkinson, eds *Reinventing Traditional Culture: The Politics of* Kastom *in Island Melanesia, Mankind* 13 (4, 1982, special issue); Bernard Narakobi, *The Melanesian Way*, Institute of Pacific Studies, Suva, 1983.

4

Britain, Germany, Australia, and New Zealand in Polynesia

Roger C. Thompson

In 1900–1901 a new colonial order was established in Polynesia. As a result of diplomatic agreement, Germany became the master of most of Samoa, leaving the remaining islands to the United States. Britain was now free to declare a protectorate over Tonga and gave New Zealand control of the Cook Islands and Niue. The last independent Polynesian island groups had succumbed to colonial control.

The colonial motives were mixed. Samoa had long been a goal for German expansionists, and it was a major centre for German economic interests in the Pacific, especially for the largest German Pacific trading company, the Deutsche Handels und Plantagen-Gesellschaft der Südsee-Inseln zu Hamburg (DHPG). However, the colony of Western Samoa was of small economic importance in a colonial empire that in 1913 consumed only 0.2 per cent of Germany's exports. In 1900 New Zealand's Prime Minister Richard Seddon had a vision of a Pacific empire that would counterbalance the coming Australian federation. But New Zealand only gained the Cook Islands and Niue. Britain was a much less enthusiastic colonial ruler in Polynesia. Tonga's main importance was its strategic relationship to Fiji.[1]

Polynesians were given little say in the imperial reorganisation. On a visit to Rarotonga in 1900, Seddon consulted with and received approval from *ariki* (chiefs) by promising them great benefits from New Zealand rule. He did not test opinion on other islands. Tonga was already an independent constitutional monarchy, but King George Tupou II was in no position to resist British pressure for a protectorate treaty. His self-indulgence had stimulated a financial crisis which, along with a marriage that departed from traditional expectations, had caused significant Tongan opposition towards him and Sateki, his prime minister. Some Samoans had sought and received German aid in civil wars. The victor from the recent conflict, Mata'afa

71

Iosefa, was rewarded with the post of highest Samoan chief, which other chiefs accepted because there was no surviving rival. But Mata'afa was now subject to the German emperor and his representatives in Samoa.[2]

Colonial rulers were paying some attention to islander interests. Britain initially took control only of Tonga's foreign and defence policies, imposed some legal jurisdiction over Europeans, and claimed the right of the British consul to offer advice. In Samoa the German Governor, Dr Wilhelm Solf, who knew more about Samoan culture than most Europeans, recognised the military power represented by Mata'afa's 2500 troops armed with modern rifles. He renounced the use of force and promised the *Malo o Samoa* (council of chiefs) to respect 'old traditions'. The British Secretary of State for the Colonies, Joseph Chamberlain, justified the transfer of the Cook Islands and Niue to New Zealand on the grounds that 'the natives are of the same race as the Maories [*sic*] with whom the [New Zealand] Colonial Government "has succeeded in establishing entirely satisfactory relations" ', though the way Maori land had been acquired by pakeha (European) settlers should have inspired less confidence.[3]

Colonial officials also had their own agendas. Walter Gudgeon, the first Cook Islands Resident Commissioner, had considerable previous experience with Maori as a Native Land Court judge. But because he initially believed that the islanders were dying out, he moved to facilitate transfers of land to European settlers by introducing a land court on the New Zealand model.[4] In Samoa, Solf was determined to break the *Malo*'s power. He started by skilfully disarming Samoans with offers of financial compensation and imposing on them copra-planting regulations and a poll tax. He was also acting in the interests of the DHPG, which dominated the marketing of Samoan-grown produce, and on which he depended for political and economic support. Consequently, Solf did not encourage individual German settlers or potential competitors to the DHPG, allowing Samoans to preserve the 81 per cent of the colony's land that they still owned.[5]

In Tonga British Consul Hamilton Hunter, a former colonial official in Fiji, held little respect for Tongans and less for their government. When the king disdained his advice, he launched a campaign against Tupou and Sateki, accusing them of corruption and nepotism. Hunter gained the support of members of the small European community and noble opponents of the Tongan government. In messages to the British high commissioner of the western Pacific in Fiji, he misrepresented this rift in the Tongan nobility as representing mass popular hostility to government tyranny.[6]

The British resident commissioner in the Gilbert and Ellice Islands Colony in 1900 also was in the process of establishing authoritarian control over the islanders. He was William Telfer Campbell, who in British New Guinea had indulged in destroying coconut trees and burning houses. In the Gilbert and Ellice Islands he was converting his predecessor's reliance on islander self-rule into an autocratic regime. With the assistance of temporary

European government agents and appointed *kaubure* (village wardens), he compelled islanders to work periodically on public projects, consolidated them into large villages, and flogged and imprisoned miscreants. When he left in 1908, he had established a system of well-ordered and clean villages under his authoritarian control. The pattern of British rule in the colony had been set for the next quarter century.[7]

Colonial officials in Polynesia generally were supported by their imperial masters. DHPG influence in Germany allowed Solf a free hand in Samoa, despite campaigns against him by German victims of his anti-settler policies. Campbell in the Gilberts received general approval from the Western Pacific High Commission (WPHC).

Hunter in Tonga received encouragement from western Pacific high commissioners (who were also governors of Fiji) for his anti-government campaign. There was some hesitation in the British Colonial Office, but in 1904 High Commissioner Sir Everard im Thurn was authorized to travel by warship to Tonga to impose a new order on its government. The result was a virtual coup d'état. Sateki was deported to Fiji. All but one of Tupou's ministers were sacked and replaced by his noble opponents. Europeans were appointed as assistant treasurer and chief justice, and future Tongan governments were required to accept the British consul's advice. Tupou signed this agreement in 1905 knowing that otherwise he faced deportation to Fiji. With im Thurn's approval and the compliance of the new Prime Minister, John Mateialona, Hunter became the de facto ruler of Tonga.[8]

Less metropolitan government support was given to Gudgeon in the Cook Islands. Seddon approved a general policy of economic development, as did Minister for Trade and Customs C. H. Mills, who assumed responsibility for the Cook Islands and Niue in 1902. His appointment reflected the government's economic agenda, though he was given no staff with which to formulate island policies. However, especially after his visit to the islands in 1903, Mills was concerned to maintain the support of the *ariki*, who had long opposed land sales to Europeans with the aid of the London Missionary Society (LMS). New Zealand allowed that policy to remain. The *ariki* were reluctant even to lease much land to Europeans. Gudgeon hoped the granting of individual titles to Cook Islanders by the land court would solve that problem. But this aim was compromised by his policy, as the court's judge, of limiting *ariki* land acquisition by granting titles to all adult members of descent families as joint owners.[9]

However, Gudgeon was given a free hand to abolish in 1904 the jurisdiction of local *ariki* courts on any island where there was a European government agent, arguing that this served the cause of the common people. Egalitarian principles had been used to justify increasing the authority of the colony's officials, who were now judges as well as administrators. The *ariki* retained some power through island councils, but all of the ordinances they passed needed the resident commissioner's assent and could be disallowed by the government in Wellington. On Niue, the New Zealand resident commissioner also became the centre of power as the president of a council composed of compliant Niueans and a figurehead king.[10]

Some islanders resisted authoritarian colonial policies. Some Samoans perceived Solf's intentions. Exploiting popular dissatisfaction with his policies and a downturn in copra prices, they launched in 1904, with the *Malo's* backing, an independent *Oloa* copra marketing venture. Solf acted quickly against this threat to the DHPG's economic dominance and to his policy to weaken the *Malo*. He did not risk a frontal assault on the movement, given Samoans' economic power as producers of copra and consumers of European goods, but he prohibited the payment of a levy imposed by the *Malo* to assist the *Oloa*. After that order was disobeyed, while he was absent in 1905 on a trip to New Zealand, Solf acted to break the *Malo's* power by stripping chiefs of their privileges. One of the deposed chiefs, Lauaki Namulau'ulu Mamoe, a skilful orator and a power-broker of the civil war era, responded by agitating for restoration of Samoan political rights and received widespread support from other chiefs. The campaign developed by 1909 into a threat of a violent Samoan uprising. Solf was careful to avoid provocation, knowing the damage Samoans could cause and the problems of fighting them in a bush war. But he organised a demonstration of German power by calling in ships of Germany's East Asia squadron. He received valuable assistance from European missionaries, who succeeded in splitting Lauaki's ranks, causing him to surrender in the knowledge that he and supporters faced only deportation to the German North Pacific Islands rather than execution for rebellion. Samoans had learned not to challenge German rule.[11]

Tupou had more success in resisting heavy-handed British policy in Tonga. The autocratic-minded Campbell gave him the opportunity. Campbell not only exceeded his authority by assuming the right to attend Tongan Cabinet meetings, but also, at the behest of European traders, he moved to suppress a new Tongan copra marketing company. This was the *Tonga Ma'a Tonga Kautaha* (Tonga for the Tongans Company), which was the brainchild of an unsuccessful businessman, Alexander Cameron, who had a part-Tongan wife and was enthusiastically supported by Tongans, who enjoyed individual land rights and produced practically all Tonga's copra. They objected to their treatment by European traders, who extracted high profits from sales of their copra and charged them up to twice the prices of goods they sold to fellow Europeans. The *Kautaha* not only offered substantial savings in the marketing of home-grown copra, but it also quickly gained cult status as a way of restoring Tongan independence.[12]

Campbell succeeded in 1910 in persuading the Cabinet to close down the *Kautaha* and seize its assets, after a European auditor alleged discrepancies in its books. But Campbell's attempt to charge Cameron with embezzlement backfired when he was acquitted by the Western Pacific High Commission's judicial commissioner. Cameron and *Kautaha* members struck back by suing the Tonga Government for £11 500 compensation for misappropriation of the company's assets plus damages. Furthermore, Chief Justice Robert Skeen, a New Zealander with Samoan experience, declared invalid the government's subsequent ordinance to protect itself. Campbell attempted to force the dismissal of Skeen, which was stubbornly resisted by Tupou, who perceived a chance to dump his hostile Cabinet. A subsequent Western Pacific High Commissioner, Sir Francis May, also failed to move the King, who in turn urged Campbell's dismissal. May backed down, and Campbell left Tonga in April 1912 to be pensioned off in London. Tupou, with the assistance of a New Zealand lawyer, had won a major victory. The *Kautaha* was revived, though it withered away by 1916, crippled by Cameron's lax management and by an economic depression in Tonga caused by a series of hurricanes after 1912, drought in 1915, and war-induced shipping scarcity. But Tupou was now able to dismiss Mateialona and most of the Cabinet, replacing them with his own supporters, while the new consul, Islay McOwan, kept a low profile.[13]

The only other Polynesians who were allowed a hand in shaping their own destiny in the early 1900s were the Maori of New Zealand. In 1900 the New Zealand Liberal Government started to provide assistance to the Maori community. Influencing this change was the Young Maori Party, consisting of educated professional men who believed that Maori should strive to emulate pakeha society. One of them, Apirana Ngata, a lawyer who was New Zealand's first Maori university graduate, expressed their sense of responsibility: 'It is ours to remove prejudice, to argue out of existence fallacious doctrines, to lay the foundations of a healthier, more compact, more powerful social opinion among our people'. Indeed, Young Maori Party leaders were conscious of the poor living conditions of the majority of their 45 330 compatriots in 1901. Many were eking out unhealthy and precarious existences on marginal land, often relying on seasonal labouring for pakeha and exhibiting signs of social demoralisation. They were in danger of becoming a permanent servant community for Europeans, who mostly treated them with a sense of racial superiority.[14]

The centrepiece of the new approach in 1900 was the Maori Councils Act, which resulted in the first major programmes to deliver medical services to Maori communities. Maui Pomare, his people's first medical graduate, was appointed in 1900 as the first Maori health officer and launched efforts to improve hygiene and sanitation. The success of these measures was limited. Maori standards of health remained much worse than those of the pakeha community into the 1930s. Nevertheless, such efforts contributed to a fall in Maori death rates, which was rescuing the Maori population from its nineteenth-century decline to reach 56 987 by 1921. In that year, Maori were still overwhelmingly rural, with educational services directed mainly to that end. Few of them moved beyond primary school. Despite attempts to preserve their landholdings, they were still selling land to pakeha buyers. Some Maori groups had tried to remain independent of pakeha rule, but the last one, led by Rua Kenana in the Urewera country, was suppressed by police in 1916. Maori were suffering much more deprivation in landowner-ship than most other Polynesians, though many Maori were retaining their old tribal loyalties and communities. A few of them had been able to rise to a professional social level in the pakeha community, and Maori elected four of the seventy-four members of parliament. From 1899 to 1912 James Carroll was the first Maori Minister for Native Affairs. However, the big majority of Maori were living on the rural margins of pakeha society.[15]

During World War One a Maori battalion saw active service in Europe. However, only 20 per cent of eligible Maori males volunteered, and some tribes, notably in the Waikato, refused to participate in the war. Tonga's government initially considered neutrality but decided to firmly support the war effort, and six Tongans served in the New Zealand Maori regiment. Tonga's wartime economic depression induced its government in 1917 to seek a £10 000 loan from Britain. This was approved, but only on the condition of future European supervision of government finances, which restored some of the British consul's former power. Some Western Samoans sided with Germany, but Solf's successor, Governor Schultz, refused their offer of military assistance on the grounds of the indefensibility of the colony. The New Zealand military administration ran a more lax regime resulting in restoration of much Samoan self-rule. But this freedom and the egalitarian attitudes of some New Zealand troops encouraged Samoan notions of equality with whites and primed a time bomb for the future, which was additionally charged by Samoan resentment about new taxes and wartime inflation. Because of the shipping scarcity, Cook Islanders also suffered from a col-lapse in the prices of the oranges, bananas, and tomatoes they grew for the New Zealand market. Some of these islanders, including one hundred and fifty Niueans, volunteered to join the New Zealand Maori regiment.[16]

In the immediate aftermath of the war, an influenza pandemic delivered a devastating blow to many Polynesians. The poor health of New Zealand Maori was demonstrated when at least 1057 of them died, nearly five times the pakeha death rate. On isolated Nauru the pandemic killed 10 per cent of 1279 Nauruans. About 8 per cent of Tongans died when the pandemic struck their islands. McOwan's tireless efforts to assist suffering Tongans helped cement his influence with the Tongan government. The pandemic had a contrary political effect in Western Samoa, where it killed over 20 per cent of 35 000 Samoans and 1000 part-Europeans. Survivors bitterly blamed the New Zealand military administrator, Lieutenant-Colonel Robert Logan, for allowing the New Zealand ship, *Tulune*, which carried the disease, to dock at Apia in November 1918. Furthermore, Logan stubbornly refused to accept from American Samoa an offer of medical assistance that might have saved many lives.[17]

Phosphate mining in Nauru. (Australian Government Publishing Service)

Economic domination

Part of the authoritarian style of colonial control in Polynesia to 1920 was economic domination. The suppression of the *Oloa* in Samoa and the *Kautaha* in Tonga not only stopped challenges to colonial authority but also favoured European traders. However, there was no automatic symbiosis of European economic interests and colonial rule. Campbell's successors in the Gilbert and Ellice Islands, to the chagrin of the ubiquitous Australian Burns, Philp & Company, were encouraging Japanese traders to the protectorate because they offered higher copra prices to islanders. Laissez-faire colonial economic policies, however, allowed Burns, Philp to make good trading profits in Polynesia. Especially valuable was Tonga, where the collapse of the *Kautaha* and recovery from wartime depression raised the company's annual profit rate in 1918–19 to a 'very satisfactory' 14 per cent. The most prominent influence of a metropolitan company in Polynesia was the British Pacific Phosphate Company, which operated on Ocean Island and on German-owned Nauru. On Ocean Island this company mined phosphate from 1902, initially for a payment to the Banaban people of a mere £50 per year. Banaban dissatisfaction resulted in 1912 in an increase to about £5000 per year to be paid into a trust fund for them. But the company was allowed to amass to 1913 profits worth more than £1.75 million.[18]

Another colonial reshuffle occurred in Polynesia in 1920, when the German islands became League of Nations mandates, with the administering nations enjoying full political and economic power. Western Samoa was granted to New Zealand, and Nauru to Australia. New Zealand, which had occupied German Samoa in 1914, thereby gained its longstanding ambition to rule Samoans, though the expansionist gloss had now worn thin, with concerns expressed in the New Zealand parliament about the cost involved. Australian Prime Minister 'Billy' Hughes had no difficulty in convincing his parliament of the benefits to be gained from phosphate-rich Nauru, arguing the need to supply Australian farmers with their 'very life blood' of phosphate supplies 'at cost price'. But Britain and New Zealand forced him to agree to British Empire control. Hughes 'pressed very strongly' for Australia to be the administering power, which was conceded for the mandate's first five years.[19]

Australian and New Zealand control of mandated islands widened the variety of colonial styles in Polynesia in the 1920s and 1930s. In appointment of administrators, Australia and New Zealand used little of their existing experience in ruling Pacific Islanders. Also in New Zealand, Ngata, now a Maori member of parliament who became Minister for Native Affairs in 1928, lamented that 'this little country cocked its head up & threw its chest out, so that nothing less than a "Department of External Affairs" under Ministers wedded to the mailed-fist kind of politics' was created to control Samoa.[20]

Consequently, the first administrator of the Western Samoa mandate was New Zealand's senior soldier, Major General George Richardson, who had no previous knowledge of Polynesians. Peter Buck, a former Maori representative in the New Zealand parliament and the medical officer of the World War One Maori regiment, wrote that it was 'well known amongst the military crowd that Richardson was shunted out of the Defence Department' to make room for someone else who had had more active service in the field, 'and the Samoan appointment was the way of solving the difficulty'. Richardson was concerned to protect Samoan rights and to introduce progressive educational and social policies. But he possessed an autocratic temperament, befitting his lifetime army career, and he had too much paternalistic zeal. He was also insensitive to proud and independent-minded Samoans, whom he characterised as 'childlike'. In particular, his ignorance of Samoan customs caused deep offence, with policies such as banning the exchange of fine mats and stripping refractory chiefs of their chiefly titles. His attempts to individualise Samoan landholdings and reorganise Samoan villages were viewed by Samoans as serious attacks on their family rights and communal autonomy.[21]

Furthermore Buck, who in his capacity as a research fellow at the Bishop Museum in Hawai'i visited Samoa in 1927, condemned New Zealand civil servants appointed to Western Samoa who 'fawned on Richardson with a corresponding inimical attitude towards the people they were supposed to be serving'. They were 'apt to look upon themselves as little kings'. They also alienated part-Europeans, who formed the majority of Samoa's local 'European' community. 'An attitude of regarding the half-caste as an inferior person was maintained in Government circles from Richardson down.'[22]

Nauru was administered by a territories branch in the Prime Minister's Department, which also supervised the New Guinea mandate and Papua. For Nauru's first administrator, Australia, like New Zealand, chose a senior military officer, Brigadier Thomas Griffiths, who had spent the previous year as military administrator of the New Guinea territory. Griffiths set about conciliating Nauruans who had shown signs of rebellion under Acting British Resident Commissioner George Smith-Rewse, a former Gilbert and Ellice official. They were being led by Timothy Detudamo, an LMS-educated chief's son, who had returned in 1918 from four years in the United States assisting in Bible translation. With the backing of Nauruan chiefs, he had tried to establish a co-operative store to compete with the one owned by the Pacific Phosphate Company. He had also threatened to demand from the company £3 million compensation 'for all your Company has robbed us of all those years . . . and the hundreds of acres of our Lands you have ruined and despoiled'. He had been sentenced to two years' imprisonment for libellous and seditious language, though was kept 'as a political prisoner' working for Smith-Rewse. Griffiths freed Detudamo and allowed Nauruans to run their own co-operative store. He negotiated increases in the royalty paid to Nauruans by the new British Phosphate Commission from a halfpenny per ton of phosphate exports to fourpence plus twopence into a trust fund. He sponsored in 1926 a tour of Australia by most of the island's fifteen chiefs, whom he had appointed to an advisory council. He also introduced compulsory primary education.[23]

In the Gilbert and Ellice Islands Colony, the most authoritarian colonial style in Polynesia continued into the 1930s. It was especially perpetuated by Arthur Grimble, who arrived there in 1914 after a British university education. As a district officer in the Gilbert Islands from 1916 to 1920, he grew to love the islanders and learned much about their culture. In later life he romanticised these experiences in popular but somewhat mythical books. He returned to the colonial administration's headquarters on Ocean Island as native lands commissioner and the acknowledged expert on islander affairs, and from 1926 to 1932 was resident commissioner. Grimble's major aim was to protect islanders from outside influences. With an authoritarian disposition that allowed no independence to members of his staff, he also imposed on islanders an extraordinarily detailed set of regulations. They were published as a single-law code for the colony in 1930, entitled *Regulations for the Good Order and Cleanliness of the Gilbert and Ellice*

Islands. Among a host of restrictions, islanders could be prosecuted for public dancing at any time except between 6 PM and 9 PM on Wednesdays and Saturdays or 'with shameful gestures', for sleeping in an eating house, or for holding feasts to welcome visitors. Based on a pattern of government control established by Campbell, and influenced by LMS puritanism, Grimble's code startled WPHC officials, because its restrictions belonged to an earlier colonial age. But it was approved on the assumption that he was the expert who knew what was best for the islanders.[24]

The style of New Zealand's administration of the Cook Islands and Niue was midway between Grimble's authoritarianism and Griffiths' permissive paternalism in Nauru. From 1909 until 1934 those New Zealand territories were controlled by Maori Ministers for Native Affairs, a unique government of colonial subjects by members of their own race. The first Maori minister, Carroll, drew on Maori experiences of problems created by rapid Europeanisation to introduce a *taihoa* (go slow) policy to protect the islanders from too rapid cultural change. This policy allowed significant freedom to the resident commissioners. Buck was unsure whether it 'was due to a profound philosophy or a natural inertia'. Pomare (1912–1928) continued the *taihoa* policy but, in keeping with his previous Maori experience, increased health services for islanders. Ngata, who took over late in 1928, also complimented Pomare on taking 'full advantage of the good times to provide the islands with essential services such as shipping, wireless and schools'.[25]

However, especially after his visit to Rarotonga in 1932, Ngata noticed significant deficiencies in the administration of the Cook Islands, which left him in 'doubt as to the applicability of Maori solutions'. Land titles were in an unsatisfactory state because relative interests of members of descent groups 'were never determined'. There had been a failure to assist islander exporters who were relying on orange trees growing wild without proper cultivation. Furthermore, he wrote, 'the experiment of combining in one person the position of R.C., Judge of the High Court and Judge of the Native Land Court has not turned out satisfactorily'. Hugh Ayson, Resident Commissioner since 1922, filled 'too many positions and is not efficient in any one of them'. There also had been appointments 'of an inferior type of official in Education, Health &c. [and] non-representation of the Native interest and a tactful repression of their wishes'. The most 'difficult factor', in Ngata's view, was 'the stratification of the people. . . . On Rarotonga the Ariki system has been stereotyped by missionary influence and confirmed by the Courts, that is the Government'. The result was neglect in agriculture and a stifling of capable non-*ariki* islanders. Ngata considered that the *taihoa* policy in the Cook Islands, compounded by poor administration, had failed for people who had experienced significant Europeanisation. He explained: 'the taste for pakeha things is increasing and must be satisfied'.[26]

The most culturally sensitive colonial style in Polynesia was in Tonga.

Sālote Tupou III, Tonga's queen from 1918, was blessed with political acumen, personal dignity, and readiness to seek advice. British consuls, McOwan and J. S. Neill (1927–1937), were among her most influential advisers. She also promoted Tonga's identity as a Polynesian kingdom proud of its traditions and independence. British influence also supported the perpetuation of Tonga's hierarchical political and social life. This included sanctioning a Christian mission-influenced decline in Tongan women's rights from their pre-colonial prominence to laws confining female land rights to marital status and relegating women to a subservient social role.[27]

Tongan commoners were quiescent under aristocratic rule, not yet experiencing the effects of overpopulation on their guaranteed landholdings. There were some signs of discontent among Tongan nobles about the degree of British influence and the government's employment of Europeans as senior public servants. A source of the dissatisfaction was the way British consuls staunchly supported Sālote's rule.[28]

New Zealand paternalism aroused no concerted protests from Cook Islanders. They enthusiastically welcomed Ngata when he was able finally to visit them in 1932. But this was a special occasion, summed up in his comment about 'the warmth in the attitude of the people towards us which Ayson confessed he had not experienced in the many years he had been on the island'. However, islanders had come to rely on the resident commissioner and his officers for their needs. When Ngata withdrew officials in 1931 because of the depression, he discovered, 'I have made myself unpopular in the Cook Group with the economies imposed'. But when one of the protesters, Makea-nui Tiniau, one of Rarotonga's five *ariki*, travelled for business and family reasons to New Zealand, Ngata convinced him that 'agitations . . . will cut no ice in the face of an unprecedented depression'. Mass public protests in the Cook Islands were a post–World War Two phenomenon.[29]

Nor were there organised protests by Gilbert and Ellice Islanders against the authoritarian nature of colonial rule, mainly because Grimble's code was less oppressive in practice than on paper. *Kaubure* and appointed islander governors usually ignored regulations that breached local customs. The one colonial official who was physically assaulted, Henry Newton, had alienated South Gilbert Islanders by imposing on them an officious work regime and by attacking LMS policies. However, there were appeals, especially from Ellis Islanders, for the repeal of Grimble's code, which many felt was an insult to their intelligence.[30]

Conversely, Nauruans welcomed Griffiths' policies. Petitions were sent to the Australian government and the British king from 'the chiefs and the people of Nauru' requesting the retention of Australian control. Britain and New Zealand therefore agreed to extend the Australian administration of Nauru beyond the first five-year term.[31]

The reactions of Samoans to New Zealand rule were a stark contrast.

Richardson's cultural arrogance, capping Samoan grievances under the military administration and evoking the spirit of opposition to German rule, provoked Samoans in 1926 to join with part-Europeans and white residents in an anti-administration campaign, which started with two public meetings in Apia. The 'Europeans' were seeking control of the administration-dominated legislature, whereas Samoans were expressing a determination to govern themselves. Another 'European' complaint was Richardson's proposed copra-marketing scheme to assist Samoan producers. Perceiving the contradiction in aims, but recognising their lack of power, Samoan leaders were willing to make common cause with 'Europeans' in a movement, they soon called the *Ola Mau a Samoa* (the firm opinion of Samoa). Also many local 'Europeans' spoke Samoan and had family ties with Samoans.[32]

Richardson could not believe that Samoans were capable of leadership in the Mau movement. It had to be a cat's-paw to serve local 'European' interests. He blamed especially Samoa's most successful local merchant, Olaf Nelson, of Swedish–Samoan descent. The New Zealand government accepted Richardson's explanation. When William Nosworthy, Minister for External Affairs, visited Samoa in June 1927 to enquire about the disturbances, he listened primarily to Richardson and met the Mau committee only to condemn the movement for seeking to foist European self-government onto duped Samoans. His boorish manner also alienated the publicly polite Samoans.[33]

Richardson and Nosworthy considered they could crush the Mau by deporting from Samoa its main 'European' leaders: Nelson, Alfred Smyth, and Australian-born Alfred Gurr. Richardson also issued banning orders—which were mostly ignored—against Samoan members of the Mau committee. Samoans responded with an escalation of opposition to the administration. Mau policemen, dressed in uniforms made by Nelson's firm and carrying thick walking sticks and clubs, started picketing Apia stores in order to deny customs revenue to the administration. Buck observed that 'the Mau police were a genial smiling lot. . . . It was really amusing to see them fraternising and laughing with the khaki clad police of the Administration. They were inordinately proud of their purple lavalava and head bands'.[34]

Richardson panicked, and Nosworthy was keen to teach upstart Samoans a sharp lesson. The New Zealand government's response of sending two warships to Samoa in February 1928 had recent Pacific precedents. In 1920 an Australian warship and New Zealand troops had been employed, at Britain's behest, against militant Indian strikers in Fiji, and in 1927 an Australian destroyer supported a search for violent Kwaio warriors in the Solomon Islands. However, the Mau had not committed any acts of violence as had occurred in Fiji and the Solomons. Mau police also did not resist their mass arrest by New Zealand marines when they defied the ban placed on wearing Mau uniforms. Other Mau Samoans gave themselves up, ensuring an overflowing of the detention centres. From the guarded encampment into which they were all herded, they went in and out at will, daring marine sentries to defy orders and shoot them. A cheeky defiance of authority was becoming a Mau hallmark. Within a fortnight an embarrassed Richardson released the prisoners, thereby weakening his authority. Whereas many Samoan villagers had not initially supported the Mau because they usually ignored administration edicts conflicting with traditional custom, the New Zealand military action against fellow Samoans had aroused clear majority Samoan support for the Mau.[35]

A new administrator, chosen to deal with the Mau, was another World War One officer, Lieutenant-Colonel Stephen Allen, though he was also a lawyer, farmer, and small-town mayor. A contingent of armed special New Zealand police replaced the marines in Samoa. Allen targeted the Samoan high chief and Mau leader, Tupua Tamasese Lelofi III, who had been banned earlier by Richardson. Convicted of not paying taxes, a common Mau tactic, he was jailed in New Zealand for six months. Because of its widespread village-based organisation, the Mau continued to thrive. Moreover, the New Zealand government, embarrassed by damaging publicity, such as an exposé of sexual abuses of Samoan women by New Zealand officials, allowed Tamasese to return home in June 1928 after serving his term.[36]

The situation in Samoa had become a stand-off between defiant Mau protesters and New Zealand police, frustrated by restraining orders. The result was Black Saturday, 28 December 1929, when Tamasese and twelve other Samoans were shot by the police, one of whom was beaten to death. The police had been waiting, with rifles and a machine-gun, for a crowd of Samoans gathering to welcome Smyth home from exile. The melee started with a police attempt, on Allen's order, to arrest a Samoan non-taxpayer who for months had been unmolested. The coroner at the inquest justified the police use of firearms against a crowd armed with no more than sticks and stones, a verdict that outraged most Samoans.[37]

This violence was followed by strong New Zealand military action to hunt down Mau leaders and imprison them. But a Mau women's movement started protesting, and non-taxpaying Samoans were bleeding the administration of revenue. The League of Nations Permanent Mandates Commission also rebuked the New Zealand government, and the opposition Labour Party was denouncing New Zealand 'oppression' in Samoa.[38]

The government took a new approach when Allen was replaced in 1931 by another old soldier, Brigadier-General Herbert Hart. But Ngata, who participated in the selection, said he was a 'likeable' person who would be able to carry on the administration while ignoring the Mau. Ngata explained: 'I have often found with our people that if you let them alone or take little or no notice of their bragging their activities will subside'. Samoan support for the Mau did diminish.[39]

Buck and Ngata condemned New Zealand government policy in Samoa as a mistaken attempt to push Samoans too quickly towards European life-styles. 'The pakeha standardised mould as applied to Samoa by Richardson was bad technique', wrote Buck. He lamented that 'the question of an anthropological approach never for one moment entered into the minds of those responsible for the appointment' of officials in Samoa. Buck and Ngata have been criticised for not appreciating that contemporary anthropology also was affected by cultural values.[40] Buck acknowledged that 'from our Maori standard, the Samoan is ignorant, self-satisfied and arrogant'. But he perceived correctly that most Samoans wished to be left alone to manage their own affairs because, despite their contact with 'missionary influence, traders, and Government servants for a large number of years ... the Samoan background is Samoan'. More modern anthropological research suggests that Samoan social conservatism was related to the widespread *matai* system of chiefs elected by their kin, giving Samoans great faith in their own social and political organisation.[41]

After Griffiths left in 1927, Nauruans also showed some dissent with Australian paternalism. It surfaced when the next administrator, William Newman, a senior public servant looking for a quiet post before retirement, appointed Detudamo in 1930 to the vacant position of head chief without consulting the council of chiefs. To Newman it was a natural promotion because Detudamo had been assistant head chief since 1927, and in 1929 he had been appointed to a new post of Superintendent of Nauruan Affairs. But ten of the other fourteen chiefs outraged Newman when they presented a letter for transmission to the prime minister of Australia protesting at Newman's failure to consult 'the Nauruan people' in the appointment and making other unspecified complaints. Those complaints were later revealed as dissatisfaction with Newman's non-fulfillment of promised policies, such as not providing shower-baths for their homes.[42]

Newman was due to take leave in Australia. An acting administrator from the Prime Minister's Department, Carl Gabel, investigated the complaints. He supported Newman's stance, despite a petition with five hundred Nauruan signatures requesting that Newman should not return because Nauruans had 'no faith or confidence in him'. Gabel nominated as the main cause of the dissatisfaction an erosion of European 'prestige'. Nauruans, in his view, had been given too much freedom, especially in 'prodigality' of expenditure. They even had been 'allowed' to own six cars, six trucks, and thirty-three motorcycles. Another sign of Nauruan discontent with European control was a large breakaway in 1930 from the island's European missionary-controlled LMS church to form the Buada Church. Ironically, Detudamo was a prominent leader of that Nauruan religious secession.[43] Newman returned with a message from Canberra that Nauru's chiefs must declare their loyalty to him or face dismissal. Only one chose the latter course, but the people of his district demonstrated their feelings by refusing to nominate a successor.[44]

The failure of their protest quietened Nauruans for the rest of the 1930s. The next administrator, naval commander Rupert Garsia, who had no better qualifications than commanding a naval boys' training institution in Sydney, but had an influential friend, looked after his own social needs rather than Nauruan interests. Canberra refused to reappoint him in 1938 because he had ignored Prime Minister's Department policy by indulging in extravagant expenditure and nepotistic hiring of staff. Nauruans responded to Garsia by calling for the return of Griffiths, but at seventy-two years of age he was too old. The next administrator was Frederick Chalmers, another World War One officer and a Tasmanian farmer with good political connections. However, he earned the satisfaction of Nauruans with his easygoing disposition and by renegotiating the phosphate royalties agreement in their favour. Nevertheless, his was still a paternalistic regime that was keeping the lid on Nauruan aspirations, which were to cause significant post-war dissension.[45]

In particular, no attempt was being made to provide employment or more self-governing opportunities for educated Nauruans, some of whom were receiving secondary education in Australia. 'There is no doubt', wrote Nauru's Director of Education William Groves in 1938, 'that the people as a whole have shown themselves capable of development in step with rather rapid Europeanization of their lives; . . . with guidance they are able to manage much of their own affairs'. The tragedy was that 'there is no European here whose job it is, or who seems to want to help put their feet on the road'.[46]

Nauruans had opposed Australian administration policy with letters and petitions rather than with sticks and stones. However, they were also showing signs of unrest about their returns from phosphate mining in tough negotiations with the British Phosphate Commission in the late 1930s. Though in 1939 the 201 landowners among the 1733 Nauruans had a combined annual income of £14 873, the exploitative imbalance was demonstrated by that year's phosphate exports to Australia worth £382 207. There, it was sold at half the world phosphate price, a saving of more than 32 shillings per ton for Australian farmers, compared with 8 pence per ton paid to Nauruans.[47]

On Ocean Island, Banabans, who numbered 691 in 1935 and were deeply attached to their disappearing land, had been attempting, without success, to halt all mining by demanding exorbitant payments. Their problem was that the British government was part-owner with Australia and New Zealand of the British Phosphate Commission. In 1937 Banabans reluctantly accepted a royalty of 10½ pence per ton of phosphate exports, from which £8 was granted annually to each Banaban adult and £4 to each child. The commission's raison d'être was to provide phosphate for Australian, New Zealand, and British consumers at the cheapest possible price, and thus services for Gilbert and Ellice Islanders were severely restricted. Western

Pacific High Commissioner Sir Arthur Richards complained in 1937 that 'far too much deference has been accorded to the views of the [Phosphate] Commissioners in the matter of Government Expenditure' and that 'the Resident Commissioner is reduced to the position of a semi-dependent' of the commission. For example, in the financial year 1936–37 only £4005 was spent on education for 30 222 Gilbert and Ellice Islanders, compared with £9318 spent on educating less than half that number of Cook Islanders.[48]

Polynesians were asserting some economic independence in the interwar years. A Burns, Philp inspector of the company's Tonga branches reported in 1921 that 'the natives' had been 'declining to make copra' because of low prices and had adopted the habit of withholding copra to force up the price. The company also bemoaned that Tongans would only work as casual labourers for ten shillings per day. In 1922 Tongans formed another independent copra marketing company and gained the support of Burns, Philp's Fiji-based competitor, Morris Hedstrom Limited. However, by 1926 the Australian company had arranged price-fixing agreements with its major overseas competitors. Nevertheless, Burns, Philp still faced competition from Japanese traders in Tonga, and its three branches there did not make a huge annual profit of 38 per cent in the period 1929 to 1932, as has been claimed.[49] The 1929 profit in Tonga was 7.5 per cent, falling to 4.5 per cent in 1932, despite a reduction of over half of the value of the branch capital, and rising to an average of 9 per cent from 1935 to 1938, which was 2 per cent higher than the net profit for the whole Burns, Philp (South Seas) Company during those years. In Samoa the company's returns were diminished by Mau direction of copra to Nelson's firm in the late 1920s. In 1936 the Nauruan co-operative store drove Burns, Philp from Nauru, and in the 1930s officials were encouraging Gilbert and Ellice Islanders to form their own copra-marketing co-operative.[50]

Changing colonial policies

During the 1930s winds of change in wider world colonial policies were starting to blow into Polynesia. A prominent advocate was Harry Maude, an anthropology graduate who arrived in the Gilbert and Ellice Islands in 1929. After Grimble's departure in 1932, Maude started to press for restoring authority to traditional leaders and allowing islanders much more freedom to run their own lives, though the changes were not fully implemented until after he became resident commissioner in 1946. Ngata decided that Cook Islanders needed more assistance to cope with their Europeanising world. He decreed exclusive use of the English language during school hours. But there were few employment opportunities for English speakers in the Cook Islands, and the main value of this policy was to equip islanders to take unskilled jobs in New Zealand during and after

World War Two. 'Having fallen upon evil times financially', Ngata was unable to add much to the colony's economic infrastructure. He had to fight hard to retain money for health and education from the New Zealand annual grant, which fell from £17 483 in 1930–31 to £11 000 in 1937–38. The New Zealand Labour government, which was elected in 1935, lifted the grant to £22 112 in 1938–39, with the additional expenditure concentrated on health and economic development. Inadequate shipping services remained a serious economic problem for the colony. The New Zealand Labour government also satisfied Samoans temporarily by sanctioning a virtual Mau takeover of local government in the mandate. However, the Labour government still operated from the culturally superior standpoint that Samoans could not aspire to national independence until their living standards and education were raised to a much higher level. This attitude was to cause post-war problems in Western Samoa.[51]

In New Zealand, the Maori battalion's good record in World War One gained more respectability for Maori in pakeha eyes. Limited contact between mostly rural Maori and white New Zealanders also directed the racist propaganda of the extreme pakeha right against Chinese and other non-English-speaking immigrants rather than towards Maori. However, most pakeha still saw Maori through prejudice-tinted glasses. 'The pakeha', explained Buck, 'regards us from the higher altitude of his culture and stresses how far we are behind'.[52]

Maori still suffered discrimination in employment, especially during the 1930s depression, when Ngata noted: 'the pakeha is looking after himself first'. Nevertheless, he was glad that 'such of our people as had come to depend on public works, gum-digging, timber work and so forth' were returning to their rural *pa*. He had been working strenuously to stimulate effective Maori land use in order to promote economic welfare and a sense of Maori identity. Another manifestation of Maori consciousness was the proclamation of Tahupotiki Wiremu Ratana, a charismatic faith-healer, that the Maori were God's chosen race. Starting in 1918, he attracted much support from people demoralised by the influenza pandemic and those searching for a way out of rural poverty. From 1922 he was backing a political Ratana movement which, in alliance with the Labour Party, captured one Maori parliamentary seat in 1932 and all four of them by 1943. The Labour leader, Michael Savage, promised 'full economic equality' for Maori while preserving their racial identity. But in 1940 Ngata feared that the Labour government's comprehensive social welfare programme was 'striking a severe blow [to] maintenance of the individuality of the Maori people'. Also in 1939 the Maori death rate was still significantly higher than for pakeha, a reflection of poorer general living conditions. Improvements to Maori living standards in the 1920s with more cash farming received a major setback during the depression.[53]

Paternalistic colonial rule from 1900 to 1939 influenced other Polynesians to varying degrees. British support for Tonga's monarchical government helped perpetuate hierarchical Tongan society. Grimble and his predecessors assisted the preservation of the cultural identity of Gilbert Islanders, but they were not being well prepared to face the rapidly Europeanising outside world. A schoolmaster who bucked the Grimble system, Donald Kennedy, was not only restoring to Ellice Islanders a pride in their own language and culture weakened by decades of teaching by Samoan LMS pastors. He also was placing great emphasis on English and academic training, which gave his pupils a head start in the post–World War Two world, and was sowing seeds of future Tuvaluan nationalism.[54]

New Zealand policy in Western Samoa was promoting nationalism for a contrary reason. Richardson's attempts to modernise Samoan society ran into the brick wall of Samoan cultural conservatism. The consequent Mau movement significantly increased Samoans' sense of national identity in a society previously divided by factional struggles. On the other hand, whereas the Maori-based *taihoa* policy would have been more acceptable to Samoans, it failed to stem the onrush of Europeanisation in the Cook Islands. Ngata's emphasis on English-language teaching equipped many Cook Islanders to become post-war overseas migrants, rather than participate in their own economic development. Indeed, New Zealand paternalism in the Cook Islands had created an islander dependency on administrators that inhibited post-war islander initiatives. Nauruans, experiencing an even more rapid Europeanisation than Cook Islanders, were initially encouraged by Griffiths but were unassisted by the paternalism and apathy of subsequent administrators. Australia in Nauru and the other colonial powers in Polynesia were to face more assertive Polynesians in the post-World War Two world.

Notes

1 Stewart G. Firth, 'German Firms in the Pacific Islands, 1857–1914', in *Germany in the Pacific and Far East, 1870–1914*, ed. John A. Moses and Paul M. Kennedy, Queensland University Press, St Lucia, 1977, 3–25; Lewis H. Gann, 'Marginal Colonialism: The German Case' in *Germans in the Tropics: Essays in German Colonial History*, Arthur J. Knoll and Lewis H. Gann, Greenwood, Westport, CT, 1987, 6. Angus Ross, *New Zealand Aspirations in the Pacific in the Nineteenth Century*, Oxford University Press, 1964, ch. 14; P. M. Kennedy, 'Britain and the Tongan Harbours, 1898–1914', *Historical Studies* 15 (1972): 252; Penelope A. Lavaka, The Limits of Advice: Britain and the Kingdom of Tonga, 1900–1970, PhD dissertation, Australian National University, Canberra, 1981, 21–22.

2 Richard Gilson, *The Cook Islands 1820–1950*, Victoria University Press, Wellington, 1980, 99–100; 'Eseta Fusitu'a and Noel Rutherford, 'George Tupou II and the British Protectorate', in *Friendly Islands: A History of Tonga*, ed. Noel Rutherford, Oxford University Press, Melbourne, 1977, ch. 10; Lavaka, ch. 2; Peter J. Hempenstall, *Pacific Islanders Under German Rule: A Study in the Meaning*

of Colonial Resistance, Australian National University Press, Canberra, 1978, 25–34.

3 Hempenstall, 32–33; Mālama Meleiseā, *The Making of Modern Samoa: Traditional Authority and Colonial Administration in the Modern History of Western Samoa*, University of the South Pacific, Suva, 1987, 47; Chamberlain to Lord Hopetoun, 22 Jan. 1902, in *Documents on Australian International Affairs 1901–1918*, ed. Gordon Greenwood and Charles Grimshaw, Nelson, Melbourne, 1977, 531.

4 R. G. Crocombe, 'Land Polices in the Dependencies', in *New Zealand's Record in the Pacific Islands in the Twentieth Century*, ed. Angus Ross, Longman Paul, Auckland, 1969, 14.

5 Hempenstall, 34–43.

6 Fusitu'a and Rutherford, 182–185; Lavaka, ch. 3.

7 Barrie Macdonald, *Cinderellas of the Empire: Towards a History of Kiribati and Tuvalu*, Australian National University Press, Canberra, 1982, ch. 5.

8 Lavaka, chs 4–5; Fusitu'a and Rutherford, 185–188.

9 Gilson, 116–118; Crocombe, 15–16.

10 Gilson, 113–132; S. D. Wilson, 'The Record in the Cook Islands and Niue 1910–45', in Ross 1969, 26–32; Leslie Rex and Young Vivian, 'New Zealand Period', in *Niue: A History of the Island*, by H. Vilitama et al., Institute of Pacific Studies and Government of Niue, Suva, 1982, 127–128.

11 Hempenstall, 43–72; Peter Hempenstall and Noel Rutherford, *Protest and Dissent in the Colonial Pacific*, University of the South Pacific, Suva, 1984, ch. 1; J. W. Davidson, 'Lauaki Namulau'ulu Mamoe: A Traditionalist in Samoan Politics', in *Pacific Islands Portraits*, ed. J. W. Davidson and Deryck Scarr, Australian National University Press, Canberra, 1970, 267–300.

12 Noel Rutherford, 'Tonga Ma'a Tonga Kautaha: A Proto-Cooperative in Tonga', *Journal of Pacific History* 16 (1, 1981): 20–26; Penelope A. Lavaka, 'The *Tonga Ma'a Tonga Kautaha*: A Watershed in British–Tongan Relations', *Pacific Studies* 4 (1981): 142–145.

13 Lavaka, Tonga, 145–163; Rutherford, 27–41; Hempenstall and Rutherford, ch. 2; Elizabeth Wood Ellem, 'Chief Justices of Tonga 1905–40', *Journal of Pacific History* 24 (1989): 22–24.

14 A. Ngata to P. Buck, 30 January 1899, in *Na To Hoa Aroha: From Your Dear Friend. The Correspondence between Sir Apirana Ngata and Sir Peter Buck 1925–50*, 3 vols, ed. M. P. K. Sorrenson, Auckland University Press, 1986, 1:15; M. P. K. Sorrenson, 'Maori and Pakeha', in *The Oxford History of New Zealand*, ed. W. H. Oliver with B. R. Williams, Oxford University Press, Wellington, 1981, ch. 7; Michael King, 'Between Two Worlds', in *The Oxford History of New Zealand*, ch. 11.

15 King, 279–288; D. Ian Pool, *The Maori Population of New Zealand 1769–1971*, Auckland University Press, 1977, 106–145, 237.

16 King, 297; Lavaka, Limits of Advice, 222–249; Meleiseā ch. 5; Hermann Hiery, 'West Samoans between Germany and New Zealand, 1914–1921', in *War & Society*, 10 (1, 1992): 53–80; Wilson, 38–39; Rex and Vivian, 129.

17 Pool, 127–128; *Nauru Annual Report*, 1920; Lavaka, Limits of Advice, 262; Meleiseā, 121–122. For subsequent problems confronted by Logan's successor as military administrator, Colonel Robert Tate, see Mary Boyd, 'Coping with

Samoan Resistance after the 1918 Influenza Epidemic', *Journal of Pacific History* 15 (1980): 155–174.

18 K. Buckley and K. Klugman, *The History of Burns Philp: The Australian Company in the Pacific*, Burns, Philp & Company, Sydney, 268; Private Report, no. 19, Burns, Philp Papers, Australian National University Archives of Business and Labour, Canberra; Macdonald 1982, 94–102.

19 Mary Boyd, 'The Record in Western Samoa to 1945', in Ross, 1969, 124–125; *Commonwealth of Australia Parliamentary Debates* 89: 12679; A. Milner to J. Smuts, 1 January 1920, Milner Papers, C703, Bodleian Library, Oxford.

20 Ngata to Buck, 9 February 1928, in Sorrenson, 1:63.

21 Buck to Ngata, 13 January 1931, in Sorrenson 2:104; Michael J. Field, *Mau: Samoa's Struggle Against New Zealand Oppression*, Reed, Wellington, 1984, ch. 5; K. S. Eteuati, '*Evaevaga a Samoa*: Assertion of Samoan Autonomy, 1920–1936', PhD dissertation, Australian National University, 1982, 57–76; Meleiseā, 126–139.

22 Buck to Ngata, 30 March 1929, 25 August 1931, in Sorrenson, 1:187, 2:211.

23 G. Smith-Rewse to C. Rodwell, 15 December 1919, and enclosures, CO 225/170, File A518, R800/1/3, Australian Archives, Canberra; *Nauru Annual Reports*, 1922–1927.

24 Barrie Macdonald, 'Grimble of the Islands: Myth and Man' in *More Pacific Islands Portraits*, ed. Deryck Scarr, Australian National University Press, Canberra, 1978, 211–229; Macdonald 1982, 125–128, 135–136.

25 Gilson, 125–126; Buck to Ngata, 4 May 1930, in Sorrenson, 2:11; Ngata to Buck, 17 September 1932, in Sorrenson, 3:24.

26 Ngata to Buck, 17 September 1932, in Sorrenson 3:24; Ngata to Buck, 20 September 1930, in Sorrenson, 2:53–54.

27 A. H. Wood and Elizabeth Wood Ellem, 'Queen Salote Tupou III' in Rutherford, ch. 11; Lavaka, Limits of Advice, 258–273, 359–363; Christine Ward Gailey, 'Putting Down Sisters and Wives: Tongan Women and Colonization', in *Women and Colonization: Anthropological Perspectives*, ed. Mona Etienne and Eleanor Leacock, Praeger, New York, 1980, 294–322.

28 Lavaka, Limits of Advice, 270–273; Elizabeth Wood Ellem, 'Salote of Tonga and the Problem of National Unity', *Journal of Pacific History* 18 (1983): 163–182.

29 Ngata to Buck, 17 September 1932, in Sorrenson, 3:26–27; Ngata to Buck, 15 May 1931, 4 April 1932, in Sorrenson, 2:140, 261; Gilson, 202. Since this chapter was written, a history of New Zealand's administration of the Cook Islands has appeared: Dick Scott, *Years of the Pooh-Bah: A Cook Islands History*, Cook Islands Trading Corporation & Hodder and Stoughton, Rarotonga & Auckland, 1991.

30 Macdonald 1982, 128–132; Noatia P. Teo, 'Colonial Rule', in *Tuvalu: A History*, ed. Hugh Laracy, University of the South Pacific, Suva, 1983, 133.

31 Head Chief to Bruce, 15 September 1926, in J. Stonehaven to L. Amery, 8 November 1926, DO 35/1; Bruce to Amery, 9 March 1927, Amery to C. Ferguson, 10 March 1927, DO 35/21, Public Record Office, London.

32 Field, ch. 6; Meleiseā, ch. 7; Eteuati, 95–97.

33 Boyd 1969, 145–151; Eteuati, 123–125.

34 Buck to Ngata, 12 March 1928, in Sorrenson, 1:73–74.

35 Field, ch. 10; Eteuati, 141–165.

36 Field, chs 12–13; Eteuati, 165–182, 192–205.

37 Field, ch. 14; Eteuati, 213–221.

38 Boyd 1969, 166–167; Eteuati, 229–259.

39 Ngata to Buck, 8 March 1931, 9 September 1931, in Sorrenson, 2:121, 218, 271–332; Eteuati, 271–332.

40 Buck to Ngata, 29 June 1930, 13 January 1931, in Sorrenson, 2:36, 104; Mary Boyd, 'Racial Attitudes of New Zealand Officials in Western Samoa', *New Zealand Journal of History* 21 (1987): 154.

41 Buck to Ngata, 9 November 1929, 25 August 1931, 4 May 1930, in Sorrenson, 1: 262, 2: 210; Lowell D. Holmes, 'Factors Contributing to the Cultural Stability of Samoa', *Anthropological Quarterly* 53 (1980): 188–196.

42 File A518, D118/6; ten chiefs to J. Scullin, 29 November 1930; W. Newman to J. McLaren, 5, 19 December 1930, A518, O800/1/2, Australian Archives, Canberra.

43 C. Gabel to B. Chifley, 8 July 1931; memorandum by J. Halligan, 9 November 1933, A518, C800/1/2, BG118/6/1, Australian Archives, Canberra.

44 Newman to McLaren, 28 May 1931, 30 June 1931; Dabe to Scullin, 24 September 1931, A518, O800/1/2, Australian Archives, Canberra.

45 File A518, BT118/12, Australian Archives, Canberra; W. Groves to A. Elkin, 8 August 1938, Groves Papers, New Guinea Collection, University of Papua New Guinea Library, Port Moresby; T. Detudamo to H. Hurst, 6 May 1938, 14 June 1938, A518, N800/1/2, file F800/1/2; Cabinet Minutes, 18 August 1938, 1 September 1938, A2694/XM, Australian Archives, Canberra; F. Chalmers to Strahan, 7 December 1939, A518, C818/1/2/3, Australian Archives, Canberra; Maslyn Williams and Barrie Macdonald, *The Phosphateers: A History of the British Phosphate Commissioners and the Christmas Island Phosphate Commission*, Melbourne University Press, 1985, 289–290.

46 Hurst to W. Hughes, 20 April 1938, A518, AE118/7, Australian Archives, Canberra; Groves to Elkin, 8 August 1938, Groves Papers.

47 *Nauru Annual Report*, 1939; Williams and Macdonald, 273, 290.

48 *Gilbert and Ellice Islands Colony Annual Reports*, 1935, 1937; A. Richards to CO, 19 March 1937, CO 225/302/86034, Public Record Office, London; Macdonald 1982, 103–110; Gilson, 241.

49 Deryck Scarr, *The History of the Pacific Islands: Kingdoms of the Reefs*, Macmillan, Melbourne, 1990, 245.

50 Inspection Reports, Nuku'alofa Branch, 31 August 1921, 12 July 1920, shelf 5, Burns, Philp Archives, Sydney; Burns, Philp (South Seas) Minutes, 1929–1938, Burns, Philp & Company, Sydney; K. Buckley and K. Klugman, 'The Australian Presence in the Pacific': Burns Philp 1914–1946, Allen & Unwin, Sydney, 1983, 139–140, 285, 296, 315; Macdonald 1982, 141–142.

51 Macdonald 1982, 137–139; Robert Langdon, 'Harry Maude: Shy Proconsul, Dedicated Pacific Historian', in *The Changing Pacific: Essays in Honour of H. E. Maude*, ed. Niel Gunson, Oxford University Press, Melbourne, 1978, 1–10; Ngata to Buck, 17 September 1932, in Sorrenson, 3:25; Gilson, 174–178, 186–191, 241; Boyd 1987, 155.

52 Paul Spoonley, *The Politics of Nostalgia: Racism and the Extreme Right in New Zealand*, Dunmore Press, Palmerston North, 1987, ch. 3; Buck to Ngata, 4 May 1930, in Sorrenson, 2:12.

53 Ngata to Buck, 11 January 1930, in Sorrenson, 2:94; Ngata to Buck, 15 July 1940, in Sorrenson, 3:245; Barry Gustafson, *From the Cradle to the Grave: A Biography of Michael Joseph Savage*, Reed Methuen, Auckland, 1986, 188–190; Pool, ch. 6.

54 Macdonald 1982, 135–137; Teo, 'Colonial Rule', 136–138.

5

Patterns of colonial rule in Micronesia

David Hanlon

Micronesia is the term that has been applied to the 2106 Pacific islands and atolls that lie essentially north of the equator and west of the international date line. As preface to the colonial future to come, early European explorers, missionaries, sea captains, traders, naval officers, and map makers gave names to these islands that commemorated their own sovereigns, ships, native lands, or themselves. Through these bestowals of names and accompanying acts of description, the otherness of the islands and their people was rendered in terms that were familiar, intelligible, and encouraging to those with an expansionist agenda. The name Micronesia, first suggested in 1831 by the French geographer Domeny de Rienzi and derived from a combination of Greek words meaning 'tiny islands', marked a major qualitative step in the transition from textual representation to physical domination.[1] The term reflected the larger, nineteenth-century, imperial world's intensified need to order, categorize, bound, and know this part of the Pacific for purposes of control. In short, the use of words to name and describe began a process of exploitation that would culminate in the establishment of formal colonial rule over the area.[2]

Violence, domination, exploitation, and racism would all characterize to varying degrees the tenures of each metropolitan power that governed Micronesia at different times between 1886 and the outbreak of World War Two. Each colonising nation would attempt to justify and enhance its rule through rituals of possession, denigrating descriptions of Micronesian societies, the usurpation of indigenous political authority, and the promotion of alien, disruptive systems of religion, education, and economy. This chapter focuses on these major patterns in the shared colonial history of the Caroline, Mariana, and Marshall Islands under Spanish, German, and Japanese rule. American control over Guam between 1899 and 1941 also receives attention for its common colonial patterns, its distinctive historical features, and its role as harbinger of the larger American presence in Micronesia that would follow World War Two.

Colonial claims

Early Spanish exploration of the Pacific in the sixteenth century provided the basis for Spanish claims over the Caroline, Mariana, and Marshall Islands. Except for Guam and the rest of the Marianas, which were formally colonised beginning in 1668, Spain showed little active interest in the area. Beginning in the latter half of the nineteenth century, expanding German commercial activity in the Pacific threatened Spain's lethargic claim to greater Micronesia and resulted in a treaty with local Marshallese chiefs that established German control over Jaluit Atoll in 1878. The raising of the German flag over the major islands of the Caroline and Marshall groups by a government-ordered naval expedition in 1885 led to riots in Madrid, denunciation of the kaiser's action from other European capitals, and near-war between Spain and Germany. On 17 December 1885, Pope Leo XIII, in a compromise decision orchestrated carefully by German Chancellor Otto von Bismarck, recognized Spanish claims to administer the Carolines and German rights to trade in the area.[3] The Marshall Islands remained under the kaiser's flag as a protectorate. In 1888, the Jaluit Company, an internationally backed commercial enterprise formed from the merger of the Robertson & Hernsheim Company and the local interests of the Deutsche Handels-und-Plantagen Gesellschaft der Südsee Inseln zu Hamburg in the Marshalls, received an administrative charter over the islands. The granting of an administrative charter to commercial companies represented the German government's early preferred strategy of rule for its Pacific holdings. In return for its willingness to assume administrative responsibility and costs, the company acquired rights and privileges that gave it a monopoly over all commercial activities in the Marshalls.

Germany's attempts to gain control over Spanish Micronesia were ultimately successful in 1899. With its defeat at the hands of the United States in the Spanish–American War of 1898, Spain was now forced to relinquish all of its Pacific territories. Secret negotiations between German and Spanish representatives in Paris resulted in the sale of the Mariana and Caroline islands to Germany for the sum of 2.5 million pesetas. As with Spain, war would also spell the end of Germany's control over Micronesia. At the outbreak of World War One in Europe, Germany's Pacific possessions were distant, isolated, and undefensible. Beginning in October 1914, Japan, allied with Great Britain against Germany and the other Axis powers through a 1902 agreement, simply sailed into the various harbors of the islands and raised its flag. This seizure of the islands was part of a larger southern movement or *nanshin* as it was called in Japanese.[4] The strongest proponents of this southward advance were Japanese naval officials whose maritime interests would be most immediately served by access to Micronesian harbours and waters. Earlier wars with China and Russia in the late nineteenth and very early twentieth centuries had revealed that although Japan's ambition to achieve world power status was primarily continental in orientation, the South Seas had not gone wholly unnoticed. As early as the 1880s, a few government officials, naval officers, and journalists were arguing for the Japanese acquisition of equatorial lands in terms of economic advantage, national security, and geopolitics. Said Japanese Diet member Takekoshi Yosaburo: 'Whoever controls the tropics controls the world.'[5] In 1919, the League of Nations formally recognised Japan's occupation of the islands through the award of a Class C Mandate. In return for the mandate, the metropolitan power promised to file progress reports with the League, forego the construction of any fortifications in the mandated territory, and guarantee the right of commerce within the territory to all nations. In effect, the fictitious guardianship on behalf of the League of Nations provided little more than a thin cover for the Japanese annexation of Micronesia.

Ceremonies of possession

Diplomatic negotiations in distant European capitals required appropriate ceremonies of possession in the lands acquired. Spain dressed the arrival of its colonising parties in the Carolines with a considerable amount of pomp, ceremony, and spectacle, all surrounded by religious rites. On Yap, the colonising party was led in procession from the shore to the Catholic church with cross, candles, and a bell.[6] On arriving at the church, built the previous year, all sang the 'Te Deum'. On Pohnpei, drum rolls, musket fire, and the music of coronets greeted the raising of the Spanish flag on 25 July 1886.[7] Lieutenant Bayo y Hernandez Pinzon of the warship *Manila* proclaimed possession of the island and its immediately surrounding atolls and islands in the name of Dona Maria Cristina de Hapsburgo Lorena, the reigning queen of Spain. To reaffirm, in their own minds at least, the credibility of their rule, the Spaniards also staged elaborate yearly celebrations of their queen's birthday.

The history of Spanish rule would reveal the hollowness of these ceremonies. On Pohnpei, violent uprisings in 1887, 1890, and 1898 would turn Spanish colonisers into hostages on the island they purported to rule. A governor wrote in 1892 that the Pohnpeians were content to leave the Spaniards 'enclosed in our polygon of 1025 meters without attacking our laws, governing themselves at their pleasure and believing themselves already with the right to impose on us their barbaric customs'.[8] On Yap, the centre of Spanish rule for the Western Carolines, local resistance would be revealed through a more general, culturally informed refusal to change. The Spaniards had little or no effect elsewhere among the islands and atolls of Micronesia, except through brief sporadic visits from officials based on Yap or Pohnpei.

German ceremonies, whether they involved acts of possession or celebrations of the kaiser's birthday, could no more preclude violence or other culturally prescribed forms of resistance than had those of the Spaniards. In his report on the official ceremonies of transfer for the Eastern Caroline Islands that took place on Pohnpei in October 1899, the governor of German New Guinea, Rudolph von Benningsen, who had ultimate jurisdiction over newly acquired Micronesia, expressed confidence in a more tranquil future for the island.[9] Albert Hahl, the resident deputy governor for the Eastern Carolines, was less sure than von Benningsen about the prospects for peace.[10] Violent rebellion against German colonial rule on Pohnpei in October 1910 would prove his doubts well founded.

Among the acts and ceremonies of possession, those of the Japanese contained the most overt threat of violence.[11] Less than two months after the official declaration of war on Germany, the Japanese navy had landed shore parties on all of the major islands of the Caroline, Mariana, and Marshall groups. On 7 October 1914, hundreds of soldiers stormed the Catholic mission grounds on Pohnpei with bayonets fixed. Machine-guns were quickly set up and trained on all foreign premises, while Japanese soldiers carried out a quick search for weapons and other instruments of resistance. On Belau, the threat of violence was even more acute when the Japanese commander threatened to execute all German officials in retaliation for the incarceration of resident Japanese nationals that had occurred just prior to the arrival of the landing party.

Japan, as had Spain and Germany, would have its own ceremonies of possession designed to intimidate and subdue. One great ceremonial occasion was the annual celebration of the emperor's birthday; the religious rites surrounding the opening of the *Kampei Taisha Nan'yō Jinja* in Belau provided another.[12] Officially dedicated in February, 1940, the shrine physically represented the power and authority of the Japanese nation in Micronesia. Somewhere in the high drama and extensive rituals of the shrine's dedication were the Belauans and other Micronesians who, by inference, had been incorporated along with their lands and waters into the greater East Asian community of nations under Japanese tutelage. This most prominent Shinto structure, like all others in the islands, was never intended as a place of worship for Japan's Micronesian subjects; rather, it served as a focus for their assumed awe and respect. One prominent Belauan said of the *Kampei Taisha* shrine: 'Though we were allowed to visit it, it was for Japanese only'.[13]

Ceremonies of possession usually sought to formalise the boundary between the coloniser and the colonised. The larger world required of the metropolitan power a more benevolent, internationally voiced justification to cloak the self-interest that usually underlay the colonisation process. In this regard, the concept of primitivism served the advocates of empire well in the early twentieth century. Moreover, the developing discipline of anthropology offered a scientific basis for primitivism and, inadvertently, a justification with which empire could be defended against its critics. The French anthropologist Lèvy-Bruhl had helped move European thinking away from the directly pejorative concept of the savage towards the slightly less hostile notion of primitivism.[14] Lèvy-Bruhl postulated that primitive peoples were not illogical in their understanding of the world, but rather 'pre-logical'. They possessed no process of causality; for primitive peoples, the natural world was guided by mystical outside forces. In short, 'primitive' peoples were deemed to be without intellectual, social, political, and religious structures that would allow them to cope with modernity. In their own ways and time, each of Micronesia's colonisers in Micronesia explained their mission as an effort to overcome this disinclination towards rational thought and to help integrate the islands' populations into the modern world. Primitivism, of course, had to be studied systematically in order to be exploited politically. The German Südsee Expedition sailed through the Caroline and Marshall Islands between August 1909 and April 1910.[15] Staffed by three ethnologists, an artist, and an official diarist and collector, the expedition, under the leadership of Augustin Krämer, sought to observe and record the last years of allegedly declining Micronesian cultures. In the spring of 1915, a Japanese research team from Tokyo University began a two-month tour of the islands.[16] Focusing their efforts in the areas of medicine, agriculture, and natural science, the team produced a massive report that, in effect, buttressed Japanese claims to Micronesia through the demonstration of knowledge and expertise in assumed critical areas.

The earliest colonial representatives were quick to identify what they thought to be the primitive aspects of Micronesian cultures. Spanish Capuchin missionaries described Belauan culture as steeped in superstition, ignorance, thievery, and unrestrained sexuality.[17] On Yap, this same group complained of polygamy, divorce, the custom of *mespil* (group wife), and the general difficulty of the language. Above all was the seeming indifference and aloofness of the people to missionary endeavours.[18] Fourteen years of Spanish rule did little to alter these assessments. German officials expressed similar sentiments. Arno Senftt, the German district administrator for Yap from 1899 to 1908, whose jurisdiction also included Belau, deplored the mournful state of mind that plagued the people of the Western Carolines.[19] Senftt blamed the exploitation of the priestly and chiefly classes on Belau for what he saw as the arrested state of moral and intellectual development there. Albert Hahl, the deputy governor of the Eastern Carolines, regarded the Pohnpeians as, by nature, distrustful, treacherous, and apathetic.[20] His successor, Victor Berg, characterised the people of the island as 'incorrigible vagabonds'.[21]

Japanese colonial officials referred to all Micronesians as *santo kokumin* (third-class people), at the very bottom of the imperial social order.[22]

Strategies for domination

All of Micronesia's colonial masters sought to legitimise their rule through the usurpation of indigenous chiefly authority. On Pohnpei, the first Spanish governor, Don Isidro Posadillo, gave each of the five paramount chiefs of the island the title of *gobernadorcillo* (little governors).[23] With proper ceremony, Posadillo provided the chiefs with the symbols of their new Spanish office, the flag and the sceptre. On Pohnpei in German times, the chiefs were given judicial powers in their respective chiefdoms for a variety of offences ranging from disrespectful behaviour to assault. The paramount chiefs in each of the five districts, the *nahnmwarki*, were given the title of *richter* (petty judge), while the German governor remained the *Kaiserliche richter* (imperial judge).[24] On Yap, Arno Senfft created an advisory council of chiefs, supplemented by elected representatives from over one hundred villages, to help implement German colonial policies.[25] A similar though more modest arrangement was created on Belau.

Micronesian chiefs were also incorporated into the system of Japanese colonial rule, but below the lowest Japanese functionary in the local government.[26] The regulations of the colonial government created two types of Micronesian leaders: the sectional chief (*sosonchō*) and a local liaison officer (*sonchō*). These chiefs served as minor functionaries in a bureaucratic structure and were charged with notifying their communities of laws, regulations, and pronouncements from the district government. They collected taxes, made reports, and appointed work parties for various public construction projects. Said one Pohnpeian *sosonchō*, 'The Japanese policeman gave the orders: I was forced to see that they were carried out'.[27] On the more remote islands and atolls of the mandate, the structures of chiefly authority were less affected. However, regular visits of Japanese colonial officials to Bikini, Woleai, Ulithi, and Satawal, reminded local chiefs quite clearly of the power of an alien order that could reach out from the district centres of the larger islands to affect their lives.

Each of the dominant colonial powers would have its particular mode or vehicle of domination. For Spain, religion, more particularly Catholicism, was the instrument of submission and control. Spanish Catholic and American Protestant missionaries had been working in the Caroline, Marshall, and Mariana islands long before the establishment of formal colonial empire. These early mission efforts had been carried out without the benefit of overt imperial backing. However, the reassertion of Spanish interests in the Carolines in 1886 brought church and state together in a close, mutually reinforcing alliance. Members of the Spanish Capuchin order now headed the mission effort in the Caroline and Mariana islands. Father Antonio de Valencia gave expression to this alliance between '*la espada y la cruz*' when, on reaching Belau in 1891, he stated his intention to help 'make Palau a real Spanish land'.[28] Indeed, Peter Hempenstall has called missionaries the 'real representatives' of colonial rule at the district and sectional levels.[29]

A change in colonial administrations ultimately led to a change in the nationality of the missionaries themselves. For a time, Spanish Capuchins continued to run the Catholic mission stations in German Micronesia. Not until 1903 did the German Capuchins from the Rhein-Westfalen Province begin replacing their Spanish counterparts.[30] Native Hawaiian missionaries worked in the Marshalls until 1889, when their places were taken by local Marshallese pastors.[31] American Congregational missionaries, though barred from Pohnpei between 1890 and 1900 by the Spanish colonial government for their alleged role in the hostilities of 1890 on the island, continued to oversee eastern Micronesia from mission stations on Kosrae and Chuuk. In 1907, the Americans yielded their work in the Carolines to members of the Jugendbund für entscheidendes Christentum, the German evangelical mission organisation based in Bad Liebenzeller.[32]

Despite the support of resident colonial governments, Spanish missionary efforts met with considerable resistance. The apostolic mission was not readily apparent to islanders, who had considerable trouble understanding the presence and purpose of priests among them. Father de Valencia wrote of the situation on Belau: 'Some take us for traders with a different uniform from the others who live here; others believed that we came to govern the land and would be followed by soldiers. But all were far from believing that we were bringing them a new teaching, a new way of life dramatically opposed to their own'.[33] In both Yap and Belau, Spanish and later German Capuchin missionaries experienced strong local resistance from those they identified as chiefs, shamans, and sorcerers. On Pohnpei, local political rivalries heavily influenced the demography of Christianity. Resistance to the introduction of Roman Catholicism proved strongest in those areas of the island with entrenched Protestant mission stations. Conversely, the sections of Pohnpei traditionally at odds with the Protestant areas often responded quickly and enthusiastically to Catholic mission efforts. In the words of a later German colonial official, 'the natives consider the churches as political institutions'.[34]

By 1936, the ebb and flow of mission efforts had produced statistics that showed 78 per cent of the total population of the Caroline, Mariana, and Marshall islands to be either Catholic or Protestant. Only on Yap and Belau did the number of Christians register at less than 50 per cent of the total population. Despite the solace provided by this arithmetic of religious conversion, missionaries of all nationalities and denominations worried over the depth of their converts' faith. During Japanese times, advances achieved by Spanish Jesuits in the Chuuk area, referred to as the Islands of Apparitions because of the numerous reports of religious visions there,[35] were offset by the generally stagnant conditions in Yap, the perennial 'Child of Sorrow' of the greater Catholic effort in Micronesia.[36] Not even the Marianas, with almost two and a half centuries of exposure to Catholicism, was exempt from the missionaries' despair. Towards the end of German rule, Father Gallus Lehmann wrote of the intellectual inferiority of the Saipanese. Their poverty of knowledge and general lack of conceptual and cognitive abilities, said the missionary, set them apart from all others. The only language they understood was that of the senses. Because of this, concluded Father Lehmann, the missionary was prevented from presenting the higher exalted secrets of religion.[37]

A shared nationality and common purpose did not necessarily make for harmony between missionaries and colonial officials. On Pohnpei, Spanish Capuchins railed in their early mission reports against the indifference and eccentricities of the first Spanish governor, Don Isidro Posadillo.[38] The 1887 assassination of Posadillo by Pohnpeians confirmed in the missionaries' minds the folly of agnostic administrators. Georg Fritz, who served as German district officer on Pohnpei from 1908 to 1909, blamed the political meddling and indiscriminate prosletysing of German Capuchin missionaries as one of the major causes behind the rebellion against colonial rule that erupted in north-western Pohnpei in October 1910.[39]

Dealings between European or American missionaries and colonial officials of a nation with a radically different set of religious beliefs and practices were not necessarily problematic. Mutual goals could be found. Tadao Yanaihara believed that the spread of Christianity in Micronesia had 'done more than any other agency to break down totemism and to free the native mind from the clutches of superstition, fear and domination of the sorcerer'.[40] The Japanese colonial scholar viewed Christianity as producing radical change that included a general improvement in the standard of living, the development of literacy, the improvement of health and sanitation standards, a greater appreciation of productive economic activity, and a check against sexual licence.

Although the Japanese navy placed severe restrictions on missions and mission activities during the war years from 1914 to 1918, Yanaihara's assessment of Christianity in the islands reflected the essentially positive light in which the Japanese colonial government came to view Christianity following the end of World War One. Father Paulo Marela, a representative from the Roman Curia, wrote of the mutually beneficial pre-war alliance between missionaries and Japanese colonial officials in his 1937 study of Catholicism in the mandate islands. Father Marela affirmed that the missions and the colonial government were engaged in a joint effort to develop islanders' talents, to elevate their minds, and to cultivate them as good, conscientious Japanese people.[41] In 1932, the Japanese government provided a ¥7000 subsidy to the Catholic mission, now staffed by Spanish Jesuits, and a ¥23 000 subsidy to the Nan'yō Dendō Dan, a missionary arm of Japanese

Protestant churches that had replaced the Liebenzeller mission to the Caroline, Mariana, and Marshall islands.[42] With the approach of World War Two, however, relations between foreign missionaries and the Japanese colonial government deteriorated badly.

How Micronesians actually regarded Christianity and whether or not they separated religious conversion from its larger colonial context remain open questions. Recent studies of the relationship between colonialism and Christianity in other areas of the Pacific suggest that conversion did not necessarily entail abject submission to colonial rule.[43] As a political strategy, religious conversion to Christianity allowed Micronesian peoples to contain the demands of foreign authority by permitting communication and negotiation with colonial representatives through a higher, mutually shared body of religious beliefs. In this way, the more oppressive aspects of the colonial presence could be blunted.

The manipulation of Christianity as leverage against general colonial intrusion was not the only religious strategy employed by Micronesians. Resistance also resulted from the rise or assertion of more indigenous systems of religious belief. German colonial accounts make repeated reference to opposition from Yapese sorcerers. In Belau, a man named Rdiall from a low-ranking family whose ancestral home was at Ngkeklau in Ngeraard began claiming direct communication with the gods of Belau.[44] By 1907 he was speaking to increasing numbers of people about a future without any foreign administration or control. This sounded highly subversive to German officials, who investigated and then banned the movement.

The *Modekngei* proved a highly visible, sometimes more formidable, form of resistance to Japanese rule in Belau.[45] Influenced by the words of Rdiall, the *Modekngei* sought to restore the worship of ancient Belauan gods. Studies of the *Modekngei* movement suggest that its members were drawn from those segments of Belauan society that received little direct benefit from Japanese rule.[46] These included members of the high-ranking clans, the elderly, and the people in areas distant from Koror, the capital of the Japanese colonial administration for Belau and all of Micronesia. Specific acts of resistance to foreign rule by the *Modekngei* included the burning of the Japanese school at Ngeraard, a prohibition on female members' marriages to Belauan men working for the colonial administration, and the singing of anti-Japanese songs. Despite these activities, the arrests of *Modekngei* leaders in 1938 resulted in large part from the urging of other Belauan groups more immediately and beneficially involved with the colonial presence.[47] The Japanese themselves tended to see the *Modekngei* as a less-than-serious threat. Kenjiro Kitayama, former governor-general of the South Seas Bureau (*Nan'yō-chō*) from 1936 to 1940, testified before a meeting of the Imperial Japanese Diet's standing committee on the budget that the *Modekngei* posed no problem to Japanese rule because Belauans' overall educational and cultural levels were low.[48]

As had efforts at religious conversion, education served the agenda of submission to colonial rule in Micronesia. In the early years of formal colonial rule, missionaries carried the burden of educating as well as proseletysing; they were not without governmental support and assistance, however. An early government report on the German administration of the Marshall Islands cited missions and their educational efforts as highly desirable because they instilled obedience in the native population.[49] Indicative of government support for mission schools were the Spanish administration's subsidies to the Catholic mission schools on Pohnpei and Yap. The German administration also gave financial assistance to both Catholic and Protestant mission schools to support German language learning.[50] In general, mission schools placed particular emphasis on basic literacy and 'practical' skills, with advanced study for those students chosen to serve as missionaries to other islands or as local mission assistants.

The most encompassing, self-serving colonial education system belonged to the Japanese.[51] With the seizure of Micronesia by Japan in 1914, the many mission schools throughout the islands were temporarily shut down. On the bigger islands, Japanese naval personnel had provided an initial rudimentary schooling system in the absence of anything more formal and structured. In 1923, with the islands now administered by the civilian-staffed *Nan'yō-chō*, there was issued a set of regulations, the *Nan'yō-chō Kōgakkō Kisoku*, that reorganized the entire school system and identified the fundamental goals of education in Micronesia as the moral guidance of students, the imparting of knowledge indispensable to the betterment of life, and training directed towards the physical development and health of the islanders. Under these regulations, education in the public schools or *kōgakkō* was to consist of three years of elementary class work, with a supplementary two-year programme of study for students of special promise and ability. By 1930, the *Nan'yō-chō* government operated some twenty-four public schools in which more than half of the school-aged children of Micronesia were enrolled. In 1935, enrollment in Japanese schools became compulsory for all Micronesian school-aged children; throughout Micronesia, the mission schools, which had been allowed to reopen in 1919 following the end of World War One, now filled only a minor supplemental role in the area of religious instruction.

For the very best male students from the supplemental two-year schools in the district centres, there was the *Mōkkō Tōtei Yoseijō* (Carpentry Apprentice Training School) in Koror, Belau. Established in 1926, the school trained young Micronesians, the majority of them Belauans, in carpentry and woodworking. Although offering a rare and desirable opportunity in many ways, the Belau school underscored the servile role for Micronesians in the colonial scheme of things. No Micronesians were trained for administrative operations involving leadership and responsibility. The highest position open to those Micronesians with five years of schooling was that of village constable.

Segregation also became a feature of the larger school system in Micronesia. Japanese children, the sons and daughters of the increasing numbers of immigrants to Micronesia, attended the separate *shogakkō*, eight-year primary schools located in the district centres of the major islands and modelled after the elementary school system that existed at the time in Japan. The segregation in education arose from differences of race and culture; colonial officials believed that younger members of backward, primitive societies had no place in a classroom with Japanese children. For most Micronesian children, their years of schooling left them with little real ability in the Japanese language. Supplies were short and work in other subjects cursory or limited. The use of vernacular Micronesian languages in the Japanese school system, first ignored, became expressly forbidden. What learning occurred generally consisted of rote memorisation and group recitation, with heavy doses of corporal punishment for incorrect answers or apparent laziness. In the words of one scholar, 'formal Japanese education for many Micronesians was at worst a cultural humiliation; for most, . . . of limited permanent value'.[52]

The economics of colonisation

As with religion and education, efforts at economic development were another vehicle through which colonial powers sought to direct Micronesian people and their resources towards the service of larger metropolitan interests. Germany and Japan were the most aggressive in this area. German commercial efforts in Micronesia began with the opening of a trading station on Yap in 1869 by the Hamburg firm of J. C. Godeffroy und Sohn.[53] By 1880, Yap was well established as the commercial center for the Western Carolines. In the same year, the Hernsheim Company, another early and major German trading firm in Micronesia, was operating stations in Belau, Yap, Woleai, and Pohnpei.[54] The Jaluit Company monopolised all trade in the Marshall Islands, where until 1907 copra remained the most profitable commodity.[55] The German Colonial Office's insistence on strict restrictions against the acquisition of land by non-native peoples led officials of the Jaluit Company to enlist the support of Marshallese chiefs in the copra production process. By the end of the nineteenth century, some of the wealthier chiefs were earning between twenty and thirty thousand marks a year from the copra trade. Of the nine ships handling the copra trade in the Marshalls in this period, five belonged to Marshallese chiefs.

These gains made in copra production lagged far behind German expectations, however. With the termination of the Jaluit Company's governing charter in 1906 and the subsequent inclusion of the Marshalls with the rest of German Micronesia under the administration of German New Guinea, colonial officials quickly came to view a declining, listless population as the major impediment to economic development in the Marshalls. Social relocation and cultural reorganisation were thought to be the cures. With restrictions on the sale of local land to non-natives lifted in 1907, colonial officials considered the purchase of Bikini, Enewetak, Rongelap, Rongrik, Alinganae, Wotho, Taka, Wotje, and Erikub, and the relocation of their populations to areas in the south.[56] As outlined in a 1912 document by the imperial governor of German New Guinea, the objectives of such a policy included lessening the effects of natural disasters, increasing the vitality of the native race through intermarriage with peoples of other islands and atolls, facilitating the task of administration, and turning over the vacated land to entrepreneurial capital and intensive plantation culture.[57] The whole programme of managed migration was eventually abandoned, however, because of the resistance of chiefs and people, and because of the problems of adjustment that often plagued the resettled communities.

Population problems were also a concern in the Marianas. German colonial officers identified general indifference and the lack of a large vigorous population as impediments to economic development. Efforts to enlist German immigrants to establish settlements never achieved any real success. In the Western Carolines, environmental impediments to economic development were more than compounded by opposition from powerful segments within Belauan and Yapese societies. Arno Senfft blamed the Belauan chiefs for their arrogance and greed. Even more powerful than the opposition of the chiefs was that emanating from those identified as sorcerers. In 1901, Senfft had threatened banishment for sorcerers interfering in the affairs of the German colonial administration in Belau. Although reporting no overt opposition from this group in 1904, he wrote that their power and influence remained formidable.[58] Senfft also sought unsuccessfully to curb the activities of the men's clubs which he felt did little more than distract Belauan men from more productive activities.

Given the political, demographic, and environmental difficulties in the Carolines and Marianas, the Marshalls remained the centre of commercial activity and profit for German Micronesia. Phosphate came to replace copra as the most profitable trade item in the period from 1906 to 1914.[59] Phosphate was found in commercial quantities on Nauru, and also on Ngeaur (formerly Angaur), Fais, Beliliou, and Tobi in the Western Carolines. On Nauru, which the Germans administered as part of the Marshall Islands Protectorate, the Jaluit Company had sublet its phosphate rights to the Pacific Phosphate Company Limited of London in return for a percentage of its stock and other considerations. The German colonial government exercised control of deposits on Ngeaur and Fais. In 1908, the Deutsche Südsee-Phosphat-Aktien-Gesellschaft (DSPAG), a consortium of German banks and other firms, was granted the phosphate rights on Ngeaur in return for an annual fee of 30 000 marks and a gradually increasing percentage of the profits over the life of the grant. In 1914, the DSPAG secured the mining rights to phosphate on Fais as well.

The acquisition of land title was the first, most necessary, prerequisite for phosphate mining in Micronesia. Relying on deceit, pressure, and modest monetary inducements, representatives of the German colonial government got the people of Ngeaur to relinquish all claims to their island 'for all time'; under the terms of this agreement, the people of Ngeaur were left with only a reservation of 150 hectares in the island's south-east corner.[60] With the land secured, labour became the most pressing concern. Unable to secure enough Chinese labourers from the Asian mainland, company officials turned to the Caroline Islands. In the Western Carolines, promises made by company officials to local chiefs were broken as islander labourers on Ngeaur found themselves forced to accept goods instead of wages, thrashed for disciplinary infractions, and provided with poor rations and insufficient rest periods. The veteran of German colonial administration Georg Fritz, district officer on Yap from 1909 to 1911, became so dismayed by the abusive treatment of island labourers that he refused to assist the company in any further recruitment drives within his jurisdiction. The colonial office eventually asserted itself over the resistance of local officials like Fritz who protested the conditions of the phosphate labour trade. Adjustments were made to extend the length of the labour contract from one to three years and to remove government officials from Ngeaur, leaving discipline and supervision to DSPAG representatives. In 1912, 600 islanders from the Western Carolines signed labour contracts. In the last years of the German colonial administration, particular emphasis was placed on the recruitment of labour from the Eastern Carolines where 774 islanders were recruited in 1913 for work on Ngeaur. Plans to recruit similar numbers the following year met with protest from Hermann Kersting, the district officer on Pohnpei, who believed that the enlisting of such relatively large numbers of young adult males threatened the well-being of the islands and atolls from which they came.

Nauru also relied on labourers from the Carolines. In 1907, 100 Chuukese, induced by the promises of the district officer on Pohnpei, agreed to work on Nauru.[61] Discipline, the nature of the work, and the conditions under which it was performed were extremely arduous. Each communication from Nauru brought reports of death, leading Chuukese chiefs and elders to insist that their young men be released from work there. While the high demand for labour ultimately drove up wages for labourers, Micronesian lands and people served ultimately as mere resources to be used and exploited in the quest for higher profits. In the estimation of one Pacific scholar, the aim of the German colonial government in Micronesia was to supply phosphate firms with land, long mining leases, low overhead, high returns, and a disciplined, underpaid work force.[62] To be sure, German trade in the greater Pacific never amounted to more than a fraction of 1 per cent of Germany's total foreign trade; nonetheless, efforts at economic development in Micronesia certainly earned profits for a very select group of resident traders, financiers and bankers back in Europe, as well as local chiefs in Micronesia.[63] German overall efforts paled, however, against the scope of Japanese economic activity in Micronesia from the mid-1920s to the advent of World War Two.[64]

The Japanese commercial presence in the islands actually began in the late 1880s when small groups of Japanese traders, lured by the prospects of profit and adventure, began to trade and barter for copra and coconut oil with the inhabitants of the Caroline, Mariana, and Marshall islands.[65] By 1906, 80 per cent of the total trade in German Micronesia was controlled by the Japanese. In 1908, the greatest commercial rivalry in the Mariana and Caroline islands was between the *Nan'yō Bōeki Hiki Gōshigaisha* and the *Nan'yō Bōeki Maruyama Gōemeigaisha*, both firms founded by Japanese traders in Micronesia.[66] These two Japanese concerns eventually merged to form the *Nan'yō Bōeki Kabushikigaisha* (South Seas Trading Company) that would become better known as *Nambō*. By 1914, *Nambō* held a leading position in the commercial life of the islands; its copra and bêche-de-mer trade, commercial fishing operations, inter-island mail service, .and freight and passenger business, all combined to give it a near monopoly over trade in the central and western parts of Micronesia. World War One, and with it the seizure of Micronesia by Japan, further enhanced the already formidable power of *Nambō*.

Investments were made in agriculture and industry as well as commerce. Through the establishment of the *Nan'yō Kōhatsu Kaisha* (South Seas Development Company), the entrepreneur Matsue Haruji was able to develop sugar on Saipan into the most profitable of all agricultural enterprises.[67] Matsue's *Nankō* inspired domestic financial support for a host of other developmental enterprises in the mandate. This private investment activity was sustained through the 1930s by the Japanese government's effort to integrate colonial territories more extensively and more quickly into the larger imperial economy. A special commission was formed to identify means to accelerate the Japanese settlement in Micronesia, speed the exploitation of island and marine resources, and promote tropical industry as a whole. There followed the formation of the *Nan'yō Takushoku Kaisha* (South Seas Colonisation Corporation), an agency of the colonial government with a board of directors drawn from government and business circles. *Nantaku*, as it was called, quickly assumed direct management of the phosphate mines in the Western Carolines; it also established a host of subsidiary companies involving electrical energy, refrigeration, aluminium mining, pearl fishing, and commercial agriculture. The activities of *Nantaku* and its subsidiary enterprises graphically demonstrated the mutually beneficial, reinforcing alliance between Japanese government and business in Micronesia.[68]

The flow of Japanese immigrants into the islands intensified dramatically with this governmental backing for economic development.[69] By 1935, there were 50 000 Japanese nationals in the islands, the majority of whom were

Uninhabitated before the Japanese, Tinian Town was built when the sugar industry was begun by Nan'yō Kōhatsu Kaisha. 1937. (From the collection of Belau National Museum)

from Okinawa. In 1940, the total Japanese population had climbed to 77 000; two years later, it reached 96 000. By the outbreak of war between Japan and the United States, Micronesians in Micronesia were outnumbered by almost twice as many Japanese, most of whom resided in Saipan and Koror.

The financial ledger of Japan's Micronesian colony dramatically reveals the extent of economic development.[70] In 1922, the islands were a drain on the imperial treasury, with administrative expenditures required to compensate for the lack of local revenues and the failure of the very first development projects. By the late 1920s, a combination of private initiative and government support, especially in the areas of sugar and phosphate production, had generated revenues that began to reverse this imbalance. In 1932, local revenues were such that grants from the Japanese national government were no longer necessary. By 1937, the colonial government in Micronesia had a reserve of close to one million yen. Within the larger context of the Japanese empire, the economic standing and contributions of the mandate islands were quite small. This tiniest of Japan's colonies provided only 1 per cent of the total value of goods produced by the empire in 1939. However, these seemingly insignificant trade figures were more than offset by the ability of this relatively active, vibrant local economy to pay for the cost of its own administration and thus serve Japan's ultimate strategic interests in the islands.

Land was, of course, a necessary component of any scheme to develop the islands economically. Spain, while claiming in theory that all land belonged to the Crown, did honour indigenous landholding practices by offering to purchase set tracts for churches, garrisons, or colonial administrative centres. The German administration, with its commitment to economic development, believed in the prerequisite of establishing a system of private landownership. In the Marianas, that process had been largely accomplished by the preceding Spanish regime, which had issued legal titles to private individuals for set parcels of land. The German administration tended to confirm these titles as well as provide lease land for commercial companies and grants of small parcels of freehold land for islander immigrants from the Central Carolines.[71]

On Pohnpei, land reform was intricately tied up with a programme to undermine what was seen to be the absolute authority of the island's chiefly system. In 1908, German Governor Georg Fritz prepared a land reform programme designed to make the island more open to economic development.[72] The rights of chiefs to require labour and produce from commoners was to be abolished, as was their control over the land. The price of this land reform effort would be the assassination of Governor Gustav Boeder, who attempted to implement it, and general rebellion against German colonial authority in the north-west chiefdom of the island in October, 1910. Not until 1912 was the German land reform programme for Pohnpei actually put into effect.

Japan initially honoured both the patchwork collection of different indigenous land tenure systems and the changes made by the previous German administration.[73] All land unoccupied or uncultivated was considered the property of the colonial government. Private land held by Micronesians was protected against the encroachments of Japanese speculators. No Japanese corporation could buy, sell, or mortgage land in Micronesia. However, there were no restrictions on the sale of land between different Micronesian parties. The leasing of Micronesian land to Japanese citizens was permitted, but for lease periods of no more than ten years. Uncertainty over both public and private landholdings led the colonial government to undertake, beginning in 1923, a land survey and registration programme. This effort did not end confusion over land title, nor did it effectively address the issue of usage patterns. The Japanese surveyors often assumed uninhabited land was unused land, hence the property of the colonial government. Traditional lands intentionally left open for general hunting, fishing, farming, or lumbering activities were thus appropriated.

The increase of Japanese immigration into Micronesia, especially in the 1930s, exacerbated the pressures on Micronesian lands. While some Chamorro families on Saipan benefited handsomely from lease agreements with Matsue

Damage caused by aerial and naval bombardment, Garapan, Saipan, July 1944. Smoke rises from a burning fuel dump near the remains of the Catholic Church. (Land Management Office, Capitol Hill, Saipan)

Haruji and the South Seas Development Company, many other Micronesians found themselves alienated from their land by the needs and demands of the foreign settlers who were arriving in ever-increasing numbers. In 1931, the Japanese colonial government lifted the restriction on the sale of land to private individuals and companies from Japan. Government approval was still required, but it was a Japanese government now increasingly attentive to the land needs of Japanese immigrants. With the militarisation of the islands just prior to World War Two, regard for Micronesian ownership of land declined drastically. All lands deemed necessary for Japanese defence of the islands were seized by the military. With the islands under siege in the latter stages of the war, there was not even a pretence of offering compensation for lands taken.

World War Two would bring Japan and the United States into open conflict. Many of the most important battles of the Pacific War would be fought on the atolls and islands of Micronesia. Long before the outbreak of hostilities, however, both countries had regarded each other suspiciously.[74] Japan resented strongly the racial discrimination and immigration quotas experienced by its citizens in Hawai'i, California, and the Pacific Northwest in the very late nineteenth and early twentieth centuries. The United States, for its part, developed a very deep-seated distrust of general Japanese expansion in the greater Pacific area. In this period of heightened tension, the United States Navy drafted Plan Orange, a strategic contingency arrangement to be implemented in the event of war with Japan in the Pacific. Access to the cable station at Yap was also of concern to American government officials who, from 1920 to 1922, worried publicly about Japanese control over the important transpacific communications facility there.[75] Japan's general secrecy on matters of administration and its severe restrictions on outsiders' contact with the islands added further to the suspicions of some American officials that military fortification of the area was the Asian coloniser's ultimate objective.[76] Although the political, economic, and ideological differences that separated the two nations were great, the physical distance between them was quite small, at least in Micronesia. In 1914, less than fifty miles of ocean lay between Japanese Rota and American Guam in the Mariana Islands chain.

America on Guam

Guam had come under American control as a result of the Spanish–American War of 1898 that had marked the United States' formal commitment to imperial expansion in the Pacific. During negotiations over the Treaty of Paris that had defined the terms of peace, American representatives had initially considered the acquisition of the Caroline Islands and later the retention of at least one of the group, preferably Kosrae, as a base for maintaining American interests in the area.[77]

Americans came relatively late to the role of formal colonial power. The history of the American presence in the Pacific, however, began with the voyage of the trading ship *Empress of China* in 1783 and included the activities of China traders, missionaries, New England whalers, and naval officers. In addition to Guam, the United States, by the start of the twentieth century, had formally acquired the Philippines, Hawai'i, and Tutuila and the Manu'a group in Samoa.[78] In Hawai'i, an 1893 revolt, led by American businessmen and missionary descendants, overthrew the government of Queen Lili'uokalani.[79] Subsequent attempts to have the United States annex the territory met with resistance in the United States Congress. Reasons for this resistance to annexation ranged from concerns over American governmental complicity in the overthrow of the Hawaiian monarchy to fears on the part of some over the 'ruinous effects' of incorporating a territory full of non-white people. However, the outbreak of the Spanish–American War led both houses of the American Congress to pass resolutions formally annexing Hawai'i. From 1900 to 1941, race would prove the pivotal issue in Hawai'i, as five major business concerns dominated all aspects of life in the islands by repressing the political rights and personal freedoms of native Hawaiians and increasing the numbers of Asian immigrants brought to work the sugar plantations of the territory.

In American Samoa, the issue was not so much race but neglect.[80] The partition of Samoa brought Tutuila and the Manu'a group to the United States in 1899. The US Navy was given jurisdiction over the islands in 1900 and, for purposes of administration, divided up its holdings in the Samoa group into three administrative districts: eastern Tutuila, western Tutuila, and the Manu'a group. For the most part, there was accommodation between the naval administration and the chiefly system in the islands; however, in matters of conflict American administrative law and policy took precedence over the *fa'a Samoa*. A local protest movement (Mau) did form as the result of a series of longstanding grievances involving poor communications between the naval administration and the people, an inadequate physical infrastructure to support economic activity in the area, limitations on broader Samoan involvement in the affairs of government, a backward school system, and problems stemming from the relationships between Samoan women and American naval personnel. Though the Mau had assumed the status of a political party in American Samoa by 1927, its effectiveness was limited by the prevailing, essentially tranquil, and mutually reinforcing relationship between Samoan chiefs and naval administrators.

Naval administration and racial issues would be two prominent features of American rule on Guam. As had other colonial powers in Micronesia, America sought to justify domination of Guam and its people through demeaning, essentially racist description. An early American observer of the Chamorro population described them as 'decimated, spiritless, and mongrolized [*sic*]'; another referred to them as 'a listless, ambitionless, unorganized mass of humanity stirred only by the hope of individual survival'.[81] Reflecting on the first twelve years of American naval rule over Guam, the editor of the *Guam News Letter* provided a glimpse of early colonial problems there:

> *Colonies were a new thing to us, dependent peoples had formed no part of our scheme of things. Many things, long a matter of course with other nations, were not only new but distasteful to us. Illiteracy, unhygienic conditions and disease are not acceptable to any civilized people; but the previous and long-continued poverty of Guam had brought about these conditions in a degree appalling to our stay-at-home eyes. . . . Our troops, new to conquest and familiar with only one race other than their own, needed a deal of controlling and correcting in matters unofficial and nonmilitary; and were in many cases lawless and turbulent.[82]*

The editor went on to describe an order addressed to all American military personnel reminding them that the people of Guam were neither 'damned dagoes' nor 'niggers'.

The arrival of the United States occupying force and the formal ceremonies of possession suggested that the application of democracy on Guam would be substantially less than was practised in the new 'Mother Country'.[83]

Captain Richard L. Leary of the USS *Yosemite*, charged with establishing naval rule on Guam, spent his first months aboard the *Yosemite* while the old Spanish governor's palace at Agaña was refurbished. On 26 November 1899, Leary, riding in an imported carriage drawn by white stallions brought from the Philippines and with a Filipino coachman, left the ship for his official residence. The *Yosemite* band, a Japanese steward, house servants, and a load of furniture and paraphernalia from the United States followed the governor's carriage.

From the beginning, the American naval presence on Guam suffered from the contradictions and tensions between the rights of the people and the strategic interests of the US Navy.[84] In the event of tension or conflict, however, the primacy of naval strategic interests would prevail. The territory was to be administered within the absolute domain of naval authority 'which necessarily is and must remain supreme in the ceded territory until the legislation of the United States shall provide otherwise'.[85] This decidedly individualistic, absolute approach to government was justified in American minds by the 'doctrine of limited incorporation', which postulated that the inhabitants of a territory acquired by the United States were not entitled to the benefits, privileges, and protection of the Constitution until Congress formally extended those rights through legislation that incorporated the territory in question into the Union.[86]

The contradiction between American domestic democracy and American colonial rule on Guam did not go unnoticed by the people of the island. As early as 1901, thirty-two citizens, using what Ranajit Guha might call the conceptual and institutional structures of their domination for counter-hegemonic purposes, petitioned the United States government for the full civil liberties and privileges of American citizenship.[87] The then governor of the island, Commander Seaton Schroeder, endorsed the petition and urged its consideration by his superiors. A bill to provide the citizens of Guam with American citizenship was passed by the United States Senate in 1905; it languished and died, however, in the United States House of Representatives.

Certain naval governors sought to provide the people of Guam with greater representation and voice in the governmental process. The governor who tried most to do something about the lack of Chamorro civil and political rights was Willis W. Bradley, Jr. He created a Bill of Rights for the people of Guam, provided for the election of representatives to the First Guam Congress, and made official requests to Washington, DC, for full citizenship for the Chamorro people.[88] But his efforts to obtain a legally recognised Bill of Rights and full citizenship for Guam's people foundered. Thereafter, the cause of more representative government declined, in large part because of the neglect and manipulation of later naval governors who followed Bradley.[89] A renewed effort to win the right to American citizenship was made in 1936 with the journey of a two-man delegation to Washington, DC, to meet with congressional leaders, government officials, and President Franklin D. Roosevelt himself.[90] The stiffest opposition to this ultimately failed effort came from the United States Navy, which argued that Guam's strategic location amid an increasingly hostile international environment precluded such changes.[91] Controlling about one-third of Guam's total land area by 1938, the navy further stated that the people of Guam were simply not prepared for self-government and that, in effect, they already enjoyed many of the privileges of citizenship without any of the accompanying responsibilities. In any event, Japan's forceful seizure of Guam from the United States on 10 December 1941 provided no relief for the people of the island. The people of Guam now found themselves suspect and oppressed because of their past association with a coloniser that practised its particular brand of democracy only at home.

A final thought on a new beginning

Much, much more needs to be written about the history of colonialism in the area called Micronesia. This brief essay has focused on a consideration of the common strategies through which different colonial powers sought to possess and control the islands and atolls there. The examination of this process of domination has revealed something of Micronesians' responses and resistance. There remains, however, the extremely important question of how Micronesians actually view their colonial past. Careful reflection is required here. Richard J. Parmentier, in a study of myth, history, and polity in Belau, has suggested that most Belauans today understand the island's different colonisers as much like the Ruschel gods of Belauan myth who came to establish a new harmonious order over the land, but turned instead to the manipulation of local political rivalries, the exploitation of economic resources, and the usurpation of indigenous leadership.[92] The accreditation of godliness to Micronesia's different colonial overlords is highly questionable. However, given the patterns of violence, exploitation, disruption, and dispossession, the analogy seems otherwise strikingly appropriate.

Notes

1 Jules Sébastien César Dumont D'Urville, 'Sur les îsles du Grand Ocean', *Bulletin de la Société de Géographie* 17 (1832): 5. See also Grégoire Louis Domeny de Rienzi, *Océanie ou Cinquième Partie du Monde: Revue Géographique de Ethnographique de la Malaisie, de la Micronésie, de la Polynésie, et de la Melanésie*, 3 vols, Firmin Didot Frères, Paris, 1863–1872. For a consideration of the artificiality of the term *Micronesia*, see David Hanlon, 'Micronesia: Writing and Rewriting the Histories of a Nonentity', *Pacific Studies* 12 (2, 1989): 1–21.
2 On the relationship between representation and domination, see Patrick Brantlinger, 'Victorians and Africans: The Genealogy of the Myth of the Dark

Continent', *Critical Inquiry* 12 (Autumn, 1985): 166–203; and Mary Louise Pratt, 'Scratches on the Face of the Country, or, What Mr. Barrow Saw in the Land of the Bushmen', *Critical Inquiry* 12 (Autumn, 1985): 119–143. There is also Edward Said, *Orientalism*, Random House, New York, 1979.

3 For an in-depth consideration of the dispute between Spain and Germany over the Caroline Islands, see Richard J. Brown, 'Germany, Spain, and the Caroline Islands, 1885–1899', PhD dissertation, University of Southern Mississippi, 1976; see also Brown's 'The German Acquisition of the Caroline Islands, 1898–1899', in *Germany in the Pacific and Far East, 1870–1914*, ed. John A. Moses and Paul M. Kennedy, University of Queensland Press, St Lucia, 1977, 137–155. Spain's position is articulated in Rafael Gracia y Parejo, *Considerations on the Rights of Spain over the Caroline Islands*, trans. and ed. Patricia M. Bieber, Pacific Islands Program, Miscellaneous Working Papers no. 1, University of Hawai'i, Honolulu, 1973; see also Francis X. Hezel, *The First Taint of Civilization: A History of the Caroline and Marshall Islands in Pre-Colonial Days, 1521–1885*, Pacific Islands Monograph Series no. 1, University of Hawai'i Press, Honolulu, 1983, 306–313. The impetus for the formal extension of Spanish colonial rule over the Caroline Islands came from clerical leaders in Manila who insisted on the primacy of Spain's civilising and Christianising mission. A number of government officials in Manila and Madrid vigorously protested the prohibitive and wasteful expense involved in administering such remote islands. The case against Spain's colonisation of the Caroline Islands is articulated by Valeriano Weyler y Nicolau, governor general of the Philippines and the Marquis of Tenerife, in his introduction to Anacleto Cabeza Pereiro's, *La Isla de Ponapé: Geograpfia, Etnografia, Historia*, Tipo-Litografia de Chofre, Manila, 1895.

4 Mark R. Peattie, *Nan'yō: The Rise and Fall of the Japanese in Micronesia, 1885–1945*, Pacific Islands Monograph Series no. 4, University of Hawai'i Press, Honolulu, 1988, 37.

5 Peattie, 37.

6 Francis X. Hezel and M. L. Berg, eds, *Winds of Change: A Book of Readings on Micronesian History*, Omnibus Program for Social Studies Cultural Heritage, Trust Territory of the Pacific Islands, 1979, 365.

7 Luis Bayo y Hernandez Pinzon, 'Actas de posesion y adhesion de la Isla de Ascensión Ponapi y adyacentes en las Carolinas y de la Proclama para su incorporacion', 26 July 1886, in Archivo Histórico Nacional, Madrid, 1970, legajo 5857, c. 1, 1–6.

8 Peter Hempenstall, 'The Spanish–Micronesian Wars', in *Protest and Dissent in the Colonial Pacific*, ed. Peter Hempenstall and Noel Rutherford, Institute of Pacific Studies, University of the South Pacific, Suva, 1984, 115.

9 Hezel and Berg, 402.

10 Peter Hempenstall, *Pacific Islanders Under German Rule*, Australian National University Press, Canberra, 1978, 81.

11 Peattie, 62–64.

12 Peattie, 225–229.

13 Peattie, 108.

14 The imperial implications of Lèvy-Bruhl's work are considered in Raymond Betts, *Uncertain Dimensions: Western Overseas Empires in the Twentieth Century*, University of Minnesota Press, Minneapolis, 1985, 52–53.

15 M. L. Berg, '"The Wandering Life Among Unreliable Islanders": The Hamburg Südsee-Expedition in Micronesia', *Journal of Pacific History* 23 (1, 1988): 96.

16 Peattie, 45–46. Later, in the early years of the American administration of the islands, similar anthropological and scientific studies of Micronesian life were carried out by the United States Commercial Company and under the auspices of such programmes as the Coordinated Investigation of Micronesian Anthropology (CIMA) and Scientific Investigations in Micronesia (SIM); the last two programmes were sponsored jointly by the Office of Naval Research and the Pacific Science Board of the National Research Council.

17 Francis X. Hezel, 'Spanish Capuchins in the Carolines', *Micronesian Reporter* 19 (3, 1971): 39.

18 Francis X. Hezel, 'The Catholic Church in Yap', typescript in University of Hawai'i at Mānoa, Hamilton Library, Hawaiian and Pacific Collection, n.d., 14.

19 Palau Community Action Agency, *A History of Palau*, vol. 2, Koror, Palau, 1978, 227.

20 Hempenstall 1978, 81.

21 Hempenstall 1978, 82–83.

22 Peattie, 112.

23 David Hanlon, *Upon a Stone Altar: A History of the Island of Pohnpei to 1890*, Pacific Islands Monograph Series no. 5, University of Hawai'i Press, Honolulu, 1988, 157.

24 Hempenstall 1978, 115.

25 Ralph Quentin McKinney, 'Micronesia Under German Rule, 1885–1914', MA thesis, Stanford University, 1947, 76–78.

26 Peattie, 75–77.

27 Peattie, 76.

28 Hezel 1971, 40.

29 Hempenstall 1978, 86.

30 Hempenstall 1978, 85.

31 Nancy J. Morris, 'Hawaiian Missionaries Abroad, 1852–1909', PhD dissertation, University of Hawai'i, Honolulu, 1987, 2.

32 Hempenstall 1978, 85.

33 Hezel 1971, 39.

34 Paul Hambruch, *Ponape*, vol. 1, *Ergebnisse der Südsee Expedition, 1908–1910*, ed. Georg Thilenius, II, Ethnographie B, Mikronesian, Bd. 7, Friederichsen, de Gruyter, Hamburg, 1932, 206f.

35 Francis X. Hezel, 'The Catholic Church in Truk', typescript in University of Hawai'i, Hamilton Library, Hawaiian and Pacific Collection, Honolulu, 1987, 14.

36 Hezel n.d., 8.

37 Capuchin Mission, Northern Marianas, *Aus den Missionen: Reports on Mission Work in the Northern Marianas, 1910–1913*, trans. and ed. Mark L. Berg, United States Trust Territory of the Pacific Islands Historic Preservation Office, Saipan, 1981, 20.

38 Hempenstall 1984, 109.

39 Georg Fritz, *Ad Majorem Dei Gloriam: Die Vorgeschichte des Aufstandes von 1910/1911 in Ponape*, Dieterich'sche Verlagsbuchhandlung, Theodore Weicher, Leipzig, 1912, 40; see also Hambruch 1932, 297.

40 Tadao Yanaihara, *Pacific Islands Under Japanese Mandate*, Greenwood Press, Westport, CT, 1976, 234.

41 Wakako Higuchi, ed., *Micronesia Under the Japanese Administration: Interviews with Former South Sea Bureau and Military Officials*, Micronesian Area Research Center, University of Guam, Agaña, 1987, 130.

42 Yanaihara, 238.

43 On this point, see, for example, Vincente Rafael, *Contracting Colonialism: Translation and Christian Conversion in Tagalog Society Under Early Spanish Rule*, Cornell University Press, Ithaca, NY, 1988.

44 Palau Community Action Agency, 232–233.

45 Arthur J. Vidich, *Political Factionalism in Palau: Its Rise and Development*, CIMA Report no. 23, Washington, DC, 1949, 84–90; also, Palau Community Action Agency, 381–385.

46 Vidich, 90–91.

47 Vidich, 91.

48 Higuchi, 124–125.

49 McKinney, 42.

50 McKinney, 125.

51 Peattie, 90–96.

52 Peattie, 95.

53 Hezel 1983, 265.

54 Hezel and Berg, 317.

55 McKinney, 22–26.

56 Mertz to Imperial Governor in Rabaul, 'Upon the decree of November 15, 1911 [no. 7188/11], of January 21, 1912 [no. 799/12] and of April 11, 1912 [no. 3410/12] concerning the land acquisition in the Marshall Islands', Jaluit, 16 May 1912, in Stewart Firth and Paula Machido, 'Translation of German Documents Relating to Micronesia', University of Hawai'i, Hamilton Library, Hawaiian and Pacific Collection, Honolulu, 1986, no. 1–5.

57 Imperial Governor Hahl to Government Station at Jaluit, 'In Response to the Report of 16 May, I. No. 492 on the Subject of Land Acquisition', in Firth and Machido, no. 2–1.

58 McKinney, 79.

59 McKinney, 115.

60 For an excellent survey of the land and labour recruiting issues surrounding phosphate mining in German Micronesia, consult Stewart Firth, 'German Labour Policy in Nauru and Angaur, 1906–1914', *Journal of Pacific History* 13 (1–2, 1978): 36–52.

61 Firth 1978, 42–43.

62 Firth 1978, 51.

63 Stewart Firth, 'German Firms in the Western Pacific Islands, 1857–1914', *Journal of Pacific History* 8 (1973): 10.

64 For an overview of Japan's efforts at economic development during its colonial administration of Micronesia, see David C. Purcell, Jr, 'The Economics of Exploitation', *Journal of Pacific History* 11 (3, 1978): 189–211.

65 Peattie, 16.

66 Peattie, 24–25.

67 Peattie, 123–132.

68 Peattie, 132–134.

69 Peattie, 157–161; see also Yanaihara, 29–49.

70 Peattie, 150–152.

71 Commonwealth of the Northern Marianas, Arts and Culture Council, *Life in the Northern Mariana Islands during the German Administration (1899–1914)*, Saipan, 1982, 7.

72 For the particulars of the land reform programme on Pohnpei, see Hempenstall 1978, 87–89. He describes the land reform effort as a subtly disguised attempt to reduce the independence of the chiefs and to bring them under the administrative control of the German colonial government.

73 Peattie, 96–100.

74 For background on the pre-war tensions between Japan and the United States, see Akira Iriye, *Pacific Estrangement: Japanese and American Expansion, 1897–1911*, Harvard University Press, Cambridge, MA, 1972; also, John Dower, *War Without Mercy*, Pantheon Books, New York, 1986.

75 For an understanding of the Yap controversy see, Sumitra Rattan, 'The Yap Controversy and Its Significance', *Journal of Pacific History* 7 (1972): 125–136; Timothy P. Maga, 'Prelude to War? The United States, Japan and the Yap Crisis, 1918–1922', *American Diplomatic History* 9 (1985): 215–231; also Peattie, 57–61.

76 Peattie, 231–251.

77 For a summary of the Micronesian issues during the Treaty of Paris negotiations, see Pearle E. Quinn, 'The Diplomatic Struggle for the Carolines, 1898', *Pacific Historical Review* 14 (3, 1945): 290–302; also Brown 1976.

78 See also Robert C. Kiste, ch. 10, this volume.

79 For a problematic but still useful overview of Hawaiian history, see Gavan Daws, *Shoal of Time: A History of the Hawaiian Islands*, University Press of Hawai'i, Honolulu, 1968. See also Noel Kent, *Hawaii: Islands Under the Influence*, New York: Monthly Press, 1983; and Haunani-Kay Trask, 'Hawai'i: Colonization and Decolonization', in *Class and Culture in the South Pacific*, ed. Anthony Hooper et al., University of the South Pacific, Institute of Pacific Studies and University of Auckland, Centre for Pacific Studies, Suva and Auckland, 1987. Also Roger Bell, *Last Among Equals: Hawaiian Statehood and American Politics*, University of Hawai'i Press, Honolulu, 1984; and Ralph S. Kuykendall, *The Hawaiian Kingdom*, 3 vols (1778 to 1893), University of Hawai'i Press, Honolulu, 1938, 1953, 1967.

80 For a naval administrator's view of the history of American Samoa since 1900, see Captain J. A. C. Gray, *Amerika Samoa: A History of American Samoa and Its United States Naval Administration*, United States Naval Institute, Annapolis, MD, 1960.

81 Quoted in Mary T. P. H. Sasaki, 'The Quest for Civil and Political Rights, Guam, U. S. A.', student paper, History 496, University of Hawai'i, Honolulu, 1988, 5; taken from United States Naval Department, *Report on Guam*, 1899–1950, Washington, DC, Government Printing Office, 1950, 3.

82 Quoted in Penelope C. Bordallo, 'A Campaign for Political Rights on Guam, Mariana Islands, 1899–1950', MA thesis, University of Hawai'i, Honolulu, 1982, 19.

83 Charles E. Beardsley, *Guam: Past and Present*, Charles E. Tuttle, Tokyo, 1964, 196–197; for another general history of Guam that includes a review of American

naval rule, see Paul Carano and Pedro C. Sanchez, *A Complete History of Guam*, Charles E. Tuttle, Tokyo, 1968.

84 This theme is emphasized most effectively in Laura Maude Thompson, *Guam and Its People*, Princeton University Press, Princeton, 1947. Thompson likened the US naval administration of Guam to that of a battleship (p. 72) and characterised American rule as far more regal and oppressive than the preceding centuries of Spanish colonialism (pp. 292–300).

85 These words, taken from President William McKinley's instructions of 12 January 1899 to the naval commander on Guam, are cited in Bordallo, 23.

86 Bordallo, 48–49.

87 Bordallo, 59–66; Ranajit Guha, *Elementary Aspects of Peasant Insurgency in Colonial India*, Oxford University Press, New Delhi, 1983, provides the theoretical framework for this interpretation of the 1901 petition drive on Guam.

88 Bordallo, 100–105.

89 Bordallo, 113.

90 For an extended account of this trip, see Bordallo, 123–144.

91 The text of the United States Navy's official response to the 1936 Washington visit of the Guam delegation and to the petition for full citizenship rights is in Bordallo, 130–131.

92 Richard J. Parmentier, *The Sacred Remains: Myth, History, and Polity in Belau*, University of Chicago Press, Chicago, 1987, 154–155.

6

France in Melanesia and Polynesia

Stephen Henningham

In the Paris of 1931, the international colonial exposition was 'the event of the year'.[1] The exposition, which comprised an 'improvised town'[2] of 110 hectares with a population of 400 000, attracted more than eight million visitors. The Netherlands, Portugal, Belgium, and Italy provided exhibits, but France took the lead in asserting the grandeur of its empire, which was second only to Britain's in size and wealth. The French presence in the Pacific Islands was given recognition: visitors could be captivated by the dancers of Tahiti and could marvel at what the right-wing press described as the 'Canaques cannibales' of New Caledonia.[3] However, most of the French exhibits and displays focused on France's vast possessions in Africa and Asia. Within its colonial empire, the French Pacific entities assumed only a modest place, although they did their bit, not least as specks on the maps studied by French schoolchildren, to stoke French pride and maintain French prestige.

In France, the French colonies and protectorates in the Pacific Islands region were generally regarded as small, poor, distant, and mostly insignificant. Especially between the wars, French opinion was preoccupied with domestic problems and with European affairs—notably the continuing threat posed by Germany. Yet by this time the French Pacific islands had already, over several decades, been subject to the imposition of French and other external influences, and were becoming increasingly integrated into the French colonial system.

Early encounters

French contact with the Pacific Islands region had begun in April 1768, when the two ships of Count Louis Antoine de Bougainville arrived at Tahiti after passing through the Tuamotu Archipelago. Tahiti had been 'discovered' for Europe the year before by England's Captain Wallis, but Bougainville and his crew did not know this when they arrived.[4] The part played by Spanish, Portugese, Dutch, and British navigators in establishing contacts between Europe and the Pacific Islands is well known. As is perhaps less appreciated in the Anglophone countries, French navigators also took part in this process of interaction, contributing to European knowledge of the region and helping pave the way for the later involvement of French missionaries, administrators, soldiers, and settlers. By the early nineteenth century French navigators had voyaged widely in the region and had visited parts of all of the various island groups that would later become incorporated into French colonies and protectorates.[5]

The Tahitians lacked a written language. Because only parts of their oral traditions have survived, we have only a general impression of their perceptions of the new arrivals. For the French, the visit was tinged with wonder. They were impressed by Tahiti's natural beauty. And they found the 'natives'—especially the women—more than friendly.[6] In mid-April Bougainville sailed on. He later reported on his brief visit to Tahiti in his *Voyage autour du monde*, the celebrated account of his expedition. His comments on Tahiti and its inhabitants in this book both reflected and helped reinforce notions prevalent in France and elsewhere in eighteenth-century Europe. In that era, philosophers and writers, keen to denounce the evils and injustices of their own civilisation, idealised and romanticised what they regarded as more natural and unspoiled societies elsewhere. They viewed those societies through a distorting lens that prevented an appreciation of them on their own terms. For example, accounts of the generally warm welcome given to the visitors in Tahiti failed to take account of Polynesian traditions of hospitality, of the Polynesian belief that the visitors were of divine status, and of the way the Polynesians had been overawed by Western naval firepower.[7]

Despite the pioneering activities of French navigators, several decades elapsed before France established a presence. Just as Bougainville had arrived second after Wallis in Tahiti, France ran second to Britain in acquiring influence and possessions in the Pacific. France was preoccupied at first by further tensions and conflicts in Europe, and by the French Revolution and the Napoleonic Wars, and later on by various colonial adventures elsewhere. In addition, although it was the strongest land power in Europe, France was disadvantaged by Britain's superior sea power. France did not capitalise on an early claim to Western Australia, and La Pérouse sailed into Botany Bay in New South Wales two days after Captain Phillip's First Fleet of British colonists. A few decades later, French settlers landed in New Zealand in 1840, only to find that Britain had annexed these islands a few months earlier.

Afraid of again being pre-empted, French naval officers established protectorates over the Marquesas group, and Tahiti, Moorea, and other islands, in 1842. French missionaries had landed in Wallis and Futuna, in the central Pacific, in 1837, and France established an unofficial protectorate there in 1842. In December 1843, French missionaries arrived in the Melanesian islands of New Caledonia. In 1853, France annexed the main island (*La Grande Terre*) of New Caledonia, mainly as a location for a penal colony. The outlying Loyalty Islands were incorporated as the 'dependencies' of New Caledonia in 1864. Also in 1864, attracted by its guano deposits, France annexed the remote, uninhabited island of Clipperton in the eastern Pacific, and later upheld its sovereignty against a Mexican claim.

Before France established a presence in some of the Pacific islands, the main influence on those that became French possessions or protectorates had been British. Supported from the British colonies in Australia and New Zealand, British missionaries and traders fanned out through the Pacific. Much of the population of the Loyalty Islands and of what would become French Polynesia was converted by British Protestant missionaries. British traders visited New Caledonia and the New Hebrides in search of sea slugs and sandalwood, for which they exchanged alcohol, weapons, fish-hooks, metal tools, clothes, and other goods. In Tahiti, with missionary support and after many vicissitudes, the Pomare dynasty established control over Tahiti and Moorea and set out to expand its influence. The British missionary and commercial presence in Tahiti and nearby islands had become firmly established by the 1840s, and the imposition of a French protectorate, largely at the initiative of an impetuous French naval officer, almost sparked a war between Britain and France.

In Tahiti and the Loyalty Islands, some of the local people became literate in their own language, using the Bible translated by the missionaries as their main text. British and German traders established themselves in Wallis and Futuna. British and American whaling boats traversed the oceans, recruiting islanders, including Tahitians, Loyalty Islanders and Wallisians, as crew. In Tahiti, Moorea, the Marquesas, and several of the other islands of what would become French Polynesia, the local people had contacts with American naval crew, traders, whalers, missionaries, and beachcombers. When French colonies and protectorates were eventually established, these influences were overlaid but never completely obscured.

In the 1880s, imperial competition heightened the world over. France confirmed its protectorate of Wallis and Futuna and incorporated—by annexation or by the establishment of protectorates—several of the island groups in the general vicinity of Tahiti into the *Etablissements Français d'Océanie*. In 1958, this entity would become the territory of *Polynésie Française* (French Polynesia). In 1887 France also signed a convention with Britain establishing a joint naval commission in the New Hebrides, whereby the two powers sought to protect and control their own nationals in these islands. This paved the way for the establishment of joint Anglo-French rule over the archipelago under the special 'Condominium' inaugurated in 1906. By the beginning of the twentieth century, the French territorial presence had taken the shape it would retain until the present, except for the New Hebrides, which attained independence as the Republic of Vanuatu in 1980.

For France, the various Pacific islands that were added to its colonial empire during the nineteenth century had only modest economic value, consisting mainly of the nickel and other minerals of New Caledonia and the phosphate of Makatea Atoll in French Polynesia. Efforts to establish plantation economies failed, as did the attempt to construct a viable settler colony in New Caledonia similar to those in Australia or New Zealand. New Caledonia did not attract large numbers of settlers and remained reliant on metropolitan subsidies. The reasons for these failures included limited resources, small scale, and remoteness from markets—all problems nowadays encountered by several of the independent Pacific Island countries. Nor did the Pacific colonies and protectorates assume much strategic or diplomatic importance for France, except insofar as possession of them contributed to French prestige. Although they were of little importance to metropolitan France, the establishment of the French presence, as part of the European expansion into the Pacific, had great and lasting implications for the indigenous peoples brought into the French sphere.

Cultural diversity

The peoples whose islands the French visited, annexed, colonised, or brought under 'protection' had diverse cultures and antecedents.[8] Before long, however, the French began to draw a broad distinction between the Polynesian peoples of the *Etablissements Français d'Océanie* and Wallis and Futuna, and the Melanesian peoples of the New Hebrides and New Caledonia and its dependencies. Indeed, French navigators and geographers in the early nineteenth century had begun the convention of dividing the Pacific Islands region into Polynesia, Melanesia, and Micronesia. French observers often exaggerated the differences between Melanesians and Polynesians, ignoring the similarities in their material cultures, the interactions in some areas between the two groupings before the European arrival, and the diversity among the Melanesians.[9]

During the colonial era many French observers idealised the Polynesians. They regarded what two French commentators have described as 'this marvellous people'[10] as taller, fairer and more open and accommodating than the Melanesians.[11] They and other foreigners regarded the stratified Polynesian societies, with their apparent equivalents of 'chiefs' and 'kings', as more comprehensible and easier to handle than the generally more diffuse and geographically circumscribed Melanesian societies, especially in what they saw as the 'anarchic' New Hebrides.[12]

For French officials and settlers, the distinctions drawn between 'Polynesians' and 'Melanesians' rested on a seldom-questioned assumption of the superiority of Western civilisation—an assumption that helped justify harsh treatment of the indigenous peoples. With untroubled consciences, and often with a patronising sense of doing good, Europeans grabbed land and coerced the 'natives' into providing free or ill-paid labour. Melanesians, defined as more savage than Polynesians, could be exploited with even fewer qualms.

The notions of 'Polynesian' and 'Melanesian' were externally imposed categories that at the time probably would have had limited, if any, relevance to the communities encountered by the French and other voyagers and colonists.[13] Among the peoples of the Pacific Islands, conceptions of identity were circumscribed. Tahiti was the largest and most populous island in what became French Polynesia. In the early nineteenth century, its population had strong links with the peoples of the rest of the Society Islands as well as connections with the peoples of the Tuamotu Archipelago. However, connections were less close with the inhabitants of the Austral and Gambier groups. The peoples of the Marquesas Islands, several hundred kilometres to the north-east, spoke a distinct Polynesian language, all but incomprehensible to the Tahitians, with whom their links were tenuous. The people of the Society Islands had closer links with the inhabitants of the Cook Islands than they had with the Marquesans.

Apart from the differences between the inhabitants of the five island groups of the *Etablissements Français d'Océanie*, differences existed between and within particular islands. The primary focus of loyalty was the small, local territorial and kinship grouping. The impressive mountain forts of Rapa in the Austral Islands attest to bitter rivalry and recurrent warfare. Similarly, in the western Polynesian cultural region in the central Pacific, society on Wallis Island was divided into several rival groups, despite the presence of a paramount chief with claims to overall authority. On Futuna, two paramount chiefs held authority, their followers locked in rivalry.

Whereas the Polynesians at least shared strong cultural and linguistic similarities, the Melanesian peoples were diverse and divided. Melanesia had larger areas and populations and had been subject to more waves of migration. Poor communications and difficult terrains had encouraged small, isolated communities to evolve distinct characteristics. The Melanesians of New Caledonia comprised nearly thirty separate linguistic-cultural groups, with no single language encompassing more than a small minority of the total. The majority of the population lived in the valleys of the mountainous main island. But the smaller islands were also inhabited, including notably the Loyalty group (Ouvea, Tiga, Lifou, and Mare) and the Isle of Pines. The communities on the smaller islands, especially Ouvea, had experienced significant contacts with Polynesian peoples.

To the north, in the twelve major and over sixty smaller islands of the New Hebrides, over one hundred distinct languages were spoken. One missionary concluded that the archipelago, the most linguistically diverse region in the world, was 'a very Babel'.[14] Before the European arrival, the key organisational unit in New Caledonia and the New Hebrides numbered only a few score people. Larger groupings for trade, war, or ceremonies were ephemeral.

Accommodation and resistance

The diversity of the island populations helps explain the varied islander responses to the new arrivals. No single type of reaction dominated. In the larger Melanesian islands, the major impact of the new arrivals was on the coastal areas, with influences passed to the interior indirectly and often only slowly. The variety of responses reflected the demands of varying kinds and intensity made by the new arrivals—naval commanders and their crews, traders and merchant seamen, missionaries and administrators, settlers, miners, and adventurers—as well as the various opportunities they offered.[15]

Although responses varied, many island communities showed a willingness to come to terms with the new arrivals, even after they had realised that, technological superiority notwithstanding, the Europeans were nothing if not human, and not returning ancestors or otherwise semi-divine.[16] Throughout the Pacific Islands, however, trouble often arose when the Europeans breached customs, encroached on the islanders' way of life, and ignored traditions of exchange and reciprocity.[17] In the Marquesas, almost all of the forty or so beachcombers killed from 1798 to 1880 'died because they flaunted some *tapu* [taboo], stole . . . property or quarrelled in their drunkenness.'[18] Even in the 'savage' New Hebrides, although many communities treated all outsiders as enemies, some attacks were reprisals for earlier European depredations.[19] On other occasions the local people attacked in order to protect their territory against the uninvited new arrivals, or in quest of their material wealth.[20] Conflict and violence were widespread. In the New Hebrides in the nineteenth century, local people attacked missionaries, labour recruiters, and planters. French or British ships several times shelled villages in reprisal.[21]

On Futuna Island in 1843, Father Pierre Chanel was killed and eaten, becoming the Pacific Islands' first saint because of this martyrdom. On Wallis Island, the French Catholic missionaries supported the winning side in an internal power struggle, in which the losers were linked to Tongan Protestant missionaries who wished both to spread the gospel and, it seems, reassert traditional Tongan overlordship over Wallis.[22] The French Catholic missionaries subsequently established themselves strongly in Wallis and Futuna, but even their own accounts indicate that sporadic dissent and resistance continued.[23]

In Tahiti, resistance to the imposition of the protectorate lasted two years, with the rebels holed up in mountain strongholds. The Tahitians had come under strong British influence. They opposed France as an interloper with few connections in Tahiti and neighbouring islands. Encouraged by British missionaries, they were hostile to the Roman Catholic church and to the French Catholic missionaries. The local people often clashed with the French in most of the other islands that would eventually become part of French Polynesia. Soon after the annexation of the Marquesas, two French officers were killed and several of their men wounded, and further casualties followed in later incidents.[24] In the Leeward Islands, the westerly islands of the Society group, which had come under strong British missionary and trader influence, the islanders resisted French annexation in the 1880s, until a punitive force visited and hundreds of the rebels were exiled.[25]

In New Caledonia, frequent conflicts with the French took place throughout the first decades of contact and colonisation. Between 1843 and 1870, over forty violent events and incidents occurred.[26] In the late 1850s and the 1860s, Melanesians resisting the takeover of land for the new colony fought with the French near the capital of Noumea, a small trading and military post.[27] Following the extension of colonisation along the west coast, a great war took place in 1878–1879, sparked by the taking over of Melanesian lands, the damage to village gardens by settlers' cattle, disputes over women, and the desecration of burial sites. Several hundred Melanesians and more than two hundred Europeans were killed, and the defeated tribes were driven from their ancestral lands.[28]

For the next few decades opposition was intermittent and small in scale, until major hostilities again erupted in 1917, when some Melanesian tribes fought back against settler encroachments and forced recruitment for World War One.[29] The disturbances began when army recruiters disrupted a customary ceremony of reconciliation between two tribes, against a background of increasing settler pressure since around 1900 on Melanesian lands in the northern highlands of New Caledonia. The Melanesians attacked the recruiters, injuring two of them. In the following few weeks, isolated settlers and miners were attacked across the area near Kone, Hienghene, Touho, and Ponerihouen. Military patrols eventually re-established French control, bringing an end to what seems to have been a series of incidents rather than a concerted revolt.

With the rise of nationalism in the French Pacific territories in recent decades, nationalist leaders have emphasised what they see as continuities with earlier conflicts. Jean-Marie Tjibaou, the leader of the New Caledonian nationalist movement until his death in May 1989, used to show visitors to his home village near Hienghene the site where in 1917 his tribe fled over the ridge under fire from a punitive force. His grandmother was killed, with his father in her arms, but his father was plucked up and carried to safety. In 1969, some of the first Melanesians to call for independence named their party *Groupe 1878*. In Tahiti in 1986, Oscar Temaru, the leader of the anti-nuclear, pro-independence *Front pour Libération Polynesien* (Polynesian Liberation Front), erected a monument to commemorate a battle in the war of 1844–1847.

Although opposition was widespread, these references by modern nationalists oversimplify the historical record. In 1844–1847 'the Tahitian resistance comprised most of the population . . .', but some Tahitian chiefs and their followers, along with other Polynesians, aided the French.[30] In New Caledonia, the French defeated their opponents in the 1850s and 1860s and in 1878 and 1917 with the aid of Melanesian guides and soldiers. In 1917, for example, the administration once again adopted the ploy of mobilising 'the traditonal opponents of those who were in rebellion'.[31] Some of the tribes whose aid was enlisted were from Houailou. Their treatment of the rebels reminded observers of the brutal repression of 1878. French victory would have been much harder to attain—and in the case of the major revolt of 1878 perhaps impossible—without this kind of help. The Melanesians who aided the French did so in pursuit of their own interests and in terms of their own values and attitudes concerning conflict and war. At times they took the opportunity to attack traditional rivals. At least until the repression of the 1878 revolt and possibly later, they often clearly regarded the French colonists as useful allies in local conflicts, rather than as an external power that ultimately would come to dominate the entire country. In 1917, Melanesians were fighting with the French army in France while Melanesians and French soldiers were clashing in New Caledonia. In the French Pacific, as elsewhere in the colonial world, Europeans profited from traditional rivalries and circumscribed local loyalties to consolidate their presence.[32] The concept of nation-state was still in the process of crystallisation in nineteenth-century Europe, whence it was exported to the colonial world.

The absence of a wider 'national' sense of identity was also demonstrated in the various 'nativist' movements that emerged at various times in the New Hebrides. In the early twentieth century the Tamata movement in the interior of Espiritu Santo sought to eradicate the damaging influences believed to result from the European presence on the coast. In the late 1930s the John Frum movement emerged on the southern island of Tanna, then gained impetus and acquired 'cargo cult' characteristics in response to the material wealth assembled by the Americans when they based themselves in parts of the New Hebrides during World War Two. Its adherents believed that by reforming their behaviour and performing certain rituals they could gain access to abundant supplies of 'cargo'—that is, Western material goods. The Malekula Native Company, of north-west Malekula and neighbouring islands, began in 1939 as a path-breaking experiment in co-operative primary production, before similarly acquiring cargo cult characteristics during the war.[33]

These movements were attempts, in reaction to Western influences, to recapture the initiative and to restructure the social, economic, and moral order in beneficial ways. Although upholding some traditions, they also expressed a willingness to break radically with the past. They were 'proto-nationalist' in their character and goals, even though the unit embraced by their vision was local rather than archipelago wide. They had much in common with the 'micronationalist' movements of Papua New Guinea and elsewhere in Melanesia, not least in their 'tendency towards disengagement or withdrawal . . . from the larger national community'.[34]

Movements such as these were part of a wide variety of responses to the new circumstances and influences present in the Condominium and in the other areas under French influence. The local peoples sought to protect their own traditions, while borrowing and adopting those elements they found useful and attractive from what Western civilisation had on offer. Oppression, blunders, and misunderstandings occurred, and the dice were often loaded heavily in favour of the Europeans, but the interaction was two-way.

Regional variations

The intensity of foreign influences and pressures on local societies varied greatly. Least affected overall were those of the New Hebrides, except in the closely settled parts of Efate and Espiritu Santo and a few other places. Most of the settlers who established themselves in the New Hebrides were French, and French speculators acquired land titles—if mostly fanciful and dubiously obtained—to over half of the archipelago. French Catholic missionaries and New Caledonia-based trading companies were active.[35]

The French settlers in Noumea looked on the archipelago as an extension of the colony in New Caledonia and available for eventual annexation. But French government interest in this idea waxed and waned. Britain stood in the way. London saw its claims to the archipelago as a useful bargaining chip, which now and again it considered exchanging with the French for a concession elsewhere, but the overseas British—the settlers in the Australian and New Zealand colonies—stiffened the resolve of the mother country. They insisted that French ambitions be challenged.[36] The result was the uneasy compromise embodied in the Anglo-French Condominium—in effect a joint protectorate—established in 1906.

The 'Pandemonium', as the Condominium was called by some because of its comic-opera ineffectiveness, depended on agreement by the administering powers—agreement that was hard to attain, except after long delays and much negotiation. Both Britain and France were reluctant to invest in an area not fully under their own control. This reluctance, along with the humid climate, the prevalence of malaria and other tropical illnesses, the uncertainties of plantation agriculture, and the scarcity of ports and safe anchorages, limited major European influence in the New Hebrides to a few locations. The interiors of some of the larger islands escaped even token condominium administrative sway right up to the 1950s. Later on, joint rule, especially because of French opposition to decolonisation, complicated and embittered the transition to independence in 1980, leaving a legacy of division.[37]

At times local communities were able to protect their autonomy to some extent and to win concessions by playing off one colonial administration against the other. But people from the archipelago also suffered greatly as plantation labourers in the New Hebrides, Queensland, and elsewhere, and as mine, plantation, and dock workers in New Caledonia. The labour trade, which began in the 1860s and continued into the early decades of the twentieth century, had important effects. About 100 000 people from the New Hebrides took part. The majority of them eventually returned home, usually after several years abroad. They brought with them new knowledge, attitudes, skills, and possessions. People from the coastal areas constituted a large proportion of these migrants, but many people from villages in the interior also went.

To the south, in New Caledonia, the disruption and transformation of indigenous societies was greater, especially on the main island. European and other immigrants arrived and were granted most of the good land. At first the French administration promised that indigenous rights to lands would be preserved. But this pledge was soon transgressed, under the pressure of settler encroachments, by successive redefinitions of what should remain in Melanesian possession. The land question was central to the 1878 war and to other resistance to colonisation. The defeated tribes had their lands confiscated and were removed to reservations.

By the end of the nineteenth century the Melanesians had lost much of their land on the dry west coast plains and had been confined to small reserves, often in the mountains where the soil was poor. On the wetter east coast, where conditions were less suitable for extensive grazing, the Melanesians retained more land, although here again settlers pushed them off the most fertile river valley flats.[38] These expropriations contributed to the 1917 revolt and continued at a reduced rate until the mid-twentieth century. Some of the Melanesians arrested during the disturbances of 1984–1985 explained their arson of settler homesteads by saying that the land held by the settlers had wrongfully been taken from their fathers only a generation ago.

On the main island of New Caledonia, Melanesian resentment over land runs deep. Land, and the people's relationship to it, are central to Melanesian culture. Clans and tribes claimed much larger areas, used in shifting agriculture, than they tilled at any one time. Apart from agricultural and other resource potential, land that seemed vacant or underused to Europeans bore rich religious and symbolic meanings. The theft of the land was a body blow to traditions and culture, not just a threat to livelihood. Its demoralising effects were reinforced by exotic diseases, alcohol, and exploitation by traders and settlers. Moreover, the Melanesians were subject to the *Régime de l'indigénat*. These 'native regulations', which had their counterparts in the other French colonies and elsewhere in the colonial world, were set in operation from 1887. The regulations established a special legal code for Melanesians, in part removing them from the scope of civil law; tightly restricted their movements and activities; subjected them to a head tax; and obliged them to provide free labour.

On the other hand, the restriction of the Melanesians to their reserves; their marginalisation from settler society; and the paternalistic but protective role played by some Roman Catholic and most Protestant missionaries contributed to the protection of their traditions and distinctiveness. In some respects 'overprotection' may have taken place, slowing the process of constructive adaption to the challenges and opportunities of the modern world.[39]

In New Caledonia, as in the other French Pacific entities, there were considerable variations. The Loyalty Islands did not attract settlers: they lacked safe habours and anchorages, and their coral plateaus lacked large areas of good soil. European beachcombers, sandalwood traders, and whaling crews visited, but the children they fathered were fully absorbed into the local kinship system. In the Loyalty Islands the social hierarchy, headed by chiefs, was more elaborate than on the mainland. The resilience of this structure helped preserve many traditions and assisted the islanders to adapt to new pressures and opportunities at their own pace. As they had done earlier in Tahiti and its neighbouring islands, the representatives of the London Missionary Society established themselves in the Loyalty Islands before French rule was imposed. They converted the majority of the population, and for some fifty years from 1842 were a dominant influence, until they handed over responsibility for preaching the Protestant faith in the Loyalties to their French counterparts. Roman Catholic missionaries, who had already been active on the main island of New Caledonia, arrived in the Loyalties after the pastors of the London Missionary Society, but made some inroads. Old quarrels transposed into new allegiances as rival chiefs and tribes became either Catholic or Protestant. Like their counterparts on the mainland, the Loyalty Islanders were devout adherents to their new faith, yet they retained many traditional beliefs and customs, interpreting Christianity in the light of their own preconceptions and needs.[40]

Unlike the other French Pacific entities, New Caledonia became a colony of settlement in which Europeans and other immigrants made up a large proportion of the population on the main island. New Caledonia was also distinctive as a penal colony, inspired in part by the British penal settlements established earlier in Australia. Between 1864 and 1897, more than 20 000 convicts arrived. During this period free settlers were outnumbered by the convicts, and the penal administration operated as a state within the state. Most of the convicts were ordinary criminals, but they included some 4500 political prisoners convicted and deported for taking part in the revolt of the Paris Commune in 1871. The *communards* were eventually repatriated to France, but the great majority of the other convicts remained in the colony after they had been freed.[41] Two societies in parallel emerged, interacting but maintaining separate identities. The committee that prepared New Caledonia's exhibition for the World's Fair of 1900 resolved not to include the Melanesians in the display, taking the view that 'the future is for the immigrants, the settlers, who will associate the aboriginals with their work, and in this way elevate the inferior race'.[42]

Much intermixing took place, encouraged by the imbalance between the numbers of male and female settlers. Traders, settlers, ex-convicts, and rural gendarmes often cohabited with Melanesian women, especially before World War One, and brief liaisons were frequent. The resulting children were assimilated into one or other major community. Those recognised as part of the European community became French citizens, subject to the common law, whereas those absorbed into the Melanesian community were merely French subjects, with a special legal status.[43] Today, James Wright, a nationalist militant from Lifou in the Loyalty Islands, traces his descent from a British trader, while Justin Guillemard, a hard-line opponent of independence, responds to claims that he is racist by pointing out that his great-grandparents included two Melanesian women.

The impact of the settlement of New Caledonia on its indigenous people resembled in some respects what happened in the British colonies of Australia and New Zealand. The immigrants came to control all the major resources and to dominate society. They shunted the indigenous peoples to one side, took much of their land, and overwhelmed or threatened the survival of their traditions and culture. The big difference was that in the two British colonies, and especially in Australia, the demographic and consequently the political balance shifted overwhelmingly in favour of the immigrants.

In the central Pacific, in the western Polynesian islands of Wallis and Futuna, foreign intrusion and influence was more restricted than in New Caledonia. French Catholic missionaries won over the paramount chief of Wallis and both the paramount chiefs on Futuna, despite the death of Father Pierre Chanel. The French Catholic missionaries on Wallis supported the winning side in an internal power struggle. Assisted by the paramount chiefs, the missionaries in due course gained the adherence of almost all the inhabitants. But it was equally true that the authority of the church, backed up by French naval visits, strengthened the authority of the paramount chiefs, which hitherto had been diffuse and often contested.[44]

The church wished to insulate the people of these islands against most other outside influences. This objective was made easier to attain because Futuna has no lagoon or other safe anchorages, while the passes through the

Wallis reef are difficult and dangerous. These islands also had little to export, apart from copra and some pearlshell. They remained off major trade routes, although some local people crewed on whaling and trading vessels. Directed by their 'kings' and chiefs, the people of Wallis and Futuna accepted the church's authority and laboured hard to build churches and presbyteries and to provide the priests with food.

In the early twentieth century tensions arose between the French residents and the Catholic Mission, which the residents thought was too powerful. The conflict focused in part on whether church or state should control the unpaid labour of the islanders, which the church had been drawing on for a grandiose building programme. Tensions waxed and waned in accordance with the fluctuating strength of the anticlerical forces in metropolitan France. The residents won, and between the wars the local people were put to work on roads and other developmental projects. The burden of forced labour was heavy, even if some of its results were to the islanders' benefit, and caused tensions. Young men bore the burden of the unpaid work, but the welfare of the women and children was affected, because the men had less time to assist the women in the gardens or to go fishing.[45]

Nonetheless, the isolation and scarce resources of these islands helped insulate their inhabitants from the disease, land-grabbing, and exploitation suffered by island communities elsewhere. The ending of tribal warfare, improved medical care, and church opposition to contraception laid the basis for a steady population increase after World War One. Meanwhile, as among other Pacific Island peoples, adherence to Christianity had a distinctive character, with elements of local tradition incorporated.

Compared with Wallis and Futuna, the effects of the European intrusion were more devastating in eastern Polynesia, in the numerous islands of the five island groups of the *Etablissements Français d'Océanie*. In Mangareva and the other islands in the Gambier group, as in Wallis and Futuna, Catholic missionaries created a theocracy and put the islanders to work. The heavy workload, the neglect of traditional subsistence activities, and imported diseases brought about substantial depopulation.[46] In the Marquesas, Western diseases, alcohol, and the introduction of firearms into tribal warfare contributed to a major population decline and a rapid break-down of traditional culture.[47] Other outer islands were more insulated from new pressures and influences, especially if their anchorages were poor or dangerous.

On Tahiti, the main island of the *Etablissements Français d'Océanie*, the effects of contact with Europeans were substantial. But like many island peoples elsewhere, the Tahitians adapted with resilience. They spoke a single language that was also spoken or understood in the closer neighbouring islands, and they shared a common culture. Tahiti did not become a settlement colony. It lacked resources, was distant from France, and was isolated from markets. In the absence of a numerous European population, some individuals of mixed extraction emerged as a privileged group. The *Demi* (literally 'half'—

half caste) community remains important to this day. Its leading members generally trace their descent from unions between European settlers and the daughters of the Tahitian aristocracy.

The Euro-Tahitian elite of *Demis* played a prominent role in the local economy, although from the early twentieth century its position was challenged by Chinese traders. The land policy of the French authorities permitted much of the prime lagoon-side land to be acquired, and created tensions and conflicts. However, substantial areas remained in Tahitian and especially *Demi* hands.[48] As events after World War Two would show, deep resentments persisted among many French Polynesians about their experience under colonialism. But until recent decades, Tahiti retained its image as an enchanted and unspoiled 'Island of Love', to quote the title of the most popular English-language book on Tahiti and its islands.[49] Although the image was primarily heterosexual, sexual behaviour and attitudes were more broad-ranging, bisexuality and homosexuality being a socially accepted dimension of traditional Polynesian culture.

New goods, values, and patterns of organisation

Despite the variations between and within the French Pacific entities, the new pressures, influences, and opportunities their peoples encountered wrought substantial changes, even in the most isolated communities, thanks to trade networks and cultural interaction. These changes were already under way before the islands became French possessions or protectorates.

Metal implements replaced those of wood and stone, easing drudgery. Islanders increasingly fished with metal fish-hooks and Western-made nets, hunted with muskets or rifles, and wore cheap Western-made clothes.[50] Most islanders continued to rely on subsistence production, but their communities also received income from the modern, European-dominated cash economy, whether through cash remittances from migrant workers, earnings from casual labour, or the sale of copra and other local products to European (and Chinese) traders. Food consumption patterns altered as trade-store flour, rice, and tinned goods partly replaced traditional foods, harming dental and general health but providing sustenance when traditional foods were scarce. Alcohol and tobacco became widely used, and often abused, many settlers setting a bad example. Recent research shows that earlier accounts of massive overall depopulation were exaggerated.[51] Nonetheless, new diseases to which islanders had no immunity caused much death and suffering, at times devastating small communities, especially those that came into frequent contact with settlers and traders.

By the early twentieth century most of the islanders of the French Pacific had become at least nominally Christian. The exception was about a third of the population of the New Hebrides, who retained their adherence to traditional *kastom* beliefs, although these were modified by Christian and other Western influences. *Kastom* (English: custom; French: *la coutume*) defies precise definiton, but refers to the traditional values, practices, and patterns of behaviour regulating Melanesian communities. The churches, especially the Protestant organisations in New Caledonia, provided a new focus for demoralised and disoriented communities. They helped people adapt to new challenges and helped train and develop local leaders. Though subject to evolution, many pre-existing values and customs, though subject to evolution, remained strong. Meanwhile the use of indigenous languages and the training and employment of local people, especially in Protestant congregations, permitted indigenous communities to regard the Christian faith and the local churches as their own, rather than as something externally imposed.

The French presence—and the joint British–French presence in the New Hebrides—established new administrative and economic linkages between diverse and formerly more or less isolated and independent local communities. In New Caledonia and the *Etablissements Français d'Océanie* the local gendarme operated as the key representative of the French state, combining law-and-order functions with a range of other duties. His role was comparable in some respects to that later played by the *kiap* (patrol officer) in Papua New Guinea. On the Melanesian reserves in New Caledonia, to which the majority of Melanesians were restricted until after World War Two, a hierarchy of traditional high chiefs (*grand chefs*, literally, big chiefs) and village-level chiefs (*petit chefs*, literally, small chiefs) fulfilled local administrative tasks under the direction of the local gendarme. Especially where tribes had been shifted after rebellions, these chiefs were often administrative appointees, with little prestige within the Melanesian communities. And where chiefs with genuine traditional status were present, their partial incorporation into the French administration at times reduced their standing among their people.

In the *Etablissements Français d'Océanie*, no attempt was made to incorporate the chiefly system, which already had been eroded by Protestant missionary and other new influences, into the French administrative structure. Nonetheless, high-ranking families retained social prestige and maintained economic power through land ownership. During the early twentieth century the French administration faced the task of integrating the various components of the *Etablissements Français d'Océanie*, which had been acquired over several decades, into a single administrative entity. However, the process of administrative rationalisation proceeded slowly, with the Leeward Islands, which hitherto had been under strong British and German influence, operating under special arrangements until World War Two.

Meanwhile Tahiti and its capital Pape'ete, which had grown up from almost nothing on the shores of the best anchorage, assumed unprecedented importance. The administration, the churches, and the economy centred on the main island and its port town. From the late nineteenth century, people from the outer islands began to move there in search of work and opportunities, a trend later accelerated from the early 1960s by the nuclear testing programme. By 1951 half of the total population of the *Etablissements Français d'Océanie* already lived on Tahiti, with another 5 per cent on the nearby, closely linked island of Moorea. Nearly a quarter of the overall total lived in Pape'ete, the only town worthy of the name.[52]

In New Caledonia, the port town of Noumea mushroomed in a formerly sparsely populated area as the key administrative, industrial, and commercial centre. As in the *Etablissements Français d'Océanie*, however, the sway of the administration was reduced outside the capital and its immediate environs. European settlers dominated Noumea and the other towns, while the indigenous Kanaks constituted most of the population in much of the interior, especially on most of the east coast, and in the Loyalty Islands. Local ties remained strong among Melanesians, but under French rule interaction between the various tribal groupings greatly increased. The indigenous languages survived, but under threat, while French became the language of communication between different Melanesian groups and between Melanesians and settlers.

In Wallis and Futuna, tribal or district rivalries became muted under the French protectorate. The two islands, which are more than two hundred kilometres apart, are both populated by Polynesians. But before the French arrival their populations had closer historical links with two western Polynesian countries—the people of Wallis with Tonga, and the people of Futuna with Samoa. French overlordship bound the futures of Wallis and Futuna together, and offered, for a handful of talented young men, leadership opportunities in the Catholic church.

In the New Hebrides, all except the most isolated communities in the interiors of the larger islands eventually came into contact with the British–French administrative and economic system. Bislama, a lingua franca developed from 'Sandalwood English' by indentured New Hebridean workers overseas, became a countrywide means of communication. In the French and British zones of influence, and in their areas of overlap, especially in and near the new towns of Vila on Efate and Luganville (later Santo town) on Espiritu Santo, many New Hebrideans acquired some French or English.

British involvement in the Condominium of the New Hebrides tempered the aggressive nationalism of Australian business and missionary interests and also helped protect the inhabitants of the archipelago from the fate of their counterparts on the main island of New Caledonia. Port areas and some of the smaller islands were much changed, in part through disease and depopulation. In contrast to New Caledonia, however, where settlement was substantial, in the New Hebrides the non-indigenous population, including planters, traders, officials, and Asian indentured workers, never formed more than a small minority of the population. As in much of the Pacific Islands region, significant aspects of the pre-contact cultures endured and evolved.

Ripples of change

By the early twentieth century, the hopes cherished by some officials and businessmen for the generation of great agricultural and mineral wealth in the French Pacific colonies and protectorates had generally been disappointed. The main exceptions were the returns, which were mostly repatriated, from the nickel and other metals of New Caledonia and from the phosphate of Makatea Atoll in the *Etablissements Français d'Océanie*. The slump of the 1930s accentuated the economic malaise of the French Pacific islands. The malaise was also social: despite some improvements after World War One, inequality and exploitation endured.

Most visitors to the French Pacific islands described them as sleepy outposts of empire. Nonetheless, beneath the generally placid surface, important changes took place during the early decades of the twentieth century. If practice of the Christian faith was one key element of the response by indigenous communities to contact with the new world, their involvement in cash cropping was another. Subsistence agriculture and fishing remained central. From the late nineteenth century, cash cropping increasingly complemented subsistence agriculture. Copra was produced in all of the French Pacific entities. In addition, other crops were produced at various times, and in New Caledonia Melanesians began to produce coffee. With official encouragement, this crop became widely grown by Melanesian farmers on the main island between the wars. Through cash cropping, and although local populations by no means benefited equally, the peoples of the French Pacific earned income with which to purchase goods, and acquired new knowledge and skills.

Another important change involved greater—although by no means complete—assimilation of metropolitan French language and culture, along with strengthened links with metropolitan France. Until World War One, external influence on the islanders was generally European rather than strictly French. British businessmen, notably James Paddon and John Higginson, played a leading part in the early contact and colonial history of New Caledonia and the New Hebrides. (Higginson, however, later acquired French nationality.) Australian stockmen established the New Caledonian grazing industry, enriching Caledonian French with words such as *le stockman*, *la station*, and *le creek*, not to mention that useful exclamation, *bagrite*! (bugger it!).

Before the French protectorate was imposed on Tahiti, only a handful of Frenchmen lived there. Up to this time the main external influence on Tahiti and nearby islands had been from British and American missionaries and traders, and from a miscellany of sailors and beachcombers. In due course French immigrants began to trickle into the *Etablissements Français d'Océanie*, totalling a few hundred by the turn of the century. The overwhelming majority of these people were male and of modest means, and many of them became more or less assimilated into the Tahitian community through intermarriage. Late in the nineteenth century, French officials complained that France was bearing the administrative costs of the *Etablissements Français d'Océanie* but that the commercial benefits were going to British and German firms. Similarly, in 1918, as Colin Newbury has pointed out, 'it was still possible for a French governor to describe the Pacific colony as a set of Polynesian and foreign communities linked by foreign trade and shipping with the outside world and administered by France without much compensation in terms of economic or strategic advantage'.[53]

In the late nineteenth century, the London Missionary Society handed over the task of spreading the faith to the French Protestant church in both New Caledonia and the *Etablissements Français d'Océanie*. Immigration by Anglophones into New Caledonia dwindled and ceased in the early twentieth century because of the lack of opportunities there. The French administration encouraged assimilation of the French language and culture. In both New Caledonia and the *Etablissements Français d'Océanie*, families of Irish or English origin, such as the Daleys and the Martins in New Caledonia, were absorbed into the Francophone population.

In the *Etablissements Français d'Océanie* and Wallis, German interests were eclipsed by World War One. German nationals were interned and their properties confiscated. After the war these properties were mostly auctioned, but with Germans excluded from the bidding. In Tahiti, a German firm, the *Société Commerciale de l'Océanie*, had become 'Tahiti's largest nineteenth-century merchant enterprise and had dominated local trade. At auction most of its properties were bought by Chin Foo [Tchung Fo Chong], a Chinese businessman who had arrived in Tahiti in the late 1890s and had established himself as a vanilla merchant and restaurant owner'.[54]

This purchase, as well as marking the end of German influence, also symbolized the increasing strength of the Chinese community in Tahiti and its islands. The origins of the community date to the arrival of about a thousand Chinese men imported by William Stewart in 1864 to work on his cotton plantation. The plantation was temporarily viable because the American Civil War had stopped cotton exports from the American South, but failed once normal conditions were re-established. Most of the Chinese left, but a few hundred remained. They married into the Tahitian community and engaged increasingly in small-scale retail commerce. In the late 1890s they numbered only about three hundred, but the size of the community increased rapidly through migration from around 1900 onwards. By 1911, the community numbered 1137, and was expanding from hawking, market gardening, and shopkeeping into banking and import-export business. Chinese women immigrants arrived from 1907, and in the following few decades the community became increasingly distinctive, with its own schools, temple, and cemeteries. With a few exceptions, the Chinese were not granted French citizenship until after World War Two, and their distinctiveness and economic dynamism—especially their banking activities—attracted prejudice and hostility among their *Demi* and European business rivals and more widely.[55]

Their French critics would have preferred the Chinese to restrict themselves to labouring and peddling instead of competing economically with French and *Demi* interests. A similar concern with protecting broader national French interests was shown, at least intermittently, by the metropolitan government. From 1922, for example, following negotiations with the Ministry of Commerce, the French line Messageries Maritimes, in return for a subsidy, connected Tahiti to a global French colonial route linking French possessions in the Indian Ocean, the Pacific, and the Caribbean.[56]

French national involvement in the Pacific colonies and their links with France were strengthened in response to the Great Depression, during which prices slumped for the narrow range of commodity exports produced in the French Pacific colonies and protectorates. Under a law passed in March 1931, the French government established a new system of protective tariffs for French colonial produce in which the French Pacific entities participated. In addition, the French government subsidised the local budgets of the *Etablissements Français d'Océanie* and New Caledonia, which had gone into deficit as a result of reduced receipts. In 1933, it was agreed that henceforth 60 per cent of the copra from the *Etablissements Français d'Océanie* would go to France in return for a system of bonus payments financed by high import duties in France on produce of foreign origin. New Caledonia and the New Hebrides benefited from similar arrangements under this scheme.[57]

In the New Hebrides, the French government encouraged an expansion of French influence despite the constraints imposed by the system of joint administration with the United Kingdom. At the time of the negotiation of the Condominium the French delegates had ensured that the responsibilities and powers of the joint administration were restricted, leaving greater freedom of action to the separate French and British administrations. They wanted to make it easier for France to expand its influence by taking advantage of Britain's lack of interest in the archipelago—a lack that continued despite intermittent Australian expansionist pressures.[58] The objective of eventually acquiring the New Hebrides as a French colony was never attained, but French influence in the archipelago became significant. In 1910 French nationals outnumbered British by 566 to 288, and by 1939 the proportion was ten to one. France was the chief market for copra, the main export crop, and French interests dominated the commercial economy.[59]

France used the land claims of French nationals as a means to expand French influence and to create grounds for a prospective French takeover. In 1887 the French government rescued the Noumea-based *Compagnie Calédonienne des Nouvelles-Hébrides*, which had extensive land claims in the New Hebrides, from bankruptcy. In 1894 the government pledged further subsidies and all but took over the company. At this time the company was renamed the *Société Française des Nouvelles-Hébrides*. By 1905 it had acquired paper title to some fifteen thousand square kilometres—well over half of the land area of the New Hebrides. French officials knew that many of the titles were bogus. But when negotiating the Condominium, the French ensured that legal challenges to titles registered before 1887 would be impossible, and that challenges to titles registered in the period from 1887 to 1904 would be difficult to sustain.[60]

Whereas British officials did little, French officials put much effort into promoting French influence and protecting the interests of French nationals. The French part of the joint administration turned a blind eye to offences against the Condominium regulations: before World War One, for example, the French Residency often failed to levy fines on French settlers found guilty of infraction of the labour code.[61] When commodity prices crashed during the Great Depression, and following drought and cyclone damage, the French authorities saved French planters from bankruptcy by subsidising French-produced copra and by advancing 5 million francs to write off debts. In return for its advances, the French government took over many of the titles of the *Société Française des Nouvelles-Hébrides*, thus consolidating its control.[62]

Although the French government and its officials worked hard to expand French influence, Anglophone influence became more widespread. By the early twentieth century, Presbyterian and Anglican missions, strongly supported by the churches in Australia and New Zealand, had converted over half of the indigenous population. These missionaries had won more converts than the French Catholic missionaries, largely because of their more extensive use of vernacular languages and their training and use of indigenous lay preachers and pastors. As a result Francophone influence among the indigenous population languished behind Anglophone influence, even though French settlers were the predominant presence on the plantations and in the two small urban centres of Port Vila on Efate and Luganville on Espiritu Santo. The first census of the archipelago, conducted in 1967, recorded that 42 per cent of the ni-Vanuatu (as the indigenous population later became known) were Presbyterian, 15 per cent were Anglican, and small numbers of other ni-Vanuatu belonged to various minor Protestant sects.[63]

Attitudes to the French were also soured by labour disputes. Some planters treated their labourers fairly, but even under a 'good master', labourers were expected to work long hours for poor wages. The condominium regulations on hours of work were consistent with the standards and attitudes

of the era concerning non-white labour, and were comparable with those
applied elsewhere in the Pacific Islands. These regulations required that
labourers should have Sunday off, except for domestic duties and the care
of animals; have one clear hour of rest each day at the time of the midday
meal; and should only be required to work between sunrise and sunset.[64]
Conditions varied from one plantation to another but, at least until World
War Two, many planters mistreated and exploited their labourers. They
underpaid them, provided substandard food and accommodation, charged
exorbitant prices in the plantation store, kept them working after their
contracts had expired, and enforced discipline with violence. Some British
planters treated their labourers badly, and many of the labour recruiters and
overseers were Britons, Australians, or New Zealanders. Nonetheless, a large
majority of the planters were French, so disputes over labour questions
reflected especially badly on France and its local representatives.[65]

Land disputes also led to anti-French feeling. The notion of individual,
absolute ownership of land is alien to Melanesian tradition, as is the idea of
its permanent sale. Instead, overlapping rights to the use and produce of
land are held jointly. A consensus on who has rights to a particular area
does not necessarily exist, and rival claims are common. Acquisition of land
by settlers was feasible, but only when endorsed by all those with an interest
in the land on the basis of a full understanding of the rights being transferred,
and of the agreed boundaries.

The French titles, most of which dated from the late nineteenth century,
were rarely acquired in this way. No cadastral survey was made and
boundaries were poorly marked, if at all. Prospective 'purchasers' sailed up
and down the coast, at times laying claim to pieces of land without even
bothering to go ashore. Agreements were reached on the ship's deck with
one or two local people, often after they had been plied with alcohol. In
many instances little attempt was made to establish that the individuals
concerned had the authority, on behalf of their communities, to enter into
agreements, or even to ensure that they belonged to the community concerned. Even when they were legitimate representatives of their communities, the illiterate islanders who made their mark on transfer documents
often thought that they were merely conceding landing and trading rights,
or else the right to use some of the lands on the shore. Unbeknown to the
local people, the titles often covered claims extending far into the interior,
into areas well outside the territory of the coastal communities.[66]

Because their attitudes to land varied so sharply, and because many of the
settlers' claims were dubious, tensions between settlers and local communities over land were chronic, but they were contained, and a more or less
satisfactory accommodation emerged between settlers and local communities. Such compromise was possible in part because, except in a few areas,
the population density in the archipelago was generally low, and there was
sufficient land for both plantation and subsistence use. Even so, these disputes

would help to provide impetus for the emergence of a nationalist movement in the years leading up to independence in 1980.

In the Condominium, the administration operated in a tenuous fashion outside Port Vila and Luganville. With the joint administrations handicapped by a lack of funds and by competition and bickering, missions and plantations assumed some administrative functions, while disputes within indigenous communities were resolved by customary means, including violence. Both the Presbyterian and Anglican churches set up schools and clinics, and assumed some administrative functions, filling the vacuum left by the Condominium authorities. After World War Two, the British employed ni-Vanuatu educated in church schools in junior administrative positions and as schoolteachers, helping create an Anglophone elite. In contrast, French practice was generally to employ metropolitan French people in even junior positions.

The consolidation and 'indigenisation' of Christianity and the new involvement of indigenous communities in cash cropping reduced the disadvantages of the indigenous peoples of the French Pacific. In addition their health standards improved, because they developed greater resistance to imported diseases and because of medical advances and improved access to modern health care. In New Caledonia, where many settlers had expected the Melanesians to 'die out', the consolidation and growth of the Melanesian population took place during the interwar period.

In the Marquesas islands in the *Etablissements Français d'Océanie*, the population slumped from five thousand to two thousand between 1880 and 1920, largely, it appears, because of female infertility caused by imported venereal disease.[67] The decline was reversed in the 1920s because of increased resistance and better health care.[68] Though the change of direction was less dramatic elsewhere in the French Pacific entities, in most areas a demographic revival took place.

In New Caledonia in the interwar period, the consolidation and growth of the Melanesian population and Melanesian participation in cash cropping coincided with the failure of French efforts to make New Caledonia a viable, self-reliant settler colony analogous to those Britain had established in Australia and New Zealand. Immigration from France slowed to a trickle. Smallholder capitalist agriculture mostly failed in New Caledonian conditions. Many small settlers were obliged to leave the land, and landholdings became concentrated. Extensive grazing rather than intensive cultivation, complemented by mining, became characteristic of European economic activity. Under Governor Guyon, whose term in the colony ran from 1925 to 1932, an ambitious programme of public works and development measures was planned. Roads and other infrastructure were expanded and improved. However, the full programme was not implemented because of budgetary restrictions resulting from the Great Depression, because of settler opposition to the costs involved and to measures benefiting the Melanesian population, and because of a loss of momentum following Guyon's departure.[69]

The failure of rural settlement and economic development in New Caledonia had long-term implications. Alain Saussol has pointed out that during the twentieth century up to 1939, 'the most important turning point in the history of New Caledonia occurred. While the colonial order—unchanged since the late nineteenth century—was gently running down, the conditions that were to challenge its legitimacy [that is, the Melanesian demographic, economic, and cultural revival] were quietly coming about'.[70]

World War Two and after

Until after World War Two, the indigenous peoples of New Caledonia and the other French Pacific entities lacked the constitutional means to express their potential political strength. In the *Etablissements Français d'Océanie* and New Caledonia, only a small minority of the indigenous population was permitted to take part in the embryonic local organs of self-government. These bodies, which were the scene of chronic bickering between the metropolitan government and local interests, were dominated by settlers and businessmen. World War Two brought changes. Hostilities did not take place on the territory of any of the French entities, but the impact of the war on them was substantial. United States and allied support bases were established on Espiritu Santo and Efate in the New Hebrides; on Wallis Island; on Bora Bora in the *Etablissements Français d'Océanie*; and at Noumea—where the former headquarters of the South-west Pacific Command later became the seat of the South Pacific Commission.

Memories of the war linger. Older generation European New Caledonians talk nostalgically of the *La guerre des américains* (the Americans' War) rather than of World War Two, while some young Wallisians proudly claim an American serviceman among their grandparents. With thousands of troops requiring provisions and services, local economies boomed. The easy-going, free-spending Americans made a favourable impression. Melanesians noted that black American servicemen occupied posts of some administrative and technical responsibility. Several hundred volunteers, comprising both indigenous people and settlers, served with distinction in the Free French Forces in North Africa, the Atlantic, and southern Europe.[71]

Immediately after the war a partial dismantling of the old colonial system took place in response to liberal and radical currents of opinion in metropolitan France. The *indigenat* and forced labour were abolished. Full democratic rights and freedoms were gradually extended to the indigenous peoples, although progress lagged in the Condominium and in Wallis and Futuna. From around 1950 the *Rassemblement Démocratique des Populations Tahitiennes* (Democratic Assembly of the Tahitian People) in Tahiti and the

Union Calédonienne (Caledonian Union) in New Caledonia championed autonomist and protonationalist sentiments. The impetus for these movements came in part from Melanesian and Polynesian veterans who had returned home with wider horizons and heightened expectations. France contained these pressures, sometimes using dubious methods.[72]

In a 1957 study, Hubert Deschamps and Jean Guiart indicated, in part by what they took for granted, that the French Pacific presence was stable, well founded, and enduring.[73] Their judgment was tested in the 1958 referendum, in which voters throughout France's overseas possessions chose between independence—with no guarantee of further aid—and continued integration with France with the status of partly self-governing overseas territories.

The peoples of the French Pacific voted clearly against independence, overwhelmingly in New Caledonia (98 per cent), and decisively (64 per cent) in the *Etablissements Français d'Océanie*. In Wallis and Futuna, in a separate plebiscite held in December 1959, an overwhelming majority of voters opted for the transformation of the protectorate into an overseas territory. No poll was held in the Condominium of the New Hebrides, the frontier of the French presence in the region, but here too the French position seemed assured. In 1957 Guiart concluded that France was not likely to leave the archipelago. He advised prospective settlers to gather sufficient capital, avoid excess drinking, and establish a good rapport with the local people.[74] Yet it was here that, some years later, France's efforts to maintain its presence in the Pacific Islands region suffered their first reversal, in a conflict between France and an indigenous nationalist movement based on adherents of the Presbyterian and Anglican churches and opposed to land-grabbing by settlers and speculators.

* * *

I AM GRATEFUL to Dr Dorothy Shineberg for her helpful comments on a draft of this chapter. Earlier versions of a considerable part of the chapter appear in my *France and the South Pacific: A Contemporary History*, Allen & Unwin, Sydney, and University of Hawai'i Press, Honolulu, 1992.

Notes

1 *Le Temps*, 6 January 1931, quoted in Catherine Coquery-Vidrovitch, 'Mythes et réalités de l'idée coloniale française entre les deux guerres', in *France: Politics, Society, Culture and International Relations*, ed. Robert Aldrich, Papers from the Seventh George Rudé Seminar in French History and Civilisation, Department of Economic History, University of Sydney, 1990, 159–197, 164.

2 Coquery-Vidrovitch, 164.

3 Coquery-Vidrovitch, 167. See also Bernard Brou, *Espoirs et réalités: La Nouvelle*

Calédonie de 1925 à 1945, Société d'Etudes Historiques de la Nouvelle-Calédonie, Noumea, 1975, 88–89.

4 John Dunmore, *French Explorers in the Pacific*, Oxford University Press, 1965, 1: 71–77. Bougainville's was the first French expedition to the South Pacific, but the first Frenchmen to enter the region were the nineteen anonymous seamen who sailed with Magellan. None survived the voyage (Dunmore, 7).

5 After leaving Tahiti and sailing more than 2000 kilometres to the west, Bougainville's expedition passed close to Wallis Island, 'discovered' by Wallis the year before. Some 1500 kilometres farther on, the expedition stopped briefly to gather fresh provisions in the northern part of the New Hebrides Archipelago, 'discovered' by the Spaniard Quiros in 1606. However, Bougainville had no contact with New Caledonia, a few hundred kilometres to the south. The first confirmed French visit to these islands, which Cook had 'discovered' in 1774, was by d'Entrecasteaux in 1792.

6 Women crowded in the canoes that surrounded the ships as they came close to shore. Bougainville recalled that one young woman found her way on board the flagship and discarded her garment, to the delight of the sailors sweating at the capstan to drop the anchor. Never was a capstan turned so quickly, he reminisced, in an oft-quoted comment that has titillated 'generations of male readers (Louis Antoine de Bougainville, *Un Voyage autour du monde*, Paris, 1771, 190. English translation by J. R. Forster, *A Voyage round the World*, London, 1772). Secondary accounts in English include Dunmore 1965; J. C. Beaglehole, *The Exploration of the Pacific*, 3rd edn, Adam and Charles Black, London, 1966; Gavan Daws, *A Dream of Islands: Voyages of Self-Discovery in the South Seas*, Jacaranda Press, Milton, QLD, 1980; and K. R. Howe, *Where the Waves Fall: A New South Sea Islands History from First Settlement to Colonial Rule*, Allen & Unwin, Sydney, and University of Hawai'i Press, Honolulu, 1984.

7 See Greg Dening, 'Ethnohistory in Polynesia: The Value of Ethnohistorical Evidence', *Journal of Pacific History* 1 (1, 1966): 23–42. See also W. H. Pearson, 'The Reception of European Voyagers on Polynesian Islands, 1568–1797', *Journal de la Société des Océanistes* 26 (March 1970): 121–154, and his 'European Intimidation and the Myth of Tahiti', *Journal of Pacific History* 4 (1969): 199–217; and Caroline Ralston,'Changes in the Lives of Ordinary Women in Early Post-Contact Hawaii', in *Family and Gender in the Pacific: Domestic Contradictions and the Colonial Impact*, ed. Margaret Jolly and Martha Macintyre, Cambridge University Press, 1989, 45–64.

8 See Howe, 3–66, for an account of the peoples of the region before and at the time of European contact.

9 Howe, 3–66; Jean Guiart, *La terre est le sang des morts*, 2nd edn, Editions Anthropos, Paris, 1985, ch. 1; Nicholas Thomas, 'The Force of Ethnology: Origins and Significance of the Melanesia/Polynesia Division', and 'Comments' by various authors, *Current Anthropology* 30 (1, February 1989): 2–41.

10 Hubert Deschamps and Jean Guiart, *Tahiti, Nouvelle-Calédonie, Nouvelles-Hébrides*, L'Union Française, Paris, 1957, 27.

11 Robert Langdon has suggested that the people of eastern Polynesia had already come under some European influences, before the Wallis and Bougainville expeditions arrived, thanks to the crew of a Spanish vessel wrecked in the Tuamotus in 1526. See his *The Lost Caravel*, Pacific Publications, Sydney, 1975, revised 1987.

12 See Howe, 59–65. Howe in part follows Bronwen Douglas, 'Rank, Power, Authority: A Reassessment of Traditional Leadership in South Pacific Societies', *Journal of Pacific History* 14 (1979): 2–27.

13 Howe, 3–24; Guiart 1985, ch. 1.

14 Quoted in Deryck Scarr, *Fragments of Empire: A History of the Western Pacific High Commission, 1877–1914*, Australian National University Press, Canberra, 1967, 307.

15 Dorothy Shineberg, *They Came For Sandalwood: A Study of the Sandalwood Trade in the South-West Pacific 1830–1865*, Melbourne University Press, 1967; Robert Aldrich, *The French Presence in the South Pacific, 1842–1940*, Macmillan, London, 1990, ch. 6.

16 See Roselène Dousset (Dousset-Leenhardt), *Colonialisme et Contradictions: Etude sur les Causes socio-historiques de l'Insurrection de 1878 en Nouvelle-Calédonie*, Mouton, Paris, 1970, chs 2 and 3. See also her *Terre natale, terre d'exile*, Maissonneuve & Larose, Paris, 1976. Madame Dousset cites the experience of Captain Tardy de Montravel, who voyaged around New Caledonia in 1853 and received a warm reception almost everywhere (1970, 99). For a detailed analysis of European–Melanesian relations in the north-eastern part of the main island, the area most affected by early interactions, see Bronwen Douglas, A History of Culture Contact in North-Eastern New Caledonia, 1774–1870, PhD dissertation, Australian National University, Canberra, 1972. See also John Connell, *New Caledonia or Kanaky? The Political History of a French Colony*, National Centre for Development Studies, Canberra, 1987, 22–23.

17 See Pearson 1969; 1970.

18 Greg Dening, *Islands and Beaches: Discourse on a Silent Land, Marquesas, 1774–1880*, University of Hawai'i Press, Honolulu, 1980, 247.

19 Scarr, 17–71.

20 See Shineberg, 1967, 200, and chs 14 and 16.

21 Scarr, 173–175.

22 See I. C. Campbell, 'Imperialism, Dynasticism, and Conversion: Tongan Designs on 'Uvea (Wallis Island), 1835–52', *Journal of the Polynesian Society* 92 (2 June 1983): 155–167.

23 See Alexandre Poncet, *Histoire de l'Ile Wallis: Le Protectorat français*, Société des Océanistes, Paris, 1972, 38, 52–53, 55, 74, 93, 197.

24 Dening, 1980, 212, 220, and chs 6 and 7.

25 For an overview of resistance in the *Etablissements Français d'Océanie* see Pierre-Yves Toullelan, 'Comment la Polynésie est devenue française', in *Annales du Centre Universitaire de Pirae*, no. 3 (1989): 56–68.

26 Dousset-Leenhardt 1970, 115–123. For incidents relating to the sandalwood trade in New Caledonia and the New Hebrides between 1842 and 1865, see Shineberg 1967, 247–249. See also Bronwen Douglas, '"Almost Constantly at War"? An Ethnographic Perspective on Fighting in New Caledonia', *Journal of Pacific History* 25 (1 June 1990): 22–46.

27 See Bronwen Douglas 'Conflict and Alliance in a Colonial Context: Case Studies in New Caledonia 1853–1870', *Journal of Pacific History* 15 (1, 1980): 21–51. The French initially called the new town Port-de-France, but reverted to Noumea, the Melanesian name for the location, because of confusion with Fort-de-France, the capital of Martinique.

28 Connell, 62–73; Guiart 1985, 71–77; Linda Latham 'Revolt Re-examined: The 1878 Insurrection in New Caledonia', *Journal of Pacific History* 10 (1975): 48–63.

29 Connell, 73–76; Jean Guiart, 'Les événements de 1917 en Nouvelle-Calédonie', *Journal de la Société des Océanistes* 29 (1970): 265–282.

30 The defeat of the Tahitians came when a man from Rapa showed the French forces a little-known track whereby they scaled the heights and dominated the key Tahitian position. Colin Newbury, *Tahiti Nui: Change and Survival in French Polynesia 1767–1945*, University of Hawai'i Press, Honolulu, 1980, 115–122.

31 Connell, 76.

32 See Douglas 1980.

33 Jean Guiart, 'Forerunners of Melanesian Nationalism', *Oceania* 22 (2 December 1951): 81–90; Jeremy MacClancy, *To Kill a Bird with Two Stones: A Short History of Vanuatu*, Vanuatu Cultural Centre, Vila, 1980; John Beasant, *The Santo Rebellion: An Imperial Reckoning*, University of Hawai'i Press, Honolulu, and Heinemann, Melbourne, 1984.

34 R. J. May, ed., *Micronationalist Movements in Papua New Guinea*. Monograph 1, Department of Political and Social Change, Australian National University, Canberra, 1982, 2, 442.

35 Howard Van Trease, *The Politics of Land in Vanuatu: From Colony to Independence*, Institute of Pacific Studies, University of the South Pacific, Suva, 1987; Scarr, 199, 212–213, 219, 230.

36 Scarr, 207; C. W. Newbury, 'Aspects of French Policy in the Pacific, 1853–1906', *Pacific Historical Review* 27 (1, Feb 1958): 45–56.

37 See MacClancy.

38 Alain Saussol, *L'Héritage: Essai sur le problème foncier mélanésien en Nouvelle-Calédonie*, Société des Océanistes, Paris, 1979.

39 Dorothy Shineberg, personal communication, November 1990.

40 See Poncet, especially chs 10, 11.

41 Dornoy, 22–23; Bernard Brou, *Peuplement et Population de la Nouvelle-Calédonie: La société moderne*, Société d'Etudes Historiques de la Nouvelle-Calédonie, n.d., 55.

42 Union Agricole Calédonienne, *Notice sur la Nouvelle-Calédonie, ses richesses, son avenir*, Société d'Editions Littéraires et Artistiques, Paris, 1900, *vi*.

43 See Brou n.d., 27–29.

44 See Campbell 1983.

45 Nancy J. Pollock, 'Doctor Administrators in Wallis and Futuna', *Journal of Pacific History* 25 (1 June 1990): 47–67.

46 Newbury 1980, 139–140. Part of this population decline possibly resulted from migration to Tahiti.

47 Newbury 1980, 140; and Daws.

48 Newbury 1980, chs 6, 8, 9, 10; Newbury, 1958, 49–50. See also Gabriel Tetiarahi, 'The Society Islands: Squeezing Out the Polynesians' 100–107, and François Ravault 'Land Problems in French Polynesia' 112–117, in *French Polynesia: A Book of Selected Readings*, ed. Nancy J. Pollock and Ron Crocombe, Institute of Pacific Studies, University of the South Pacific, Suva, 1988.

49 Robert Langdon, *Tahiti: Island of Love*, 5th edn, Pacific Publications, Sydney, 1979.

50 Shineberg 1967, ch. 12.

51 See Dorothy Shineberg, 'Un nouveau regard sur la démographie historique de la Nouvelle-Calédonie', *Journal de la société des Océanistes* 39 (1983): 33–43.

52 Newbury 1980; Deschamps and Guiart, 51–52.

53 Newbury 1980, 268.

54 Newbury 1980, 283–284.

55 Guy Guennou, François Merceron, Michel Lextreyt, and Pierre-Yves Toulellan, *Terres et Civilisations Polynésiennes*, Nathan, Paris, 1987, 134, 136, 161–164; Newbury 1980, 170–172, 263, 275–278, 284, 286–288.

56 Newbury 1980, 289.

57 Newbury 1980, 289, 294–298.

58 See R. C. Thompson, *Australian Imperialism in the South Pacific: The Expansionist Era, 1820–1920*, Melbourne University Press, 1980.

59 Scarr, 210; MacClancy, 86. See also Aldrich, 306.

60 Cyril S. Belshaw, *Island Administration in the South West Pacific: Government and Reconstruction in New Caledonia, the New Hebrides, and the British Solomon Islands*, Royal Institute of International Affairs, London and New York, 1950, 60; Edward Jacomb, *France and England in the New Hebrides: The Anglo-French Condominium*, George Robertson, Melbourne, 1914, 22–26; Scarr, 183, 198–205, 212–213, 219, 223–227.

61 Scarr, 232–234; Jacomb, 77; MacClancy, 82.

62 MacClancy, 91.

63 Norma MacArthur and J. F. Yaxley, *Condominium of the New Hebrides: A Report on the First Census of the Population 1967*, New South Wales Government Printer, Vila and Sydney, 1968, 66–67.

64 Article 45 of the Convention Respecting 'The New Hebrides', London, 27 February 1906. The convention is reprinted as Appendix 2 to Jacomb.

65 See R. J. Fletcher (pseud.), *Isles of Illusion: Letters from the South Seas*, Century, London, 1986; first published 1923.

66 Jacomb, ch. 9; Scarr, 198–205; Van Trease.

67 The Marquesans seemed destined for the tragic fate of the Tasmanian Aborigines and of other Australian Aboriginal groups that had disappeared as distinct communities because of imported disease, conflicts with settlers, and demoralisation.

68 Jean-Louis Rallu, The Historical Demography of the French Pacific Territories, seminar, Demography Department, Research School of Social Sciences, Australian National University, 14 August 1990.

69 See Brou 1975, especially 242–247.

70 Alain Saussol, 'The Colonial Chimera: From Annexation to the Re-emergence of Kannak Identity', in *New Caledonia: Essays in Nationalism and Dependency*, ed. Michael Spencer, Alan Ward, and John Connell, University of Queensland Press, St Lucia, 1988, 50.

71 See, for example, Stephen Henningham, 'How the Men of Maré Went to War', *Pacific Islands Monthly* (January 1989): 36–37.

72 Connell, ch. 11; Langdon 1979, 253–258.

73 Deschamps and Guiart.

74 Deschamps and Guiart, 297–299.

Part 2
Towards decolonisation

7

World War Two

Hugh Laracy

The fighting that erupted in the Pacific during World War Two flowed not from Germany's invasion of Poland in 1939, but from Japan's invasion of China in 1937. Admittedly, Germany in late 1940 and early 1941 had made the first offensive moves, when marauding German warships attacked British targets in the Pacific. Several merchant ships (and possibly the Australian warship *Sydney*) were sunk, Nauru was bombarded, and mines were laid in New Zealand waters. For a while there was also a likelihood that New Caledonia might side with the pro-German Vichy regime in France.[1] However, that threat to Allied security in the region was dissolved in September 1940, when a colonial official named Henri Sautot defied his superiors and rallied his compatriots in support of the Free French movement of Charles de Gaulle. Not until 7 December 1941, with the Japanese raid on the United States naval base at Pearl Harbor in Hawai'i did the war begin to impinge heavily on the Pacific Islands. Almost simultaneously (although a day earlier because of the east–west time difference) Japanese land forces also attacked Hong Kong and began the action that led them in February 1942 to capture the British base at Singapore. With these events the Asian and European streams of war converged, and the conflict became truly global. With these attacks—as blatant acts of aggression as have ever set nations fighting (despite expressions of an opinion to the contrary)—Japan unambiguously reaffirmed its alliance, proclaimed in the tripartite pact of September 1940, with the Axis powers of Germany and Italy.[2] At the same time, the United States was prompted to enter the war formally, on the side of Britain as one of the Allies.

Already in mid-1941 Japanese forces had begun to extend their operations from China into South-East Asia, and in March 1942 they captured their main objective there—the Indonesian oilfields, which are the largest in Asia. Japan needed to control them in order to secure its long-standing ambition for a victory in China, which had been threatened in July 1941 when the British, American, and Dutch governments had sought to restrain Japan's aggression by blocking its oil supply. For the longer term, Japan's policy envisaged organising the nations from Burma eastward to New Guinea and adjacent Pacific islands into a grouping to be known as the Greater East Asia Co-Prosperity Sphere. Such an arrangement, it was believed, would be of twofold benefit to Japan: economically it would provide a vast and guaranteed market for Japanese manufacturers as well as reliable sources of raw materials; militarily, it would block the route by which China might be supplied by the Allies and thereby assisted to resist Japanese imperialism. The outer limits of the proposed sphere were never clearly defined, but by mid-1942, striking from bases in Micronesia, which they had begun fortifying in 1940, the Japanese had occupied much of New Guinea and the Solomons as well as the Gilbert Islands (now part of Kiribati). They appeared to be on the way to Fiji, New Caledonia, and Australia. Yet already they were beginning to stumble.

In attacking Pearl Harbor the Japanese made three serious miscalculations. First, they underestimated the ability of America to strike back and the readiness of President Franklin Roosevelt to commit his country to war. (It has been argued that Roosevelt and certain of his senior officials were only waiting for an excuse to enter the war and that they did not, therefore, pass on to the commanders in Hawai'i information they had of the impending Japanese attack.)[3] The second flaw was that although they destroyed a number of aged battleships of the US Pacific Fleet, the Japanese missed its core—the three aircraft carriers that were exercising at sea at the time of the attack (a fact of particular significance to proponents of the 'waiting-for-an-excuse' theory). The third weakness was that instead of merely attacking Pearl Harbor the Japanese did not also occupy the lightly defended island of O'ahu. The move had been considered—and rejected—by Admiral Isoroku Yamamoto, the supreme naval commander, two months before the attack. As a result the Japanese had aroused the United States from its isolationism, incurred its enmity, but let slip an opportunity to obtain an inestimable strategic advantage by capturing its main Pacific base. Their willingness to take such a risk was based on the expectation that Japan could make a rapid advance through the western Pacific and then obtain a negotiated peace, and not be drawn into a war of attrition.[4]

The implications of the defeats in Japanese strategy soon became apparent. Within six months of the attack on Pearl Harbor Japan suffered heavily in two crucial engagements. In the Battle of the Coral Sea (7–8 May 1942), westward of the Solomons, US carrier-borne aircraft turned back an invasion force heading for Port Moresby, and in the Battle of Midway Island (3–6 June), north-west of Hawai'i, Japan lost four aircraft carriers. These were the first naval battles in history in which the opposing vessels not only did not fire at each other, but never even saw each other. Although American losses were high, Japan was also weakened by these clashes, to the extent of

Shell craters and foxholes at Kakambona Beach, Guadalcanal, the day after the US bombardment forced the Japanese to retreat. The First Battalion, 27th Infantry, is converting the area to a supply dump and bivouac area, 25 January 1943. (US Army Signal Corps, National Archives)

being unable to sustain the momentum of attack. From June 1942 the Americans began to develop naval and air superiority in the Pacific, although it was another six months before their advantage became clear, and even then it was not unequivocal. Meanwhile the Japanese had landed on many islands and had to be forced out of them in a series of bitter battles, fought mostly on land.

Restrained by the setbacks at sea, Japan's southward advance was finally halted at Guadalcanal in the Solomon Islands. American troops landed there on 7 August 1942 to capture an almost-completed airfield. From this, re-named Henderson Field after a hero of the Battle of Midway, the Japanese would have been able to reach Fiji and New Caledonia. Their retaliation for the challenge to their drive for dominance in the south-west Pacific was swift and savage. In a battle off neighbouring Savo Island on 8 August, a Japanese fleet destroyed four Allied heavy cruisers and forced the with-drawal to New Caledonia of the rest of the naval force, which had been intended to support the landing. Indeed, mindful of the damage done by Japanese torpedoes in earlier engagements, Admiral F. J. Fletcher had withdrawn much of his fleet, including the aircraft carriers, before the counterattack began. Ten thousand US Marines on Guadalcanal and another six thousand on nearby Tulagi were left in a precarious position. Without sea or air protection, and bereft of most of their equipment, they faced an enemy that was being rapidly and, for the moment, more easily reinforced. The ensuing contest was a bitter one, but after a campaign that lasted six months the Japanese retreated from Guadalcanal in February 1943. Meanwhile, in July 1942 the Japanese had renewed the attack on Port Moresby, this time from the north by way of the Kokoda Trail across the Owen Stanley Range. By October they had come within 30 miles (48 km) of their goal. Then they found themselves opposed by fresh Australian veterans brought back from the Middle East and were forced to retreat, although Papua was not cleared of Japanese until late January 1943.

Within the broad extent of the Japanese-occupied Pacific in early 1943, the reverses in Papua and Guadalcanal were small affairs. Still, they were precedents that would be followed by many other retreats over the next two and a half years, as the tide of war was made to flow inexorably, if slowly and haltingly, back towards Japan. Advancing northwards through the Solomons, the Allies invaded New Georgia in June 1943 and Bougainville in November. In June they also launched a fresh offensive in New Guinea; and in the Gilbert Islands, the easternmost group occupied by the Japanese, the heavily fortified atoll of Tarawa was captured by the Americans in November 1943. The following February the fortress islands of Kwajalein and Enewetak in the Marshalls were liberated, and in June Saipan and Tinian in the Marianas. A month later Guam, also in the Marianas, but American territory since 1898, was reclaimed, having been in Japanese hands since two days after Pearl Harbor. In the final months of the war, moving ever closer to Japan, the Americans captured Iwo Jima in the Bonins in February 1945 and Okinawa in June. In all of these landings the losses on both sides were massive. Meanwhile, in the wake of the advance, various other Japanese-held positions, such as the bases at Rabaul and Chuuk (Truk), had been bypassed, left isolated and cut off from supplies. Though still subjected to bombing raids, they were tactically neutralised and not worth the cost of a more direct assault. Then, on 6 August 1945 an American B24 bomber, the *Enola Gay*, took off from Tinian and dropped an atomic bomb on the Japanese city of Hiroshima. On 8 August the city of Nagasaki was likewise bombed. Shocked by these events and recognising the futility of continued fighting, despite a readiness among their forces to continue dying, the Japanese Supreme Council was forced to abandon the dream of imperial conquest. Accordingly, it reluctantly—though realistically, since Japan was economically and militarily debilitated—accepted the Emperor's proposal to capitulate. World War Two came to a formal end in the Pacific on 2

September 1945, when the instrument of surrender was signed aboard Admiral Halsey's flagship, the USS *Missouri*, in Tokyo Harbour.

The military history of the war has been exhaustively documented. The combatants, especially on the victorious Allied side, have been and continue to be well served by their scribes. The policies and diplomacy of governments, the course and costs of campaigns, the strategies and disputes of generals and admirals and the exploits and experiences of the military units— and of many of the individuals—under their command have been narrated, analysed, and assessed at length and in detail. Participants and other firsthand observers, as well as commentators safely separated by time and distance from the events they describe, have all contributed to this work. Library shelves and bulky bibliographies attest their industry. Comprehensive accounts are readily accessible of, for example, incidents such as the tragic fiasco of the US landings on Tarawa and the aerial ambush of Admiral Yamamoto. In the first, the landing-craft entered the lagoon at low tide instead of at high tide, so that the Marines had to advance, wading through the shallows into a barrage of Japanese fire instead of being landed on the beach, as intended; in the second, Yamamoto, having left the safety of Chuuk to inspect the south-eastern corner of Japan's defence perimeter was shot down over southern Bougainville on 18 April 1943, after a radio message outlining his flight plan had been intercepted and decoded by the Americans. American cryptographers had broken the secret Japanese codes in the years before the war.[5]

A myriad of other well-chronicled items and episodes could be cited to make the point about the assiduity of those who have written about the war, including, for example, the following random list of topics: the fear of young men going into battle; the experience of Lieutenant John F. Kennedy (later president of the United States) and his crew after their vessel PT109 was rammed by the Japanese destroyer *Amarigi* in the Solomons in August 1943; the beheading of forty-two civilians, most of them German Catholic missionaries, aboard the Japanese destroyer *Okikaze* in New Guinea waters on 17 May 1943; the extraordinary achievement of American submarines in destroying more than 1100 Japanese merchant ships and 201 warships, for the loss of only 52 of their own craft; the mass suicide of thousands of Japanese civilians—mostly women and children—who hurled themselves off the cliffs at Marpi Point on Saipan on 7 July 1944; the two-month-long battle for tiny Pelelieu in Palau, where 10 000 Japanese were killed in futile but savage defence late in 1944; the assaults of Kamikaze suicide planes on American naval forces westward of the Marianas during the first half of 1945; the desperate resistance of the Japanese during 1944 and 1945, which provided the Americans with an excuse (though not by August 1945 a need) to finish the war by dropping the atom bomb. Solid descriptions and commentaries are easily available on all these matters.[6]

In contrast to those concerning the belligerents, published accounts of

Pacific Islanders' involvement in the war are very few and less abundantly informed. So, too, are the relevant documentary sources. Moreover, the oral record of their experience was eroded sharply during the 1980s as the generation of those with wartime memories began to die out at a steadily accelerating rate. As a telling indication of the fragility of that record, within a year of their contributing to a research project conducted during 1987 and 1988 on indigenous recollections of the war, three of the principal Solomon Islands informants—George Maelalo, Bill Bennett, and Jonathan Fifi'i—were dead. Nevertheless, there is still material enough—photographic, oral, physical remains—to illustrate the range and complexity of what the conflict meant for the Pacific peoples. They were not only profoundly and enduringly affected by the war that had come unbidden to their islands, but many of them contributed in a variety of ways to the waging of it. Admittedly, certain stories are already well known, such as that of Jacob Vouza who in August 1942 preferred to be bayonetted and left for dead by his Japanese captors than tell them about American defensive positions on Guadalcanal. Another is that of the 'Fuzzy-Wuzzy Angels', the Papuan villagers who assisted Australian troops as carriers, stretcher bearers, and comforters on the Kokoda Trail. The publicity attracted by these episodes should not obscure the many other, no less important, facets to the islanders' experience of the war.

The first widespread phase of that experience was a mingling of fearful expectation and confusion as, from December 1941, the Japanese loomed ever nearer. Intensifying those feelings, in coastal New Guinea and the Solomons especially, was the dissolution of the colonial leadership structure with the hurried evacuation of most of the European traders, planters, missionaries, and officials shortly before the Japanese were expected to arrive. Referring to Normanby Island in Papua New Guinea, one writer commented that 'approaching war brought about the collapse of an entire social universe'.[7] In some places law and order broke down as old scores were settled and abandoned houses and stores were looted; in some, millenarian excitement broke out; in some the people feasted while they still had the chance and the food; in some they just waited with apprehension, and in others with hope. In Port Moresby undisciplined Australian troops engaged in looting. In the Louisiade group a man named Buriga inspired several murders by prophesying that if the islanders killed the remaining white and mixed-race people their ancestral spirits would come back to them to deliver a ship full of cargo that had allegedly been misappropriated by Europeans.[8]

By late 1942, however, such uncertainties were largely resolved. The battle lines were clearly drawn and provided a basis on which Pacific Islanders could be broadly classified according to the way they would experience the war. Some of them lived within the area of Japanese occupation, and some did not. Those who did were destined to have the much harder time of it,

One of the 'fuzzy-wuzzy angels' lights a cigarette for a wounded Australian soldier being evacuated. Faria Valley, Papua New Guinea, October 1943. (Australian War Memorial, negative number 059014)

especially when their islands were turned into battlefields in the course of the Allied drive northwards. Disease, hunger, danger, and abandonment of coastal villages for refuges inland were commonly the lot of these people, which became increasingly painful the longer they had to wait for Allied liberation. For many of the people of Japan's mandated territories, acute suffering began as early as 1939, when Japan started militarising Micronesia and harshly recruited local labour to assist in construction work. In the Marshalls, for instance, 'whole villages [were] swept for adult males, who were then shipped from atoll to atoll as the navy's labor requirements dictated. Thus', continued Peattie, in his study of the Japanese regime, 'began the increasingly insensitive and ultimately brutal exploitation of the indigenous population by the Japanese military, an activity that was eventually to corrode whatever loyalties the Micronesians held toward Japan'.[9] In southern Bougainville by 1944 the Allies had achieved the same effect by cutting enemy supply lines. Desperate with hunger the Japanese then resorted to cannibalism and to raiding local gardens in order to survive, so incurring the wrath of the villagers. As Eric Feldt commented in a history of coastwatching operations, the villagers might have been prepared to accept Japanese, Australian, or German overlordship, but they did not surrender their vassals' right to secure their own subsistence. Adam Mueller, a German missionary who stayed on Bougainville, dated the rise of a guerrilla war there from July 1944, when two Japanese patrols were wiped out by aggrieved villages.

> *In some places . . . practically all the pigs of the natives were killed, [and] the coconut palms and sago palms cut down. In some few cases whole gardens of whole villages were stripped . . . and even not-bearing plants were uprooted. There was now a question of life and death for the natives. And when here and there a case of cannibalism became known there was no more holding them. 'Ju Tink Mipela kilim nating ol Japan? Mi no kilim nating', I was told. [That is, 'Do you think I killed Japanese for no reason at all? Not so.']*[10]

In contrast to those whose homes lay within Japanese-held territory for all or much of the war years, people who spent that time within the sphere of Allied occupation experienced the war no less profoundly, if in more congenial ways. For them the war became a time of excitement and bustle and material abundance. Their islands were abruptly exposed as never before to new influences from outside. Their harbours were used by fleets of warships, while onshore bases were built to house troops, and landing fields were constructed to service a suddenly created aircraft traffic. These developments gave islanders unprecedented opportunities to acquire imported goods: by working for money, selling curios, receiving gifts. They also offered chances for learning more of life beyond the islands and made possible a degree of fraternisation with Europeans hitherto unknown but eagerly accepted. As a missionary on Malaita commented early in 1944 'the people speak only of dollars and Americans'.[11]

Whether victims or beneficiaries, Pacific Islanders were for the most part observers of the war and the activities it generated rather than participants. Nevertheless, significant numbers of them were actively involved in the conflict, especially on the Allied side. One clearly significant indigenous contribution consisted of support for the coastwatchers. The most important of these was an Australian-organised surveillance network of, mainly, former colonial officials and traders who served behind or near enemy lines in New Guinea and the Solomons. Their number included one woman, Ruby Boye, who was based on Vanikoro in the Santa Cruz group. The task was to report by teleradio on the movements of Japanese forces and on weather conditions. It was dangerous but necessary work. The information the coastwatchers transmitted gave warning of impending Japanese attacks as well as assessments of Japanese strength and estimates of aircraft losses—information that was crucial in the battle for the Solomons. Coastwatchers' reports of the near-completion of a Japanese airfield on the Guadalcanal plains precipitated the attack on that island; reports on the numbers of ships and planes the Japanese attackers were desperately flinging against it from their base in Rabaul assisted the Americans to counter those raids and, ultimately, to hold the island. Hence the famous comment of Admiral William Halsey, US naval commander in the South Pacific (October 1942 to June 1944), 'the coastwatchers saved Guadalcanal, and Guadalcanal saved the Pacific'. Not stated, however, was that without the co-operation of islanders—as messengers, as carriers, as scouts, as guerrillas, and above all as neighbours who were generally not disposed to divulge their whereabouts to the Japanese—the coastwatchers could not have survived. Still, their position remained precarious. On Bougainville, for instance, intensifying Japanese control of the island not only increased the likelihood that the coastwatchers would be captured, but that they might be betrayed, as villagers grew more inclined to obey new masters than to protect fugitive remnants of the former colonial order. Accordingly, the pair, Paul Mason and Jack Reid, were evacuated by US submarine in July 1943.[12]

Another notable Solomons coastwatcher, whose career also illustrates the proposition that while the system could not function without indigenous support that support could not be taken for granted, was D. G. Kennedy. He was based first on Santa Isabel, but his security was threatened after a local man named George Bogese, a Suva-trained medical practitioner who had a grudge against him, assisted the Japanese to locate his camp. Kennedy then shifted to a less accessible spot named Seghe in neighbouring New Georgia. From there he not only reported on the movements of enemy forces but also mobilised a powerful indigenous force, which he directed in guerrilla actions against the Japanese. In addition, he oversaw an extensive network of scouts, who also helped rescue American pilots and sailors who had come to grief behind Japanese lines. One beneficiary of this service was Lieutenant John F. Kennedy.[13]

In view of the broad sympathy of the islanders for the Allies and the many dangers that D. G. Kennedy faced in his coastwatching, it is noteworthy that the attempt to kill him that came nearest to succeeding was made not by the Japanese but by his own lieutenant. This was Bill Bennett, a Solomon Islander who, in May 1943, exasperated by Kennedy's bullying manner, attempted to kill him during the confusion of a skirmish with a party of Japanese, but only managed to wound him. His personal affairs attended to, Bennett then took command and concluded the action, which left eight Japanese dead. Militarily, this episode, the 'Battle of Morovo', was of slight importance; its significance is in the assassination attempt (which did not become publicly known until 1987), which epitomises the complexity of islander loyalty: 'loyalists' and 'traitors' may not be as easily categorised as many histories suggest. Ironically, while Bennett has been unequivocally regarded as a war hero, Bogese has been excoriated as a collaborator. Further illustrations of the ambiguity of loyalty abound in other places, with islanders generally showing a pragmatic tendency not to antagonise, if not necessarily to assist, whatever forces had invaded their territory.

Failure to assist could bring harsh retribution, as in the case of a Papuan named Emboge. A traditional leader from Buna, at the northern end of the Kokoda Trail, he sought in the disruption of war an opportunity to reclaim autonomy for himself and his people. He began in August 1942 by betraying a number of Australians attempting to flee from the Japanese. Later he severed relations with the Japanese as well, but in November, before he could be made to pay for that piece of temerity, the Australians reoccupied Bura. They captured Emboge and, regarding his short-lived assertion of autonomy as treasonous, hanged him in August 1943.[14]

Whether the people were motivated by self-interest or by deeper loyalties, the sustained military advances of the Allies from early 1943 ensured that they would be in an increasingly better position than the Japanese to cultivate and draw on indigenous goodwill, as they already did in areas under their control. This even extended to the formal military enlistment of Pacific Islander volunteers. In American Samoa the Fitafita Guard, a kind of police force, was deployed as a defence force in 1941. In the Solomon Islands at the end of the Guadalcanal campaign, a more active force was formed to supply scouts for the American troops. From this was formed a smaller unit, which served in the front line of the advance until the close of the Bougainville campaign at war's end. Of the twenty-three men originally in this unit only seven survived to return home. A somewhat better survival rate befell the much larger contingent Fiji contributed to the war. Recruited with the ardent support of the chiefs, especially Ratu Sukuna, himself a World War One veteran, almost 6500 Fijians were under arms when numbers were at their peak in mid-1943. Of this force more than 2000 were deployed in the Solomons between late 1942 and mid-1944, serving with distinction and earning a high reputation for bravery and bushcraft. Forty-two of them died, but the casualty list would have much larger had a battalion of 500 men, which in February 1944 was in danger of being cut off by the Japanese, not been led to safety across the Crown Prince Range to Torokina by the Reverend Usaia Sotutu. He was a Fijian Methodist missionary who had worked on Bougainville for twenty years and knew the jungle trails well. In another incident a Fijian corporal, Sefanaia Sukunaivalu, killed while covering the retreat of his platoon, won the Victoria Cross, the highest British award for valour. A Tongan platoon was also associated with the Fijians. In Papua, too, a military unit that came to be named the Pacific

Thirty islanders haul a 75mm mountain gun up Ulupu Ridge, Papua New Gunea, July 1945. (Australian War Memorial, negative number 093952)

Islands Regiment was formed in 1940. Members of it were in the force that resisted the Japanese on the Kokoda Trail, and by 1945 4000 men had served in it. Several were decorated and some killed large numbers of Japanese; Sergeant Matri was credited with shooting more than a hundred of them. Fifty-seven Papua New Guinea soldiers (and twenty-eight police) were killed in the war.[15]

Less dramatically than soldiers, but probably more usefully, Pacific Islanders also contributed to the Allied war effort as labourers, working at the bases built by the Americans as they took up positions—at first defensive and then offensive—against the Japanese. Admiral E. J. King's strategy was to safeguard the lines of communication between Hawai'i and Australia by creating a 'series of strong points' along the route. Between December 1941, when the United States adopted that strategy by deciding to hold Australia, and March 1942, 79 000 US troops embarked for the South Pacific—four times the number that had been despatched to the European theatre at that time. The first major US establishment was in New Caledonia, which by March 1942 was garrisoned by 17 000 troops. That same month several companies of troops occupied Efate in Vanuatu (then the New Hebrides). In May Tonga was occupied, and in June construction of a big base began at Santo in Vanuatu, nearer to the Japanese-occupied Solomons. From Vanuatu and New Caledonia, American land, sea, and air forces were deployed for the occupation and defence of Guadalcanal, which in turn became the site of a major base as the war's front line moved farther north.[16]

And so the pattern continued. In October 1942 the Americans occupied Tuvalu (forestalling the Japanese, whose losses at the Battle of Midway impeded their intended advance southwards from Kiribati). There they built three airfields, which were to be used by aircraft engaged in the battle for Tarawa a year later. Again, early in 1944 the Americans killed over 3000 Japanese to capture Manus Island, to the north of the New Guinea mainland, and proceeded to transform it into a base through which more than one million servicemen would pass in the next eighteen months, pressing towards Japan.[17]

At all of these posts, and at numerous others scattered throughout the Pacific, islanders found employment and also discovered a market for handicrafts, fruit, building materials, and personal services. To many who had the good fortune to be behind the line of Allied advance, the war brought unprecedented prosperity. It also brought enlarged opportunities for fraternising with Europeans; the chance to develop a taste for ice-cream, beer, ready-made cigarettes, and movies; and ready access to supplies of shirts, blankets, lanterns, tools, and canned meat. In enjoying the company and generosity of the servicemen, in sharing food or a joke, and sometimes danger, with white men for the first time, islanders received an insight into a new order of human life. Figures give some indication of the scale of labour recruitment (which was usually for a term of three or six months): in October 1943 in New Caledonia the US military was employing 1500 Kanaks, in Vanuatu a total of 2000 men worked on US bases, in the Solomons 3700 were so employed, and in Papua New Guinea the monthly labour strength employed by the Australians peaked in June 1944 at nearly 38 000 men.[18]

The openhandedness and warmth that engendered wartime friendships are richly illustrated by nostalgic comments recorded by Robert King, a US Peace Corps volunteer who collected oral testimonies in the Solomons in the 1980s. Jim Bennett, brother of the guerrilla fighter Bill Bennett, recalled that:

The Americans were generous with the rations—they said the people were helping them so they gave us food and sometimes they would exchange for grass skirts and carvings. . . .

[But there was more than that]. Before the war finished I was in Honiara—it was like nothing I had ever seen—all the service clubs, cinemas. . . . You could take a bus anywhere along the main road day or night. Since I was working in the post office I knew which movies were on where—boxing ones, cowboy etc. The officers wouldn't recognise us if we put our minds to dressing up like the coloured soldiers. We would go to the PXs, Navy and Army—my word, that's the time we all started to drink and smoke. Three dollars was a carton of beer.

The service clubs—you could dance every night with the band playing. The army nurses were the main partners. New Zealand and American both. . . . All the food, too—doughnuts, ice cream, hot dogs. . . . We had a good time—it was top. I mean when the danger was over. And we learned to know white people for the first time—talk to them, have a smoke.

Robert Bule, a driver at Munda, also had cherished memories:

One day I had a flat tire, but no jack. I got a spanner and [then] noticed a man smiling at me. 'What's wrong, kid?' he asked. I explained. 'So what are you going to do?'
'Oh, I don't know,' I said. Then he lifted the jeep up and said to take off the wheel. I hurried to the job, but he just said 'Go ahead, take it easy'. The American troops were very kind and we had friendly times.

So, too, did Esau Hiele:

In 1944 I went to Tenaru and worked with wireless and radio operations there. And I had a look at KEN [the radio control centre], too. I was surprised—it was such a big place, underground. I went and enjoyed the service, clubs, movies and boxing bouts—I never missed those. There were plenty of PXs. Everything was so easy to get if you had dollars.

Hiele went on to comment on the effect of the war on himself and his followers:

The war brought a very big change. People's minds were open, eyes were open, brains were open to outside things. People no longer found it difficult to understand new things.[19]

And, he might well have added, 'they began to want new things'.

The implications of such changes were enormous and were early manifest in a greater readiness among Pacific Islanders to challenge the authority of their colonial rulers. Conversely, for those rulers a greater need arose than had existed before the war to cope with—be it by repressing or by accommodating—a more restive and demanding citizenry. In such circumstances, tensions could scarcely be avoided. Often the islanders' demands, which frequently had deep pre-war roots, were expressed through orchestrated social movements, such as the John Frum cult on Tanna in Vanuatu. It first manifested itself in 1940 as a rejection of the authority of the Presbyterian mission, but soon also attracted, and reciprocated, the hostility of the government authorities. The coming of the American troops seemed to offer fulfilment of John Frum hopes for greater prosperity and a more benign regime—many Tannese worked as labourers—and the movement has continued to be sustained by the messianic belief that the Americans will one day come again as benefactors, as they did in 1942.[20]

Another large-scale movement similar in its objectives to John Frum, but less inclined to political and religious separatism and driven more by a secular than a millenarian impulse, was the one begun by Paliau Maloat on Manus in New Guinea in 1946. A former police sergeant under the Australians, and a man with notable organising ability and a talent for oratory, Paliau had spent the war in Rabaul assisting the Japanese in civilian administration. Already before the war he had shown an interest in social reform. Returning to Manus in 1945 he found a population ready for change. The US presence on the island had aroused among the people acute aspirations for economic modernisation and for racial equality with Europeans. Ironically, the latter ambition was fed—as it was at various other US posts— by the sight of black servicemen apparently enjoying the same conditions of service as their white fellows. They wore trousers, smoked tailor-made cigarettes, and rode in jeeps, providing a heady example that contrasted with the deprivations of the islanders in pre-war colonial society. (Islanders appear to have been so dazzled by the contrast that they consistently failed to notice that the African–American soldiers were themselves organised into segregated units and regarded as social inferiors by white Americans; racial segregation in the US military forces lasted until 1953.)

For the Manus, the American occupation was 'the time without taboos'. Under Paliau's direction Manus people, especially in the south of the island, formally abandoned many of the customs of the past. They also set up village councils to promote such things as good neighbourliness, large-scale economic co-operation, better housing, village hygiene, and more businesslike management of community finances. Furthermore, they attempted these things independently of the government (even to the extent of boycotting it), even though Australia's post-war reconstruction policy was based on a broader view of its responsibilities to its subjects than had prevailed before. More improvements in education, health services, agriculture, trade, water supply, and local government were intended. That the Australian tax-payers were willing to finance these changes owed much to the widespread appreciation of the assistance given to Australian soldiers by Papua New Guineans, especially the 'Fuzzy-Wuzzy Angels' of Kokoda Trail fame. As for Paliau, after being imprisoned for obstructiveness, he adopted a more pragmatic approach and urged his followers to co-operate with the government rather than resist it in their quest for modernisation. During 1951 his movement was steadily and peacefully absorbed into the government-controlled programme.[21]

About the same time in the Solomon Islands, supporters of the Maasina Rule movement were also in the process of abandoning their resistance to the British colonial administration, which was then seeking to re-establish its authority. Although born of the war, Maasina Rule, which was centred on Malaita, had strong pre-war roots of discontent. These included lingering disappointment at the expulsion of Kanaka labourers from Queensland a generation before, and resentment at the way in which the colonial regime seemed to discriminate against indigenes in favour of *araikwao* (Europeans). More recent factors were dismay at the evacuation of most of the white population, hitherto seemingly invincible, and a sense of betrayal at the inability of the administration to offer any protection against the advancing Japanese. In April 1942 people in north Malaita, feeling themselves abandoned and due for destruction, feasted extravagantly lest the Japanese deprive them of the chance to enjoy their pigs and gardens. They need not have worried since it was Japanese policy to treat the islanders in a considerate manner, at least in the early stages of their occupation. In any case, Malaita was not overrun by the Japanese and, following the campaign on neighbouring Guadalcanal, found itself fixed securely—and prosperously—within the orbit of American operations. The most populous island of the Solomons, and before the war the main supplier of labour for plantations throughout the protectorate, Malaita was the principal source of recruits, providing more than two thousand men to the Labour Corps. The material rewards of this work, together with the opportunities it offered for novel and congenial experiences, ill disposed the labourers to return to the position of subordination and poverty of pre-war colonialism. The war had generated a nationalism aimed at breaking the hold of the British regime.[22]

This was Maasina Rule (the rule of brotherhood), which sprung up on Malaita among demobilised Labour Corps members during 1944. It was not just a reaction to the impending end of good times. Giving point to the movement's demands for a greater measure of indigenous autonomy and a higher level of well-being was an ideology that owed much to Christian influence. Missionary teaching, particularly that the of the Bible-centred South Sea Evangelical Mission (SSEM), which was strong on Malaita, proved to have definite political implications. The New Testament provided criteria by which the British could be judged and found wanting. This is clear in a document written in 1949 by an SSEM teacher named Ariel Sisili and circulated widely through Malaita. 'The Scriptures [God's word] says man was created equal and God shared his love toward all mankind equally, whatever the colour or race; yet,' commented Sisili, 'the law in the Solomon Islands seems to be of two different kinds, one for the white race and the other for the natives. . . . They have never shown [us] any sign of real friendship.' Then, with the outbreak of war, the British were deemed to have completely broken faith with their charges. 'We believed we would be safely protected and safeguarded by them. But when the enemy came they all evacuated . . . "the hireling seeth the wolf coming, leaveth the sheep and fleeth because they are not his own" (John 10, 12).'

The Americans, in contrast, were seen as living up to Biblical ideals. 'With the natives' hopes utterly gone, a new dawn breaks, the USA arrives and bravely plunges into war against the advancing enemy and drives them back, which freed us from our fears. . . . Until they came here we never knew', said Sisili, 'the true love and friendship mentioned in Bible.' Again he quoted St John (13:15) to reinforce his argument: 'greater love hath no man than this that a man lay down his life for his friends'. As liberators and benefactors, the Americans won the esteem of the islanders. They also provided new and stimulating information about freedom. In criticising British opposition to Malaita aspirations, Sisili's document also appealed to the 'four freedoms'—of speech, of religion, from want, from fear—cited by President Franklin Roosevelt in February 1941 as common entitlements of humanity. In December 1950 Sisili even went so far as to promulgate 'The Malaita Declaration of Independence', and was soon afterwards tried and convicted for sedition.[23]

In the first stirrings of what was to become Maasina Rule a few Malaitans on Guadalcanal explored the possibilities of having the Americans replace the British as their rulers. In 1943 a man named Kabini collected contributions from labourers for American Red Cross funds in an attempt to 'buy' American rule. On learning the reason for this generosity the American authorities denied the likelihood of any such eventuality, and returned the contributions. Even so, rumours of a change continued to flourish, and on several occasions during 1945 the American commander on Guadalcanal had not only to deny there was any truth in them, but also to decline requests to eject the British. Meanwhile, the malcontents were not to be deterred from going it alone. In June 1945 various streams of unrest coalesced when an ex-labourer named Nori led a patrol three hundred strong through the central districts of Malaita to urge support for a programme of social improvement and indigenous autonomy that he had worked out with another Labour Corps man named Aliki Nono'ohimae.

By early 1946 Maasina Rule had spread throughout Malaita and by the end of the year it had begun to spread to neighbouring islands. Determined to re-impose their authority, in August 1947 the British began a series of mass arrests of Maasina Rule supporters. In June 1949, for instance, there were more than two thousand men in prison on a variety of charges ranging from non-payment of the poll tax to sedition. By the end of 1949, however, popular enthusiasm for Maasina Rule was beginning to fade. No material benefits had been achieved; bush people were suffering from malaria in the coastal villages to which they had migrated in search of an improved way of life in large communities modelled on the US camps; and the large-scale jailings were upsetting village economies and domestic arrangements. Although pockets of resistance remained until 1955, by the end of 1951 Malaitans were moving back towards the pre-war order of things; some were paying their tax, and labourers were starting to recruit for the works of reconstruction. However, co-operation was not unqualified acquiescence. Accordingly, over the following decade the government, recognising their restiveness, began to prepare the islanders for political development, but at its own pace.[24]

A similar situation existed in the New Zealand-ruled Cook Islands. There, too, wartime experience generated a new assertiveness among the local people. There, too, the immediate response of the authorities was to crush the movement for a greater indigenous say in the running of affairs. Yet by the late 1950s the administration itself was orchestrating political change.[25]

In the French territories, in contrast, the pattern of events was different. Unrest inspired by contact with the Americans occurred in Uvea (Wallis), but suppression was not followed by measures designed to end colonial rule.[26] Nor was it in French Polynesia. There, 200 survivors of the 300-strong Tahitian battle unit that had fought with distinction in North Africa and Europe returned to Pape'ete early in 1946. Disillusioned at the hollowness of a heroes' welcome, they desired more tangible rewards for the dangers they had endured. In this they obtained support and leadership from Pouvana'a a O'opa, a World War One veteran already well known for championing indigenous interests and as a critic of the colonial regime. To back up their demands in 1947 they organised two mass protest rallies. After the second one Pouvana'a and six of his closest collaborators were arrested on a charge of 'conspiracy against the security of the State'. They were held in prison for five months pending trial, but were acquitted when the court at length convened.

His involvement with the veterans, one of whom was his son Marcel, quickly helped establish Pouvana'a as the outstanding spokesman for the indigenous population generally. During the 1950s, when for a time it seemed as if French policy might be directed towards decolonisation in the Pacific, he was a prominent member of the Territorial Assembly for French Polynesia. However, any illusions he may have had about the likelihood of political concessions to local demands were dashed in October 1958, after Pouvana'a had urged his followers to vote (in a gerrymandered referendum on the matter) for independence from France. By order of President Charles de Gaulle, Pouvana'a and his associates were summarily dismissed from the Government Council, the executive arm of the Assembly. Then, in a replay of his misadventure in 1947, after being held in confinement for a year, Pouvana'a was convicted of trumped-up charges of plotting to burn down the town of Pape'ete. This time he was sentenced to a long prison term.[27]

Although for a time assertive, agitation such as that organised by Maasina Rule, or by Pouvana'a or Paliau, did not exert a decisive influence on the political evolution of the modern Pacific. The transition from colonial dependency to independent nationhood was not a product of war-born nationalism. Nevertheless, the impact of the war endured in many ways. Relics of it, both material and otherwise, abound and conspicuous among them are the wartime airfields scattered through the islands. Most are now abandoned—as at Torokina and Palmyra—or used by aircraft much smaller and for flights less frequent than those for which they were designed; much formerly productive garden or plantation land lies lost beneath a layer of compacted crushed coral or concrete. But others have become international airports, their country's main gateway to the outside world: New Caledonia, Vanuatu, the Solomons, Papua New Guinea, Fiji, Tonga, Western Samoa, and Tuvalu all offer cases in point. Likewise, port facilities, roads, and even buildings erected during the war (such as the hospital in Honiara) have in many places continued in use, contributing decades later to the infrastructure of modernity in the Pacific.

Another visible, indeed indelible and living, result of the war has been the boost it gave to migration from the Pacific Islands. In Samoa, for instance, the acquisition of new skills during the war helped in a particular way to generate an eagerness to succeed in overseas labour markets.[28] This was just the beginning of what was to grow into a self-sustaining movement, as people came routinely to look further afield for the betterment they desired— to New Zealand, Australia, and the United States. And it was not just a Samoan movement, but was Pacific-wide, although more marked in Polynesia than elsewhere.

Other links between the war and later events are substantial if less direct. For instance, the Fiji and Papua New Guinea military forces that came into being in 1940 were disbanded after the war, but the prowess they had shown in combat contributed to their rebirth in 1949 and 1951 respectively. Initially these forces were intended to fit in with the then-current military designs of Britain and Australia, but they were destined to endure as permanent armies and to become significant players in indigenous politics. It was the army that overthrew a democratically elected government in Fiji in 1987. Earlier, in 1980, the Papua New Guinea military had intervened in Vanuatu to put down a revolt on the island of Santo. In 1990 units of the same force were again poised for such an action, only this time to maintain the unity of their own nation. Equipped with Australian helicopter gunships, they spent much of that year on Nissan ready to invade the secessionist islands of Bougainville and Buka, standing by at an airfield built in less than a month by American 'Seabees' forty-six years before to serve the bombing of Rabaul and Chuuk.[29] From there in 1991 they began a systematic and brutal reconquest, forcing the would-be Republic of Bougainville to remain the North Solomons Province of Papua New Guinea.

World War Two has cast a long shadow in the Pacific, and with it goes a warning. There may be more than a touch of irony in the erection of

Japanese peace monuments (in contrast to Allied war memorials) near many of the major battlefields, but that ought not to blind cynics to the costs involved when the Pacific has not lived up to its name.

Notes

1 John Lawrey, *The Cross of Lorraine in the South Pacific: Australia and the Free French Movement 1940–1942*, *Journal of Pacific History*, Canberra, 1982.

2 In 1988 a senior Japanese cabinet minister, Seisuke Okuno, was forced to resign his position after creating a furore by saying that Japan was not an aggressor in World War Two. *Honolulu Star-Bulletin*, 13, 19 May 1988; *Honolulu Advertiser*, 19 May 1988.

3 BBC, 'Sacrifice at Pearl Harbor', television documentary, 1989.

4 John J. Stephan, *Hawaii under the Rising Sun: Japan's Plans for Conquest after Pearl Harbor*. University of Hawai'i Press, Honolulu, 1984.

5 Robert Sherrod, *Tarawa: The Story of a Battle*, Ruell, Sloane & Pearce, New York, 1944; Burke Davis, *Get Yamamoto*, Random House, New York, 1969; Gordon W. Prange, *Miracle at Midway*, Penguin, New York, 1982, 17–20. Although the literature on World War Two in the Pacific is vast, it is still markedly uneven. Admittedly, the military history has been thoroughly documented (at least for the Americans and their Allies), but concise authoritative surveys of the conflict remain few. In marked contrast to that of the main combatants, the Pacific Islanders' experience of the war (be it direct or indirect, individual or collective) has received little serious attention from researchers and writers. As yet there is no comprehensive account of the war as a major event in the overall history of the Pacific. Such a work would provide a broad context within which the partial and fragmented data that is available on the islanders' experience might be more fully understood. John Costello, *The Pacific War* (Collins, London 1981) is a useful survey of military history, while John Dower, *War Without Mercy: Race and Power in the Pacific War* (Pantheon, New York, 1986) is a stimulating analysis of the racial hatred that intensified military hostility. Several works place the war firmly in its political and diplomatic settings: Saburo Ienaga, *The Pacific War, 1931–1945,* (Pantheon, New York, 1978); and Edwin P. Hoyt, *Japan's War: The Great Pacific Conflict,* (McGraw-Hill, New York, 1986), discuss Japanese involvement; and Ronald H. Spector, *Eagle Against the Sun: The American War with Japan,* (Free Press, New York, 1985), deals with the United States.

On the Pacific Islands' dimension of the war, useful chapters may be found in the general histories of the various island groups and in the biographies of a number of their leaders. For the beginnings of a more systematic recording and analysis of the war from a local perspective see: Neville Robinson, *Villagers at War: Papua New Guineans in World War Two,* (Australian National University Press, Canberra, 1981); Geoffrey White et al, eds, *The Big Death: Solomon Islanders Remember World War Two* (University of the South Pacific, Suva, 1988); *'O'O: A Journal of Solomon Islands Studies* 4 (1988—special issue *Taem Blong Faet: World War Two in Melanesia*, edited by Hugh Laracy and Geoffrey White); Geoffrey M. White and Lamont Lindstrom, eds, *The Pacific Theater: Island*

Representations of World War II (University of Hawai'i Press, Honolulu, 1989); and Geoffrey M. White, ed., *Remembering the Pacific War,* (Center for Pacific Islands Studies, Honolulu, 1991).

6 William Manchester, *Goodbye Darkness: A Memoir of the Pacific War*, Joseph, London, 1981; Robert J. Donovan, *PT 109: John F. Kennedy in World War II*, McGraw-Hill, New York, 1961; Ralph M. Wiltgen, 'The Death of Bishop Loerks and His Companions', *Verbum* 6 (1964): 363–397, *Verbum* 7 (1965): 14–44; Trevor Nevitt Dupuy, *The Naval War in the Pacific: On to Tokyo*, Edmund Ward, London, 1966; Mark R. Peattie, *Nan'yō: The Rise and Fall of the Japanese in Micronesia, 1885–1945*, Pacific Islands Monograph Series no. 4, University of Hawai'i Press, Honolulu, 1988, 257–310.

7 Carl E. Thune, 'The Making of History: The Representation of World War II on Normanby Island, Papua New Guinea', in White and Lindstrom, 237.

8 Maria Lepowsky, 'Soldiers and Spirits: The Impact of World War II on a Coral Sea Island', in White and Lindstrom, 210–213.

9 Peattie, 251–252.

10 Eric Feldt, *The Coast Watchers*, Oxford University Press, Melbourne, 1946, 135; Mueller, quoted in Hugh Laracy, *Marists and Melanesians: A History of Catholic Missions in the Solomon Islands*, Australian National University Press, Canberra, 1976, 116–117.

11 Laracy 1976, 123.

12 Walter Lord, *Lonely Vigil: Coastwatchers of the Solomons*, Viking Press, New York, 1977, 292; D. C. Horton, *Fire over the Islands: The Coast Watchers of the Solomons*, A. H. & A. W. Reed, Sydney, 1970, 247; James Griffin, 'Paul Mason: Planter and Coastwatcher', in *Papua New Guinea Portraits: The Expatriate Experience*, ed. James Griffin, Australian National University Press, Canberra, 1978, 151–161; Feldt 1946, 285; Suzy Baldwin, 'Coastwatcher Ruby Boye,' *Australian Women's Weekly*, February 1988, 193–195 (monthy).

13 James A. Boutilier, 'Kennedy's "Army": Solomon Islands at War', in White and Lindstrom, 329–352; Hugh Laracy, 'George Bogese: "Just a Bloody Traitor"?', in White, 1991, 59–75.

14 Hugh Laracy and Geoffrey White, 'Editorial Introduction', *'O'O: A Journal of Solomon Islands Studies* 4 (1988): 3–4; William Bennett, 'Behind Japanese Lines in the Western Solomons', in White et al., 1988, 133–148.

15 Hank Nelson, *Papua New Guinea: Black Unity or Black Chaos?* Penguin, Ringwood, VIC, 1972, 80–88; Asesela Ravuvu, *Fijians at War*, South Pacific Social Sciences Association, Suva, 1974; White et al, 1988, 175–196; Noel Rutherford, ed., *Friendly Islands: A History of Tonga*, Oxford University Press, Melbourne, 1977, 201.

16 M. P. Lissington, *New Zealand and the United States, 1840–1944*, Government Printer, Wellington, 1972, 42–43; Lawrey, 94; Charles J. Weeks, 'The United States Occupation of Tonga, 1942–1945: The Social and Economic Impact', *Pacific Historical Review* 56 (3, 1987): 404–405.

17 Hugh Laracy, ed., *Tuvalu: A History*, University of the South Pacific, Suva, 1983, 140–144; Nelson 1972, 82.

18 Lamont Lindstrom, 'Working Encounters: Oral Histories of World War II Labor Corps from Tanna, Vanuatu', in White and Lindstrom, 398; Lamont Lindstrom and Geoffrey White, 'War Stories', in White and Lindstrom, 32.

19 'Of Food and Friendship: Selected Comments', *'O'O: A Journal of Solomon Islands Studies* 4 (1988): 109, 112, 114–115.

20 Peter Worsley, *The Trumpet Shall Sound: A Study of 'Cargo' Cults in Melanesia*, Paladin, London, 1970, 162–171.

21 Worsley, 193–204.

22 Hugh Laracy, ed., *Pacific Protest: The Maasina Rule Movement, Solomon Islands, 1944–1952*, University of the South Pacific, Suva, 1983, 1–38.

23 'Ariel Sisili's Movement', in Laracy 1983, 162–176.

24 Laracy 1983, 1–38; Judith A. Bennett, *Wealth of the Solomons: A History of a Pacific Archipelago, 1800–1978*, Pacific Islands Monograph Series no. 3, University of Hawai'i Press, Honolulu, 1987, 292–299.

25 Richard Gilson, *The Cook Islands, 1820–1950*, Victoria University of Wellington, 1980, 192–199; Kathleen Hancock, *Sir Albert Henry: His Life and Times*, Methuen, Auckland, 1979, 59–61, 65–75.

26 Alexander Poncet, *Histoire de l'île Wallis*, Musée de l'Homme, Paris, 1972, 162–181.

27 Bengt Danielsson and Marie-Thérèse Danielsson, *Moruroa Mon Amour: The French Nuclear Tests in the Pacific*, Penguin, Harmondsworth, 1977, 22–43.

28 Robert W. Franco, 'Samoan Representations of World War II and Military Work: The Emergence of International Movement Networks', in White and Lindstrom, 373–374.

29 *Pacific Islands Monthly*, June 1990, 17.

8

Britain

Barrie Macdonald

In the 1960s, the trend towards the decolonisation of dependent territories that had begun with the independence of India reached into the Pacific Islands. With very few exceptions, most notably Western Samoa and Nauru, the initiative lay with the colonial powers, though the timing and shape of political developments were often the product of local wishes and pressures. For Britain, which had ruled over the largest of all the modern colonial empires, decolonisation in Oceania meant a staged withdrawal that drew on policies and models developed in Asia and Africa over the preceding half-century. Britain's first step towards withdrawal from Oceania followed closely on the decolonisation of Black Africa and the celebrated United Nations Resolution 1514 of 1960, which declared that a lack of social and economic preparedness was no barrier to self-determination.

For a decade, as Britain managed the transfer of power in its smaller territories, it seemed that the planned destination was some form of self-government in free association with Britain. However, from the early 1970s independence was the only option offered—and, because of Britain's own economic difficulties and diplomatic priorities in the mid-1970s, it was to be independence sooner rather than later. To achieve these goals, compromises in other areas were necessary, particularly in the acceptance of constitutional innovation and in the willingness to offer unprecedented financial settlements at independence. In the late 1970s, Britain ushered (some might say 'rushed') to independence a series of small nations that were politically fragile, strategically vulnerable, and increasingly dependent on foreign aid for their economic survival.

While the decolonisation of British Oceania might have been initiated more by imperial withdrawal than anticolonial nationalism, the final outcome had a distinctive Pacific character. Faced with the realities of decolonisation, island leaders responded quickly to its challenges and opportunities, modifying constitutional precedents to meet local circumstances, and building new relationships within and beyond the region to compensate for the withdrawal of Britain and to promote the economic and social development of the new Pacific microstates. In essence, the process meant the gradual introduction of representative assemblies, proceeding to a form of responsible government, with the executive becoming subject to the control of the legislature and, ultimately, with the severing of all power of the British government but with the retention of ties to the Crown. Able to accommodate an infinite variety of forms, this 'Westminster model' became the basis for the evolution of the British Empire into the British Commonwealth of Nations.[1]

At first, the British dependencies in the Pacific—the Colony of Fiji, the British Solomon Islands Protectorate, the Gilbert and Ellice Islands Colony, and Pitcairn—together with the British–French Condominium of the New Hebrides and the Kingdom of Tonga, were deliberately set apart from this process. They were, after all, small, remote, and economically vulnerable— the last being particularly important in the post-war era when self-sufficiency was still seen as an essential prerequisite to sovereign independence—and there were few signs of political awareness. Occasional demands for change had surfaced, as from the Maasina Rule movement in Solomon Islands, but such incidents were localised and muted; after the disruption of war, there was more interest in reconstruction than revolution.

The background to decolonisation

Between the wars, Britain's main concern had been with trusteeship and gradual development in its colonial dependencies. At the centre of this policy was the evolution of India towards responsible parliamentary government with, surprisingly perhaps, a concurrent belief that colonial tutelage for the rest of the empire would continue well into the twenty-first century.[2] Not until the late 1930s, with the growing acceptance of the inevitability of Indian independence, widespread economic distress elsewhere in the empire, and a sensitivity to international criticism over social conditions in the empire, was there a serious reappraisal of British colonial policy.[3] Then the war impoverished Britain and raised further questions about the future viability of empire. The British public at home had grown disenchanted with the idea of colonial possessions, as much as with their cost; abroad, the United States in particular adopted an anti-imperial stance, subsequently modified just enough to accommodate its own need for military bases in the north and central Pacific. The Atlantic Charter of 1941 gave little comfort to imperialists, and the newly formed United Nations Organization provided a forum in which anticolonial forces from both East and West were soon joined by the new Asian nations in calling for the liberation of colonial peoples.

In response to some of these pressures, and in anticipation of others, the

British government had already made considerable modification to its colonial policy by the end of World War Two.[4] By that time, India was firmly on the path to independence, and the passing of the first Colonial Development and Welfare Act in 1940 had marked the abandonment of the principle that colonies should be economically self-sufficient and the beginning of modern policies for development assistance.[5] By early 1947, Colonial Office planners had concluded that most of British Africa would have responsible government within a decade, and that in the future any significant economic development would depend on the creation of centralised and democratic political institutions. The basic thrust of British colonial policy had changed 'from one of jealously conserving imperial power in alliance with African kings and chiefs to one of building up independent nations hand in hand with modern elites'.[6]

Even though the new policies seemed in tune with the international mood reflected in the United Nations, they were out of step with the realities of the other European empires. At the Brazzaville Conference in 1947, for example, France reiterated its determination to further integrate its empire into the republic and ruled out future self-government for its colonies.[7] Again, in 1959, when Harold Macmillan declared that the 'wind of change' was blowing through the African continent, he was merely pointing to the realities of Britain's policy of accelerated decolonisation and showing the way to the other European powers.[8]

Although the dismantling of empire may have originated in Europe, events on the periphery were no less important. Partition and independence in India weakened Britain's strategic position in Asia, for example, and the independence of Israel and Britain's gradual loss of influence in the Middle East, as much as Egyptian nationalism, made the withdrawal from Suez inevitable. This, in turn, reduced the importance of Cyprus and Malta. As the fabric of strategic and economic interests was gradually unravelled in the 1950s, and the integrity of the whole further threatened by colonial nationalism, it was difficult to find any rationale for keeping the remaining territories.

These developments in Asia, the Middle East, Africa, and the Caribbean established the framework for decolonisation in the Pacific, but they had little immediate impact on the British Pacific islands. When local government systems were reshaped after the war, with a view to revitalising traditional authority structures rather than creating new ones, little reference was made to political development or to any future transfer of power. Britain (and to some extent Australia and New Zealand) sought to offer a 'new deal' to island peoples after the war, and to promote social development, but in terms of their long-term future, the Pacific Islands were still perceived by the British government as a special case.[9] Until well into the 1950s Britain was convinced that 'In the case of the smaller territories there can, *a priori*, be no question of [a] journey towards sovereign government'.[10]

In the two decades after World War Two, the colonial empires of the Western powers were all but dismantled. In 1960 alone, seventeen newly independent countries joined the United Nations, and the changing mood of world opinion was reflected in the UN General Assembly's passing of Resolution 1514. Although the world body had seen a dramatic change in its membership and had provided a forum for anticolonial rhetoric, its overall importance in the 1950s should not be exaggerated. Smaller powers, like New Zealand and Australia, had always been more sensitive to world opinion than the major powers and had taken a strong joint stand on trusteeship immediately after World War Two. In New Zealand's case, sensitivity on trusteeship had been heightened by a strong Samoan nationalist movement and the Mau's resistance to colonial rule in the 1920s and 1930s.

Not surprisingly, the model of decolonisation established by Britain was first taken up in the Pacific by New Zealand and applied to Western Samoa, which became independent in 1962. The momentum was maintained with the decolonisation of the Cook Islands, which achieved full internal self-government in free association with New Zealand in 1965. In Nauru, despite reluctance from Britain and opposition from Australia, New Zealand's willingness to contemplate independence combined with powerful Nauruan nationalism and pressure from the United Nations to bring independence to the Pacific's smallest republic in 1968. Britain joined the other colonial powers in making the 1970s the decade of decolonisation for the Pacific Islands, with the severing of imperial ties with Fiji and Tonga in 1970, the independence of Papua New Guinea and self-government for Niue in 1975, independence for Solomon Islands in 1978, partition and subsequent independence for the Gilbert and Ellice Islands Colony as Kiribati (1979) and Tuvalu (1978), culminating in 1980 in the independence of the New Hebrides as Vanuatu—the last of the British Pacific territories to be decolonised and the first of the French.[11]

Fiji

Not until 1960, on the eve of Western Samoa's independence, did Britain take its first serious step towards the decolonisation of Fiji, marking the initiation of a process that for the most part would be stimulated by metropolitan initiatives but shaped to meet the demands of Fiji's plural society and its inherent racial tensions. The move came very much as an afterthought to the decolonisation of the rest of the empire. In the fifteen years since the end of World War Two, the number of people living in the dependencies of the British Crown had dropped from about 630 million to less than 30 million, the remaining territories being cases where the rights of minorities posed difficulties or, as in the Pacific Islands, smallness had hitherto been seen as an insuperable barrier to sovereign independence.[12]

In November 1960, the governor of Fiji served notice that 'the time has come to consider some modifications of the present Constitution' and followed three months later with proposals that spelled out the various stages of the Westminster model of constitutional development. The initial response from each of Fiji's three racial communities, Fijians, Indians, and Europeans, was predictable in terms of communal interests, but also confirmed that most of the country's leaders had continued to believe, or hope, that the wind of change would be no more than a gentle breeze when it reached Fiji at some time in the remote future. Ratu Kamisese Mara, a high-ranking chief from Lau who emerged as unchallenged leader of the Fijians in this period, rejected the suggested changes on the grounds that 'Any proposal for constitutional changes that ignores and does not take into consideration the Deed of Cession is ill-conceived [and] will not be on stable ground'.[13] Mara maintained that in 1874 Fijian chiefs had ceded their lands to be 'part and parcel of Britain'. Constitutional development would only be acceptable to the people, he said, if it recognised this and provided for Fiji a status akin to that of Malta, the Channel Islands, or the Isle of Man.[14] This conservatism was predictable, as was the insistence of the Indian members that any constitution 'must also be brought round the promise made by Lord Salisbury's despatch [of 1875] with regard to the Indian people when the right of permanent settlement and equality in all respects with other races were granted to the people'.[15] European support for an eventual, but limited, transference of power was predictable, but there was also recognition that the basis on which Europeans had previously claimed a share in government—as protectors of the Fijians—was no longer sustainable. Increasingly the disproportionate representation of the European community was defended on the basis of protecting minority rights and the substantial European role in the economy. The Europeans moved from being the protectors of the Fijians to being their partners, reaffirming a close association that permitted the British government to promote the idea of equivalent treatment for the two major races in the knowledge that, by acting in concert with the Europeans, the Fijians could always prevail.

In practice, this partnership helped Britain to resolve a serious dilemma. Since the 1920s, it had rejected any notion of democracy through a common electoral roll as incompatible with Britain's more fundamental obligation to the paramountcy of Fijian interests. Britain had thus become the arbiter among the races, each of which was seen as having a distinct role. The image used by Ratu Sir Lala Sukuna, the first Fijian to be a member of the Executive Council, portrayed Fiji as a three-legged stool, balanced on the separate contribution of the races—land from the Fijians, labour from the Indians, capital and management from the Europeans.[16]

The government's difficulties were exacerbated by trends in the population. By 1946, Indians had narrowly outnumbered Fijians; in 1956, this trend had been confirmed with 49 per cent of the population being Indian, 43 per

Left: The Right Honorable Ratu Sir Kamisese Mara (Government Printer, Fiji)   Right: Ratu Sir Lala Sukuna (Government Printer, Fiji)

cent Fijian, and the other races—European, part-European, Chinese, non-Fijian Pacific Islanders—accounting for a mere 8 per cent. Despite these disparities, decolonisation proceeded on the basis of an 'equality of races'; in 1963 the franchise was widened to include Fijians and women of all races, and the ministerial membership system—the first step towards cabinet government—had been introduced with three members, one from each racial community, given responsibility for communications and works, social services, and natural resources.

More changes were to follow. In 1964, the Wilson Labour government made clear its intention to reduce its commitments 'east of Suez' and, in the same year, the remnants of the Colonial Office were absorbed into the Foreign and Commonwealth Office. In Fiji, Governor Sir Kenneth Maddox, who had served in Nigeria through the decolonisation years, had already stated that 'it would be wise to move slightly in advance of public opinion rather than to lag behind it'.[17] He was reiterating the principle first learned in Mountbatten's 'forced march to independence' in India, and subsequently applied throughout Africa—that for an orderly decolonisation, it was essential for the colonial power to seize and hold the initiative so that the momentum would be maintained, frustration would not build, and competing groups within the colonial society would be preoccupied with protecting their own interests in an environment of rapid change.

Elections in 1963, and a constitutional conference in 1965, foreshadowed the introduction of ministerial government, the appointment of Mara as chief minister, the introduction of an elected majority in the Legislative Council, and the rapid evolution of political parties.[18] The conference, held in London, did little to grapple with the fundamental problems of constitution-making in a plural society. Indian leaders reiterated the demand for a common electoral roll first made by their predecessors in 1929, and any hopes that they might compromise were destroyed by the governor's statement, reported in the Australian press, that 'it is inconceivable that Britain would permit the Fijians to be placed politically under the heel of an immigrant community'.[19]

With a common roll unacceptable to Fijians and Europeans, the British government's compromise was eventually adopted. Henceforth, Fijians, Indians, and General Electors (comprising Europeans, part-Europeans and Chinese) returned nine, nine, and seven members respectively to the new legislature. In addition, there were nine members, three from each of the ethnic groupings, elected on a cross-voting system by electors of all races, and two representatives from the Council of Chiefs. Momentum towards independence was established with an electoral system whose main features were an emphasis on ethnic divisions, a slight numerical advantage for Fijian members over Indians, and a significant overrepresentation of the European-dominated General Electors, who secured 27 per cent of the seats in parliament though constituting less than 5 per cent of the population.[20]

While the 1966 constitution did not commit Fiji to any particular constitution for independence, few doubted that the future lay with a two-party system. The Indian community, especially in western Viti Levu, had a long history of political organisation, strengthened in the late 1930s by the formation of cane-farmers' unions and again in 1960 by a bitter cane-cutting strike over the price paid to growers. The founder of the Federation Party was A. D. Patel, an Indian-born lawyer who had established his credentials with cane farmers as a radical leader in the 1960 strike and was at the same time closely aligned with the Gujerati professional and business community. Although initially based in the west, the Federation Party quickly became the leading voice in Indian politics, with its strident demands for a common roll and its condemnation of European privilege.[21]

The Alliance Party, under the leadership of Mara, was based on the Fijian Association, a conservative body founded in 1956 to mobilise Fijian labour in the event of a cane strike. Having been dormant for some years, from 1963 the organisation began to adopt a higher political profile, demanding not merely the protection of Fijian land ownership and the status of the Council of Chiefs but, significantly for post-independence developments, that the prime minister of Fiji must always be a Fijian and that, in any future legislature, Fijians must always have an absolute majority over all other races.[22] In 1964, it had made a commitment to multiracialism while upholding the principle of Fijian paramountcy. In 1965, the association became the dominant element in the newly formed Alliance Party, which also included the General Electors' Association, the Muslim Political Front, the Chinese Association, and the Rotuman Convention.[23]

The Alliance made a strong showing in the 1966 elections, winning 22 seats (effectively increased to 27 with the support of three independents and the two nominees of the Council of Chiefs) to the 9 seats of the Federation Party. With the move to full ministerial government in 1967, with Mara as chief minister, the Federation Party boycotted parliamentary sessions, forcing by-elections for the nine Indian communal seats in September 1968. In these, the Alliance won just 22 per cent of the vote; the Federation Party, which had secured 65 per cent of the vote in 1966, now won a landslide 78 per cent and increased its majority in all seats.[24] While the result was greeted with jubilation by the Federation Party, the results provoked a conservative backlash among Fijians, with mass meetings demanding the deportation of Indians and the Fijian Association declaring its willingness to use force in defence of Fijian interests. Rioting occurred in some centres, and assaults on Indians were staged by Fijians.[25]

The events surrounding the 1968 by-elections starkly emphasised the realities of Fijian politics and the fundamental conflict, reflected in the economy no less than in politics, that existed among the various ethnic communities. This plural society, which owed its origins to the essential incompatibility of policies designed to protect Fijian society and the demands of the sugar economy, was the central feature of Fiji's colonial heritage.[26] Within such a society, with minimal intermarriage, political status legally defined by race, and economic roles defined, in practice, with only slightly less rigidity, the realities of nearly a century of colonial rule were laid bare.

The 1968 by-elections reflected these realities, but the threat of communal violence had a sobering effect on the leaders of all races as they contemplated future independence without the mediation of Britain. The only way forward was to find a compromise that recognised the importance of ethnicity but eased the fears of both races. The Alliance's answer was an uneasy commitment to multiracialism, vulnerable to attack as tokenism on one side, and as a selling out of Fijian interests on the other. For its part, the Federation Party endorsed the notion of a Fijian head of state with power to veto legislation that endangered Fijian interests, and tried to build a wider support-base by championing the grievances of Fijian landowners against both their chiefs and the government.

The 1968 by-elections had provided one warning of the dangers of communal politics; race riots in Malaysia in May 1969 provided another, and gave impetus to moves for constitutional talks. The Alliance leadership was conscious that its current strength might be undermined in the longer term, as the Indian majority in the population grew and Britain came under increasing pressure in the United Nations. The Federation Party had been made sharply aware of the dangers of communal politics and its inability to attract votes among non-Indians. The way towards a compromise was eased by the death of A. D. Patel in 1969 and his replacement by S. M. Koya—like Patel, a radical leader in the 1960 cane strike, but Fiji-born, a Muslim, and by inclination more conciliatory.

In confidential talks late in 1969, rapid progress was made as politicians took over the initiative from Britain and sought local solutions to local problems. The Alliance accepted the principle of full independence; the Federation Party gave way on the common roll. With these barriers removed, and agreement on constitutional protection for Fijian interests, the path to a settlement was cleared.[27]

In the end, the constitutional conference in London in May 1970 was an anticlimax, concentrating on means and details rather than ends and principles. The electoral system remained. There would be 27 communal seats (12 Fijian, 12 Indian, 3 General) in which Fijian, Indian and General voters would each vote for members of their own racial community. There would also be 25 national seats (10 Fijian, 10 Indian, 5 General) in which representatives of each racial community would be chosen by electors of all races voting on a combined electoral roll. Each elector thus cast four votes—one for a representative of the voter's own racial community and three further votes in a national constituency in which candidates contested seats designated by race but with a multiracial electoral roll. The representation of General Electors was reduced, but remained disproportionately high relative to population. The Senate, with nominees from the prime minister, the leader of the opposition, and the Council of Chiefs, reflected Fiji's ethnic composition, and, with entrenched legislation and veto powers in the Senate, it was believed that the protection of Fijian interests was assured. The constitution thus protected the long-term interests of the Fijians and guaranteed the basic economic and political rights of Indians, but left the General Electors effectively holding the balance of power.[28]

What the constitution-makers did not recognise was that Fiji's society was changing and that the assumptions of monolithic communal voting on which the constitution was based would be undermined by conservatives who rejected multiracialism in favour of 'Fiji for the Fijians', by urban wage and salary earners who rejected the domination of the Fijian chiefly elite, and by rural Fijians too apathetic or too disenchanted to vote. In the social and economic changes that prompted these defections lay the seeds of post-independence political instability, because any significant departure from a communal voting pattern opened the possibility of defeat for Alliance candidates in national constituencies.

Events throughout the decade of decolonisation in Fiji, from the governor's first indication of change in November 1960, to sovereign independence on Cession Day, 10 October 1970, with Ratu Sir Kamisese Mara as Fiji's first prime minister, showed that Fiji's political future, like its colonial past, was to be determined primarily by matters of race. It also showed that the future, like the past, was based not so much on the balance of interests symbolised by the three-legged stool, as on the competing interests of the three races. With independence, the role of mediator that had been a primary function of the colonial power fell on the constitution, with the prospects for political stability directly linked to the future willingness of all races to behave in accordance with the assumptions on which it was based. However, this could not be guaranteed, because the constitution sought to maintain Fijian paramountcy through indirect means, and because the underlying assumption was that existing patterns of political behaviour would not change.

Tonga

In a process much less complicated than for Fiji, Britain also relinquished formal responsibility for Tonga in 1970. From the turn of the century, the relationship between the two had been governed by a treaty of friendship, modified formally from time to time, but with the relationship more often shaped in practice by the pressures of the time and by the personalities of the leading figures in the Tongan government and their British counterparts locally and in the Western Pacific High Commission.[29]

After a major revision of the treaty in 1958, and further modifications a decade later, Tonga enjoyed self-government in internal affairs and participated in the benefits of the Colonial Development and Welfare Scheme, while Britain retained responsibility for internal security and foreign affairs. With a strong sense of cultural identity, and with the unifying force of the monarchy, Tonga had never lost the sense of nationalism that had been a potent force in the building of a strong Tongan government in the nineteenth century. Strictly speaking, Tonga had never been a colonial possession, nor had Tongans been colonial subjects, but the world-wide movement towards self-determination saw Tonga anxious to reassert its sovereignty, only to find as late as 1967 that the British government still favoured some form of free association as the preferred outcome of any constitutional change.[30] In February 1968 the Tongan government informed Britain of its intention to seek independence, and from then, in the light of Britain's stated policy on decolonisation, it was only a matter of time.[31] In a process that Tongan leaders insisted on describing as Tonga's 're-entry into the Comity of Nations', and with timing that owed something to the decolonisation of Fiji, Tongan returned to full independence in June 1970.

Western Pacific High Commission dependencies

In the Western Pacific High Commission (WPHC) territories, as for Fiji, there was evidence of a strong British initiative towards decolonisation after 1960.

All three, the British Solomon Islands Protectorate, the Gilbert and Ellice Islands Colony, and the New Hebrides, with 1960 populations of 125 000, 45 000, and 60 000 respectively, had been considered too small for separate administrations at the end of the nineteenth century; for each, including the British 'share' of the New Hebrides, a resident commissioner was made responsible to the High Commissioner for the Western Pacific, an office usually held conjointly with the governorship of Fiji until 1952, and separately established in Honiara from that time. Now, with decolonisation, the difficulties posed by geographical fragmentation, cultural divisions, economic dependence, and the absurdities of the Condominium, all complicated the transfer of power and prompted an unusual degree of constitutional experimentation that was accepted, and sometimes encouraged, by the British government in its bid for disengagement.

In the 1940s and 1950s, the WPHC territories shared in the British government's Colonial Development and Welfare Scheme. In keeping with the official view that saw self-government as only a distant possibility and economic self-sufficiency as no more than a pipe-dream, the emphasis was on the creation of infrastructure, particularly in the areas of communications and transport, and the provision of social services, with a special emphasis on secondary education, teacher training, and hospital services. But because all three entities were composed of scattered archipelagos, and smallness initially meant only a single government high school, teachers' college, or hospital, these services were increasingly concentrated at the respective colonial headquarters, thus accelerating urbanisation, encouraging migration, and creating an ever-increasing gulf between the centre and the periphery. Political awareness spread only slowly and was largely confined to urban-based educated elites. It followed that there were few political parties; political activists were generally seen as representing their own interests or at most a specific district or faction, but that was all. For much of the 1960s and the first part of the 1970s, most people remained preoccupied with local issues and, seeing the government as a source of funds as well as authority, judged their representatives on their capacity to capture resources for the constituency. Accordingly, a fear that decolonisation might cause a loss of aid funds added to a general rural conservatism. Little sense of national identity existed in any of the WPHC countries, though there was a strong growth of anticolonial nationalism in the New Hebrides in the 1970s, prompted by grievances over land and sharpened by the French reluctance to withdraw.

Solomon Islands

In Solomon Islands, the 1960 British initiative towards a transfer of power meant the replacement of the Resident Commissioner's Advisory Council by legislative and executive councils dominated by government officials. In 1965, the first elections were held, though most constituencies returned members from electoral colleges of local body representatives rather than by direct election, and in 1967 the first general election was held. Despite earlier political movements, like Maasina Rule of the 1940s, the cultural diversity and geographical fragmentation of Solomon Islands ensured that political awareness spread only slowly. With only a brief history of colonial local government, few Solomon Islanders had experience in Western political systems, and only a small elite, in government or the churches, had a Western education. Because of this, almost all initiatives in policy-making and legislation remained with government officials, leaving Solomon Islands members, unskilled in parliamentary procedures, with a limited role for the most part confined to raising local issues and complaining about the price of copra.[32]

Towards the end of the decade, elected members took a greater role in policy-making, but there was little progress towards collective responsibility as Solomon Islands politicians tended to see themselves as being in opposition to the colonial government. In the minds of officials at least, the Westminster system seemed inappropriate to the personal and faction-based politics of Solomon Islands, and they believed they could overcome these difficulties with a constitution based on a Ceylon precedent from thirty years before. This involved the introduction of a single governing council based on a series of committees, rather than ministers, that took responsibility for various aspects of government activity. Advocates for the new constitution argued that as well as reflecting Melanesian decision-making procedures based on discussion and consensus, it would provide training in policy formation and parliamentary procedure. Critics have argued that the pragmatic issue of securing co-operation between elected members and officials was more important, and even that came second to the imperative of maintaining the momentum of decolonisation.[33]

At this time, too, the situation was clouded by the lack of any clear direction as to the future constitutional status of Solomon Islands. Neither elected members nor officials spoke openly of independence—the former fearful that independence might bring an end to aid grants and the latter, aware of this, anxious to maintain the momentum of change. An underlying assumption was that the options were still open, and considerable interest was shown in the arrangement reached between New Zealand and the Cook Islands whereby the Cook Islands were given full internal self-government but with New Zealand citizenship, the right to declare themselves independent in the future, and the promise of substantial financial assistance—in short, the type of constitution that, at least as late as 1967, Britain still favoured for Tonga. By mid-1971 British attitudes had hardened, however; independence was now to be the target, even for the WPHC territories, and any that chose a constitution granting less than independence would be forced to accept something less than self-government. Such a strategy was designed to ensure that the inevitable pressures and frustrations of responsibility without power would soon generate a demand for independence.

With local politicians frustrated by the operations of the committee system, and officials now determined on independence, there were pressures on both sides that brought a return to Westminster orthodoxy. The governing council was reconstituted as a legislative assembly and Solomon Mamaloni elected as chief minister. Mamaloni, Western-educated, former public servant, successful entrepreneur, and, in the context of Solomon Islands politics in the mid-1970s, a radical, had been one of the strongest critics of the Governing Council. The return to a Westminster system encouraged the growth of political parties in the pursuit of power, but, as before, these were based more on personality and friendship than on ideology.

Developments just after Mamaloni had taken office showed just how firmly Britain was determined on independence for Solomon Islands. The complications of its own entry into the European Community, the implications of imminent independence for neighbouring Papua New Guinea, and the potentially destabilising effects of Bougainville secessionism all contributed to the down-hill rush towards independence. At negotiations in May 1975 it was agreed that Solomon Islands would move to self-government at the end of the year and to independence within a further twelve to eighteen months. In practice, it would take twice that long, with the delay caused not so much by the basic constitutional structure or the ultimate outcome, but by issues peculiar to the colonial history of Solomon Islands.

The constitutional structure was largely settled by the work of a committee in 1975–76. In a constitution that broadly followed the Westminster model, but with modifications for local circumstances, Solomon Islands opted for a parliamentary democracy with the Queen as head of state and her representative, the governor-general, elected by parliament; there was to be a single-chamber legislature and, recognising the hazards of party government in Solomon Islands, the prime minister was to be elected by and from the members of parliament and could be removed only by a motion of no confidence. In another significant modification that reflected the underlying scepticism about political motivations, parliament could be dissolved and an early election called only by parliamentary resolution.[34]

Although taking time, all of these issues proved straightforward in practice. The critical issues were over a financial settlement for independence, citizenship, land ownership, and threats to a unified independence posed by secessionism in the western Solomons. The financial settlement for the first five years of independence was reached only after long negotiations and broke new ground for the British Pacific islands because it involved substantial budgetary assistance towards the recurrent costs of government.

In the course of negotiations, Solomon Islands managed to secure the conversion of a proposed £18 million development loan into a grant, the change reflecting the leverage that Solomon Islands could exert by threatening to delay independence unless the financial future was secure.

The citizenship issue focused particularly on the rights of Gilbertese resettled in Solomon Islands in the 1950s as a way of dealing with perceived overpopulation on their own barren atolls. Solomon Islands preferences were to restrict citizenship to indigenous Solomon Islanders only, with residents of other races to be given belonger status. The British government, beset by racial and immigration problems of its own, sought a broader definition of citizenship that would embrace virtually all long-term residents irrespective of race. In the end, indigenous Solomon Islanders automatically became citizens at independence, and others were given citizenship on application providing they met stated criteria. This created a differentiation among citizens over land rights; the Solomon Islands position that only indigenous Solomon Islanders should be allowed to own land prevailed, modified only to protect existing freehold titles held by Gilbertese. Other alienations were to revert or be restricted to long-term leasehold.

Inevitably in a country like Solomon Islands, where levels of development and politicisation varied widely across the country, the finer constitutional issues were understood by only a minority, most of whom resided in Honiara. But this did not signify a lack of concern with local rights and interests. The breakaway movement in the western Solomons emerged on the eve of independence to defend such interests. Westerners particularly compared themselves with Malaitans, who were seen as dominating the government and as having a recent past—and to some extent a present—characterised by violence and paganism. The western islanders felt they were missing out in the distribution of government funds. Overall, the breakaway movement was based on 'the westerners' strong sense of identity and apartness. Their blackness, their Roviana lingua franca, their Christian religious affiliations, their beautiful and influential women, and their pride in being smallholder producers rather than migrant laborers marked them off as a distinct group from their brown neighbors. Their confidence in themselves was reinforced by the model of the thriving indigenous Christian Fellowship Church and their successful creation of a single Western Council in 1972 ... '.[35]

In addition, the westerners were witness to secessionist attempts in Bougainville just across the border, they had grievances over land, and they feared that their substantial contribution to the national economy would be captured for the benefit of others. Above all, they were nervous of a central administration led by a Malaitan—Peter Kenilorea had replaced Solomon Mamaloni as chief minister in 1976—and a bureaucracy dominated by a strong Malaitan presence. The westerners therefore boycotted the independence celebrations in July 1978, but did not seek to secede; their stance was a reminder that a devolution of responsibility to the provinces would have to be high on the post-independence agenda if national integration were to be achieved.

Despite threats to withhold or reject independence and difficult negotiations over a financial settlement, citizenship, and land, the final transition of power was relatively smooth. Perhaps the most important reason was that once the impetus towards decolonisation had been provided by the British government, the Solomon Islanders accepted the challenge on their own terms and were able to exert sufficient leverage to secure conditions that met their own goals, both for the immediate shape of independence and for the longer-term future.

The Gilbert and Ellice Islands

Not until 1960, as part of its wider initiative on decolonisation in the Pacific, did Britain try to develop central political institutions in the Gilbert and Ellice Islands Colony, a dependency hitherto regarded as too small, too poor, and too fragmented even for self-government. Developments through the 1960s and 1970s showed not only the primacy of loyalties to kin and to home island but an overriding division of Gilbertese versus Ellice, Micronesian versus Polynesian, majority versus minority. These realities served to modify the traditional Westminster model of constitutional development and led, against the wishes of the British government, to partition before independence.[36]

The conditions prevailing in the colony in the late 1950s created little local demand for political change. In addition to the cultural diversity, practical restraints on the development of political consciousness included a population living on small islands scattered across thousands of miles of ocean, and infrequent and expensive shipping that made it difficult either to overcome local loyalties or to bring representatives together on a regular basis. Insofar as it encouraged indigenous participation at all, the government concentrated its efforts on consultation with the leaders of local governments.

The decolonisation initiative was launched in 1960, although little progress was made with a new constitution until 1963, when an advisory council was appointed for the first time. Because such a start was thought to be too little as well as too late, and because the government was anxious to emphasise that a genuine transfer of power was taking place, an executive council with legislative power was established from 1964. Composed of four appointed islanders, four expatriate officials, and presided over by the resident commissioner, it was always an instrument of the colonial government, but it did permit consultation and provide some guidance in Western forms of government. Because of a requirement that all members should be fluent in English, Gilbert and Ellice Islander membership was largely confined to local civil servants.

Despite some awareness of wider political developments in the Third World, local issues were much more important. Since World War Two, aid funds had been used to build up the infrastructure and to expand social services which, because of the costs and inconvenience of decentralisation, were concentrated on South Tarawa, the colony headquarters. This strategy denied Ellice Islanders the secondary education in their own islands that they had enjoyed before the war, and meant that for education and employment their young people had to move to Tarawa. Moreover, because of their attitude towards Christianity and social change, Ellice Islanders had always responded strongly to the opportunities for secondary education. Now, though they accounted for no more than 15 per cent of the population, they held nearly half of the positions in the upper levels of the civil service and, under a policy of merit selection, were winning nearly 40 per cent of overseas scholarships and secondary school places. Ellice Islanders saw themselves as progressive, outgoing, and keen to seize the opportunities of Westernisation. They saw the Gilbertese as culturally conservative, personally reserved, and with a propensity for violence. The Gilbertese, on the other hand, condemned the Ellice Islanders for giving away their culture and ingratiating themselves with expatriate officials for advancement, and resented the Ellice Islanders' success in securing educational opportunities and wage employment in government service and in the phosphate industry. Largely in response to this situation, the Gilbertese National Party was formed by a group of civil servants in 1965; nationalistic in outlook, the party raised the spectre of the colony's politics being dominated through the decolonisation years by the issues of culture and religion, the latter reflecting sharp divisions between Catholic and Protestant within the Gilbert Islands.[37]

The next constitutional step towards self-government involved the introduction of a largely elected House of Representatives with an advisory function and a governing council on which officials outnumbered elected members. In this new environment there was a lessening of overt tension between Gilbertese and Ellice Islanders, partly because of a deliberate policy by Reuben Uatioa, the chief elected member, but also because of increasing awareness of constitutional issues. The House of Representatives, with 19 Gilbertese and 4 Ellice Island members, showed the way of the future. Whereas it had previously been widely assumed among the islanders that any future legislature would operate on the principle of 'equal' representation for both races, it now became clear that 'democracy' meant dominance for the Gilbertese majority.

The new constitution lasted for three years; it provided some training in parliamentary procedure, but frustrations were caused by rigid rules of debate, the expectation that the English language would be used, and inexperience on both sides of the House. In the light of the numerical smallness of the educated elite, local civil servants were permitted to stand for election to the House, and several future cabinet ministers, including Naboua Ratieta, the first chief minister, served among its ranks.

More important in this period was the transformation of the rivalry between the two cultures. With the Gilbertese soft-pedalling, the initiative passed to the Ellice Islanders, and the concerns of those resident on Tarawa soon spread to the outer islands. Ellice Islanders took note of the Gilbertese numerical superiority and their advocacy of racial quotas on scholarships and employment, and saw a bleak future for themselves. Their stance of 'separation before self-government' emerged in these years and determined their attitude towards constitutional changes from then on.

In 1969 a select committee on the constitution was established at the initiative of the government and produced recommendations that would return the colony to the orthodoxy of the Westminster model. There would be an elected majority in the Legislative Council but a majority of government officials in the Executive Council; ministerial members would be appointed by the governor in consultation with a leader of government business. And in a belated attempt to defuse ethnic rivalry it was agreed that, irrespective of size, each of the islands of the Gilbert and Ellice groups would return at least one member of parliament—a change that doubled Ellice representation to eight but left them heavily outnumbered by Gilbertese.

Despite these continuing concerns, the Legislative Council worked much better than its predecessor; members were more familiar with parliamentary procedure and the workings of government; select committees provided the opportunity for participation in policy formation; slowly, but only slowly, colonial officials were getting used to the idea of relinquishing power.

The colony had undergone significant constitutional change in 1963, 1964, 1967, and 1971, but while the path was clear the destination was not. At meetings with Anthony Kershaw, Britain's parliamentary under-secretary for foreign and commonwealth affairs, local members of parliament who had looked towards some form of self-government in free association with Britain realised that Britain intended them to become independent. The Ellice Islanders' demand for separation again surfaced, and, with the Anguilla Crisis a recent memory, British officials acknowledged for the first time that no Bill of Rights or legislation for minority protection would remove the concerns of the Ellice Islanders.

The creation of Tuvalu

A special commissioner was appointed to consider the secession issue and his recommendations, which failed to grasp either the determination of the Ellice Islanders or the extent of their support, were intended to frighten them into acceptance of unitary independence. Should a referendum of their people endorse it, they were to be permitted to secede, but with no share of the colony's reserves or assets except for a single, small, aging ship. There was no promise of future aid. The subsequent referendum brought a high turnout and a 92 per cent vote in favour of secession. Ellice Islanders ignored the conditions of secession believing, correctly as it turned out, that they would be able to attract sufficient aid in the future. The referendum was observed by the United Nations—partly because of a changed policy towards it on the part of the Wilson Labour government, partly to give international credibility to colonial partition. The Ellice Islanders welcomed the involvement of the world body, associating it with development assistance and international goodwill, but they were bewildered by questions that assumed their oppression and exploitation by the forces of colonialism. Equally, the UN delegates were bewildered by answers that asserted that colonialism and Christianity had brought the Ellice Islands out of darkness into light, and that Britain had always been a caring parent to its colonial children.[38]

With separation effected in January 1976, each part of the divided colony could move to independence. First Tuvalu (meaning 'eight together', a traditional name for the Ellice group), moved to dominion status within the British Commonwealth in October 1978, having full independence but acknowledging the Queen as head of state. Having effectively managed its affairs since separation, Tuvalu needed no intervening period of self-government. Recognizing its smallness—a population of 7200 living on a chain of islands with a total land area of a mere 25 square kilometres—the Tuvalu legislature had only twelve members. Because there were no political parties, the prime minister was elected by members of parliament, and ministers were appointed on his advice by the governor-general. At independence, Toaripi Lauti, a former teacher and labour officer in the phosphate industry, and chief minister since separation, was elected Tuvalu's first prime minister.

Tuvalu's achievement of independence represented a triumph for the nationalist spirit that had driven its politicians and united its people for more than a decade. But nationalism would not pay the bills, and despite an income from philatelic sales that matched all other sources of government revenue, the country suffered at independence from both a lack of infrastructure and a substantial annual deficit. Its earlier declarations notwithstanding, Britain paid a substantial development grant and provided budgetary assistance during the early years of independence.

From Gilbert Islands to Kiribati

For Kiribati (pronounced Kiribas, the local rendition of Gilberts), the transition to independence proved more difficult. With the establishment of a separate Tuvalu administration from 1975, Ellice Islanders began to leave Tarawa in significant numbers, creating new opportunities for Gilbertese but at the same time affecting the performance of the public service. Late in

1976, the country moved to self-government with the appointment of the first local minister of finance and the withdrawal of the governor from the executive council. However, the expectation that independence would follow in mid-1978 was upset by the revival of 'the Banaban issue' by the prime minister of Fiji. The Banaban people, resettled on Rabi Island in Fiji after World War Two, had outstanding claims over land rights and phosphate royalties for which they had unsuccessfully sought redress through the courts. They now demanded the secession of Banaba (Ocean Island) from the Gilbert Islands for a self-governing Banaban nation—a demand that became more strident once it became clear that Britain was prepared to sacrifice territorial integrity to meet the strength of Tuvaluan nationalism. The willingness of the British government even to entertain the Banaban claim in the face of strong Gilbertese opposition caused resentment in Tarawa that remained long after the claim had been rejected, though a parliamentary seat for a Banaban representative was created.

The issue was considered, among others, by a widely representative constitutional convention called in 1977 to establish the principles for a 'home-grown' constitution. The convention decided on a single legislature with provision for run-off elections where any candidate failed to win a majority of all votes in the general election. In a move that showed a determination to make politicians accountable, there was provision for the recall of a member through an electors' petition. The selection procedures for the presidency showed a similar concern with popular participation and accountability. The members of the House of Assembly were to nominate from among their number a slate of candidates for a national election. The president, both head of state for the republic, and head of government, was to choose ministers who were members of the House. The subsequent election carried these same concerns into practice, and there was a high turnout for both the Assembly and presidential elections. Success in the latter fell to Ieremia Tabai, a twenty-nine-year-old commerce graduate who had adopted a stance strongly critical of the previous administration and, in travelling throughout the country, had established his credentials as a supporter of 'the people' rather than 'the government'—a reflection of the popular belief that even at the stage of self-government, the country had still been ruled by a colonial regime.

Vanuatu

Given the political history of the New Hebrides, it was to be expected that decolonisation would add to existing tension between the two condominium powers. From the 1960s, Britain tried to treat the New Hebrides as it did the other WPHC territories and to move it towards self-government, then independence. France, seeing any form of autonomy for the New Hebrides as the first of its dominoes to fall in French Oceania, opposed then obstructed the transfer of power. Meanwhile the manoeuvring of the metropolitan powers, together with a major legacy of colonial grievances, saw the emergence of a powerful New Hebridean nationalism in the 1970s that, combined with British policy, gave an irresistible momentum to the demand for decolonisation and a distinctive local shape to independence once it was achieved.

The condominium structure meant that progress was always slow, and at every step there had to be an exact balancing of national interests. When the Advisory Council was first established in 1957, therefore, there were four British, four French, and four New Hebridean members. Through the 1960s, the unofficial membership of the council was gradually increased, with the number of New Hebrideans matching the combined British and French representation from 1964. A limited franchise was introduced, with members being returned by electoral colleges of local government representatives and the Chamber of Commerce. Though having no formal power, the council gradually acquired increasing influence through the opportunity to comment on draft legislation and the condominium budget.[39]

Because of the inhibitions of the condominium system, however, and the presence of a strong settler presence, the council was incapable of dealing with the land issue that was the focus of New Hebridean grievances over large tracts (amounting to nearly 40 per cent of the territory) alienated early in the colonial period to foreign, mostly French, interests.

In the late 1960s, protesters on Espiritu Santo led by the charismatic Jimmy Stevens had confronted settlers and brought the land issue into the political arena. The particular source of grievance was the ownership of 'Dark Bush Land'—in essence bush land that was alienated but uncleared. Since the mid-1960s, the Nagriamel movement, led by Stevens, had been demanding the return to New Hebridean ownership of all such land. (The name Nagriamel is derived from the name of two forest plants commonly associated with bush land.) Nagriamel attracted several thousand members across tribal, linguistic, and religious boundaries but drew its strongest support from Espiritu Santo, on which the largest alienations had been made. Nagriamel's strength demonstrated that a nationalist base might be built on a foundation of anticolonial grievance, land issues in particular, but the movement was essentially separatist, with some resemblance to a cargo cult, and its leadership was politically naive. From 1970 the challenge was taken up by the indigenous elite, which soon proved adept not only at confronting the colonial administration in its own terms, and had thus shifted the focus to a demand for independence, but also at drawing on a broad-based sense of nationalism that had developed over the land issue.[40]

In 1971, the New Hebrides National Party (NHNP) was formed by a group of young Western-educated New Hebrideans who were concerned to protect and promote their culture and saw land at the heart of any cultural development. From their first protests at land alienation in 1971, they not only tapped a well-spring of national discontent but directed their efforts at achieving independence, which, they argued, was the only way to safeguard New Hebridean culture. The development of the NHNP prompted the formation of other political associations, notably the French settler-dominated *Union de la Population des Nouvelles Hébrides* and, later, the *Union des Communautés des Nouvelles-Hébrides*, which attracted both settler and New Hebridean support.[41]

Initially, the NHNP was strongly urban based, with its leading members holding positions with the government or churches. Prominent among them were Barak Sope, a graduate of the University of the South Pacific, and Father Walter Lini, an Anglican priest. The organisation was dominated by English speakers and thus, bearing in mind British encouragement of political participation, was also damned in some quarters for being anglophone as well. The NHNP's land policy, formulated in 1974, provided for the nationalisation and leasing of all foreign-owned developed land and the return to custom ownership of all foreign-owned bush land. This allowed the party to develop rural strength from the mid-1970s and thus broadened its appeal. Britain was increasingly anxious for disengagement, but France was reluctant to abandon its policy, reiterated as late as 1970, that it intended to remain in the New Hebrides 'for a long time' because it had a mission of New Hebridean development to complete.[42] However, in the face of British pressure and New Hebridean protest, France had little choice and, at a ministerial conference in 1974, agreed to the establishment of a Representative Assembly with 29 seats filled on universal suffrage, but with 4 seats reserved for chiefs and 9 for the representatives of the Chamber of Commerce.

The NHNP won a majority of universal suffrage seats in national elections in 1975. It won nearly 60 per cent of the Melanesian vote but still found the Assembly evenly divided because of the distribution of special-interest seats. There was, not surprisingly in the light of the mood of the times, some suspicion that the condominium powers had intervened to undermine the NHNP in the year of delay between the elections and the first session of the Assembly. In January 1977 the NHNP, now renamed the Vanua'aku (Our Land) Pati, boycotted the Assembly and in November declared the People's Provisional Government, which effectively took control of large areas of the country.[43] Thus the Vanua'aku Pati rejected not only the French government, which was known to oppose independence, but also the British, which, despite public pronouncements to the contrary, was seen to be protecting its own relationship with its European ally rather than giving whole-hearted support to the New Hebridean cause.

With each administration, and the churches and political parties associated with them, encouraging divided loyalties among Melanesians, it was difficult to generate a united Melanesian response on political issues. But with mounting pressure through public demonstrations, street violence, and the activities of the People's Provisional Government, the condominium powers had few options and, in April 1978, they agreed to move towards independence. This decision brought the Vanua'aku Pati back into the formal political process and led to the formation of a Government of National Unity pending new elections and constitutional negotiations.[44]

As Melanesians came together in the late 1970s, it was possible to reach agreement on the land issue with an endorsement of custom ownership and a provision for regional assemblies to counterbalance the power of the national government. Vanuatu (Our Land) was to be a republic, headed by a president as head of state but with a prime minister as head of government. In November 1979, when the Vanua'aku Pati won 26 of the 39 seats in the Assembly, with 62 per cent of the popular vote in a 90 per cent turnout, it could claim a mandate for its policies and that, with Walter Lini as prime minister, it had won the right to lead the country to independence, which was scheduled for July 1980.

Although the Vanua'aku Pati had widespread support among Melanesian New Hebrideans, it was vehemently opposed by French settlers and significant numbers of francophone Melanesians. To some extent, too, its support was regionally based, and there was strong opposition to it from some of the northern islands, most notably Espiritu Santo, where Jimmy Stevens, with the surviving members of his Nagriamel movement, had entered into a bizarre alliance with French settlers and American land speculators. These groups rejected the new constitution and all it stood for and in May 1980 declared Espiritu Santo to be the independent republic of Vemarana. The high drama of the next few weeks was prompted largely by the complicity of the local French administration in the rebellion and the determination of the British administration to sit on its hands. Lini was faced with a rebellion that the colonial powers made only token gestures to quell, while he had neither the power nor the means to take action himself. A meeting of the South Pacific Forum in Tarawa applied strong regional pressure for keeping to the independence schedule and offered troops from Papua New Guinea as soon as independence was declared.[45]

To the metropolitan press, at least, the Santo rebellion was farce rather than high drama—a fitting end to the 'Pandemonium', as the Condominium had often been called—with rebels armed with everything from bows and arrows to the latest automatic rifles. Putting down the Santo rebellion, which the condominium powers had been either unable or unwilling to do, did help to establish the legitimacy and authority of the Lini government. But it also soured independence and destroyed any chance of co-operation between anglophone and francophone elements, and carried into independence a heightened awareness of the difficulties caused by the rivalries that had been inherent in the condominium structure throughout its existence. While Vanuatu's independence had a decidedly local flavour, it also showed again, if it was necessary, that new nations cannot escape their colonial heritage.

Conclusion

For Britain, the decolonisation of its Pacific Islands dependencies did not merely reflect a revised governmental relationship with the remnants of empire, but was symptomatic of a changing attitude towards the region as a whole. Since embarking on its campaign to join the European Economic Community in the 1960s, Britain had steadily withdrawn from its more remote entanglements. After decolonisation, it continued its aid commitment to its former dependencies in the Pacific Islands, but only at a minimal level. All remained members of the British Commonwealth of Nations, but that did not involve direct financial assistance commensurate with the increase in the costs of government and development from Britain or guidance in foreign affairs. The costs of maintaining government services and levels of development assistance that would help to preserve political stability it left to nations with a more direct strategic or economic interest in the region—the United States, France, Australia, and New Zealand.

Notes

1 For general accounts, see Nicholas Mansergh, *The Commonwealth Experience*, Weidenfeld and Nicolson, London, 1969; W. D. McIntyre, *Colonies into Commonwealth*, Blandford Press, London, 1966; V. Wiseman, *Britain and the Commonwealth*, Allen & Unwin, London, 1965.

2 See, for example, John Gallagher, 'The Decline, Revival and Fall of the British Empire', in *The Decline, Revival and Fall of the British Empire*, ed. John Gallagher, Cambridge University Press, Cambridge, 1982, 142–143.

3 D. J. Morgan, *The Official History of Colonial Development*, vol. 1: *The Origins of British Aid Policy, 1924–1945*, Humanities Press, Atlantic Highlands, NJ, 1980.

4 For a general discussion, see David Goldsworthy, *Colonial Issues in British Politics 1945–1961: From 'Colonial Development' to 'Wind of Change'*, Oxford University Press, Oxford, 1971.

5 See Morgan 1980, vol. 1.

6 Ronald Robinson, 'Andrew Cohen and the Transfer of Power in Tropical Africa, 1940–1951', in *Decolonisation and After: The British and French Experience*, ed. W. H. Morris-Jones and Georges Fischer, Frank Cass, London, 1980, 63.

7 See William Roger Louis, *Imperialism at Bay: The United States and the Decolonization of the British Empire*, Oxford University Press, 1977, 43–47; for another view, see Rudolph Von Albertini, *Decolonization: The Administration and Future of the Colonies, 1919–1960*, Doubleday, Garden City, NY, 1971, 366–369.

8 See Goldsworthy, 361–372.

9 H. E. Maude, 'South Pacific: Independence and Regionalism in the South Sea Islands', *The Round Table*, July 1971, 369–381.

10 Quoted in Dennis Austin, 'The Transfer of Power: Why and How', in Morris-Jones and Fischer, 6.

11 For general surveys of decolonisation in Oceania, see Peter Larmour, 'The Decolonisation of the Pacific' and Yash Ghai, 'Constitutional Issues in the Transition to Independence', in *Politics in the Pacific Islands*, vol. 4, *Foreign Forces in Pacific Politics*, ed. Ron Crocombe and Ahmed Ali, Institute of Pacific Studies, University of the South Pacific, Suva, 1983.

12 The figures are given in a speech of 11 October 1961 by Iain Macleod, Secretary of State for the Colonies, reprinted in A. N. Porter and A. J. Stockwell, *British Imperial Policy and Decolonization 1938–64*, vol. 2, Macmillan, London, 1989, 558.

13 Fiji, *Legislative Council Debates*, 1961, 133.

14 Fiji, *Legislative Council Debates*, 1961, 135.

15 Fiji, *Legislative Council Debates*, 1961, 173.

16 See Deryck Scarr, *Fiji, the Three-Legged Stool: Selected Writings of Ratu Sir Lala Sukuna*, Macmillan, London, 1983.

17 Fiji, *Legislative Council Debates*, 1961, 4.

18 On the 1963 election, see Norman Meller and James Anthony, *Fiji Goes to the Polls: The Crucial Legislative Council Elections of 1963*, East-West Center Press, Honolulu, 1968.

19 *Pacific Islands Monthly*, March 1965, 9.

20 See J. W. Davidson, 'Constitutional Changes in Fiji', *Journal of Pacific History* 1 (1966): 165–168.

21 Robert Norton, *Race and Politics in Fiji*, University of Queensland Press, St Lucia, 1977, 77–83; Roderic Alley, 'The Emergence of Party Politics', in *Politics in Fiji*, ed. Brij V. Lal, Allen & Unwin, Sydney, 1986, 40–47.

22 Alley, 33.

23 Norton, 84–98; Alley, 40–47.

24 James M. Anthony, 'The 1968 Fiji By-Elections', *Journal of Pacific History* 4 (1969): 132–135; Norton, 120–125.

25 Norton, 126–128.

26 Bruce Knapman, *Fiji's Economic History, 1874–1939: Studies of Capitalist Colonial Development*, National Centre for Development Studies, Australian National University, Canberra, 1987, 1–8.

27 Ahmed Ali, 'Political Change: From Colony to Independence', in Ahmed Ali, *Plantation to Politics: Studies on Fiji Indians*, University of the South Pacific and Fiji Times and Herald, Suva, 1980, 159–163.

28 Brij V. Lal, 'Politics since Independence: Continuity and Change, 1970–82', in Lal 1986, 76–81; R. K. Vasil, 'Communalism and Constitution-making in Fiji', *Pacific Affairs* 45 (1972–73): 21–41.

29 See Penelope A. Lavaka, 'The Limits of Advice: Britain and the Kingdom of Tonga, 1914–1970', PhD dissertation, Australian National University, 1981.

30 Lavaka, 353.

31 Lavaka, 357.

32 Francis Saemala, 'Constitutional Development', in *Solomon Islands Politics*, ed. Peter Larmour and Sue Tarua, Institute of Pacific Studies, University of the South Pacific, Suva, 1983, 1–6; Judith A. Bennett, *Wealth of the Solomons: A History of a Pacific Archipelago, 1800–1978*, Pacific Islands Monograph Series no. 3, University of Hawai'i Press, Honolulu, 1987, 319.

33 The main defence of the Governing Council is in T. Russell, 'The 1970 Constitution for the British Solomon Islands', in *The Politics of Melanesia*, ed. Marion

Ward, Research School of Pacific Studies, Australian National University, Canberra, 1970, 225–238; the main critic of Russell's view is Warren A. Paia, 'Aspects of Constitutional Development in the Solomon Islands', *Journal of Pacific History* 10 (1975): 81–89.

34 For a detailed discussion of the constitution and its creation, see Yash Ghai, 'The Making of the Independence Constitution', in Larmour and Tarua 1983, 9–52.

35 Bennett, 328.

36 Unless otherwise indicated, the material that follows is based on Barrie Macdonald, *Cinderellas of the Empire: Towards a History of Kiribati and Tuvalu*, Australian National University Press, Canberra, 1982, 220–275.

37 The background to this issue is discussed in detail in Barrie Macdonald, 'Secession in the Defence of Identity: The Making of Tuvalu', *Pacific Viewpoint* 16 (1975): 26–44; for an Ellice Islands viewpoint, see Tito Isala, 'Secession and Independence', in *Tuvalu: A History*, ed. Hugh Laracy, Institute of Pacific Studies and Extension Services, University of the South Pacific, Suva, 1983, 146–177.

38 Keith Chambers and Anne Chambers, 'Comment: A Note on the Ellice Referendum', *Pacific Viewpoint* 16 (1975): 223–224.

39 See A. G. Kalkoa, 'The Political Situation in the New Hebrides', in Ward 1970, 207–224.

40 A. L. Jackson, 'Towards Political Awareness in the New Hebrides', *Journal of Pacific History* 7 (1972): 155–162; Howard Van Trease, *The Politics of Land in Vanuatu: From Colony to Independence*, Institute of Pacific Studies, University of the South Pacific, Suva, 1987, 127–168; Jimmy Stevens, 'Nagriamel', in *New Hebrides: The Road to Independence*, ed. Chris Plant, Institute of Pacific Studies, University of the South Pacific, Suva, 1977, 35–40.

41 Van Trease, 206–246; Barak Sope, *Land and Politics in the New Hebrides*, South Pacific Social Sciences Association, Suva, 1974.

42 Jackson, 156.

43 Christopher Plant, 'New Hebrides 1977: Year of Crisis', *Journal of Pacific History* 13 (1978): 194–204.

44 Van Trease, 232; see also Grace Molisa, Nikenike Vurobaravu, and Howard Van Trease, 'Vanuatu: Overcoming Pandemonium', in *Politics in Melanesia*, ed. Ron Crocombe and Ahmed Ali, Institute of Pacific Studies, University of the South Pacific, Suva, 1982, 92–96.

45 Jeremy MacClancy, 'From New Hebrides to Vanuatu, 1979-80', *Journal of Pacific History* 16 (1979): 92–104; for a more popular account see Richard Shears, *The Coconut War: The Crisis on Espiritu Santo*, Cassell, Sydney, 1980.

9

Australia and New Zealand

Terence Wesley-Smith

World War Two marked the beginning of the end for Australian and New Zealand colonial rule in the Pacific. The disruption and destruction of war caused discontent among some of the colonised and obliged the colonial powers to take a much more active interest in their dependencies than they had before. More important, the war and its aftermath forced Australia and New Zealand to redefine their roles in a rapidly changing international order. International considerations and pressures, more than the needs and demands of the colonised, caused Australia and New Zealand to withdraw from their Pacific territories in the decades after World War Two.

The global and metropolitan contexts

Post-war foreign policies in Australia and New Zealand were conditioned by the ongoing realities of small size, lack of military and diplomatic resources, and isolation from global centers of political and economic power. In a search for collective security, considerable diplomatic energy was devoted to creating new international and regional organisations. In the course of this work, the leaders of both countries took a special interest in the fate of the colonised peoples of the world.[1]

In the 1940s, Australian and New Zealand international initiatives on colonial questions were structured by the ideological orientation of the labour parties in power in both countries. They took the moral position that the interests of the colonised were paramount and that colonial powers should be held internationally accountable for their actions. This trusteeship principle was reluctantly accepted by the great powers and became a key part of the provisions for dependencies in chapters 11 and 12 of the Charter of the United Nations.[2]

Australia and New Zealand also expressed an early commitment to the principle of self-determination for colonial peoples. One of the stated purposes of their own South Seas Regional Commission initiative of 1944, for example, was to help develop Pacific colonies towards eventual self-government. They had no difficulty supporting Article 73*b* of the United Nations Charter, which obliged powers administering 'non-self-governing' territories to bring them to self-government. Similarly, they supported without reservation the new international trusteeship system provisions, even though Article 76*b* mentioned independence as an additional future option for the peoples of trust territories.[3]

Australia and New Zealand soon demonstrated their commitment to the principles that they had helped enshrine in the United Nations Charter. Australia entered into a trusteeship agreement for the former mandated territory of New Guinea in December 1946 and in the following year started submitting annual reports of conditions in neighbouring Papua, now designated a non-self-governing territory. New Zealand officials established a trusteeship agreement for Western Samoa, a former League of Nations mandated territory, which was approved by the United Nations in 1946. At the same time, they decided to make the Cook Islands and Niue subject to the United Nations provisions for non-self-governing territories, even though these islands were legally integral parts of the New Zealand state.[4] After some squabbling, Australia, New Zealand, and Britain agreed to continue the partnership arrangement established when Nauru was a League of Nations mandate, and jointly submitted a trusteeship agreement for the island in 1947.

These voluntary actions were generally congruent with Australia's and New Zealand's national interests at the time, despite the consequent loss of unencumbered colonial control. Both countries put much store in the promise of post-war internationalism, and opening up their dependencies to United Nations scrutiny was a small price to pay for international respectability. Furthermore, before 1960 the United Nations did not require these countries to do much more in their territories than other considerations already decreed, even in the more closely monitored trust territories.

Australia's primary policy aim in Papua and New Guinea had always been to deny the area to potentially hostile powers. Before World War Two it was sufficient simply to possess the territories arching across its northern approaches. In light of the traumatic effects of the Japanese occupation, however, officials believed that programmes for political, economic, social, and educational advancement were necessary in order to restore and maintain Australian influence.[5] They were also well aware that the trusteeship agreement afforded them considerable freedom of action, including the right to administer New Guinea as if it were part of Australia, to form an administrative union with neighbouring Papua, and to maintain military establishments there. What was a 'sacred trust' under the terms of the United Nations Charter was also a mandate for Australian national self-interest.

New Zealand had even less reason to shun the sacred trust with respect to its dependent territories. Even the jewel in its imperial crown, Western Samoa, had produced little but headaches for Wellington since it was first occupied by New Zealand forces in 1914. Economic and strategic interests there were now assessed as 'negligible', and pre-war sentiments that New Zealand should 'cut [its] losses' as soon as possible were reinforced by a post-war resurgence of Samoan nationalism.[6] Although the administrative problems were less severe in New Zealand's other territories, the rewards of colonialism had been no more significant. It made good sense to co-operate fully with the United Nations' decolonisation efforts.

On the other hand, Australia and New Zealand were acutely aware of the potential threat that international supervision posed to their economic interests in phosphate-rich Nauru. They managed to negotiate a trusteeship agreement that allowed them to maintain those interests, at least in the short term.

After about 1960, international and domestic attitudes towards decolonisation began to diverge, and the key issue was timing. Although New Zealand moved rapidly in Western Samoa to head off nationalist pressures, officials in both Australia and New Zealand generally believed that the decolonisation process should be orderly, progressive, peaceful, and evolutionary, and that certain levels of economic, social, and political development were prerequisites of self-government. These gradualist policies may have sprung from a genuine concern for the welfare of the colonised, but they also reflected the strategic needs of the colonisers. It was important that these new self-governing neighbours in the Pacific be politically and economically stable and well disposed towards their former colonial rulers. However, new attitudes towards decolonisation in the United Nations made an incrementalist approach increasingly difficult to sustain.

The global process of decolonisation accelerated rapidly during the 1950s, and by 1960 more than forty new states had joined the United Nations. Mounting anticolonial sentiment was reflected in General Assembly Resolution 1514(XV) of 1960, which condemned colonialism in no uncertain terms and demanded that immediate steps be taken to eliminate it in both non-self-governing and trust territories. The blunt statement that 'inadequacy of political, economic, social or education preparedness should never serve as a pretext for delaying independence' effectively rendered gradualist policies unacceptable.

The new climate of opinion in the United Nations did not surprise New Zealand officials, who had followed international trends very closely. By 1960, they had already set a date for independence for Samoa and were actively exploring future political options for the Cook Islands. However, the new international attitudes served to strengthen New Zealand's determination to dissolve its remaining colonial relationships as soon as possible.

The rising tide of anticolonialism in the United Nations posed more serious problems for Australia, whose minister for territories had expressed the opinion in 1951 that Papua and New Guinea might not be ready for self-government for another century.[7] Political decolonisation proceeded there at a snail's pace. For a decade, officials managed to ignore the call in Resolution 1514 for an immediate transfer of power, emphasising instead the right of the colonised to set the pace of political change. In the early 1970s, however, the international costs of delaying independence finally overtook the strategic and political benefits of waiting until appropriate internal conditions had been achieved. Australian leaders decided that independence should come as soon as possible, regardless of what the people wanted.

The final political outcome of the decolonisation process was also heavily influenced by changing attitudes in the United Nations. General Assembly Resolution 1541(xv), passed shortly after Resolution 1514 in 1960, indicated that a territory could shed its colonial status by becoming independent, integrated with another state, or 'freely associated' with another state. Nevertheless, it was clear from subsequent actions and statements in the United Nations that complete sovereign independence was the preferred future status for all dependencies, regardless of their size, resources, or level of development. When other options were proposed, they tended to be regarded with suspicion and scrutinised for evidence of colonial manipulation.

This climate reinforced an official preference in New Zealand for loosening the political ties with its colonies as soon as possible. The alternative of bringing the territories into a closer political relationship with New Zealand was discussed, but firmly rejected. Officials argued that integrating the islands directly into New Zealand's highly centralised political system would mean considerable loss of local autonomy and cultural identity. The possibility of altering the existing system to accommodate the special cultural and economic needs of the islands was never seriously considered.[8]

The absence of the integration option did not pose any problems in Western Samoa, where local opinion was strongly in favour of self-government. In the other territories, however, extremely small size, lack of resources, and strong local sentiment in favour of continued close ties with New Zealand made complete independence problematic. The idea of self-government in 'free association' with New Zealand was attractive. Such a constitutional arrangement would allow for the complete local autonomy that full integration would have denied, and would permit the continuation of citizenship rights, budgetary support, and provisions for defence and foreign affairs that full independence could not easily accommodate.

Best of all, from New Zealand's perspective, free association was recognised in Resolution 1541(xv) as one way in which a colonial relationship could be extinguished. In arguing that the obligation to transmit information to the United Nations ceased when the Cook Islands, and later Niue, achieved the status of self-government in free association with New Zealand, officials emphasised that the peoples of these territories had a continuing right of self-determination. But the underlying assumption was that the future option was full independence rather than political integration with New Zealand.

Australia was rather more reluctant to move its territories in the direction of full independence but, in the end, found this outcome more acceptable than the alternatives. Unlike New Zealand, Australia had the federal structure necessary to integrate Papua and New Guinea politically while allowing for local autonomy, and its strategic interests would have been best served by this outcome. However, full integration, as well as most conceivable forms of association, would have allowed Papuans and New Guineans equal access to federal political institutions, to the social welfare benefits enjoyed by other Australian citizens, and to any part of the Australian continent. Integration under these circumstances was simply out of the question in the race-conscious Australia of the 1960s.

Australia's and New Zealand's determination to retain control of Nauru and its phosphate resources was effectively stymied by the new international norms regarding decolonisation, exploited to the full by Nauru's nationalist leader, Hammer DeRoburt. The partners eventually conceded full independence because, in the final analysis, they were not prepared to defy United Nations support for this outcome.

Although Pacific Islanders in these territories were never entirely in control of their own decolonisation, they were able to exert varying degrees of influence on the process. Local attitudes were particularly important in hastening the decolonisation of Western Samoa and Nauru, and were responsible for delaying New Zealand's withdrawal from Niue and Tokelau. Some of the Pacific peoples colonised by Australia or New Zealand, such as the New Zealand Maori, remained outside the international system of supervision altogether.[9] In their cases there was less immediate pressure on the coloniser to reconcile its interests with those of the colonised.

The following case studies illuminate the interplay of internal and external factors affecting the decolonisation process in each of Australia's and New Zealand's colonies.

Dealing with faʻa Samoa

When New Zealand submitted a draft trusteeship agreement for Western Samoa in 1946, before consulting Samoan leaders, they responded by petitioning the United Nations for immediate self-government.[10] New Zealand quickly regained the initiative with a dual strategy. First, efforts were made to enlist the support of the United Nations, which was invited to send a mission to the territory.[11] Second, Pacific historian J. W. Davidson was commissioned to advise on new policy directions. When a bold new policy for Western Samoa, which included plans for eventual independence, was endorsed by the United Nations in 1947,[12] New Zealand was back in control of the decolonisation process—and remained in control until Western Samoa achieved independence in 1962.

The provisions of the Samoan Amendment Act of 1947 reflected the British evolutionary approach to self-government that New Zealand itself had experienced. However, some important innovations and concessions were considered necessary to avoid the possibility of Samoan resistance. Nationalist aspirations were acknowledged by skipping several steps along the 'normal' road to self-government and establishing immediately a legislature with a Samoan majority and extensive domestic authority. The New Zealand preference for democratic institutions was also compromised by recognising traditional Samoan forms of political authority in the new Council of State and the legislature.[13]

When Samoan leaders agreed to participate in the 'new set-up', they were effectively turning away from their long-standing demands for immediate self-government based entirely on Samoan institutions. What they were helping to establish was not 'genuinely Samoan',[14] but a centralised, representative, Western form of government that incorporated some Samoan features.[15]

All sections of the Samoan community were represented at a constitutional convention that deliberated for six weeks late in 1954. Most of the recommendations placed before the convention by a working committee had originally been suggested by the New Zealand government. However, the leaders did add some provisions of their own, notably a condition that only those with chiefly or *matai* titles should vote for *matai* candidates in elections. They also decided that New Zealand should continue to provide protection and advice after self-government, as Britain did for Tonga.[16] With the election of Fiame Mata'afa Faumuina Mulinu'u II as Western Samoa's first prime minister, Samoan leaders began to exert much more control over their own political destiny.[17] Nevertheless, they did so in the context of the basic structures of government already in place, and the shape and direction of political development continued to be heavily influenced by the New Zealand government, the United Nations, and sundry foreign advisers.

A draft constitution produced by a new working committee, this one advised by Professor Davidson, was presented to a second constitutional convention in August 1960. Despite vigorous debate and many proposed amendments, it was accepted in its original form. The constitution provided for full, unqualified independence for Western Samoa, rather than the 'Tongan' relationship advocated earlier. This change in direction was initiated in 1959 by New Zealand officials concerned that anything less than full independence might arouse suspicion in the United Nations and put New Zealand's international reputation at risk. The offer of a treaty of friendship that would ensure continuing New Zealand financial support and technical assistance, especially in external affairs, helped persuade Samoan leaders that this was the best approach. To forestall any accusations of neo-colonialism in the Trusteeship Council, they were further persuaded to postpone the actual treaty-making until after independence.[18]

New Zealand was particularly anxious about the issue of suffrage, because any restrictions might attract opposition in the Trusteeship Council. However, those Samoans who supported universal suffrage were apparently not prepared to push the issue, and the constitutional convention decided to retain *matai* suffrage.[19] The price of this significant concession to *fa'a Samoa* (Samoan custom) was a United Nations requirement for an explicit act of self-determination, based on universal suffrage, to gauge the people's views on independence and the constitution.

In contrast, New Zealand took a more detached stand on the equally difficult head-of-state issue. Because this was of little interest to the Trusteeship Council, the working committee was left to reconcile traditional concepts of high office with modern constitutional needs. In the end, the office itself was defined as a largely ceremonial one, and the committee recommended that the two *tama-a-aiga* (royal sons) who held the office of *fautua*, Tupua Tamasese Mea'ole and Malietoa Tanumafili II, should occupy the position together for life. The legislature would elect a successor after both were dead. In May 1961, 83 per cent of voters in a plebiscite supported the new constitution, and 79 per cent agreed that Western Samoa should proceed to independence on this basis.[20] The General Assembly took note of the 'freely expressed will and desire' of the people and unanimously agreed to the termination of the trusteeship in July 1961. Western Samoa achieved independence on 1 January 1962, and its leaders signed the Treaty of Friendship with New Zealand seven months later.

Although New Zealand had no compelling reason to stay in Western Samoa, the decision to leave was finally precipitated by nationalist agitation. Samoan pressure was also responsible for accelerating the pace of change and for some local modifications to the imported institutional structure of the new state. However, New Zealand managed to retain overall control of the decolonisation process, whose outcome owed much more to foreign values and expectations than to *fa'a Samoa*.

The Cook Islands solution

Although Cook Islanders had an important influence on developments in their islands immediately after World War Two, New Zealand officials firmly controlled the pace and direction of change after about 1955, and after 1960 their actions were heavily influenced by the expectations of the United Nations.[21] A series of local protests over economic conditions in the 1940s and 1950s eventually led New Zealand to formulate a policy of accelerated political, economic, and social development for the Cook Islands.[22] Inspired by a 1955 economic survey, the new philosophy was to help Cook Islanders help themselves.[23] If development were to be achieved, officials argued, Cook Islanders must be encouraged to take more responsibility for their own economic and political affairs.

The idea that the Cooks should have more political autonomy, rather than be more fully integrated into New Zealand, was reinforced by C. C. Aikman, then professor of constitutional law at Victoria University College in Wellington. In his reports on future constitutional development, Aikman argued that full political integration would not be appropriate, because of the group's geographic isolation from New Zealand, its lower standard of living, and the people's relative lack of sophistication in Western forms of politics. Furthermore, Cook Islanders' interests would be neglected in the New Zealand parliament because they would be entitled to 'no more than one or two' representatives there. He advocated increased political autonomy for the Cook Islands, while making it clear that full independence was not a realistic goal.[24] Aikman's reports led to the establishment in 1958 (by means of the Cook Islands Amendment Act, 1957) of a legislative assembly with limited legislative and financial powers, an executive committee that advised the resident commissioner, and an expanded role for the island councils.

Anticolonialism at the United Nations after 1960 posed something of a dilemma for New Zealand officials contemplating the political future of the Cook Islands. It was quite clear that the United Nations expected a firm timetable for the decolonisation of a dependent territory, and preferably one that led to full independence. It was equally clear that Cook Islanders did not want, and would resist, such radical solutions to their problems. Some 20 per cent of all Cook Islanders were already living in New Zealand, and most were anxious not to lose their access to New Zealand citizenship, subsidies, and markets.[25]

New Zealand responded to these pressures by granting full financial autonomy to the legislative assembly in March 1962, bringing the Cook Islands very close to internal self-government. Four months later, the minister of island territories asked the legislative assembly to choose among four options: independence, integration with New Zealand, a federation of Polynesian countries, or self-government in free association with New Zealand. From the negative way in which the other options were presented it was clear that the minister considered only the last one appropriate. He asked the leaders to consider the many difficulties facing newly independent Western Samoa, and 'how much more difficult it would be for the Cook Islands to operate as an independent country'. He said that integration with New Zealand would mean giving up their own legislative assembly in favour of a single representative in the New Zealand parliament, to be shared with Niue and Tokelau. Further, he did not think that the idea of a Polynesian federation could be 'seriously considered at the present time'. He concluded that 'it would be in the best interests of the Cook Islands people to keep the present link with New Zealand, but to have full internal self-government'.[27] On 13 July the legislative assembly, after deliberating for only thirty minutes, duly requested the 'fullest possible' internal self-government consistent with retaining the New Zealand connection.

The new relationship was defined initially in the Cook Islands Constitution Bill of 1964, drafted with the help of C. C. Aikman, J. W. Davidson, and J. B. Wright, and tabled simultaneously in the New Zealand and Cook Islands legislatures. Several amendments were made, some by the New Zealand parliament and some at the initiative of Albert Henry's Cook Islands Party after it gained control of the legislature in the general elections of April 1965. These were included in the Cook Islands Constitutional Amendment Act of 1965, to which the constitution itself was attached as a schedule. The act was passed by the New Zealand parliament and the Cook Islands Assembly, and came into force on 4 August 1965. The legislation was designed in part to persuade the United Nations that the new arrangement, while not full independence, represented a genuine transfer of 'all powers to the peoples' of the Cook Islands as required by the 1960 declaration on colonialism, Resolution 1514 (xv). More particularly, officials wished to demonstrate compliance with Resolution 1541(xv), which recognised the legitimacy of continued association with the former colonial power, provided that the people concerned had made a 'free and voluntary choice', that their cultural integrity was respected, and that they retained the right to opt for a different status in the future.[27]

In order to demonstrate that Cook Islanders were acting freely, the United Nations was invited to observe the 1965 elections and the subsequent constitutional debate in the legislature. The Minister for Island Territories indicated in 1962 that a plebiscite would be held on constitutional issues, but by 1964 a general election was regarded as a sufficient test of public opinion. Some critics argued that 'the opinion of the Cook Islanders in relation to the Constitution cannot be tested by a general election when other issues will inevitably influence the voters'.[28] Addressing the other concerns, officials pointed out that New Zealand could no longer legislate for the Cook Islands, and that Cook Islanders were free to modify their constitution—and the relationship with New Zealand—unilaterally at any time. New Zealand's assiduous attention to United Nations requirements was rewarded when the Committee of Twenty-Four quickly voiced its approval, and the General Assembly terminated New Zealand's obligations under the United Nations Charter.

If New Zealand officials had to emphasise the autonomy of the Cook Islands in order to 'get off the UN hook', they also had the contrary task of assuring Cook Islanders that the ties with New Zealand were strong and ongoing. The enabling legislation reaffirmed citizenship rights, promised financial assistance, and provided that New Zealand would retain responsibility for foreign affairs and defence.

The new status of the Cook Islands as 'self-government in free association' with New Zealand was ambiguous.[29] The territory had ceased to be
non-self-governing, but there was general agreement that it had not achieved
full sovereign independence. The key issue in this respect was the nature
and extent of the Cook Islands' international legal capacity. The constitution gave the Cook Islands full legislative competence and did not limit its
jurisdiction to internal affairs. The only apparent limitations were not in the
constitution itself, but in Section 5 of the Cook Islands Constitution Act,
which stated: 'Nothing in this Act or in the Constitution shall affect the
responsibilities of Her Majesty the Queen in right of New Zealand for the
external affairs and defence of the Cook Islands, those responsibilities to
be discharged after consultation by the Prime Minister of New Zealand
with the Premier of the Cook Islands'.

Section 5 was inserted by the Island Territories Select Committee of the
New Zealand parliament with the clear intention of reserving matters of
defence and external affairs to New Zealand. As drafted, however, Section
5 does not appear to have that effect. It merely confirms what the constitution states elsewhere, that the Queen is the head of state of the Cook
Islands.[30] According to well-established principles of British constitutional
law, the Queen discharges her responsibilities for external affairs and defence,
as for other matters, only on the advice of her ministers. The question is,
Which ministers—those in New Zealand or those in the Cook Islands—are
to advise Her Majesty regarding the defence and external affairs of the
Cook Islands? According to Alex Frame, Section 5 does not answer that
question one way or the other.[31] It does not affect the constitutional ability
of the Cook Islands government to act on its own behalf in international
affairs and defence.

This ambiguity was not fully recognised in the early years of self-
government, because leaders on both sides had agreed that New Zealand
would handle all foreign affairs and defence issues. The nebulous legal
position proved to be an advantage when Premier Albert Henry, with the
encouragement of New Zealand Prime Minister Norman Kirk, explored the
option of full independence in the early 1970s. Unable to muster any enthusiasm for the idea at home, Henry settled for a new interpretation of the
relationship that gave the Cooks more freedom of action. An exchange of
letters between the two leaders in 1973, as well as numerous official
statements since then, confirmed that the Cook Islands was fully competent
to act on its own account in international affairs and that it was free to
develop its own international personality. The Cook Islands has since
demonstrated its international competence by negotiating numerous bilateral agreements, including a treaty of friendship with the United States.[32]

Amendments to the constitution in 1981 and 1982 served to further
emphasise the Cook Islands' sovereignty. In case any ambiguity remained,
a clause was inserted stating that no act of the New Zealand parliament

would henceforth apply in the Cook Islands. Another provided for appeals to be heard in the Cook Islands, rather than in New Zealand courts. To signify equal status with the independent states of the region, the *legislative assembly* was renamed the *parliament*, and the *premier* became the *prime minister*. Most significant, the old position of *high commissioner*, ambiguously designed to represent both New Zealand and the Queen, was replaced by a separate *queen's representative*.[33]

Any impediments to the political independence of the Cook Islands arise, not from the constitution itself, but from the 'special relationship' that exists between New Zealand and its former colony. Although financial and administrative support are important elements in this relationship, Cook Islanders' status as citizens of New Zealand lies at its heart. New Zealand has made clear its view that citizenship bestows obligations as well as rights and places implicit limits on how the Cook Islands conducts its internal and external affairs. Whereas both parties recognise that such limits exist, the power to decide when they have been reached lies squarely with New Zealand.[34]

The Niue solution

New Zealand did not formulate long-term policies for Niue until anticolonial pressures began to build at the United Nations in the early 1960s. Even then, policies developed for the Cook Islands were simply extended to Niue without prior consultation or concessions to local conditions and attitudes.[35]

The Cook Islands Amendment Act of 1957, designed to establish a legislative assembly in the Cooks, provided for a similar representative body in Niue. In 1962, just two years after its inauguration, the Niue Assembly was asked by New Zealand to choose one of four future political options: independence, integration with New Zealand, a Polynesian federation, or self-government. It was as clear to Niueans as it had been to Cook Islanders that New Zealand had only one 'option' in mind. In fact, unknown to Niueans, the New Zealand cabinet had already approved a timetable that provided for self-government for Niue in 1965. The proposed timetable was rejected by the Niue Assembly when it was finally presented there in 1963. In 1965, two visiting consultants, Professor Aikman and J. M. McEwen, found that Niueans were not necessarily opposed to eventual self-government, but that they did not feel ready for it yet. They were particularly concerned that self-government would mean the end of financial assistance from, and the severing of ties with, New Zealand. The government reluctantly accepted the consultants' recommendation that Niueans henceforth set the pace of change.[36]

For the remainder of the decade, officials in the Department of Island Territories could only encourage Niueans to assume more of the considerable executive powers still exercised by the resident commissioner, while their colleagues in external affairs dealt with anticolonial criticism in the United Nations as best they could. Their patience was rewarded in January 1970 when Young Vivian introduced a motion in the Niue Assembly calling for a discussion of constitutional development.[37] The next year, New Zealand's remaining executive power was transferred to an executive committee headed by the new leader of government, Robert Rex. In early 1973, more than ten years after the idea was first proposed, the New Zealand government and a delegation from Niue negotiated a timetable that would lead to an act of self-determination in 1974.

As in the Cook Islands, the final stages of the decolonisation of Niue were carefully managed to satisfy conflicting domestic and international interests. First, there was an urgent need to reassure Niueans that the ties with New Zealand would continue. This was reflected in the provisions in the Niue Constitution Act 1974 confirming New Zealand citizenship, making New Zealand responsible for foreign affairs and defence, and guaranteeing financial and administrative assistance from New Zealand. Perhaps most important, none of these crucial provisions could be altered without the support of two-thirds of Niuean voters in a referendum. Convincing the United Nations that the people of Niue were not being dragooned into accepting a qualified form of independence was relatively easy.[38] Even to the casual observer it was obvious that most Niueans favoured less rather than more independence. It was also relatively easy to demonstrate that the new constitution gave Niueans full control of their internal affairs. Perhaps most reassuring to skeptics was the fact that Niueans had a continuing right to self-determination and could unilaterally sever their ties to New Zealand at any time.

Unlike the Cook Islands, Niue has shown no inclination to exploit the ambiguities of its constitutional situation and exercise a greater degree of independence from New Zealand. Indeed, the major concern since the mid-1980s has been to maintain Niue as a 'living community' in the face of rapid population decline resulting from migration to New Zealand.[39] This situation has put its own strains on the special relationship, since New Zealand is obliged to foot most of the bill for efforts to resuscitate the Niuean community in Niue. Funding for the financial year 1990–91, for example, amounted to about NZ$10 million, 70 per cent of which was earmarked for budgetary support.[40] The financial and political costs to New Zealand of decolonising Niue have proved much higher than could have been anticipated in 1962.

Tokelau: Defiant colony

New Zealand's attempts to rid itself of the colonial taint met most resistance in the tiny atoll territory of Tokelau. For more than three decades Tokelauans have made it clear that they do not wish to alter their status as a dependency of New Zealand and are not interested in a formal act of self-determination. Nevertheless, a series of New Zealand initiatives over the years has succeeded in edging a reluctant Tokelau some way along the road to self-government.[41]

Despite efforts to improve educational and other services after the passage of the Tokelau Islands Act of 1948, there was little consideration of the group's political destiny until the 1960s. New Zealand first suggested that Tokelau form a political union with either Western Samoa or the Cook Islands. Local leaders duly visited both places in 1964, but emphatically rejected the proposal. At the first ever general *fono* later that year, elders from the three atoll communities of Fakaofo, Nukunono, and Atafu stated clearly and unambiguously that they wished to retain the existing relationship with New Zealand. The next New Zealand initiative, a scheme to resettle Tokelauans in New Zealand, was greeted with more enthusiasm. The programme made sense to leaders in Tokelau, who were aware of the pressure that expanding population was beginning to place on the extremely limited resources of the territory. For some New Zealand officials, the novel prospect was that the Tokelau problem might literally disappear if there were no Tokelauans left to be decolonised. This was not to be. The resident population dropped from a peak of 1900 in 1966, when the resettlement scheme began, to about 1600 when it effectively finished in 1971. Population has remained fairly stable since then, with the 1986 census showing a total of 1690 residents.[42]

With Niue's passage to self-government in 1974, Tokelau became New Zealand's last remaining colony. Responsibility for Tokelau was transferred to the Ministry of Foreign Affairs, precipitating further consideration of its future political status. Officials decided to invite the United Nations to become involved, and a fact-finding mission visited the atolls in 1976. It found universal support for continuing as a dependency of New Zealand, and a reluctance to even discuss the idea of eventual self-government.[43] Nevertheless, the next year New Zealand tried to interest Tokelauans in an act of self-determination and proposed 1979 as the target date. The leaders responded negatively. By the time a second United Nations mission visited the territory in June 1981, all parties seemed to accept that a change of status was unlikely to occur in the foreseeable future. Satisfaction with the status quo was reiterated by Special Representative Falani Aukuso in testimony to the small territories subcommittee of the United Nations Committee of Twenty-Four in May 1990.[44]

Statements by New Zealand officials in the 1970s and 1980s consistently recognised the right of Tokelauans to set the pace of their own decolonisation. Yet at the same time New Zealand continued to initiate institutional changes on the assumption that one day Tokelauans would 'choose' self-government. In 1967 a Tokelau public service, firmly based on the New Zealand bureaucratic model, was established and became the principal provider of services and wage employment in the territory. In 1978, when the public service had expanded to about one hundred and fifty positions, New Zealand officials began to promote the idea that it should become the instrument of the *fono* rather than of the New Zealand government. With the establishment of the budget advisory committee in 1979 as a cabinet-like body, the stage was set for a rapid transition to a fully responsible Westminster system of government when the time came. Tokelau inched closer to this goal in 1988, when it formally adopted its own symbols of nationhood—a flag and a national anthem.

Decolonising New Zealand

Although New Zealand was spurred by changing international norms and attitudes to decolonise its Pacific Island territories, there was no immediate pressure to dismantle colonial structures within New Zealand itself. Dispossessed of most of their land in the nineteenth century, Maori tribes remained dominated politically, economically, and culturally by the pakeha (European) majority. Dissident Maori movements had been intermittent and localised, and posed little threat to pakeha hegemony. With no compelling reason to change its paternalistic ways, the Department of Maori Affairs continued to espouse an ideology of 'one people' that envisioned the eventual assimilation of Maori people into the cultural mainstream.[45]

Pressure for change came from Maori movements that became increasingly aware, assertive, and politically mobilised in the decades after World War Two. Dramatic demographic changes provided an important impetus for the post-war Maori resurgence. Not only was the Maori segment of the population growing rapidly, but it was becoming increasingly urbanised. Before World War Two, about 90 per cent of the Maori population lived in rural areas; by 1990, the Maori population had quadrupled to more than 400 000, 75 per cent of whom lived in urban areas.[46] Urbanisation heightened Maori awareness of the unequal distribution of economic and political power in New Zealand and facilitated political mobilisation. Given the significance of land for Maori culture and identity, land issues were the natural catalyst for the Maori mobilisation of the 1970s. The massive land rights protest march from the north of the North Island to Wellington in 1975, the ongoing conflict over the ownership of the Raglan golf course, and the occupation of disputed land at Bastion Point in Auckland between January 1977 and May 1978, were among the events that served to raise Maori political consciousness. Some land grievances concerned the historical alienation of Maori land, while others involved more recent incursions by the state. All drew attention to the state's failure to honour the terms of the Treaty of Waitangi, by which Maori chiefs had ostensibly accepted the sovereignty of the British Crown in 1840 in return for the protection of their property rights and culture.

As Maori dissent gathered strength in the 1980s, highly educated and articulate Maori leaders made the Treaty of Waitangi the focus of their activism. By continually drawing attention to the treaty, groups like the Waitangi Action Committee appealed to an emphasis on legalism and justice in pakeha political ideology. No one was surprised when Mana Motuhake, a political party formed by a disaffected former Minister of Maori Affairs, Matiu Rata, in 1980, made ratification of the treaty one of its central policy objectives.[47]

Focusing on the treaty gave moderate Maori leaders an opportunity to seek redress within pakeha legal and political structures, but it also allowed more radical leaders to denounce as fraudulent the process by which Britain had acquired sovereignty over New Zealand in 1840. In the English language version of the treaty, the purpose of the first article is clearly to transfer sovereignty over New Zealand from the Maori chiefs who signed to the British Crown. However, in the Maori language version the neologism *kawanatanga* is used for 'sovereignty', even though its literal meaning is closer to 'governance'. As Ward has noted, it is likely that the chiefs in 1840 understood this *kawanatanga* to be 'a kind of overarching authority, intended mainly to protect their chieftainships and their lands'.[48] It is highly unlikely that they would have signed the treaty if the full meaning of sovereignty had been represented. For radicals like Donna Awatere, this was a further justification for the full restoration of Maori sovereignty.[49]

By the early 1980s, the movement for Maori self-determination had gained considerable ideological coherence and was fast becoming a force to be reckoned with in New Zealand politics. In the face of competition for voters from Mana Motuhake, the Labour Party committed itself to some fundamental reforms in Maori affairs before the 1984 general election. After being elected, the Labour Party introduced legislation to greatly strengthen the Waitangi Tribunal, a body established in 1975 'to provide for the observance and confirmation of the principles of the Treaty of Waitangi'. By extending the jurisdiction of the tribunal retrospectively to 1840, and making considerable resources available to it, the Treaty of Waitangi Amendment Act 1985 'opened the whole of New Zealand's colonial history to scrutiny, on terms laid down by the Maori'.[50]

Although the tribunal had only recommendatory powers, some of its findings were given the force of judicial precedent by the superior courts. The landmark decision in this respect came in June 1987 when the Court of Appeal found in favor of the Maori Council in a case concerning the State Owned Enterprises Act of 1986. The court noted that Section 9 of the act had invoked the principles of the Treaty of Waitangi, and concluded that this had 'the impact of a constitutional guarantee' within the field covered by the act.[51] The Court of Appeal also argued that the principles of the treaty would have to be defined, since they had been given the full force of law in this and other statutes. In 1989 the government announced a set of five principles by which the state would act 'when dealing with issues that arise from the Treaty of Waitangi'. The principles reflected and formalised recent government practice on such matters, but were greeted with outrage by many Maori leaders.[52]

The first three of these principles arose from the wording of the treaty itself and from the findings of the courts and the Waitangi Tribunal. The *Kawanatanga* Principle (Principle of Government), confirmed that the basis of the treaty was an exchange of sovereignty, which gave the government the right to make laws for protection of *rangatiratanga* (chieftainship). *Rangatiratanga* was defined in the Principle of Self-Management to mean a guarantee to Maori *iwi* (tribes) of 'the control and enjoyment of those resources and *taonga* (possessions) which it is their wish to retain'.[53] The Principle of Equality defined equality in terms of the actual enjoyment of social benefits, as well as equality before the law.

The most significant practical expression of these three principles was the 1988 proposal to radically restructure the mechanisms by which government services were delivered to Maori communities.[54] This involved the devolution of the bulk of the power and resources of the Department of Maori Affairs to a plethora of self-governing *iwi* authorities representing the various tribes.[55] For some, the empowerment of *iwi* authorities represented a genuine attempt to make government more responsive to Maori aspirations and needs. For others, however, it represented an abrogation of the state's responsibility to address Maori grievances and a threat to pan-Maori solidarity.

Although the final two principles identified by the government had been foreshadowed in the pronouncements of the tribunal and the courts, they owed more to political pragmatism than to the substance of the treaty. The Principle of Co-operation suggested that the two communities were united by a sense of common purpose and appealed to them to exercise good faith, reason, and balance in the resolution of issues. Finally, the Principle of Redress imposed a responsibility on the Crown to provide a process for the resolution of grievances. However, the provision of redress 'must take account of its practical impact and the need to avoid the creation of fresh injustice'. These two principles were of crucial importance because they effectively set limits on the social and economic revolution that might result from the full implementation of the Treaty of Waitangi.

The limiting effect of these two principles was clearly demonstrated in the resolution under the Treaty of Waitangi of tribal claims to ownership of the whole of New Zealand's fisheries. These rights were effectively confirmed in 1987 by the Court of Appeal, which ordered the government to reach a settlement with the Maori claimants.[56] After considerable negotiation, the parties agreed to a fifty-fifty split of the disputed fishing quotas, but with the tribes' share being transferred over a twenty-year period. However, the government was forced to retreat from even this position in the face of considerable opposition from the fishing industry and the pakeha electorate. It offered instead 10 per cent of the fisheries, to be transferred over a four-year period, along with an immediate grant of NZ$10 million to develop the Maori commercial fishing industry. The fate of the remaining 90 per cent was deferred, to be fought over in the courts. In this instance, Maori rights under the Treaty of Waitangi were substantially modified by appeals to the Principle of Co-operation and by the pragmatic need to take account of the 'practical impact' of government actions on the entrenched interests of the pakeha majority.

Events since the war, especially since the mid-1980s, have transformed the Maori community into an effective political force, 'awakened, articulate and assertive'.[57] Maori aspirations are no longer seen in terms of concessions to be wrung from a paternalistic and pakeha-dominated state, but in terms of indigenous rights arising, in the first instance, from the Treaty of Waitangi. The struggle is for the systematic dismantling of structures, institutions, and ideologies that have insured the domination of Maori by pakeha since the nineteenth century.

The decolonisation of New Zealand is incomplete. By the time the Labour government lost office in 1990, the initial enthusiasm for its reform efforts had given way to widespread frustration. Few Maori leaders believed that the government's version of the principles of the Treaty of Waitangi would deliver the desired true partnership with the pakeha. More radical leaders saw the principles as yet another cynical attempt to maintain the colonial status quo. If aroused Maori expectations are not realised in the future, alternative visions of a separate Maori nation, or even full Maori sovereignty over Aotearoa, may acquire broader significance and support. Another factor likely to keep the momentum going is the increasing recognition accorded to 'indigenous rights' in international bodies such as the International Labour Organization and various agencies of the United Nations. New Zealand has played an active role in the development of these emerging norms of international law and is likely to take them just as seriously as it did earlier formulations of the principle of self-determination.[58]

Changing Australian priorities in Papua New Guinea

In 1946, Australian Prime Minister J. B. Chifley told parliament that New Guinea was 'of such importance to the safety of this country that nothing but absolute control' could form the basis of the proposed trusteeship agreement with the United Nations.[59] Nevertheless, other terms of the agreement for New Guinea, as well as United Nations provisions applicable to the non-self-governing territory of Papua, ensured that Australia's 'absolute control' of these territories would eventually cease.[60]

The pace and direction of change in Papua New Guinea in the post-war period were profoundly influenced by the philosophy and priorities of Paul Hasluck, minister for territories from 1951 to 1963.[61] Hasluck's policy of 'uniform development' was based on the premise that all Papua New Guineans should benefit equally from development efforts. He committed significant resources to improvements in public health and towards the goal of universal primary education.[62] He also initiated the rapid expansion of administrative control, especially into the great highland valleys, whose large populations had only been 'discovered' in the 1930s.[63] Hasluck's views on economic and political development were extremely conservative. He was determined to avoid the social disruption that might accompany rapid economic development, and encouraged Papua New Guineans to participate in the 'modern' economy, either as small peasant farmers or as contract labourers for expatriate enterprise.[64] He paid almost no attention to secondary education, and actively discouraged the creation of a national political elite.[65] Much effort was devoted to establishing a comprehensive network of local government councils. However, the councils were used mainly to implement administration policy, rather than to encourage Papua New Guineans to assume responsibility for their own affairs.

Under Hasluck, government control was extended over most of the territory. The administration grew enormously in size, was staffed in all but the lowest echelons by Australians, and decision-making was increasingly centralised in Port Moresby and Canberra. The modern economy expanded significantly, but remained firmly under expatriate control. Even at the end of the Hasluck era it was widely assumed (by Australians and Papua New Guineans alike) that Australia would be in Papua New Guinea for many years to come.

By the early 1960s, international and local pressures were making the uniform development approach increasingly difficult to sustain. An important impetus for change came from an escalating dispute over the future of neighbouring West New Guinea, a Dutch colony claimed by the emerging state of Indonesia.[66] The Dutch responded to the Indonesian challenge by embarking on a crash programme to develop West New Guinea to early independence.[67] This activity made it more difficult for Australia to justify its relatively modest efforts in neighbouring Papua New Guinea. More important, the conflict forced Australian officials to re-evaluate their long-held belief that control of New Guinea was vital to the defence of Australia.

Concern over the strategic implications of an Indonesian takeover of West New Guinea led Australia to support the Dutch in the early stages of the dispute. However, Australia had little option but to endorse a transfer of sovereignty when it became clear that Britain and the United States were not prepared to support the Dutch militarily. The diplomatic intervention of the United States resulted in the so-called New York Agreement of 1962, which provided for the transfer of West New Guinea to Indonesia under

United Nations supervision. Strategic considerations remained important in the subsequent debate about the political future of Papua New Guinea, but they no longer dominated it. For the first time, officials were prepared to contemplate independence as an option, if a remote one, for Papua New Guinea.

Pressure for change was also building up at the United Nations. The leader of a visiting mission to Papua New Guinea in 1962, Sir Hugh Foot, warned that Australia was heading for a serious crisis at the United Nations because of its attitude towards decolonisation. The mission's report represented a comprehensive indictment of Hasluck's policy of uniform development and ushered a new era of accelerated development into Papua New Guinea.[68] The defining feature of the new approach was an emphasis on economic growth, especially after the release of the 1964 World Bank report on the territory's resources.[69] The World Bank challenged Hasluck's emphasis on providing equal economic opportunities for all Papua New Guineans, recommending instead that 'expenditures and manpower ... be concentrated in areas and on activities where the prospective return is highest'.[70] The vigorous push for economic development was backed by a greatly increased commitment of Australian resources. During the 1960s, the annual grant more than trebled, reaching nearly A$100 million by 1970.

Foreign individuals and businesses were the primary beneficiaries of the surge in economic activity during this period.[71] Nevertheless, the increased pace of change produced rumblings of discontent in many parts of the territory and precipitated organised protest in places where European activity was especially intense. By 1969 the Tolai people of the Gazelle Peninsula of New Britain, long bothered by land and population pressures, had formed the Mataungan Association to demand more local political and economic control. In the same year, an organisation known as Napidakoe Navitu was established in Bougainville to challenge the administration's programme of land acquisition for the huge copper-mining project at Panguna.

Political awareness among Papua New Guineans was also spurred by a new emphasis on secondary education. More than sixty secondary schools were established during the 1960s, and by 1970 more than twenty thousand secondary students were enrolled.[72] The introduction and expansion of tertiary education was even more impressive.[73] By the end of the 1960s, Papua New Guineans trained in these institutions of higher learning were beginning to make their presence felt in national politics. Nevertheless, the administration continued to downplay political development. Whereas Hasluck had restrained political progress to avoid the creation of an oligarchy, his successor, Charles Barnes, did so to maintain a favourable climate for foreign investment and economic growth. Spontaneous local political or economic self-help movements were discouraged, and authoritarian tactics were employed to deal with the growing dissent on the Gazelle Peninsula and in Bougainville. A representative sixty-four-member House of Assembly was established in 1964, but was effectively dominated by expatriates during its first four-year term.

In 1966 a small group of young, educated Papua New Guineans began to demand early self-government and the next year accused the Australian government of failure 'to prepare us for self-government and to fulfil its obligations as a member of the General Assembly of the United Nations'.[74] The shocked response to such statements, which one senior official described as 'impertinent', indicated that the administration had no intention of accelerating the pace of political change.[75]

Papua New Guinea's future political status was effectively determined in 1966 as the result of a visit to Canberra by members of the Select Committee on Constitutional Development.[76] In his submission to cabinet prior to the visit, Barnes argued that Australia's defence interests would be best served by 'an eventual close association' between the two countries. However, statehood should be ruled out because of the problems associated with allowing 2.5 million Melanesians free access to Australia. Although cabinet rejected his submission by declining to define any specific political goals for Papua New Guinea, individual members of the government made it clear to the visiting delegation that they considered any form of future constitutional association highly unlikely.[77]

After the Canberra meeting, members of the select committee reluctantly concluded that it would be futile to further explore the options of integration or association.[78] They concentrated instead on identifying constitutional changes that would bring Papua New Guinea closer to self-government and eventual independence. Their report was accepted by the administration, and the suggested changes were implemented after the 1968 elections. In the Second House of Assembly, which convened in 1968, the recently formed Pangu Pati, whose members favoured early self-government, organised opposition to the administration, but was usually unable to command a majority. The main impetus for early self-government came from the Labor Party in Australia.

During a well-publicised visit to the territory in late 1969 and early 1970, Leader of the Opposition E. Gough Whitlam announced that a Labor government would grant immediate self-government to Papua New Guinea if it won power in the 1972 election. He argued that the international community would no longer tolerate Australia's colonial presence in Papua New Guinea and that Labor would accelerate the pace of constitutional change regardless of the views of the people of the territory. The Whitlam visit forced the Australian government to take a stand. In July 1970, Prime Minister John Gorton publicly abandoned his party's long-held view that Papua New Guineans should set the pace of change, and advocated independence as soon as practicable. For the first time, there was a bipartisan commitment in Canberra to a speedy end to Australian colonial rule in Papua New Guinea. In 1971, detailed plans were drawn up to transfer all power, except over foreign affairs and defence, to an indigenous government by 1 December 1973.

With Australia's intentions finally clear, the struggle for control of the Third House of Assembly that convened in 1972 took on new significance. By far the largest group in the new 107-member House was the conservative United Party, whose members sought to delay independence until 'backward' areas, especially in the highlands, had had time to 'catch up'. However, the more progressive Pangu Pati, led by Michael Somare, seized the initiative and formed a National Coalition government with support from a number of other parties and individuals.[79]

The coalition included the more radical elements of Papua New Guinea politics, but their views were not widely shared. The major test for radical politics came through the work of the Constitutional Planning Committee appointed by the House of Assembly in June 1972. The all-party committee was dominated by its deputy chairman, Father John Momis, a reformist priest from Bougainville, and John Kaputin, an outspoken representative of the Mataungan Association. For nearly two years the committee listened to expert advice, considered numerous submissions, and consulted people in all parts of the country, before attempting to define a 'home-grown' constitution 'uniquely suited to Papua New Guinean needs'.[80] The committee proposed a set of 'national goals and directive principles' as the ideological underpinnings of the new state. These emphasised national sovereignty, equality, and self-reliance, made a commitment to 'integral human development', and advocated the use of 'Papua New Guinean forms of social, political and economic organization'.

Despite this intensely nationalistic ideology, the institutional structures proposed by the committee displayed few 'home-grown' qualities. It advocated a Westminster form of government that built upon the structures already transplanted from Australia, with some important innovations and modifications. Most important, the committee recommended the establishment of a network of provincial governments that would give Papua New Guinea 'a flexible, participatory and fully decentralised system of government within a unitary state'.[81] If the constitution that the committee proposed was not exactly home grown, it certainly sought to control ongoing foreign influences. It included a foreign investment code to regulate the entry and activities of foreign companies, and a leadership code that limited national leaders' involvements with such companies. It took a strong line on the issue of citizenship, recommending that only those born in Papua New Guinea before independence, and who had at least two indigenous grandparents, would become citizens automatically. Most foreign citizens would become eligible to apply for citizenship only after eight years of post-independence residence in Papua New Guinea. These provisions were explicitly designed to hasten the redistribution of wealth from foreigners, who dominated the modern sector of the economy, to Papua New Guineans.

While the Constitutional Planning Committee was exploring ways of reversing what it called the 'huge tidal wave' of colonialism, Chief Minister Somare was practising more pragmatic politics. The exigencies of coalition-building, the need to appeal to a largely conservative public, the inertia of the expatriate-dominated public service, and the sheer weight of the foreign economic presence, strongly favoured continuity rather than fundamental change. By the time the committee's final report was released in 1974, Somare and the committee were at loggerheads. As ex-officio chairman of the committee, Somare joined forces with veteran politician John Guise to produce a minority report that challenged some of the committee's key proposals. Amid considerable acrimony, members of the committee formed the Nationalist Pressure Group to fight for their version of the constitution in the House of Assembly. In the often-bitter debates that followed, however, the Nationalist Pressure Group was consistently outmanoeuvred by Somare and outvoted by the House.

The constitution that was finally adopted in August 1975 had been stripped of many of its innovative features. Although the national goals and directive principles and the leadership code remained, the foreign investment code was omitted. Provisions for naturalisation remained strict, but the required eight years of residence could now include time spent in Papua New Guinea before independence. The idea of decentralisation received widespread support, but the Constitutional Planning Committee's detailed provisions for provincial government were excluded from the constitution.[82]

If the constitutional debate was about how Papua New Guinea should be governed, there were also some difficult questions about the jurisdiction of the new state. The colonial experience had done little to create a sense of national unity, and imported state institutions sat uneasily on top of a mass of competing local interests and loyalties. In the absence of mechanisms for mass political mobilisation (or coercion), groups throughout the country showed a low level of commitment to national institutions. In some places, such as East New Britain and, to a lesser extent, the Highlands, political movements emerged to protect and promote regional interests within the emerging state. Meanwhile, regional movements in Papua and Bougainville developed secessionist tendencies, and their leaders expressed the desire to break away from Papua New Guinea altogether.[83]

The secessionist movement in Papua was unable to press its demands and had to make do with a symbolic declaration of independence in March 1975.[84] The movement in Bougainville, on the other hand, was able to mount a strong challenge to state authority.[85] Bougainville was culturally and linguistically diverse, but extremely dark skin color gave the people a powerful symbol of identity to distinguish them from the 'redskins' of other parts of Papua New Guinea. Most important, they had on their island the giant Bougainville copper and gold mine that went into production in 1972. The mine had caused considerable disruption among landowning communities in central Bougainville, and generated considerable resentment towards outsiders. It was also an asset that could sustain an independent Bougainville, and one the emerging state of Papua New Guinea could ill afford to lose.

The establishment of the Bougainville Interim District Government in early 1974 temporarily silenced the clamour for independence. The new government was highly effective in operation, but its commitment to national unity was relatively short-lived. On 30 May 1975 the Assembly voted to secede after a dispute with the national government over the size of the capital works budget. The 'Republic of the North Solomons' was declared independent on 1 September 1975 with District Commissioner Alexis Sarei as president. The move was a popular one in Bougainville, and won the support of two of the Bougainvillean members of the national parliament, John Momis and Raphael Bele, as well as the Catholic bishop in Bougainville, Gregory Singkai.

Bougainville's leaders reluctantly abandoned their bid for sovereign independence in August 1976, after failing to attract international recognition. However, they did manage to negotiate a considerable degree of autonomy within Papua New Guinea, to be exercised through the North Solomons Provincial Government. As a direct result of the settlement, the Constitutional Planning Committee's far-reaching recommendations on decentralisation were revived and implemented (in modified form) through the 1977 Organic Law on Provincial Government. The systematic transfer of power initiated by Australia in 1972 continued inexorably despite these debates and upheavals. De facto self-government was achieved in Papua New Guinea some months before the official date of 1 December 1973. Formal independence was delayed by the constitutional debate, which dragged on until August 1975. When independence was finally celebrated on 16 September 1975, Papua New Guinea had been in control of all of its own affairs, including foreign affairs and defence, since the previous March.

Australia's decision to actively withdraw from its northern colonies was prompted by international pressures, which had begun to outweigh long-standing security concerns by the late 1960s. Decolonisation was closely managed by Australia, and Papua New Guineans were not actively involved in the process until very late in the day. When political power was finally thrust on them, leaders opted for continuity rather than radical change. Although Australia no longer exercised direct political control of Papua New Guinea after 1975, it retained considerable influence there. At independence, the economy was still largely controlled by Australian companies, and nearly half of the budget of the Papua New Guinea government was funded by an Australian grant-in-aid.

Self-determination in Nauru

Australia's post–World War Two policy in Nauru was driven by its interest in the island's extensive phosphate deposits. After retaking Nauru from

Japan in 1945, Australia worked hard to maintain the monopoly control of the phosphate industry it shared with New Zealand and Britain under the terms of the Nauru Island Agreement of 1919. It reluctantly conceded the phosphate monopoly in 1967, and control of Nauru itself in 1968, primarily because of pressure from the people of Nauru, supported by the United Nations.[86]

The partner governments submitted a draft trusteeship agreement for Nauru in 1947, despite clear conflicts between the provisions of the Nauru Island Agreement and those of the United Nations Charter.[87] British officials expressed grave doubts about this attempt to reconcile the irreconcilable, but Australian and New Zealand leaders took the view that 'it would be better to have no Trusteeship Agreement at all rather than have the Phosphate Agreement jeopardized in any way'.[88] In Nauru, apparently, the economic stakes were sufficiently high to override questions of principle. The expected challenge to the phosphate monopoly at the United Nations did not eventuate, and the trusteeship agreement was approved with only minor modifications. It was to provide a useful framework for Nauruans when they began to challenge all aspects of colonial dominance in the 1950s and 1960s.

Nauruans provided the main impetus for the decolonisation of Nauru, and by 1965 their major demands were clear. Economic demands were the first to emerge. In 1956, the new Head Chief and Chairman of the Local Government Council, Hammer DeRoburt, argued for the first time that the phosphate resource did not belong to the partners, but to Nauruans, and that compensation was not a matter of goodwill but of right. He proposed that the current system of royalty payment, based on the perceived needs of the community, be replaced by one based on a fair market price for phosphate. The culmination of these efforts was a bid to purchase the phosphate operation from the partner governments a decade later.

Nauruan political aspirations took rather longer to crystallise and were complicated by the issue of resettlement. By the late 1950s, Nauruans had been persuaded that the limited life of the phosphate industry made re-settlement elsewhere inevitable. But they were determined to retain their integrity as a community at any new site, and accordingly rejected plans for relocation to Australia, New Zealand, or Britain. When Australia proposed Curtis Island off the coast of Queensland as the new homeland, the Nauruans demanded full internal self-government there, as well as their own citizenship. In 1964, DeRoburt turned his attention to securing sovereign independence for Nauru itself and abandoned the idea of resettlement altogether. The last major demand was added in 1965, when Nauruans began to actively pursue the rehabilitation of the worked-out land so that their island would be capable of supporting an expanding population.

The trusteeship agreement provided a firm structure for the decolonisation of Nauru to proceed. The various United Nations committees and visiting missions introduced few initiatives of their own, but they offered strong support for Nauruan aspirations.

Each of the partner governments reacted differently to the mounting pressure to decolonise Nauru. Australian officials tried to identify a strategy that would head off demands for full independence, pave the way for termination of the trust, and maintain the phosphate monopoly. New Zealand shared Australia's keen interest in the phosphate monopoly, but was not prepared to lose its hard-won international reputation protecting it. New Zealand advocated an early grant of self-government and some permanent form of association with Australia. But it was prepared to concede full independence and control of the phosphate deposits, if these proved necessary to win United Nations approval for the termination of the trust, and would ensure long-term supplies of phosphate. Britain did not share its partners' overriding interest in cheap supplies of phosphate, but shared their opposition to full independence. In the mid 1960s, it was still concerned about the security implications of granting independence to a state whose population numbered less than three thousand, as well as the precedent this might set for its other small dependencies.

These differences were revealed when the partners failed to agree on an appropriate response to DeRoburt's demand in 1964 for sovereign independence by January 1967. When talks were finally held with the Nauru Local Government Council in June 1965, Australia agreed to the establishment of legislative and executive councils in 1966, but refused to establish a target date for independence. By 1966, the partnership was in further disarray. Acutely aware of their deteriorating situation at the United Nations, New Zealand urged the partners to concede independence and move quickly to terminate the trusteeship. This was still unacceptable to Britain and Australia.

During talks in June 1966, Nauruan negotiators declined the partners' offer of a long-term agreement that would have doubled the Nauruan share of phosphate revenues and spoke confidently of independence in 1968. When Nauru's position received strong support in the Trusteeship Council, with even the United States appearing sympathetic to its demands, the partners had little option but to reconsider their positions. In early 1967, Australia proposed that the partners attempt to trade concessions on the phosphate industry for Nauruan acceptance of a limited form of independence. Britain was generally sympathetic to this approach, but New Zealand had already made it abundantly clear that it was not prepared to defy the United Nations on economic or political issues.

During negotiations with Nauruan leaders in 1967, the partners were forced to concede much more on the phosphate issue than they had planned. In June, they agreed to sell the assets of the British Phosphate Commission to the Nauru Phosphate Corporation for A$21 million over a three-year period. The partners insisted that this was a final settlement and refused to agree to Nauruan demands for an additional A$90 million to rehabilitate mined-out land. Hammer DeRoburt reluctantly agreed to put the matter aside for the moment, but made it quite clear that he considered it unresolved. The partners' hopes that settlement of the phosphate issue would create some room for manoeuvre on the issue of political status were dashed later in 1967. After Nauru rejected an offer of self-government in June, the partners indicated that they might be prepared to concede independence if Australia retained control of foreign affairs and defence under a treaty of friendship. However, with private encouragement from New Zealand, the Nauru delegation stuck to its demand for unqualified independence. This was finally conceded in October 1967, and approved by the Trusteeship Council in November.

After some rapid work by expatriate advisers, most notably Professor J. W. Davidson, a provisional constitution was adopted on 29 January 1968, with a final version in place by May. When Nauru became an independent republic on 31 January 1968, all of the Nauruan demands had been met except the one concerning the rehabilitation of the worked-out land. Their success owed much to the support of the United Nations, and to the disunity of the partners in the phosphate monopoly.

Conclusion

New Zealand's decolonisation policies were acclaimed in the United Nations largely because they were carefully designed to achieve that result. With no compelling strategic or economic interests at stake in Western Samoa, the Cook Islands, Niue, or Tokelau, New Zealand could afford to be flexible and accommodating of local needs. Its attitude towards the decolonisation of phosphate-rich Nauru, on the other hand, was notably less generous, at least initially. The real test of its commitment to the high principles of justice and self-determination for colonised peoples was in New Zealand itself. Here the political and economic costs of decolonisation were much higher, and the process took much longer to get under way.

Australia was less decisive than New Zealand in decolonising its Pacific territories, and attracted more international criticism as a result. Not only were there many more internal obstacles to decolonisation in Papua New Guinea than in any of the New Zealand territories, but Australia had important interests to protect there. Policy makers in Canberra were eager to enhance Australia's international reputation, but they were equally concerned with the strategic implications of decolonising Papua New Guinea and with the economic implications of withdrawing from Nauru.

The effects of Australia's and New Zealand's colonial manoeuvres, if not the manoeuvres themselves, were quite unusual in the history of global decolonisation. In Papua New Guinea, Niue, Tokelau, the Cook Islands, and to a lesser extent Western Samoa, the coloniser rather than the colonised set the pace of change. In all cases except Nauru, the colonial power bestowed a greater degree of political autonomy than the people themselves sought at the time. Political freedom was returned to these colonial peoples in the 1960s and 1970s essentially for the same reason it was removed in an earlier era—to meet the needs of the colonial power.

Notes

1. W. J. Hudson, *Australia and the Colonial Question at the United Nations*, Sydney University Press, 1970; J. Henderson, K. Jackson, and R. Kennaway, eds, *Beyond New Zealand: The Foreign Policy of a Small State*, Methuen, Auckland, 1980.
2. Chapter 11 deals with 'non-self-governing' territories, and Chapter 12 provides for an international trusteeship system.
3. M. Boyd, *New Zealand and Decolonisation in the South Pacific*, New Zealand Institute of International Affairs, Wellington, 1987, 8–17.
4. Tokelau joined the Cook Islands and Niue as 'part of New Zealand' with the passage of the Tokelau Islands Act of 1948 but, because of its extremely small size, was not officially designated a non-self-governing territory until much later.
5. In 1945, Minister for External Affairs H. V. Evatt noted that the people's goodwill must be fostered 'not only because their co-operation is essential to good administration in their own interests, but because they inhabit a vital strategic area'; I. Downs, *The Australian Trusteeship: Papua New Guinea 1945–75*, Government Publishing Service, Canberra, 1980, 5.
6. M. Boyd, 'The Record in Western Samoa to 1945', in *New Zealand's Record in the Pacific Islands in the Twentieth Century*, ed. A. Ross, Longman Paul, Auckland, 1969, 182–187.
7. Paul Hasluck, quoted in J. W. Wootten, 'New Guinea and the Outside World', in *New Guinea: Future Indefinite?* ed. J. Wilkes, Angus & Robertson, Sydney, 1968, 73.
8. I. G. Bertram and R. F. Watters, *New Zealand and Its Small Island Neighbours: A Review of New Zealand Policy toward the Cook Islands, Niue, Tokelau Islands, Kiribati and Tuvalu*, Institute of Policy Studies, Victoria University of Wellington, 1984.
9. This category also includes the peoples of the Torres Strait Islands, which remain part of the Australian state of Queensland, and Norfolk Island, which remains a territory of Australia. See H. Burmester, 'Outposts of Australia in the Pacific Ocean', *Australian Journal of Politics and History* 29 (1983): 14–25.
10. For accounts of the decolonisation of Western Samoa, see, for example, J. W. Davidson, *Samoa mo Samoa: The Emergence of the Independent State of Western Samoa*, Oxford University Press, Melbourne, 1967; Boyd 1969; and Mālama Meleiseā, *The Making of Modern Samoa: Traditional Authority and Colonial Administration in the History of Western Samoa*, Institute of Pacific Studies, University of the South Pacific, Suva, 1987.
11. This was the first such request to the United Nations by a colonial power.

12 This reflected the 'very close consultation' between officials and mission members that had taken place in Samoa and New Zealand; see J. W. Davidson, 'The Transition to Independence: The Example of Western Samoa', *Australian Journal of Politics and History* 7 (1, 1963): 24.

13 The high title-holders of the office of *fautua* (council of advisers) were to be included in the council of state, while the Samoan members of the legislature were to be *matai* (chiefs), elected by their peers.

14 Boyd 1987, 18.

15 Meleiseā, 151–154.

16 Boyd 1969, 226–228.

17 The New Zealand government had set a tentative timetable for self-government late in 1955, restructured the executive council in 1956, and introduced full cabinet government in October 1959.

18 Boyd 1969, 251.

19 However, this provision was not entrenched in the constitution, leaving future parliaments free to alter it.

20 Boyd 1969, 269.

21 For accounts of the decolonisation of the Cook Islands, see, for example, S. D. Wilson 'Cook Islands Development 1946–65', in Ross 1969, 60–114; J. F. Northey 'Self-determination in the Cook Islands', *Journal of the Polynesian Society* 74 (1965): 112–124; David Stone 'Self-government in the Cook Islands 1965', *Journal of Pacific History* 1 (1966): 168–178; Boyd 1987, 23–28; and D. Scott, *The Years of the Pooh-Bahs: A Cook Islands History*, Auckland, 1991.

22 In 1946, the Cook Islands Progressive Association was formed by future premier Albert Henry. In that year, strike action on the Rarotonga waterfront supported the association's demands for higher wages, improved shipping facilities, and representation in the New Zealand parliament. Another round of bitter protest in 1954 was sparked by an attempt to enforce New Zealand income-tax regulations in the islands.

23 H. Belshaw and V. D. Stace, *A Programme for the Economic Development of the Cook Islands*, Department of Island Territories, Wellington, 1955.

24 C. C. Aikman, *First Report on Constitutional Survey of the Cook Islands*, Department of Island Territories, Wellington, 1956; Aikman, *Second Report on Constitutional Survey of the Cook Islands*, Department of Island Territories, Wellington, 1957; discussed in Wilson, 84–86.

25 By 1966, more than 30 per cent of all Cook Islanders lived in New Zealand. Ten years later, more than 50 per cent lived there.

26 L. Gotz, speech to Cook Islands Legislative Assembly, reproduced in *Cook Islands News*, 11 July 1962.

27 C. C. Aikman, 'Constitutional Development in New Zealand's Island Territories and in Western Samoa', in Ross 1969, 337–339.

28 N. P. McKegg and J. F. Northey, *Submission in Respect of the Cook Islands Constitution Bill*, Select Committee on Island Territories, 15 September 1964.

29 For discussions of the constitutional status, see, for example, C. C. Aikman 'Constitutional Developments in the Cook Islands', in *Pacific Constitutions: Proceedings of the Canberra Law Workshop VI*, ed. P. Sack, Law Department, Research School of Social Sciences, Australian National University, Canberra, 1982, 87–96; Bertram and Watters, 31–74.

30 The phrase 'Her Majesty the Queen in Right of New Zealand' simply indicates that the queen referred to is New Zealand's queen.

31 Alex Frame, 'The External Affairs and Defence of the Cook Islands: The "Riddiford Clause" Considered', *Victoria University Law Review* 17 (1987): 141–151. Frame reviews Professor Quentin-Baxter's important unpublished 1969 analysis, in which he argued emphatically that New Zealand retained no legislative or executive powers over the Cook Islands. At that time, the New Zealand Crown Law Office was arguing that New Zealand could resolve an impasse in negotiations with the Cook Islands over civil aviation matters, specifically landing rights, by using a presumed ultimate power under Section 5.

32 However, it was not allowed to accede to the Lomé Convention on the grounds that it was not an independent state. Aikman 1982, 93–94.

33 Constitution Amendment Act 1980–81 (no. 9) and Constitution Amendment Act 1981–82 (no. 10), Government Printer, Rarotonga.

34 Bertram and Watters, 60–63.

35 For accounts of the decolonisation of Niue, see, for example, T. M. Chapman, *The Decolonisation of Niue*, Victoria University Press, Wellington, 1976; Aikman 1969; Boyd 1987, 23-28; and Bertram and Watters, 31–74.

36 C. C. Aikman and J. M. McEwen, *A Report to the Minister of Island Territories on the Constitutional Development of Niue*, Department of Island Territories, Wellington, 1965; discussed in Chapman, 21–25.

37 Chapman, 41.

38 A referendum was held on 3 September 1974, and 64 per cent voted in favour of self-government in free association with New Zealand (Chapman, 73).

39 The population of Niue was about 4000 in 1974, but by October 1987 it had dropped to 2414 (S. Levine, 'Niue', *The Contemporary Pacific* 2 [1990]: 173–175).

40 S. Levine, 'Niue', *The Contemporary Pacific* 4 (1992): 203.

41 Sources on the decolonisation of Tokelau include Aikman 1969, 316–318; Bertram and Watters, 31–74; Antony Hooper, *Aid and Dependency in a Small Pacific Territory*, University of Auckland, 1968; Antony Hooper, 'Tokelau, New Zealand, and the United Nations, 1948–1986', in *Migration and Health in a Small Society: The Case of Tokelau*, ed. Albert F. Wessen, Clarendon Press, Oxford and Oxford University Press, New York, 1992, 77–86.

42 Hooper 1992, 81–83. Bertram and Watters, 212; S. Levine, 'Tokelau', *The Contemporary Pacific* 2 (1990): 175–176.

43 Hooper 1992, 85.

44 Aukuso told the committee that the relationship with New Zealand 'feels right and we wish [it] to continue' (S. Levine, 'Tokelau', *The Contemporary Pacific* 3 [1991]: 207).

45 Recent works on Maori issues include Ranginui Walker, *Ka Whawhai Tonu Matou: Struggle Without End*, Penguin Books, Auckland, 1990; Claudia Orange, *The Treaty of Waitangi*, Allen & Unwin, Wellington, 1987; J. Kelsey, *A Question of Honour: Labour and the Treaty, 1984–1989*, Allen & Unwin, Wellington, 1990; and R. Vasil, *What Do Maori Want? New Maori Political Perspectives*, Random Century, Auckland, 1990.

46 Population figures refer to those with some Maori ancestry who identify themselves as Maori.

47 Walker, 227–229.

48 Alan Ward, 'Interpreting the Treaty of Waitangi: The Maori Resurgence and Race Relations in New Zealand', *The Contemporary Pacific* 3 (1991): 91.

49 Donna Awatere, 'Maori sovereignty', *Broadsheet*, Auckland, 1984.

50 Ward, 98, 100.

51 The purpose of the act was to 'privatise' certain state activities. The council was concerned that disputed crown lands could pass into private ownership under the terms of the act before Maori claims on them had been settled (Walker, 263–265).

52 'The Crown and the Treaty of Waitangi: A Short Statement of the Principles on Which the Crown Proposes to Act,' Department of Justice, Wellington, 1989 (reproduced in Vasil, 146–149).

53 *Taonga* were defined to include 'language and other cultural treasures'.

54 'Partnership Response', policy statement, Government of New Zealand, November 1988 (reproduced in Vasil, 150–162).

55 Since that time the department has been abolished altogether and replaced by a 'policy-forming' ministry.

56 The Maori Council and others had challenged the government's right to issue transferable fishing quotas to individuals and companies under a new fisheries management system. The quotas were worth some NZ$50 million a year (Ward, 105).

57 Vasil, 141.

58 S. J. Anaya, 'Indigenous Rights Norms in Contemporary International Law,' *Arizona Journal of International and Comparative Law*, 8 (2, 1991): 1–22.

59 W. J. Hudson, *Australia and Papua New Guinea*, Sydney University Press, 1974, 7.

60 For material on the decolonisation of Papua New Guinea, see, for example, Downs 1980; J. Griffin, H. Nelson and S. Firth, eds, *Papua New Guinea: A Political History*, Heinemann Educational, Richmond, VIC, 1979; D. Woolford, *Papua New Guinea: Initiation and Independence*, University of Queensland Press, Brisbane, 1976; and the political chronicles published periodically in the *Australian Journal of Politics and History*. The name Papua New Guinea is used throughout this section although the two colonial entities retained separate legal identities until self-government in 1973.

61 See P. Hasluck, *A Time for Building: Australian Administration in Papua and New Guinea 1951–1963*, Melbourne University Press, Clayton, VIC, 1976.

62 The number of government schools expanded rapidly, but enrollments in mission and government primary schools totalled less than 160 000 in the mid-1950s (Hasluck, 94–95).

63 In the five years to 1956, some 400 000 people, representing about one quarter of the estimated total population, were 'contacted' and subjected to government influence for the first time (Hasluck, 79).

64 Peasant production was meant to supplement, rather than displace, subsistence activities, and to use existing socio-economic relationships and institutions. Hasluck insisted that native labor policy should have as its central aims 'the preservation of the village and the continued attachment of natives to their villages' (161).

65 As late as 1962, less than 300 Papua New Guineans were receiving post-primary education.

66 See, for example, W. Henderson, *West New Guinea: The Dispute and Its Settlement*, Seton Hall University Press, South Orange, NJ, 1977.

67 A representative territorial assembly began operating in 1961.

68 United Nations Trusteeship Council, *Report of the United Nations Visiting Mission to the Trust Territory of New Guinea 1962*, United Nations, New York, 1962. For a discussion of the so-called Foot Report, see Downs, 239–251.

69 International Bank for Reconstruction and Development. *The Economic Development of the Territory of Papua and New Guinea*, Johns Hopkins University Press, Baltimore, MD, 1965.

70 The idea of 'building on the best' was embraced enthusiastically by Hasluck's successor as minister, Charles Barnes, and formed the basis of the administration's first five-year development plan introduced in 1968.

71 The expatriate population rose from 23 870 in 1960 to 48 960 in 1970 (Downs, 319). The number of Papua New Guineans producing crops for export increased dramatically, especially in the Highlands, but the vast majority continued to depend on subsistence systems for most of their material needs. The urban economy remained firmly under expatriate control.

72 Downs, 403.

73 By 1970 tertiary education was being provided by the University of Papua New Guinea and the Administrative College in Port Moresby, the University of Technology in Lae, and Goroka Teachers' College. More than seventy other technical and vocational institutions were operating.

74 Downs, 386.

75 Griffin, Nelson and Firth, 134.

76 The committee had been appointed by the House of Assembly in 1965.

77 Downs, 362–375.

78 These options would probably have won considerable support from Papua New Guineans.

79 Pangu was joined by the People's Progress Party, the Mataungan Association, Napidakoe Navitu, the New Guinea National Party, and a number of independents.

80 Constitutional Planning Committee, *Final Report*, Government Printer, Waigani, 1974, 1–2.

81 Other significant proposals were that there be no head of state and that permanent parliamentary committees be established to curb executive power.

82 The provisions for powerful parliamentary committees were also omitted. The Queen was installed as head of state, to be represented in Papua New Guinea by a governor-general.

83 See R. R. Premdas, 'Secessionist Politics in Papua New Guinea', *Pacific Affairs* 50 (1977): 64–85; R. J. May, ed., *Micronationalist Movements in Papua New Guinea*, Research School of Pacific Studies, Australian National University, Canberra, 1982.

84 See R. R. Premdas, 'Secession and Political Change: The Case of Papua Besena,' *Oceania* 47 (1977): 265–283.

85 See, for example, A. Mamak and R. D. Bedford, *Bougainville Nationalism: Aspects of Unity and Discord*, University of Canterbury, Christchurch, 1974; Leo Hannett, 'The Case for Bougainville Secession', *Meanjin Quarterly* 34 (1975):

286–293; and R. R. Premdas, 'Ethnonationalism, Copper, and Secession on Bougainville,' *Canadian Review of Studies in Nationalism* 4 (1977): 247–265.

86 Accounts of the decolonisation of Nauru include Barrie Macdonald, *In Pursuit of the Sacred Trust: Trusteeship and Independence in Nauru*, New Zealand Institute of International Affairs, Wellington, 1988; N. Viviani, *Nauru: Phosphate and Political Progress*, Australian National University Press, Canberra, 1970; and J. W. Davidson, 'The Republic of Nauru', *Journal of Pacific History* 3 (1968): 145–150.

87 The partners were aware that difficult questions could be raised about the apparent subordination of indigenous economic interests and about the obligation under Article 76d of the Charter to establish an 'open door' trade policy.

88 Prime Ministers Evatt and Fraser, quoted in Macdonald, 27.

United States

Robert C. Kiste

At the close of World War Two in 1945, the United States had three island territories all of which had been acquired around the turn of the century. American rule was never challenged in American Samoa and Hawai'i during the war, but Guam had fallen to the Japanese immediately after Japan's attack on Pearl Harbor and was recaptured by the United States in 1944. A fourth territory soon came under American control. During the war, America had seized the bulk of Micronesia, an area administered by Japan as a League of Nations mandated territory between the two world wars. In 1947, it became the US Trust Territory of the Pacific Islands, within the framework of the United Nations.

Beginning with the acquisition of its first possessions in the region, American involvement in the Pacific Islands has predominantly been motivated by strategic and security concerns. Both American Samoa and Guam were coveted by the US Navy as strategically located coaling stations in the south and far western Pacific, and while economic concerns (particularly the sugar industry) were involved, the strategic value of Pearl Harbor figured into American calculations.

The nature of American interests was quite clear in the immediate postwar years. In reference to Guam and the rest of the Mariana Islands, one naval officer reflected: 'Military control of these islands is essential as their military value far outweighs their economic value. The economic development and administration of relatively few native inhabitants should be subordinate to the real purpose for which these islands are held'.[1]

American perceptions of strategic necessity were essentially those of the Western world. The experience of World War Two had convinced the American and European metropolitan powers that ruled the islands that any intervention by potentially hostile powers could not be tolerated. Because the primary concern was with the Soviet bloc and Communist regimes in Asia, 'strategic denial' became the cornerstone of a Western policy. There was no acceptable alternative.

Traditional leaders embrace symbols of foreign authority: Chief Agrifaru of Pique Island, Faraulap Atoll, with American Flag. Photograph from US Navy Rear Admiral Wright's inspection trip to Caroline Islands, 1946. (Trust Territory Archives, Pacific Collection, University of Hawai'i Library)

Strategic concerns have been paramount for the United States, but other perceptions and sentiments have also influenced American behaviour in the region. First, most Americans have never understood that their nation has been a colonial power, and that misunderstanding in conjunction with a strong ideological commitment to democracy led to ambivalence and inconsistency in America's involvement in the region. Second, and beginning with the early days of American involvement in the Pacific, many islanders have seen advantages to their affiliation with the United States and have had no desire to sever it. To the contrary, some have opted for a closer relationship. Third, apparently for reasons of inertia, preservation of turf, and perhaps indecisiveness, the Congress and federal bureaucracies have been reluctant to let go of their island territories.

Also of importance, certain myths about their own nation are deeply ingrained in the psyche of the American people and have obscured their understanding of their nation's role in both the Pacific and the larger world.

If colonialism is defined as 'control by one power over a dependent area or people',[2] the United States has undeniably been a colonial power. However, most Americans firmly believe the opposite. At least until recent times, the collective consciousness of most Americans, influenced by textbook accounts of their own war of independence, held that their nation had only fought in defence of freedom and democracy. Colonialism is an evil committed by others, and the notion that America also has a colonial record is usually met with strong denial.

The American inability to see itself as a colonial power had significant consequences. The United States never saw a need to create a colonial service, train administrators to work abroad, or develop an explicit colonial policy. From the American point of view, decolonisation was the business of others, and the United States did not anticipate the need to prepare for the process that formally began when Western Samoa achieved independence in 1962.

The US Trust Territory of the Pacific Islands

The immediate problem for the United States at the end of the war was Micronesia. Initially, the navy administered the islands while their future was debated in Washington, DC. The Department of War (later Defense) and a good portion of Congress demanded annexation. The 'blood on the sands' argument was popular: American casualties in the islands had been large, and thus they rightfully belonged to the United States. More sensitive to international opinion of the time, the US Department of State realised that the era of colonial expansion was over, and the acquisition of new possessions was no longer respectable. Reflecting the American myth, the Secretary of War argued that acquiring Micronesia would not be an act of colonialism. Rather, the islands were necessary for the defence of the free world, and 'To serve such a purpose they must belong to the United States with absolute power to rule and fortify them. They are not colonies; they are outposts.'[3]

The UN trusteeship system provided a compromise. In 1947 the islands became a 'strategic' trust territory, the only strategic trust of the eleven trusteeships created by the United Nations. Under the terms of the arrangement, the area could be used as the United States considered necessary for defence. The Department of War had won the day. Although the United States was given the responsibility for the administration of the islands, it had not added to the number of its outright possessions in the Pacific. The strategic trust was unique, but it was not unlike the other ten trusteeships; under Article 76 of the UN Charter, as the administering authority, the United States was pledged 'to promote the political, economic, social, and educational advancement of the inhabitants of the trust territories, and their progressive development towards self-government or independence as may be appropriate to the particular circumstances of each territory and its peoples and the freely expressed wishes of the peoples concerned'.

For administrative purposes, the trust territory was initially divided into six, and later seven, administrative districts. Beginning in the east and moving west, the districts were: the Marshall Islands, Kosrae (formerly Kusaie), Pohnpei (formerly Ponape), Chuuk (formerly Truk), the Northern Marianas, Yap, and Belau (formerly Palau).

The trusteeship arrangement did not end interdepartmental squabbles in Washington, DC. The turf battles that followed also included American Samoa and Guam, but the focus was on the trust territory as the Departments of Interior, State, and War each manoeuvred to gain control. The matter was ended when President Truman decided in favour of Interior in 1951.

The initial phase of American rule in Micronesia is often referred to as an era of 'benign neglect' in which the United States governed the islands as an 'ethnographic zoo'.[4] In reality and except for strategic concerns, there was no overall policy. There is no evidence of any real concern for the preservation of indigenous cultures (which in any event had been radically altered by three previous colonial regimes), and decisions were made in far distant Washington, where little knowledge about or interest in the islands existed. For security reasons, there was a stringent policy of 'strategic denial', a fact the ethnographic zoo theorists conveniently advance in support of their theory. Entry to the islands was restricted, and the relatively few Americans who gained access were required to have security clearances. Those admitted were mainly administrators, researchers (mostly anthropologists), and members of the defence community.

Two parts of the trust territory were of primary strategic concern. In the north-east, the Marshallese atolls of Bikini and Enewetak were used as nuclear test sites between 1946 and 1956. With tragic consequences, the inhabitants of both were relocated to make way for nuclear testing.[5] Also in the Marshall Islands, Kwajalein Atoll was a logistical base for the nuclear programme; it later became an important ballistic-missile test site and is now a part of the Strategic Defense Initiative (Star Wars) programme. In the north-west, beginning in the early 1950s and continuing for approximately a decade, the northern Marianas (with the exception of Rota) were returned to navy rule, and the largest island, Saipan, was used by the Central Intelligence Agency to train Nationalist Chinese troops.[6]

Elsewhere, the territory was on a caretaker status. For the most part, areas devastated by the war were left without rehabilitation. No plans were made for the long-range future of the territory. No substantive programmes for economic development were initiated. Financial support for the territory was meagre, with an annual budget ceiling of US$7.5 million, a sum that barely kept the administrative apparatus afloat. Americans occupied all important administrative positions. The high commissioner, the territory's chief executive, was appointed by the president and, in turn, he appointed the head administrators for the several districts. Some rudimentary initiatives were taken in the political arena. Elected district legislatures were introduced, but only as advisory bodies.[7]

The early 1960s ushered in a new phase of the US trusteeship of Micronesia. In 1961, a report of a UN visiting mission offered damning criticism of the American administration. In its view, development in education, health, and the economic and political arenas had been inadequate. President John F. Kennedy ordered immediate action, launching what would eventually become massive budget increases and a vast array of federal programmes. Within two years, the territory's budget was doubled, and by the mid-1980s, annual appropriations exceeded US$115 million with approximately another US$35 million for federal programmes. The sums were without parallel for an island territory with a population of less than 160 000.[8]

In 1962, Kennedy appointed an investigative commission headed by economist Anthony Solomon. The commission assumed that the US Trust Territory of the Pacific Islands had to remain closely tied to the United States, and its report appeared within a year. It advised that if Micronesians were to be persuaded to stay within the American sphere of influence, substantial improvements were mandatory. The Solomon Report recommended increased efforts in economic development, with an emphasis on agriculture, improvements in education and health, and an ambitious capital improvement programme to upgrade the territory's entire infrastructure.

Trust territory administrators welcomed the report as a long overdue plan of action. However, recommendations on the territory's future political status were classified, and critics of the American administration charged that the Solomon Report was nothing less than a plan to manipulate Micronesians into a permanent relationship with the United States.[9] In reality, the report was of little consequence. After Kennedy's assassination, it was shelved; the administration of Lyndon B. Johnson was intent on setting its own agenda and attention was focused elsewhere. The United States soon became more deeply involved in Vietnam, and Johnson's efforts to create the 'Great Society' were launched.[10]

What had begun under Kennedy escalated during the Johnson years, and in a very real sense, events in the trust territory ran amok. In 1966, a large contingent of Peace Corps volunteers was sent there. Well-intentioned but poorly informed members of the US Congress amended social legislation to make overseas territories eligible for welfare measures originally designed for the American poor and disadvantaged. By the late 1970s, 166 separate but uncoordinated programmes were operating in the territory. Many were inappropriate for small subsistence-based island societies, including such measures as large-scale food subsidies for the impoverished (with a subsistence economy, most islanders were below the cash income level that defined the American poor); a variety of assistance programmes for the elderly (in societies that traditionally honoured and provided for the aged); and employment training and other programmes mostly designed for urban America.

The programmes were culturally and socially destructive, and along with the enormous territorial budget, Micronesians became heavily dependent on the United States. An American-style education system became the largest industry in the trust territory. A large number of expatriates were involved, creating a huge bureaucracy that became the largest employer of Micronesians. Almost everywhere, islanders flocked to the administrative centers of the territory's seven districts with the hope of obtaining education, employment, or other supposed benefits of the federal programmes. A massive welfare state was created.[11]

Other developments beginning in the 1960s have also had far-reaching consequences. The several district legislatures gained law-making capacities, and Micronesians evidenced a clear liking for self-determination. In 1965, the Congress of Micronesia was established and within two years had created a political status commission. It examined political arrangements elsewhere in the Pacific and the Caribbean, and four options for the future were considered: free association, independence, integration with the United States, and the status quo. The commission recommended the first of the four, an option suggested by the arrangement created between the Cook Islands and New Zealand in 1965. Negotiations with the United States began in 1969. America rejected free association and proposed commonwealth status (integration with the United States). So began a stalemate that would last more than a decade.

At the outset, it was assumed that the districts of the trust territory would have a common political future. However, the territory was a political entity only as an artefact of colonial history; it was an externally created amalgamation of at least a half-dozen cultural groupings with eleven separate languages (thirteen, some linguists claim). Additionally, the various parts of Micronesia had vastly different colonial histories.[12]

When negotiations became prolonged, any hope of achieving a Micronesian unity failed. The Chamorro (a term denoting both the language and people of the Marianas) people of the Northern Marianas and Guam had had the longest colonial history of all Pacific Islanders, and consequently were the most Westernised of all Micronesians and certain of their own superiority. Further, during the Central Intelligence Agency's use of Saipan in the 1950s, the Chamorros of the Northern Marianas enjoyed employment and had greater contact with Americans than did other Micronesians. Their goal was a permanent union with the United States; they wanted and were granted separate negotiations.

During the early 1970s, the United States relented and agreed to consider the option of free association for the rest of the trust territory. In 1972, momentum for further fragmentation occurred when the Department of Defense made known its desire to retain rights in Belau, the Marshall Islands,

Palauan traditional leaders in Saipan at High Commissioner Johnston's conference room, 1973. (Trust Territory Archives, Pacific Collection, University of Hawai'i Library)

and the Northern Marianas. As before, American concerns were focused in the eastern and western portions of the territory, and the strategic interest in the three districts increased their bargaining power. The position of the Northern Marianas was enhanced, and both Belau and the Marshalls advanced their own demands for separate negotiations.[13]

As a consequence, the trust territory became partitioned into the 'haves' and 'have nots'. Belau, the Marshalls, and the Northern Marianas had special strategic value to the United States, but the other four districts, Kosrae, Pohnpei, Chuuk, and Yap, were of less concern. Some separatist sentiments for further fragmentation surfaced among the 'have nots', but the United States had achieved its purposes and refused to enlarge the number of negotiating parties. The 'have nots' had no alternative but to remain together, and they eventually became the four states of the Federated States of Micronesia. In 1975, the Northern Marianas voted overwhelmingly in favour of a covenant to become the Commonwealth of the Northern Mariana Islands. The following year, the treaty was ratified by the US Congress, and President Gerald Ford gave executive approval. The Chamorros of the Northern Marianas thereby became American citizens, and their islands were integrated with the United States.

In 1979, the Republic of the Marshall Islands and the Federated States of Micronesia formed constitutional governments, and two years later the

Republic of Belau followed suit. In the process, the three acquired major responsibilities for internal self-government, and each was negotiating a Compact of Free Association. (The three compacts are much the same, but each has a set of subsidiary agreements concerned with the particulars of its own case.)

The compacts are long, legalistic, and complex documents, and they have been analysed at some length elsewhere. [14] Essentially, they define an arrangement in which the island nations grant the United States strategic prerogatives in exchange for financial subsidies and certain federal services. With free association, the islanders are citizens of their respective freely associated states, but they are also 'habitual residents' of the United States, a status allowing them to enter and work there without visas or work permits. They are not, however, American citizens.

The freely associated governments have authority over their internal and foreign affairs except as they might interfere with American strategic requirements. The prerogatives of the United States are carefully defined, and in the last analysis, the United States has the final authority to determine what does or does not constitute a matter of defence. Essentially, the United States may act with respect to its own strategic interests, but at the same time it has the responsibility for the defence of the freely associated states. The United States retains the right of strategic denial (prohibiting the presence of third-party nations). Potentially, the compact provisions give the United States considerable latitude in its activities in and relationships with the island nations.

Among the federal services guaranteed under the compacts are the weather service, aviation agencies, international postal service, disaster relief, and access to certain other assistance programmes. Some of the agencies involved have regulatory as well as service functions and provide for continuation of the American presence and influence in the islands. For disaster relief, the freely associated states are treated as equal to the fifty states of the Union.

For the Federated States of Micronesia and the Republic of the Marshall Islands, the compacts have a duration of fifteen years, after which they may be renegotiated. In the case of Belau, the term of agreement is fifty years. The financial subsidies and support services provided under the compacts are without parallel in other Pacific nations. However, because the costs of the services rendered by US agencies cannot be precisely calculated, it is not possible to determine the true magnitude of the overall economic package. The figure commonly quoted for the Federated States of Micronesia and the Republic of the Marshall Islands is US$2.5 billion; for Belau, US$1 billion. [15]

In 1983, Micronesians voted on the compacts. In each of the three areas, a majority of voters favoured the new political arrangement. In the Federated States of Micronesia and the Marshall Islands, the legislative and executive branches of government quickly approved, and the US Congress followed in 1985. In the following year, President Ronald Reagan signed the legisla-

'Vote No' parade at the time of the Micronesian constitutional referendum in Palau, 1978. (Trust Territory Archives, Pacific Collection, University of Hawai'i Library)

tion and decreed that the compacts were in effect. Belau's history has been quite different. Although the passage of the compact requires only a simple majority, it is incompatible with the constitution of Belau. The compact would allow the presence of nuclear weapons in a case of military emergency. However, Belau's constitution prohibits all nuclear and toxic materials without 'the express approval of three-fourths of the votes cast in a referendum submitted on this specific question'.[16] Including the initial vote in 1983, Belauans have gone to the polls seven times, and the results have been consistent. The compact has always been approved by a majority of voters, but not the required 75 per cent. The Belauans could alter their constitution, but this too would require the apparently unachievable three-quarters majority. The Republic of Belau remains in limbo, the last remnant of the trust territory.[17]

The new political entities

The new political entities that have emerged from the US Trust Territory of the Pacific Islands are attempting to cope with a number of internal and external circumstances. Internally, urbanisation, growing populations, and economic development are primary concerns. Externally, the new entities are exploring the ramifications of their new political statuses on the international scene.

The urbanisation that began in the 1960s has continued. Today, two-thirds of all Micronesians live in urban centres, and they are among the most urbanised of all Pacific Islanders. Like many other urban areas in the Third World, most in Micronesia lack the infrastructure necessary to provide for their populations. Water, sewage, and electrical systems cannot meet demands and often fail. Adequate housing is in scarce supply. Overcrowding and a shortage of recreational outlets are common. Health systems leave much to be desired, and preventive medicine is largely absent. A reliance on imported foods has resulted in dietary disorders and malnutrition among the young. The Marshall Islands may be the most extreme case. Imports account for over 90 per cent of the food supply, and in 1991 the nation's president reported that two-thirds of Marshallese children suffer from malnutrition.[18]

The movement to urban centres has created major demographic dislocations. In the Federated States of Micronesia and the Marshalls, and to a lesser extent in Belau, communities are widely scattered on islands far distant from one another and the urban centres. The appeals of the urban life have attracted a disproportionate number of working-age adults and youth of secondary-school age. A correspondingly large number of older people and young children are left at home in communities severely depleted of their productive work forces. Life in urban areas has also contributed to a loss of traditional skills, and many younger islanders could no longer sustain their existence in a subsistence economy.

Urbanisation, wage labour, Western education, and the incongruities between federal programmes and traditional cultures have all served to undermine traditional forms of social control. The importance of extended kin groupings has declined, and traditional leaders have lost much of their authority. Teenage delinquency and alcohol abuse are common facts of urban life. Suicide rates for young Micronesian males are among the highest in the world. Rapid increases in population also pose a serious problem for the near future. The number of Micronesians has increased more than three-fold since World War Two, and in some instances, such as the Marshalls, the population has quadrupled.[19] Family planning is virtually non-existent. Employment opportunities are far short of the number of school graduates or dropouts, and unemployment contributes further to problems of delinquency and substance abuse.

At the same time, aspirations are higher than at any time in the past. Modern communications, movies, in some cases television, the ubiquitous videos, and Western education have all created desires for a more affluent and Western life-style. The discontent of youth may be expected to continue, and as population pressures continue to grow in the face of limited opportunities, greater numbers of Micronesians will take advantage of their right to migrate to the United States or its territories. Already, there is a steady flow of citizens from the Federated States of Micronesia, particularly Chuuk, to Guam.

Although Belau remains in limbo, the Federated States of Micronesia and the Republic of the Marshall Islands are in the process of attempting to secure their status as sovereign independent states in the international community. The path has not been easy. The political arrangement of free association is not widely understood, and complications have plagued the termination of the trust territory. The other ten UN trusteeships were ended with the sanction of the UN Trusteeship Council. In the same year that President Reagan decreed that the Compacts of Free Association had simply been implemented, the council also gave its approval.

As noted, the US Trust Territory of the Pacific Islands was unique among the post-war arrangements as the only 'strategic trust'. Article 83 of the UN Charter indicates that all functions of the United Nations relating to strategic areas, 'including the approval of the terms of the trusteeship agreements and of their alteration or amendment, shall be exercised by the Security Council'. Because of concern over the provision of the UN Charter and a fear of a Soviet veto, the United States declined to seek the approval of the Security Council. As a result, some international opinion held that the trusteeship had not been terminated. As a counter argument, the United States maintained that there was no precedent for the ending of a strategic trust. Further, the United States asserted that it and the two Micronesian states were alone entitled to terminate the trusteeship, in terms mutually agreeable to themselves.

Disregarding such arguments and using behind-the-scenes diplomacy, the United States and the Micronesian states gained a commitment from the Soviet Union not to exercise its veto power. The termination of the trust territory, except for Belau, was taken to the Security Council in late 1990. Reflecting both the radical changes within the Soviet Union and its new stance in global affairs, the Soviet representative to the Security Council opined that the Micronesians have 'freely exercised their right of self-determination', and approval was achieved on 11 December 1990.[20] According to one observer, the Americans and Soviets had decided to 'clear away the underbrush of the Cold War'.[21] A more important development soon followed. On 17 September 1991, the Federated States of Micronesia and the Republic of the Marshall Islands were admitted to the United Nations along with North and South Korea and the Baltic states of Estonia, Latvia, and Lithuania, an event that 'would have been unthinkable at the height of the Cold War'.[22]

The Federated States of Micronesia and the Marshall Islands have had considerable success in achieving international recognition. Despite some initial hesitancy, the South Pacific Forum recognised both as self-governing states and invited them to membership in 1987, and another dozen or so countries, including Japan, have accorded diplomatic recognition. The United

States has embassies with resident ambassadors in both nations, and in turn, they have embassies and resident ambassadors in Washington, DC. The position of all three parties is that both nations are independent and sovereign states.

The matter remains somewhat less than clear-cut, however. Some observers question whether the status of the Micronesian states has been compromised by the strategic provisions of the Compacts of Free Association. An opinion sometimes heard in Washington is that the two freely associated states are sovereign but not independent, and not all Micronesians are certain that they have achieved either status. One line of reasoning is that the Micronesians exercised their sovereignty in deciding to relinquish independence in certain areas (those pertaining to the strategic interests of the United States) in exchange for the large financial packages and the provision of federal services. Looking at Belau, one may wonder what alternative they really had. Because it has been unwilling to accommodate American strategic interests, the small country of less than 20 000 people remains the last trust territory in the world.

Since achieving commonwealth status, the Northern Marianas has proceeded on its own course and is experiencing an economic boom that is a somewhat mixed blessing. Saipan is the primary destination of a burgeoning tourist industry that began in the late 1970s and early 1980s. The vast majority of visitors are Japanese, and by the late 1980s, the annual visitor count was approaching one-quarter of a million. The tourist industry has created a construction boom, fuelled wild land-speculation schemes, and been largely responsible for the importation of several thousand workers, primarily Filipino. The primary investors in the tourist industry are Japanese, and Nevada gambling operations have shown an interest in extending their operations to the Northern Marianas. In addition, a thriving garment-manufacturing industry developed during the 1980s, bringing thousands of workers from South Korea, Taiwan, and Sri Lanka, as well as the Philippines and other South-East Asian nations. The indigenous Chamorro population of about 18 000 is being overwhelmed by the massive influx of outsiders. The total population of the commonwealth has exploded to about 50 000 people in the last decade, 80 per cent of whom reside on Saipan. Understandably, tensions exist between local residents and the hordes of outsiders, and the Chamorro people are fearful, and very much in danger, of losing control over their own affairs.[23]

Given the nature of the economy, the people of the Northern Marianas are primarily urban, and the majority of the work force is employed by the tourist industry, other business enterprises, and local government. Economically, the commonwealth could stand on its own, but nonetheless it receives substantial sums from the United States. Covenant funds amount to about US$30 million per year, and another US$15 million is available through federal programmes. With commonwealth status, the Northern

Marianas received considerable local autonomy, retains funds derived from federal income-tax legislation, and controls immigration. Citizens of the commonwealth elect their own governor, and their bicameral legislature is derived from the trust territory era. Other American political forms have been adopted, including local Democrat and Republican party organisations.

While eagerly sought, commonwealth status has not been without disappointments. The feeling is widespread that the federal government is 'colonialist in its basic mentality to the Commonwealth,' insensitive to island needs, inflexible, too interfering, and 'insists that the Commonwealth is nothing more than another territory'.[24] In contrast to the freely associated states, the Commonwealth of the Northern Mariana Islands is part of the United States, and consequently has only belatedly realised that it does not have the same rights and privileges as the Federated States of Micronesia and the Republic of the Marshall Islands. The United States and not the commonwealth controls the two-hundred-mile exclusive economic zone surrounding the island chain (see map 2). The commonwealth would like to have its own relations with other governments, particularly those within the Pacific region, but like the fifty states of the union and the American territories, it cannot conduct its own foreign affairs. In addition to resentment over issues of autonomy, there is also some envy of the financial subsidies to the freely associated states. The question of precisely who is eligible for American citizenship has arisen. Other grievances fester, and there is a growing sentiment that the Covenant of Commonwealth should be renegotiated. The deed has been done, however. The commonwealth is part of the United States, and the US Congress is under no obligation whatsoever to re-examine the matter.

Guam

Guam, the southernmost of the Mariana Islands, is the largest island in the northern Pacific, and its location has given it strategic value since the beginning of European times. After more than two hundred years of Spanish colonial rule, it was acquired by the United States in 1898 and has remained an American possession ever since. Although large in terms of the northern Pacific, it is only about fifty kilometres long and varies from six to fifteen kilometres in width.[25] Apra Harbor has served the Spanish and American navies, and during the Vietnam War, Guam was an important air base. With the withdrawal of American forces from the Philippines, it has gained renewed strategic importance.

As in the trust territory, American rule of Guam may be divided into three eras, but the actual time periods are different. The first era spanned four decades, from 1898 until the Japanese invasion in late 1941, when Guam was under the complete control of the US Navy, with a navy officer as

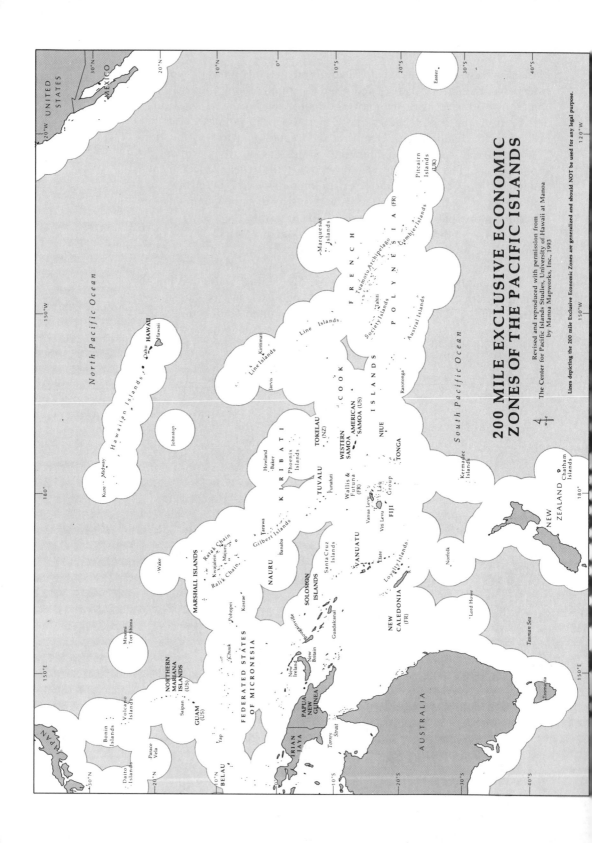

200 MILE EXCLUSIVE ECONOMIC ZONES OF THE PACIFIC ISLANDS

Revised and reproduced with permission from
The Center for Pacific Islands Studies, University of Hawaii at Manoa
by Manoa Mapworks, Inc., 1993

Lines depicting the 200 mile Exclusive Economic Zones are generalized and should NOT be used for any legal purpose.

governor. Change was gradual, and the period was marked by the maintenance of the status quo. At the turn of the century, Guam's population was
only around 10 000; the vast majority was of indigenous Chamorro descent,
and the naval garrison was small. Most Chamorros were subsistence agriculturalists and fishers residing in small rural villages. Although little of the
Chamorro pre-contact culture had survived Spanish rule, extended families
and kinship networks were basic to the social fabric, and the Chamorro
language remained alive. Reflecting the long period of Spanish rule, Roman
Catholicism was a dominant and integral part of twentieth-century Chamorro
life. The local cathedral was the focal point of most villages, and the island
landscape was reminiscent of parts of Latin America and the Philippines.

The Americans and Chamorros formed two quite separate communities,
with the navy personnel very much in the role of overlords. Gradually,
more Chamorros became employed by the navy, and by the early 1930s about
one-third of Chamorro males were wage labourers.[26] A decline in agricultural activity had begun, and with it a movement of Chamorros to Agaña,
the main military installation and administrative centre. At the outbreak
of World War Two, the population of Guam had increased to a little over
22 000. About 91 per cent were Chamorros, and about half of the island's
population resided in or near Agaña. Nonetheless, Guam was a rather sleepy
backwater in the far western Pacific, and the United States was unprepared
to defend it when war broke out.

With their invasion in December 1941, the Japanese quickly occupied the
island. Their rule was often brutal, and Chamorros suffered greatly. They
were used as forced labourers and, towards the end of Japan's hold on the
island, many were placed in concentration camps. The American invasion
brought both relief and disaster. Civilians as well as military personnel were
killed; Agaña was reduced to rubble, and most housing on the island was
destroyed. Refugee camps were hastily constructed to house the majority of
the Chamorro population, and Guam was transformed into a major US
military installation. In the haste of the effort, scant or no attention was
given to matters of land rights and ownership, and the military acquired
land at will. Substantial amounts of land were alienated, and much of the
resulting litigation remains unresolved. Some land has been returned to
local government, and the distribution of land on the island today reflects
its wartime history; the US Federal Government, the Government of Guam,
and private citizens each has about one-third of the island.

The population structure of Guam was radically altered in the immediate
post-war years. In addition to military personnel who remained, American
mainlanders flowed in. In 1949, the population had increased to slightly
over 27 000, of whom Chamorros constituted only 60 per cent, or about
16 000. For the first time, they were threatened with the possibility of becoming a minority in their own homeland.[27]

From the outset of America's rule over Guam, an unavoidable tension existed between the objectives of the Chamorro people and those of the navy administration. From the viewpoint of Washington, DC, Guam was essentially a military installation and was to be governed as such. The Chamorros did not object to the navy's presence, but they wanted recognition as loyal members of the American family. As early as 1902 and again in the mid-1920s and early 1930s, they petitioned to become American citizens, only to be met with denial. The navy opposed citizenship on the grounds that it was incompatible with the military presence. In 1917, the navy governor appointed the members of a Guam Congress, but it was advisory only. By 1931, the congress was so ineffective that it was replaced by an elected body, the Second Guam Congress, which also had only advisory powers.[28]

Further political change occurred in 1950 when the US Congress passed the Guam Organic Act, under which Guam became an unincorporated territory of the United States, its people achieved their wish to become American citizens, and some constitutional protections were extended to the new citizens.[29] As would occur with the trust territory in the following year, the administration of Guam was tranferred from the Department of Defense to the Department of Interior. As an unincorporated territory, Guam belongs to but is not an integral part of the United States. No promise of eventual statehood is implied.

The Organic Act transformed the Guam Congress into a law-making body, but the governor of Guam became an appointee of the US president. The right to an elected governor was delayed until a 1968 amendment of the Organic Act, and the first election occurred in 1970. The political structure of Guam resembles that of the United States, with Democratic and Republican parties, and Guamanian politics has always been noted for its heated contests. The Organic Act is a creation of the US Congress and differs significantly from the constitutions of the fifty states or commonwealths such as the Northern Mariana Islands and Puerto Rico. In the last analysis, Guam lacks local autonomy. Its legislation is subject to the will of Congress which may act on local issues as it sees fit. The governor of Guam is required to submit an annual financial report to the Congress and the Department of Interior. The Organic Act itself does not provide for congressional representation, but separate federal legislation in 1972 gave Guam a non-voting delegate to the US House of Representatives. The Guam representative belongs to and votes in House committees, but has no vote on the floor.

Other developments in the fifteen years following World War Two on Guam corresponded to events in the trust territory in the same period, the initial era of the US administration of Micronesia. After the passage of the Organic Act, the navy continued to exercise total control over access to Guam. Guamanians and other American citizens alike needed military permission to enter or exit Guam, a policy that brought deep and lasting resentment. It severely restricted outside investment, no other significant efforts were made to improve Guam's economy, and a parallel may easily be drawn with the era of benign neglect in the trust territory.

Paralleling the new initiatives launched in the trust territory in the early 1960s, restrictions of movement were eliminated on Guam in 1962, and the island began a period of rapid economic growth, population increase, and social change. A renewed military expansion occurred with the escalation of American involvement in Vietnam. Modest offshore banking service operations were launched, and a fledgling tourist industry gained ground. A real turning point came in 1967, when direct flights between Tokyo and Guam precipitated a dramatic expansion of the tourist industry and the number of visitors multiplied exponentially. As in the Northern Marianas, and fuelled by large-scale Japanese investment, land speculation and a building boom followed, housing costs skyrocketed, and the overall economic expansion attracted a large number of Filipinos to immigrate as labourers and employees in the service industries. Today, Guam is almost entirely urban, reflecting in miniature much of unplanned urban America. McDonald's and other fast-food chains are everywhere. Traffic congestion is routine. American movies, television, supermarkets, and shopping malls flourish. The massive tourist industry, dominated by Japanese visitors, is omnipresent.

Military and other federal expenditures are the largest source of revenue. Approximately half of the civilian work force is employed by government, both federal and local. In the private sector, tourism is the largest industry and second-largest revenue source. By 1990, the annual visitor count had surpassed three-quarters of a million, almost 80 per cent of whom were Japanese.[30] The industry had a 5 per cent annual growth rate, and employed one-third of civilian workers. Since the war, Guam has imported most of its food, and today agriculture's role is minimal, with less than two hundred workers. Manufacturing is negligible.

By 1970, Guam's population numbered about 85 000. The figure rose to 106 000 by 1980, and 133 000 by 1990. By then the Chamorros had become a minority in their own homeland, constituting less than 40 per cent of the population. Caucasians represented about 15 per cent, and Filipinos had reached slightly over 22 per cent.[31] Military personnel and their dependents accounted for most of the remainder. Out-migration has also had an impact on Guam. Since World War Two, the military has become an attractive profession for many Chamorros, and others have migrated to pursue other opportunities. The number of Chamorros living abroad is equal to about 60 per cent of those on Guam, with about 20 000 in California alone.

The overall structure of Guam's population is a source of anxiety for Chamorros, and as in the Northern Marianas, concern that they will be overwhelmed by outsiders is real and is reflected in recent political and other developments on Guam. An attempt to gain more control of local affairs occurred in 1969–70, when an initial effort was made to draft a constitution. Much debate about Guam's future political status took place, with few tangible results.

Disquiet over Guam's relationship with the United States continued to grow, and in 1974 the Guam legislature created the Political Status Commission. Increasing impatience with the federal government and the negotiations that were unfolding with the US Trust Territory of the Pacific Islands suggested that the alternatives of commonwealth or free association should be explored. The commission recommended the former. Popular sentiment held that commonwealth status might provide more control over local affairs and an opportunity to design a constitution appropriate for Guam's needs. Commonwealth was perhaps viewed as an interim arrangement under which Guam's future political status could further evolve.

In 1976 a second attempt to provide a constitution was made. A second constitutional convention was held, and a draft constitution prepared. It received both presidential and congressional approval, only to be rejected by the voters of Guam.[32] Important elected officials had not been included in the process, and the draft became a pawn in local politics. Guamanians resident in the United States were opposed to some of the draft's provisions and, more important, it did not resolve the issue of Guam's future political status.

In 1980 the Guam legislature created the Commission on Self-Determination.[33] It reviewed a number of options, and in a 1982 referendum, Guamanians voted overwhelmingly in favour of commonwealth status. A Commonwealth Draft Act was completed in 1987 and submitted to the US Congress in the following year. Essentially, the people of Guam want more control over local legislation, immigration policies, regulations pertaining to air and surface transportation, and economic relations with the United States and foreign nations. Further, Guam wants consultations with the United States prior to any new initiatives by the Department of Defense or new agreements with foreign nations that may affect Guamanian affairs.

Discussions with federal officials followed, and in December 1989 congressional hearings were held in Honolulu. It was evident, if not surprising, that the United States was reluctant to substantially reduce its authority, especially in relation to potential strategic issues. The patience of Chamorros has long been tried, and the governor of Guam made the Chamorro case quite clear:

> By any definition of the word . . . Guam is a colony. In the late sixteen hundreds, it was a Spanish colony. In 1898, it became an American colony. It is a colony today. But it must be a colony no longer. . . . The people of Guam will no longer tolerate being treated as less than other people throughout the world. We will no longer tolerate living, as we have, bereft of natural rights that we enjoyed for thousands of years

*before there was a Spanish Empire . . . for thousands of years before
America was even a dream in Columbus' eye. We must have our sovereignty restored.*[34]

Discussions between the Commission on Self-Determination and the
United States continue. Nothing of substance has been resolved. The people
of Guam might be wise to look to their fellow Chamorros in the Northern
Marianas and learn about their experiences as a commonwealth.[35]

American Samoa

As early as the 1870s, the United States showed interest in Pago Pago Bay
on Tutuila Island, one of the best natural deep-water harbours in the Pacific, as a potential coaling station for its navy. About the same time, embroiled in internal squabbles and problems with European powers, Samoans
approached the United States about some kind of protective status. Negotiations between Britain, Germany, and the United States in the late nineteenth century led to the partition of Samoa in 1899. The United States took
Tutuila along with the six smaller islands in the east that were to become
American Samoa, and President McKinley made the US Navy the administrative authority. Germany acquired the larger part of the archipelago,
now the independent nation of Western Samoa. Ironically, the ranking chiefs
of the eastern islands did not formally cede their homelands to America
until 1900 and 1904, some months and years after McKinley's fait accompli.[36]
The US Congress was somewhat nonchalant and did not approve the
cessions until 1929.

When the navy took control of American Samoa, its population was less
than 6000. After World War One the coaling depot became obsolete when
oil replaced coal as the fuel for naval vessels. The territory became a small
backwater, of little importance to Americans. More or less by default, the
navy remained the administering authority, and in contrast to Guam, naval
rule was not directly related to military interests. The officer in charge gained
the title of governor, and the number of naval personnel was never large.
From the outset, American policy recognised the vitality and validity of the
fa'a Samoa, (Samoan custom, or the Samoan way of life), and protected the
matai (chiefly) system and the Samoan communal ownership of land. Between the two world wars, modest improvements were made in health care,
and the population increased to just over 8000 in 1920, and almost 13 000
in 1940.[37] Education was mainly at the elementary level, by Samoan teachers who had little formal training. By and large, the Samoans were left to
themselves.

Each Samoan village was autonomous and each was composed of several
aiga, (extended families). The *aiga* was a landholding corporation headed by
a *matai* (titled chief). Sons often suceeded their fathers, but there were no

formal rules of succession to titles. Rather, *aiga* members selected their *matai* on the basis of leadership ability, maturity, wisdom, and knowledge of the *fa'a Samoa*. The *matai* consulted with senior kinsmen in the management of *aiga* activities, land, and resources. The *matai* and *aiga* constituted local authority and were the major forces of socal control. No greater indigenous political authority existed. The *matai* titles of each village were ranked, and each village had its own *fono* (governing council), composed of several *matai*.

Samoan culture was marked by an elaborate system of protocol, concern with prestige, respect for age, and a rich ceremonial life centred around the *fono*, the *matai* title system, and life-crisis celebrations. All Samoans were well provided for by an affluent subsistence economy. Samoans had great pride and confidence in themselves and the correctness, if not superiority, of their culture. The *fa'a Samoa* was quite flexible and resistant to outside influences. Christianity, other Western practices, and European material goods were either absorbed and modified to fit Samoan ways or rejected. Samoan culture, although inevitably modified by Western contact, remained an integrated whole.

Compared to Micronesia, World War Two had few consequences for American Samoa, but nonetheless it brought change. In anticipation of the war, a crew of more than a thousand American civilians was engaged on various construction projects on Tutuila. They were replaced with military personnel after the attack on Pearl Harbor and a marine training base was established near Pago Pago. The military upgraded the island's infrastructure with vastly improved roads, airfields, and other facilities. The size of a small local Samoan marine guard, *fitafita*, was increased, and employment opportunities attracted men to Tutuila from all over the territory. Local employment and military spending meant an unprecedented involvement in the cash economy. The closing of military operations in 1945 was traumatic. Members of the *fitafita* were given the option of transferring to the navy. Many did, and a tradition of careers in the US military began. The territory's physical plant had been improved, but a lack of funds allowed it to fall into disrepair. Most employment opportunities vanished, but many Samoans had acquired a taste for a more American life-style, somewhat free from traditional authority.

In 1951 the administraton of American Samoa was transferred to the Department of Interior.[38] Little change immediately ensued. As Congress had shown little interest, no organic act had ever been passed for American Samoa, and it remained an unorganised and unincorporated territory. Similarly, the status of Samoans was unchanged. With cession, American Samoans had become US nationals, but not citizens. As nationals, they had freedom of movement to and could find employment in the United States, but they did not have the rights of citizens, nor were they covered by the provisions of the Constitution.

The secretary of the interior claimed ultimate authority over the affairs of the territory, and the shift to Interior did not bring any measure of local civilian government to American Samoa. The secretary appointed the territory's governor. The *Fono*, a territory-wide advisory body of 24 *matai*, had been created by the naval governor in the first decade of American rule. In 1948 and remaining an advisory body only, it had been reconstituted as a bicameral body composed of an upper house of 24 *matai* and a lower house of 24 representatives.

In earlier times and immediately prior to the end of navy rule, the *Fono* had resisted any suggestion of an organic act. Samoans feared that any legislation enacted by Congress would bring them under some or all of the provisions of the Constitution, thereby eroding the *matai* system and Samoan ownership of land. In 1950, the *Fono* had gone on record as opposed to a closer political relationship with the United States. In 1951, and in order to speak with greater authority against an organic act, it demanded law-making powers. That change did not occur, but in 1952 the *Fono* reorganised itself into a more manageable body with a 12-member Senate (*matai* selected by *matai*) and an 18-member House of Representatives elected by secret ballot.

The first civilian governor appointed by the secretary of the interior assured his new charges that 'no unacceptable organic act would be rammed down the throats of the Samoans'.[39] The streamlined *Fono* asked a subsequent governor for the power to prepare a constitution. Granting approval, he opined that a constitution 'would have many of the benefits of organic legislation and at the same time permit the people of Samoa to maintain traditional systems of land tenure and their traditional social organisation so long as it meets their needs'.[40]

As with the US Trust Territory of the Pacific Islands and Guam, the 1960s ushered in a new era of change for American Samoa.[41] In the political arena, and after six years in the making, the Constitution went into effect in 1960 and was revised in 1966 to provide Samoans with more control over local affairs. The powers of the secretary of interior and the appointed governor were decreased, and the *Fono* became a true law-making body. Its numbers were again altered to give the Senate 18 and the House 20 members. In 1969, the American Samoa Political Status Commission reaffirmed the *Fono*'s earlier stance, for the same reasons, and recommended that the territory remain unorganised and unincorporated.[42] A few years later a second status commission again opted for the status quo. The Samoans were content with their status and did not want to risk any encroachment by the federal system.

In the process of realigning its relationship with Washington, the Government of American Samoa also gained control of its own immigration and emigration policies. Permanent residency for non-Samoans, including American citizens, is difficult to obtain, and the right of outsiders to engage in commerce is subject to even greater restrictions. Like Guam before it, the

Fono created and financed its own delegate to Congress, who had no official status and was in essence a lobbyist in the cause of American Samoa. In 1978, Congress granted the Samoan delegate the right to a vote in committees but not on the floor of the House of Representatives. The first election of the official representative occurred in 1980, a full eighty years after cession.

On three occasions between 1972 and 1976, proposals by the appointed governor that Samoans elect their own chief executive were met by staunch resistance. Rightly or wrongly, it was feared that an elective governor would upset the balance of local politics and undermine the *matai* system. In 1977, there was a change of heart, and a gubernatorial election was held.[43] The first elected governor, a non-*matai*, took office in 1978, and the selection of the territory's chief executive officer came under the control of the Samoans themselves. Younger and more Westernized Samoans had insisted that candidates not be restricted to *matai* title-holders. Today, as in the Northern Marianas and Guam, politics in Samoa is organised along American lines with Democratic and Republican parties.

Major change had begun somewhat earlier in the economic sector than in the political arena. In 1954, a US firm opened a tuna cannery in Pago Pago, and a second followed in 1963. Both operations were encouraged by tax and other incentives from the Government of American Samoa. In the early 1960s, like the Micronesian territories, American Samoa was greatly affected by increased attention from Washington. Congressional appropriations were tripled, scores of federal programmes were made available, and between 1961 and 1967 the appointed governor initiated other measures intended, from Washington's point of view, to bring the territory into the twentieth century. As in the trust territory, the education system was greatly expanded. Secondary education was made available to all, more schools were built, and every community was equipped with electricity and educational television to upgrade instruction in English. In an attempt to launch a tourist industry, a major hotel was constructed. Television had other Westernising consequences, when American entertainment programmes also became available.[44]

Although Samoans have largely resisted greater integration into the federal political system, employment opportunities, participation in federal programmes, and increased budgetary support have inevitably brought American Samoa into a closer and more dependent relationship with the United States. By the mid-1980s, the annual budget of the Government of American Samoa was averaging around US$75 million, three-quarters of which was derived from Congressional appropriations and federal programmes. The number of such programmes was reportedly at the same level as in the trust territory. Tuna constituted 90 per cent of all exports, most of which went to the United States, whence came almost all imports.

Today, the largest employer is the public sector, with the canneries second. Because of limited airline service, tourism has been a disappointment and remains a minor industry. Wages in the territory are much higher than in neighbouring countries, and employment in the two canneries has never been popular with American Samoans. As a consequence, American Samoa has become a magnet to outsiders, many of whom are in the territory illegally. One-half of the labour force in the canneries consists of aliens. At the same time, American Samoans themselves have taken advantage of their status as American nationals, have joined the US armed services, and have migrated to the United States in search of higher wages, education, and other opportunities. One-half of all high school graduates depart each year. The Samoan economy has been transformed from affluent subsistence to one that requires imports for food and clothing. It is heavily dependent on the public sector for income and employment and on remittances from relatives living abroad.

The population of the territory has also undergone continued rapid growth and major alterations in its demographic structure. By the mid-1980s, the population was about 36 000, of whom 16 000 were aliens, mostly from Western Samoa, Tonga, and other Polynesian islands. About 92 per cent of the population resides on Tutuila, with the majority in and around Pago Pago. Although the precise figures for outmigration are highly suspect, the number of American Samoans in California is estimated at 65 000 with another 20 000 in Hawai'i.

Compared to previous times, since World War Two American Samoa has experienced radical social and economic change. The traditional *matai* and *aiga* systems have been weakened, and there has been a shift towards a greater number of nuclear families as units of production and consumption. Nonetheless, Samoan culture has remained resilient, and much of what is distinctively Samoan remains. The land-tenure system continues to provide a foundation for the *fa'a Samoa*, with 92 per cent of all land remaining in communal ownership held by traditional kin groups.

Hawai'i

Hawai'i and Guam were annexed in the same year, 1898, but Hawai'i's Organic Act was quick to follow, enacted by the US Congress in 1900, fifty years before Guam's.[45] The two pieces of legislation were much alike, however. The governor of Hawai'i was appointed by the president. The territory's legislature was elected, but all laws and executive decisions were subject to the will of Congress, including veto power.

The population of Hawai'i at the turn of the century was about 154 000. The indigenous Hawaiians had already experienced severe depopulation, and Hawaiians and part-Hawaiians had become a minority in their own homeland, accounting for slightly less than a quarter of the territory's people. Asians originally brought to Hawai'i as plantation labourers had increased in number to well over half of the population: Japanese were a little less than 40 per cent and Chinese just under 17 per cent. Approximately 19 per cent were Caucasians.[46] Included in the last group was a relatively small *haole* (Caucasian) elite largely descended from the early New England missionaries who had arrived in the islands during the first half of the nineteenth century. In the middle of that century, a redistribution of land had divided almost all land among the Hawaiian monarch (Crown land), the numerous Hawaiian chiefs, and the government. The bulk of the population, the commoner class, had received only about 1 per cent of Hawai'i's land. Much of the chiefly and some of the government's holdings were soon alienated, and before the turn of the century, Westerners had control of three-quarters of the land. The indigenous people had been dispossessed.[47]

For the first four decades of the twentieth century, Hawai'i was essentially a plantation society. Agriculture was the mainstay of the economy: sugar was king, and pineapple was second. Political and economic power was firmly concentrated in the hands of the *haole* elite, and its members formed the conservative vanguard of the Republican Party. A few *haole* families controlled five large corporations, known as the Big Five, which dominated sugar. The corporate boards of the Big Five had interlocking memberships, and the controlling families were also linked by marriage. They sent their children to private schools, belonged to the same private clubs, and, in short, formed an all-powerful local oligarchy.[48]

The decade of the thirties foreshadowed events to come. In 1936, Pan American Airlines' China Clippers (seaplanes) commenced the first commercial air flights between San Francisco and Hawai'i, and the islands were brought closer to the American mainland.[49] The 1930s also witnessed a military buildup in Hawai'i, and by 1941 defence had replaced agriculture as the largest sector of the economy.[50]

The demography of Hawai'i was also indicative of things to come. By 1940, the population had increased by a factor of 2.75 to about 423 500, but the number of Hawaiians and part-Hawaiians had declined to 15.2 per cent of the total. The percentage of Japanese had remained about the same (over 37 per cent), while the number of Caucasians had increased to more than 25 per cent of the population. Filipinos were recent immigrants and had gained a firm foothold in the islands with about 12.5 per cent of the total. The proportion of Chinese had slipped to less than 7 per cent.[51]

World War Two precipitated changes that would alter Hawai'i forever. Beginning with the Japanese invasion of Pearl Harbor and as never before, the islands were thrust onto the main stage of world events and were soon transformed into the primary staging point for the American war effort in the Pacific. The military presence was further enlarged, and hundreds of thousands of young Americans transited the islands on the way to the Pacific and Asia.

The war was also a watershed for Hawai'i's Japanese. As it had for those resident on the west coast of the United States, the allegiance of the local

Japanese came under suspicion. In contrast to the mainland, however, internment of the entire Japanese population was out of the question. Hawai'i's Japanese were needed for the islands' labour force, and, ironically, the war effort. Only a relative few (about 1500) suffered incarceration. Anxious to demonstrate their loyalty to America, several thousand Japanese volunteered for the military and served with distinction on the European front.[52] The war experience served as a catalyst for change. Inspired by their accomplishments abroad, the young veterans returned home and began to challenge the status quo. With their veterans' benefits, many attended the University of Hawai'i, and they soon moved into education, other professional fields, and the political arena.

Although it was not a major issue prior to the war, sentiments favouring statehood had been resisted by vested interests in Hawai'i. Any change in political status, particularly in the direction of greater democratisation, was a threat to the ruling elite, and the Republican Party was firmly committed to the existing order. Impatient with the status quo, however, the Japanese, particularly the returned veterans, were the main post-war advocates of statehood and found their political home with the territory's fledgling and more liberal Democratic Party. In 1950 they were a large part of a movement that resulted in the drafting of a constitution for the future state that was overwhelmingly approved by Hawai'i's electorate.[53] The Democratic Party was well on the way to becoming the dominant force in Hawaiian politics, with a concomitant decline of the old power structure.

Statehood for Hawai'i, however, was not a new issue and had been much debated in the US Congress. The primary arguments against admission to the union were: Hawai'i was too distant from and not contiguous with the other forty-eight states, its population was too small, and it was alleged that its labour movement had been infiltrated by Communist sympathisers. In the last analysis, however, and in spite of the war record of Hawai'i's Japanese, race was the crux of the matter. Many members of Congress, especially from the American South, could not accept the notion of a state in which Caucasians were only a minority, and their numbers were sufficient to delay statehood.[54] In the end, statehood was not to be denied. Alaska's admission to the union in 1958 helped break the barrier, and in 1959 Hawai'i was granted statehood.

At that time, Hawai'i's population had increased to about 620 000, and the state was one of the most urbanised of all America. About 90 per cent of its people lived in urban areas, mostly Honolulu. Military expenditures accounted for about one-half of the economy, while the total agricultural contribution had declined to about one-third. Tourism was just entering a new era, with commercial jet travel coming to Hawai'i in the same year as statehood.

The 1960s and 1970s were decades of rapid change. Statehood brought closer integration with the rest of the United States and attracted outside investment. Mainland enterprises introduced competition on the local business scene, increased tourism precipitated a movement of permanent emigrants from the mainland, and suburbs and freeways began to spring up in and around Honolulu. High-rise development came to dominate downtown Honolulu and Waikiki Beach, and their skylines were altered forever. Internationally syndicated television, particularly the long-popular 'Hawaii Five-O' series, brought Hawai'i into the living rooms of millions of Americans and others around the world. Hawai'i was no longer such a foreign place.

The growth in tourism was phenomenal. In 1960, the number of tourists reached almost 300 000. The one-million mark was reached within seven years. Two million visitors arrived in 1972, and their numbers were doubled by 1979. Reaching into the next decade, six million were counted in 1988, and about seven million tourists now visit Hawai'i each year. The economy is dominated by tourism, with the military and agriculture ranking distant second and third places.

Beginning in the late 1960s, Japanese joined the flow of tourists to Hawai'i. Their numbers increased at a rate faster than the overall growth of the tourist industry, and, in recent years, Japanese have accounted for one out of every seven visitors. In the 1970s, Japanese investment in Hawai'i began to parallel the growing number of Japanese visitors. Purchases of hotels and resorts over the last two decades, and large-scale purchases of residential homes in the 1980s, caused alarm and some backlash among Hawai'i residents.

The 1990 census revealed that Hawai'i's population had almost doubled since statehood, with a total of 1 108 229 residents.[55] Although the major racial groups had all experienced a numerical increase, their proportions within the population had changed. The numbers of Caucasians and Filipinos had continued to grow, with Caucasians now 33 per cent and Filipinos a little over 15 per cent of the population. Japanese and Hawaiians had declined to about 23 and 12.5 per cent respectively, and the proportion of Chinese had remained about the same. An influx of Vietnamese, other Asians, and Pacific Islanders, particularly American Samoans, accounted for a small proportion of the total population.

Of all Hawai'i's major ethnic groups, the indigenous Hawaiians, dispossessed and increasingly outnumbered, are the most disadvantaged. They rank at the bottom of the socio-economic scale, are low in relative educational achievement, suffer from a wide variety of health problems, and have the shortest life expectancy. Beginning in the 1970s and gaining momentum in the 1980s, however, Hawaiians have taken a renewed interest in their own history, language, music, dance, and other elements of Hawaiian culture. By the late 1970s, a Hawaiian renaissance was discernibly underway. Pride in Hawaiian identity and a sense of a special connectedness between the people and their ancestral land are integral parts of the movement.

In recognition of the plight of the indigenous people, the Office of Hawaiian Affairs was created by an amendment to the state's constitution in 1978.[56] The office is managed by a board of directors elected from and by the ranks of Native Hawaiians with the mandate to 'provide Hawaiians the right to determine priorities which would effectuate the betterment of their conditions and welfare and promote the protection and preservation of the Hawaiian race'.[57] The Office of Hawaiian Affairs and several activist groups are energetically pursuing claims for the return of alienated lands, seeking redress and compensation for past injustices from the federal and state governments, lobbying for changes in the state educational system, and initiating other efforts for the improvement of their own people. Following the example of Native American Indian nations on the US mainland, some Hawaiians advocate the creation of a sovereign Hawaiian nation within the State of Hawai'i. A very visible Center for Hawaiian Studies has developed at the University of Hawai'i.

Hawaiians are more politically active today than at any time since annexation. The majority are supporters of the Democratic Party which revolutionised Hawai'i politics after World War Two. The first part-Hawaiian to serve as the state's chief executive, John Waihee, was elected governor of Hawai'i in 1986. In 1982 Daniel Akaka was the first Hawaiian to be elected to a seat in the US House of Representatives, and in 1990 he was elected as a US senator. Waihee and Akaka are the first Polynesians to serve as governor of a state of the union or as a member of the US Congress. Hawaiians may take pride in their achievements, but their struggle as a people for a more equitable place in their own homeland is in its infancy.

New regional linkages

New relationships continue to develop between the United States and the Pacific islands with which it has had historical ties. When other island entities were gaining independence or some form of self-government, the Commonwealth of the Northern Mariana Islands opted to break with the rest of the US Trust Territory of the Pacific Islands and, despite later reservations, for commonwealth status, that is, political integration with the United States. Although its historical relationship with the United States was quite different, at an earlier time the Territory of Hawai'i had also opted for closer political integration, in the form of statehood. The remaining two US territories, American Samoa and Guam, have achieved greater local autonomy over the last three decades. Nonetheless, Guam is far from being satisfied with its current status and is demanding a renegotiation of its place within the American political family. Only American Samoa is content with the status quo.

Within the last decade, new linkages have been created. In 1980 and with the support of federal agencies, particularly the Department of Commerce, the Pacific Basin Development Council was formed as an American club with headquarters in Honolulu. Its membership is composed of the governors of the four 'American flag islands'—American Samoa, the Northern Marianas, Guam, and Hawai'i. The council promotes economic development, sponsors relevant research, serves as a liaison among its members, and assists with the coordination of their relations with the US Congress and federal agencies in Washington, DC. It has created some sense of unity and common cause among the four governors, and their recent discussions about future economic efforts in the larger region have included representatives of Asian countries. The Pacific Basin Development Council is incorporated as a private, non-profit, tax-exempt organisation. Most of its operating costs are provided by member contributions, but other funds are derived from federal and other granting agencies.

The relationship between the United States and the Federated States of Micronesia and the Republic of the Marshall Islands is still evolving. While the Compacts of Free Association provide the two new states with sovereignty over both internal and external affairs, some would argue that their sovereignty is compromised by the strategic provisions of those compacts. To date, the United States has found no reason to exercise its strategic prerogatives, and the freely associated states have been left very much alone to pursue their own affairs. However, it is an understatement to suggest that the Federated States of Micronesia and the Republic of the Marshall Islands are heavily dependent on the financial arrangements provided by the compacts. Given their financial dependency, limited resources, rapidly expanding populations, and the access of their citizens to the United States, it is most unlikely that either state will desire to terminate its relationship with the United States. Both have expressed interest in membership in the Pacific Basin Development Council, but its current four members desire to preserve the composition of their American club. The future of Belau remains uncertain, but there are indications that suggest some movement towards a revision of the country's constitution that would remove obstacles to free association.

Certain of the new linkages in the islands involve Japan and represent some of the greatest ironies in Pacific history. The Japanese attack on Pearl Harbor in early December 1941 abruptly reawakened American interest in the Pacific, and the ousting of Japan from the region was one of the main objectives of World War Two. In a twist of fate, Japan has returned with great strength and dynamism to become a major influence in the very islands that were among the bloodiest battlegrounds of the war. Japanese investment and tourism are now important in the economy of Hawai'i and are the major engines behind the economic development of Guam and the Commonwealth of the Northern Mariana Islands. In addition to establishing diplomatic ties with the Federated States of Micronesia and the Marshall

Islands, Japan is also emerging as an aid donor and an economic force to be reckoned with in these new Micronesian states. If and when its political status is resolved, a similar turn of events may be expected in Belau.

Notes

1 Richard H. Wyttenbach, 'Micronesia and Strategic Trusteeship: A Case Study in American Politico-Military Relations', PhD dissertation, Fletcher School of Law and Diplomacy, Tufts University, 1971, 390. Document on microfilm, TTPI Archives, V10001, Reel 0118, Hamilton Library, University of Hawai'i.

2 *Webster's Ninth New Collegiate Dictionary*, Merriam-Webster, Springfield, MA, 1986, 261.

3 Grant K. Goodman and Felix Moos, eds, *The United States and Japan in the Western Pacific: Micronesia and Papua New Guinea*, Westview Press, Boulder, CO, 1981, 68.

4 Carl Heine, *Micronesia at the Crossroads*, University of Hawai'i Press, Honolulu, 1974, *xv*.

5 Robert C. Kiste, *The Bikinians: A Study in Forced Migration*, Cummings, Menlo Park, CA, 1974.

6 Gary Smith, *Micronesia: Decolonisation and US Military Interests in the Trust Territory of the Pacific Islands*, Peace Research Centre, Research School of Pacific Studies, Australian National University, Canberra, 1991, 20.

7 Norman Meller, *The Congress of Micronesia*, University of Hawai'i Press, Honolulu, 1969, 58–72.

8 Robert C. Kiste, 'Termination of the U.S. Trusteeship in Micronesia', *Journal of Pacific History* 21(3–4, 1986): 128–129.

9 Roger Gale, *The Americanization of Micronesia: A Study of the Consolidation of U.S. Rule in the Pacific*, University Press of America, Washington, DC, 1979, 106–125.

10 David Nevin, *The American Touch in Micronesia*, W. W. Norton, New York, 1977, 125–127.

11 Robert C. Kiste, 'New Political Statuses in American Micronesia', in *Contemporary Pacific Societies*, eds Victoria S. Lockwood, Thomas G. Harding, and Ben J. Wallace, Prentice Hall, Englewood Cliffs, NJ, 1993, 72.

12 Leonard E. Mason 'Unity and Disunity in Micronesia', in *Political Development in Micronesia*, eds Daniel T. Hughes and Sherwood Lingenfelter, Ohio State University Press, Columbus, Ohio, 1974, 203–262.

13 Francis X. Hezel, 'Looking Ahead to the End of Trusteeship, Trust Territory of the Pacific Islands', *Journal of Pacific History* 13 (3–4, 1978): 204–207.

14 Robert C. Kiste, 'The Fine Print of the Compacts', *Pacific Islands Monthly*, November 1983, 22–23.

15 'FSM Analysis of Free Association Compact', *Pacific 86*, Guam, February 1986, 14–15.

16 Howard R. Penniman and Austin Ranney, *Democracy in the Islands: The Micronesian Plebiscites of 1983*, American Enterprise for Public Policy Research, Washington, DC, 1985, 28.

17 *Report of the United Nations Visiting Mission to Observe the Plebiscite in Palau, Trust Territory of the Pacific Islands, February 1990*, Trusteeship Council, Official Records: Fifty-Seventh Session (May–June 1990), Supplement no. 1, United Nations, New York, 1990.

18 'Marshalls Hosts PREL Conference', *Pacific Education Updates* 3 (3, June–August 1991): 1 (Pacific Regional Educational Laboratory, Honolulu).

19 US Department of State, *Report on the Administration of the Trust Territory of the Pacific Islands to the United Nations*, July 1948, 76; Norman Douglas and Ngaire Douglas, eds, *Pacific Islands Year Book*, 16th edn, Angus & Robertson, 1989, 69, 325, 401.

20 United Nations Security Council, Resolution 683.

21 Ian Williams, 'Freedom at Last', *Pacific Islands Monthly*, February 1991, 10–12.

22 'U.N. General Assembly Admits 7 New Members', *Honolulu Star-Bulletin*, 17 September 1991.

23 Samuel F. McPhetres, 'Commonwealth of the Northern Mariana Islands', *The Contemporary Pacific* 2 (1990): 149–151; 3 (1991): 182–184; 4 (1992): 181–183; McPhetres, 'Elements of Social Change in the Contemporary Northern Mariana Islands', in *Social Change in the Pacific Islands*, ed. Albert B. Robillard, Kegan Paul International, London and New York, 1992, 241–263.

24 Froilan Cruz Tenorio, *1988 Annual Report*, Office of the Resident Representative for the United States of America for the Northern Mariana Islands, Washington, DC, 1989.

25 Arnold H. Leibowitz, *Defining Status: A Comprehensive Analysis of United States Territorial Relations*, Martinus Nijhoff, Dordrecht–Boston–London, 1989, 314, 315.

26 Laura Thompson, *Guam and Its People*, Institute of Pacific Relations, New York, 1941.

27 Leibowitz, 313, 325–326.

28 Paul Caraño and Pedro Sanchez, *A Complete History of Guam*, Tuttle, Tokyo, 1964, 228–238.

29 An organic act is essentially Congressional legislation creating a body of laws that govern a territory; it is comparable to the constitution of a state of the union. A territory governed by an organic act is said to be organised.

30 Government of Guam, *Quarterly Economic Review*, 14 (3, 1992): 29.

31 US Department of Commerce, Bureau of the Census, *1990 Census: Social, Economic, and Housing Characteristics, GUAM*, February 1992, 19.

32 Robert F. Rogers, *Guam's Commonwealth Effort 1987–1988*, Educational Series no. 8, Micronesian Area Research Center, University of Guam, Mangilão, Guam, 1988, 8.

33 Rogers, 9.

34 Joseph F. Ada, 'Testimony: Commonwealth Hearings, December 11, 1989', *Report of the Guam Commission on Self-Determination 1989*, Guam Commission on Self-Determination, Agaña, 1990, 1, 13.

35 Jon M. Van Dyke, *The Evolving Legal Relationships between the United States and Its Affiliated U.S. Flag Islands*, paper prepared for Pacific Basin Development Council, Honolulu, 1990.

36 Leibowitz, 414–416; Edward J. Michal, 'American Samoa or Eastern Samoa? The Potential for American Samoa to Become Freely Associated with the United States', *The Contemporary Pacific* 4 (1992): 137–160.

37 Captain J. A. C. Gray, *Amerika Samoa: A History of American Samoa and Its United States Naval Administration*, United States Naval Institute, Annapolis, MD, 1960, 233.

38 Leibowitz, 417, 426.

39 Gray, 261.

40 Gray, 263.

41 Lowell D. Holmes, *Samoan Village*, Holt, Rinehart & Winston, New York, 1974, 93–108.

42 Leibowitz, 461.

43 Leibowitz, 455.

44 Holmes, 97.

45 Roger Bell, *Last among Equals: Hawaiian Statehood and American Politics*, University of Hawai'i Press, Honolulu, 1984, 39.

46 Eleanor C. Nordyke, *The Peopling of Hawai'i*, 2nd edn, University of Hawai'i Press, Honolulu, 1989, 178–179.

47 Gavan Daws, *Shoal of Time: A History of the Hawaiian Islands*, University of Hawai'i Press, 1968, 124–128; Lawrence H. Fuchs, *Hawai'i Pono: A Social History*, Harcourt, Brace & World, New York, 1961, 14–17.

48 Linda Menton and Eileen Tamura, *A History of Hawai'i*, College of Education, University of Hawai'i, Honolulu, 1991, 169–174.

49 Stan Cohen, *Wings to the Orient*, Pictorial Histories Publishing Company, Missoula, MT, 1985, 158–187.

50 Menton and Tamura, 315.

51 Nordyke, 178–179.

52 Bell, 78–83.

53 Bell, 180–191.

54 Menton and Tamura, 283; Gavan Daws, *Hawai'i 1959–1989*, Publishers Group Hawai'i, Honolulu, 1989, 3.

55 'Census Bureau Releases 1990 Census Counts on Specific Racial Groups', *United States Department of Commerce News*, Washington, DC, 12 June 1991.

56 Daws, 202.

57 Jon Van Dyke, 'Constitutionality of the Office of Hawaiian Affairs', *University of Hawai'i Law Review* 7 (1, 1985): 68.

France

Paul de Deckker

Even though New Caledonia, French Polynesia, and Wallis and Futuna, the three Overseas Territories of France in the South Pacific, each had developed according to its own geographic, economic, and cultural environment, their destinies have all been, and still are, affected by decisions made in Paris.

Five years before Western Samoa became constitutionally independent in 1962, Paris had decided to pave the way to independence for New Caledonia and French Polynesia by decreeing a law providing for self-government: the *loi-cadre* of 23 June 1957. Each of the two territories elected its 'governmental council' and its own territorial assembly, while each governor, appointed by Paris, continued to represent the French state in the territory. However, the decolonizing process was arrested in 1958 after General de Gaulle became the leader of the Fifth Republic.

In 1939, France had been invaded and partly occupied by German troops, with the forced approval (after the armistice) of the Vichy government and its head, Marshall Philippe Pétain. From London, General de Gaulle, refusing to accept defeat, made a BBC radio appeal on 18 June 1940, calling on French patriots to resist the Nazi. This appeal generated diverse movements of resistance, not only in metropolitan France but also in the French colonies, from which de Gaulle obtained strong support (especially in Africa and the Pacific) for his *France libre*. In Noumea and Pape'ete the World War One Pacific battalions were re-formed and sent to the Middle East. New Caledonians and Tahitians fought at Bir-Hakeim, El-Alamein, and in Italy before being involved in the liberation of France in 1944. Twenty-five per cent of them lost their lives.

In the Pacific theatre after Pearl Harbor, de Gaulle and *la France libre* declared war on Japan. Noumea became an essential American military base harbour of the Pacific, second only to Pearl Harbor, while Bora Bora and Wallis became outposts where thousands of American soldiers were based for the duration of the war. Operations in the Solomons and in the Philippines were organised from Noumea by Admiral Nimitz, chief commander of the American Naval Forces in the Pacific.

Up to 1945, the two French colonies were governed by delegates from General de Gaulle, and the Vichy representatives were either imprisoned or evicted.[1]

World War Two was a landmark for all the French colonies. Aspirations towards freedom from the Nazi and the Japanese invaders, shared by most of the colonies, implied that, strictly speaking, obsolete colonial statutes could no longer be maintained. Foreseeing the inevitable wave of change and persuaded that it was better to go with it than be submerged by it, de Gaulle organized a conference in February 1944 in Brazzaville, capital of the Congo. Eighteen governors of French colonies attended that meeting as well as former ministers and trade unionists. The aim was to prepare reforms, to be applied to the French empire after the war, in different fields such as economics, education, welfare, customs, and administration. Decolonisation as such was not envisaged at Brazzaville. On the contrary, the conference, calling for more equality among individuals, more self-government, and a progressive social and economic assimilation of the populations into metropolitan France, excluded all political evolution outside France.

The French Constitution of 1946, founding the Fourth Republic, took into account the necessary *evolution* proclaimed at Brazzaville and, under the influence of socialist ideas, recognised for the first time the existence of 'Overseas Peoples and Nations with the right to develop their civilization, to self-government and to democratically manage their own affairs within a Union based on equality of rights and duties with France'. The word *indigène*, then considered a degrading term, disappeared thenceforth from official texts, to be replaced by its Greek equivalent *autochthon*, while *colony* was replaced by *overseas territory*.

Dealing specifically with overseas territories, the 1946 Constitution included articles that took their interests into account, providing for general franchise, elected territorial assemblies, and the election of senators and representatives to the national parliaments in Paris, on an evolving basis.

The *loi-cadre* of 1957 took into account events in Indochina, Morocco, and Tunisia. It allowed for the first statute of self-government in French overseas territories with real autonomous decision-making powers. Executive councils of government, with ministerial portfolios, were instituted.[2] Implemented by the last governments of the Fourth Republic, this law was a cornerstone for the decolonisation of overseas territories,[3] that would be realised under the Fifth Republic.

Charles de Gaulle wanted to replace the French Union by a sort of Commonwealth: *la Communauté française*. In Brazzaville again, in August 1958, he gave an address in which he explained the underlying principles: through the formation of a vast political, economic, and defensive network, including all French overseas territories wishing to participate, the *Communauté* would provide full self-government and free self-determination through referenda, which would soon be organised. De Gaulle defined new institutional structures that would link France with its former colonies and, above all, would clearly delineate the question of independence. Overseas territories, if their populations wished, could immediately obtain independence by voting 'No' in the constitutional referendum. Moreover, having voted positively, members of the *Communauté*, could later negotiate their respective statutes of independence with Paris.[4]

Gaining self-government

La Nouvelle-Calédonie et Dépendances

In 1945 New Caledonia was peopled by 31 000 Melanesians, 18 000 Europeans and some 13 500 others, mainly Javanese and Indo-Chinese indentured workers. At that time, Melanesians lived in tribal settlements, did not possess real civil status, and were just beginning to enter the cash economy via coffee plantations encouraged by the colonial administration in the late 1920s and 1930s.[5] Among the Europeans, civil servants and the Noumea petty bourgeoisie were well off, while the majority of the people lived in the bush as subsistence cultivators. The US military presence could have advanced the development of the colony, but the Noumea administration refused an American offer to help.[6] The Asiatic indentured workers, whose five-year contracts were terminated during the war, could not be repatriated to their homelands because no ships were available. As far as education was concerned, in 1945, 40 per cent of the European colonists then being drafted into the army were illiterate; schooling in the bush, if it existed, was inadequate, and for the Asians was non-existent. Mining activities were at a low ebb because of the lack of sea transport.

The French government granted the right to vote to some 11 per cent of the Melanesians in August 1945: high chiefs and small chiefs, pastors, catechists, civil servants, and military veterans (1444 out of a total of 9500 voters), and the 1946 French Constitution conferred French citizenship on all Melanesians along with the other indigenous populations of the French empire. In 1953, exactly a century after the French takeover of New Caledonia, general franchise was implemented in New Caledonia and, for the first time, some Kanaks were elected to political positions in the Territorial Assembly. Shortly after the war, the Catholic UICALO and the Protestant AICLF[7]—two Christian organisations favouring racial harmony—formed a political movement, the *Union Calédonienne* (Caledonian Union), which was to become, under its motto 'Two colours but a single people', the leading political party. It aimed at gradually producing a Caledonian identity that would unite both Melanesians and Europeans as well as urban and rural people. These religious organisations also wanted to promote Melanesian rights and interests. In the 1950s, promoting Melanesian rights implied maintaining reservations, defending traditional values, acknowledging customary justice, and reinforcing the power of customary chiefs. While wishing to isolate Melanesian communities and their traditional cultures from external influences, which were considered negative, leaders of the Caledonian Union believed that a progressive and constructive adaptation of Melanesian tribes to New Caledonian society would allow their successful integration into it. The Caledonian Union also advocated a more equitable share of economic resources and the extension of reservations into lands underexploited by colonial concessionary companies.

In the July 1951 election for New Caledonia's deputy to the French national parliament, the Caledonian Union presented a candidate who paid attention to Melanesian and European common people: Maurice Lenormand, a metropolitan pharmacist married to a Lifou woman. He won the election.

In all public declarations, the Caledonian Union wanted to maintain 'perpetual' links with France as they were thought necessary on the one hand to protect Melanesians and, on the other, to develop the territorial economic and trade sectors. Ninety-eight per cent of the votes cast at the time of the 1958 constitutional referendum were against independence.

Le Protectorat de Wallis et Futuna

The archipelago of Wallis and Futuna is located more than two thousand kilometres north-east of Noumea and three thousand kilometres north-west of Tahiti. Its three main islands are Wallis, or Uvea, and, some two hundred kilometres to its south-west, Futuna and Alofi. According to local oral tradition, Uvea (later called Wallis and not to be confused with Uvea in the Loyalty Islands) was settled around the fourteenth century by Tongan navigators. The Wallisian dynasty was founded by Tauloko by the end of that century and still exists today. Few dates exist for Futuna's settlement, which seems to have occurred from Samoa. Strong links exist between the Tongan and Wallisian languages, whereas the Futunan language very much resembles Samoan. Dutch navigators reached Futuna and Alofi in 1616, and Captain Samuel Wallis reached Uvea in 1767. French Catholic missionaries settled both Wallis and Futuna in 1837. Because of a shortage of fresh water, Alofi has never been permanently inhabited. Wallis and Futuna officially became a French protectorate in 1888, having been a *de facto* one from the mid-1850s.

Under Catholic rule, the archipelago remained entrenched in tradition and customs. Three distinct 'kingdoms' still exist today. In Wallis, the king (*lavelua*) is the overall customary ruler and is attended by a prime minister (*kivalu*) and six ministers. The island is divided into three districts—Hihifo, Hahake, and Mua—each ruled by a *faipule* (district chief). The island of Futuna is divided into two 'kingdoms', Sigave and Alo. The customary leaders of Alo (*tuiagaifo*) and Sigave (*tuisigave*) are each attended by five ministers. In 1960, Wallis and Futuna were peopled by some seven thousand inhabitants, more than two-thirds of whom resided in Wallis. A French resident, generally a physician, represented the French state in the archipelago.[8] Very few Europeans lived in Wallis and Futuna where, as in Tonga, they could never own land. Under the authority of their respective chiefs, people were mainly involved in agriculture and fishing for subsistence purposes, there being no cash economy at that time. Wallis and Futuna were in fact ruled by a French bishop who held considerable authority, religious as well as civil, over all the inhabitants, including customary chiefs and monarchs.[9] Having become a French protectorate in the 1880s, Wallis and Futuna were not concerned by the 1946 Constitution, but at the time of the 1958 referendum (which took place in December 1959 in the archipelago) 94 per cent voted in favour of the French *Communauté*, thus deciding to become an overseas territory.[10]

Les Etablissements Français de l'Océanie

At the time the Pacific Battalion was sent from Tahiti to Bir-Hakeim and Italy in 1940, Pape'ete, at that time capital of the so-called French Settlement of Oceania, had two factions in constant opposition to each other, one supporting Pétain, the other de Gaulle. While the numerous French civil servants based in Tahiti were very active in political intrigues, successive palace revolutions would jail or deport the faction not in power to remote islands until the next palace revolution. When the Pacific Battalion returned to Tahiti in 1945, the veterans told of their disgust at what they had observed in black-market France. Anti-French feelings emerged—especially against civil servants—and in that peculiar context crowds of Tahitians tried in 1947 to stop the disembarkation of newly arriving civil servants, who were already considered too numerous. Usually, after wars, veterans enjoy special status within their society because of their patriotic attitude and their direct confrontation with death. They form a specific group within the community and, neither fearing to confront civil authority nor to affront profiteers after their return home, veterans are often willing to bring change to their society if it no longer corresponds to the ideas they had of it while on the battlefield.

That was the case in Tahiti under the leadership of a World War One veteran who co-founded the Tahitian committee of de Gaulle's *France libre*: Pouvana'a a O 'opa, a carpenter. Pouvana'a was jailed during the war for denouncing administrative abuses in food supply; he escaped and, sought by the authorities, went from Huahine to Bora Bora in a canoe. Perceived both as hero and martyr, Pouvana'a led, when the 1946 Constitution offered the possibility of setting up proper political parties in Tahiti, the first populist party, called *Rassemblement des Populations Tahitiennes*. Nationalistic in essence, this party was founded on strong opposition to both the *popa'a farani* (French), who dominated institutional and economic structures, and the *Tinito* (Chinese), who dominated trade.

Pouvana'a's political ideas were twofold: on the one hand, he wanted Tahitians to master their own destiny, and advocated that all levels of public affairs and government be in the hands of Ma'ohi people; on the other, through his biblical upbringing, he advocated more social justice and collective land tenure in opposition to private land ownership, in order to protect Ma'ohi land. Pouvana'a considered the Bible and the rules it dictated to Christian people as the first of all laws. Moreover, he constantly made reference to the Sacred Book, equating the Ma'ohi with the Hebrews in captivity under Egyptian rule. Although his command of French was inadequate to address the French parliament, Pouvana'a had sufficient French to get by, and was first elected to the French national parliament as *député* in 1949 and re-elected until 1960.

The 1957 *loi-cadre* increased the number of territorial councillors from twenty to thirty and set up a Council of Government with six to eight ministers from whom a deputy-president was elected, the president of the Council of Government being *de jure* the governor of the territory. Extended decision powers were given to the Council of Government by the *loi-cadre* which established a very high degree of internal self-government and much juridical power was given to each minister.[11]

At the time of the 1958 referendum, Pouvana'a, like Sekou Touré of Guinea, advocated a 'No'. But he was not followed by the churches and the other political parties, and only one-third of the voters followed his refusal that his country become a member of the *Communauté*. Feelings ran high in Pape'ete at that time and the governor dissolved the Council of Government. Rumours of a plot, supposedly organised by Pouvana'a (who apparently wanted, by the end of October 1958, to set fire to the town of Pape'ete) ended with his arrest, and he was condemned one year later by a criminal court in Tahiti to eight years' jail and fifteen years' banishment.[12]

Pouvana'a was a charismatic leader, and his moral authority was to influence Tahitian political life right up to the present. As approved by the 1958 referendum, the French Settlement of Oceania became the Overseas Territory of French Polynesia. Ministerial positions disappeared after a reform decided by Paris in December 1958 returned all executive powers to the French governor, who again became the state representative in the territory as well as its overall executive head.

Returning to power in 1958, General de Gaulle was more pragmatic than he had been during World War Two. The *Communauté* organised under his 1958 Constitution became unworkable in the early 1960s as most of the self-governing states and French overseas territories achieved independence. According to the Constitution it was not possible for an overseas territory to become independent just by legal decree. Its institutions must first evolve, either within the structure of an overseas territory[13] or by becoming a French department. As integral parts of France, overseas territories could not secede. Later, however, in the 1970s, Djibouti and the Comores were granted independence soon after general elections in each territory affirmed their desire. Thus, the official position of the French government is that an overseas territory may become independent when the majority of its inhabitants wishes, through democratic elections. This amounts to recognition of self-determination.

General de Gaulle was especially pragmatic in dealing with Algeria. Under pressure, and forgetting his promises to French settlers there in 1958, he decided to let Algeria go, and with it his ideas of *Communauté* for the former French empire. Wanting to pursue the nuclear testing programme started under the previous republic, de Gaulle saw the need to find another place to conduct atomic tests, as Algerian independence would not permit continuing them at Reggane in the Sahara Desert.

From a reading of his *Memoirs*, it is quite clear that General de Gaulle was determined to let the French empire (or whatever it might have been called) go. He was searching for a new source of glory for the Fifth Republic, not only for the French people, whose historical past is part of their psyche, but also for the army (especially its senior officers) whose morale had been strongly affected by defeat by the Indo-Chinese at Dien Bien Phu in 1956 and the Algerian events—never recognised as a war, only as an 'operation to maintain order'.

This desire to reassert the glory of France and regain its world rank and prestige was to be realised through the implementation of the nuclear deterrent. In developing such a 'defensive' weapon, France would assure not only its autonomy of decision in national defence, but also place itself among the very few nations that possessed the nuclear deterrent, which would have important consequences for international relationships and the economy (with the non-military use of nuclear energy). Not surprisingly, through all the different governments under the Fifth Republic, there has been a general consensus on nuclear deterrence as well as a continuity of thought among the four French presidents, despite their political differences. If François Mitterrand was opposed to deterrence and nuclear tests as leader of the opposition (up to 1981), his position rapidly turned about after he became president of France. Nuclear deterrence is pivotal for the Fifth Republic. But the problem of glory would be solved in, and by, the French Polynesian islands.

Withering of statutes

For obvious strategic reasons and with a political logic internal to France, Charles de Gaulle could not permit any movement for autonomy to develop in French Polynesia. This is the main reason that ministerial positions were abolished in the Council of Government. A little later, foreign diplomatic delegations in Tahiti were forced to close, in order that only diplomatic missions based in Paris would be accredited to French Pacific territories.[14] In taking this action, de Gaulle knew that there would be few diplomatic missions to investigate the situation in Polynesia because few foreign diplomats would be able to justify the cost and necessity of travelling eighteen thousand kilometres from Paris to visit the archipelago.

After an attempt by some American companies to invest and become shareholders in the Caledonian nickel-mining business, de Gaulle decided that New Caledonia should be treated like French Polynesia and in 1963 abolished all ministerial portfolios in the territorial government. Although France had been a progressive colonial power from the end of World War Two, it became a reactionary one under the Fifth Republic, for purely internal political reasons. The first French atomic bomb exploded on 2 July 1966 in the sky above Moruroa.

New Caledonia, 1960–1990: A society without communal projects

In the 1960s the Caledonian Union favoured Melanesian inclusion in Caledonian society as much as possible. But few Kanaks achieved local political positions. The search for a separate Kanak identity merged with the birth of the nationalist Kanak movement in the early 1970s. The students' revolution of May 1968 in metropolitan France, with its ideals of freedom and questioning of bourgeois values within French society, was an important element in this process. Another was the reconsideration and questioning by Kanak priests—the first Kanaks to receive a Western education—of their involvement in their own traditional societies. Eventually, the fear by Kanaks of too many new metropolitan French in their country, aiming at land occupation and future electoral balances, reinforced the need to politically structure the search for a stronger Kanak identity.[15] The influx of Wallisians to work in the nickel-mining industry from the late 1950s contributed to Kanak fears. By the mid-1970s, the cultural festival organised by Jean-Marie Tjibaou, 'Melanesia 2000', had taken place, as had the setting up of the 'Popular Kanak Schools' by Andrea Gopea and others. Each was intended to revive traditional Melanesian values, which were perceived as the only possible response to the Kanaks' need to reaffirm their cultural identity.[16]

This Kanak search for cultural identity may conceal the fundamental problem in New Caledonia, the deep-rooted conflict between two antagonistic sets of societal values: on the one hand, the Western socio-economic model (symbolised by Noumea), and on the other, the traditional and customary Melanesian way of life (symbolised by tribal settlements). The writings of Kanak leaders suggest a rejection of Western urban values and an unconditional will to return to traditional, customary, and rural values. The serious problem New Caledonia has been faced with for over two decades is surely rooted in two opposing conceptions of life, or two antagonistic mind-sets that go beyond simple ethnic cleavages. Attempting to understand the situation solely in terms of the ethnic dimension is inadequate. For example, some Kanak leaders, like Senator Dick Ukeiwe or MP Maurice Nenou on the urban or Western side, hold Western political and socio-economic values, whereas Jean-Marie Tjibaou, Eloi Machoro, and Yeiwene Yeiwene positioned themselves on the rural or Kanak side. Instead of this rural–urban, Western–Kanak dichotomy, it might be instructive to examine New Caledonian society by looking at the two communities of people divided according to their thought processes, which are often radically different, but not necessarily antagonistic.

The Kanak psyche includes the remembrance of past colonial abuses, which are perceived as still existing. Central to its vision, which is essentially customary and rural, are aspirations for future social projects based on radical changes in present conditions. Its rhetoric emphasises a Melanesian identity shared with peoples who have already gained political independence (Papua New Guinea, the Solomons, Vanuatu). It also incorporates the long list of broken political promises and the history of double-talk from Paris, especially the ten or so changes of statutes New Caledonia has witnessed since the *loi-cadre*. These are the main elements of Kanak determination to radicalise and strengthen their nationalism, which they believe will lead to a better future.

The common denominator in the second group's mind-set, obviously less homogeneous than the first, is a conviction of the necessity to pursue development with France. It is considered that the majority of Pacific Island states that have gained constitutional independence are still economically dependent, and a beggar's mentality towards former colonial powers has emerged among their leaders, disguising what is essentially a continuation of the power relationships that existed prior to independence. Recognising the futility of this independentist illusion, the second group rejects the adversary dualism of 'independence versus dependence', preferring interdependence within a freely chosen partnership with France. This does not imply, for some people within this group, an unwillingness to both modify interethnic relationships inherited from the past and encourage an enhanced Caledonian identity. Because of the apparent incompatibility of these two societal options, however, no immediate solution has been evident, exacerbating the inflexible entrenchment of some Western pressure groups in their socio-economic positions, assets, and interests.

Identification with mutually antagonistic societal goals is at the heart of internal Caledonian oppositions. The fragmentation of this country is rooted in its peculiar past: at the 1983 census, for example, not a single Kanak was counted among the learned professions. Feeling excluded from a system that could not or would not integrate them, the majority of Melanesians believe the Kanak egalitarian model of life to be the only solution for a better future.

New Caledonia is a multi-ethnic society, with, according to the 1983 census, roughly 62 000 Melanesians (43%), 54 000 Europeans (37%), 12 200 Wallisians (8.4%), 5600 Tahitians (3.8%), 5400 Indonesians (3.7%), 2400 Vietnamese (1.6%), 1200 ni-Vanuatu (0.8%), and 2900 Others (2%).[17] Each community derives its identity from its own past. Wallisians, for example, rapidly became integrated into the modern productive sector of the economy, forming the nickel's proletariat. At the same time they have preserved their traditions and customs, thereby achieving a special place in New Caledonian society. Born in New Caledonia, the second-generation Wallisians perceive the country as their own and are less concerned about their links with their parents' archipelago.[18] This second generation is in trouble, especially in Noumea suburbs. Adolescent deviance is a major social problem that includes school problems, alcoholism, violence, cultural inadequacy, and so on. They no longer speak the Wallisian language and have great difficulty adapting to an urban culture.

As much a colonial product as the Wallisian migrants, the *Caldoche* (people of European or mixed extraction) likewise feel that their roots are in the country in which, as in Australia or New Zealand, they are sometimes fifth- or sixth-generation settlers. The *Caldoche* no longer identify with the metropolitan French; on the contrary, they perceive themselves as having more in common with white Australians, sharing a similar cultural history, although they were ambivalent about the attitude of Australia during the political events of 1984–1988 in New Caledonia.[19]

That in the foreseeable future no particular ethnic group will be able to hold an overall majority was taken into account by Michel Rocard after the Uvea disaster in 1988, upon his appointment as the new prime minister in Paris. For far too long New Caledonia has been a purely political problem, inflaming passions in France when violent events hit the headlines, only to fall back into oblivion as soon as quiet was restored. These intermittent appearances have not facilitated a real understanding of the country, especially when French politicians, in either the parliament or the Senate, tended to invert their usual ideological stance when dealing with New Caledonia. For instance, many would advocate the implementation of a multiracial society in France while rejecting the same programme for New Caledonia, and, at the other end of the political spectrum, many pleaded for the return of North African migrants in France to their home countries while rejecting the same programme for French migrants in New Caledonia. This lack of consistency perhaps reflects a characteristic ideological contradiction and certainly betrayed a continuing ignorance of a French overseas territory that has often been the subject of passionate political debate in Paris.

Despite its relatively small population, New Caledonia is a very complex political entity similar to countries with several million inhabitants. Journalists and writers usually present its political problems in dualistic terms— 'loyalist *Caldoches*' versus 'FLNKS Kanaks'—a simplistic perception that conceals the true complexity.

In the late 1970s and in the early 1980s, under Jean-Marie Tjibaou's leadership, the Caledonian Union programme to promote Melanesian identity evolved from the position that more self-government should be granted by Paris (as was the case with the 1957 *loi-cadre*) to the search for independence through an institutional framework. After the agreement at Nainville-les-Roches collapsed in 1984, the Independentist Front, chaired by Tjibaou, became the Kanak Socialist National Liberation Front (FLNKS), grouping together several political parties. These included the old Caledonian Union chaired by Tjibaou; PALIKA (Kanak Liberation Party, advocating Kanak revolutionary socialist independence, collective ownership of the essential means of production, and power to the Kanak people and not to the Kanak bourgeoisie); FULK (United Front for Kanak Liberation, led by Yann Céléne Uregei, Minister of Foreign Affairs of FLNKS until his dismissal, and well known in religious and academic circles in Australia and New Zealand, as well as in Libya); UPM (Melanesian Progressive Union, sharing the French Revolutionary Communist League's options and instigator of the Kanak schools movement); and PSK (Kanak Socialist Party, based in Noumea, looking for an alliance between trade unions and all Caledonian workers, whatever their ethnicity). To these political parties must be added USTKE (Trade Union of Exploited Kanak Workers) and GFKEL (Fighting Group of Exploited Kanak Women). Under irrelevant directives from Paris, the FLNKS would increasingly radicalise its political positions, until the dramatic events of April 1988 ended in a nineteenth-century-style colonial massacre at Uvea. Too many Kanak youths and French gendarmes lost their lives.

According to the Matignon Accord, signed in Paris in August 1988 under the personal impetus of Prime Minister Michel Rocard by the principal New Caledonian leaders, all New Caledonians will choose, in a referendum to be organised in 1998, constitutional independence *or not* for New Caledonia, to be implemented from then on. After five years of violent trouble and unrest, the Matignon Accord not only gives time to Kanak leaders to prepare for independence, but also gives the country the chance to regain some calm. The president and the deputy-president of the FLNKS, Jean-Marie Tjibaou and Yeiwene Yeiwene, were killed just one year after the Uvea massacre by some Kanaks who could not accept the futility of the Uvea youths' deaths and what they perceived as the FLNKS leaders' treason in relation to their previous political commitments. New FLNKS leaders have since been elected but it is questionable whether young Kanak people will wait for ten years before resuming active political involvement.

Wallis and Futuna (1961–1990): Custom and tradition in transition

Following the wish expressed by the voters in the referendum of 27 December 1959, a law was promulgated on 29 July 1961 making Wallis and Futuna a French Overseas Territory.

The existing system of government, as defined by the 1961 statute, is based on the 1957 *loi-cadre* and subsequent amendments and decrees, and largely reflects the customs and religious affiliation of the territory and its inhabitants as well as its geographic isolation and lack of resources. For instance, the third article of the statute allows for the free exercise of the Roman Catholic religion in the archipelago and for the metropolitan state to continuously pay for the salaries and recruitment, decided by the Wallisian Roman Catholic bishop, of all local and metropolitan secondary schoolteachers coming to the archipelago. Such liberality exists nowhere else in French overseas territories or departments, or in the Fifth Republic.

Under the Constitution, the territory elects one member (or *député*) and one senator to the national parliament in France. As head of the territory, the superior administrator represents the French government in the territory and is included with governors of overseas territories or high commissioners when representing his territory in legal and defence matters. The Territorial Assembly, elected through general franchise every five years, comprises twenty members. The archipelago is subdivided into three areas, each with its own council presided over by its own king. Wallisians and Futunans are French citizens, but the great majority of them follow customary practices rather than French civil laws, except that the French penal laws are applicable to everybody residing in the territory. Land tenure in Wallis and Futuna is defined by custom and validated by the Territorial Assembly.[20]

Administratively, the archipelago represents, strictly speaking, not only a legal contradiction within the unified French sphere (according to which every French citizen is under the same rules and laws), but also the flexibility France can use, when the political will exists, in dealing with an overseas territory. This flexibility weakens the frequent legalistic assertion of the impossibility of providing specific rules or laws for New Caledonia in order to take Caledonian peculiarities into account. For example, by acknowledging in the 1961 statute the existence and permanence of three monarchical powers in Wallis and Futuna (and giving each of them a civil list), France officially recognises that the republican model might not always be applicable to all French citizens. So much the better!

Wallis and Futuna are inhabited today by around 12 000 people. No more than 200 expatriates (most of them French civil servants and their families) live there, where they normally cannot own land.

Wallis and Futuna live harmoniously under a dual-power system that combines elements of the traditional customary structure and the modern French state. The system has a number of implications for the everyday life of Wallisians and Futunans. Territorial civil servants account for about 1000 people today compared to only 120 in the late 1970s. Health care has been entirely the responsibility of the French state since 1972, while education, financed by Paris, is totally free of charge at the primary and secondary levels.[21] France also provides university scholarships to tertiary students, and retirement benefits for every person over fifty-five years of age.

The economy continues to be based on traditional subsistence food production (taro, sweet potato, bananas, and the like), with pigs, chicken, and lagoon or coastal fish to provide protein. Coconut plantations (4000 hectares or so) do not produce copra any longer because of transport costs, lack of international demand, and depressed world prices. Exports are non-existent. Traditional food used to be sent to Wallisians living in New Caledonia in return for remittances.[22] Handicrafts produced by women are sold overseas or to the few local tourists.

The essential infrastructure (electricity, roads, water system, public build-ing construction, fuel depots, hospitals, air transport, radio and television stations, and so forth) is financed by the French state as are social and health services and education. The territorial budget (supplemented by philatelic and tobacco sales, customs duties, and import taxes) only partly covers spending, the deficit being offset by yearly French aid.

Having achieved some modernisation while remaining essentially tradi-tional, the archipelago is almost completely dependent on France financially.[23] In the long term, a movement towards independence seems unlikely to emerge in the territory, because Wallis and Futuna would not think of separating itself from its prime source of income. However, the status quo between traditional and modernising forces might change. Young people who have completed military service in France have tremendous difficulties readjusting to the traditional life-style and tend to regret their incursion into modernity. With the nickel-mining depression in New Caledonia,[24] they encounter difficulties finding jobs in Noumea and rapidly become critical of the nobility, the traditions, and their strict societal rules. These young people could become a force for change in Wallis and Futuna. Prime Minister Rocard visited the archipelago during August 1989 and at once understood the problem. He set up a programme to pay wages to hundreds of young people for planting trees and flowers along the roads in Wallis so that they can learn horticultural techniques. This example illustrates the disequilibrium often existing between modernity and tradition.

French Polynesia, 1961–1990: Modernity inflicted

In 1960, the main resources of the territory were agricultural (copra and vanilla) and phosphates from Makatea in the Tuamotus, which was exhausted in the early 1960s. The shooting of the film *Mutiny on the Bounty* in Tahiti and Moorea by Metro-Goldwyn-Mayer in 1961 with Marlon Brando had a tremendous psychological effect. Hundreds of film technicians stayed in Tahiti for months. People rented out accommodation and were employed as film extras. They realised that incomes did not have to come from agricultural work. In 1963, the completion of Fa'a'a international airport linked Tahiti with the external world and tourism began to be an important activity, creating a demand for hotels.

However, the major modernising factor arose from the decision to use two Tuamotu atolls—Fangataufa and Mururoa—to conduct nuclear tests, together with the necessity to use Hao Island as well as Pape'ete as military bases. Thousands of French engineers, technicians, and military personnel came to Tahiti, often with their families, to live for a few years. The need for immense military construction compounds, European-standard accommodation, and French food had a double impact: not only did French Polynesian people from all the islands leave their rural plantations to offer labour to the new construction sector, but also the territorial budget increased tremendously through new customs duties and taxes on all the imported materials and products from France. Tahiti very rapidly gained the appearance of a rich country, in part because French salaries, civil or military, are doubled while metropolitan people live in French Polynesia. Local salaries soon followed, to avoid discrepancies in incomes. Although there is no income tax in French Polynesia, the cost of living is very high because of import duties. Consequently, without strong budgetary support, agricultural activities would have entirely disappeared because they could no longer offer reasonable incomes to producers. For this reason, even today, producers in French Polynesia are paid more for their copra than it sells for on the world market, in an attempt to keep people in the islands and discourage them from going to the already overcrowded town of Pape'ete and its suburbs.

Another example that demonstrates the artificiality of this type of economy is the production of potatoes in the Austral Islands, which have a suitable climate. Someone who owns a piece of land in Rurutu, for example, is eligible to receive free of charge from the territorial agricultural ministry all machinery and drivers necessary to flatten, plough, and furrow the land. The landowner then places in the furrows the potato seeds provided gratuitously by the agricultural ministry, and the machines cover the seeds. When the potatoes are mature, other machines with specialised technicians come to harvest them, and the ministry, from its own budget, sends the produce to Pape'ete to be sold. However, because the Tahitian market is usually well supplied by Australian and New Zealand potato exporters, the Rurutu potatoes, not finding buyers, often end up rotting in Pape'ete's dockside sheds. The ministry then provides financial compensation to the unlucky Rurutu potato producer. This example reflects what is too often called *development* and the very high degree of artificiality through which the French Polynesian economy works.[25]

As the entire French Polynesian economy came to depend heavily on military expenditure, its solvency was also at the mercy of the military. In the last few years, the French government has reduced the numbers of army people sent to Tahiti, mainly for budgetary reasons because costs initially engendered by the nuclear testing activities were inflationary and, after twenty years of operation, became too high for the Ministry of Defence. As a consequence, military personnel or engineers and technicians are now often sent from Paris without their families, for shorter periods. The effects on commerce, house rents, import taxes, and so on have been so negative that French Polynesia is now in a very difficult financial situation. The overall debt of the territory amounts to several million US dollars, and Paris seems to have decided not to continue supplementing the deficit to the same extent as in the past. The suspension of nuclear testing in 1992 can only exacerbate this situation and reflects not only the increasingly high cost of conducting the tests (one test costs around one billion French francs or US$250 million) but also the political decision not to increase the budget for them. Another reason that might explain why Paris remains unwilling to carry on supplementing the territorial budget is the self-governing status the territory gained in 1984.

Since then, French Polynesia has been ruled by a president and ten ministers elected by the 42 Territorial Assembly members, themselves elected by general franchise every four years. All portfolios are in the hands of the territorial government except justice, defence, and treasury. In foreign affairs the president of the territorial government is fully able to sign conventions with other Pacific Island states officially recognised by France. Without going into details, French Polynesia has a self-governing status similar to that of the Cook Islands with New Zealand.[26] Because of this status, Paris thinks that French Polynesia should also organise its spending within the limits of the large transfer of public money France makes every year (well over one billion US dollars). Like a spoiled mistress soon to be abandoned by her lover, French Polynesia's attitude has evolved from one of willing acceptance of largesse to concern that the polluting effects of the relationship may, after the lover is long gone, threaten its very existence.

French Polynesia experienced major trouble in October 1987, when Pape'ete was set on fire during a night of rampage. Some have explained the uprising in terms of inequalities between economic classes. While it is true that Chinese shops were ransacked, loot-worthy shops in Pape'ete are nearly all Chinese anyway. It is also true that French Polynesia is a class society: the richest are the top metropolitan civil servants, the Chinese, and the *Demis* (persons of mixed French and Polynesian descent), who hold the financial and productive means.[27] The remaining classes are the employed wage workers, who have a general education; and the poor and uneducated who are ill-at-ease in the Tahitian consumer society because their lack of resources excludes them. All of them want a share of today's prosperity and all the status symbols that go with it. Pape'ete is surrounded by slums, especially on its western edge. Inside the slum dwellings are the modern consumer items generated by Western societies: refrigerators, televisions, videos, and so forth. Often children in Tahiti may have no food to eat at home because their parents have to make payments on loans for the four-wheel-drive car, the last video, the engine-powered boat, and the rest. Young children starve in Tahiti during school holidays because they are not fed at home, the only meal they are used to being the free midday one at school. Artificial economies engender artificial habits and, for a part of French Polynesian society, there has been a cultural transfer to what is perceived as modernity.

French Polynesia has a per capita gross national product a little higher than that of New Zealand, but its wealth distribution is much more uneven. Official figures that would show the composition of this society according to such indicators as purchasing power are not available to depict the plight of the system's leftovers.

Conclusion

It may be argued that, strictly speaking, colonial rule is not maintained in these French overseas territories because each of them may attain constitutional independence by simply voting for it at election time and because they already have, or will soon have, some degree of internal self-government. However, at all levels, the economic, social, and even cultural systems are permeated by remnants of colonial domination. But the Hegelian relationship between masters and slaves, the latter in fact masters of the former, also applies. In financial terms, Tahitians and Wallisians probably more than New Caledonians excel in contriving that Paris increase aid flows on the basis of the colonial past and the guilt it engenders in Paris ministries. The game is not necessarily only one way, although it cannot be played by constitutionally independent countries because the former colonial power turned that page when it granted independence. Moreover, Great Britain and New Zealand and Australia—the last two being *Pacific powers*—too often forget their obligation towards their former colonies. That Pacific Islanders aspire to one form or another of modernity is evident in the incredible numbers of Pacific Island migrants to New Zealand, Australia, and the United States. Strict restrictions are imposed on Samoans, Tongans, and others. Only Cook Islanders and Niueans have free access to the cities of Auckland and Wellington because of the free association of their respective countries with New Zealand.

Will France change its attitude towards its three territories in the Pacific in the foreseeable future? Since 1986 Paris has wanted them to be more involved in the Pacific Islands region in terms of trade and economic relations as well as in political and cultural matters. Such integration is not easy to achieve because of differences in standards of living as well as language. But dialogues with their neighbour countries are becoming an increasing reality of daily life in New Caledonia and French Polynesia. Any sudden change in the level of financial transfers from Paris could, paradoxically, reinforce the cohesion within the region between the French territories and the constitutionally independent Pacific Island states. New partnerships will emerge, and old ones may be maintained, but not necessarily on the same bases.

*   *   *

I EXPRESS my thanks to Peter Crowe and to an anonymous reviewer for helpful comments.

Notes

1 The Protectorate of Wallis and Futuna was also administered from Noumea under the executive authority of Thierry d'Argenlieu (1889–1959), who was instructed to find all means to protect and assure the defence of the French Pacific colonies with the help of the Allies. Emile de Curton became the French governor in Tahiti for the duration of the war.

2 Was the *loi-cadre* an undeniably significant advance in preparing the two French territories for independence, or was it instead a means to encourage them to maintain their links with France by making major concessions and reforms?

  Loi-cadre number 56–619 of 23 June 1956 was applied in the two territories through a decree signed the following year by the French prime minister. For example in French Polynesia, 'Decree numéro 57–812 portant institution d'un Conseil de gouvernement et extension des attributions de l'assemblée territoriale dans les Etablissements français de l'Océanie (22 July 1957)', *Journal Officiel de la Polynésie Française*, 15 August 1957, 446–455; and 'Decree numéro 57–817 portant déconcentration administrative par transfert d'attribution des services centraux du Ministère de la France d'outre-mer', *Journal Officiel de la Polynésie Française*, 15 August 1957, 453–455. See also Jean Pérès, *Histoire de l'évolution des institutions politiques: De Tahiti à la Polynésie Française*, 2nd ed, Pape'ete, 1987, mimeo, 19–23; Albert Daussin-Charpantier, 'L'expérience polynésienne d'autonomie interne: Avatar de la décentralisation ou étape vers l'independance association, *La Vie Départementale et Régionale*, number 45, 1988, 21; and Charles Cadoux, 'L'accès de la Polynésie Française à l'autonomie interne: Point d'aboutissement ou nouvelle base de départ', *Revue de Droit Public et International*, number 2, Paris, 1989, 360–361, from which I quote (my translation): 'From the simple administrative decentralisation (statute of 1946) we were starting towards "political" decentralisation. There was here a dynamic that could evolve into real autonomy'.

In fact, the governor of French Polynesia who then became the chief of the territory, possessed competence only in national and international affairs. See Michel Lextreyt, 'Il y a trente ans: La Loi-cadre Défferre (1956) ou: Comment la Polynésie a échoué dans sa première expérience d'autonomie interne', *Bulletin de la Société des Etudes Océaniennes*, number 237, vol. 20, no. 2, 1968, 26; and Christian Gleizal, ed., *Encyclopédie de la Polynésie Française: La Polynésie s'ouvre au Monde (1842–1960)*, vol. 7, Pape'ete, 1987, 48, 'to provide a council which sits around the Governor and which is, in some ways, a Council of Ministers'. In French Polynesia, Pouvana'a a O'opa was then called Prime Minister.

The concepts of *autonomie interne* and *self-government* do not possess the same meaning in the English and the French languages. *Autonomie interne* in French (usually translated into English as 'self-government' means that the territorial government or assembly deals statutorily with all areas of competence that do not have national or international implications such as Foreign Affairs, Defence, Treasury, and so on. In other words, *autonomie interne* means in the French language 'self-administration' or 'internal self-government'. In English, the definition of self-government (Webster's 1985) is 'government under the control and direction of the inhabitants of a political unit rather than by an outside authority', *autonomy* being 'the quality or state of being self-governing'.

As independence, on a constitutional level, means political separation, even though *autonomie interne* and *self-government* (whether in free association or not) do not have identical meanings, both terms imply dependency.

The *loi-cadre* applied in New Caledonia in the same way as in French Polynesia. See V. Thompson and R. Adloff, *The French Pacific Islands: French Polynesia and New Caledonia*, University of California Press, Berkeley, 1971, 303–305; Bernard Brou, *30 ans d'histoire de la Nouvelle-Calédonie, 1945–1977*, Société d'Etudes historiques de la Nouvelle-Calédonie, Noumea, n.d., 48–49; Alain Christnacht, *La Nouvelle-Calédonie*, 2nd edn, La Documentation Française, Notes et Documents, 1990, 40; and Stephen Henningham, *France and the South Pacific: A Contemporary History*, Allen & Unwin, Sydney and University of Hawai'i Press, Honolulu, 1991, 55.

3 Decolonisation means 'to free from colonial status'. There are three options for doing this, as stipulated by the United Nations: granting independence; integrating into the metropolis (departmentalisation, like Martinique in the West Indies, or Hawai'i becoming the fiftieth state of the United States); or self-government in free association with the metropolis (like the Cook Islands or Niue).

4 Only Guinea in Africa voted a massive 'No' at the time of the referendum and became independent under Sekou Touré. All links with France were cut immediately. Under the sway of Pouvana'a, one-third of French Polynesia's electors voted 'No', giving the unsatisfied de Gaulle the impression that the territory had mixed feelings about his referendum. On this point, see Henningham, 120–126;

and Philippe Guesdon, *L'évolution statutaire de la Polynésie Française ou le mouvement autonomiste face à ses contraintes*, Mémoire de Sciences Politiques, Poitiers, 1976, 28–39.

The independence of Algeria (full political separation) was perceived by Charles de Gaulle as the only solution to end the war. Once Algeria had gained its independence, it was logical that the other African colonies should follow suit, although retaining strong neo-colonial links with France.

5 Missionaries had previously engaged Melanesians to cultivate coffee and copra plantations. Melanesians, especially from Lifou and Mare, had also begun to come to Noumea and to European plantations on the main island to find paid employment.

6 The American forces offered to develop basic rural infrastructures such as roads, schools, and so on. The French authorities refused. All infrastructure necessary for the American presence had been built as part of the war effort (Tontouta airport and a road to link it to Noumea, as well as jetties). See Henry Daly, 'La guerre du Pacifique: Les hôpitaux américains en Nouvelle-Calédonie', *in Bulletin de la Société d'Etudes Historiques de la Nouvelle-Calédonie*, 1989, no. 79, 42–52. When the American forces left in 1946, orders were sent from Paris to refuse their offer to sell all army material except weapons at a nominal price. On the orders of the French government, jeeps, bulldozers, trucks, corrugated iron sheets, and the like were dumped in lagoons around New Caledonia and in Lake Lano on Wallis. New Caledonia was to favour the re-emerging French economy by buying French products. See Jacqueline Senès, *La vie quotidienne en Nouvelle-Calédonie de 1850 à nos jours*, Hachette, Paris, 1985, 284; and Bernard Brou, *Espoirs et réalités: La Nouvelle-Calédonie de 1925 à 1945*, no. 9, Société d'Etudes Historiques de la Nouvelle-Calédonie, Noumea, 1975, 187–188.

7 Union des Indigènes calédoniens amis de la liberté dans l'ordre: Union of Caledonian Indigenous Peoples, Friends of Liberty within Order, and Association des Indigènes calédoniens et loyaltiens français: Association of French Caledonian and Loyalty Islands Indigenous Peoples.

8 See Jean-Claude Roux, *Espaces coloniaux et sociétés polynésiennes de Wallis et Futuna*, thesis, Université de Paris 1; see also Nancy Pollock, 'Doctor Administrators in Wallis and Futuna', *Journal of Pacific History* 25 (1, 1990): 47–67, a paper largely inspired by and based on Jean-Claude Roux's thesis.

9 The king of Wallis and the bishop—the present one, Monseigneur Lolesio Fuahea, the first indigenous bishop—are usually addressed as *Aliki* (Lord) or *Te Hau*. The bishop holds the spiritual power while the king holds the customary power. Before Bishop Lolesio, French bishops in Wallis were the pivotal link between French administrators and the various chiefs. Because French administrators very rarely speak Wallisian, they are automatically in an inferior position to the church. Up to very recent times the bishop selected the French nationals who came to Wallis and Futuna to teach in secondary schools and were paid by the French Ministry of Education. This is an example of the dominance of the Roman Catholic church. Of course the *Administrateurs supérieurs* asserted the influence of the French state, but the influence of the Catholic church remains essential to an understanding of past and present life on Wallis and Futuna. See Jean-Claude Roux, 'Pouvoir religieux et pouvoir politique à Wallis et Futuna', in *Etats et Pouvoirs dans les Territoires Français du Pacifique*, ed. Paul de Deckker and P.

Lagayette, L'Harmattan, Paris, 1987, 54–80; and Frédéric Angleviel, *Wallis et Futuna (1801–1888): Contacts, Evangélisations, Inculturations*, thèse-ès-lettres, Université Paul Valéry, Montpellier III, 1989.

10 With 4307 voting 'Yes' and only 257 voting 'No', Wallis and Futuna decided overwhelmingly in favour of becoming a French Overseas Territory. The status of the territory is defined by statutory law (no. 61814 of 29 July 1961), and in Article 3 the customary powers and the Roman Catholic religion of the inhabitants are expressly recognised and respected.

11 See note 2, above.

12 For years the French government was asked to review the conclusions of the criminal court, considered in Tahiti completely unjustified because they were politically influenced. A statue of Pouvana'a now stands in Tarahoi Place in Pape'ete, just in front of the offices of the territorial government and the high commissioner. An association, which includes Polynesian and French politicians and lawyers, was founded years ago to lobby both the French Senate and the parliament for a new trial.

13 The 1958 Constitution of France remains ambiguous and unclear on the question of overseas territories proceeding to independence. According to article 2, 'France is an indivisible. . . . Republic', and article 53 states, 'treaties . . . which concern cession, exchange or adjunction of a territory can only be ratified or approved by a law. . . . No cession, no exchange, no adjunction of territory is valid without the consent of the interested populations'. Thus, for a territory to attain sovereignty and secede from France, two guarantees are necessary: the Republic must enact a law, and the interested populations must consent. However, in political terms independence is generally presented as the achievement of decolonisation. When Djibouti and the Comores sought independence, the Constitutional Council in Paris validated their respective referendums on the basis of article 53 and then extended the interpretation of the 1958 constitution, thereby avoiding a political crisis. See Jean-Yves Faberon, *Le statut des Territoires d'Outre-Mer*, Centre Territorial de Recherche et de Documentation Pédagogique, Noumea, 1992, 5–27.

14 On 30 April 1965, after only three months of activities, US Consul George Gray closed the American Consulate in Pape'ete following instructions from Washington at the request of the French government. In 1948, Harry Truman had closed the original American Consulate after 112 years, for economic reasons. Its reopening coincided with the implementation of atomic testing. Argon Kuan, the Consul General of Taiwan, left Tahiti the same year, following a decision of the French government in Paris, and the Consulate General of Taiwan was closed. See Philippe Mazellier, *Tahiti: De l'atome à l'autonomie*, Hibiscus Editions, Pape'ete, 1979, 129–130.

15 See Olivier Apikaoua, *Eglises et aspirations indépendantistes mélanésiennes en Nouvelle-Calédonie de 1840 à 1984*, Mémoire de DEA, Université Française du Pacifique, Noumea, 1993.

16 See Jean-Marie Kohler and Patrick Pillon, *Adapter l'école ou réorienter le projet social: Le problème d'un enseignement spécifique pour les Mélanésiens*, Direction d'Enseignement catholique, Noumea, 1982; and Jean-Marie Kohler and Loïc Wacquant, 'La question scolaire en Nouvelle-Calédonie: Idéologies et sociologie', *Les Temps Modernes*, no. 464 (1985): 1654–1685.

17 For precise figures, see Alain Christnacht, *La Nouvelle-Calédonie*, La Documentation Française, Paris, 1987, 25–26.

18 Quite a few Wallisians became self-employed during the nickel boom as drivers who owned their own truck. This lasted a few years (1969–1972). As wage employees, Wallisians could send remittances to help their extended families at home obtain consumer products such as corned beef, wine, tinned fish, and the like. Paita, north of Noumea, is a Wallisian town that tries to recreate a Wallisian environment. See Sylvette Boyer, *Les Wallisiens de Paita*, Mémoire de maîtrise, University of Bordeaux 2, 1985.

19 They have a similar ambivalence in their attitude to France, because they identify with France in terms of language, culture, shared history, sometimes family connections, and so on, but they feel that their cultural roots are in the Pacific. Attitudes to France might in some respects be compared to those of fifth- and sixth-generation Australians and New Zealanders to Britain.

20 This *code coutumier* or *droit civil particulier* also applies in New Caledonia, covering Melanesian customary law. For example, if a Frenchman has an affair with a Melanesian woman and they have a child whom the man does not legally recognise, throughout its life this child will come under the *code coutumier*. If, two years after the child's birth, the Frenchman marries the mother and they have a second child, because they are now married under French law, their second child will not be covered by Melanesian customary law but by the French civil code. If at the time of his death the Frenchman leaves money to his two children, the money the first child receives will be diffused to the clan, while the second child, without clan obligations, may become a prosperous capitalist.

21 Since 1991 it has been possible for Wallisian pupils to sit for their baccalauréat in Uvea, and in 1993 the *Institut Universitaire de Formation des Maîtres* (teachers' training college), a branch of the *Université Française du Pacifique*, will open there.

22 Fewer and fewer remittances are sent to Wallis and Futuna by Wallisians in New Caledonia, as more and more of them decline to follow the traditional duty of supporting their relatives left at home. This of course implies both a greater involvement in the Western economy and a lesser concern with family matters in the remote archipelago. Frequently, they wait for their parents' death at home before finally cutting off their customary obligations. In 1983 Wallisians sent remittances from New Caledonia to their families at home to the value of at least US$200 000. See Benoit Anthéaume and Joël Bonnemaison, *Atlas des îles et états du Pacifique sud*, GIP Reclus and Publisud, Montpellier and Paris, 1988, 82.

23 See Karl H. Rensch, 'Wallis and Futuna: Total Dependency', in *Politics in Polynesia*, ed. R. Crocombe and A. Ali, University of the South Pacific, Suva, 1983, 4–17.

24 After World War Two, Wallisians and Futunans began to migrate to New Caledonia, peaking between 1968 and 1972 during the nickel boom. Today, the numbers of Wallisians in New Caledonia are about the same as in Wallis, that is 13 000. More than 50 per cent of them are under twenty years of age. Politically, the Wallisians and Futunans in New Caledonia tend to be on the side of the non-indigenous communities, even though a political party, l'Union Océanienne, was recently formed by Wallisians on the grounds that they should not appear to oppose Kanak aspirations for independence.

25 On this, for Tubuai Island, see an in-depth analysis by Victoria Lockwood, 'Development, French Neocolonialism, and the Structure of the Tubuai Economy', *Oceania* 58 (3, 1988): 176–192; and 'Welfare State Colonialism in Rural French Polynesia', in *Contemporary Pacific Societies: Studies in Development and Change*, eds Victoria S. Lockwood, Thomas G. Harding, and Ben J. Wallace, Prentice Hall, Englewood Cliffs, NJ, 1993, 81–97.

26 An in-depth analysis of the Cook Islands' and French Polynesia's statutes has been done by Jean Chevrier, 'Note (2254) au Haut-Commissaire de la République Française en Polynésie Française: Statut des îles Cook et Perspectives d'évolution de la Polynésie Française', Pape'ete, 31 October 1985, mimeo, 27 pages (with annex).

27 See the excellent work by Michel Panoff, *Tahiti métisse*, Denoël, Paris, 1989, which offers a constructive approach to the contemporary history of French Polynesia; and, for future prospects, Bernard Poirine, *Tahiti: Du melting-pot à l'explosion?* L'Harmattan, Paris, 1992.

Part 3
Uncertain times

Regionalism and nationalism

R. A. Herr

Regional organisation in the Pacific Islands is both a product of the colonial era and a mechanism for dealing with the post-colonial international environment. What began as a convenient administrative device for the reconstruction of the possessions of the colonial powers in the war-ravaged Pacific has now become a major instrument of foreign policy for the independent and self-governing states of the region. However, this transformation from colonial tool to instrument of independence has been evolutionary rather than revolutionary. An understanding of the historical context is essential to a full appreciation of the course of recent developments in Pacific regionalism. Equally, the challenges to Pacific regionalism cannot be understood without looking beyond the region to its rapidly changing international environment, especially since the late 1980s.

A few central themes have dominated regional co-operation in the Pacific Islands virtually from its origins. A preoccupation with economic development, introspection, dependence on external support, and a limited scope have been characteristic. Because all colonial governments were anxious to avoid unnecessary expenditure, they were prepared to co-operate in areas where a reduction in the cost of administration could be expected. Following independence, the new microstates hoped to achieve economies of scale through co-operation in pursuit of their developmental aspirations. That colonial regimes would steer regionalism towards introspection is no surprise. The metropolitan powers saw few gains in broadening the diplomatic horizons of their territories. The dependence on non-island funding to pay for the costs of co-operation was similarly predictable, given the sparse economic resources available to the Pacific Islands and the relatively low cost of these services to outside donors. Finally, the limited scope of regionalism in the Pacific can be explained substantially by the interaction of these factors over the years.

The logic of overcoming the islands' obvious economic and geographic limitations by means of some form of co-operative effort seemed so compelling that little serious critical assessment of the alternatives to regionalism has been made. Global mechanisms, particularly those associated with the United Nations, have been influential, as have other multilateral devices operating at either the subglobal or subregional levels. Nevertheless, in practice, the principal alternative has always been what it remains today— national self-reliance.

National interest stands out as a critical influence on Pacific regionalism at several levels. It has strongly influenced the agenda for co-operation, particularly in focusing developmental activities on export-enhancing projects. National interest has profoundly affected the structure of regionalism in the Pacific, as was perhaps most destructively evident in the issue of creating a single regional organisation, which dominated infrastructure decisions for more than a decade. National interest has also played a significant role in such procedural matters as the selection of staff and the assessment of contributions. It has even been a factor in subregionalism insofar as this impediment to regionalism is grounded in ethnically motivated loyalty to a Polynesian, Melanesian, or Micronesian cultural grouping.

The capacity of the Pacific Islands to regionally coordinate their international position has been impressive despite the constraints of nationalism. Arguably, given the islands' long-term support, multilateral co-operation at the regional level has achieved at least the minimum of hopes it engendered. Externally, Pacific regionalism can be seen as even more successful. It has surprised many external states that might have expected less resistance to the pursuit of their own interests in the region. Important examples are the regional regimes regulating nuclear materials, access to fisheries resources, and the protection of the marine environment.

In this chapter, the contemporary position of Pacific regionalism in terms of its evolution, extent, purposes, and relevance to changing circumstances both within the region and in the wider international order is reviewed. In particular I shall argue that, ironically, as the Pacific Islands have moved to reform regionalism internally, external changes may have overtaken their efforts. Pacific Island governments may well find that regional co-operation is no longer an optional addition to their statecraft, but an international necessity in a world increasingly dominated by large macro-regional trading blocs and the exigencies of a new international order.

Pacific regionalism in historical review

Contemporary intergovernmental regional co-operation dates from the establishment of the South Pacific Commission (SPC) in 1947.[1] By 1944, Australia and New Zealand were anxious to contribute to the 'new world order' of the post–World War Two era by advancing regional arrangements in their own corner of the globe. In the ANZAC Pact of that year, the two powers proposed two regional associations to coordinate post-war reconstruction in the Pacific—one to guarantee the security of the region and a second to promote the welfare of the indigenous people. The mutual security proposal never attracted the level of additional support that would have made it viable, but the humanitarian body did garner adequate interest to proceed, perhaps because, although focused on the Pacific Islands, the South Pacific Commission drew more broadly for its inspiration. It was intended, among other objectives, to implement the idealistic goals of the Atlantic Charter regarding the rights of dependent peoples to development.

However, national interest blocked the highest aims of regional co-operation when the six colonial powers with administrative control of the Pacific Islands met in Canberra in February 1947 to negotiate the establishment of the South Pacific Commission. The proposed regional body was denied a role in political development. Instead, it was given fairly broad responsibility for the limited mandate of coordinating research on economic, health, and social development. These modest aims enabled American, Australian, British, Dutch, French, and New Zealand colonial administrators to maintain a working consensus at an operational level—at the cost of the political ideals of the Atlantic Charter.

Maintaining the integrity of national colonial systems became a major impediment to regional integration through the South Pacific Commission, both substantively and in terms of the organisation's image in subsequent years. Nevertheless, in the context of the late 1940s, the commission did much to advance the cause of regionalism in the Pacific. It virtually defined the scope of the region—from the Northern Marianas to Minerva Reef; from Palau to Pitcairn. By its experience, the commission proved the viability of intergovernmental co-operation at the regional level. It also established a commitment among a set of external powers to fund and otherwise support Pacific regional institutions. And, most important, through the creation of an auxiliary advisory body composed of delegates from the islands themselves—the South Pacific Conference—it involved the peoples of the islands in regionalism.

Successful as the South Pacific Commission has been within its limited terms of reference (and it has been highly successful by almost any objective criterion), the bar to political activity prevented it from playing the sort of decolonising role that many islanders hoped for. This qualm became apparent in 1965 when three regional polities—Fiji, Tonga, and Western Samoa—were forced to go outside the commission's framework to pursue their common economic ambition of higher commodity prices for their agricultural exports. The resulting Pacific Islands Producers' Association was the region's first indigenous intergovernmental organisation.[2] Despite its pathbreaking significance as an organisation, it was entrusted with only a relatively narrow economic brief to assist in securing improved prices, primarily in New Zealand, for members' bananas. Although scarcely a failure, the producers' association was not an unqualified success in practice. It perhaps made a greater impact as an alternative venue to the South Pacific Conference, where islanders could gain experience in the operation of regional co-operation.

Dissatisfaction with the South Pacific Commission mounted during the 1960s as the pressures for decolonisation increased. Contributing factors included the loss of West New Guinea to the regional system in 1962; metropolitan resistance to Western Samoa's attempt to accede to the Canberra Agreement from 1962 to 1964, and metropolitan refusal to reform the internal procedures of the commission to accommodate more influence from the islands. Moreover, French objections to discussion of the environmental hazards of nuclear testing served to remind the islands regularly throughout the 1960s of the limitations of the South Pacific Commission as well as the dominance of the Western colonial powers over all of its organs. Matters came to a head in 1970 with the independence of Fiji. A review of the commission in that year concluded against reform and the newly independent government determined to strike out on an independent course.

The experience of collective action through the Pacific Islands Producers' Association gave focus to the search for a political alternative to the commission's hamstrung South Pacific Conference. Five independent or self-governing countries met with Australia and New Zealand in Wellington in August 1971 to consult at a heads-of-government level on the entire gamut of regional issues. This meeting gave rise to the South Pacific Forum which, although not technically an international organisation, had a profound influence on regional affairs in the 1970s and 1980s.[3] The Forum redressed the deficiencies of the South Pacific Commission, but at some cost to its founders' own aspirations. Its capacity for unfettered political debate constrained membership to only independent or self-governing countries, thereby restricting its geographic scope to something less than the comprehensive coverage of the commission. Second, the Forum had no formal treaty to give it legal personality. This limitation is not requisite organisationally, but it undoubtedly helped at Wellington that the participants in the first Forum did not have to agree to a set of binding legal obligations in order to meet again.

The Forum's lack of legal personality may have been a factor at the second meeting in Canberra in February 1972, however, when the members decided to establish a new economic body to support its development aims. The resultant South Pacific Bureau for Economic Co-operation (SPEC) was not initially intended to serve as the Forum's secretariat, although this responsibility ultimately devolved on it some years later.[4] The bureau's primary mandate was to assist the export capacity of member states. The independent regional states found themselves in control of two regional economic development agencies with very little in terms of formal responsibilities to distinguish one from the other. The Pacific Islands Producers' Association's days were clearly numbered by the decision to create the South Pacific Bureau for Economic Co-operation, but the question of why it was not revamped instead of creating a new body remains an enigma. Personality issues and concerns over the Pacific Islands Producers' Association's rather broader membership probably figured in the Forum decision. The association was incorporated into the new organisation in 1974.[5]

The amalgamation of the two organisations may have inadvertently set in train a process that would dominate the institutional dimension of regionalism in the Pacific for the next fifteen years—the concept of a single regional organisation. The idea of transferring the functions of the South Pacific Commission to the South Pacific Bureau for Economic Co-operation appealed to a number of the bureau's members on the grounds of economic and administrative efficiency, but primarily because this would eliminate the colonial vestiges of the commission. The mechanism of institutional merger, however, threatened the interests of other regional states, particularly the smaller, less well-endowed ones. It also created difficulties for its proponents by putting at risk the geographic scope of the region, because even the most ardent advocates of a single regional organisation did not wish to see fellow islanders still living in dependent territories excluded from the regional processes.

Astonishingly, the South Pacific Forum itself demonstrated the impracticality of the concept in 1979, when it moved to create a new regional organisation under its own aegis but independent of the bureau for economic co-operation. The catalyst for this development was the United Nations Third Conference on the Law of the Sea. The prospect of effective control over offshore resources had a magnetic attraction for the region's small countries lacking natural land endowments. The creation of the Forum Fisheries Agency in 1979 not only implicitly challenged the concept of a single regional organisation but also reaffirmed the introspective orientation of Pacific regionalism. An early agreement by officials to include distant-water fishing nations within the proposed regulatory body was repudiated by the prime ministers when they met at the 1978 Forum on Niue.[6] Distrust of the motives of these nations, especially their potential influence on the decision-making processes of the Forum Fisheries Agency, made a number of Forum states sufficiently uneasy to block extraregional membership.

Superficially it might appear that the control of marine resources sparked by the UN Third Conference on the Law of the Sea was responsible also for the establishment of a second offshore agency—the Committee for Coordination of Joint Prospecting for Mineral Resources in South Pacific Offshore Areas (CCOP/SOPAC). However, technically this committee was founded in 1972, before the UN conference began. Uncertainties about its legal status, raised in 1982, were a consequence of Cold War rivalries rather than an indigenous desire to regulate offshore minerals. Confirming the status of the body as an intergovernmental organisation in 1984, a memorandum of understanding gave the islands control over the involvement of extraregional states in it. (The Soviet Union was the state in question in 1982–1983.) In a practical sense the rationale for the committee on joint prospecting was a throw-back, closer to the South Pacific Commission than either the South Pacific Bureau for Economic Co-operation or the Forum Fisheries Agency. It was created more to transfer technology and to generate knowledge of potentially exploitable marine resources for export than to promote the development of known resources. In 1989, the committee shortened its acronym to the simpler sopac by changing its name to the South Pacific Applied Geo-Science Commission.

The historical context of Pacific Islands regionalism reveals how thoroughly imbued its origins were with the process of decolonisation. Given the political status of the islands and their Third- (and fourth-) World standing this situation is scarcely surprising. Nevertheless, their historical experience arguably had the effect of distorting the intended consequences of regional co-operation for many years. What was almost a conspiracy of mutual ignorance existed between the 'producers' and 'consumers' of Pacific regionalism during the 1970s and early 1980s. The islands found in regional organisation a mechanism for international bonding that distinguished their interests from those of outsiders. The non-island governments that funded (and continue to fund) approximately 90 per cent of all the costs of Pacific regional organisation felt these multilateral mechanisms would enable the regional microstates to better meet the traditional obligations of statehood.[7]

The process of political bonding among the remote, disparate, and financially strapped small island polities undoubtedly served many useful functions early in their experience of decolonisation. Certainly both the islands and their extraregional backers demonstrated by their actions that they found more than passing utility in regionalism. However, their common support for regionalism tended to disguise the extent of the contrast in the basic aims the two groups held for regional co-operation, especially with regard to the influence of national interest as a factor in the consensus on the value of the concept.

The eagerness of non-island contributors to pay the costs of Pacific regionalism encouraged the islands to maintain collectively organisations that they may not have been able, or willing, to afford individually had they had to cover all the real costs from their national exchequers. Sensibly, from the point of view of national self-interest, therefore, the individual island members have tended to accept, without undue introspection, claims of significant benefits from regional co-operation. For their part, the non-island donors were not as concerned with the institutional efficiency of the organisations as they were that the maintenance of these bodies would secure their national objectives in the region, which ranged from security and political stability to humanitarianism and preservation of the state system.

Material support for the concept of multilateralism was not the only area where national self-interest played a noteworthy role in Pacific regionalism. Probably the earliest of the major signs of the paramountcy of national interest occurred in 1976 with the 'More Effective Aid' review by the South Pacific Bureau for Economic Co-operation. This review of the aid patterns of the islands concluded that it would be to the Pacific Islands' advantage to develop a collective regime (through the bureau) to manage the huge aid flows into the region. However, this recommendation appeared to challenge the fundamental interests of the SPEC membership on several grounds. Bilateral aid transfers provided a significant proportion of the governmental income for a number of the members. A regional clearinghouse for aid might insulate the small states from undue donor influence, but the loss of direct negotiations for these funds would also jeopardise opportunities for special pleading by the recipients. Further, a central administrative organ for distributing aid could seek to impose on the members development objectives contrary to their national priorities. Conceivably, individual development plans might be dominated by regional programmes.

Aid management was perhaps the most sensitive issue the regional states refused to refer to regional processes in the early years but it was not the only significant one. Consistently, throughout the two decades from the advent of the Pacific Islands Producers' Association, the islands declined every opportunity to establish any regional mutual security regime, despite some recognition of the desirability of such an arrangement. Papua New Guinea even formally proposed a regional security force following the success of its intervention in the Vemarana rebellion on Espiritu Santo in Vanuatu in 1980. Yet the potential mischief such a collective mechanism might wreak weighed more heavily on regional states than the claimed benefits, particularly in terms of the capacity of a regional force to intervene in the internal affairs of member states.

The twenty years from the mid-1960s, when the South Pacific Commission began to experience significant indigenous pressure for reform, to the mid-1980s could scarcely be characterised as solely concerned with ritualistic decolonisation or preserving the broadest possible scope for national interest. Many substantive achievements were recorded by all Pacific regional bodies in these years. Beside the establishment of the South Pacific Forum, the Forum Fisheries Agency, and the Committee for Coordination of Joint Prospecting for Mineral Resources, notable regional breakthroughs included the creation of the South Pacific Regional Environment Programme, conclusion of the South Pacific Area Regional Trade and Economic Co-operation Agreement, the establishment of the Pacific Forum Line, and negotiation of the South Pacific Nuclear Free Zone Treaty. Other events or projects might be equally significant as exemplars of effective multilateral co-operation. Nevertheless, whatever progress was made during these years, the regional processes of the Pacific Islands expended much energy unnecessarily

Macu Salato, former Secretary-General of the South Pacific Commission and citizen of Fiji, with Frank Brosnahan, Acting Vice-Chancellor of the University of the South Pacific outside the Fono, *American Samoa, at a South Pacific conference, early 1980s. (Robert C. Kiste)*

on the concept of a single regional organisation in order to 'decolonise' this process. The primary consequence of this preoccupation was an introspective orientation to Pacific regionalism.

The relationships linking decolonisation, the development of independent national foreign policies, and the growth of indigenous instruments for regional co-operation may have led ineluctably to the preoccupation with removing the vestiges of colonialism in the minds of many island policymakers. Nevertheless, the device of a single regional organisation could not have been seriously contemplated unless internal political rectitude took precedence over almost everything else. After all, its chief purpose was to expel the South Pacific Commission's three metropolitan great powers—France, the United Kingdom, and the United States—from formal access to the region. Such a drastic step would make sense only if the commission were somehow an essential element in the Pacific's regional ecology, which in at least one sense it was. The one resource the commission had, and that the proponents of a single organisation wanted to preserve, was its comprehensive geographic scope. Supporters of the concept wanted to control the political structures of the region, not just to regulate the affairs of the independent states (which could control their external relations in any case), but to manage the entire region as they conceived it, as defined by the scope of the commission.

Reform and restructuring

Islanders' expectations for regional co-operation matured with experience throughout the 1970s and early 1980s, but a fundamental shift occurred around 1987. The reasons for this change are complex, ranging from internal policy adjustments in the wake of the May 1987 military coup in Fiji, through Australian ambitions for its national role in the region, to the first harbingers of the new world order. The critical feature of the new island attitude towards regional co-operation was the recognition that the introspective orientation of earlier years would have to be abandoned. Rather than using its regional structures to hold the extraregional order at bay, the Pacific Islands leadership came to accept that its regional resources would have to be mobilised to engage the rest of the world. A new pattern of regionalism had to be considered.

The 1987 South Pacific Forum met in Apia, Western Samoa, in an atmosphere of heightened tension and drama, because it convened within weeks of the Fiji military coup. Much of the discussion at this Forum took place against the backdrop of prospective collective intervention in national affairs. Fiji had the most to fear in this regard because Australia and New Zealand clearly hoped sanctions against the military regime would be agreed, but countries that saw the coup as a reassertion of Fijian indigenous rights were almost equally concerned. As with the earlier proposal for a regional defence force, these states recognised that any capacity to enforce sanctions against one member state could be used later against others. In terms of both the issue and the procedure, a majority of the island members of the Forum had strong reasons for resisting collective action against Fiji.

And not just Fiji. Australia persisted with a pre-coup intention to raise the risks of the Libyan presence in the region at the Apia Forum. Vanuatu's Prime Minister Walter Lini had objected previously at inclusion of this topic on the agenda, perceiving quite reasonably that it would provide the occasion for an admonitory lecture. Again, the protection of national interests tended to override regional collective action. As it turned out, a compromise was reached: a briefing on Libyan involvement in the region was offered rather than a full Forum debate. Agreement was also reached on the establishment of a committee to consider how sensitive security information might be handled regionally in the future.

Ironically, in light of the assertions of national interest at the Apia Forum, the 1987 meeting was to be a watershed in regional relations. It prepared the way for a restructuring of regional organisation as comprehensive as anything envisaged by proponents of a single organisation. By 1987, the Forum wanted to extend its influence beyond the boundaries of the Pacific Islands. It delegated the task of investigating the means by which appropriate extraregional actors might engage the Pacific Islands, through the Forum as the area's paramount regional body, to the recently created Committee on Regional Institutional Arrangements.[8] Because the focus of the Forum's interests had shifted 180 degrees, the reforms proposed by the new committee diametrically reversed the aims of the proposed single regional organisation. Where the latter was intended to secure greater internal control for the islands through regionalism, the committee's arrangements were designed to make regional mechanisms more effective in treating with outside interests.

The heart of the reforms was a concept borrowed from the Association of South-East Asian Nations—the idea of 'dialogue partnerships'. A dialogue partner was to be an extraregional actor invited to attend a post-Forum meeting with elements of the Forum to discuss issues of mutual relevance. In keeping with the earlier aims of a single regional organisation, the initiative for participation in the dialogue process rested entirely with the Forum. The extraregional actors concerned did not volunteer for dialogue on the basis of their interests, but were identified by the Forum as those with whom the Forum wished to talk about matters of current moment to the islands.

The intention was apparently to be fairly liberal in the longer term regarding dialogue participation, but at least initially the numbers were restricted to those states most directly involved with the regional economies. Cosmetically, limiting the number of dialogue partners was facilitated by the holding of the first Forum to include the dialogue arrangement (1989) on Tarawa, where accommodation was scarce. The Forum could quite reasonably claim that space at this meeting could be found for only six governments—Canada, China, France, Great Britain, Japan, and the United States. In the event, only five attended after New Zealand's Prime Minister David Lange withdrew an offer of air transport to China in the wake of the Tiananmen Square massacre.

The dialogue arrangement has proved a balm for old wounds but has also opened some new issues. Differing expectations of dialogue partnership by the respective sides of the dialogue have surfaced. The Forum is represented by senior politicians and the dialogue partners by senior bureaucrats. The differing status of the two sides caused early comment and some concern, which still has not been entirely resolved despite the obvious difficulties in either side changing the pattern of its representation. It is not even clear that the Forum would be able to cope with a significantly upgraded representation from its dialogue partners. Were these countries to send senior politicians, they would almost certainly expect to enjoy prequisites proportionate to their status—probably close to those of full membership.

Cementing the more outward-looking orientation of the new arrangement, the Committee on Regional Institutional Arrangements implicitly accepted that the concept of a single organisation should be abandoned with a suggestion for a mechanism to coordinate the multiplicity of regional bodies. In one sense the proposal only recognised the reality of what the Forum itself had done in 1979 when it established the Forum Fisheries Agency as an organisation separate from the South Pacific Bureau for Economic Co-operation. Nonetheless, the gesture was more than symbolic. The proposal that was ultimately endorsed by the Forum under the name South Pacific Organisations Coordinating Committee effectively ended the long-running campaign by some regional states—mainly the Melanesian members of the Forum—to expel France, the United Kingdom, and the United States from the South Pacific Commission. But the implications of the new coordinating committee quickly went well beyond the issue of existing extraregional involvement in the islands. It offered Japan a new and unexpected avenue into Pacific regional processes.

The continued existence of the South Pacific Commission not only opened an opportunity for Japan to seek full membership in one of the only regional organisations where this might be a real possibility, but, through such membership, the process instituted by the South Pacific Organisations Coordinating Committee gave rise to formal participation in all regional organisations. De jure membership in a regional body clearly had had significant advantages for the other three great powers because they maintained SPC membership throughout the entire controversy over a single regional organisation. Japan has long felt itself entitled to similar recognition of its regional interests. Tokyo appreciates that membership in the region by right offers more avenues for influence than are available either through the Forum's dialogue mechanism or through the other informal channels it enjoys in the Forum Fisheries Agency and the South Pacific Applied Geo-Science Commission. Of course, the islands also appreciated this legal nicety and this was why a number of them had supported the concept of a single regional organisation. Japan, however, has not been bereft of regional advocates and by the end of 1991 seemed to be on the verge of success in the South Pacific Commission.

A third element of the reforms of the Committee on Regional Institutional Arrangements focuses on the institutional limitations of the Forum itself. The South Pacific Forum is not technically an international organisation, because it has no legal personality. No formal treaty or charter exists to give it legal status. Like the Commonwealth of Nations, the Forum is a very exclusive political club. To circumvent this genuine limitation on its capacity to act internationally, the relationship between the Forum and the South Pacific Bureau for Economic Co-operation was clarified. The bureau was renamed the Forum Secretariat (following the model of the Commonwealth Secretariat) to ensure that this arm of the Forum would be accepted internationally as the legitimate agent of the Forum. Legally, the situation has not changed for the Forum itself, however, and much will depend on how effectively the Forum Secretariat moves from the bureau's original economic focus to a wider policy role, as well as on the international reaction to this cosmetic change.

Another consequence (albeit unintended) of the reform process of the Committee on Regional Institutional Arrangements may be the proliferation of regional intergovernmental organisations. Although the reforms logically removed the formal regional qualms about multiple intergovernmental organisations, the elimination of the political resistance to the creation of new organisations might have been expected to take time. However, this restraint has already been relaxed and two new organisations have been established in recent years. During 1990 and 1991 member governments and the three sponsoring organisations—South Pacific Commission, Forum Secretariat, and United Nations Environment Programme—reached agreement on a proposal to establish the South Pacific Regional Environment Programme as an autonomous body with legal personality. By the end of 1991, it was moving out of its wing of the SPC headquarters in Noumea to new premises in Apia as a new regional intergovernmental organisation.

Although the standing of the South Pacific Regional Environmental Programme in this capacity cannot be gainsaid, there is some dispute about the claims of the Tourism Council of the South Pacific. Rather like the environmental programme, the council was essentially a programme within another body (although there were external antecedents) and, after a period of growth, a decision was made to act independently. Whether the council is a Forum programme under the Forum Secretariat or an independent intergovernmental organisation depends substantially on the legal character of its putative charter. If its 1988 Memorandum of Association is a treaty, the council is an intergovernmental organisation. This issue has yet to be resolved.[9]

Contemporary regionalism and the new world order

Change in the latter half of the 1980s was not limited to Pacific regionalism. Significant changes in the international environment began to alter global perspectives from the mid-to-late 1980s, most notably with Mikhail Gorbachev's reform of what was then the Soviet Union. Gorbachev's *perestroika* fundamentally reshaped not only public attitudes and policy in the Soviet Union but also the geopolitics of international order. However, even without Gorbachev, changes were already in train that would profoundly influence global affairs, including the increasing unification of the European Community, the emergence of Japan as a claimant to great-power status, the growing coherence of Asia and the Pacific as an economic region, and the emergence of environmentalism as an important item on the world agenda. Important as these and other developments might have been with-out the collapse of the Cold War, the ending of East–West rivalry has overshadowed all else.

Given its origins, many of the key features of the new world order are, not surprisingly, characterised by the dismantling of the Cold War.[10] Per-haps three of the four pillars of the new world order can be attributed to that event:

the end of ideological rivalry (and, concomitantly, a reassertion of national interest) as the core element in the foreign policy of the great powers;

a return to hierarchically structured international politics with the United Nations Security Council serving as an arena for a concert of powers globally;

increasing multipolarity (particularly a renewed emphasis on economic regionalism) in the organisation of global politics to replace the bipolarity of the Cold War; and

the identification and acceptance of economic advantage as the primary indicator of national interest.

Somewhat ironically, several of the elements of the new world order will tend to work against Pacific regionalism despite others operating to vindicate its original aims. The new world order legitimates the basic thrusts and directions of Pacific regionalism in several ways. By its emphasis on economic priorities, it validates the economic development strategy that has long underpinned Pacific regionalism. The new world order is working also to elevate regional association as a major mechanism in international relations because the collapse of the Cold War bipolarity leaves a power vacuum that must be filled. Regional organisations have been a significant factor in facilitating the movement towards global multipolarity. Theoretically, even the reassertion of power-based national interest might be seen as positive for Pacific regionalism, for two reasons: first, national interest is a major rationale for the history of intergovernmental co-operation in the islands; second, the islands collectively have more power than they have individu-ally. At this point the structure of the new world order begins to pose genuine problems for a Pacific community facing the realities of the twenty-first century.

The end of ideological rivalry will strike most in the islands, with con-siderable justice, as a real advance in world politics. Yet on the negative side, for all small powers, including the micro-powers of the South Pacific, ideological value during the Cold War was never fully related to strategic or economic strength. In the later years of the struggle, incremental ideo-logical gains involved escalating economic or aid costs in the two camps as smaller and smaller entities were drawn into their rivalry. Politically (and prudentially) this was a dangerous game, but it did give the objects of Cold War rivalry disproportionate influence at some levels. Today, despite some inertia in the international system, more pragmatic, hard-headed considerations influence the positions of the great powers in their relations with smaller powers.

Even collectively, the islands do not control significant amounts of global resources. One might more fairly say 'especially collectively' because the region's collective resources are essentially the marine environment and its wealth. Other resources with global or extraregional significance tend to be located in individual countries, such as Papua New Guinea's gold and copper, New Caledonia's nickel, and Nauru's depleting store of phosphate. The region's constituent members are too small in area and population and too dispersed across the world's largest ocean to create an effective regional internal market or to establish a powerful export cartel.[11] In reality, the islands have not pooled their collective efforts regionally to share strength so much as to share weakness. The emphasis of the new world order on national and international strength will not enhance the islands' regional capacity to influence world trends or events.

Related to this aspect of the new world order is the hierarchical structuring of international politics. The Congress of Vienna made a virtue of necessity following the defeat of Napoleon Bonaparte by establishing the Concert of Europe at the apex of a hierarchically structured world system. The League of Nations sought to reverse this situation by treating all states as equal, regardless of size or power. The failure of the League brought a partial return to the Concert system with the establishment of permanent membership of the UN Security Council for great powers. Whatever idealism one reads into the United Nations, the permanent membership of the Security Council demonstrates the resilience of power politics. The Cold War prevented the wartime concert from operating in the Security Council for most of the history of the United Nations, but without this impediment, deference to great-power interests appears again to be ascendant. The more the international agenda is dominated by the great powers, the less attention the interests of the Pacific microstates will be able to command—collectively or individually.

Although the multipolarity of the emerging international system favours the creation of regional associations, the demands and expectations of the new world order on states will also apply to these international organisations. That is, the pursuit of national interest as defined by economic rationality will be paramount. Taken together, the region's natural and human assets do not figure as prominently today in the economic plans of other nations or regions as did the strategic value of the islands in the strategic assessments of the Western allies during the Cold War. This perhaps cynical interpretation flows from both the apparent logic of the new world order and the early indications of the effects of the post–Cold War order in the Pacific

Islands. By late 1989, aid patterns were already beginning to show signs that the loss of strategic relevance could prove costly.[12] Although new aid do-nors may be forthcoming to offset expected declining strategic interests, few seem likely to match the aid growth of the 1970s and 1980s. The current global economic decline, combined with the huge amounts of international capital and liquidity being absorbed in the reunification of Germany, the reconstruction of Eastern Europe, and the dismantling of the Soviet Union, make the prospects of finding new aid sources remote. The one exception is Japan.

The global multipolarity of the new world order is creating an oppor-tunity for an Asia-Pacific leader to emerge. Japan sees itself as the logical candidate, although the claims of China may be pressed more vigorously in future years. Despite its own economic woes at present, Japan is perhaps the only major power to have large amounts of disposable international capital. In many circles this circumstance redresses the imperfect Japanese claim to great-power status arising from its lack of usable military force. The Pacific Islands will be affected by Japan's emergence as a regional leader in at least two important ways: Tokyo is seeking to achieve a de jure presence in Pacific regionalism in large part to pursue new political ambitions in the area. Perhaps more important, however, Japan seems likely to favour the macro-regional processes of the Pacific Economic Co-operation Confer-ence and the Asia Pacific Economic Co-operation Group as the stage for playing out its hegemonic role. Pacific Island involvement in both these arenas is currently limited to regional organisations such as the Forum and the Forum Fisheries Agency. If the islands are to enjoy any influence in the hierarchically structured multipolarity of the new world order, regional rather than national channels are almost certain to be required.

Conclusion

Regionalism has undergone significant changes over the past fifty years in the Pacific Islands. From an administrative convenience for a few colonial powers to preserve their national interests in the area at a minimum cost, regional co-operation has become a key tool of diplomacy for more than a dozen independent or self-governing states through the Forum family of agencies. Perhaps as important in historical terms, regionalism has served as a cultural cement for all Pacific Island polities, whether dependent or in-dependent, through the South Pacific Commission. Nevertheless, national interest has always played a significant role in the dynamics of Pacific Island regionalism, but arguably no more than in other parts of the world.

One major point of contention arose precisely because of national inter-est—the issue of a single regional organisation. States that felt able to pro-tect and project their national interests effectively, both within and outside the region, tended to support the concept. The smaller, more vulnerable, more dependent polities that believed they needed a regional prop (that included Britain, France, and the United States) for the pursuit of their interests were loath to put these regional structures at risk. Although the extraregional states that would have been expelled from regional circles by the success of the proposal for a single regional organisation were scarcely passive bystanders in the debate, it was largely resolved by the islands in terms of their assessments of the relevance of regionalism for their separate national interests. In this case at least, national interest meant more engagement, not less, with the extraregional environment. Hence the reforms of 1988 by the Committee on Regional Institutional Arrangements.

The emerging international order is likely to propel the islands towards further engagement with the rest of the world, particularly the countries of the Pacific rim. Given the asymmetries of power that exist between the microstates of the Pacific Islands and the rest of the world, the uncertainties surrounding effective influence in the new world order, and the likely progress towards further Asia-Pacific co-operation, the islands are also likely to find it necessary to rely more on their regional institutions to pursue this engagement. In both the Pacific Economic Co-operation Conference and the Asia Pacific Economic Co-operation Group, islands' access to Asia-Pacific processes, insofar as this exists, is limited to representation through regional agencies. The largest states, Papua New Guinea and perhaps Fiji, may aspire·to separate national representation, but if they were to succeed, the smaller states would have a very hard task in achieving credibility within the Asia-Pacific processes and might well be excluded altogether.

On balance, Pacific Island regionalism has proved valuable and valued over the years. While the contribution of regionalism has tended to be esteemed for the support regional organisations have given to national interests, the record is clear that many compromises have been necessary to maintain the current levels of association. Regional organisations and regional processes have also proved fairly adaptive, though in this area questions for the future arise. The world is in such dramatic flux that adaptation and change have become requisites for survival. The momentous shifts in global political structures since 1989 are certain to reduce the salience of microstates for the immediate future. Increasingly, the islands will have to use their regional associations more fully than in the past as avenues of access to the wider world.

Notes

1 General treatments of the growth and development of South Pacific regionalism can be found in: M. Margaret Ball, 'Regionalism and the Pacific Commonwealth', *Pacific Affairs* 46 (1973): 232–253; Gregory E. Fry, 'Regionalism and International Politics of the South Pacific', *Pacific Affairs* 54 (1981): 455–484; R. A. Herr,

'Organisations and Issues in South Pacific Regionalism', in *New Zealand and the Pacific*, ed. Roderic Alley, Westview Press, Boulder, CO, 155–180.

2 Uentabo Fakoofo Neemia, *Co-operation and Conflict*, University of the South Pacific, Suva, 1986, 25.

3 An intergovernmental organisation is characterised by three key elements—a membership of three or more states, legal personality (established by treaty or similar charter), and a permanent secretariat.

4 Neemia, 27.

5 Herr, 165.

6 R. A. Herr, 'Cross-cutting Pressures in Contemporary South Pacific Regionalism', *World Review* 18 (August 1979): 18–19.

7 See Neemia, 50–69, for indicative contributions to various South Pacific intergovernmental organisations. However, these figures do not detail the increasing proportion of expenditure by intergovernmental organisations under the category of 'extra-budgetary projects'. These costs are virtually all carried by non-island donors and consequently bring normal totals from external sources to the very high levels estimated here.

8 Richard A. Herr, 'The Region in Review: International Issues and Events, 1988', *The Contemporary Pacific* 1 (1989): 142–145, describes the process and reforms of the Committee on Regional Institutional Arrangements.

9 Trevor Sofield, 'Regional Tourism Development: The Tourism Council of the South Pacific (TCSP)', manuscript supplied by author, 1991.

10 While some may attribute the concept and interpretation of the new world order to President George Bush, the usage here does not assign it any specific substantive content. It is assumed that the new pattern of post–Cold War relations is still unfolding, and that no final form can yet be discerned, although some predictions are offered here.

11 Feleti Sevele, 'Inter-regional Trade: Limited Potential', *Pacific Perspective* 11 (1, 1983): 23–27. See Te'o I. J. Fairbairn, *Island Economies: Studies from the South Pacific*, Institute of Pacific Studies, University of the South Pacific, Suva, 1985, 241–254, for a contrasting assessment.

12 'Fisheries Aid: Patterns and Sources', in *The Forum Fisheries Agency*, ed. Richard Herr, University of the South Pacific, Suva, 1990, 188.

13

Strategic and nuclear issues

Stewart Firth

'Strategy'—the protection and advancement of the military interests that nation-states identify with their self-preservation—is the focus of this chapter. History suggests that the leaders of nation-states regard such 'strategic' interests as fundamental, for to neglect them is to place the state itself at risk. Because strategic forces in the Pacific Islands have almost all come from outside the region, and still do, the external strategic framework within which islanders have had to make their history is of central concern, and requires an assessment of the power of outsiders. In the nuclear age, strategic interests have come to encompass the ability to experiment with nuclear weapons, both bombs and missiles, and the Pacific Islands have provided vital locations for such testing. Despite the end of the Cold War and the collapse of the former Soviet Union, the Pacific is where the United States tests intercontinental ballistic missiles and where, for more than a quarter of a century until 1992, France exploded nuclear bombs. The nuclear politics of the region in the recent past are also examined here.

The map of the islands at the beginning of this century is a stark reminder that the Pacific has been caught up in the strategic manoeuvrings of external states ever since it became part of the wider world. In the Spanish–American War of 1898 the United States, then a rising power with a growing navy, had just acquired the island of Guam along with the much richer prize of the Philippines. The Americans had made Hawai'i a US territory and arranged with the British and the Germans to acquire American Samoa, subsequently administered by the US Navy. In an age when international prestige and colonies went together, Germany was determined not to be left out. Embarking on the massive expansion of its naval fleet, Germany had bought the Caroline Islands and the Northern Marianas from Spain and could now add these to its existing colonial possessions in the Marshall Islands, the Solomons, and New Guinea, as well as its new colony of German Samoa, where the black-white-red flag of the Fatherland was raised in 1900.

The far-flung territorial interests of Britain, the greatest colonial and maritime power in the world, were well represented in the Pacific. Apart from the self-governing settler colony of New Zealand, acquired in 1840, the British held the Crown Colonies of Fiji and British New Guinea, together with the protectorates of the British Solomon Islands and the Gilbert and Ellice Islands, a supervisory role in the Kingdom of Tonga, and, through New Zealand, control of the affairs of the Cook Islands, Niue, and Tokelau, not to mention a half-stake in the New Hebrides (now Vanuatu), soon to be formalised as a system of joint rule by the British and the French.[1]

France held its five eastern Polynesian archipelagos under the title of French Oceania, was the ruler of more Polynesian islands in Wallis and Futuna, and, then as now, was administering its colony of New Caledonia.[2] The easternmost of the Dutch possessions in South-East Asia, and the westernmost Pacific territory, was Dutch New Guinea, part of the Melanesian culture area.

As the global strategic balance changed during the century, so did the disposition of Pacific Island territories. Australia and New Zealand succeeded to the German territories south of the equator after Germany's defeat in World War One, Australia taking New Guinea and New Zealand Western Samoa. Nauru, a rich prize for its phosphate deposits, went in theory to the British Empire and in practice to Australia. Under an agreement with the British, Japan invaded and administered the German territories north of the equator.[3] Then, defeated in battle in the 1940s, Japan too was removed, this time by one of the two superpowers that World War Two created, the United States. The Americans, who had become the greatest military and economic power, found themselves administering some of the world's smallest island territories.

The strategic needs of external states had played a large part in determining how the islands would be divided and redivided between colonial powers in the first half of the century, and they were to be just as significant in influencing the character of decolonisation in the 1960s and 1970s.

Decolonisation

New Zealand, a small state with limited and local strategic interests, initiated island decolonisation by granting independence to its former trusteeship territory of Western Samoa in 1962, and self-government to the Cook Islands in 1965 and Niue in 1973.[4] The Dutch, whose colonies in the East Indies were an anachronism surviving from an earlier age of maritime supremacy, were succeeded by the Indonesians as rulers of west New Guinea in 1963, a change supposedly confirmed by the west New Guineans in a farcical 'act of free choice' in 1969. In what is now the Indonesian province of Irian Jaya, one kind of foreign rule over Melanesians was followed by another, as Asians replaced Europeans in positions of authority. The British, a spent force east of Suez by the late 1960s, created the majority of independent Pacific countries—Fiji, Tonga, Solomon Islands, Kiribati, and Tuvalu—by lowering the Union Jack there during the 1970s and leading the Anglo-French withdrawal from Vanuatu in 1980. Meantime Australia, which had given Nauru its independence in 1968, created the largest Pacific Island country by surrendering its territory of Papua and granting independence to the trusteeship territory of New Guinea in 1975.[5] Papua New Guinea, which owes its borders to the European strategic logic of the late nineteenth century and to World War One, is the only Pacific country that does not fall into the category of 'microstate'.

The strategic needs of the colonising powers differed. Those of the Netherlands and Britain, powers in decline, were best served by withdrawal. Indonesia, needing foreign adventures as symbols of national integration, was eager to acquire the former Dutch territory in Melanesia and, as a new state, could do so without incurring the odium of the international community for being a colonial power. Australia and New Zealand were small powers with regional interests; France was a great power, nuclear armed, with aspirations to play a global role; and the United States was a nuclear superpower with military forces stationed across the north Pacific and in East Asia.

The Pacific policies of each of these external states were expressions of their differing strategic needs. Australia and New Zealand, wanting the Pacific Islands to serve regional defence requirements by being politically stable, encouraged the emergence of new states in the Western image as a way of forestalling radical nationalism. France resisted, and continues to resist, the decolonisation of its Pacific territories, because their loss would undermine France's claim to be a world power and create a gap in the global string of French military installations.[6] The United States, too, needed the Pacific to serve its global defence strategies and therefore insisted on a cast-iron guarantee of future military access to the islands of Micronesia, coupled with permanent denial of the area to other military forces.

The unusual character of Micronesia's decolonisation arises from its strategic value to a nuclear superpower with global interests, as well as from the hard bargaining that was done—within that political context—by the Micronesians over many years of negotiations with the Americans. Three of four earlier parts of the former Trust Territory of the Pacific Islands changed their political status under arrangements that came into effect from 1986 and were finally approved by the United Nations Security Council in 1990. The Northern Marianas became a US commonwealth. The Republic of the Marshall Islands (RMI) and the Federated States of Micronesia (FSM) entered into free association with the United States. But Palau remained as the residuum of the former trust territory with a resident director appointed by the United States Department of the Interior in 1991. Under their

Compacts of Free Association with the United States, the Marshalls and the Federated States of Micronesia receive large amounts of American aid until the year 2001; in return, the two countries have signed mutual security agreements that guarantee the United States a monopoly over military access to their territory for as long as the Americans want it. Both were admitted as full members of the United Nations in 1991 and have been widely recognised as sovereign. As Edward J. Michal has argued, they are best seen as 'protected states', countries that have surrendered certain sovereign powers to another state, with a status rather like that of Tonga between 1900 and 1970.[7] American global interests also explain why Palau has not been decolonised. A nuclear-free Palau, as would be required by Palau's still unchanged constitution of 1979 if it were ever to go into effect, would hinder the transit of American military forces with whatever weapons they might be carrying, a right that the United States insisted on throughout its negotiations with Micronesian leaders.[8]

The decolonisation of a dozen island territories between 1962 and 1990 obscured a number of factors. One was that independence did not arise from nationalism. None of the colonial powers was compelled to withdraw by the pressure of local opinion, with the possible exception of the French in Vanuatu. Instead, political independence was bestowed by the colonisers for their own reasons because it suited them. They left because they wanted to leave. Another factor was that, except in phosphate-rich Nauru, political independence in the islands was not accompanied by economic independence, indeed quite the reverse. A third was that more Pacific Island territories remained territories than became independent, even though the majority of Pacific Islanders now lived in independent states.[9] The transfer of constitutional power to Pacific Islanders in the thirty years following Western Samoa's independence in 1962 was far from complete, and the transfer of economic power was minimal. Hawai'i remained a state of the United States, the Torres Strait Islands and Norfolk Island parts of Australia, Irian Jaya a province of Indonesia, Easter Island part of Chile; Guam and American Samoa were still United States territories; Palau was still a UN Trust Territory; and French Polynesia, New Caledonia, and Wallis and Futuna stayed as overseas territories of France. Having been the testing ground for some of the most remarkable applications of the doctrine of national self-determination, as for example in tiny Tuvalu, the Pacific Islands emerged from the age of decolonisation only partly decolonised.

Nationalist movements

Now that the high tide of decolonisation has receded, and in a far less favourable political climate, ethnically focused nationalisms are emerging in the Pacific. In Irian Jaya, New Caledonia, French Polynesia, Guam, Hawai'i, New Zealand, and the Torres Strait Islands groups of people see themselves as subject to colonial domination—by the Indonesians, the French, the Americans, the pakeha New Zealanders, and the white Australians in turn.[10] Melanesian, Kanak, Chamorro, Hawaiian, Maori, and Torres Strait Islander identities are seen as having been suppressed by foreigners and are reasserted and celebrated in the anticolonial cause. On the island of Bougainville, a North Solomons nationalism within the new state of Papua New Guinea has served to justify secessionism provoked by the dissatisfaction of local landowners with their treatment by the copper mine. The secessionists identify the central government in Port Moresby—other Papua New Guineans—as foreign and oppressive.

Only in the Indonesian and French territories and in Papua New Guinea can these nationalist movements be said to have put independence or secession on the political agenda. Elsewhere—in Hawai'i, Guam, or New Zealand, for example—indigenous nationalists may dramatise the subordination of colonised peoples and influence government policy, but they have no prospect of taking control of the state. For this reason I focus on Irian Jaya, Bougainville, and the French territories, where nationalism is a potent political force and has provoked armed conflict. Yet even in these places nationalist movements are highly unlikely to succeed in bringing new states into being. Just as independence came to the Pacific because the colonisers of the 1960s and 1970s wanted to leave, so it will now be resisted because the colonisers of the 1990s—so defined at least by their opponents—want to stay.

The Indonesians are determined to stay in Irian Jaya. The recent history of the rest of the region, Fiji included, seems benign indeed alongside that of Irian Jaya, where numerous Melanesians have been killed by the Indonesian armed forces since the 1960s, in their continuing conflict with the *Organisasi Papua Merdeka* (Movement for Free Papua). No one knows precisely how many have died in this forgotten war of independence, but they certainly number in the tens of thousands. Measured by the yardstick of deaths in armed conflict, the struggle for an independent West Papua is the most significant movement for independence in the Pacific Islands, yet it is almost certain to fail. For the Indonesian government the issue is one of maintaining the territorial integrity of the nation and avoiding a precedent that might encourage secessionist movements elsewhere in the outer islands of the Indonesian archipelago. With a population of 180 million, and armed forces numbering 300 000, the Indonesian state operates on a scale characteristic of South-East Asia rather than the Pacific Islands, and Indonesian leaders clearly regard the suppression of the Movement for Free Papua as one among many military tasks that must be undertaken in the nation's interest. The fate of a million Melanesians in a remote province is not a high priority. And the prospects for the movement are further dimmed by the ineluctable fact that no other country, except for powerless Pacific states such as Vanuatu, has any practical reason to support independence for Irian Jaya.

Ever since the suppression of Indonesian Communists in 1966, Australia has sought friendship with Jakarta at almost any cost and will not jeopardise that friendship for the sake of the Irianese, any more than it was willing to intervene on behalf of the people of East Timor when their country was forcibly incorporated into Indonesia in 1975, or to do much more than offer criticism when soldiers shot dead scores of East Timorese in Dili in 1991.[11] The Australian calculation is a strategic one: Indonesia could one day be an enemy; Indonesia should therefore be placated. Papua New Guinea, with armed forces one hundredth the size of Indonesia's and a land border with its giant neighbour, also puts its relations with Jakarta ahead of sympathy with the Melanesians of Irian Jaya. Working together with Indonesia is now Port Moresby's aim, one that has developed, since the 1987 Treaty of Mutual Respect, Friendship and Cooperation, into direct military co-operation be-tween the two countries, as agreed in the Papua New Guinea–Indonesia Status of Forces Agreement of 1992. Under this agreement, troops of each country may enter the territory of the other.[12]

Papua New Guinea is determined to stay in Bougainville. The Papua New Guinea government faced a political crisis from 1989 onwards, as land-owners from Panguna on Bougainville, the site of the country's huge copper mine, turned a peaceful protest about compensation and pollution into an armed rebellion against the central government. In the years following Papua New Guinea's independence in 1975, the mine had substantially under-written the Papua New Guinean economy. Bougainville Copper, 53 per cent owned by Conzinc Riotinto Australia, provided 40 per cent of Papua New Guinea's exports and 19 per cent of government revenues at the time of its forced closure because of sabotage in 1989. Until the Bougainville mine closed down, the national government got 63 per cent of the profits generated by the mine, the provincial government got 4.8 per cent, and the local land-owners, who have lost land and seen pollution of the air, water, and soil, got 0.2 per cent.[13]

By early 1990 the Papua New Guinea Defence Force was in action against the rebels, now called the Bougainville Revolutionary Army, in an ill-disciplined campaign—sometimes little more than a rampage—that had the principal effect of uniting Bougainvilleans against the national government. Australia supplied the force with four Iroquois helicopters that were used, against Australia's expressly stated conditions, as gunships equipped with machine-guns. The soldiers were soon withdrawn. But when the rebels declared independence for the North Solomons in May 1990, the national government responded with a blockade that deprived the Bougainvilleans of telecommunications, food, oil, and health services and soon caused a serious deterioration in living conditions. Schools closed. Children remained unvaccinated. Avoidable deaths from childbirth and common diseases multiplied.

In this situation the secessionists agreed to negotiate with the national government, but accords reached between the two sides in 1990 and 1991 failed to settle the fundamental issue of sovereignty in the North Solomons Province, and by 1992 the Bougainville Revolutionary Army was once again asserting its authority by seizing a ship on charter to the International Red Cross.[14] In the meantime, however, popular support for the secessionist movement was waning, especially in areas away from the copper mine such as Buin, North Bougainville, and Buka, where the majority of villagers seem to have welcomed the return of the Papua New Guinea Defence Force and the national government.[15] By early 1993 the government was claiming that its troops, backed by air support, had reclaimed the township of Arawa in central Bougainville from the rebels. The new prime minister elected in 1992, Paias Wingti, had still not proposed a political settlement of the Bougainville problem, the only way it would ever be solved. The Bougainville independence movement appeared likely to last in some form for years, to represent a continuing challenge to the rule of the national government in that part of Papua New Guinea, but not to succeed in creating an independent republic of the North Solomons or to precipitate the disintegration of the Papua New Guinean state as some observers had earlier feared. The Bougainville crisis nevertheless served as a reminder of the fragility of Papua New Guinea as a nation-state and of the possibility that Australia, the former colonial power, might be drawn into internal conflicts as the military guarantor of that state.

France is determined to stay in the Pacific, as is evident from the tenor of French Pacific policy since the 1970s. In New Caledonia the political strength of the independence forces has declined rather than grown since the contending forces reached an interim agreement in the so-called Matignon Accords of 1988. According to the formula devised at that time, only those whose 'place of main residence' since 1988 has been New Caledonia will be permitted to vote in the independence referendum now planned for 1998. Meanwhile France hopes to wean a minority of Kanaks away from independence and attach them to a French future for the territory by a programme of more widely shared economic development. New Caledonia's Land and Rural Development Agency redistributed 15 000 hectares of land to Kanaks in 1989, and more in 1990. Training programmes for Kanaks, although less generous than originally promised, have been instituted. And, with a loan from the French government, the northern province government, which is in Kanak hands, bought a nickel-mining and tourism company in 1990.[16]

At the same time, political divisions multiplied within the FLNKS (Kanak Socialist National Liberation Front), the coalition of parties that has represented the independence movement in New Caledonia since 1984. With the assassination of Jean-Marie Tjibaou by Kanak extremists in May 1989 the FLNKS lost its most experienced leader, a man who had acted as a powerful symbol of movement unity. The expected meeting of the Congress of the FLNKS was delayed for months after the assassination, and when it finally took place early in 1990, the dissident Kanak group FULK (United Front for Kanak Liberation) was excluded. In 1991 the moderate independence party LKS (Kanak Socialist Liberation Party), under Loyalty Islands Chief Nidoish Naisseline, withdrew its support for the Matignon peace process and accused the FLNKS of abandoning the goal of independence, a charge that seemed to be justified later in the year when some FLNKS leaders were reported as proposing a compromise with anti-independence politician Jacques Lafleur. Rock Wamytan, Vice President of the FLNKS, was left to try to explain away the movement's internal tensions as 'a natural phase three years after the signing of the Matignon Peace Accords'.[17] As the midterm review of the Matignon Accords approached in 1993, the results of development expenditure were beginning to be seen in the northern and islands provinces in the form of rural electrification, new roads, telephones, sanitation, piped drinking water, and better health care. In the hands of pragmatic Kanak politicians like Léopold Jorédié, president of the Northern Province, such advances in the Kanak standard of living were becoming powerful arguments for sticking with France after 1998 in a qualified form of independence. A vote for outright independence in 1998 seemed increasingly unlikely.

Strategy and development

After more than a quarter of a century of continuous nuclear testing in the Tuamotu Archipelago of French Polynesia, France announced in April 1992 that it would suspend its tests for the rest of the year. Since 1966 France had exploded 177 bombs in the Pacific, 44 in the atmosphere in the early years of the test programme and a further 133 after regional protests forced the explosions underground in 1975. French Polynesia's population is only marginally greater than New Caledonia's, but in the 1980s France was spending more than twice as much there. Most of the extra money was to support nuclear testing.[18] Deep in their pits, the bombs fed France's appetite for new warheads for its programme of nuclear modernisation and spread radioactive contamination in amounts claimed to be negligible but known only to the French military. With nuclear test sites at Moruroa and Fangataufa atolls, a support base on Hao Atoll, and headquarters in Pape'ete, the Centre d'Expérimentation Pacifique attracted military francs in quantities that substantially subsidised the French Polynesian economy. During the 1980s, 57 per cent of state spending in the territory came from the military.[19]

French Polynesia and the Marshall Islands are extreme cases of island economies sustained by massive external subsidy. They are 'strategic value economies', in which France and the United States pay a price for strategic benefits: a nuclear test site for the French; an intercontinental ballistic-missile and Star Wars test site for the Americans. Even if French Polynesia were one day to follow the Marshalls' example and enter some form of free association with France, the power relationship that derives from dependence on military money would continue for as long as the French wanted to make use of its military facilities in the territory.

In stark and dramatic form, the strategic value economies exemplify the relationship between strategy and dependent development in the Pacific Islands. Less obvious, however, is the extent to which dependent development throughout the entire region—whether in sovereign, semi-sovereign, or colonial political entities—has arisen from the price that external states are willing to pay Pacific Islanders for the protection of strategic interests. Strategy and aid in the islands have gone hand in hand. Aid donors, especially Australia, have been willing to invest in the political stability of the Pacific Islands as a form of strategic insurance for themselves—a policy that was not necessary as long as the islands were securely under the political control of the colonial powers, yet became an urgent matter once island territories gained independence and were free to make their own decisions about friends and enemies. The consequence has been a massive inflow of aid to the region since the mid-1970s, making the Pacific Islanders, per capita, the recipients of the largest amounts of overseas development assistance in the world.

Strategic insurance is not the only advantage that aid givers seek. Japan has been giving aid in increasing amounts to Pacific countries in recent years, with the obvious intention of smoothing the way for Japanese investment in mining, forestry, and tourism. Japan was the single largest aid donor to Kiribati and Western Samoa as early as 1987, and in 1988 Japanese grants and technical assistance to the Pacific Islands were worth US$75.04 million, of which $30.47 million went to Papua New Guinea and $13.84 million to Solomon Islands.[20] The island states, Papua New Guinea above all, will continue to be among the beneficiaries of Japan's rapidly expanding programme of overseas development assistance which, world-wide, was worth more than US$50 billion in the five years 1988 to 1992, or more than double the aid disbursed in the previous five-year period. Japan's insurance is economic in character.

With the end of the Cold War, the need for external states to take out strategic insurance has diminished. American and Australian politicians were slow to recognise it. When a United States congressional delegation visited the Pacific Islands in 1989 it conceded that the Soviet Union, mired in internal problems, was 'hardly likely . . . to utilize force in the South Pacific', yet still felt bound to reassert the vital importance of 'strategic denial vis-à-vis the Soviet Union in the region' as a central aim of United States policy.[21]

The delegation called for United States accession to the South Pacific Nuclear Free Zone Treaty, more diplomats, more aid, and more Voice of America broadcasts, as ways of making friends, creating influence for the United States in the region, and preserving strategic denial of the region to the Soviet Union. President Bush's meeting with Pacific Islands leaders in Honolulu in 1990 appeared to be undertaken in the same spirit. And the Australian government's regional security statement of December 1989 argued that in the Pacific 'we should expect continued manifestations (for the most part opportunistic) of Soviet attempts to gain influence and supporters and to erode the strong pro-Western bias of the region'.[22] Yet by 1992 the Soviet Union no longer existed, its successor republics were desperate for Western assistance, and the idea of a Russian threat in the Pacific seemed implausible. The Cold War had been the unspoken premiss behind virtually every strategic calculation by external states in the Pacific Islands since the 1940s; now it was gone.

Although the collapse of the Soviet Union might have weakened the United States' interest in the islands, it did not have that effect in Australia, traditionally the largest and politically most influential aid donor to the region as a whole; Canberra saw one kind of threat—an external one—overtaken in the late 1980s by another—internal in origin—in the form of political instability in the island states. The Pacific, an influential Australian parliamentary committee concluded in 1989, 'is "pacific" no more'. The committee had in mind the Fiji coups of 1987, unrest in Vanuatu in 1988, and the growing militancy of the secessionist movement in Bougainville in 1989.[23] In his 1989 regional security statement the Australian Minister for Foreign Affairs, Senator Gareth Evans, raised the possibility of using Australian military force in the South Pacific 'in pursuit of security interests not immediately affecting the defence of our national territory', and attempted to define in advance the 'unusual and extreme circumstances' in which such military intervention might be appropriate.[24] This was an admission that the logic of Australian policy in the Pacific was being undermined by forces of island origin, above all by the emergence in a number of island states of an exclusivist politics of race, land, and identity. The logic had long been that aid and diplomacy, together with generous support for regional institutions, were all that was needed to produce political stability, which in turn would create a regional consensus on security favourable to Australia. It now transpired that Pacific Island countries had unique histories of their own and unique political problems, which the mere injection of aid and diplomatic assistance could not solve.

To critics of the government in Australia, the regional security statement was evidence of a 'new militarism' in Australian foreign policy and a readiness to secure Australian strategic objectives in the region by fair means or foul—by aid and diplomacy if possible, but by military force if necessary. The government was accused of perpetuating an Australian Monroe Doctrine in the region. In reply, the minister for foreign affairs claimed that in raising the whole issue he had sought not to encourage the use of military force but to set limits for it and to pursue a 'balanced middle course' between opponents of military intervention and those 'who are already comfortable with the idea of such Australian military intervention in a range of situations'.[25] In a separate but related development, Australia's Defence Co-operation Programme with Pacific Island states, particularly Papua New Guinea, expanded swiftly in the late 1980s and early 1990s. In response to the Bougainville crisis, Australia's defence assistance to Papua New Guinea almost doubled between 1988–89 and 1990–91. And in an effort to check growing lawlessness in the towns of Papua New Guinea, sometimes on a scale which suggested that the national government had lost all authority, Australia promised to give Papua New Guinea extra equipment, training, and infrastructure for the Royal PNG Constabulary and the PNG Defence Force.[26]

By 1993 the Pacific Island states seemed likely to free themselves from some of the external pressures that had accompanied the Cold War, such as the opposition that tiny Kiribati encountered from Washington and Canberra when it concluded a fisheries agreement with the Soviet Union in 1985. On the other hand, the end of the Cold War signified the end of any chance of playing East off against West, or of using the risk of Soviet political gains in the islands as a lever to extract financial assistance from Western countries. New external pressures were replacing the Cold War ones. Australia, with its policy of 'constructive commitment' to the South Pacific, appeared to be openly committed to the defence of political stability as defined by Canberra. Japan was set on a course of ever-increasing economic involvement. The web of island entanglements with external powers seemed as great as ever.

A 'nuclear-free Pacific'

What were the origins of the idea of a nuclear-free Pacific? In the mid-1980s, at a time of renewed tension between the United States and the Soviet Union, some observers claimed that outsiders had brought nuclear-free ideas to the Pacific Islands in order to discredit the West and foment anti-Western feeling among the islanders. The concept of a nuclear-free Pacific was seen as an alien import to the region.

This notion is far from the truth. Rather than adopting foreign ideas, Pacific Islanders were responding to their own historical experiences when they espoused freedom from nuclear tests, nuclear waste dumping, and nuclear ship visits. In one way or another, whether as sites for the explosion of nuclear bombs in the atmosphere, test centres for underground blasts, or splashdown points for experimental missiles, the Pacific Islands have had a continuous nuclear history since 1946.[27] As in Japan, anti-nuclear feeling is strong because of what people have personally experienced. In addition, many Pacific Islanders associate their nuclear history with the humiliations of colonialism.

A 1989 report to the United States House of Representatives Committee on Foreign Affairs described a 'depth of aversion in the region to all nuclear activities' in the islands and said that islanders were determined 'to press this point as an expression of their independence and sovereignty'. The writers of the report, staff serving the Republicans on the Congressional committee, explained the 'broad sympathy in the region for anti-nuclear positions':

> *The tendency toward support for anti-nuclear positions has a complex foundation resting on the damage that was actually done in the Pacific—primarily by the U.S.—by bomb tests; a fear that nuclear activities, especially dumping, could cause pollution that might endanger marine resources which are viewed as important sources of national wealth and livelihood; and a desire to confront French activities as a result of the perceived colonial or even imperial attitude of the French.*[28]

From one end of the Pacific Islands region to the other, governments and people alike have a tradition of being anti-nuclear. At the regional level, nuclear issues have been on the agenda of the South Pacific Forum ever since it first brought seven independent and self-governing countries of the region together in 1971. On that occasion the Forum condemned French nuclear testing, a view endorsed by the eight countries that have subsequently achieved independence or self-government and become members of the Forum: Niue, Papua New Guinea, Solomon Islands, Kiribati, Tuvalu, Vanuatu, the Marshall Islands, and the Federated States of Micronesia. Yet it would be a mistake to conclude that everyone in the Pacific meant the same thing by the phrase 'nuclear-free Pacific'.

Almost everyone wanted the waters of the Pacific pure and free from nuclear pollution, and almost everyone saw French testing as colonialist. This form of anti-nuclearism was environmental and anticolonial in inspiration and enjoyed almost universal support outside the French territories and considerable support within them. But a more radical current of opinion influenced government policy in a few countries. This was the idea that Pacific countries should comprehensively denuclearise themselves, whatever external states might think. The advocates of this more thoroughgoing anti-nuclearism were not merely environmentalist and anticolonial, but also opposed nuclear alliances, the presence or transit of nuclear weapons, and the potential use of nuclear weapons in defence of Pacific countries. They called for a truly nuclear-free Pacific.

The regional nuclear politics of the Pacific in the 1980s—now superseded by other concerns such as driftnet fishing—centred on the question of how Pacific countries would respond to these two broad forms of nuclear-free sentiment, the moderate and the radical.

For its own strategic reasons, Australia sought to exploit the differences between these two forms of anti-nuclearism during the 1980s. The Australian view was that nuclear-free sentiment in the South Pacific was too strong and widespread to be ignored, as the Americans wished, and was likely to become more radical unless it found political expression. The South Pacific Nuclear Free Zone Treaty initiated by Australia in 1983 was intended to achieve a number of objectives at once, all with long-term Western interests in mind: to put regional pressure on the French to stop testing; to preserve rights of passage for American ships and aircraft; to protect American communications facilities in Australia and New Zealand; to allow the Americans to test missiles south of the equator if they wished; and, by the very act of creating something *called* a 'nuclear-free zone', to guide rising anti-nuclear sentiment in the Pacific in directions safe for the United States. The aim was to direct attention towards the French and away from the Americans.

The chief Australian negotiator of the South Pacific Nuclear Free Zone Treaty was reported as telling a visiting Congressional delegation from the United States in 1986 that Australia had

> *assumed a leadership role in the Forum in order to provide a rational and responsible guide in developing the South Pacific Nuclear Free Zone Treaty. It feared that some of the more emotional nations might take a more radical position in opposing French testing. The aim of Australia ... was to channel the efforts of the Forum into a constructive program.*[29]

From the perspective of the Australian government, the strategy was a success, reining in those countries that wished to go much further than the treaty in denuclearising the region. The South Pacific Nuclear Free Zone Treaty has now been signed by eleven of the fifteen Forum countries and ratified by all of those except Papua New Guinea and Solomon Islands. Solomon Islands, which at first argued that the treaty did not create a truly nuclear-free zone, signed at the May 1987 meeting of the South Pacific Forum. Vanuatu remains isolated as the one state in the South Pacific that has refused to sign the treaty on the grounds that it is too weak. The Kingdom of Tonga, strongly pro-American, has not signed for the opposite reason. The Marshall Islands and the Federated States of Micronesia could not sign without first consulting the United States, which at present would not agree.[30]

Under the terms of the treaty, the states possessing nuclear weapons were invited to sign its protocols. So far only China and the former Soviet Union have signed. France has not because it may resume its nuclear tests in French Polynesia, and the United States has not because of the precedent that the treaty might create. Both the Reagan and the Bush administrations feared a proliferation of nuclear-free zones in the oceans of the world, with the potential to hamper the free movement of the US Navy. Yet disagreement over the issue exists in Washington. The US House of Representatives passed a 'sense of the Congress' resolution in 1987, urging President Reagan to reconsider his decision. The Congressional resolution declared that signing and ratifying the protocols to the treaty would be in the national interest of

Left: Former Prime Minister of Fiji, Dr Timoci Bavadra (Ministry of Information, Fiji)   Right: Colonel Sitiveni Rambuka (John Fairfax)

the United States. Another such resolution passed by the House of Representatives in 1989 argued that signing the protocols 'would not prejudge United States policy with respect to proposals for nuclear-weapon-free zones in other regions'.[31] In the light of dramatic advances in nuclear arms control, the new Clinton administration may yet accede to the treaty protocols.

A further expression of moderate regional anti-nuclear sentiment is the 1988 Convention for the Protection of the Natural Resources and Environment of the South Pacific Region, which, among other things, prohibits the dumping of nuclear waste in the Pacific. This convention has been signed not only by many Pacific countries, but even by the region's two nuclear-weapons states, France and the United States.

Despite Australia's conservative influence on regional nuclear-free policies during the 1980s, however, the more thoroughgoing version of the nuclear-free idea by no means disappeared at the national level. In different parts of the Pacific nuclear issues took on an intensely local character, arising from particular nuclear histories or the mobilisation of anti-nuclear opinion under the banner of nationalism.

On 12 April 1987 the people of Fiji elected a government pledged to a strong anti-nuclearism that had the potential to disrupt the security arrangements of the United States. The new prime minister, Dr Timoci Bavadra, committed his government to a nuclear-free Pacific and promised to ban port visits by nuclear warships. A month later, on 14 May 1987, the democratically elected government was overthrown in the region's first military coup and replaced by a military regime that reversed the nuclear-free policy. The leader of the coup, Colonel Sitiveni Rabuka, thought that banning nuclear ships and becoming non-aligned would harm the interests of the United States.[32]

The causes of the military coup lie in Fijian politics, not in the nuclear-free stance of the short-lived Bavadra government. Although the Americans were privately relieved to see a nuclear-free government put out of office, they did not mastermind the coup. Indeed, the conservative and pro-American government of Fiji, a recipient of French aid, told the United Nations in 1989 that French nuclear tests in the South Pacific were threatening food resources and deserved strong condemnation.[33] The coup leaders and their conservative allies put an end to a radically nuclear-free government in Fiji, and espoused instead the moderate anti-nuclearism that is characteristic of all independent Pacific states.

French Polynesia

In French Polynesia, opposition to the tests reached a high point during the government of territorial President Alexandre Léontieff from 1987 to 1991. A minority saw testing as an issue of political principle, tied to the question of the territory's colonial status, and in August 1988 the moderate pro-independence party *Ia Mana te Nunaa* began its campaign for a local referendum on whether or not France should continue to test, and for independent studies on the medical and environmental impact of the tests. As the bicentenary of the fall of the Bastille approached, the bomb became the focus of protest. Youth activists of the radical Polynesian Liberation Front went on a hunger strike outside the Catholic cathedral in Pape'ete until President Léontieff promised a public debate on nuclear tests. Fearing what might happen if such a debate were to proceed without direction from Paris, French Prime Minister Michel Rocard flew to French Polynesia in August 1989 and ruled out a referendum in the territory on the future of the nuclear-testing programme. He wanted to put a stop to talk in Tahiti about the people of the territory themselves making the decision on nuclear tests. French defence policy would be made by the whole of France, he said, not by one of its overseas territories. At Moruroa Atoll he sought to reassure people by promising that the number of nuclear explosions each year would be cut from eight to six.[34]

The French authorities organised a week-long conference with local leaders in October 1989 and took a group to see the Moruroa test site. Churches, trade unions, and political parties were represented, but the talks, the first ever between the French military and Polynesian representatives, were boycotted by the Polynesian Liberation Front and the Evangelical Church,

both of which are strongly anti-nuclear. The military men argued that testing was safe for the health of French Polynesia's 190 000 people, an argument that failed to convince Jacqui Drollet, leader of *Ia Mana te Nunaa*.
Statistics compiled by the French Army, he said, failed to tell the story, and
he renewed his call for an independent team of doctors to survey the population of French Polynesia.[35]

Critics of the French tests continue to argue that radioactive plutonium,
cesium, and strontium could easily escape through fissures in the volcanic
rock of Moruroa Atoll, where more than a hundred underground explosions
have taken place since 1975. Perhaps because the atoll was indeed cracking,
or perhaps as a purely political move, France conducted the two final explosions of 1989 at its old test site on Fangataufa Atoll, and adopted the
practice of testing all larger weapons there rather than on Moruroa.[36]

Under the 1984 statute of autonomy and again in its modifications of
1990, Paris devolved certain powers to the territorial government in Tahiti,
adding to the authority of the territorial president elected by the assembly
and diminishing the role of the resident French high commissioner.[37] French
Polynesia has been permitted to play a more active regional role and join
some regional organisations such as the Forum Secretariat. But on key issues the final say rests with the French state: France retains full control over
the nuclear test programme, should it resume, and over all related matters
of health and environmental protection; it permits the territory the right to
exploit the islands' two-hundred-mile exclusive economic zone but may
reclaim that right at any time; and whatever political autonomy the government in Tahiti may enjoy is bestowed by French statutory law and may be
withdrawn by changes to that law.

'The one who pays', Rocard said on his visit in 1989, 'is the one who
controls'. Just as France consulted none of its citizens in French Polynesia
before deciding to test its nuclear weapons there, so it ignored them in the
decision to suspend the tests. The suspension after twenty-six years took
everyone by surprise, including military personnel at Moruroa who were
preparing for the 1992 series. The independence parties, which gained only
four of the forty-one seats in the Territorial Assembly elections of 1991, were
delighted. Many others feared for the territory's economy if the suspension
should prove permanent. By August 1992 the test suspension had already
cost French Polynesia more than five billion CPF (A$77 million) in financial
transfers from France, and the territorial budget had been cut by one billion
CPF (A$15 million). According to one official estimate, seven thousand of the
territory's fifty-four thousand wage earners would lose their jobs if the
nuclear testing centre were to be closed. Having come to depend for jobs
and livelihoods on the strategic value of their island, the people of French
Polynesia now faced a future with that value and its political leverage
suddenly removed. Even if the conservatives were to win the French elections
of March 1993 and resume testing as the military wanted, the economic

reprieve for French Polynesia would probably be temporary in a situation where nuclear testing by Russia and the United States was likely to have stopped altogether by 1997.[38]

Nuclear-free Palau

Just as French strategic interests have determined the destiny of many islanders south of the equator, American strategy has been at the heart of arrangements for the future of many islanders to the north. The Palauans' nuclear-free constitution of 1979 has been a sticking point in negotiations with the United States for more than a decade. In return for aid, the Americans have insisted that they must be free to bring nuclear weapons into Palauan waters if they choose. The American calculation is that, sometime in the fifty years covered by the Palau Compact of Free Association, the armed forces of the United States might need the islands of the Palauan archipelago for training or for military bases. For their part, the Palauans have had a constitution that requires the approval of 75 per cent of voters before it may be changed, and the constitution remained unchanged in this respect until Palauans voted to amend it in November 1992. The stalemate has given the Palauan leaders leverage in negotiating a better deal with the United States under the Compact; it has brought the Palauans into conflict with the United States; it has endlessly delayed the termination of the United Nations Trusteeship in Palau; and it has inflamed political divisions within Palauan society.[39]

By the end of 1986 the people of Palau had voted four times in plebiscites on the Compact of Free Association, the agreement that would determine their future relationship with the United States, and on each occasion the vote had failed to reach the 75 per cent needed to override nuclear-free provisions in the Palauan constitution so that the Compact could come into effect. Under the Compact, the United States would be able to bring nuclear weapons on board their ships and aircraft into and out of Palauan territory.

Since then, Palau has held more plebiscites and endured more political dispute. When a vote in June 1987 failed to get the required majority, President Lazarus Salii, who wanted the Compact to come into effect, suspended nine hundred of the territory's thirteen hundred public servants, saying that there was no money left to pay their wages. He was hoping that economic distress would convince people to vote for the Compact. A further vote, in August 1987, purported to change the Palauan constitution so that a simple majority of 50 per cent plus one would be enough to pass the Compact and override the nuclear-free provisions; a subsequent plebiscite on the Compact under this supposedly altered constitution was then held to have passed. For the United States, the problem seemed to have been solved.

*Lazarus Salii of Palau,
1970s. (Trust Territory
Archives, Pacific
Collection, University of
Hawai'i Library)*

But a group of Palauan women who intended to challenge this decision in court were intimidated into withdrawing their case. Someone shot dead the father of an anti-nuclear activist, and in early 1988 a delegation from the International Commission of Jurists claimed that violence had prevented due process of law in the territory. The case was allowed to come to the Supreme Court of Palau, which ruled in April 1988 that the constitutional amendment of 1987 was 'null, void and of no effect'.[40] Judge Robert A. Hefner commented in his verdict that the plaintiffs had brought the case under what appeared to be 'stressful and adverse conditions'.[41] In other words, the constitution had never been changed, and a 75 per cent majority was still needed for the acceptance of a nuclear Compact with the United States.

After allegations of corruption, President Salii committed suicide in August 1988. A 1989 report on Palau by the United States General Accounting Office revealed that the Palau administration had spent nearly US$2 million trying to ensure that people voted in favor of the Compact.[42] On the American side, high hopes were held that the Palauans would accept a revised Compact that paid off some of their debts and provided additional compensation for land the United States might use in the future for military purposes. American and Palauan negotiators agreed on the new terms in Guam in May 1989. But when the people cast their ballots in February 1990, the vote once again failed to reach the majority necessary to accept the

Compact in its nuclear form. With most ballots counted, only 60.5 per cent had voted in favour of the Compact, a lower margin than ever before. The aid package they would get was bigger than ever before, but the price was that they would have to allow nuclear vessels and aircraft into their country and be ready to make land available for the US military if it should be needed at any time. In essence if not in detail, the dispute between Palau and the United States had not changed in a decade. In the two years after that vote, the United States reasserted administrative control over Palau, in particular through the Department of Interior's Secretarial Order no. 3142, which limited the financial powers of the Palau government. The headquarters of the Trust Territory of the Pacific Islands and its director are now located in Palau, a territory that has in large measure reverted to its former colonial status.

The referendum of 1992 was a re-run of recent Palauan history. By a margin of six to four, the Palauans amended their constitution so that a simple majority would be enough to approve the Compact when a new plebiscite is held. As happened in 1987, the constitutionality of this change was challenged in court by a group of Palauan women; and, as happened in 1989, Palauan legislators said they wanted further modifications to the Compact.

The Palauans' nuclear-free sentiment has always been inseparable from their attachment to land, and many Palauans remained concerned that the existing Compact would allow the United States to take any area of land over a fifty-year period. Expressing concern that 'under the Compact every inch of Palauan land is vulnerable to United States military use', an anti-Compact group told the UN Visiting Mission in 1992:

> *As you are well aware, the political climate around the world is changing; we watch the CNN and we know that; the cold war is over; the Soviet Union is no longer a threat; the European community is talking about uniting . . . the strategic value of Palau as perceived ten years ago is now obsolete.*[43]

Nowhere in the Pacific has the promise of post-independence aid had so many strings attached as in Palau. Whether the Clinton administration would at last remove those strings remained to be seen.

A radioactive legacy

The people of the Marshall Islands still live with the radioactive legacy of American nuclear tests of the 1950s. The history of the testing programme is no longer a secret, though people will continue to disagree about the exact course of events at Bikini Atoll on 1 March 1954, when the Americans triggered a gigantic thermonuclear explosion that spread fallout over some

An area of Bikini Atoll showing the scars of nuclear testing, 1968. (Trust Territory Archives, Pacific Collection, University of Hawai'i Library)

atoll populations in the northern Marshalls. The time is long past when it could be argued that the United States had done nothing to make amends for the destructive effect of nuclear testing on islanders' health and on the natural environment. Unlike France, which has never wholly lost traditions of absolutism in government, and which has successfully hidden its nuclear testing from public scrutiny, the United States is a liberal society—if a flawed one—in which sympathetic lawyers and legislators have spent more than two decades prising the truth from the authorities, representing the islanders' case in court and in Congress, and ensuring that something was done.

Section 177 of the Compact with the Marshalls established a trust fund of US$150 million for distribution to the people of the four 'radiation atolls'. Islanders had been removed from Bikini and Enewetak to make way for the tests, and Rongelap and Utrik were exposed to fallout from the Bravo test. At the same time the United States government, appealing to the legal doctrine of 'espousal', blocked all further litigation by ensuring that Section 177 constituted 'the full settlement of all claims, past, present and future, of the Government, citizens and nationals of the Marshall Islands which are based on, arise out of or are in any way related to the Nuclear Testing Program and which are against the United States'. Lawyers for the islanders contested the espousal doctrine, but their suits were dismissed, a federal appeals court upholding the dismissal in 1989.[44]

The resettlement of island homelands by the northern Marshallese has had a chequered history. A group of Bikinians returned to Bikini Atoll in the mid-1970s, only to be moved off again in 1978 because of official fears that they were absorbing dangerous amounts of radionuclides. A long-promised clean-up of Bikini, funded by the US Congress, has been in progress since 1988. Scientists have blanketed the entire island of Eneu with potassium fertiliser in an attempt to block the movement of radioactive cesium 137 into coconuts and other plants. Enewetak Atoll, centre of the test programme in the 1950s, was cleaned up—as much as that is possible—in the late 1970s, and some Enewetak Islanders have been living in the safer, southern part of the atoll since 1980. The people of Rongelap, exposed to fallout in 1954 and suffering from the health effects ever since, were moved to an uncontaminated island in Kwajalein Atoll by the Greenpeace organisation in 1985. Studies of the safety of Rongelap were still being conducted in 1990.

The officially recognised test victims are a small minority of the Marshallese who, as a people, are far more affected by the activities of the US Army at Kwajalein Atoll, a major testing centre for American intercontinental ballistic missiles since 1959. Under the Compact, the tests continue. Kwajalein Missile Range, now known as the US Army Kwajalein Atoll facilities, represents an investment of about US$500 million and is the principal site for testing anti-missile missile and space experiments under the Strategic Defense Initiative or Star Wars programme initiated by the Reagan administration during the 1980s.

The army base on Kwajalein Island in the south-east corner of the atoll has long played a central role in Marshallese life. Thousands of Marshallese began to settle on the 40 hectares (96 acres) of Ebeye Island during the 1960s after being forced off their home islands in Kwajalein Atoll so that the United States could fire its missiles into the lagoon; they were soon joined by thousands more, who were attracted by the menial jobs available across the water at Kwajalein Island, the centre of army operations. As eight thousand people jostled for space on the treeless strip of atoll land, a slum of broken sewers, polluted water, and epidemics grew up, in striking contrast to the vacation resort conditions on Kwajalein, where the Americans lived. Ebeye was a scandal.[45]

Repeated sail-ins by Kwajalein landowners, in 1969, 1979, 1982, and again in 1985–86, when groups of people occupied islands in the missile-splashdown zone, focused attention on the issue of the lease moneys paid by the United States for its use of the atoll; under the Compact of Free Association the United States now pays about $9 million a year to some five thousand atoll landowners. Bitter legal battles over customary rights to Kwajalein land have been conducted for years. Since 1983, conditions on Ebeye have gradually improved as local leaders have taken the initiative through their elected council and the Kwajalein Development Authority, funded by lease moneys, rebuilds the water, sewerage, and electricity systems. Eventually urban congestion on Ebeye will be relieved by the construction of a causeway across the reefs to South Loi, North Loi, Ebwoj, and Gugeegue islands to the north.[46] By 1993, living conditions on Ebeye had improved considerably.

The Marshall Islanders have paid a heavy price for living on islands that happened to be of strategic value to the United States, above all in radioactive contamination of land and people—now being redressed or compensated for—and in a markedly dependent form of urbanised economic development that has largely superseded the older, outer-island subsistence economy.[47] Like Pacific Islanders elsewhere, though, most Marshall Islanders are likely to regard life in an urban centre such as Ebeye as an advance on life in the isolated outer islands.

Nuclear-free sentiment, at its peak during the 1980s, took different forms in different parts of the Pacific: almost universal opposition to French testing, even by independent states that were accepting French aid, such as Fiji; radical anti-nuclearism in Vanuatu and Palau, which both sought to be completely nuclear-free; an anticolonial movement in French Polynesia; and continuing demands for compensation and assistance in the Marshall Islands.

Conclusion

By 1993 the Cold War was a thing of the past. A dramatically changed strategic situation in eastern Europe, the collapse of the former Soviet Union, and momentous arms control agreements between Russia and the United States suggested that a turning-point had been reached in twentieth-century history. All US sea-based tactical nuclear weapons had been withdrawn from overseas bases, ships, and submarines, and general US policy was not to deploy them. The United States had committed itself to stop all nuclear testing by the end of 1996. The START agreement between Russia and the United States provided for drastic reductions in the most dangerous weapons, the long-range strategic weapons whose development owed so much to testing in the Pacific.

The implications for the Pacific Islands could be profound. The Western nuclear powers, after all, had tested their bombs and missiles in the Pacific Islands in order to maintain a nuclear deterrent against attack from what used to be the Soviet Union; the United States had the old Soviet threat in mind when it insisted on nuclear access to Palau. That threat no longer existed. France had exploded its bombs in the Tuamotu Archipelago for the sake of an independent nuclear deterrent in a world at risk of nuclear war between two superpowers. That risk was now radically diminished. Australia's aid to the islands had flowed freely since the mid-1970s as a response, at least in part, to the possibility of Soviet influence. That possibility was now gone. The strategic map was now changing as the superpowers retreated to pay the bills for their military competition.

For half a century, the strategic ambitions of outsiders had worked against

Pacific Islanders—or at least that was their most obvious effect in the form of military experiments, radioactive damage, and demands for nuclear access. As external powers began to lose strategic interest in the islands, however, islanders became aware of another side of the argument. Strategic importance had brought foreign assistance to the Pacific on a massive scale. The task of island governments would now be to find new ways of meeting the economic demands of their people.

Notes

1 The Cook Islands and Niue were annexed to New Zealand in 1901. W. P. Morell, *Britain in the Pacific Islands*, Clarendon Press, Oxford, 1960, 296–297.

2 Virginia Thompson and Richard Adloff, *The French Pacific Islands: French Polynesia and New Caledonia*, University of California Press, Berkeley, 1971, 15.

3 Mark R. Peattie, *Nan'yō: The Rise and Fall of the Japanese in Micronesia, 1885–1945*, Pacific Islands Monograph Series no. 4, University of Hawai'i Press, Honolulu, 1988.

4 Peter Sack, ed., *Pacific Constitutions*, Department of Law, Research School of Social Sciences, Australian National University, Canberra, 1982.

5 Ian Downs, *The Australian Trusteeship: Papua New Guinea 1945–75*, Australian Government Publishing Service, Canberra, 1980.

6 Bengt Danielsson and Marie-Thérèse Danielsson, *Poisoned Reign: French Nuclear Colonialism in the Pacific*, Penguin Books Australia, Ringwood, VIC, 1986; Stephen Henningham, *France and the South Pacific: A Contemporary History*, University of Hawai'i Press, Honolulu, 1992, 231.

7 Stewart Firth, 'Sovereignty and Independence in the Contemporary Pacific', *The Contemporary Pacific* 1 (1989): 77–83; Edward J. Michal, ' "Protected States": The Political Status of the Federated States of Micronesia and the Republic of the Marshall Islands', *The Contemporary Pacific* 5 (2, 1993).

8 Gary Smith, *Micronesia: Decolonisation and US Military Interests in the Trust Territories of the Pacific Islands*, Peace Research Centre, Australian National University, Canberra, 1991, 43–60.

9 Barrie Macdonald, 'Self-determination and self-government', *Journal of Pacific History* 17 (1982): 51–61.

10 Robin Osborne, *Indonesia's Secret War: The Guerilla Struggle in Irian Jaya*, Allen & Unwin, Sydney, 1985; Stephen Henningham, 'Keeping the Tricolor Flying: The French Pacific into the 1990s', *The Contemporary Pacific* 1 (1989): 97–132; Laura Souder-Jaffery and Robert A. Underwood, eds, *Chamorro Self-Determination: The Right of a People, I Derechon I Taotao*, Micronesian Area Research Center Education Series Publication no. 7, University of Guam, 1987; George Hu'eu Sanford Kanahele, *Ku Kanaka Stand Tall: A Search for Hawaiian Values*, University of Hawai'i Press and Waiaha Foundation, Honolulu, 1986; Michael Kioni Dudley and Keoni Kealoha Agard, *A Call for Hawaiian Sovereignty*, Na Kane O Ka Malo Press, Honolulu, 1990; Robert Macdonald, *The Fifth Wind: New Zealand and the Legacy of a Turbulent Past*, Bloomsbury Publishing, London, 1989; Sandra J. Kehoe-Forutan, *Torres Strait Independence:*

A Chronicle of Events, Department of Geographical Sciences, University of Queensland, Research Report no. 1, St Lucia, QLD, 1988.

11 'The Strategic Basis of Defence Policy', *The National Times*, Sydney, 30 March to 5 April 1984; Osborne; R. J. May, ed., *Between Two Nations: The Indonesia–Papua New Guinea Border and West Papua Nationalism*, Robert Brown & Associates, Bathurst, NSW, 1986; Harold Crouch, 'Indonesia and the Security of Australia and Papua New Guinea', in *Security and Defence: Pacific and Global Perspectives*, ed. Desmond Ball and Cathy Downes, Allen & Unwin, Sydney, 1990, 378–397.

12 'Indonesia Finds a New Ally Just Down the Road', *Sydney Morning Herald*, 18 January 1992.

13 Information supplied by Dr John Connell.

14 *Sydney Morning Herald*, 17 January 1992.

15 Leigh Neighbour, 'The Bougainville Crisis and the Legitimacy of the Papua New Guinea State', BA honours thesis, Macquarie University, 1991, 37.

16 Henningham 1992, 108.

17 *Pacific Report*, 2 May and 21 November 1991.

18 Henningham 1989, 100.

19 Karin von Strokirch 'Constraints on Autonomy in French Polynesia', paper presented to Third Conference of Pacific Islands Political Studies Association, December 1991.

20 Economic Cooperation Bureau, Ministry of Foreign Affairs, *Outlook of Japan's Economic Cooperation*, Tokyo, February 1990.

21 *Problems in Paradise: United States Interests in the South Pacific: Report of a Congressional Delegation to the South Pacific August 5–16, 1989*, Washington, DC, 1990, 6, 10.

22 Ministerial Statement, December 1989, reproduced in *Australia's Regional Security*, ed. Greg Fry, Allen & Unwin, Sydney, 1991, 173.

23 The Parliament of the Commonwealth of Australia, Joint Committee on Foreign Affairs, Defence, and Trade, *Australia's Relations with the South Pacific*, March 1989, xxii.

24 Ministerial Statement, paragraphs 88 and 90, in Fry 1991, 191.

25 Graeme Cheeseman and St John Kettle, *The New Australian Militarism: Undermining Our Future Security*, Pluto Press Australia, Sydney, 1990; Fry 1991, 85–95, 120–137, 149.

26 Department of Foreign Affairs and Trade, *Backgrounder*, 26 January 1990.

27 Stewart Firth, *Nuclear Playground*, South Sea Books, University of Hawai'i Press, Honolulu, 1987.

28 *Regional Security Developments in the South Pacific. Report of a Minority Staff Study Mission to Honolulu; Fiji; Vanuatu; Auckland and Wellington, New Zealand; Sydney and Canberra, Australia, November 28–December 13, 1988, to the Committee on Foreign Affairs U.S. House of Representatives*, Washington, DC, 1989, 12–13, 26.

29 United States Congress, 99th Congress, *House of Representatives Armed Services Committee: Report of the Delegation to the South Pacific*, Washington, DC, 1986, 15, quoted in Michael Hamel-Green, *The South Pacific Nuclear Free Zone Treaty: A Critical Assessment*, Peace Research Centre, Australian National University, Canberra, 1990, 61.

30 Michal, 1993.

31 *Problems in Paradise*, 128.

32 Michael Hamel-Green 'Regional Arms Control in the South Pacific: Island State Responses to Australia's Nuclear Free Zone Initiative', *The Contemporary Pacific* 3 (1991): 59–84.

33 *South Pacific: Radio Australia News Summary*, 2 October 1989.

34 'Islanders Force French to Face Up to Risks in the Business of the Nuclear Bomb', *Sydney Morning Herald*, 28 October 1989; *South Pacific: Radio Australia News Summary*, 27 August 1989.

35 *South Pacific: Radio Australia News Summary*, 7 October 1989.

36 'Era of Blasts May Be Over for the Atoll of Mururoa', *Sydney Morning Herald*, 28 October 1989.

37 Henningham 1992, 148–150.

38 For information in these two paragraphs I am indebted to two papers by Karin von Strokirch, 'Constraints on Autonomy in French Polynesia' and 'Suspension of Nuclear Testing: The Implications for French Polynesia', paper presented at Pacific History Association conference, Christchurch, December 1992.

39 Richard J. Parmentier, 'The Rhetoric of Free Association and Palau's Political Struggle', *The Contemporary Pacific* 3 (1991): 146–158.

40 Associate Justice Robert A. Hefner, *Order and Judgment in the Supreme Court of the Republic of Palau Trial Division*, 22 April 1988.

41 *Fritz v. Salii*, Civil Action no. 161–187, in the Supreme Court of the Republic of Palau Trial Division, 22 April 1988.

42 General Accounting Office, *U.S. Trust Territory: Issues Associated with Palau's Transition to Self-Government*, Washington, DC, 1989.

43 *Pacific Daily News*, Guam, 11 February 1990; *Pacific News Bulletin*, Sydney, October 1992, November 1992, January 1993.

44 Smith 1991, 73–77.

45 Giff Johnson, *Collision Course at Kwajalein: Marshall Islanders in the Shadow of the Bomb*, Pacific Concerns Resource Center, Honolulu, 1984.

46 'The Reconstruction of Ebeye', *Pacific Magazine*, January–February 1990, 30–69.

47 John Connell, 'The New Micronesia: Pitfalls and Problems of Dependent Development', *Pacific Studies* 14 (1991): 87–117.

14

Economic development and dependency

Bruce Knapman

'Tiko can't be developed,' Manu declared, 'unless the ancient gods are killed.'

'But the ancient gods are dead. The Sabbatarians killed them long ago,' countered the ancient preacher.

'Never believe that, sir. Had they died Tiko would have developed long ago. Look around you,' Manu advised.

The ancient preacher looked around and saw nothing; he looked at himself, his tattered clothes, his nailed-in second-hand sandals, and nodded rather dubiously. He wished to be developed. 'And how do you slay the ancient gods?' he inquired cautiously.

'Never try, sir, it's useless,' Manu replied. 'Kill the new ones.' And that, in short, is what Manu does. . . . He pedals his bicycle to the International Nightlight Hotel, to the Bank of Tiko, and all over Tulisi, shouting his lonely message against Development, but the whole capital is as a cemetery.

Epeli Hau'ofa, Tales of the Tikongs

First and fleeting contact between Pacific Islanders and the West was followed sooner or later by permanent linkage. During the nineteenth century, foreign trade and investment to varying degrees transformed island economies into raw materials (and in some cases labour) suppliers on the extreme periphery of an expanding capitalist world market. Between 1883 and 1913 the Pacific Islands became 'top fliers' of a rapidly developing tropical world,[1] largely because of sugar growth in Fiji and nickel growth in New Caledonia. Almost everywhere trade provided a 'vent' for surplus productive capacity in subsistence economic systems that were 'ecologically robust' and thus brought into being mixed subsistence–cash cropping economies (table 1).[2] Colonial rule brought law and order and public services.

In consequence of this opening up of island societies and its consolidation

Table 1   *Exports from the Pacific Islands, 1883–1913*

(us$ *million*)

	1883	1913
Fiji	1.7	6.9
French Polynesia	0.7	2.2
New Caledonia	0.6	3.1
Papua	0.1	0.3
Other	2.0	5.0
Subtotal	5.1	17.5
Total Tropics[a]	1020.0	2768.5

Note: *a* Countries between 30 degrees north and 30 degrees south.

Source: Charles C. Stover, 'Tropical Exports', in *Tropical Development 1880–1913: Studies in Economic Progress*, ed. W. Arthur Lewis, George Allen & Unwin, London, 1970, 46–63.

in the twentieth century, two major changes occurred. First, Pacific populations were no longer 'blissfully unaware of the higher standards of living in the outside world'.[3] Second, provision of public health services eventually reduced death rates. Today, islanders' aspirations for material goods and services are rising towards American, Australian, or New Zealand levels (though they are neither uniform across or within countries, nor the same as European aspirations in respect of the trade-off with non-material 'goods' like leisure and culture), and island populations are increasing at natural rates of around 2–4 per cent annually, with urban populations growing faster.[4]

The fundamental economic development problem confronting Pacific Island states and territories is how to prevent a widening of what Mishan calls the 'margin of discontent' between wants and their satisfaction—in a situation where even if wants were static, annual total income growth would have to be 2 per cent or more in order to maintain average standards of living for growing populations.[5] As Lewis wrote in a classic text on economic growth, 'raising total output by 2 per cent per annum is no mean feat. It requires considerable expenditures on education and other public services, a doubling of current capital formation, and many changes in beliefs and institutions'.[6] It is, moreover, a process incompletely understood: 'We do not really know why some countries are more dynamic than others'.[7] There is no simple formula for guaranteed success. If the capacity to produce does not expand to match the capacity to consume, only two broad alternatives are available: either the budget constraint is eased by income transfers in the form of aid flows or migrant remittances; or consumption per head falls and frustration rises.

Table 2   Pacific Islands basic indicators

State/ Territory	Land (sq. km.)	Sea (ooo sq. km.)	Population[a] (ooo)	GNP[b] (us$m.)
American Samoa	197	390	33	
Cook Islands	240	1,830	17	20
Federated States of Micronesia	701	2,978	95	
Fiji	18,272	1,290	723	1,091
French Polynesia	3,265	5,030	186	1,370
Guam	541	218	121	
Kiribati	690	3,550	66	32
Marshall Islands	181	2,131	39	42
Nauru	21	320	8	70
New Caledonia	19,103	1,740	154	860
Niue	259	390	3	3
Northern Marianas	471	1,823	20	
Palau (Belau)	494	629	18	
Papua New Guinea	462,243	3,120	3,494	2,555
Solomon Islands	28,530	1,340	293	123
Tokelau	10	290	2	1
Tonga	699	700	99	72
Tuvalu	26	900	8	4
Vanuatu	11,880	680	145	83
Wallis & Futuna	255	300	11	
Western Samoa	2,935	120	166	110

Notes: *a* Figures are for 1987 except for Federated States of Micronesia and Guam (1986), Palau (1985), and American Samoa and Wallis & Futuna (1981).

b Gross national product: figures are for various years in the 1980s.

Sources: ESCAP, *Statistical Yearbook for Asia and the Pacific 1986–1987; Pacific Economic Bulletin* 3 (Dec. 1988), Australian National University; *Pac Facts*, University of New South Wales, 1988; *Marshall Islands Statistical Abstract 1988*, Office of Planning and Statistics, Majuro.

This chapter is about the fundamental and related economic problems confronting twenty-one Pacific countries (table 2). Growth potential and performance, and development options are discussed; and generalizations that occupy the middle ground between complete relativism and universalism are offered. The islands are as diverse economically as they are politically, socially, and culturally, but they do share many characteristics and can be subgrouped.

The general conclusion is that growth prospects are limited in a minority of countries and virtually non-existent in most, and that in both cases rising material living standards necessarily imply continued 'dependence', whether on trade in goods and services, foreign investment, resource rents, aid, or remittances. Self-reliance, which is listed in development plans as a major development objective, therefore should be recognised as conflicting with the other major objective of raising living standards—which is only to say that there is a trade-off and a difficult choice to be made. Relatively more economic self-sufficiency may be an objective of value in its own right according to the tenets of Buddhist economics.[8] It may be an objective that, if attained, is expected to contribute to a perfectly legitimate broader goal of national independence, which is presumably what President Tabai of Kiribati had in mind when he stated that 'perpetual dependence on others . . . obviously cannot be regarded as development'.[9] But the objective ought not to be pursued under the illusion that there are no economic costs or, 'even worse, under the wishful fantasy that short-run economic conditions will actually improve if trade with other . . . countries is curtailed'.[10] In this connection, it is noteworthy that according to a study of seventeen Pacific countries using 1970s data, 'official development aid was found to be positively associated with GDP per capita and with the quality of life indices' (life expectancy, infant mortality, population per doctor, population per hospital bed, and access to education), and that a 'safe generalization does seem to be that aid received per head is related to political dependency'.[11]

Development potential

An examination of the basic indicators in table 2 establishes that Pacific Island states and territories are small by any of the conventional criteria of land area, population, and gross national product. Using the commonly accepted population criterion of fewer than five million, which generally correlates well with other measures of size, all but Papua New Guinea are very small, with populations under one million.[12] Thirteen of the twenty-one countries covered have populations under one hundred thousand.

Additionally, land areas are often not only small in total, but also fragmented, dispersed, and distant from world markets in terms of kilometres and economic accessibility. Tuvalu's 26 square kilometres, for example, is made up of nine coral atolls scattered north to south over 560 kilometres of ocean, with the capital of Funafuti lying 1100 kilometres north of Suva, Fiji, which in turn lies 3215 kilometres north-east of Sydney, 2113 kilometres north of Auckland, and 8816 kilometres south-west of San Francisco.[13] More generally, using the crow-flying distance between extreme points of a country divided by population as an indicator, dispersion is found by the United Nations Council on Trade and Development (UNCTAD) Secretariat to be 'particularly acute' in the Pacific, even by comparison with other island regions: 'The mean dispersion for the small Pacific island countries was 28.4 metres in 1981; for the Caribbean it was 3.6 metres, and in the African and Indian Ocean region 6.1 metres'.[14] As to distance from world markets, the South Pacific Commission estimates that nineteen countries of the Pacific region are on average 2900 kilometres from a population centre of 500 000 people or more, compared with 700 and 1800 for the Caribbean and the Indian Ocean, respectively.[15] Outer island remoteness from capitals, and the capitals' remoteness from the metropolitan cities, particularly distinguishes the Pacific Islands from the general body of small nations.[16]

Geography is reinforced by economics and technological change: isolated island communities supply and demand little cargo, so that frequent and regular shipping services are not commercially sustainable, and high internal and external transport costs are a constraint on the development of domestic markets and export opportunities, while technical changes in sea and air transport favour long-haul traffic and marginalise outer islands and even entire countries.[17]

The locational disadvantage of Pacific Island economies is clear-cut: they must bear high transport costs on export and import goods whose prices they cannot influence precisely because they are small. The other economic consequences of smallness have been much discussed since Simon Kuznets' 1960 suggestion that 'small countries are under a greater handicap than large in the task of economic growth'.[18] At base the handicap is greater because small countries are characterised by limited resource endowments and small domestic markets. Together these characteristics severely constrain production and trading possibilities and dictate a pattern of specialisation that makes for vulnerability to external economic forces, though as always 'much depends on the circumstances and characteristics of particular countries'.[19]

Taking natural resources first, a distinction must be drawn between those Pacific countries made up largely or entirely of volcanic or continental islands and those made up substantially or entirely of atolls (Federated States of Micronesia, French Polynesia, the Cook Islands, Kiribati, the Marshall Islands, Nauru, Niue, Tokelau, and Tuvalu).[20] Only a few metres above sea level at their highest points, the atolls have extremely poor soil, experience great rainfall variability, and in times of drought or flooding suffer salination of any groundwater lens that exists. The coconut palm, some taro varieties, and a few vegetables and fruits are all that can be cultivated, and they are susceptible to pests and diseases. Marine resources are of crucial significance, but are not as varied as is often supposed and were never so continuously bountiful as to prevent subsistence from being something of a struggle. It is well established that population pressure on fixed natural resources led to abortion, infanticide, warfare, and forced migration.[21]

Moreover, the resource base has always been highly vulnerable to natural hazards such as hurricanes, tidal waves, and storm surges. In 1946 a hurricane 'reduced the atoll of Suwarrow in the northern Cook Islands from 21 separate islets to 7: the rest were swept away'.[22] In 1960 a hurricane made 4000 of Niue's 4780 people homeless and wiped out copra production for two years.[23] Tidal surges in a two-week period in 1979 destroyed hundreds of homes on Majuro in the Marshall Islands.[24] Erosion is a general problem, and prospects are grim because of the greenhouse effect, which is 'likely . . . to lead to a substantial decline in agricultural production, a possible decline in fisheries production, and a loss of vital water, timber and firewood resources, thus reducing the potential of the few areas in which the atolls and atoll states currently demonstrate a degree of self-reliance'.[25]

Fortuitous economic deposits of phosphate expand, or did expand, production possibilities in a few cases (Nauru, Banaba, Christmas), but by definition are non-renewable, so that much depends on the uses to which export income is put. Tellingly, investments by the governments concerned have been placed overseas. Other mineral resources have been discovered in the exclusive economic zones of atoll states. Polymetallic nodules at depths of 4000 to 6000 metres are found in promising densities in the northern Cooks and are present in Marshallese, Kiribati, French Polynesian, and Tuvaluan waters. But existence is not synonymous with economic accessibility: many legal, technological, and commercial issues must yet be solved.[26]

The fisheries resource of the exclusive economic zones (see map page 240) is more promising, for world-wide they contain 90 per cent of known commercially exploitable fish stocks. Of the world's tuna, 70 per cent is caught in the Pacific (40 per cent in the west). However, though atoll states have rights over vast expanses of ocean (table 2), they are not necessarily in a position to farm the sea themselves because of the capital and technological requirements of distant-water fishing, or because of a scarcity of baitfish resulting from limited lagoon and shelf areas—as Tuvalu's unsuccessful attempt in the 1980s bears witness. Nor are they in a position to extract appropriate rental income by licensing foreign fleets and guaranteeing exclusive use of their waters. Under the 1987 Multilateral Fisheries Treaty between the United States and South Pacific Forum nations, some license fees are now paid where once they were not, and such crumbs from the negotiating table may be crucial revenue to island governments. But Japan and Taiwan do not pay fees, and their 'wall-of-death' drift-netters poach and threaten overexploitation of stocks, largely immune from the efforts of a handful of patrol-boat captains.[27] 'The general conclusion must be that the treasure chest of living and non-living marine resources is likely to remain either locked or prove empty for many small island developing countries'.[28]

The tourist-attracting resources of sun, sea, and sand may possess some untapped potential in atoll states, but relative to other islands, let alone other tourist destinations, the attractions are limited. The islands are less accessible, and poor water and sanitation can be a problem—as anyone who has visited an atoll knows.

The volcanic island countries, and in particular the larger states of the western Pacific, have a wider range of natural resources. Total land areas are a poor guide to agricultural potential because 'landforms, drainage or soil conditions severely restrict the proportion of land which can be used for permanent agriculture': 30 to 50 per cent in Papua New Guinea, probably a similar percentage in the Solomon Islands, 62 per cent in Fiji, 50 per cent in Western Samoa, and 40 per cent in Vanuatu. The proportion is likely to fall as commercialisation of agriculture proceeds, because steepland soils suitable for subsistence cropping are unsuitable for cash cropping.[29] Nonetheless, the agronomic potential of these countries is much greater than that of the atolls. Their village agriculture was the inspiration for the well-known economic model of 'subsistence affluence' which formalised a British colonial official's remark that in Fiji 'the earth need only be tickled to laugh back in harvest'.[30] Their more fertile soils support commercial cropping of sugar cane, rice, passionfruit, a variety of vegetables, and other crops. Significant forestry resources exist in the Melanesian countries also.[31]

Additionally, the larger volcanic islands are better endowed with both mineral and marine resources, as well as tourist attractions. New Caledonia has the third largest nickel deposits in the world; Papua New Guinea has enormous deposits of copper and gold; and Fiji and the Solomons produce gold. The last three of these countries have the capacity to generate hydro-electric power. More extensive lagoon and reef areas make for greater potential in artisanal fishing and aquaculture, and the richest pelagic waters surround Papua New Guinea and the Solomon Islands.[32] Natural hazards do not discriminate in favour of the better endowed, however. Volcanic eruptions in Tonga in 1946 and Vanuatu in 1960 forced evacuations of village populations. In May 1986, Cyclone Namu made 90 000 Solomon Islanders homeless, destroyed 22 000 hectares of coconut groves and two-thirds of subsistence gardens on Malaita and Guadalcanal, cut oil palm output by a third, and destroyed the forestry resource in South Malaita.[33] Hurricanes are intermittent occurrences in Fiji and Vanuatu, laying to rest at least temporarily the best of development plans.

Natural resource poverty sets a particularly sharp limit to output growth in the atoll states, while imposing constraints of varying severity on the prospects of the non-atoll countries. Smallness of human resource endowments strengthens these constraints in a number of ways. First, decision-making in small societies is more personalised, with consequent 'reluctance to carry through vigorously any official act which might offend some person or group', and 'advancement of the meritorious employee tends to be at par with the mediocre'.[34] Second and related, though more contentious, Lowenthal has suggested that 'any state requires an irreducible minimum of infrastructure, and the smaller the state the larger its government looms in its economy and society', with the result that bureaucracy is intrusive and stifling of individual initiative and innovation.[35] Third, it has been suggested that a small labour force implies a small pool of human potential skills, though, fourth, the restrictions placed on expanding the skill base by small size are more important.[36] Demand is insufficient to sustain the local provision of education and training facilities at manageable cost levels, so that there is not only an absence of educational opportunity for the young, but also of the research and advice usually available from universities (though regional co-operation can help here).

This last-mentioned development constraint is just one aspect of the general problem of diseconomies of scale that afflicts small economies. The observation that 'the smallest unit of a great number of necessary facilities is larger than a small community can fully utilize' applies to human resources, physical facilities, and government administration in general.[37] People with high-level skills are often underused and are therefore relatively expensive because of low domestic demand. For the same reason there is no justification for training back-ups. Consequently and paradoxically, the economy appears to have both an overabundance and a deficiency of skills simultaneously. A person with medical training may take on a number of non-medical functions, for example, leaving another medically trained person of the same age unemployed and gradually losing learned skills; if the employed person leaves temporarily or permanently, a serious skills gap opens (that may or may not be filled by technical assistance). Rescue launches may act as police vessels, pilot boats, and politicians' private nocturnal fishing vessels, and be irreplaceable at short notice in the event of breakdown. Even allowing for the possibility that island governments have been saddled with some inappropriate functions and structures by departing colonial governments or persistent patrons, the 'irreducible minimum' referred to earlier in relation to limited consumption capacities of small populations means high unit costs of public services are unavoidable.

Similarly, the extremely small domestic markets of Pacific economies prevent the realisation of economies of scale in manufacturing and ensure that any production will be high in cost. This situation limits import substitution to a narrow range of consumer goods naturally protected by distance, and reduces the chances of export. Although conventional economic wisdom usually has it that a small economy can realise economies of scale by selling in large world markets, the realities are that export often follows successful production and sale on a domestic market, and small, remote economies are severely disadvantaged in the areas of technology and marketing. Large economies generally have a wider range of industries and a greater learning base, and are therefore in a better position to design and develop manufacturing technologies, as well as to discover, win, and service foreign markets. Manufacturing for export in small economies is only likely to occur as a result of direct investment by transnational corporations that bring technology and marketing skills with them. Most Pacific Island countries lack the location, infrastructure, skills, and (not unfortunately) relatively low wages to be competitive in this regard. The alternative of economic integration is probably unworkable for political reasons, but has little economic rationale where the degree of complementarity between economies is very low.[38]

Diseconomies of scale occur in banking and finance also, making efficient financial intermediation difficult if not impossible without a foreign bank presence, and making financial management more costly. Small economies face higher unit charges for managerial services, information, exchange cover, and borrowing, and find it harder and more expensive to diversify their financial portfolios.[39] The diseconomies in transport have already been mentioned.

In sum, smallness and remoteness place formidable constraints on the growth of Pacific Island economies. However, some actual and potential compensating advantages do exist: 'Isolation can protect human, floral and faunal populations from disease or other unwanted arrivals; small island populations rarely experience the social or environmental problems . . . of larger urban centres; and small size can make complete coverage by a service or innovation readily achievable once the initial barrier of distance has been bridged'.[40] It is sometimes suggested that the alleged 'greater social cohesiveness' of small societies facilitates the various social, political, and cultural adjustments demanded by the development process,[41] including the administration of development: 'Smallness can facilitate administrative co-ordination and integration. It can promote responsiveness of officials and employees to the public will'—though as noted earlier this has a potentially negative aspect as well.[42] Wace has suggested that the biological advantages of remoteness can be exploited for the purposes of quarantine, gene pool conservation, rare tropical flower, fruit, and hardwood cultivation, and research; but he noted that such activities are likely to be supplementary to 'traditional forms of livelihood [and] would, if adopted, hardly lead to spectacular increases in the standard of living of islanders'.[43] Whether for economic or technical reasons, few of the activities have been adopted.[44]

The more conspicuous use of remoteness has been military. Nuclear weapons testing may permit increases in material living standards of compensated or displaced populations and may generate substantial demand for local goods and services. But sooner or later it effectively destroys the very asset being exploited and leaves an unhappy legacy: 'The fate of the Bikinians . . . miserable in alien refuges after forty years, reminds us how crucial are the ties between particular lands and particular lives'.[45] Military installations are less physically destructive and can in effect bring an export market to small islands' doorsteps, as well as *de facto* rental payments. In Micronesia, location is 'of such value strategically that it is worth millions to the United States to keep it out of the hands of other, potentially unfriendly countries'.[46] It may also be worth hundreds of thousands of dollars to some American companies to use remote islands as dumping grounds for various waste products, but this depressing option is hardly developmental.

Small states may have a relative advantage in the provision of logistic services (e.g. siting of communication and observation facilities), offshore financial and administrative services (tax havens, flags of convenience), and other services like philately. These options should not be dismissed out of hand—indeed they have been picked up by some Pacific countries—but they are not peculiarly open to island economies alone. The market is very competitive in the second and third categories (with Caribbean suppliers especially well established); supplying the services can make heavy human resource demands (not least in the area of preventing penetration by international criminal organisations); and the problem of vulnerability remains. Vanuatu's flag of convenience legislation has not been successful, and Tuvalu's stamp sales have been victim to the vagaries of the international philatelic market.[47]

On balance, the disadvantages of small size and remoteness outweigh any advantages, shrinking the range and quantities of goods and services that can be produced. For all their acknowledged heterogeneity, island economies are characterised by a concentration of output in a few industries, an absence of internal economic linkages, and heavy dependence on foreign trade with relatively few partners: 'goods which are produced tend to be exported, goods which are sold ... tend to be imported, and the commodities which are both produced and consumed within the mini-state tend to be services [though] even a substantial amount of these services may be purchased by foreigners in a mini-state which specializes in tourism, offshore banking, offshore insurance or tax avoidance facilities'.[48] In this way, trade hopefully reconciles the 'severe incompatibility' between islands' patterns of consumption and production.[49] For the Pacific region, merchandise exports plus imports per head in 1978 averaged 45 per cent of gross national product per head.[50]

Dependence on trade creates its own problems, and by itself is often unable to complete the reconciliation referred to. All Pacific Island exports are primary products, with coconut products the most important export commodity for all economies except Papua New Guinea (copper), American Samoa (tuna), Fiji (sugar), New Caledonia (nickel), and Nauru (phosphate). The price for coconut products depends on vegetable oil prices established in a world market dominated on the supply side by soya bean production in Brazil, soya bean and maize production in the United States, olive oil production in Europe, and palm oil production in Malaysia. Like primary product prices in general, it is subject to occasional changes in trend and considerable instability.[51] An exhaustive study of commodity markets has concluded that primary product exporters have probably experienced a terms-of-trade decline in the period 1868–1970, and that without doubt commodity export prices have been and are 'considerably more unstable than those of manufactured products'. During the period 1951–1980, sugar ranked first of eighteen commodities in terms of price instability, with copper and copra in the middle of the group.[52]

Price instability contributes to wide, sometimes violent, fluctuations in export earnings. Developing countries in general suffer more than the developed in this respect, and Pacific countries suffer even more, as is evidenced

Table 3   *Export instability in Pacific economies, 1960–84*

	Standard deviation around log trend
Fiji	0.23
Kiribati	0.34
Papua New Guinea	0.39
Solomon Islands	0.26
Tonga	0.25
Vanuatu	0.28
Western Samoa	0.28
Malaysia	0.20
Sri Lanka	0.13
Australia	0.15
New Zealand	0.15
United States	0.16
World exports	0.19

Source: Bruce J. Smith, 'Some Aspects of Economic Adjustment in Small Island Economies', in *Economic Adjustment: Policies and Problems*, ed. Sir Frank Holmes, International Monetary Fund, Washington, DC, 1987, 241.

by the data in table 3. Such variability may hinder economic growth by causing unpredicted swings in savings, government revenue, and the capacity to import investment goods, and by creating uncertainty in the minds of planners and potential investors. It definitely makes for major problems in macroeconomic management. These can be handled, but either 'stop–go' policies must be put in place or an expensive level of external reserves maintained—and in any event scarce skilled human resources must be diverted from other tasks. The very existence of the International Monetary Fund's Compensatory Financing Facility and the European Community's STABEX scheme is testimony to the potential harm export instability can cause. As to price support, many Pacific island countries would readily accept an arrangement like Fiji has to sell its major export at a guaranteed above-world price under the European Community's Lomé Convention.[53] Some refer to this as 'aid with dignity', but it is actually partial compensation for the damage caused by the Community's Common Agricultural Policy (specifically in this case the subsidised production of beet sugar by European farmers).[54]

On the subject of trade reconciling incompatible patterns of production and consumption, it is clear that exports of goods do not cover imports. In 1979 the imports to exports ratio for thirty-four island economies was 366 per cent, while for Pacific economies the average merchandise trade deficit in 1981 stood at A$236 per head, ranging from A$3071 for French Polynesia to a solitary recording of a surplus (A$2200) for American Samoa because of tuna exports. The discussion of development performance that follows details how the gap was and is covered by invisible receipts and official aid. A general indication is given by the fact that aid per head in 1980 was A$217 (against gross national product per head of roughly A$1500), ranging from zero to Nauru to around a thousand dollars to American Samoa, French Polynesia, New Caledonia, Niue, Tokelau, and the US Trust Territory of Micronesia.[55]

Clearly, the dependence of island countries on trade in goods and services and on aid is extreme.[56] Viability, understood as the ability to satisfy consumption demands, implies vulnerability. No wonder, then, that 'it is in the sphere of present-day trade and economic relations that the Island states feel particularly disadvantaged by their small size and isolation'.[57]

An overall summary assessment commanding wide agreement would be that, of the twenty-one Pacific Island groups listed in table 2, only Fiji and Papua New Guinea clearly have the resource endowments and location that will permit long-term economic growth, while French Polynesia, New Caledonia, Solomon Islands, Tonga, Vanuatu, and Western Samoa have limited potential. Even in the 'clear' cases, growth is tenuous because of its dependent nature. The rest of the countries have no real potential for generating sustained growth in output.[58] In the next section what has actually been happening is examined.

Development performance

Not surprisingly, after the initial growth of the 1880–1913 period referred to in the opening paragraph, the atoll economies have not expanded output significantly unless in possession of exploitable mineral deposits (see table 4 for Nauru's 1970s record). Real commodity exports per head of the Cook Islands population averaged NZ$361 annually in 1920–1929, peaked at NZ$480 in 1960–1969, and dropped to NZ$296 in 1980–1983. The respective figures for Niue are NZ$145, NZ$203 (in 1950–1959), and NZ$189. Tokelau exported WS$91 per head in real terms in 1926, but averaged just WS$40 in 1980–1983. Only Kiribati exhibits export expansion, with exports per head averaging A$271 in 1925–1929 and reaching A$643 in 1970–1979. After the exhaustion of phosphate on Banaba in 1979, exports per head fell to A$56 in 1980–1983. Real total output fell 47.8 per cent in 1980, and grew at a miserable average of only 0.8 per cent in 1981–1985, implying a fall in real income per head of 1.3 per cent per year.[59] This followed on from an uninspiring 1.8 per cent real growth in gross national product and virtual stagnation in income per head in the 1970s (table 4). For Tuvalu also the growth story since independence is not encouraging: real gross domestic product per head fell 15 per cent between 1981 and 1985.[60]

Although these economies did not experience export-led growth, they certainly increased levels of consumption, at least until the 1980s. Real imports per head in the early 1980s were fourfold, eightfold, and sevenfold higher than 1920s levels for the Cook Islands, Niue, and Tokelau, respectively. For Kiribati, the increase was threefold. The major stimulus for this import growth came from a public sector heavily financed by the New Zealand government in the case of the Cooks, Niue, and Tokelau, and (less heavily) by Britain in the case of Kiribati and Tuvalu: 'During the last four decades ... government has been a "leading sector" in the growth of living standards in all these societies, and has accounted for the bulk of the wage employment expansion in the Islands'.[61] Budgetary and project aid constitute the engine, with remittances auxiliary. For the five economies mentioned, annual imports in the early 1980s averaged around $50 million. Exports of goods and services totalled NZ$10 million, whereas aid and remittances added to NZ$40 million.[62] Disaggregating, the much larger flows per head of aid and remittances to the Cooks and Niue compared with those to Kiribati are reflected in the growth rates of the 1970s (table 4).

A similar story of aid-funded, public sector–led growth in consumption can be told of the other atoll economies of Micronesia and Polynesia. Taking the Marshall Islands as an example, annual production of copra in the 1980s is about what it was in 1913, and commodity exports only bring in a few million US dollars; yet imports increased substantially in the interim, with the annual trade deficit averaging US$20 million in 1979–1987—or US$582 per person—*exclusive* of government imports! Of Marshallese in paid employment in 1987, 35 per cent were in the public sector, and a further 16 per cent were employed at the Kwajalein missile-testing base. Only one-fifth of US$61 million in government recurrent expenditures was funded from domestic sources in that year; the rest came from US grants. Capital expenditures of US$44 million were funded entirely from foreign grants and borrowings. Obviously, aid was crucial to growth in real income per head averaging 4–5 per cent per year in 1982–1984, and to the provision of services. Income per head was around US$1300 in 1984, life expectancy had increased to 66 years in 1980, and the infant mortality rate had declined from a reported 48 per thousand live births in 1973 to 33 in 1984.[63]

Aid has also been an engine of consumption growth in French Polynesia. According to Barry Shineberg, 'the coming of the nuclear testing agency, the c.e.p. [Centre d'Expérimentation du Pacifique], brought great prosperity to the bulk of the population', though the data he reports imply an implausibly high annual average per capita income growth of 11.5 per cent in the period 1962–1982. The 1970s figure of 1.5 per cent given in table 4 is more likely. Public sector expansion provided jobs in urban centres and for people in the Tuamotu atolls. Over the thirty years to 1988 the infant

Table 4   Growth, income per head, and aid per head

Country	Real GNP growth 1970–1980 (%)		GNP per head US$		Aid per head US$
	Total	Per head	1986	1980	1986
Cook Islands	2.5	3.6	1360	1090	1553
Fiji	5.5	3.5	1510	1850	59
French Polynesia	4.1	1.5	7849	6530	1376
Kiribati	1.8	0.1	480	730	203
Marshall			1307		1900
Nauru	6.6	6.6	9091	5300	0
New Caledonia	−3.5	−0.4	5760	7000	1387
Niue		7.2	1080	1100	1400
Papua New Guinea	2.6	0.3	730	780	73
Solomon Islands	4.7	1.2	420	460	106
Tokelau			560	550	1000
Tonga	2.4	0.9	720	480	139
Tuvalu			570	550	550
US Pacific Islands				920	
Vanuatu	2.5	−1.1	530	520	171
Wallis & Futuna				990	
Western Samoa	4.1	3.1	660	850	142

Sources: OECD, *Development Co-operation Review*, Paris, 1982, 254–256. *Pacific Economic Bulletin* 2 (Dec. 1987): 28; 3 (Dec. 1988): 44–45; Republic of the Marshall Islands, *First Five Year Development Plan 1985–1989*, Office of Planning and Statistics, Majuro, 1987, 18.

mortality rate dropped from 86 per thousand live births to 27, life expectancy rose from 54 to 67 years, and the rate of infectious diseases dropped dramatically.[64]

Data in tables 4 and 5 are consistent with the view that in terms of income per head and some standard quality of life indicators, atoll and other ultrasmall economies are likely to be better off if they are politically dependent in some form or other. Guam, the Northern Marianas, and American Samoa are part of the United States, while the Marshalls, the Federated States of Micronesia, and Belau are in association with it. Tokelau is an overseas territory of New Zealand, with which the Cooks and Niue are in association. Wallis and Futuna is part of France, which retains a firm grip on French Polynesia. Individuals in these island groups have rights of access to the metropolitan countries that are unavailable to the politically independent states of Tuvalu and Kiribati, and receive subsidised services in greater degree. Residents of Tuvalu and Kiribati have the knowledge of their greater sovereignty, and the associated freedom to set their own economic policies,

Table 5   Social indicators

Country	Life expectancy 1986	Life expectancy 1970	Infant mortality 1986	Infant mortality 1970	Population per physician 1980	Literacy % 1980
Cook Islands	70	65	26	36	916	75
Fiji	68	61	26	50	2,232	79
French Polynesia	69		27		698	95
Guam	70				1,335	
Kiribati	52	54	38	49	1,953	90
Marshall Islands	66		33	48	3,709	90
New Caledonia	68	61				91
Niue					1,650	100
Palau					1,479	
Papua New Guinea	54	46	62	133	15,625	32
Solomon Islands	59	52	38	52	7,412	13
Tokelau						97
Tonga	65		36	8	2,310	93
Tuvalu	68		38			98
Vanuatu	63		38		4,269	20
Western Samoa	64		24		2,476	98

Sources: Pacific Economic Bulletin 3 (Dec. 1988): 44; Economic and Social Commission for Asia and the Pacific, *Statistical Yearbook for Asia and the Pacific 1986–1987.* Bangkok; Republic of the Marshall Islands, *First Five Year Development Plan 1985–1989,* Office of Planning and Statistics, Majuro, 1987, 18; Emmanuel Vigneron, Symposium on Health and Development at 26th Congress of the International Geographical Union, University of Sydney, 21–26 August 1988, reported in Australian Development Studies Network Newsletter, Canberra, 11 November 1988, 9–10; Christopher Browne and Douglas A. Scott, *Economic Development in Seven Pacific Island Countries,* Washington, DC, International Monetary Fund, 1989, 162.

make their own tax laws, issue their own stamps, rent out fishing rights, and so on.[65]

The opportunity to emigrate and heavy aid flows are not unmitigated blessings, however, whatever the precise political status of the country concerned may be. Aid flows that dominate the balance of payments have a crowding-out or 'booming sector' effect on traditional tradeable goods production, by causing appreciation of effective exchange rates. Such flows sustain relatively large public sectors and therefore underpin rapid urbanisation, the associated emergence of bureaucratic elites, and growing inequalities of income distribution between and within urban and rural areas. To take the Marshall Islands as an example again, 60 per cent of the population live in urban areas, where the average income is more than four times higher than in rural areas. The average figure disguises substantial inequality and unemployment, with the poorest 25 per cent of income earners in Majuro in 1984 receiving less than 3 per cent of total income and the richest 6 per cent of income earners receiving more than 25 per cent. The unemployment rate is above 20 per cent in a situation where further public employment expansion is impossible because of the recurrent cost burdens imposed by past and present welfare programmes, services, and projects. Additionally, the incidence of non-communicable degenerative 'diseases of affluence', to which Pacific Islanders seem genetically predisposed, is on the increase because of overnutrition and nutritional imbalance associated with urbanisation: about 50 per cent of patients attending hospitals are treated for diabetes.

Aid and remittances also reduce the overall capacity to produce, insofar as unearned assistance tends to undermine thrift, effort, and enterprise; the more human resources are diverted from agriculture, the less robust that sector becomes as traditional skills and knowledge are progressively lost. This last point applies with even greater force if and when the young who have left the village for the urban centre subsequently leave for an overseas destination. Emigration erodes the human resource foundation of local production while simultaneously easing the budget constraints of resident populations. Aid and remittances, in short, transfer a claim on goods and services; they do not increase the ability of small, resource-poor economies to generate increased income. This is why dependence on aid and emigration is likely to be permanent, and why project aid is, in many instances, a wasteful method of assistance that would be better replaced by lump-sum capital donations that generate interest income for island governments—like the Tuvalu Trust Fund.[66]

Where resource endowments do not impose extremely sharp limits on production possibilities, aid may do what it is in theory supposed to do, namely promote growth by (temporarily) augmenting domestic supplies of people, money, and goods. Aid receipts per head in Western Samoa, Vanuatu, Tonga, and the Solomon Islands do not approach the levels of the atoll states and dependencies, but in the 1980s nonetheless constituted 20–30 per cent of gross national product per head. The figures for Papua New Guinea and Fiji are predictably lower at 10 and 4 per cent, respectively (table 4). In these two cases, and in the Solomon Islands, export of goods and services has been the engine of growth—copper and gold in Papua New Guinea; sugar and tourism in Fiji; copra, cocoa, palm oil, fishing, and timber in the Solomons. In the 1970s, real gross national product increased at annual average rates of 5.5 per cent for Fiji, 4.7 per cent for the Solomons, and 2.6 per cent for Papua New Guinea (table 4). Imports, largely consisting of intermediate goods, capital equipment, and food and beverages, were financed without difficulty.[67]

In Vanuatu 2.5 per cent annual growth was achieved in the 1970s because of expansion of copra and beef exports, and the development of tourism and offshore banking. However, exports declined as a proportion of imports, and reliance was placed on aid, which was around 32 per cent of gross national product and accounted for nearly half of total government revenue at independence in 1980. The same decline in the merchandise export–import ratio characterised Tonga and Western Samoa, which in addition to aid relied on workers' remittances equivalent to one-third of gross domestic product to cover the deficit. These remittance flows add to aid's booming sector effects and help to explain stagnation in agricultural output, but simultaneously permit income to grow faster than domestic output: in Western Samoa real gross national product (income received by residents) grew at 4 per cent in the 1970s whereas real gross domestic product (output produced by residents) increased at around 2.5 per cent.[68] A reverse process was evident in New Caledonia where, in the context of low nickel prices following the boom of the 1950s and 1960s, income from investments and employment was being transferred abroad (table 4).

The reasonable growth achievements of the 1970s largely reflected faster expansion in the early part of the decade and slowdown following OPEC I in 1973–74 and the associated world recession. OPEC II in 1979 and another recession, plus natural disasters and, in some cases, domestic economic management problems, have combined to make the growth record of the 1980s less impressive. The story is one of sluggish, erratic growth in total output and declining incomes per head. The average annual percentage increases in real gross domestic product in 1980–1987 were 0.5 for Fiji, 1.7 for Papua New Guinea, and 1.4 for the Solomons. Figures in 1983–1987 were 1.9 for Vanuatu and 1.9 for Western Samoa, while Tonga in 1982–1987 recorded a slightly better result of 2.3. Only in Tonga, was even *nominal* income per head higher in 1986 than in 1980 (table 4).[69] New Caledonia has clearly experienced a decline in living standards, though in this case average income is essentially meaningless.

Overall, on the positive side, it is possible to agree with Browne and Scott's assessment of the economic performance of Fiji, Papua New Guinea, the Solomon Islands, Tonga, Vanuatu, and Western Samoa:

> [They] have made considerable economic progress ... despite deep-seated impediments to growth associated particularly with geographical location and difficult topography. High public investment has helped to create infrastructure, mainly in the fields of transport, communications, health, and education. Fiscal and monetary policies have served to ensure domestic financial stability and sound balance of payments positions.[70]

Quality of life indicators reveal general improvements in the period 1970–1986 (table 5).

On the negative side, the 'deep-seated impediments' remain precisely that; production is still concentrated on a few industries vulnerable to external shocks, and growth is consequently tenuous. Meanwhile populations and labour forces continue to expand at rapid rates, demanding services and jobs. Additionally, recent events have shown that political stability cannot be taken for granted. The 'model' Fiji economy has been undermined by the 1987 coups, and a secessionist movement on Bougainville threatens the nation's main export earner and source of government revenue.[71] Dommen once wrote that 'island countries . . . are particularly fortunate places, where life is longer and nature is bounteous though the menu may be short. Politics are friendlier. Hurricanes are more dangerous than social unrest'.[72] The last two statements can no longer be made without heavy qualification. And the first one concerning bounteous nature still meets with a retort that Dommen was aware of: if the islands are so fortunate, why then do so many islanders leave like a shot if given an emigration opportunity? In the final section of this chapter, this question is reconsidered in the context of a discussion of development options for the future.

Development directions: A conclusion

The economic problem confronting Pacific Island communities is the classic one of scarcity. Limited means are available to satisfy a widespread increase in wants: 'Pacific Islanders living in rural villages now tend to seek very much the same improvements in living conditions and material goods as do urban dwellers—better housing, electric power, clean water supplies and access, usually by road, to markets, shops and services'.[73] Urban dwellers acquire their taste patterns from direct and vicarious experience of countries where the economic problem is stood on its head: 'Our enormously productive economy [USA] demands that we make consumption our way of life, that we convert the buying and use of goods into rituals, that we seek our spiritual satisfactions, our ego satisfactions, in consumption'.[74]

In this chapter I have argued that the prospects for expanding production capacity to keep pace with consumption capacity are severely limited by island remoteness and narrowness of resource endowments; and that for most island economies growth in consumption of private and public goods and services has only been possible because of official aid transfers and private remittances from the many individuals who prefer the inner-city areas of Sydney, Auckland, Honolulu, and Los Angeles to the 'tropical paradise' of the tourist brochures. For the few economies with growth potential, performance depends crucially on external demand, has been sluggish recently, and in some cases is threatened by political instability.

Economic viability in the sense of ensuring an 'acceptable' standard of living requires ongoing dependence in one form or another, and in all cases is menaced by population growth that presses on natural resources and prevents financial resources from being used to improve physical and social infrastructures and equipment for those already born. According to one assessment, 'some countries, such as Papua New Guinea, Solomon Islands

Motifs on the walls of the Bank of Papua New Guinea, Port Moresby, acknowledge traditional art forms. Early 1990s. (Robert C. Kiste)

and Vanuatu, which are subject to serious pressures from population growth, are heading to a breakdown in their school systems'.[75] Unfortunately, inasmuch as falling birth rates seem to follow rising living standards, the island economies are caught in a vicious circle.

Even if the circle were broken by economic growth, it does not follow that economic or social welfare would increase. Accepting for the moment that growth is a necessary condition for increased economic welfare on the Western premise that more goods are better than less, growth may throw up an unacceptable income distribution and involve unacceptable private and social costs (such as deteriorating working conditions and environmental degradation), in which case growth is not a sufficient condition for improving economic welfare. Further, whether or not it is sufficient, growth 'need not also promote social welfare . . . since the process of development has a profound impact on social institutions, habits, and beliefs. Some aspects of human welfare might suffer if relations that were once personal become impersonal, the continuity in one's way of living is disrupted, and the support and assurance of a stable community disappear'.[76]

Pacific Islanders and their governments are acutely aware of this last point of course. Development plans talk of the need to preserve 'traditional' values, culture, and social institutions as far as is possible. But the trade-off between development and tradition is difficult to specify in operational terms and usually is put in the 'non-economic', too-hard basket—from which it is retrieved by anthropologists whose position is unambiguous: 'Civilization, practically identical to the free market and its results, threatens happiness and dissolves community'.[77] These social scientists do not have influence with politicians and planners, however, and the reality is that sheer isolation does more to preserve neo-traditional society than the rhetoric of the urban relatively well-to-do (which rhetoric can serve as an ideological smokescreen to mask inequality and privilege). After all, the subsistence sector, typically undervalued and neglected by policy makers, still employs more than 50 per cent of the work force in most island economies.[78]

The impression remains that 'any threat of an enforced withdrawal towards a more self-reliant, subsistence lifestyle and decrease in services prompts increased demands for emigration rather than exhilaration at the prospect of a return to the "Pacific Way"'.[79] Some pitfalls of higher incomes may be pointed out: Nauruan males in their twenties drink the alcoholic equivalent of ten ounces of whisky a day and die young; Papua New Guinean highlanders spend one-third of their annual coffee income on beer, and thus help transform a situation of subsistence affluence into one of 'subsistence malaise'.[80] Evidence may be advanced to show that the consumer society produces anxiety, not happiness, as desires for new and quickly obsolete goods are created in order that appetites should constantly run ahead of, or at least keep pace with, the means for their gratification.[81] The pressure and strain of trying to maximise consumption can be demonstrated, and the benefits of maximising human satisfaction through an optimal pattern of consumption argued.[82]

In the end, though, the ascetic idea that more is not better, gains as small a number of adherents in the Pacific as it does anywhere. The ancient Chinese equation that happiness equals results divided by expectations is given a materialistic interpretation; the emphasis is on raising the numerator to match a rising denominator.[83] Achieving this, and thereby containing the margins of discontent, will continue to be the difficult task it has been, and will require ongoing dependency and emigration.

Notes

1 W. Arthur Lewis, *Growth and Fluctuations 1870–1913*, George Allen & Unwin, London, 1978, 215.

2 Vent for surplus is explained in H. Myint, 'The "Classical Theory" of International Trade and Underdeveloped Countries', in *Economic Policy for Development*, ed. I. Livingstone, Harmondsworth, Penguin, 1971, 85–112. The phrase 'ecologically robust' comes from R. Gerard Ward, 'Reflections on Pacific Island Agriculture in the Late 20th Century', *Journal of Pacific History* 21 (October 1986): 217–226.

3 H. Myint, *The Economics of the Developing Countries*, Hutchinson, London, 1973, 18.

4 Epeli Hau'ofa, 'A Pacific Islander's View', in *South Pacific Agriculture: Choices and Constraints*, ed. R. Gerard Ward and Andrew Proctor, Asian Development Bank and Australian National University Press, Canberra, 1980, 485; H. C. Brookfield with Doreen Hart, *Melanesia: A Geographical Interpretation of an Island World*, Methuen, London, 1971, 414–416; R. Gerard Ward and Epeli Hau'ofa, 'The Demographic and Dietary Contexts', in Ward and Proctor, 27–29, 34; R. V. Cole and T. G. Parry, eds, *Selected Issues in Pacific Island Development*, Australian National University, Canberra, 1986, 5.

5 E. J. Mishan, *The Costs of Economic Growth*, Harmondsworth, Penguin, 1967, 150.

6 W. Arthur Lewis, *Theory of Economic Growth*, George Allen & Unwin, London, 1955, 314–315.

7 W. Arthur Lewis, *Development Planning: The Essentials of Economic Policy*, George Allen & Unwin, London, 1966, 23.

8 E. F. Schumacher, 'Buddhist Economics', in *Toward a Steady-State Economy*, ed. Herman E. Daly, W. H. Freeman, San Francisco, 1973, 231–239.

9 Quoted in John Connell, *Sovereignty and Survival: Island Microstates in the Third World*, Research Monograph no.3, Department of Geography, University of Sydney, 1988, 80.

10 Salvatore Schiavo-Campo, *International Economics: An Introduction to Theory and Policy*, Winthrop Publishers, Cambridge, MA, 1978, 10.

11 Dennis A. Ahlburg, 'Is Population Growth a Deterrent to Development in the South Pacific?', Islands/Australia Working Paper no. 87/6, Australian National University, Canberra, 1987, 7; UNCTAD Secretariat, 'Examination of the Particular Needs and Problems of Island Developing Countries', in *States, Microstates and Islands*, ed. Edward Dommen and Philippe Hein, Croom Helm, London, 1985, 145.

12 P. J. Lloyd and R. M. Sundrum, 'Characteristics of Small Economies', in *Problems and Policies in Small Economies*, ed. B. Jalan, Croom Helm, London, 1982, 17–38.

13 Government of Tuvalu, *Tuvalu, National Development Plan IV 1988–1991*, Funafuti, 1988, 47; Ward and Proctor, 24.

14 UNCTAD Secretariat, 123.

15 South Pacific Commission, *South Pacific Economies 1981: Statistical Summary*, Noumea, 1984, 3.

16 R. G. Ward, 'The Consequences of Smallness in Polynesia', in *Problems of Smaller Territories*, ed. Burton Benedict, Athlone Press, London, 1967, 96.

17 See UNCTAD Secretariat, 126–127; Andrew S. Proctor, 'Transport and Agricultural Development', in Ward and Proctor, 157–180; Peter Forsyth, 'Economic Problems of International Transport for the South Pacific Island Economies', in Cole and Parry, 176–207; Harold Brookfield, 'The Transport Factor in Island Development', in *The Island States of the Pacific and Indian Oceans: Anatomy of Development*, Australian National University Press, Canberra, 1980, 201–238.

18 Quoted in Bimal Jalan, 'Introduction', in Jalan, 3.

19 A. D. Knox, 'Some Economic Problems of Small Countries', in Benedict, 43.

20 John Connell, 'Population, Migration, and Problems of Atoll Development in

the South Pacific, *Pacific Studies* 9 (1986): 41–58; Stephen Pollard, 'Pacific Atoll Economies', *Asian-Pacific Economic Literature* 3 (1989): 65–83.

21 Ward 1967, 82–84; François Doumenge, 'The Viability of Small Intertropical Islands', in Dommen and Hein, 80–82; Peter Roy and John Connell, '"Greenhouse": The Impact of Sea Level Rise on Low Coral Islands in the South Pacific', Research Institute for Asia and the Pacific, Occasional Paper no. 6, University of Sydney, 1989, 19–22.

22 Ron Crocombe, 'Some Problems Facing Pacific Islands Countries', *Pacific Perspective* 14 (1988): 1.

23 Ward 1967, 83.

24 Republic of the Marshall Islands, *First Five Year Development Plan 1985–1989*, Majuro, Office of Planning and Statistics, 1987, 3.

25 Roy and Connell, 35.

26 Russell Howarth, 'Mineral Resource Potential of Southwest Pacific Island Nations', paper presented at Australia and the South Pacific, 1988, conference at University of New South Wales, December 1988; Bruce G. Karolle and Dirk Anthony Ballendorf, 'Prospects for Economic Self-Sufficiency in the New Micronesian States', Centre for Southeast Asian Studies, Occasional Paper no. 25, James Cook University of North Queensland, 1986, 12.

27 Michael King, 'Fisheries Development', mimeo, Australian Maritime College, Launceston, 1984; Antony J. Dolman, 'Paradise Lost? The Past Performance and Future Prospects of Small Island Developing Countries', in Dommen and Hein, 59; Karolle and Ballendorf, 15; Connell 1988, 49; R. Gerard Ward, 'The Environmental Context', in Ward and Proctor, 5; *The Economist*, 5 August 1989, 62.

28 Dolman, 60.

29 Ward in Ward and Proctor, 8–12; United Nations, *Special Economic and Disaster Relief Assistance: Special Programmes of Economic Assistance, Assistance to Vanuatu*, Report of the Secretary-General, document A/39/388, 1984, 7.

30 Basil H. Thomson, *The Fijians: A Study of the Decay of Custom*, Heinemann, London, 1908, 83. For the formal models see E. K. Fisk, 'The Response of Nonmonetary Production Units to Contact with the Exchange Economy', in *Agriculture in Development Theory*, ed. Lloyd G. Reynolds; Te'o I. J. Fairbairn and Clem Tisdell, 'Subsistence Economies and Unsustainable Development and Trade: Some Simple Theory', in Te'o I. J. Fairbairn, *Island Economies: Studies from the South Pacific*, Institute of Pacific Studies, University of the South Pacific, Suva, 1985.

31 Fairbairn, 7.

32 Howarth; Fairbairn, 9–12.

33 Doumenge, 74; *Courier*, March–April 1987, 46–59.

34 UNITAR, United Nations Institute for Training and Research, *Status and Problems of Very Small States and Territories*, UNITAR Series no. 3, New York, 1969, 168, 171.

35 David Lowenthal, 'Social features', in *Politics, Security and Development in Small States*, ed. Colin Clarke and Tony Payne, Allen & Unwin, London, 1987, 43.

36 Lloyd and Sundrum, 29.

37 UNCTAD Secretariat, 144.

38 Lloyd and Sundrum, 27; William G. Demas, *The Economics of Development in Small Countries with Special Reference to the Caribbean*, McGill University Press, Montreal, 1965, 49–52; Ian Thomas, 'The Industrialisation Experience of Small

Economies', in Jalan, 103–124; Sanjaya Lall and Surojit Ghosh, 'The Role of Foreign Investment and Exports in Industrialisation', in Jalan, 143–163; Connell, 69–73.

39 Maxwell J. Fry, 'Financial Sectors in Some Small Island Developing Economies', in Jalan, 185–207; G. K. Helleiner, 'Balance of Payments Problems and Macro-Economic Policy in Small Economies', in Jalan, 179–180.

40 Ward in Ward and Proctor, 25.

41 Knox, 44.

42 UNITAR, 162.

43 Nigel Wace, 'Exploitation of the Advantages of Remoteness and Isolation in the Economic Development of Pacific Islands', in Shand, 112.

44 UNCTAD Secretariat, 140.

45 D. Lowenthal, 'Islands Today: Conservation and Innovation', mimeo, University College, London, 1987, quoted in Connell, 10.

46 Karolle and Ballendorf, 38.

47 Dommen and Hein, 165–169; Crocombe, 6; Government of Tuvalu, 13.

48 Deena R. Khatkhate and Brock K. Short, 'Monetary and Central Banking Problems in Mini States', in *Islands*, ed. Edward Dommen, Pergamon Press, Oxford, 1980, 1018.

49 Dudley Seers, 'The New Role of Development Planning', in Jalan, 79.

50 South Pacific Commission, 7, 9.

51 Graeme S. Dorrance, Maureen Liu, and Berhann Woldekidan, 'Pacific Island Commodity Markets', *Pacific Economic Bulletin* 3 (1988): 15.

52 Alasdair J. MacBean and D. T. Nguyen, *Commodity Policies: Problems and Prospects*, Croom Helm, London, 1987, 98, 115, 347.

53 The Lomé Convention provides the main framework within which aid and investment from Community members are channelled to sixty-six African, Caribbean, and Pacific (ACP) states. It first came into force in April 1976. The third convention expired on 28 February 1990, to be replaced by Lomé IV.

54 MacBean and Nguyen, 148–149; Helleiner; see also Ross Garnaut, 'Economic Instability in Small Countries: Macroeconomic Responses', in Shand, 313–331; Bruce J. Smith, 'Some Aspects of Economic Adjustment in Small Island Economies', in *Economic Adjustment: Policies and Problems*, ed. Sir Frank Holmes, International Monetary Fund, Washington, DC, 1987, 237–262; Bruce Knapman and Salvatore Schiavo-Campo, 'Growth and Fluctuations of Fiji's Exports, 1875–1978', *Economic Development and Cultural Change* 32 (1983): 97–119. 'Aid with Dignity' features in Michael Taylor, 'Issues in Fiji's Development: Economic Rationality or Aid with Dignity?', in *Fiji: Future Imperfect?* ed. Michael Taylor, Allen & Unwin, Sydney, 1987, 1–13.

55 UNCTAD Secretariat, 136–137; South Pacific Commission, 7, 9, 23.

56 Compare E. C. Dommen and P. L. Hein, 'Foreign Trade in Goods and Services: The Dominant Activity of Small Island Economies', in Dommen and Hein, 152–184.

57 Muriel Brookfield and R. Gerard Ward, eds, *New Directions in the South Pacific: A Message for Australia*, Academy for the Social Sciences in Australia, Australian National University, Canberra, 1988, 14.

58 Compare Joint Committee on Foreign Affairs, Defence and Trade, *Australia's Relations with the South Pacific*, Canberra, Australian Government Publishing

Service, 1989, 59–60; Leslie V. Castle, 'The Economic Context', in Ward and Proctor, 107–136.

59 Geoffrey Bertram, '"Sustainable Development" in Pacific Micro-Economies', *World Development* 14 (1986): 811; Christopher Browne and Douglas A. Scott, *Economic Development in Seven Pacific Island Countries*, Washington, DC, International Monetary Fund, 1989, 70; S. J. Pollard, 'The Viability and Vulnerability of a Small Island State: The Case of Kiribati', Islands/Australia Working Paper no. 87/14, Australian National University, Canberra, 1987, 2.

60 Government of Tuvalu, 14.

61 Bertram, 812.

62 Bertram, 815.

63 Karolle and Ballendorf, 7; Republic of the Marshall Islands, *Marshall Islands Statistical Abstract*, Office of Planning and Statistics, Majuro, 1988, 15, 73, 88; Republic of the Marshall Islands, 1987, 11–12.

64 Barry Shineberg, 'The Image of France: Recent Developments in French Polynesia', *Journal of Pacific History* 21 (July 1986): 154, 159; Emmanuel Vigneron, Symposium on Health and Development at 26th Congress of the International Geographical Union, University of Sydney, 21–26 August 1988, reported in *Australian Development Studies Network Newsletter*, Canberra, 11 November 1988, 9–10.

65 See Mike Faber, 'Island Micro States: Problems of Viability', *Round Table* 292 (1984): 372–376.

66 For a fuller discussion see Brookfield and Ward, 53–60; Bruce Knapman, 'Aid and the Dependent Development of Pacific Island States', *Journal of Pacific History* 21 (July 1986): 139–152; and E. K. Fisk and C. S. Mellor, *Tuvalu Trust Fund Appraisal Study*, Pacific Regional Team Report no. 16, Australian Development Assistance Bureau, Sydney, 1986. Marshall Islands data are from Republic of the Marshall Islands, 1987, 17–18. On nutrition see R. R. Thaman, 'Health and Nutrition in the Pacific Islands: Development or Underdevelopment?', *GeoJournal* 16 (1988): 211–227.

67 Browne and Scott.

68 Browne and Scott; Fairbairn, 303.

69 Growth calculations are based on data in Browne and Scott.

70 Browne and Scott, 29.

71 For details on Fiji see Bruce Knapman, 'Economy and State in Fiji before and after the Coups', *The Contemporary Pacific* 2 (1990): 59–86. On Papua New Guinea see Australian International Development Assistance Bureau, *Papua New Guinea: Economic Situation and Outlook May 1988*, Australian Government Publishing Service, Canberra, 1989.

72 Edward Dommen, 'Some Distinguishing Characteristics of Island States', in Dommen, 931.

73 Brookfield and Ward, 51.

74 Marketing consultant Victor Lebow in the mid-1950s, quoted in Vance Packard, *The Waste Makers*, Harmondsworth, Penguin, 1960, 33.

75 C. D. Throsby, ed., *Human Resources Development in the Pacific*, Australian National University, Canberra, 1987, 15.

76 Gerald M. Meier and Robert E. Baldwin, *Economic Development: Theory, History, Policy*, John Wiley & Sons, New York, 1957, 7–8.

77 Allan Bloom, *The Closing of the American Mind: How Higher Education Has Failed Democracy and Impoverished the Souls of Today's Students*, Penguin, London, 1987, 362.

78 Fairbairn, 31.

79 Brookfield and Ward, 36.

80 Thaman, 222; Larry Grossman, 'The Cultural Ecology of Economic Development', *Annals of the Association of American Geographers* 71 (June 1981): 230.

81 Tibor Scitovsky, *The Joyless Economy: An Inquiry into Human Satisfaction and Consumer Dissatisfaction*, Oxford University Press, New York, 1976.

82 Schumacher, 235.

83 Schiavo-Campo, 58.

Social change

Penelope Schoeffel

The colonial era in the Pacific Islands, lasting for the greater part of the twentieth century, can now be seen as a period in which social change was restrained by a combination of paternalism, physical isolation, and, prior to the 1950s, neglect. From the 1960s, moves towards granting political independence or, conversely, greater degrees of incorporation, were made by the dominant foreign powers in the region. Since then the pace of social change throughout the region has been rapid, and the small, isolated, self-contained societies of the Pacific Islands have been drawn rapidly into the margins of a complex international system racing towards global interdependence.

The stereotype of a remote Pacific Island village is likely to have radio–tape recorders on which elders listen to the world news and youths play the latest hit songs. In towns around the Pacific urban squatters, as well as the middle class, have video players and tune in to the same entertainment diet of romance and aggression as do other urbanites around the world. People in remote corners of Papua New Guinea, experiencing disorienting influxes of wealth as new discoveries of gold and oil are made on their land, regard helicopters as a normal means of transportation. People on isolated atolls and islands regularly socialise and trade with Asian tuna fishers. In Tonga and Western Samoa, village families typically have members living in Australia, New Zealand, and the United States, and their influence conditions expectations about what constitutes 'the good life'. People from all over the world visit the main centres of the Pacific Islands, whether on business, as tourists, or as aid personnel, from places as diverse as Helsinki and Madras. The process of integration has been accelerated by the broadening of the range of possible choices open to people about how and where they will live—by migrating to towns or foreign lands, or by staying in their villages to live in new ways. The agents of change are not just the various transportation and communication technologies of the late twentieth century, but the opening up of the region to global influences.

As well as containing social change for over half a century in most of the Pacific islands, the effect of the colonial era was to segregate the islands into artificial regions of European influence, separating the Pacific Islands from South-East Asia, with which throughout human history they had had connections, if remote ones. The smallness of the Pacific Island colonies allowed the European powers (including Australia and New Zealand) and their various agents to exert a degree of cultural influence that had not been possible in Asia. This too has changed rapidly since the decolonisation period of the sixties and seventies and the abandonment of Asia-phobic policies by Australia and New Zealand. In the contemporary Pacific Islands, the ex-colonial powers and those that still hold Pacific Island territories are still prominent as aid donors and technical advisers, pulling political strings from Paris, Washington, Canberra, and Wellington; but evidence is everywhere of the growing dominance of the new commercial powers of the Pacific rim—Japan,[1] Taiwan, Hong Kong, Korea, Malaysia, and Indonesia. Most of the few money-making enterprises in the islands, such as fisheries, forestry, and tourism, are now dominated by investors from these countries, although the old established powers still dominate the mining industries.

Regions

Today the Pacific Islands form a number of subregions that have similar socio-economic characteristics and cross-cut the ethno-linguistic culture regions of Melanesia, Polynesia, and Micronesia (see map page 5). The broadest division within the region, with the most striking economic differences (see Knapman, chapter 14), is between those island countries that remain connected, to a greater or lesser extent, to a metropolitan power, and those that have full political independence. The first group comprises the former American Trust Territory of Micronesia and American Samoa; the French territories of New Caledonia, Wallis and Futuna, and French Polynesia; the New Zealand–associated states of Niue and the Cook Islands; and the New Zealand territory of Tokelau.

The way of life of the peoples of these states and territories has been largely transformed by what might loosely be called the 'modernising' effects of high and recurrent levels of aid. Most of their people live in houses constructed of non-traditional materials such as concrete blocks and corrugated iron, wear imported clothing, and regularly consume imported foods and beverages. They have universal primary education and access to basic medical care and secondary education. Unemployment is high, but those who have paid work earn wages that are high in comparison with most independent developing countries. They watch television programmes from the metropolitan country with which they are linked, and their right to emigrate there is unimpeded. Overall, there is no great difference between the situations of the majority of the peoples in these states and territories and those of the poorest groups in New Zealand, France, and the United States. The direction of change in these islands is one of gradual assimilation to the values and aspirations of the dominant power.

The politically independent countries form three subregions. The first comprises the Melanesian states of Papua New Guinea, the Solomon Islands, and Vanuatu—the largest in terms of land and population. These countries are characterised by their great diversity of languages and subcultures and great contrasts between the way of life of the people who are flocking in increasing numbers to the modern, reasonably well-serviced towns and the rural majority, who live in small villages, in houses built mainly of bush materials, and devote most of their time to subsistence agriculture and exchange. Except for a few well-endowed areas of Papua New Guinea, little cash is earned by most rural people in Melanesia, and that mainly by growing and selling copra, coffee, or cocoa, for which prices have been severely depressed since the late 1980s. Such money as can be earned is spent mainly on extra food, liquor, school fees, local travel, and a few consumer goods. Health services and primary education are not accessible to all, and in many areas children have to board away from home in order to attend school. Secondary schooling is even less accessible. For example, in Papua New Guinea, with a population of around 3.5 million, there are only five national government-run senior high schools.

Paradoxically, Papua New Guinea is the richest country in the region in terms of its natural resources, but life expectancy is the lowest and infant mortality rates are the highest in the region. The situation in the Solomon Islands and Vanuatu is marginally better in terms of life expectancy and considerably better in terms of infant mortality[2] (see Knapman, chapter 14). These countries are all cursed with endemic malaria, which kills babies and young children and weakens the health and shortens the lives of those who survive childhood. Nonetheless, all three countries have experienced fertility and population growth rates that are among the highest in the world. The consequences of population growth are beginning to have profound effects in Papua New Guinea, the Solomon Islands, and Vanuatu, because these countries have been unable to export their surplus populations as most other island countries have done in the last quarter of this century. At the present rate of increase, it is estimated that the population of Papua New Guinea will grow from around 4.5 million in the year 2000 to 37 million by 2090, that of the Solomon Islands will grow from 463 000 to over 10 million, and that of Vanuatu from around 195 000 to around 2.5 million.[3] Already population growth is outstripping the capabilities of these countries to provide employment and services in education and health that are essential for national goals of modernisation and human development.[4] Fortunately, demographers predict a decline in birth rates leading to more moderate growth rates[5] (around 6 million for Papua New Guinea, 0.6 million for the Solomon Islands, and 0.3 million for Vanuatu by 2090).

The second subregion comprises the former British Gilbert and Ellis Islands Colony, now the separate states of Kiribati and Tuvalu. Both of these micro-states are made up of atolls, and what sets them apart as a distinctive subregion is the lack of supportive ties with their former colonial ruler (unlike other atoll countries such as Tokelau and the Marshall Islands) and their lack of resources other than the tuna fishery. Both now rely on aid from a variety of sources, and contributions from Australia and Japan exceed those from the United Kingdom. The I-Kiribati are Micronesian, with a Polynesian admixture in some of the southern atolls, while the Tuvaluans are Polynesian, with linguistic and cultural affinities to Samoa. Despite their cultural differences, the way of life of their rural populations is very similar. The lack of resources and of easy avenues for emigration make the possibilities for social change more limited than in most other Pacific island countries.

The two urbanised atolls, Funafuti in Tuvalu and Tarawa in Kiribati, are extremely overcrowded, and development plans are aimed at increasing the attractiveness of outer-island life in order to reduce movement to the urban areas. Both have experienced outbreaks of cholera in recent years as a result of water pollution, are short of land for further housing or other development use, and depend almost entirely on food imported from outside the island. Most Tuvaluans and I-Kiribati still live in rural villages, in thatched houses constructed from mangrove and coconut palm materials. The populations of the inhabited islets of each of the atolls are close-knit socially, and usually religiously. Leadership is provided by male elders and the centre of community life is the church and its associated large communal meetinghouse. Subsistence is based on fishing, cutting toddy (the sap of the coconut palm, which is drunk as a beverage or boiled to a syrup), coconuts, bananas, breadfruit, and laboriously cultivated atoll taro. Fresh water is scarce, as is cultivable soil, so that on the less well endowed atolls fish, toddy, and coconuts are the main food sources.

Cash is obtained from the sale of copra and for some, from remittances from relatives who have jobs in Nauru or on foreign ships. It is spent on foods such as rice, sugar, flour, and tinned meat, cloth or clothing, and occasionally on coveted consumer goods such as radio–tape recorders and bicycles. Atoll populations, particularly those of Tuvalu, are fairly well served in terms of basic health services and primary education, but higher education is available to very few. As evidenced by their relatively higher life expectancy and lower levels of infant mortality (see table 5, page 339), Tuvaluans have higher standards of living than I-Kiribati.

The third subregion comprises Fiji, Tonga, and Samoa. The historical experiences of these three central Pacific Island nations and their economic situations—Fiji's relatively developed economy and Western Samoa and Tonga's migrant remittance economies—have produced certain features in common. All have near-universal primary education and high rates of participation in secondary education. Except for Indo-Fijians, the rural majority in all three countries live in villages under some form of neo-traditional chiefly system and practice mixed subsistence and cash cropping. Beyond the kin group, the church community is the most important social attachment. Villages may contain several different church communities of different Christian denominations. Most Tongans, Samoans, and Indo-Fijians live in houses built from permanent building materials, and increasing numbers of rural Fijians are exchanging thatched *bure* for concrete-block or weatherboard houses with iron roofs.

Fiji has more, and larger, urban centres, while in Tonga and Samoa, rural communities are becoming more urbanised in their life-styles as the result of emigrant influences and remittances. All three countries have basically literate, well-fed, generally healthy populations with reasonably high life expectancies and low infant mortality rates. In Tonga and Western Samoa high fertility rates have been counterbalanced by high rates of emigration so that overall population growth rates have declined since the 1970s. Traditionally, each country was homogeneous in terms of the ethnicity, culture, and language of the people; now in Fiji indigenous Fijians are slightly less than half the population, the remainder comprising predominantly urban minorities of Indo-Fijians, part-Europeans, other Pacific Islanders, Chinese, and Europeans. Indigenous Tongans and Samoans remain the great majority of the population in their countries, and the main sources of cultural change and modernisation are their emigrant populations in the United States, New Zealand, and Australia.

Urbanisation

For the first half of the twentieth century, migration was circumscribed by the subject status of most Pacific peoples. Except when it was desirable to recruit Pacific Islanders as labourers, colonial policies were paternalist and aimed to keep islanders in their villages. From about the 1950s rural–urban migration began to gain momentum throughout the region. At first this process was formally coordinated by governments. One of the driving forces was the growth in education, particularly secondary education, with the setting up of national high schools with boarding facilities in one central location. This growth was accompanied by an increase in infrastructural spending and the size of the expatriate bureaucracy. Associated with these developments was an increase in investment in urban centres, a growth in retailing through shops and produce markets, and expanded mechanical, building, and banking services. A number of small manufacturing ventures also began at this time in Papua New Guinea and Fiji. These operations required labour, not organised gangs as in the case of the plantation and mining industries, but individual workers with at least a few years of formal education.

The authorities did not plan for urban development, however, and only very large-scale employers provided housing for their workers, so that migrants from rural villages had to fend for themselves. Squatter settlements began to pop up around Pacific towns. In Western Samoa low-income part-Europeans had long occupied areas of swampy land around Apia that were disdained by local village landowners. Villagers moving to town to work swelled the numbers of small, rickety *fale* and the area of land that was being patiently reclaimed with coral rubble, sand, and refuse. On Tarawa, I-Kiribati workers who could not find space to build on plots of government-owned land, negotiated with landowners in various customary ways for tenancy rights. In Tonga the process of urbanisation was facilitated in 1876 by land reform that allocated town allotments as well as blocks of farmland to commoners.

By the 1960s squatter settlements were becoming a recognised problem in Papua New Guinea. The indigenous landowners in urban areas, who had already suffered the alienation of large portions of their land, now found the little they had left occupied by strangers from other parts of the country. Although many settlements were overcrowded and insanitary, and the houses in them were in most cases inferior to village houses, they evolved into village-like communities of people from the same ethno-linguistic background. Settlements founded by established workers soon began to swell with new settlers from their home areas seeking work and a more interesting way of life. The response of the administration, as in some other parts of the Pacific, was to subdivide government-owned land under low covenants, supplying the blocks with access roads, electricity, and water. These met the needs of the small but growing numbers of skilled and white-collar workers, but were beyond the means of most migrants to the towns.

Urbanisation has proceeded fastest in Papua New Guinea. Only 3 per cent of the indigenous population lived in towns in 1960, but by 1980, 28 per cent had moved to town, and at the present rate of migration more than half the population will be living in urban areas within the next ten years.[6] The lack of economic opportunities and services 'pushes' people to leave rural villages, while the desire for wage employment and a modern life-style 'pulls' them to town. Urbanisation is the main factor behind Papua New Guinea's notorious law-and-order problem. In the anomie of urban life, men and youths without employment or other sources of amusement formed gangs involving integration of the tribal warrior tradition on a larger social scale.[7] The *raskols*, as they are known locally, began to rob houses, plunder small stores, and steal and strip cars on an organised basis in the early 1970s. Initially the problem was more or less confined to the capital, Port Moresby, which is like an island, inaccessible by road to the most populous provinces, which can only be reached by air. Over time these gangs graduated to more horrendous crimes of gratuitous violence. Now *raskol* gangs operate in all urban centres and a good many rural areas as well, where they have taken to

Above: Downtown Avarua, capital of Cook Islands, late 1980s. (Robert C. Kiste)

Below: Vila street scene, 1992. (Robert C. Kiste)

Main street, Honiara, capital of Solomon Islands, June 1992. (Robert C. Kiste)

highway robbery on the country's main roads. Middle-class urban residents have been forced to live behind high fences topped with razor wire, and lower-income groups who cannot afford such deterrents have become the most frequent victims of urban crime. In some provinces *raskol* gangs are part of the political system and are used by politicians or aspiring politicians to intimidate their opponents.

In Micronesia urbanisation has been stimulated by population movements, which gained momentum from the 1960s, from the outer islands to provincial centres and main towns. In Palau and the Marshall Islands over half the population lives in urban areas, and in the Federated States of Micronesia (FSM) the populations of the main islands in each state, Yap, Chuuk, Pohnpei, and Kosrae, include increasing numbers of outer islanders. The US administration, while well funded for such recurrent expenses as salaries and various federal welfare programmes, had little money to spare for capital works. Consequently the towns of the three new island states—Palau, the Federated States of Micronesia, and the Marshall Islands—present an appearance of dilapidation and, in some cases, squalor that is surprising in view of the wealth and power of their former ruler. Most school and college buildings are constructed of galvanised iron sheets, and there are few roads or good public buildings aside from a few new hotels in Koror and the new FSM central government buildings on Pohnpei. The most astonishing juxtapositioning of urban poverty and Western consumerism occurs in the Marshall Islands, where rickety little shacks, jammed side-by-side in alleys strewn with drink cans and candy wrappers, are equipped with air-conditioners, television sets, and washing machines. Urbanisation in the Marshall Islands has contributed to social breakdown in rural areas and high incidences of alcoholism, teenage pregnancy, and venereal disease in both rural and urban areas.[8]

Emigration

In some Pacific Island countries, urbanisation has been slowed because more people are moving overseas than into towns. The people of Tokelau, the Cook Islands, and Niue have New Zealand citizenship and may move freely to and from that country, and the majority of able-bodied adults from all three countries live in New Zealand. According to population data for New Zealand in 1990, there are 23 000 Cook Islanders and 8000 Niueans[9] resident in New Zealand. Eastern Samoans, as inhabitants of an American territory, have the right to reside in the United States, and like Cook Islanders and Niueans with New Zealand, most do. The international border between western and eastern Samoa is a colonial artifact drawn in 1900, and most Samoan extended families (*'aiga*) have branches on both sides of it. Through their family connections, thousands of Western Samoans have been able to reside in American Samoa long enough to gain residence rights that enable them to enter and work in the United States. Smaller numbers of Tongans have also managed to migrate to the United States, some via American Samoa. Large immigrant Polynesian communities now exist in California and Hawai'i; more than 46 000 are Samoan and 11 000 are Tongan.[10] Micronesians do not appear to migrate to the United States on the same scale, but increasing numbers are moving to Guam and Saipan to take advantage of the job market created by a tourist boom. Similarly, it appears that relatively few people from the French Pacific territories migrate to France, but fairly large numbers of Tahitians and people from Wallis and Futuna have jobs in Noumea.[11]

About 4 per cent of New Zealand's population are Pacific Island Polynesians.[12] More than 50 000 are Samoan, and 9000 Tongan. Western Samoa, a former New Zealand dependency, lacks the felicitous arrangements of Niue and the Cook Islands, but during a period of rapid economic growth in New Zealand in the 1960s, New Zealand began to welcome large numbers of Samoan 'guest workers'.[13] Smaller numbers of guest workers from Tonga and Fiji were also accepted. Many overstayed their permits, while others returned home and applied formally to emigrate to New Zealand. This was easiest for Samoans because under a treaty of friendship between Western Samoa and New Zealand, New Zealand agreed to accept a quota of 1100 migrants from Samoa each year. New Zealand's economy began to slow down in the mid-1970s, by which time thousands of islanders, mainly Samoans, were residing illegally in New Zealand. In the good times it had been convenient to ignore this fact, but as unemployment rates began to climb and the presence of large numbers of brown-skinned people with unfamiliar customs in New Zealand cities and towns began to be seen as a 'social problem', public opinion became concerned about Polynesian immigration.[14] Unpleasant scenes ensued of police 'dawn raids' on islanders' homes and street arrests to apprehend overstayers. Islanders and liberal-minded white New Zealanders were justifiably outraged, pointing out that when the islanders had played an essential role in the economy doing jobs disdained by New Zealand citizens they had been welcome enough, and that they had earned residence rights. Subsequently an amnesty was granted to island overstayers, and many were granted resident status. Samoans are now New Zealand's second largest ethnic minority, after the Maori. Under a reciprocal arrangement, New Zealand citizens are entitled to reside freely in Australia, so growing numbers of New Zealanders of island origins have settled in Australia[15] to form the nucleus of communities that now attract direct migration from their home islands.

Large-scale emigration has profound effects on the culture of the migrants' home islands. New Zealand, Australia, and the United States are seen as 'promised lands', and the perceived affluence of migrant relatives is deeply envied. The fact that most island migrants are relatively poor and of low socio-economic status in their new lands is seldom understood by those back home. Goals of local economic development become secondary to the goal of trying to migrate or of assisting relatives to migrate. Some scholars[16] have concluded that Pacific Islander emigration has had largely negative consequences, subverting economic development by siphoning off and proletarianising the most physically and intellectually able members of island populations, skewing development aspirations unrealistically, and accelerating and perpetuating the peripheral, dependent situation of many Pacific Island countries. More positive evaluations take account of the effects of migration in reducing population pressure and the negative social and environmental consequences, and the effects of remittances in improving the quality of rural life for islanders.[17] Bertram and Watters have argued that prevailing models of development do not apply to emigration-dependent Pacific Island mini-states, which have their own unique characteristics as 'MIRAB economies'.[18] MIRAB is an acronym derived from their key characteristics of dependency on *Mi*gration, *R*emittances, foreign *A*id, and *B*ureaucracy, the last providing the major source of national employment and economic activity.

Remittances have become important in most Pacific village economies. In Kiribati and Tuvalu they are earned by workers on temporary contracts to mine phosphate in Nauru, or seamen working on foreign ships, while in Papua New Guinea, Solomon Islands, and Vanuatu they are earned by urban migrants. Some countries, notably Tonga and Western Samoa, have become economically dependent on migrants' remittances at national as well as village levels. The pattern of Samoan remittances is typical of Pacific Island migrants; in their first few years overseas they send regular amounts home, constituting a large proportion of their income, to finance a family project such as a new house. Remittances then taper off to intermittent contributions to family ceremonial obligations (e.g., funerals, weddings, title bestowals, church donations, church openings, and the like) and to fund-raising activities for their home villages and churches.[19] New migrants are absorbed into large Samoan communities in most New Zealand towns and cities, where they develop new sets of financial obligations mainly associated with church membership. The churches serve island migrants as a centre of social and ceremonial as well as religious activity and produce a new form of collective identity, so that individuals come to identify themselves as Samoan Methodists, Congregationalists, Catholics, Mormons, and so on, instead of by their home villages or islands.

The rapid growth in overseas emigration since the 1960s has had revolutionary effects in the emigrants' homelands. Overseas migrant communities have stimulated export industries in coconut products and taro that have eclipsed the traditional export commodities of cocoa and copra. The social and economic effects of emigration are having 'urbanising' effects on rural communities. For example, in 1960 the great majority of Western Samoans lived in villages of houses built in the traditional style out of local materials, clustered around central meeting grounds (*malae*) on the coasts of the main islands. Today the great majority live in houses with cement floors and iron roofs, each in its own compound dispersed along the main roads encircling the islands. Most villages have churches and primary schools of modern design and materials. This transformation has been almost wholly financed by the remittances from migrants to New Zealand, the United States, and most recently, Australia.

In MIRAB societies there appears to be an overall trend away from the extended family household structure towards a more nuclear type of family structure. Referring again to a Samoan example, a study of change between 1976 and 1986 in a village on the south coast of Upolu in Western Samoa showed that while the population barely grew in ten years, due to emigration, the number of households increased over the same period, indicating that households were becoming based on smaller groups of people.[20] Changes in social and family structure appear to be contributing to a number of social problems, including epidemics of suicide and increased domestic violence.[21]

Beliefs

The social transformations created by the introduction of Christianity were largely complete in Polynesia and much of Micronesia in the nineteenth century, but many areas of Melanesia did not experience this change until the early twentieth century, and in some areas, such as the New Guinea highlands, until the late twentieth century. Nor did Christianity always have so profoundly transforming an effect in Melanesia as it did in Polynesia, perhaps because it did not always coincide with the first sustained contact with Europeans and the outside world.

In most of Polynesia and Micronesia people devote considerable resources to their churches. In Polynesia, particularly, the practices of the established churches[22] have become syncretically interwoven with older institutions, beliefs, and values. For example, nothing could be further from the humble lifestyle of Christ than that of the Samoan *faifeau* (Congregational or Methodist pastor). When the Samoans became Christians, they placed ministers of religion in the same conceptual category as their most sacred order of chiefs, the *ali'i pa'ia*. They interpreted the Bible in much the same way as did the medieval Church of Europe, acknowledging the divine right of kings or the God-given moral right of rulers to exercise secular authority. The authority of God over humans parallels that of the *matai* (chief) over his household or the council over the village, as a popular song asserts:

> *Ua tofia nei e le Atua Samoa ina ia pulea e matai*
> *Aua o lona suafa ua vaelua i ai. . . .*
>
> *God has willed that Samoa be controlled by* matai
> *Because He has shared His authority with them. . . .*[23]

Clergy are obeyed in spiritual matters; however, they are expected to remain aloof from village politics, other than those of direct concern to their ministry, and may not sit in the village council without a special invitation from its members. The sacred status of the *faifeau*, and the honour of the village, are reflected in the large house and the good food, monetary gifts, and personal services provided by the congregation.

The social changes deriving from the effects of emigration and urbanisation are presenting challenges to tradition, which includes the established churches. As people turn away from aspects of traditional life such as communal conformity, they do not turn away from religion itself as in many Western nations, but turn instead to new religions, particularly those emanating from the United States which emphasise individuality and personal experience or Christian rebirth. The Church of Jesus Christ of the Latter-Day Saints (the Mormon church) began its missions in the Pacific in the late nineteenth century but met with limited success until the 1970s, when it began to make significant inroads on the membership of established churches in Polynesia and Micronesia. Cynics attribute this to the opportunities offered by the Mormons for higher education in the United States, with the attendant possibilities of emigration (there are around ten thousand Tongans living in the Mormon capital, Salt Lake City, Utah). But the Mormons have a discourse of modernisation interwoven with the doctrines of their church.[24] Their neo-Protestant ethic enshrines nuclear family life, inner-directedness and self-reliance, industry, and abstemiousnes—the antithesis of the traditional values of Polynesia. The church offers a 'new way' that has great appeal for many islanders.

The Assemblies of God, which also has strong American cultural resonances, is probably the fastest growing church, overall, in the Pacific region. It is particularly attractive to youth with its Gospel–pop music and emphasis on participation and fellowship. There has also been a proliferation of smaller, evangelically oriented Christian religious movements, some of local inspiration and some the result of international evangelism. The Baha'i faith is also gaining ground in the Pacific and has built a magnificent regional temple in Western Samoa as part of its strategy towards the realisation of its global vision of a prosperous, united, peaceful world under a single government. In Kiribati and Tuvalu women were prominent among the early converts to the faith, attracted by the Baha'i commandment that the sexes must be equal, in sharp contrast to the patriarchal structure of the established churches.[25]

Food

In all Pacific Island states dietary change has resulted from changes to the traditional food production systems brought about by the introduction of commercial cash-crop agriculture and by urbanisation.[26] In many parts of the Pacific Islands rapid population growth is beginning to put pressure on land resources, and the prevailing system of shifting agriculture is becoming less viable and productive. Economic patterns based on the production of exportable agricultural commodities, established during the colonial period, persist to the present day, but a shift from plantation to smallholder production has occurred. Large-scale plantations are still found in some of the Pacific Islands, but the main producers of exports are rural smallholders who augment their subsistence livelihood with small plantations of cash crops.[27] Cash cropping combined with population growth has affected traditional food production systems by occupying land that was once used for food production, by absorbing labour once devoted to food production, by decreasing the diversity and extent of food crops planted, and by substantially increasing the workload of women in countries where women are the primary food producers.

Traditional Pacific Island diets were high in complex carbohydrates from root crops, bananas, and breadfruit, and low in fat, salt, and sugar. Pacific Islanders now increasingly eat diets based on imported refined rice and flour, and supplementary foods that are high in sugar, salt, and fat.[28] Throughout the Pacific Islands countries a rising incidence of non-communicable diseases appears to be linked to changes in diet, eating habits, and child-

A nakamal *(kava shop) in Vila, Vanuatu, serves* kastom *followers who prefer kava rather than beer. (Lamont Lindstrom)*

feeding practices.[29] Nutrition-related conditions include diabetes, cardiovascular diseases, gout, alcohol-related diseases, tooth and gum disease, certain types of cancer, kwashiorkor, marasmus, slow infant growth rates, and diseases caused by deficiencies of vitamins and minerals in the diet. The onset of diabetes occurs at an early age in some Polynesian and Micronesian populations, and the disease often leads to blindness, kidney disease, gangrene, and diseases of the heart and arteries.

The incidence of some of these nutrition-related diseases is very high in the Pacific Islands. Nauru has the highest incidence of diabetes in the world, and incidences are abnormally high in most of Polynesia and 'American' Micronesia;[30] for example, in the Marshall Islands, over half the patients treated or admitted to hospital are diabetic. Studies among children in the Federated States of Micronesia and Kiribati in 1990 show that the incidence of vitamin A deficiency, which can cause blindness and other diseases, is among the highest in the world. Heart disease is among the top four leading causes of death in almost all Pacific Island countries.[31]

One of the major economic consequences of dietary change has been increasing dependency on imported food in all the Pacific Islands.[32] Food and beverages account for between 17 and 28 per cent of the value of total imports in most Pacific Island countries, and the proportion of food imports as a component of total exports has been rising steadily over time.[33]

The problem is particularly acute in the American Pacific because since the 1950s, most islanders in US jurisdictions qualified for federal programmes established in the United States under Lyndon Johnson's push for a 'Great Society'. Food programmes designed for America's inner-city poor, such as school breakfasts and lunches, meals for the elderly, and food stamps for families, were made available in Micronesia and American Samoa. The result has been a shift in food preferences to imported foods and a decline in subsistence production. In countries where there have been no food subsidies, one reason why consumers are increasingly dependent on imported cereals such as rice and flour and low quality meats is that these foods are often cheaper than local produce. Production and marketing of local food in most Pacific Island countries is lagging because it is linked to the underdeveloped subsistence sector. Little effort is being made to develop this sector, and national development resources tend to be used to support production for export. At the same time, the price of food is increasing sharply relative to wages; for example, the prices of basic food items in Fiji increased from 30 per cent to 200 per cent between 1986 and 1990, while wages increased by only about 18 per cent.[34]

Gender

Gender relations vary greatly in Pacific cultures. The New Guinea highlands offer an extreme example of gender inequality. Men are ranked according to their ability to accumulate and redistribute wealth items such as pigs and pearlshells, from 'big men' down to 'rubbish men', but women are effectively treated as property to be transferred between kin groups to grow food crops, rear children, and raise pigs.[35] In contrast, in western Polynesian cultures, although different roles are assigned to men and women, status inequality operates in favour of women as sisters, whose rank is usually higher than that of their brothers.[36] The division of labour is also reversed in Tonga compared to the New Guinea highlands, for in Tonga agricultural work has always been considered men's work.

In Melanesia and many parts of Micronesia, women were primarily responsible for growing and preparing food, with varying degrees of assistance from men. In western Polynesia, particularly in Tonga and Western Samoa, food production was included among male roles; women helped with chores such as weeding from time to time, but their primary role was to produce manufactured objects such as mats, tapa cloth, coconut oil, and many other items for domestic use and exchange. In eastern and southern Polynesia—Hawai'i, French Polynesia, the Cook Islands, and New Zealand—women of lesser rank appear to have been more involved in agriculture than was the case in western Polynesia. The great differences between Melanesia and Polynesia in terms of the relative status of women and men may be measured in rates of participation in secondary and higher education and wage employment. On each count the situation for women in relation to men is one of increasing parity in Polynesia and great inequality in Melanesia. Sex ratio and life expectancy statistics for Papua New Guinea indicate that women there are on a par with the women of the Indian subcontinent; the ratio of males to females recorded in the 1980 census of Papua New Guinea indicates, contrary to the demographic norm, a higher death rate and shorter life expectancy for females than for males. Although statistical data indicate that nationally women's life expectancy of 50 years is slightly longer than men's, the figures for the rural populations of most provinces show that men's life expectancy is two or three years longer than women's. In contrast, sex ratios and life expectancy for Polynesia are not so far removed from the rates in Australia and New Zealand, where women have a greater life expectancy.

Christianity has had a profound effect on gender relations, with both positive and negative effects on the contemporary status of women. Missionaries, both Europeans and islanders, tended to see their own social institutions as more befitting to a Christian way of life than those of the island societies they wished to convert. In particular, customs associated with marriage and domestic arrangements seemed, to the missionaries, greatly in need of reform. In almost all Pacific societies men of high status were usually able to acquire more than one wife, and sometimes many wives, while men of low status were lucky to find even one. The exchange of women was central to the social structure of all Pacific societies and was linked to the exchange of highly valued goods. Missionaries tended to interpret these arrangements as the buying and selling of women by men; they took their ideal of Christian marriage from St Paul, that a man should have one wife over whom he had the right of command but the duty to care for and protect. In many Pacific societies husbands occupied separate living quarters from their wives, and in Samoa, unmarried women lived together in their own dwelling-house. Missionaries taught that husband and wife should share the same dwelling, along with their children, and that men should be the providers and women their helpmates. In Samoa, where cooking was done by young men, the missionaries taught women to cook, leading to the present-day division of labour in which men do traditional forms of cooking and women cook introduced dishes using saucepans. The Protestant churches educated men to be ministers and women to be their wives so that the couple could provide a role model of proper Christian marriage and family life to the congregations they were sent to serve.

The transformation of domestic life in Polynesia and much of Micronesia was more or less complete by the turn of the century, but in Melanesia evangelical work continues among people following traditional religions to the present time. For example, colonial and missionary contact with the million inhabitants of the New Guinea highlands did not begin until the

1930s and few changes were brought to the area until the 1950s. Although the highlands have been widely evangelised in the past sixty years, in many highland provinces polygyny is still regarded as an important means of attaining a political career. Having several wives provides aspiring politicians with a larger number of affinal kinship connections that can be used for political support; furthermore several wives can plant more crops and raise more pigs, thus creating more wealth with which to attract political support.

Very few women are parliamentarians in the Pacific Islands. However, in Polynesia there are many female chiefs. In Samoa growing numbers of women now hold *matai* titles, a phenomenon of the twentieth century. The remarkable increase in recent decades of female *matai* is related to the success of a significant proportion of Samoan women in attaining higher educational qualifications. Such achievements have in many cases been rewarded by the extended family by bestowing titles on their outstanding daughters. In the Cook Islands most of the high *ariki* titles are now held by women, and even in Fiji, where Melanesian values concerning the inferiority of women outweigh Polynesian influences on gender relations, Adi Lady Lala holds one of Fiji's paramount titles, *Rokotui Dreketi*.

In the 1970s international agencies began to acknowledge the need to recognise the role of women in development. The tendency for much of this century had been for colonial officials and development planners to assume the existence of universal sex roles in which men carried out productive work while women did unproductive domestic work. For example, the 1971 Census of Western Samoa classified only 5189 women as 'economically active'.[37] Of these, 3928 women were 'working primarily for money' and 1261 were growing, gathering, and catching food. In the classification of 'not economically active', aside from children and schoolgirls, 24 807 women were described as 'home makers'. Such figures ignore the fact that, aside from the multitude of economic and service activities Samoan women perform through their village committees, every rural Samoan 'home maker' produces a variety of goods that are essential to the subsistence economy. These almost universally include sleeping and floor mats, food mats, house blinds, thatch pieces, brooms, fans, coconut and kava strainers, coconut oil, herbal remedies, green vegetables and fruit, sewn garments and household linen using imported cloth, gathered reef seafoods, poultry and eggs, and many other items.[38] In Melanesian societies women play, in addition, a major role in agricultural production, and throughout the Pacific Islands women predominate as sellers of produce in municipal markets, contributing significantly to household incomes.[39]

Most Pacific Island societies did not have formal organisations specifically for women in pre-colonial times. Samoa appears to have been an exception. There the *aualuma o tama'ita'i* was a formal institution into which young women were ritually received at puberty. It included all women who

Town market, Apia, early 1990s. (Robert C. Kiste)

were members, by virtue of descent, of the extended families that made up the local polity.[40] However, all Pacific Island societies had a division of labour between men and women, and gender groups were further subdivided according to age, rank, status, and so on. In the pre-colonial Pacific most production was carried out on a household basis and involved co-operating groups of men and women working within their own specialised spheres of activity.

The Christian churches introduced formal women's organisations to most Pacific islands when they became established in the mid-nineteenth century. These were women's auxiliary groups who convened for religious study, to decorate the village church, to raise funds for the church, and to learn what missionaries deemed appropriate womanly arts, such as sewing and cooking. Such organisations have been strong throughout the twentieth century and include organisations such as the Anglican Mother's Union, the Methodist Women's Fellowship, the Seventh Day Adventists' Dorcas Society, Catholic Women's leagues, and so on. During the colonial period, some island groups developed national, secular women's organisations, and those that did tended to have hierarchical traditional political structures to which these were attached—*Soqosoqo Vakamarama* of Fiji, *Lagafonua* of Tonga, and the National Council of Women in Western Samoa, are examples. These organisations drew their leadership from among the wives of leading chiefs. The organisations of Fiji and Tonga placed particular emphasis on the maintenance of cultural traditions and of women's arts and crafts within those traditions. Fiji also formed a National Council of Women, which started in the early 1970s and aimed to act as an umbrella for church and secular women's organisations in order to represent to government the concerns of women, as delegated by member organisations, through its president and executive. In Western Samoa, the situation was somewhat different. From the 1920s on, village women's committees had evolved, with the encouragement of colonial health authorities, out of the traditional *aualuma* societies and the church women's auxiliaries. The *komiti tumama* 'sanitation committees' were village based and were led by the wives of the leading chiefs and orators of the village, thus mirroring the political structure of the village Council of Chiefs. Their main orientation was towards the improvement of public health, by supervising drinking-water supplies, village sanitation, household hygiene, mosquito eradication, and first aid. By the 1970s the *komiti* had evolved into multi-purpose organisations, playing social, ceremonial, and economic as well as health-promotion roles. When Western Samoa became independent in 1962, the wife of the outgoing administrator and the wife of the new prime minister encouraged the establishment of a national women's organisation to be led by the wives and sisters of Samoa's paramount chiefs; however, this organisation never flourished in the same manner as the village *komiti*.[41]

In many Pacific countries the colonial authorities established during the 1950s and 1960s what were termed 'social development' programmes for rural women. These programmes were usually attached to the departments responsible for administration from the district level down and employed female officers with titles such as 'women's interest assistant' or 'social development assistant', whose job it was to offer instruction to village women's organisations in subjects such as nutrition, cooking, sewing, childcare, and public health. The South Pacific Commission set up a Community Education Training Centre to train women through one-year courses for positions such as these, and Papua New Guinea established a small national training programme within the Administrative College. Two non-sectarian internationally linked non-government offices were also active in the region prior to the decade—the Young Women's Christian Association and the Pacific South East Asia Union of Women. These organisations aimed to promote women's roles as wives, mothers, and home-makers, and to represent women's perspectives to governments almost entirely composed of men. Their leadership was largely made up of the wives of prominent men at village, district, and national levels, although many were also women of exceptional achievement in their own right.

Insofar as any of these organisations sought to promote the representation of women's concerns, it was in relation to the home, the welfare of children and young women, and on special issues such as the restriction of liquor licensing. More feminist programmes have been espoused by university-educated Pacific women since the 1970s. These have aimed to raise the status of women through education and by getting greater numbers of women into senior, decision-making positions in order to institute measures to prevent violence against women.[42] Unfortunately these programmes have not gained the strong support from village-based women necessary to make them politically significant. This is partly because new urban-based, feminist-oriented women's organisations have been perceived as rivals for the few resources and opportunities available to women by the long-established and conservatively oriented church and neo-traditional women's groups. Another reason is that in Melanesia, rural women are likely to see such idealistic agendas as too far removed from the realities and hardships of their lives.

Identity

In the late twentieth century, women tend to be seen as the keepers of traditional culture in the Pacific Islands and tradition is the frequently invoked rationale for criticising women who attempt to adopt modern lifestyles and values. While men may freely embrace modern economic activities, education, political institutions, mores, and fashions, women must do so with caution, particularly in Melanesia. Baluwe Umetrifo, a university graduate from a region first contacted by Europeans in the 1930s, regretfully compares his changing Eastern Highlands Province to a woman adopting modern styles and attitudes in his poem, '*Yupela Meri I Senis Hariap Pinis*'[43] (Woman, You've Changed So Fast):

> *Not long ago I used to go up the Heklaka hill.*
> *When I looked below over the green valley*
> *I could see smoke popping up here and there—*
> *From amongst the jar trees and kunai grass,*
> *And I could see you young girls*
> *Working very hard in your gardens,*
> *In your traditional* pulpuls*
> *With pig grease reflecting in the sun*
> *From your beautiful skin.*
>
> *But now*
> *When I go up the Heklaka hill*
> *And look below over the beautiful valley*
> *I can see grey smoke popping out of mills and factories*
> *From among the huge ugly lumps of metal*
> *And I can see you young girls*
> *In blue jeans and jackets*
> *With high heel shoes and stinky perfumes*

* Fibre skirts

Purses in one hand and newspapers in the other.
As you walk from shop to shop gardening
With your breasts sweating the breast bags.

O yupela i senis hariap pinis!†
Not long ago your names used to be Urakume, Mohoe and Ilaie
You never looked at boys nor talked to them
Always eyes were on the ground
With bilums‡ *on your heads*

But now
All your names have changed
To Marys, Bettys, Jennys, and Roses
And you go around hand in hand
With your mangi poroman§ *without* bilums
O yupela ol meri i winim
Pinis misis *Queen!*
Na yu Goroka yu laik winim *Tokyo and New York!*‖

In Vanuatu there are many revitalisation movements known as *kastom* in the lingua franca, Bislama. The term, deriving from the English word *custom*, implies an adherence to traditional cultural insitutions, particularly those that regulate gender relations. For example, the *kastom* movement also has a fairly widespread following on the island of Tanna. In some areas, whole villages adhere to *kastom* in the sense of eschewing church membership, and in a few of them the *kastom* movement has included the revival of the traditional penis wrapper as male dress, and the rejection of schooling for children, particularly girls. In other villages one or two households may be ideologically committed to *kastom*—to the extent that they define themselves that way (although they may dress as others do and send their children to church schools). Most Christians adhere to *kastom* insofar as it can be accommodated within the particular ideological tenets of their sect or denomination. Those who espouse *kastom* as a primary ideology are particularly concerned about the maintenance of what they consider proper gender relations. They see *kastom* as the means of asserting absolute male dominance, rejecting ideologies that assert the rights of women, and opposing organisations that try to raise the status of women or increase the choices available to them.[44] Grace Mera Molisa voices such concerns in her poem 'Custom':[45]

'*Custom*'
misapplied
bastardized

---

† Oh you have changed so fast!; ‡ string carry bags; § Young friends; ‖ Oh you women beat the Queen! / and you, Goroka, want to beat Tokyo and New York!

murdered
a frankenstein
corpse
conveniently
recalled
to intimidate
women

The tension between modern values and tradition in Melanesia is particularly linked to the issue of women's sexual freedom, since the right to
control the marriages of their womenfolk and to receive bride-price for
them is still strongly asserted by kin groups throughout Papua New Guinea,
the Solomon Islands, and Vanuatu. The contradictions felt by many young
Melanesian women who adopt fashionable clothing, hairstyles, and makeup—
which are seen in the Pacific Islands as symbols of foreign female modernity
and liberation—while remaining bound by the traditional values of their
people are expressed by Jully Makini Sipolo from the Solomon Islands in
her poem, 'Civilised Girl':[46]

Cheap perfume
Six inch heels
Skin-tight pants
Civilised girl

Steel-wool hair
Fuzzy and stiff
Now soft as coconut husk
Held by a dozen clips

Charcoal-black skin
Painted red
Bushy eye-brows
Plucked and penciled

Who am I?
Melanesian Caucasian or
Half-caste?
Make up your mind

Where am I going—
Forward, backward, still?
What do I call myself—
Mrs Miss or Ms?

Why do I do this?
Imitation
What's wrong with it?
Civilisation.

Throughout the 1970s and 1980s there was an optimistic belief that development could occur within the framework of traditional Pacific Island cultures and land-tenure systems. This hope has been most coherently expressed by the Australian-educated lawyer Bernard Narakobi, a Papua New Guinean. His treatise on 'the Melanesian Way' celebrates the egalitarianism, the emphasis on kinship and community, the consensus decision-making, and the spiritual values of traditional Melanesian cultures.[47] Another writer, Kumalau Tawali of Papua New Guinea, also celebrated traditional knowledge and skills versus arrogant foreign attempts to promote change in these lines from his poem 'The Bush Kanaka Speaks':[48]

> *The kiap shouts at us*
> *forcing the veins to stand out in his neck*
> *nearly forcing the excreta out of his bottom*
> *he says: you are ignorant.*
>
> *He says: you are ignorant,*
> *but can he shape a canoe,*
> *tie a mast, fix an outrigger?*
> *Can he steer a canoe through the night*
> *without losing his way?*
> *Does he know when a turtle comes ashore*
> *to lay its eggs?*

The quest for dignity and pride in a national identity has had some negative aspects, however. Nationalist rhetoric has tended to inhibit internal criticism of the political system and status quo, and those who point out unpleasant truths through academic or literary means may be accused of 'thinking like foreigners' and of having in some sense sided with the outside world. Albert Wendt's poem 'The Faa-Samoa is Perfect, They Sd'[49] denounces the elite version of tradition:

> *The faa-samoa is perfect, they sd*
> *from behind cocktail bars like pulpits*
> *double scotch on the rocks, i sd*
>
> *we have no orphans, no one starves.*
> *we share everything, they sd*
> *refill my glass, i sd*
>
> *and we all have alofa*
> *for one another, they sd*
> *drown me in your alofa then, i sd*
>
> *its true they sd, our samoa*
> *is a paradise, we venerate our royalty,*
> *our pastors and leaders and beloved dead*

god gave us the faa-samoa and
only he can take it away, they sd
amen, i sd

their imported firstclass whisky
was alive with corpses: my uncle
and his army of hungry kids,
malnutritioned children in dirty wards,
an old woman begging in the bank,
my generation migrating overseas
for jobs, while politicians
and merchants brag obesely
in the RSA, and pastors bang
out sermons about the obedient
*and righteous life—aiafu**
all growing fat in
a blind man's paradise

The emphasis of many cultural nationalist ideologies in the Pacific Islands on the forms and institutions of the past, even revising the past and cloaking it in great and glorious colours, has political dimensions.[50] Such ideologies may disguise and perpetuate inequality and legitimate privilege, and may also be a way of diverting attention away from unpleasant realities, but *kastom*, the *fa'a Samoa*, 'the Melanesian Way', and so on also bestow collective dignity, uniqueness, and worth. They ameliorate the pain of realisation by Pacific Islanders that they are sometimes perceived by the outside world as primitive curiosities or backward inhabitants of the Third World.[51]

Corruption and nepotism are also accepted or at least tolerated as a feature of 'tradition'. In Samoa it was the practice of chiefs to materially reward those who provided them with political support,[52] as it was under the 'big man' system of Melanesia. The style of democracy common to the politically independent Pacific states has fostered an adaptation of this practice, in which most members of parliament, particularly if they are in ministerial positions, feel obliged to deliver aid projects—no matter how poorly conceived—to their electorates, or to use even more dubious means to win the favour of their constituencies. In those countries where Asian enterprises are significant—which is in most of the politically independent states and Micronesia—established practices of 'favours for favours' have been imported from South-East Asia. In a number of these countries this practice has compromised high-level policy decisions about rights to exploit natural resources, to the benefit of foreign interests and highly placed local individuals, but to the disadvantage of the nation and the owners of the resource. The apparently rapid spread of corrupt practices in Pacific Island

* Sweat-eaters

countries since independence—for example 'tipping' public servants who provide assistance in some way is now said to be a common practice in Western Samoa—cannot simply be blamed on outsiders, or on low wages, but must also be linked to the mores of societies that are still fundamentally kin based, where relatives, *wantoks*,[53] or friends are expected to favour one another and where, conversely, people who are not relatives are seen as likely to be less helpful unless given some form of reciprocal favour.

Despite the vast amounts of aid that have been lavished on the Pacific Islands since the late 1960s, economic growth has been disappointingly slow (see Knapman, chapter 14). In the absence of industrialisation, the only sector in which mass participation is possible is the agricultural sector. Although the 'traditional' way of life offers security and identity to the majority of the population, many of its features discourage villagers from engaging in a greater degree of commercially oriented agricultural specialisation.[54] The perennial tree crops that have been grown in small plots by village people throughout the 'independent' Pacific Islands since the beginning of the twentieth century, and that are still the mainstay of the rural cash economy, yield very modest returns, because of fluctuating or chronically depressed world prices. The production of these commodities does not offer people the quantum leap in incomes that usually motivates very rapid social change.[55] Disputes over customary land rights, which are ubiquitous in Melanesia and Western Samoa and to some extent in Fiji, also inhibit the practice of commercial agriculture. In Melanesia inflated claims for compensation, by landowners looking for alternative sources of wealth to the unrewarding practice of agriculture, frequently hold up or undermine development projects ranging in magnitude from village water-supply projects to hydro-electric dams. A Samoan proverb says 'We want the yams but fear the stones' (in Samoa yam cultivation involves the laborious removal of stones from the ground to make a growing pit), reflecting the universal human preference for rewards without sacrifice. Rural people want a higher standard of living but are justifiably unwilling to abandon the security of their established way of life for uncertain new directions. They look to their governments and to the outside world to present answers to their dilemma.

Directions

All the trends of the twentieth century have been towards increasing dependency based on unequal bargaining power between the Pacific Islands and other countries so that the Pacific Islands have become exemplars for a dependency or world-systems theory of development.[56] Yet, paradoxically, the more dependent the relationship between a Pacific Island country and a stronger power, the better off its population is, in terms of access to basic services and social indicators such as life expectancy. Dependency is a problem for the Pacific Islands mainly in terms of the *insecurity* of their links with the outside world. The small island countries that are building their links to larger, wealthier countries through emigration may ultimately have more durable and useful ties than those linked by the strategic concerns of the dominant powers. For example in New Zealand, a country with a population of just over 3 million people, over a million dollars was raised directly from the public in a twenty-four-hour telethon to fund relief after a devastating tropical cyclone in Western Samoa just before Christmas 1991. This occurred in a time of deep economic recession and heightened racial tension, a time when one in three Polynesian adults were unemployed, yet people of all ethnic backgrounds made donations because New Zealanders feel connected to Western Samoa—not because of the former colonial links, but because Samoans are now New Zealand's third largest ethnic group after the Anglo-Irish and the Maori.

Scholarly conclusions about change in the Pacific Islands have been almost unremittingly negative since the 1970s. They have emphasised the emergence of class relations disguised in tradition,[57] the emergence of regional elites who have more in common with one another than with ordinary people of their own lands,[58] the incorporation of Pacific Island economies into the global capitalist order and the pre-eminence of multinational corporations,[59] the proletarianisation of populations moving into urban environments, and the transformation of independent subsistence producers into a marginal peasantry.[60] Without getting into philosophical debate about the notion of progress, the question could be asked: Are the peoples of the Pacific Islands better or worse off today than they were a century ago? The Rousseauesque myth of the Pacific Islands as a 'paradise'[61] has tended to conjure up a falsely idyllic picture of the past in the minds of those unfamiliar with the realities of 'subsistence affluence'. People paid a heavy price in the past for the economic independence born of isolation; life in small-scale societies was often oppressive, cruel, and unequal; isolated islands had few resources and were vulnerable to a range of natural disasters; and disease, famine, and warfare were regular and often interconnected events. Human happiness is difficult to measure objectively, but there are some grounds for optimism about the changes of the past century. Vitality and dynamism as well as social problems are observable in the burgeoning towns of the South Pacific. So far most Pacific island states have retained a commitment to democratic forms that recognise individual human rights to a far greater degree than in the past, despite the frequent subversion of these systems made possible, even inevitable, by the wide difference in knowledge and understanding between educated elites and the unsophisticated majority. The process of incorporation of the Pacific Islands into a global economic system during the twentieth century has been disruptive, often destructive and exploitative, but it has also brought what most islanders would regard as advantageous changes. These include a wider range of choices, a greater degree of individual rights and personal security, reduction of disease, and increased life expectancy.

Notes

1 See James A. Boutilier, 'Hungry Sharks: Japanese Economic Activity in Melanesia 1960–1980', *Pacific Studies* 8 (1, 1984): 71–94.

2 Some recent interpretation of social indicators are provided in Penelope Schoeffel, *Women In Development: Papua New Guinea*, 1987; and her *Women in Development: Fiji*, 1988; also Shireen Lateef, *Women in Development: Solomon Islands*, 1989; and her *Women in Development: Marshall Islands*. These country papers were published for in-house use by the Country Programmes (East) Division of Asian Development Bank, Manila, from which they are available on application.

3 Martin L. Bakker, *Populations of the South Pacific: An Overview of Demographic Levels, Patterns and Trends*, United Nations Population Fund and University of the South Pacific, Suva, 1990.

4 Dennis Ahlburg, 'Demographic Pressure on Health, Education, and Employment Resources in the South Pacific Region', *Pacific Studies* 12 (2, 1989): 23–31.

5 Bakker, 72.

6 Some 58 per cent of the population will be living in towns by the year 2000 according to an ESCAP estimate in *Urbanisation in Papua New Guinea*, Economic and Social Commission for Asia and the Pacific, n.d.

7 Marc Schlitz, 'Rascalism, Tradition and the State in Papua New Guinea', in *Domestic Violence in Papua New Guinea*, ed. Susan Toft, Law Reform Commission of Papua New Guinea Monograph no. 3, Port Moresby, 1985, 141–160.

8 For a recent overview of development issues in Micronesia see John Connell, 'The New Micronesia: Pitfalls and Problems of Dependent Development', *Pacific Studies* 14 (2, 1991): 87–120. See also Larry W. Mayo, 'U.S. Administration and Prospects for Economic Self-Sufficiency: A Comparison of Guam and Select Areas of Micronesia', *Pacific Studies* 11 (3, 1988): 53–75; and D. Nevin, *The American Touch in Micronesia*, Norton, New York, 1977.

9 New Zealand Department of Statistics, 1991.

10 Michael J. Levin, 'Patterns and Implications of 1980–90 Immigration from Asia and the Pacific to the United States', paper presented to the 17th Pacific Science Congress, Honolulu, May 1991.

11 A series of country reports on migration, employment and development for the Cook Islands, Niue, Tokelau, and Western Samoa was commissioned and published by the International Labour Organisation and the South Pacific Commission. An overview of the studies is presented in John Connell, *Migration, Employment and Development in the South Pacific*, General Report on the SPC/ILO series, South Pacific Commission, Noumea, 1984.

12 For a detailed overview see Richard Bedford and Katherine Gibson, *Migration, Employment and Development in the South Pacific: New Zealand*, Country Report no. 23B, International Labour Organisation and South Pacific Commission, Noumea, 1986. See also D. W. Boardman, 'Polynesian Immigrants: Migration Process and Distribution in New Zealand', in *New Zealand Society:*

Contemporary Perspectives, ed. S. D. Webb and J. Collette, John Wiley & Sons, Sydney, 1973, 318–324; E. M. K. Douglas, 'New Polynesian Voyagers: Visitors, Workers, and Migrants in New Zealand', in *Circulation in Third World Countries*, ed. R. Mansell Prothero and Murray Chapman, Routledge & Kegan Paul, London, 1985, 414–435; and Ian Fairbairn, 'Samoan Migration to New Zealand: The General Background and Some Economic Consequences for Samoa', *Journal of the Polynesian Society* 70 (1, 1961): 18–30.

13 For a discussion of the social effects of Samoan emigration to New Zealand see D. C. Pitt and A. J. C. Macpherson, *Emerging Pluralism: The Samoan Community in New Zealand*, Longman Paul, Auckland, 1974; also A. J. C. Macpherson, 'The Polynesian Migrant Family: A Samoan Case Study', in *The Social Structure of the New Zealand Family*, ed. P. G. Koopman Boyden, Methuen, Wellington, 1978; A. J. C. Macpherson, 'Polynesians in New Zealand: An Emerging Eth-class?' in *Social Class in New Zealand*, ed. D. C. Pitt, Longman Paul, Auckland, 1979, 99–112.

14 Bedford and Gibson 1986, 17.

15 John Connell, *Migration, Employment and Development in the South Pacific: Australia*, Country Report no. 23A, International Labour Organisation and South Pacific Commission, Noumea 1985.

16 Paul Shankman, *Migration and Underdevelopment: The Case of Western Samoa*, Westview, Boulder, CO, 1976.

17 See L. F. Vaʻa, 'The Future Impacts of Island Emigration on Migrants' Home Communities and Their Home Countries', paper presented to 17th Pacific Science Congress, Honolulu, May–June 1991, also *Remittances and Rural Development: Migration, Dependency and Inequality in the South Pacific*, Development Studies Centre Occasional Paper no. 22, Australian National University, Canberra, 1980.

18 I. G. Bertram and R. F. Watters, 'The Concept of the MIRAB Economy in Small South Pacific Countries', *Pacific Viewpoint* 26 (3, 1985): 497–519.

19 Cluny Macpherson, 'The Ways Migrants and Their Children View Island Homelands', paper presented at 17th Pacific Science Congress, Honolulu, May–June 1991.

20 Unpublished data on Poutasi village collected by P. Schoeffel and P. Solomona, 1976–1986.

21 See Francis X. Hezel, 'Suicide and the Micronesian Family', *The Contemporary Pacific* 1 (1989): 43–74; and Cluny Macpherson and Laʻavasa Macpherson 'Suicide in Western Samoa: A Sociological Perspective', in *Culture, Youth and Suicide in the Pacific: Papers from an East West Centre Conference*, ed. Francis X. Hezel, Donald H. Rubinstein, and Geoffrey M. White, Working Paper Series, Pacific Islands Studies Program, University of Hawaiʻi, Honolulu, 1985, 36–73; Susan Toft, ed., *Domestic Violence in Urban Papua New Guinea*, Law Reform Commission of Papua New Guinea Occasional Paper no. 19, Boroko, 1986; Karen Nero, 'The Hidden Pain: Drunkenness and Domestic Violence in Palau', 63–92, and Dorothy Ayers Counts, 'Domestic Violence in Oceania: Conclusion', 225–254, both in *Domestic Violence in Oceania*, ed. Dorothy Ayers Counts, special issue of *Pacific Studies* 13 (3, 1990).

22 See Ron Crocombe, *The South Pacific*, 5th revised edn, University of the South Pacific, Suva, 1989, 72–89; also John Garrett, *To Live Among the Stars: Christian*

Origins in Oceania, University of the South Pacific and World Council of Churches, Suva and Geneva, 1982.

23 Quoted by Mālama Meleiseā in *The Making of Modern Samoa*, University of the South Pacific, Suva, 1987, 230.

24 Tamar G. Gordon, 'Inventing Mormon Identity in Tonga', PhD dissertation in anthropology, University of California, Berkeley, 1988.

25 This was told me by Baha'i converts in both countries. The status of Tuvaluan women is lower than the norm in Western Polynesia. According to Mālama Iati, a missionary on Nukulaelae in Tuvalu in the 1950s, she and her husband had tried to introduce the Samoan cultural idea of *feagaiga*, which confers dignity on women and engenders respect for them, through the special status of women as men's sisters. She said their attempts were strongly rejected by Tuvaluan church leaders (Mālama Meleiseā, personal communication).

26 Michael Hamnett, 'The Pacific Islands in the Process of Change: Critical Issues for Health and Nutrition', in *The Pacific Conference: Nutrition in a Changing World, Proceedings*, ed. M. Bruss, University of Hawai'i, Honolulu, 1987, 16–17; Michael Hamnett, 'Major Social, Economic, and Political Trends with Implications for Health and Nutrition', in Bruss 1987, 18–21.

27 Te'o Fairbairn, 'Subsistence Economy and Policy Options for Small Island Economies', in *Class and Culture in the South Pacific*, ed. Antony Hooper et al, Centre for Pacific Studies, University of Auckland, and Institute of Pacific Studies, University of the South Pacific, Suva, 1987.

28 R. Thaman, 'Deterioration of Traditional Food Systems, Increasing Malnutrition and Food Dependency in the Pacific Islands', *Journal of Food and Nutrition* 39 (3, 1982): 109–121. For an account of early colonial influences on dietary change, see Nancy Pollock, 'The Early Development of Housekeeping and Imports in Fiji', *Pacific Studies* 12 (2, 1989): 53–82.

29 T. Coyne, J. Badcock, and R. Taylor, eds, *The Effects of Urbanization and Western Diet on the Health of Pacific Populations*, South Pacific Commission Technical Paper no. 186, Noumea, 1984; see also Epeli Hau'ofa, *Corned Beef and Tapioca: A Report on the Food Distribution System in Tonga*, Development Studies Centre Monograph 19, Australian National University and Centre for Applied Studies in Development, University of the South Pacific, Suva, 1979.

30 Paul Zimmet, 'Epidemiology of Diabetes and Its Macrovascular Manifestations in Pacific Populations: The Medical Effects of Social Progress', *Diabetes Care* 2 (March–April 1976): 144–153.

31 Data provided by UNICEF regional office, Suva, Fiji.

32 T. G. McGee, 'Food Dependency in the Pacific: A Preliminary Statement', Working Paper no. 2, Development Studies Centre, Research School of Pacific Studies, Australian National University, Canberra, 1975.

33 Kofe Siliga, 'Household Food Security in the Pacific Island: A Desk Study', paper prepared for South Pacific Commission–UNICEF Household Food Security Project.

34 Kevin J. Barr, *Poverty In Fiji*, Fiji Forum for Justice, Peace and the Integrity of Creation, Suva, 1990.

35 Marilyn Strathern, *Women in Between: Female Roles in a Male World: Mount Hagen, New Guinea*, Seminar Press, London, 1972.

36 For example, A. Kaeppler, 'Rank in Tonga', *Ethnology* 10 (1971): 171–193; Julia

Hecht, 'The Culture of Gender in Pukapuka. Males, Females and the Mayakitanga Sacred Maid', *Journal of the Polynesian Society* 86 (1977): 183–206; Judith Huntsman and Antony Hooper, 'Male and Female in Tokelau Culture', *Journal of the Polynesian Society* 84 (1975): 415–430; Penelope Schoeffel, 'Gender, Status and Power in Western Samoa', *Canberra Anthropology* (1978): 169–181; Bradd Shore, 'Incest Prohibitions and the Logic of Power in Samoa', *Journal of the Polynesian Society* 85 (2, 1976): 275–295; Garth Rogers, 'The Father's Sister is Black', *Journal of the Polynesian Society* 86 (1977): 183–206.

37 Western Samoa 1971 Census of Population and Housing, Table 39, Department of Statistics, Apia, 1971.

38 For a discussion of women and development issues in Papua New Guinea see S. Stratigos and P. J. Hughes, eds, *The Ethics of Development: Women as Unequal Partners on Development*, papers from the 1986 Waigani Seminar, University of Papua New Guinea, Waigani, 1987. See also papers on women's roles in Peter King, Wendy Less, and Vincent Warakai, eds, *From Rhetoric to Reality? Papua New Guinea's Eight Point Plan and National Goals after a Decade*, papers from the 1984 Waigani Seminar, University of Papua New Guinea, Waigani, 1985. For the Pacific region, see *Women in Development in the South Pacific: Barriers and Opportunities*, papers presented at a conference held in Vanuatu, 11–14 August 1984, Development Studies Centre, Australian National University, Canberra, 1985.

39 See, for example, the case study in Jeanette Dickerson-Putman, 'Women's Contribution to the Domestic and National Economy of Papua New Guinea', *Research in Economic Anthropology* 10 (1988): 201–222.

40 Penelope Schoeffel, 'The Origins and Development of Women's Associations in Western Samoa, 1830–1977', *Pacific Studies* 3 (1, 1977): 1–21.

41 Schoeffel, 1977.

42 See Counts, 1990.

43 Onebondo Poster Poem no. 10, National Arts School, University of Papua New Guinea, 1980.

44 These observations derive from my 1991 field work in Tanna, but see also Lamont Lindstrom, 'Leftamap Kastom: The Political History of Tradition on Tanna, Vanuatu', *Mankind* 13 (4, 1982): 316–329.

45 Grace Mera Molisa, 'Custom', in her *Black Stone*, Mana Publications, Suva, 1983, 24.

46 Jully Makini Sipolo, 'Civilised Girl', from the anthology of the same name, South Pacific Creative Arts Society, Suva, Fiji, 1981, 21.

47 Bernard Narakobi, *The Melanesian Way*, Institute of Papua New Guinea Studies and Institute of Pacific Studies, Port Moresby, 1983.

48 Excerpt from Kumalau Tawali, 'The Bush Kanaka Speaks' in *Signs in the Sky*, Papua Pocket Poets no. 19, Port Moresby, 1970 (no pagination).

49 Excerpt from Albert Wendt, 'The Faa Samoa is Perfect, They Sd', from *Inside us the Dead*, Longman Paul, Auckland, 1976, 46.

50 See Roger M. Keesing, 'Creating the Past: Custom and Identity in the Contemporary Pacific', *The Contemporary Pacific* 1 (1989): 19–42; Sione Latukefu, 'Noble Traditions and Christian Principles as National Ideology in Papua New Guinea: Do Their Philosophies Complement or Contradict Each Other?' *Pacific Studies* 11 (2, 1988): 83–96; Jocelyn Linnekin, 'The Politics of Culture in the

Pacific', in *Cultural Identity and Ethnicity in the Pacific*, ed. Jocelyn Linnekin and Lin Poyer, University of Hawai'i Press, Honolulu, 1990, 149–173.

51 Mālama Meleiseā, 'Ideology in Pacific Studies: A Personal View', in *Class and Culture in the South Pacific*, ed. Antony Hooper et al, Centre for Pacific Studies, University of Auckland and Institute of Pacific Studies, University of the South Pacific, Auckland and Suva, 1987, 140–152.

52 Mālama Meleiseā discusses the perception of legitimacy as a recurrent theme of tension between high-ranking Samoans and German and New Zealand authorities throughout the twentieth century, using a Weberian paradigm. Whereas the colonial officials had a rational-legal understanding of power and authority, Samoan chiefs, whose attitudes were shaped within the framework of traditional authority, expected to be able to use offices bestowed on them by the colonial administration to further their own interests and those of their relatives, village, and district. See Meleiseā *The Making of Modern Samoa*, University of the South Pacific, Suva, 1987.

53 A Melanesian pidgin term for a person of the same language group, which is now used of people from the same island or province, or even country, in certain contexts.

54 Macpherson denies that this is the case in Western Samoa, citing examples of entrepreneurial families and individuals who have succeeded in commercial ventures within the context of village life. He argues that the constraining factor is that more attractive choices for advancement exist for village people than that of village agriculture, such as emigration. See Cluny Macpherson, 'The Road to Power Is a Chainsaw: Villages and Innovation in Western Samoa', *Pacific Studies* 11 (2, 1988): 1–24. See also Tim O'Meara's excellent study of village farmer motivation in *Samoa Planters: Tradition and Economic Development in Polynesia*, Holt, Rinehart & Winston, Fort Worth TX, 1990.

55 For an unparalleled analysis of the problems of agricultural development in a historical context see Stephen J. Duggan, 'The failure of Economic Reform in the Sepik: The Role of Church and State in Economic Development', *Pacific Studies* 14 (2, 1991): 1–28. Duggan's case study of West Sepik, with regional variations, broadly reflects what has occurred in most of the Pacific islands.

56 For example, see I. Wallerstein, *The Modern World System*. Academic Press, New York, 1974.

57 For example, Keesing 1989.

58 For example, Epeli Hau'ofa, 'The New South Pacific Society: Integration and Independence' and Ray Watters, 'MIRAB Societies and Bureaucratic Elites' in Hooper 1987, 1–12.

59 For example, Geoff Bertram, 'The Political Economy of Decolonisation and Nationhood in Small Pacific Societies', in Hooper 1987, 16–29. For a more polemical view see Michael C. Howard, Simione Durutalo, N. Plange, and R. Witton, *The Political Economy of the South Pacific*, South-East Asian Monograph Series 13, James Cook University, Townsville, 1983.

60 For example, Diana Howlett, 'Terminal Development: Tribalism to Peasantry', in *The Pacific in Transition: Geographical Perspectives on Adaptation and Change*, ed. Harold Brookfield, Edward Arnold, London, 1973, 249–273.

61 See, for example, A. Grove Day, *Mad About Islands: Novelists of a Vanished Pacific*, Mutual Publishing, Honolulu, 1987.

16

Political institutions

Peter Larmour

Analysis of political institutions in the Pacific Islands has been preoccupied with written constitutions and the achievement of independence. This approach remains important for understanding places like Palau, Guam, and New Caledonia, where different types of nationalists, and those opposing them, argue and negotiate about the provisions of future constitutions. However, events there and elsewhere since the late 1980s suggest a need to broaden the scope to include unconstitutional change, and changes in countries that have been independent for a long time. Fiji's coups, the arrest and trial of Vanuatu's president, and the attempted secession of Papua New Guinea's North Solomons Province are examples of the former; moves towards greater democracy in Tonga and Western Samoa are examples of the latter.

In this chapter political institutions are treated as part of a system, relating to each other, and to the society, territory, and economy that they govern. The types of institution are familiar: the executive, the legislature, political parties, the bureaucracy, the judiciary, and (in Fiji and Papua New Guinea) the army. The last two are included despite arguments that the army and the judiciary should 'keep out of politics'. They can be excluded only on a very normative or narrow definition of politics as the activity of elected officials.

Although these types of institution are more or less universal, they come in different packages: as independent states; as territories in 'free association' with New Zealand or signing a 'Compact of Free Association' with the United States; as 'overseas territories' of France; as a commonwealth and unincorporated territories of the United States; and as several other smaller entities, variously defined (see map page 382).

Many of the differences and similarities between the polities have to do with the relationships between these institutions, rather than the institutions themselves. For example, the relationship between metropolitan and territorial institutions distinguishes independent states from colonies. The relationship

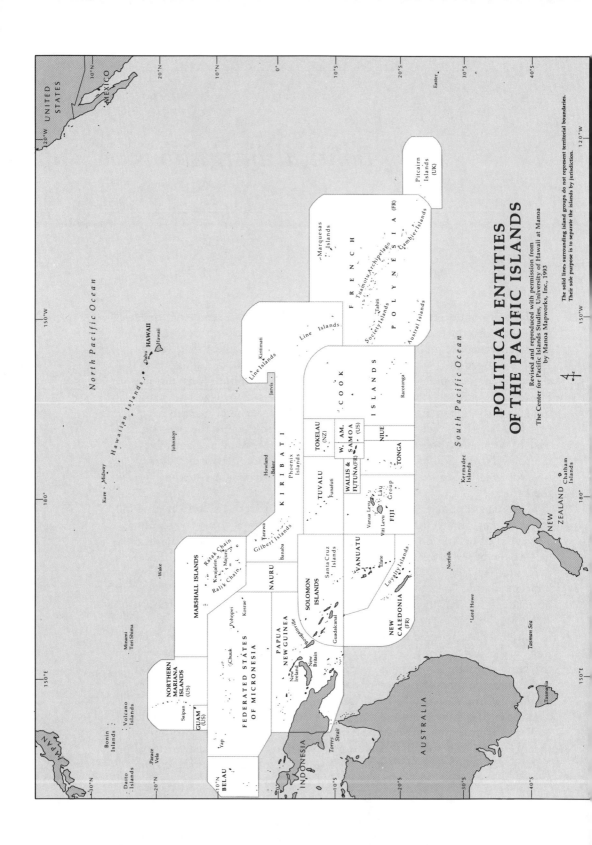

POLITICAL ENTITIES
OF THE PACIFIC ISLANDS

Revised and reproduced with permission from
The Center for Pacific Islands Studies, University of Hawaii at Manoa
by Manoa Mapworks, Inc., 1993

The solid lines surrounding island groups do not represent territorial boundaries.
Their sole purpose is to separate the islands by jurisdiction.

between executive and legislature distinguishes the 'Westminster' systems of former British, New Zealand, and Australian colonies from most of the former US and other territories. It also distinguishes Tonga, where the monarch may veto legislation, from the other constitutional monarchies, like Solomon Islands, where she may not.

The political system

These institutions do not operate in isolation. Acting together as a political system, they relate downwards to the society, territory, and economy that they govern, sometimes through intermediate layers of state, provincial, and local government (themselves divided into legislature, executive, and so on). Political institutions in the US commonwealth, US unincorporated territories, and French overseas territories also relate upwards to metropolitan legislatures and government departments. American Samoans, for example, elect a non-voting delegate to the US Congress, while New Caledonians vote in elections for the French National Assembly and Senate (and even the European parliament).

The political systems also relate sideways to their counterparts in other territories, through foreign ministries and regional agencies such as the South Pacific Forum and the South Pacific Commission, as well as wider international organisations, such as the Commonwealth or the International Air Transport Association. These international relationships are discussed elsewhere in this volume.

To emphasise the relationships between political institutions is not to imply that the relationships are harmonious, or that the separate institutions necessarily work together. Whether political institutions add up to a coherent 'political system' is to some extent an empirical question. They may add up to incoherence, contradiction, or paralysis. Papua New Guinea's political system often seems at war with itself: the legislature at war with the executive, expressed in frequent parliamentary votes of no confidence; the centre at war with the provinces, expressed in frequent suspensions of provincial governments; and the judiciary at war with the executive, in for example, the Rooney affair, described later.

However Papua New Guinea is a reminder that conflict between institutions may be a matter of design, and a mark of success rather than failure. The system of 'separation of powers', and the notion of 'checks and balances' are based on the idea that a political system at war with itself is less likely to oppress its citizens. Oppositions, ombudsmen, commissions of enquiry, and independent judges are supposed to criticise the executive: that is their job. Critics doubt that such liberal, conflict-ridden systems can deliver 'development', or argue that they contradict traditional values of consensus and respect for leaders.

Traditional versus introduced institutions

One fault line through Pacific political institutions lies between those regarded as 'traditional' and those 'introduced'. The issue is complicated, for several reasons. First, most traditional institutions, such as chieftaincy, have been redefined or repositioned by social and economic changes, colonial rule, and independent governments. Introduced institutions have likewise adapted to, or acted through, traditional institutions. They are interconnected, and neither exists in a pure form.

Second, confusion often exists about what counts as the opposite of such traditional institutions: is it 'modern', in the sense of up-to-date? metropolitan, as in Britain, Australia, or France? or simply introduced? For example, colonial rule introduced some metropolitan political institutions, but also created specifically colonial ones: there are no 'district officers' in Britain, or *kiaps* in Australia.

Third, a defining characteristic of 'modern' institutions is often said to be their specialisation. Traditional institutions—such as village meetings of elders—typically combined several functions that are now carried out by separate agencies: courts, police, and parliament.

Fourth, existing differences between traditional and introduced institutions would make substitution of one for the other difficult. Introduced institutions generally have a much wider geographical scope, enclosing a number of separate and possibly rivalrous traditional systems. Another kind of scope is involved when traditional and introduced institutions disagree about what matters count as 'public' or 'political', and what as 'private' or 'non-political'.[1]

In practice, various degrees of institutional dualism persist in most countries—as they do to some degree in metropolitan countries, where people rely on family and neighbours for help in resolving some problems, and police keep clear of others. In some circumstances, traditional and introduced institutions may have become confused, as Vanuatu's prime minister has argued.[2] Or use of the two systems may simply be opportunistic, as Meleiseā has complained about Western Samoa: 'once *papalagi* law was no longer an instrusive system to be reacted against, but part of the law of independent Western Samoa, people began to use the two systems selectively depending on the interests involved'.[3]

In places like Western Samoa and Tonga, modern adaptations of traditional institutions have been incorporated into the colonial and post-colonial state, and it is easy to explain away traditionalism as the self-interest of conservative elites. When traditionalism comes from politicians in Melanesia, where traditional institutions have usually been regarded as more egalitarian, it is less easy to explain away. Again there are differences. Father Lini of Vanuatu argues, in spite of Fiji, that traditional institutions are often more democratic than introduced ones and so form a bulwark against coups.[4]

Solomon Mamaloni of Solomon Islands, a master of modern parliamentary politics, argues for recognition of the 'wisdom and authority of chiefs' as part of a defence of ethnic interests and identity against foreigners.

In Fiji it was mainly a group of commoners—the *taukei*—who were pressing hard for the restoration of chiefly prerogatives. The issue of traditionalism could not simply be reduced to one of self-serving ideology. Modernising elites sometimes find themselves under fire from traditionalist masses, just as elites may use tradition to demobilise threatening mass action. It may be better to treat 'tradition' and 'modernity' as legitimating rhetorics, rather than categories of analysis, and to pay more attention to the dualistic structure of government—another kind of 'separation of powers'—than the precise content of either pole.

Ideas, individuals, and institutions

Institutions do not exist independently of the people leading, staffing, and using them. To say a Pacific Island country has a Westminster system of government is a statement not only about its constitutional provisions (that prime minister and Cabinet are also members of the legislature) but also about the ideas and expectations of its politicians, and other potentially powerful actors like the army, who may—or may not—'respect its conventions'. These expectations may be set out in written constitutions, or unstated (for example, that there should be a regional balance in senior appointments). Ordinary citizens' expectations also shape institutions: one function of the broadly based processes of consultation that took place before independence in Western Samoa, Kiribati, Tuvalu, and Melanesia (except Fiji), was to increase popular commitment to the institutions adopted at independence.

People may bring quite different ideas and expectations to similarly titled institutions. Differences in expectations may not become clear until there is a crisis: part of the shock that followed the Fiji coups came from the demonstration that different groups within and outside Fiji had very different expectations about its institutions. In the Pacific Islands, the role of governor general, or president, has been a particular focus of different expectations[5] and is discussed further later.

Fiji also showed that some people had quite different ideas about the values that should be embodied in institutions, a difference expressed most stridently in the Taukei movement's submission to the Great Council of Chiefs: 'The two principal ideas of democracy—liberty (or freedom) and equality are foreign values, and indeed contrary to the Fijian way of life where liberty exists only within one's social rank and equality is strictly constrained by a fully developed social hierarchy'.[6]

In the rest of this chapter political institutions are considered one by one, and then the relationships between them and the society, territory, and economy they govern are examined.

The executive

The executive is the person, or small group of people, attempting to lead or manage the political system. Typically they include a president or prime minister, their close advisers, ministers, and heads-of-government agencies (particularly when these are appointed by the Cabinet, as in Papua New Guinea, rather than the public service). If parties are institutionalised, their officials may form part of the executive, as when the Vanua'aku Pati appointed party officials to ministers' offices in Vanuatu in the early 1980s.

In the Pacific Islands, members of the executive may be elected to the position or appointed. They may inherit it or seize it by force. Typically, there is a mixture of methods. The prime minister or premier in four of the five Westminster systems—Papua New Guinea, Solomon Islands, Tuvalu, and Niue—is elected by the legislature and then formally appointed by the Queen's representative. In the fifth, the Cook Islands, no formal election is held, but the Queen's representative appoints as prime minister the member of parliament 'who is likely to command the confidence of a majority of the members of the Assembly'.[7] Fiji's appointment provisions were similar until Colonel Rabuka arrested the Cabinet in May 1987. They were restored in the 1990 constitution, but with the provision that the person selected must be an ethnic Fijian.[8]

A mixture of methods of appointment also characterised traditional systems of government. Chiefly titles in Samoa, for example, were bestowed by a process of consultation and selection by the *aiga potopoto*, or family group, but were confirmed at a meeting of other title-holders.[9] In a famous article, Marshall Sahlins argued that inheritance dominated in the selection of chiefs in Polynesia, while personal achievement dominated in the selection of big men in Melanesia.[10] Recent scholarship finds the contrast too sharply drawn and cites examples of inheritance in Melanesia, and achievement in Polynesia.[11]

In colonies, the executive—high commissioner, governor, administrator—was typically appointed by the metropolitan government, but in both the French and the American territories a more complex mix of local election and metropolitan veto is now found. Since 1984 in French Polynesia, the elected leader of the Territorial Assembly has replaced the high commissioner as president of the Governing Council. However, the high commissioner remains directly responsible for public services provided by the metropolitan, rather than the territorial, government and has a retrospective veto over Governing Council decisions.

In the American territories of Guam and American Samoa, governors are locally and directly elected, but do not have executive authority over all the

The Royal Palace of Tonga, Nukuʻalofa, early 1990s, with guard. (Robert C. Kiste)

government agencies operating within their respective territories (notably, in Guam, the military controls one-third of the land area).[12] The governors' actions are subject to veto by the metropolitan Secretary of the Interior, just as local legislation may be overridden by Congress.

Tonga is a monarchy, governed under a constitution that dates back to 1875. The king personally presides over a privy council, appoints ministers to Cabinet (which is presided over by a prime minister, who happens to be his younger brother), and appoints regional governors. He decides when the Legislative Assembly will sit, and vetoes legislation of which he disapproves.

Some such monarchical powers exist in a formal and attenuated way in the constitutions of the former New Zealand, Australian, and British colonies that decided to retain the British monarch as the titular head of state: Niue, Cook Islands, Tuvalu, Papua New Guinea, Solomon Islands, and Fiji until 1987. In these countries the Queen is represented locally by a governor general or high commissioner, whose role is largely symbolic and procedural—though occupants who have been politicians, like Sir John Guise in Papua New Guinea, tend to interpret their powers as widely as possible. Constitutional provisions, and conventions, put executive power in the hands of the prime minister and Cabinet. In Fiji, however, the governor general—who also had Fijian traditional legitimacy—emerged as an active, if vacillating, participant in the political manoeuvring that followed the first of the 1987 coups.

Other former Australian, British, and New Zealand colonies—Nauru,

Kiribati, Western Samoa, and Vanuatu (the last jointly ruled by Britain and France)—became republics, and substantial republican sentiment remains in Solomon Islands. Following Ghai, these polities can be divided into those that combine the role of head of government—prime minister—and head of state (Nauru, Kiribati) and those, like the monarchies, that separate the two roles (Western Samoa and Vanuatu).[13] Conflict between the president and the prime minister of Vanuatu led in 1988 to the arrest of the president, his conviction on charges of incitement to mutiny, and his subsequent release on appeal.

Of the former American colonies, the Federated States of Micronesia (FSM) and Palau combine head of state with head of government, the former elected by parliament, the latter elected directly. The Republic of the Marshall Islands and its neighbour, Kiribati, part of the former British Gilbert and Ellice Islands Colony, provide contrasting cases of crossover between colonial political traditions. The Marshall Islands adopted a constitution with a president elected from and by parliament, along the Westminster model, whereas Kiribati provided for the direct election of a president from a shortlist consisting of members of parliament.

Fiji's 1990 constitution insists that key positions in the executive and the judiciary are held by indigenous Fijians, rather than Fiji Indians or other racial groups. In practice, rather than law, and with occasional exceptions, executive offices throughout the Pacific Islands tend to be held by men rather than women.

Legislatures

Colonial legislatures often had much longer traditions of local, and particularly indigenous, participation than other branches of government. Where popular mass-based movements for independence were absent, legislatures became the centres of opposition to colonial rule—and their members often the greatest beneficiaries of its ending.

As has been shown, the relationship between executive and legislative branches differentiates the Westminster system adopted by most of the former British, Australian, and New Zealand colonies, from the 'Washington' system adopted by most of the American colonies (except the Marshall Islands). The Westminster principle of executive responsibility to parliament is formalised in Papua New Guinea's constitution through a mechanism of parliamentary votes of no confidence in particular ministers or in the government as a whole. The constitution provides some political restraints on the exercise of such votes,[14] but it does not give the prime minister the power to deter them by threatening to precipitate a general election. In the event, votes of no confidence, threats of them, and deals stitched up to forestall them, have become a permanent feature of Papua New Guinea

Parliament House, Papua New Guinea, June 1992. (Robert C. Kiste)

politics. Papua New Guinea governments have changed three times between elections, as a result of votes of no confidence.[15] Frustration with this situation led Prime Minister Namaliu, after getting his budget passed in November 1989, simply to adjourn parliament until the following July.

Of the independent states, only Fiji has a bicameral legislature. Ghai has suggested that the absence of bicameral legislatures is surprising, given constitutional commitments to federal, quasi-federal, or decentralised systems of government—second chambers in federations often represent state interests.[16] A number of constitutions, however, provide for separate chambers or councils to represent traditional or chiefly interests, which the legislatures may, or are required to, consult over matters such as land and custom. These are the House of Arikis (Cook Islands), the Great Council of Chiefs (Fiji), Malvatu Mauri (Vanuatu), and the Council of Iroij (Marshall Islands). In normal times these bodies may seem token, but the Great Council of Chiefs emerged as the centre of political manoeuvring and the fount of ethnic Fijian legitimacy after the coups in Fiji and is given an enhanced and fundamental role in the 1990 constitution (its own constitution being unspecified, though there has been discussion in the interim government of reducing and 'purifying' its membership).

Most legislatures are elected by universal adult suffrage. From 1962, Western Samoa restricted the franchise to family heads, *matai*, but universal adult suffrage was introduced after a referendum in 1990. Most countries adopted a first-past-the-post system, in which the person with the largest vote became the winner. In Papua New Guinea particularly, this system has led to some odd results: because the vote was divided evenly among many candidates in the 1987 election the winner in Kerowagi got only 8 per cent of the votes cast.[17] Kiribati and Vanuatu aim for proportional representation through multi-member electorates, in Vanuatu to ensure that the French-speaking minority is represented in parliament.

Fiji divides its voters according to race. The 1970 constitution provided for both communal and cross-communal voting. The 1990 constitution is simpler: voting is entirely within one's own ethnic group. It reserves 37 seats for indigenous Fijians (1:9500), 27 for Indians (1:12 500), 1 for Rotumans, and 5 for other ethnic groups.[18]

In Tonga the electoral bias is in favour of noble families, reserving nine parliamentary seats for 33 noble families (1:4), and nine for 100 000 commoners (1:11 000).

Parties

Political parties in the Pacific Islands provide good examples of the problems (for analysts) of defining and (for activists) of creating and maintaining political institutions. They tend to be created and abandoned with great rapidity: the Papua New Guinea backbencher, Theo Tuya, may have set a recent record, having been a member of four parties in the three years since he was elected.[19] Numbers of members are typically uncertain, and differences in their platforms and regional or class composition are often more apparent to enthusiasts than to outsiders.

Ghai suggests a continuum.[20] In Fiji, the Cook Islands, and Vanuatu parties have played a relatively strong role in candidate selection, campaigning, and formation of governments. At the weak end of the continuum are Kiribati, Tonga, Niue, the Marshall Islands, and Nauru. In the middle are Papua New Guinea, Solomon Islands, and Western Samoa. The difficulty with this approach is the waxing and waning of party strength. In Western Samoa no parties were formed from independence until the 1980s. The Alliance Party in Fiji has practically dissolved since the coups, and the Vanua'aku Pati has been steadily losing popular support and its share of the popular vote, while factions spun off into opposition during the 1980s.

In Solomon Islands every government since independence has been a coalition of parties, until in 1989 the new prime minister announced that his Peoples Alliance Party had become the first single-party government in the country's history. Yet this was achieved by some members of his Cabinet changing parties after the election, and the achievement was somewhat undermined when in October 1990 he sacked five ministers, announced that henceforth he was an 'independent', and appointed opposition members in their place.[21]

In Papua New Guinea's 1987 election, only 37 per cent of candidates were endorsed by a party, and they received only 59 per cent of votes cast. A series of academic election studies has tried to tease out the independent effect of 'party' on voter choice or candidate wins in general elections, with little success. The hunt for parties may also reflect metropolitan biases among politicial scientists (and many islanders). The absence of parties is treated as a deficiency to be made up, or a remedy to be imported from overseas, rather than a normal feature of Pacific politics.

Yet Papua New Guinea's 'Pangu Pati' clearly refers to something: its candidates in 1982 won 34 per cent of the national vote and almost half the seats in parliament.[22] It has some institutional existence, separate from its parliamentary members; it pays a few officials, and has a 'business arm'. Sometimes the institutional autonomy of parties has been maintained by their role as channels for corruption: the polarisation of Cook Islands society into 'Cook Islands Party' and 'Demos' during the 1970s was partly sustained by a flow of official resources such as housing, loans, jobs, and scholarships towards supporters of the Cook Islands Party. A minor version of the same circumstance was observed in Solomon Islands in the mid-1980s and is described later.

The party deficit in the Pacific Islands is sometimes compared with the mass-based nationalist movements in Africa[23] and at other times with parties in modern Westminster systems (rather than the weaker and perhaps more appropriate models of Republicans and Democrats in the United States). Clearly the Westminster system can and has operated without strong political parties—it did for much of the nineteenth century in Australia, for example.

The 'need' for parties is typically discussed in legal constitutional or managerial terms. However, the European experience suggests another focus —on the rise of Labour parties and the coalescence of conservative and Christian democratic opposition to them. A number of examples of attempts to form Labour parties in the Pacific Islands may be cited: the *Botakin Karikirakean Aroia Tan Makuri* (BKATM) in Kiribati and Nationalists in Solomon Islands in the 1970s, and most significantly, the Labour Party in Fiji in the mid-1980s, whose victory in coalition with the National Federation Party in 1987 provoked the reaction that destroyed the constitution. To the extent that 'Labour' emerges as a distinct and oppositional interest, and trade unions form the extraparliamentary infrastructure for a party, they may provoke conservative and Christian interests to form new kinds of parties in opposition.

Bureaucracies

Some pre-colonial systems of government, particularly the 'protostates' that were emerging from chiefly systems in what are now French Polynesia and

Hawai'i, employed permanent officials. Colonial rule was not necessarily or immediately 'bureaucratic' in the Weberian sense of hierarchy, specialisation, rules, careers, and a strong distinction between public office and private life. Some early colonial administrators governed in a highly personal and arbitrary way (while some of Papua New Guinea's *kiaps* ran their own businesses on the side). However, in the Cook Islands, for example, metropolitan appointment gradually replaced local elections in the choice of officials, and written laws replaced unwritten customs.[24] The separation of colonial officials from the society they governed was emphasised by racial exclusivity. Highly detailed codes of 'native regulations' testify to the bureaucratic supervision of daily life.

A world-wide expansion of state activity after World War Two had its Pacific counterpart in 'welfare colonialism', expressed in trusteeship agreements and still reflected in the worthy work programme of the South Pacific Commission. Increasing involvement of the government in infrastructure and social services drew in specialised professionals and technicians. The Papua New Guinea public service, for example, grew in size from 1300 public servants in 1950, to 29 000 at independence in 1975, going on to peak at 51 000 in 1980, before entering a period of restraint and reductions in the 1980s.[25] In Western Samoa, there were about 350 positions in the Western Samoan 'native administration' when New Zealand took the country over, or 1 for every 110 people.[26] By the mid-1980s the 'public sector' had grown to about 4700 people, or 1 for every 34 people.[27] On that basis, Western Samoa had become about three times as intensively governed.[28]

Bureaucracies in the Pacific Islands are now regularly and dogmatically criticised by local politicians, international aid agencies, and banks as being 'too large'. Though they loom large in the countries' cash economies, they are nevertheless thin on the ground, particularly in Melanesia. On average, public sector employees amount to 3.5 per cent of population in the independent states, or about the same as in other developing countries (3.7 per cent), but less than half the number in advanced industrial countries (9.05 per cent).[29] In the largest country, Papua New Guinea, the public service—central and provincial—amounts to only 2.2 per cent of the population (and of those a national manpower assessment found that 42 per cent failed to meet the qualifications set down for their positions by the Public Service Commission).[30]

Relations between permanent officials and elected ministers are frequently tense, in the Pacific as elsewhere. In Papua New Guinea the courts have become involved in several rows, notably between Police Minister Warren Dutton and Commissioner of Police Philip Bouraga, where the court found awkwardly that the minister had no constitutional powers of 'direction and control' over department heads, other than those set out in specific legislation, or delegated by Cabinet (though Cabinet could sack department heads, which threat might induce co-operation).[31] Westminster systems seem to make particularly heavy weather of the relationship between agency heads and politicians, trying to draw imaginary lines through inevitably shared tasks. In the Pacific Islands the similarity of roles between ministers and heads of departments is often underlined by the identity of occupants: senior officials resign (as late as possible) to become politicians, and defeated politicians slip back into the public service.

Judiciary

On a number of occasions, judges have successfully held up their interpretations of the law against the executives of Pacific Island governments. In the Cook Islands in 1978 a decision by the chief justice to disallow the votes of supporters flown in from New Zealand ended thirteen years of rule by Albert Henry. Because their votes had been enough to decide the election, the chief justice reversed the results, giving the opposition 16 seats to the Cook Islands Party's 6, and making Dr Tom Davis premier.

In Papua New Guinea in 1979 a minister, Nahau Rooney, was briefly jailed in a confrontation between the executive and the judiciary over a deportation decision. She had written to the High Court, criticising it for setting aside the deportation order. In her letter and a subsequent broadcast she argued that it was the right of the executive, and particularly Papua New Guineans rather than foreign judges, to decide which foreigners could stay in the country. She was charged and convicted for contempt of court, but released on the licence of the prime minister. The chief justice resigned. The Papua New Guinea government has been rebuffed by the courts on a number of other matters, but Papua New Guinea's judicial institutions have not been able to come to grips with well-documented examples of abuse of power by security forces on Bougainville, the subject of criticism from Amnesty International.

In 1988 in Vanuatu, when the president announced the dissolution of parliament, and swore in an alternative interim government, parliament continued to sit, and Prime Minister Walter Lini declared the interim government illegal. The president appealed to the police for support, but was silenced by an order of the Supreme Court while parliament passed a vote of no confidence in him. He was arrested on charges of incitement to mutiny, conferring an illegal oath, and making a seditious statement.[32] He and the five members of his alternative government were tried and convicted, but were acquitted in April 1989 on appeal to the Supreme Court.

A brief show of judicial independence of the exceutive in Fiji immediately followed the first coup, when Governor General Ratu Sir Penaia Ganilau seemed to lean towards accepting the overthrow of the government. Chief Justice Sir Timoci Tuivaga, and several other judges, wrote reminding him that 'the purported suspension of the Constitution of Fiji by the military regime which has assumed de facto power is illegal and invalid'.[33]

The army

Fiji and Papua New Guinea inherited armies when they became independent, and Tonga has a smaller military force whose loyalty may become significant in a crisis. Fiji's armed forces numbered 2500 at the time of the first coup, and grew to 6000 by the end of the year.[34] Papua New Guinea's number about 3400.

Saffu has described how, when Papua New Guinea's constitution was being drawn up, some people argued that the army should be given a direct role in government in order to forestall the possibility of coups.[35] Similar proposals for the institutionalisation of military political influence were made in Fiji after 1987. The 1990 constitution provides more conventionally for a minister responsible for defence and security, but also gives broad responsibility directly to the army.[36] Proposals have been made for the creation of military forces in Kiribati and Solomon Islands, and Papua New Guinea's former Prime Minister Sir Julius Chan has proposed a regional peacekeeping force.

Several confrontations between the executive and the army in Papua New Guinea have generally arisen out of military frustration with government policy or pay. In 1977 Commander Ted Diro held an unauthorised meeting with Seth Rumkorem, a leader of the anti-Indonesian guerrillas in Irian Jaya. Anticipating his dismissal by a Cabinet fearful of offending the Indonesian government, senior officers plotted to kidnap the Cabinet members and hold them hostage until they reconsidered their policies towards Indonesia. In the event, Diro was reprimanded rather than dismissed, and his supporters called off 'The Coup that Never Was'.[37]

In 1988, the army flew troops to Lae and cordoned off the airfield to prevent its closure by the Department of Civil Aviation, implementing a Cabinet decision to shift civil and military operations to a larger airport farther out of town. In 1989 about four hundred soldiers in Port Moresby rioted, ignored their officers, and marched on parliament over a long-running dispute about pay and conditions. The police too have protested about government policy, particularly on Bougainville. In March 1989, a squad turned up outside the house of Minister for Decentralisation Father Momis, pressing him not to sack Police Commissioner Paul Tohian, who had just publicly criticised the government for its 'indecisiveness' in dealing with the Bougainville rebels.[38] When the security forces were withdrawn from Bougainville after the ceasefire another rumour of his sacking provoked Tohian to leave a barbecue and summon his officers by radio to meet him outside parliament—the so-called 'Bar Be Coup'. But the army and the deputy police commissioner remained loyal.

Military and police interventions in the Papua New Guinea political system have concerned threats of dismissal, pay, and military and police policy. By and large, the perpetrators have been pursuing their own institutional interests, including exempting themselves from the rules applying to other government agencies and private citizens. The army's intervention in Fiji's politics in 1987 was much more ambitious. The policies of the newly elected coalition government were not particularly threatening to the institutional interests of the military (though Colonel Rabuka did invoke the excuse that the army would have been reluctant to get involved in putting down Fijian violence against the new government).

In May 1987, soldiers arrested and sequestered the newly elected Fiji Labour–National Federation Party Coalition Cabinet. The governor general, though sympathetic to Rabuka and his aspirations, backed away from recognising the coup. The Cabinet members were released, but Rabuka and former Alliance Party politicians were appointed to a Council of Advisers. In September they stepped in once again to prevent the implementation of a compromise between the Alliance and the deposed Coalition engineered by the governor general. The soldiers' goals were substantially achieved in the new constitution promulgated in 1990, which provided for a permanent predominance of ethnic Fijians in Parliament, and in the executive. During this period the army grew in numbers and budget autonomy. Rabuka proposed that it might go into primary production on its own behalf (and so—by implication—depend less on the executive or the legislature for funding).

Society, territory, and economy

The ways in which the constellation of institutions relates to the wider society, territory, and economy are examined in this section. Each of these relationships has been problematic in the Pacific Islands.

Society

The relationship between the political system and society may be considered in several ways: first by asking how accurately its composition mirrors the composition of the society it governs; second by looking at the degree of participation of ordinary members of society in the political system (measured, say, by voter turnout); and third by looking at intermediary institutions, such as the press and—particularly in the Pacific Islands—churches.

Colonial political systems were typically unrepresentative of the societies they governed, though some mutual adjustment took place. They were staffed by outsiders and operated under laws and assumptions that often differed from those prevailing in the local society. Decolonisation promised more local people in senior positions, laws that reflected local customs, and services provided to where people lived in rural areas, rather than mainly to the towns. Achievement of this closer correspondence has been slow, and an 'organic' relationship between state and society may not be achievable any-where. In Papua New Guinea, for example, naturalised citizens continue to be overrepresented in parliament, and senior technical and professional positions continue to be held by foreigners, though the overall percentage of foreigners in the public service fell from 14 per cent at independence to 6 per cent in 1984.[39] Despite a series of reports from the Law Reform Commission, customary principles have made little impact on the law. An urban bias persists in the provision of services throughout the Pacific.

Colonial history often also provided a distinctive regional face to particu-lar political institutions. Papuans in Papua New Guinea, for example, were overrepresented in senior ranks of the army and parts of the bureaucracy at independence.[40]

Of course, political leaders may not see that a statistical representation of society is necessary or relevant: chiefs lead, they might say, rather than follow. Tonga's political system is a distorted reflection of Tongan society, biased in favour of the nobility, while Fiji's 1990 constitution provides that whatever the demographic situation, the political system will reflect a pre-dominantly Fijian face (particularly *rural* Fijian). And in every country, though no constitutional barriers to women exist, the face presented by the political system is overwhelmingly masculine.

Participation in the political systems can be measured by such elements as numbers of candidates standing for election, and voter turnout. In most countries, both measures seem high. In Papua New Guinea in 1987, for example, an average of 14 candidates campaigned for each seat, an increase of 35 per cent over the last election.[41] In Vanuatu in 1979, 92 per cent of registered voters went to the polls.[42] Levels of turnout have been particu-larly crucial in Fiji elections.[43] Other measures of participation include turnout in referenda, and at meetings organised by the select committees enquiring into constitutional status, land policy, or decentralisation that have become a feature of politics in Melanesia. Solomon Islands 1987 Constitution Review Committee reported the activities of fourteen differ-ent subcommittees that held public meetings in villages throughout the country.[44]

Other institutions mediate between the political system and the society. The influence of newspapers is circumscribed by problems of distribution outside cities as well as limits on literacy. They depend heavily on capital and stories from overseas owners. In their local political news they tend to stick closely to the comings and goings of politicians, judges, and senior officials. To that extent it may be more sensible to treat them as insiders in the political systems of Pacific Island states, rather than as major social institutions linking the political system to the wider society. But as insiders they are often knowledgeable and critical of hypocrisy and abuse of power, and governments have shown increasing impatience with unflattering reports. Fiji's daily press has been self-censored since the coups.

In the former British, Australian, and New Zealand colonies, radio has been kept firmly under the control of the executives. Television has posed a dilemma for independent governments. The Papua New Guinea government has repeatedly toyed with government ownership of television, through the National Broadcasting Commission, or more recently as a shareholder in an established broadcast network. However, the logic of large investment and running costs, facilitation by some politically astute appointments to boards, and appeals to the courts have led to foreign ownership. Nevertheless, licensing, work permits, and the cost of gathering news outside press conferences and lobbies have kept the political reporting of these media determinedly bland. Meanwhile, direct broadcasting from satellite, retailed through private cable networks, has circumvented national government regulation.

The Christian churches have come to play a distinctive role in relating political system to society in the Pacific Islands. Christian missions were influential in state-building in Polynesia and continue to provide public services such as education and hospitals that are elsewhere provided by governments. The Roman Catholic bishop in Tonga provides a focus for liberal democratic criticism of the executive. Roman Catholic church members have been closely involved on both sides in the Bougainville secession, with the bishop becoming a minister in the secessionist government, and Father Momis the national minister responsible for decentralisation. Papua New Guinea churches support the liberal-campaigning *Times of Papua New Guinea*, which circulates among the elite. The Roman Catholic church was prominent in the campaign against the fishing treaties with the Russians in Kiribati in the early 1980s. Support for the Fiji coups had strong undertones of Methodism: a decree protecting the sabbath was one of the first promulgated after the second coup. A new wave of evangelical churches has played an active, politically conservative role in political campaigns, being significant in the general election in the Papua New Guinea Highlands in 1982.

Territory

The relationship between the political system and territory is particularly problematic in Melanesia, where it is reflected in separatist movements like that on Bougainville, and in Micronesia, where it has led to the adoption of decentralised or federal systems of government like those of Palau or the Federated States of Micronesia. There are several reasons.

First, colonial states typically incorporated a number of smaller political systems: separatist leaders could claim that independence should restore their traditional autonomy, rather than resubjugate them to a distant capital, or a different ethnic group.

Second, whatever their geographic scope, colonial governments were typically more centralised than their predecessors. Centralisation tended to privilege those who lived around the colonial centres of power and got earlier access to jobs and education. These privileges in turn created resentment among more distant, or more lately incorporated, populations. Tensions between Highlanders and Papuans, and the protection of earlier Papuan privileges was one of the factors behind the drive for Papuan separatism at independence.

Secessionist movements surfaced at independence in western Solomon Islands, on Santo and Tanna in Vanuatu, on Banaba in Kiribati, and in Rotuma after the Fiji coups, but the most persistent and violent secession movement has been on Bougainville. The first attempt was at Papua New Guinea's independence, which Bougainville leaders refused to acknowledge while they petitioned the United Nations for separate independence, blockaded airfields, and took over government buildings. They were persuaded to return by promises to change the constitution to provide for a greater degree of devolution to the provincial government already in place in Bougainville, and to provide constitutional entrenchment of its autonomy.

The second round began in a dispute between Bougainville landowners, the national government, and the mining company, Conzinc Riotinto of Australia, the main owners and operators of the Bougainville copper mine. In late 1988, when landowners first turned to sabotage to press their claim for compensation for environmental damage, the provincial government sided with the national government. As repression by the security forces increasingly alienated public opinion on Bougainville, the attacks on the mine spread into a broader rejection of government authority and foreign presence on the island, culminating in the declaration of independence and the withdrawal of government security forces in March 1990. After one round of negotiations in August, government forces retook the offshore island of Buka, but the mainland of Bougainville remained isolated.

While the Melanesian colonial territories became independent more or less united, the US Trust Territory of the Pacific Islands has systematically divided itself up, through a series of referenda, at the level of colonial districts and (on Palau) subdistricts. A proposed federal constitution for the whole trust territory was accepted by only three districts, which now form the Federated States of Micronesia (one district subsequently divided itself into two). Such separatism is not simply a transitional anxiety of independence, to be dissolved into future national unity. It is a continuing theme in constitutional reviews: Solomon Islands Constitution Review in 1987 recommended a federal system, and the majority of submissions to the second FSM constitutional review favoured greater decentralisation.

Economy

Theories of imperialism explain the extension of colonial government to the Pacific Islands in fundamentally economic terms. Contemporary promoters of colonialism promised economic benefits, and German colonial rule was introduced through trading companies that took on the powers of governments. The French government was itself a shareholder in the *Société Française des Nouvelles-Hébrides*, the largest foreign landowner in colonial Vanuatu. Colonial officials may have conceived of their own role in more high-minded terms, but they were compelled by budgetary pressures to promote agricultural production for export to generate revenue they could tax to fund government operations. Big companies like the Colonial Sugar Refining Company in Fiji and Unilever in Solomon Islands were influential in colonial politics, initiating a strong colonial tradition of interventionist policy.

Nevertheless, the ability or willingness of political executives to influence local economies seems to have become more limited. The islands' domestic markets are small, and the countries that became independent between 1962 and 1980 were faced with an increasingly interdependent world economy. Indigenous sources of capital were limited, and management skills stretched. Even if there was scope, many lost the will to intervene, coming under the influence of doctrines of deregulation and privatisation promoted by donor governments, banks, and lending agencies throughout the Third World.

The relationship between the political system and the economy has several dimensions. First is the question of the state itself as producer or distributor. In default of private enterprise, or as a matter of policy, colonial governments involved themselves in agriculture, mining, trading, and tourism. In New Caledonia, a pro-independence provincial government has bought into a nickel-mining company, and in Papua New Guinea political parties and provincial governments possess 'business arms'. Economic nationalism encourages the extension of such activities. Doctrines of privatisation, and the provision of openings for indigenous capitalists (who are often politicians themselves), favour their divestment. In Papua New Guinea in the 1980s the executive often spoke in two voices: some ministers on occasion favouring nationalisation, and others opting for privatisation and deregulation. Fiji's economic policy since the coups has been similarly driven in two directions: the atmosphere of crisis and the absence of parliamentary opposition has allowed officials to introduce deregulatory, wage-cutting policies that have encouraged private foreign investment. Yet the press of Fijian nationalism demands greater intervention for affirmative action on behalf of indigenous Fijians, and the army itself has gone into business.

Second, short of public ownership, is the use of regulatory powers to give particular groups advantage over others, domestic or foreign. Colonial governments were often accused of using regulations to favour European commercial interests over those of indigenous people. Indigenous politicians continue to complain that banks favour foreigners, or non-indigenous citizens, in their lending policies. State and provincial governments are often under pressure to adopt hiring and contracting policies that will favour people and companies from their own state or province.

Third is the issue of official corruption. Regulation, public ownership, and privatisation all provide opportunities to divert government resources to personal, clan, or party use. Tradition or custom often provides a convenient cloak. Examples often come to light only with changes of government, as in the Cook Islands in 1978, or when specific institutions like Papua New Guinea's Ombudsman Commission, whose job includes enforcement of a Leadership Code, are created and continuously staffed and funded to uncover them. Papua New Guinea provides itself with the most documented examples of official corruption—in the granting of forestry licences, in preferences given to senior ministers in the purchase of shares, in the purchase of official appointment diaries, in grants of land in the capital city. Similar enquiries in Solomon Islands have uncovered corruption in the sale of government housing and in forestry licensing. In New Caledonia, the newly created Land Reform Agency has been found to have transferred land not to its traditional Melanesian owners, but cheaply to European supporters of the government. In less open and self-critical political systems, accusations of corruption are stifled, or discounted as rumour, disrespect, or lack of patriotism.

Fourth, in the relationship between the political system and the economy are two aspects of the politics of budgeting. On the one hand, most island governments continue to rely on foreign aid to fund part of their budget expenditure (even if it is described as public investment). Fiji's budget is more self-sufficient than most, though the artifically high price paid for its sugar exports is foreign aid in a more dignified form.[45] The intergovernmental aspects of aid dependency are outside the scope of this chapter, except to note that the alternatives to foreign aid are increased local taxes or lower standards of public services. The level and incidence of taxation are highly political questions, with potentially sharp impacts on the relationship between political system and society. Vanuatu and French Polynesia, for example, still have to face the political trauma of introducing an income tax. Taxes on exports fall disproportionately on rural producers, whereas taxes on imports fall disproportionately on urban workers: in imposing them, political executives must make political calculations about the levels of unrest they can tolerate, as well as judgments about their economic impact.

Finally, questions about state and economy raised by Marxist accounts of Pacific Island politics must be considered. Simple versions reduce the relationship between economy and political system to a determination by the former of the latter. More recent accounts grant the political system some 'relative autonomy'. One element, the issue of the political conditions for, and consequences of, the formation of economic classes, has already been noted in the discussion of Labour parties.

Class analysis is notoriously difficult in developing countries, with their multiplicity of overlapping and intermediate class positions (and powerful actors often absent internationally). That the most well organised workers are often public servants, who may be running businesses on the side, complicates relationships between class and politics. Actors may not recognise themselves in the class analyses made by organisers or academics: objective classes 'in themselves' often disappointingly fail to become subjective classes 'for themselves'.

Contrary to views that little difference exists between party policies in Papua New Guinea, S. MacWilliam has explained divisions and alliances between coalition partners in governments in the 1980s,[46] and their policies towards manufacturing as against agriculture, in terms of the different interests of indigenous and international capital—differences between factions of the bourgeoisie, rather than between bourgeoisie and proletariat.

Several accounts of the Fiji coups emphasise their class as well as their ethnic character, noting the formation of the Labour Party in response to the wage freeze of the mid-1980s, the progressive character of its manifesto, the small but crucial shift of urban Fijian votes from the Alliance, and the economic interests of the Alliance Party politicians who were restored to power by the first coup.[47] A class analysis, however, has less purchase on the motivations of Rabuka and the *taukei* who actually carried out the coups. Nevertheless, the Fijian nationalism to which they successfully appealed had strong economic undertones, expressed in the proposals for job reservation and affirmative action for Fijians. There is also a strong class content to the policy of economic recovery followed by the post-coup regimes, for example in wages and working conditions in its tax free-zones.

Conclusions

Society, territory, and economy act together on the political system in what is one of the defining characteristics of the region: its relatively high rate of labour migration, inward and outward. The political consequences of immigration are expressed in the three violent crises of the late 1980s. Tensions created by the influx of migrant and contract labour to Bougainville helped generalise specific grievances about the mine to a province-wide revolt and the expulsion of nearly all non-Bougainvilleans. Tensions between indigenous Fijians and the descendants of Indian and other immigrants provided popular Fijian sympathy for Rabuka's coups. Tensions between traditional landowners around Port Vila and migrants from other parts of Vanuatu contributed to the unrest that culminated in the arrest of the president and his proposed prime minister (also his nephew), who came from villages with rights over land in the capital. Some of these immigrations have been so large as to withdraw the territories from regular modern consideration as 'Pacific Islands' (e.g., New Zealand, Hawai'i, and often Guam).

Emigration has also had political consequences, leaving behind people who are relatively undereducated, very old, or very young, and creating influential émigré groups, concerned to influence the politics back home. The fly-in voters in the Cook Islands are a good example, and a special overseas seat in parliament has since been created for Cook Islanders resident in New Zealand and elsewhere in the world. The Tongan nobility is rightly nervous of the power of relatively richer and better educated Tongans overseas to influence events back home. Emigrés from Fiji since the coups also maintain pressure on foreign governments to keep up their criticism of the new constitutional arrangements.

The last territory to become constitutionally independent was Vanuatu as long ago as 1980, while the protracted political status negotiations between the United States and the former Trust Territory of the Pacific Islands, begun in the 1960s, are still unresolved in relation to Palau. Palau's adopted constitution prohibits nuclear weapons, and the United States insists that the Compact of Free Association requires their presence. Late in 1990 the United States seemed to be restoring some kind of direct rule over Palau. Meanwhile, the political crisis in New Caledonia has been defused by another kind of direct rule from Paris, precisely by putting off until 1998 any further decisions on decolonisation. To use the language of postmodernism, the 'grand narrative' of decolonisation seems to have broken down into a series of more local, and contradictory, resolutions.

Related is the question of violence. Analysts and journalists used to join regional and metropolitan leaders in celebrating the peacefulness of change in political institutions in the Pacific Islands (forgetting, for example, the violence on the Gazelle Peninsula that precipitated Australia's withdrawal from what became Papua New Guinea). Events of the late 1980s—the kidnapping of soldiers, seige, and massacre of Kanak nationalists at Ouvea in New Caledonia; Fiji's coups; Papua New Guinea's crime problems; and Bougainville's secession—have encouraged a counter myth, of 'trouble in paradise'. Given the diversity of the region, any assessment of the prospects for stability and change in political institutions depends heavily on the assumptions brought to bear. These necessarily include assumptions about what (if anything) drives history. Facts do not speak for themselves, and evidence can be found for quite contradictory generalisations.

* * *

I AM GRATEFUL for comments on an earlier draft by Ron Crocombe, Yaw Saffu, and Scott MacWilliam, but remain responsible for remaining errors.

Notes

1 Payback is a good example: wrongs such as killing or adultery were often regarded as political matters, involving collisions between groups, whereas introduced legislation treats them as criminal matters, between individuals and the state.

2 'At the moment there's confusion between legal, constitutional rights that the chief and every person has, and the distinct authority of the chief, which doesn't have the support of the constitution or the legal system' (Walter Lini, *Pacific Islands Monthly*, September 1990).

3 Mālama Meleiseā, *The Making of Modern Samoa*, University of the South Pacific, Suva, 1987.

4 Lini, 1990.

5 As it was when the governor general dismissed the Australian prime minister in 1975.

6 Quoted in R. Robertson and A. Tamanisau, *Fiji: Shattered Coups*, Pluto Press, Sydney, 1988, 81.

7 Section 13 (2) (b) of 'The Constitution of the Cook Islands', in *Selected Constitutions of the Pacific Islands*, Extension Services, University of the South Pacific, Suva, 1980, 21–54, 28.

8 Section 83 (2) of *Constitution of the Sovereign Democratic Republic of Fiji*, Government Printer, Suva, 1990, 80.

9 Meleiseā, 114.

10 Marshall Sahlins, 'Poor Man, Rich Man, Big-Man, Chief: Political Types in Melanesia and Polynesia', *Comparative Studies in Society and History* 5 (1962): 285–303.

11 B. Standish, 'The Big-Man Model Reconsidered: Power and Stratification in Chimbu', Discussion Paper no. 22, IASER, Port Moresby, 1978; Bronwen Douglas, 'Rank, Power, Authority: A Reassessment of Traditional Leadership in South Pacific Societies', *Journal of Pacific History* 14 (1, 1979): 2–27; see also Lamont Lindstrom, '"Big-Man": A Short Terminological History', *American Anthropologist* 83 (1981): 900–905; and Lindstrom, 'Doctor, Lawyer, Wise Man, Priest: Big-Men and Knowledge in Melanesia', *Man* 19 (1984): 291–301, on the 'big-man' category.

12 Laura Souder-Jaffrey, 'A Not So Perfect Union: Federal-Territorial Relations between the United States and Guam', in *Chamorro Self-Determination*, ed. Laura Souder-Jaffrey and Robert Underwood, Chamorro Studies Association, Guam, 7–32; P. Souder, 'Guam', in *Land Tenure in the Pacific*, ed. R. Crocombe, 3rd edn, Institute of Pacific Studies, Suva, 211–225, 218.

13 Yash Ghai, 'Systems of Government: I' and 'Systems of Government: II', in *Law, Politics and Government in the Pacific Island States*, University of the South Pacific, Suva, 1988, 54–105.

14 The executive is protected during a six-month honeymoon period, by the provision that successful votes of no confidence towards the end of the parliamentary term simply bring forward a general election, and by requiring its movers to nominate an alternative prime minister.

15 From Somare to Chan in 1980, Somare to Wingti in 1985, Wingti to Namaliu in 1988; see S. Dorney, *Papua New Guinea*, Random House, Sydney, 1990, 62–82.

16 Ghai, 61–62.

17 Dorney, 58.

18 The *Sydney Morning Herald* of 13 December 1989 quoted the Fiji Bureau of Statistics, and gave the following population figures: Fijians, 351 966; Indians 337 557; total, including Rotumans and others 727 104. During the year 8500 people had left; more have probably done so since.

19 *Islands Business*, December 1990.

20 Ghai, 69.

21 *Islands Business*, November 1990. This was a repeat of a similar tactic used in the mid-1970s.

22 Dorney, 66.

23 The Vanua'aku Pati has been the nearest thing to a mass-based nationalist movement on the African model.

24 R. Gilson, *The Cook Islands 1820–1950*, University of the South Pacific and Victoria University Press, Suva and Wellington, 1980.

25 O. Diwedi, 'The Growth of the Public Service in Papua New Guinea', in *The Public Service of Papua New Guinea*, ed. O. Diwedi and N. Paulias, Administrative College of Papua New Guinea, Boroko, 1986, 72–89.

26 Meleiseā, 107.

27 Asian Development Bank, *Economic Survey on Western Samoa*, Report no. SAM:Ec-85, Asian Development Bank, Manila, 1988, 13.

28 There would also be a number of expatriate officials constituting the colonial government, partly counterbalanced by expatriate advisers that may not be counted under the 'public service' after independence.

29 Country statistics for 1988–1989 from national development plans held in the National Centre for Development Studies, Canberra. Average figures are for 1979–1981, in P. S. Heller and A. A. Tait, *Government Employment and Pay: Some International Comparisons*, Occasional Paper no. 24, World Bank, Washington, DC, 1983, Table 1.

30 P. Berlin, 'Public Sector Management in Papua New Guinea: An Adminstrative Overview', mimeo, no. SR104345/J111942/D3851/41, World Bank, Washington, DC, 1983.

31 Yash Ghai and David Hegarty, 'Ministerial and Bureaucratic Power in Papua New Guinea: Aspects of the Bouraga/Dutton Dispute', in *Pacific Constitutions*, ed. Peter Sack, Law Department, Research School of Social Sciences, Australian National University, Canberra, 1982.

32 *Islands Business*, January 1989.

33 Brij V. Lal, *Power and Prejudice: The Making of the Fiji Crisis*, New Zealand Institute of International Affairs, Wellington, 1988, 82.

34 Yaw Saffu, 'Changing Civil–Military Relations in Fiji', *Australian Journal of International Affairs* 44 (2, 1990): 159–170; 164.

35 Yaw Saffu, 'Military Roles and Relations in Papua New Guinea', paper presented to conference, The Armed Forces in Asia and the Pacific: Prospects for the 1990s, Department of Political and Social Change, Research School of Pacific Studies, Australian National University, Canberra, 1989.

36 Sections 85 (2), and 94 of *Constitution of . . . Fiji*, 1990, 82, 86.

37 Dorney, 201.

38 Dorney, 139.

39 Dwivedi, 74.

40 Dorney, 206.

41 M. Turner 'Gender, Age and Education of Candidates and Members', in *Eleksin: The 1987 Election in Papua New Guinea*, ed. M. Oliver, University of Papua New Guinea, Port Moresby, 1989, 5.

42 Turner, 5.

43 Brij V. Lal, ed., *Politics in Fiji: Studies in Contemporary History*, Institute for Polynesian Studies, Lāʻie, Hawaiʻi, 1986, 89.

44 Solomon Islands, *1987 Constitution Review Committee Report*, Solomon Mamaloni, Chair, Government Printer, Honiara, 1988.

45 M. Taylor, 'Issues in Fiji's Development: Economic Rationality or Aid with Dignity', in *Fiji: Future Imperfect*, ed. M. Taylor, Allen & Unwin, Sydney, 1987.

46 S. MacWilliam, 'Shifts in Post-Colonial Political Power: Papua New Guinea 1972–87', paper presented to Australian Political Studies Association, University of New South Wales, September 1989.

47 See, for example, Robertson and Tamanisau 1988.

17

Representations of
cultural identities

Vilsoni Hereniko

Like eunuchs, they grace the shoreline of Waikīkī. Coconut palms without coconuts. Symbols of lost identities. Exotic images as a backdrop for semi-naked tourists lounging on the beach.

Coconut palms have grown at Waikīkī since the first Hawaiians arrived in their magnificent canoes some two thousand years ago. Originating in the South-East Asian–Melanesian region, coconuts were carried in the canoes of early long-distance navigators of the Pacific Ocean. Coconut palms were much valued then—for the many different uses of their roots, trunks, and leaves, but mainly for their nuts, which provided a reliable source of sustenance. Coconut flesh was scraped and its cream used for cooking; coconut juice was refreshing and nourishing—ideal for a tropical climate. But all that has changed forever, at least at Waikīkī, where tourists now reign. There, coconut palms are merely decorative, essential to complete the picture of Paradise—a tropical world of pleasure and personal happiness. To maintain this illusion, coconuts are removed so that dreams of Eden may remain intact.

Robert Muldoon, a former prime minister of New Zealand, once referred to the Pacific Islands as having little to offer apart from coconuts. Likewise, in Auckland, where Polynesians are increasingly visible, the pakeha (white) population sometimes refers to islanders as 'coconuts', a metaphor with connotations akin to 'nigger'. Migrants who return to the islands only to behave in a European fashion are also labelled 'coconuts' by their compatriots—like coconuts, they are brown outside but white inside. Despite such pejorative use, however, among Melanesians, Micronesians, and Polynesians the word *coconut* continues to evoke feelings of a shared identity.

Similarly, literature and art are symbolic expressions of cultural identities, embodying their creators' visions of who they were, are, or could be. These visions encompass one or more aspects of culture, such as ethnicity, geographical context, gender, and politics. Although foreign scholars tend to view each of these as discrete entities, Pacific Islanders regard all aspects of life as inseparable parts of who they are.[1] Although the focus here is primarily on the way literature and art embody and express cultural identities, I also discuss significant cultural, historical, or political events that have dramatically affected the formation of those identities. Just as explicit expressions of identity may or may not accurately reflect internalised notions of self at the personal level, our views of who we are may or may not coincide with other people's views of us. Our cultural identities are therefore always in a state of becoming, a journey in which we never arrive; who we are is not a rock that is passed on from generation to generation, fixed and unchanging. Yet, like Maui who tried to snare the sun as it journeyed across the sky (so he thought), I shall snare a metaphorical sun, hold it still for a moment that we may see it more clearly, then set it free again to continue its journey. After all, cultural identity is process, not product.

Signposts exist along the way to help us understand who we are. The oral histories, imaginative literature, and the visual and performing arts of the Pacific Islands indicate significant moments in the evolution of cultural identities. At the national level, these moments may or may not reflect what actually happens at the level of everyday behaviour in rural villages. However, because the ruling elite at the national level are in a position to impose on the people their official versions of the national identity (but not the other way round), their views affect national policies and influence international thought. Besides, the educated elite who live in urban areas or in metropolitan countries are becoming increasingly influential in shaping cultural identities in their home islands through remittances. Most of the indigenous sources I use, then, are primarily the views of the educated or ruling elite. It is their view of what makes them different from or similar to other groups of people—their cultural identities—that I analyse and discuss.

To help analysis and discussion, I divide Pacific history into three phases using a Rotuman standpoint that corresponds to the perspective of other Pacific groups: *ao maksul ta* (time of darkness), *ao taf ta* (time of light), and *ao fo'ou ta* (new time). These three phases coincide with the Euro-American categories of pre-colonial, colonial, and post-colonial. Although these two different ways of discussing history are similar in that they appear to use European intrusion into the Pacific as their basic point of departure for categorisation (missionisation in the Rotuman view; colonialism in the European), there is an essential difference. The Rotuman, or what I shall refer to from now on as the islander perspective, highlights the importance of Christianity in the shaping of Pacific cultural identities, revealing, in a nutshell, that cultural identity was contested during the time of darkness, transformed (with certain elements suppressed) during the time of light, and negotiable during the new time.

At the 1989 Festival of Marquesan Arts in Taioha'e, Marquesan drummers played Tahitian rhythms on Tahitian drums and wore tapa stained with 'ena (turmeric) and adorned with motifs associated with Marquesan tattooing. They also wore pandanus garlands and mother-of-pearl headdresses to which carved coconut medallions were attached. Guitar playing followed the drumming. (Jane Moulin)

Ao maksul ta: *Time of darkness*

Pacific Islanders shared a circular view of life. Donna Awatere has written of Maori notions in which 'past and present merge in the cyclic rhythm of nature and the ancestors' rhythm of life and death'.[2] Albert Wendt, the Samoan poet and novelist, referred to this period in history as the time of 'Pouliuli, the Great Darkness out of which we came and to which we must all return'.[3] This circle of life has no beginning and no end, and each living thing is part of that circle. At the centre are the gods of the ancestors. These gods maintain the unity of the circle from within, as well as attract attention from the periphery. This non-linear view of life contrasts with the Western view of the evolution of civilisation, marked by development and progress. Using this yardstick as a way of judging Pacific cultures, the *papalagi* (skybreakers) regarded the islanders as 'primitive' or 'uncivilised', at the low end of the civilisation continuum. Further, this linear perspective designated the time of darkness as one that was relatively static and simple. Such a view is not shared in the oral histories of the islands.

Darkness in Polynesian conception was fluid and ambiguous: Hine Nui te Po (literally, the Lady of Darkness) was originally the Lady of Light, an embodiment of double identities, with a vagina that is the site of birth and the locus of death.[4] Such ambivalence is evident in many of the creation myths, including the Hawaiian *Kumulipo*, which includes both natural and supernatural forces in its evolutionary account of creation.[5] Further, many of the myths, legends, chants, and songs of the Pacific contain complex accounts of sea exploits and navigational feats that suggest a dynamic period of contact between islands, conflict, and settlement. For example, the oral history of Pohnpei in Micronesia reveals conquests by successive groups of people from outside, with accompanying changes in social practice and the introduction of new skills and knowledge. 'Polynesians' in Pohnpei and Kosrae in perhaps the twelfth or thirteenth century produced enormous changes in social structures, introducing *kava* and other Polynesian elements, and leaving the islands with massive stone ruins that are a notable tourist attraction today.[6] On Pohnpei, attempts were made to extend domination island-wide; the same was true of Samoa and the Marshall Islands.[7] New Caledonia was deeply divided, with 'warring tribes speaking mutually unintelligible languages',[8] and on Santa Isabel in the Solomon Islands an extensive military capacity was reported by the first Spanish explorers.[9]

This phase in Pacific history produced some of the most dynamic and imaginative art forms, testimony to a time of fervent attempts to understand the universe, religious preoccupation, and territorial expansion, particularly within island entities. Witness, for example, the elaborate and magnificent war clubs, spears, canoes, carvings, statues, and ceremonial objects of this period that still exist in museums and private collections around the world. This artistic excellence was most marked in the larger continental or volcanic islands of Melanesia and Polynesia, where tribal conflict was a dominant feature. Instead of hindering artistic production, political rivalry and conflicting ideologies probably acted as catalysts for the production of art. Contemporary developments in the Pacific indicate that during times of conflict, the artists and the arts become a focal point for cultural and spiritual sustenance.

Drawing from their surroundings, artists created objects or songs and dances that served practical or religious purposes. The weaving of fine mats for ceremonial exchange, the carving of ritual objects, the building of spirit houses, the preparation of costumes for dramatic performances—all these and many more activities embodied 'aspirations, visions, fears, hopes and dreams',[10] not just of the immediate and known environment, but of the lands and peoples beyond the seas. For example, Micronesian art reveals influences from Indonesia and Melanesia. Evidences of contact include the loom weaving of the Caroline Islands, the dance masks from Satawan in the Mortlock Islands (Chuuk), and pearlshell inlay in Belauan bowls.[11] Many songs, dances, plants, and fruit trees maintain the names of islands whence they came. Some plants and fruit trees in Rotuma bear Tongan or Samoan names, and accounts of Samoan storytelling performances attribute the existence of rats, thornbushes, nettles, and noxious weeds to Fiji.[12] Such evidence indicates much borrowing from other islands and an awareness of cultural difference—that which makes individuals or groups distinct from each other—long before European or American ships appeared on the horizon.

The arrival of Europeans was not a total surprise to the islanders. For example, a seer in Tahiti predicted the arrival of foreigners who would possess the land and put an end to existing customs;[13] a prophet in Hawai'i recounted a revelation from heaven and the subversion of the *kapu* of the country;[14] a prophet from Kwaio of Malaita and John Frum of Tanna also foretold the arrival of Americans.[15] Though prophetic, these warnings of European or American colonialism and hegemony could not have anticipated the onslaught on island cultures that was soon to follow, brought ashore by 'skybreakers' or 'ghosts of the open ocean', white men who came in sailing ships carrying guns, weapons, diseases, iron tools, and strange ideas.

Ao taf ta: *Time of light*

Explorers, whalers, and beachcombers arrived in the sixteenth century. Islanders' reactions to these early Europeans ranged from fascination to indifference, from fear to adulation, from envy to contempt. The missionaries who followed saw many of their compatriots revelling with the 'natives' in the 'darkness'. For example, many of the whites on Pohnpei in Micronesia 'smoked, drank, cursed, had several wives, and were generally indifferent to piety in all its forms'.[16] The missionaries saw these Europeans as having succumbed to the 'pagan' life of the islanders, which they associated with darkness and therefore saw as needing to be dispelled by the Light, Jesus Christ and his teachings. A 'cosmic struggle between Light and Darkness' ensued.[17]

Many of the cultural practices of the Pacific Islanders were relegated by the missionaries to the time of darkness and therefore had to be eradicated. The complex past of island life became a simple struggle between good and bad, Christian and pagan, light and dark. A new sense of order was introduced, with the ancestral gods banished and the Christian God instituted in their place. Converts relinquished 'heathen' practices that contained overt violence, sexuality, and joy: in short, 'natives' were converted to an alien culture and religion, and adopted new customs such as the wearing of clothes, hymn singing, and sexual restraint. With their backs to the old ways, islanders focused on a new identity based on Christian values. A strict code of morality reinforced by promises of an uncertain afterlife in heaven or hell ensured that islanders were constantly sinning and forever seeking redemption. What Oppenheim has written of the Maori is typical of what happened in the rest of the Pacific: 'The introduction of Protestant Christianity, with its values of suffering, vicarious atonement, sin and forgiveness and its customs of moderation, thrift, prudence and deferred gratification—above all its nonviolence and sexual prudishness—presented the antithesis of almost everything that Maoris valued'.[18] As missionaries steered islanders further along the path of progress, a linear perception of history replaced the cyclic view of the past. In time, islanders came to think of their history in terms of 'the time of darkness' and 'the time of enlightenment.'[19]

From 1840 to the end of the nineteenth century, European countries scrambled for colonies. Ill-prepared for another onslaught from a more developed technology and a radically different philosophy of life, most island cultures submitted to colonial government. Working hand in hand, Christianity and Western capitalism almost succeeded in reducing Pacific Islanders to caricatures of the colonisers—be they French, American, German, British, or Spanish. From the arrival of the missionaries in the nineteenth century to World War Two, Pacific Islanders were taught to emulate the dress, language, behaviour, and customs of the colonisers. Missionary teachings and education were devoted to 'civilising' the islanders, to cutting them away from the roots of their cultures, 'from what the colonisers viewed as darkness, superstition, barbarism, and savagery'.[20] For many, this process of 'castration'[21] or 'physical and spiritual dismemberment'[22] meant the loss of dignity and pride.

Along the rocky road of piety, many islanders satirised Europeans and the new religion even as they appropriated it and refashioned it to suit their social and political needs. Numerous accounts reveal that Europeans were often mocked or satirised in comedic performances.[23] Donald Sloan wrote of *fale 'aitu* (houses of spirits) comic sketches that parodied European behaviour;[24] Richard Dana described *oli* (chants) by a noted Hawaiian improvisator that derided Americans and Englishmen;[25] James Chalmers wrote of young Rarotongan men parodying military manoeuvres and engaging in drunken orgies to flout and undermine the church.[26] Apart from these symbolic representations, more dramatic ways of resistance were found: millenarianist movements in Samoa and Aotearoa, cargo cults, military rebellions, and armed resistance to European encroachment in various places, including Papua New Guinea. In Rotuma, for example, religious wars between Catholics and Methodists in 1871 and 1878 created further and new divisions among the people; some of the negative effects of these wars are still evident today. Christianity's impact varied from island to island, although uniformity was apparent in the way islanders accommodated what the colonisers imposed yet resisted it at the same time, by infusing it with cultural elements that made it an indigenous institution, different from its foreign counterpart.

In his novel *Leaves of the Banyan Tree*, Albert Wendt has explored the effects of this complex process of colonisation on the individual and on the community.[27] Pepe refuses to 'sell' his soul to the Christian faith and to emulate his father, who madly pursues the way of religion and the *papalagi*. Pepe dies, alone and without friends, but at least with his self-respect intact—he was true to himself. On the other hand his father, Tauilopepe, spends a lifetime manipulating the church, his village, and his people to prop up his ego and his insatiable materialism, only to lose it all to Galupo, a more Westernised, calculating young upstart. As he dies Tauilopepe hears his son Pepe shouting 'Guilty!'. In pursuit of the 'dream' Tauilopepe and his followers had 'pushed the bush back to the range'; they had also 'forsaken things pagan, things belonging to the Darkness before the coming of the Light'.[28] In their place, a Samoan version of Christianity (as taught by a Solomon Island pastor) was installed.

The Christian church, like most social or cultural institutions, is both restrictive and malleable. In the early stages, the restrictive nature of Christianity maintained a stranglehold over converts in order to clearly differentiate them from their 'pagan' compatriots. This did not last long, however. A religious revival swept the Pacific some years after islanders had bowed to Christianity, causing them to seek a type of religion that embraced Pacific symbols of expression and Pacific sensibilities. Thus Aiavao of Samoa wrote of a happy marriage between Samoan culture and Christianity.[29] He noted that traditional meetings in Samoa always end with some reference to God or some examples from the Bible; he also described Christian services that featured Samoan music, Samoan dancing, and formal presentation of food and Samoan fine mats. In both Samoa and Tonga, buffoonery has made its way into church-related activities, as both entertainment and a means of criticising the church and its clergy. In the Cook Islands, *nuku* (biblical pageant) day is held once a year. Hundreds of children dressed in colourful costumes meet to perform biblical pageants, march around with banners, and sing songs. In short, islanders recognised the malleability of Christianity and the need to modify Christian practices to suit their cultures. In Samoa, as in many other parts of the Pacific today, Christianity is regarded as an integral part of life.[30]

World War Two helped transform the ambivalent views of Europeans and Americans about the Pacific and its inhabitants, though there is some evidence that islanders occasionally exploited stereotypical images of the 'native' or 'savage' to their advantage.[31] For example, war narratives on Santa Isabel contain 'an ironic mixture of humorous self-deprecation and superior cunning . . . the image of "savage" is accepted on one level to be denied on another, establishing an ironic counterpoint characteristic of much of the war's oral literature'.[32] Further, the war forced soldiers from Japan, Australia, New Zealand, and the United States to experience the difficult terrain, climate, vegetation, and tropical diseases such as malaria and yaws. In the tropics, foreigners were ill-prepared. As Papua New Guineans, and elsewhere Fijians and Solomon Islanders, helped them to overcome their difficulties—by acting as soldiers, carriers, riflemen, stretcher bearers, or guides, and as human beings struggling together to win a war against a common enemy—'fuzzy-wuzzy devils' became 'fuzzy-wuzzy angels'. The success of the Maori Battalion during the same war also enhanced the prestige and pride of Maori.[33] Firsthand experience with islanders helped in a small way to dispel ignorance, fear, and prejudice, particularly among soldiers.

Representations of Pacific Islanders from the eighteenth century to the 1980s became the domain of Europeans, whose views of the Pacific and its inhabitants were ethnocentric at best and racist at worst.[34] The general trend during this time had been for fiction writers such as Somerset Maugham, Jack London, Herman Melville, and James A. Michener to portray Polynesia as a paradise where simplicity, beauty, and innocence reigned, and Melanesia as a dangerous jungle where death and evil lurked. Polynesians were usually depicted as light-skinned and beautiful, Melanesians as black and inferior specimens. Missionary and anthropological accounts were usually just as distorted, revealing *'papalagi* fantasies and hang-ups, dreams and nightmares.'[35] These representations of islanders are important because they shape attitudes of foreigners about the Pacific and its inhabitants. Negative or positive stereotypes reduce islanders to two-dimensional figures, not fully human, resulting in the erosion of the self-esteem and dignity of the colonised. They must then contend with identities that are not of their own making but nonetheless become regarded over time as their distinctive characteristic, that which makes them different from others. A stereotypical cultural identity, once stuck, is almost impossible to shake off completely.[36]

The period after World War Two, until independence, was one of cultural reconstruction and political development. Western education was becoming more and more important. High schools were established, followed by colleges. The University of Papua New Guinea opened its doors in 1966, and its students, with the help of Ulli and Georgina Beier who arrived from the University of Nigeria in 1969, started writing imaginative literature. The university's language department also encouraged creative writing, and soon poems, stories, plays, and novels were being written in English.[37] No longer were Pacific Islanders content to allow representations of themselves in print to be the preserve of foreigners. Many saw it as their mission to restore full humanity to their people.

Colonialism was the pervasive theme in those early works from Papua New Guinea. Those writing in the 1960s were born in the 1940s, and had suffered from the imposition of a foreign view of the world and themselves. Sensing that the possibility of self-determination was in sight—former British colonies world-wide were either fighting for or had gained independence—these early writers became fearless. A university education (either overseas or at home) had restored their pride and raised their confidence.

Now that they had acquired the tools of their oppressors, they were suitably armed for psychological and intellectual combat. No longer content to remain oppressed, these Western-educated islanders condemned the injustices within Christianity and Western capitalism in their writings. Their ultimate goal was political and cultural independence.

The most powerful metaphor for the effects of the colonial experience on the indigenous Pacific peoples is that of a forced and unequal marriage, the subject of a play by Leo Hannet of Papua New Guinea.[38] In *The Ungrateful Daughter*, Ebonita, a young Papua New Guinean girl adopted by an Australian couple, is forced to marry an Australian against her wishes. Her compliance leads her to the altar, where she suddenly reverses her marriage vows and screams 'I don't!', tears off her white wedding dress to reveal her grass skirt underneath, flicks her hips, and dances a tribal number. Accompanied by wild drumming and similarly attired dancers, she and her troupe chase away the Australian wedding guests who flee off-stage. The University of Papua New Guinea thus led the way in what may be termed the creation of protest or resistance literature and theatre.

Two years after that university was established, the University of the South Pacific enrolled its first students. By bringing future leaders into contact with one another, and through its Pacific Week programme and the influence of individuals such as Albert Wendt, Marjorie Tuainekore Crocombe, Epeli Hau'ofa, Konai Helu-Thaman, Pio Manoa, Subramani, and Raymond Pillai, the university began to produce imaginative literature. Albert Wendt started teaching creative writing classes in 1975, and the South Pacific Creative Arts Society started publishing the best of the new writing that was being produced within the region covered by the university. Creative writing workshops were also held in Tonga, Samoa, Tuvalu, Vanuatu, and the Solomon Islands; the best from these workshops were published in local publications such as *Faikava* (Tonga), *Moana* (Samoa), *Sinnet* (Fiji), *Pacific Islands Monthly*, and later on in *Mana*, the literary journal of the South Pacific Creative Arts Society.

As in Papua New Guinea, a lot of the writing generated at the University of the South Pacific was anticolonial and anti-European. Most of these writers straddled two worlds: that of the rural villages in which they grew up, and the urban world in which the colonisers' values and customs reigned supreme.[39] Marginalised from their own societies and feeling their loss and alienation acutely, their literary attempts were suffused with anger and a rejection of Christianity and Western values, as evident in this poem by Albert Leomala of the New Hebrides (now Vanuatu):

> *Cross I hate you*
> *You are killing me*
> *You are destroying*

> *My traditions*
> *I hate you Cross . . .*
>
> *Cross run away*
> *Run away from me*
> *I hate you*
> *Take your ideas*
> *And your civilisation*
> *And go back to where you belong.*[40]

The same or similar sentiments are echoed by other Pacific writers. For example, in Vincent Eri's novel *The Crocodile* (the first Papua New Guinean novel), the protagonist Hoiri 'wasted' all his years 'carrying the white man's cargo'.[41] Makiuti Tongia of the Cook Islands ended his poem entitled 'Missionary' with these lines:

> *Today I think of my Maori identity*
> *and wonder if I should stay in this*
> *Christian land.*[42]

In Vanessa Griffen's short story 'The Concert', Miss Renner takes a group of Fijian schoolgirls from a rural village to see a quartet in the city in the hope that they will 'become more cultured'.[43] But the girls either fall asleep or clap at the wrong places, leaving her very disappointed. On the way back to school in the bus the girls sing spontaneously and beautifully. 'But then,' thinks Miss Renner, again with that same feeling of regret, 'they're only Fijian songs.'[44] These early examples were symptomatic of a growing wave of resistance to colonialism and Western values, as islanders sought cultural identities that were more in tune with their ethnic heritage.

The sense of loss that is a direct result of Western education is aptly captured in the poetry of Konai Helu-Thaman of Tonga. One of her most popular poems, 'Reality', is about an educated boy who graduates from school only to find that there are no available jobs. As he ponders what to do with his life, an old man close by whispers:

> *Come fishing with me today*
> *For you have a lot to learn yet.*[45]

A Western education often results in alienation from the land and the community, an erosion of an identity that is rooted in the indigenous culture. Many islanders educated overseas discover on their return home the need to learn or re-learn traditional skills in order to become part of a community again and re-attain an indigenous identity.

Christianity, like formal Western education, endeavoured to impose values and beliefs that were supposed to prepare islanders for life in a modern world. Although islanders often appeared to have totally rejected certain ancestral beliefs that came under censure by the missionaries, this mask was often thin. At times of crisis, many reverted to the ancestral spirits for assistance. Albert Maori Kiki's observation in 1968 that many of the Orokolo people are 'Christian and church-goers, but they put the Bible aside on week-days'[46] is still valid today, though the degree of reliance on the old gods and remedies continues to vary from place to place, depending on the impact of missionisation and the effectiveness or otherwise of Christian faith.

The cultural reawakening of the 1960s and 1970s was not confined to literature. In their attempts to mould a nation-state, island leaders organised national art and craft festivals to encourage the revival of art forms that hitherto had been suppressed. The tourism industry was also taking a keen interest in the revival of local dances and crafts. As a result of better transportation by land, sea, and air, more and more artists were gaining access to new tools, raw materials, and ideas. The missionaries relaxed their strict rules on dancing and similar customary practices, even as islanders infused Christianity with Pacific images and symbols that were no longer offensive. The culmination of this cultural renaissance was the first South Pacific Festival of Arts (now Festival of Pacific Arts), held in Suva in 1972.

The Suva festival was a turning point in the restoration of dignity and pride for all Pacific countries, except Guam and Tahiti, which did not participate (but joined the second festival four years later in Rotorua, New Zealand). Individual and isolated attempts to revive local art forms—particularly in the visual and performing arts—were brought together in an arena where they were celebrated. The result was a cultural explosion on a scale previously unheard of in the Pacific. Islanders became aware of the essential differences between themselves and their neighbours, as well as what they have in common. The success of the first festival reverberated far and wide; since then, this festival brings together artists of all kinds every four years—to dance, sing, laugh, learn from one another, and celebrate their Pacific identities.

Today, some Pacific islands are independent, some are self-governing, and some islanders are minorities in their own countries. In Hawai'i, New Zealand, New Caledonia, and French Polynesia, the shackles of colonialism still hold fast. In all these islands, however, Christianity has shed its 'light' for at least a hundred and fifty years; elements of local cultures that are being revived are therefore usually those reconcilable with Christian beliefs. These reconstituted forms that fuse selected elements from the time of darkness and the time of light have become, over the years, traditional. In line with the Western view of development and progress, Pacific cultures—including arts—are continually evolving and taking on more and more elements from European, Asian, American, and other Pacific cultures. The final mix is therefore quite different from 'the real ways of life that prevailed in the Pacific on the eve of European invasion'.[47] Nevertheless, these new identities are valid and necessary, as Pacific Islanders continue to struggle towards self-determination in all spheres of their lives.

Ao fo'ou ta: *New time*

A selected and politicised synthesis of the past and present is characteristic of contemporary expressions of identity in the period that Euro-American scholars call post-colonial. The term *post-colonial* is problematic as there are evidences of neo-colonial practices even in independent or self-governing nations. In the French colonies, New Zealand, and Hawai'i, where indigenous people are still struggling for sovereignty in their own land, the term is meaningless. The Rotuman word *fo'ou* is a more accurate description of this new phase in history. It is an adjective that means 'new', suggesting strangeness and unfamiliarity. In Rotuma, it is usually used in the context of shifting allegiances between foreign and local ways. Someone who behaves in an 'un-Rotuman' fashion may be mocked for having 'sold out' to foreign ways and ideas. Sometimes the same term is used to justify certain kinds of dress or behaviour, to impress on others the realities of living in the present and the evolutionary nature of culture. These uses of the word *fo'ou* to censure or to justify dress or behaviour suggest that in the contemporary Pacific, cultural identity has become negotiable.

A century or more of foreign domination, missionisation, depopulation (in the case of Hawai'i, New Zealand, New Caledonia, and the Marquesas), urbanisation, money economies, intermarriage, Western education, and mass tourism have irreversibly altered the social and cultural fabric of Pacific life. Attempts to preserve traditional cultures have led to charges of 'invented traditions' and 'inauthenticity' by Western scholars.[48] As may be expected, these 'outsider' views are met with counter-arguments, by both Pacific Island scholars and non-indigenous academics.[49] Quite often the focus of these arguments is blurred, for the wrong questions are being asked, and the answers offered are muddled and unhelpful. More and more, indigenous scholars prefer that outsiders refrain from pontificating about indigenous identities. It is unlikely, however, that non-indigenous scholars will stop writing about the constructions of identity among political activists and nations in the evolving Pacific; a more realistic approach would be for all concerned to focus on issues that will lead to the restoration of equality and human dignity between races. To understand the cultural, historical, and political reasons for the essentialist stance that present-day political movements have taken, and the reasons for the projection of selected images and symbols that highlight cultural differences, is more important than whether or not these symbols are 'authentic'. Seeming inconsistencies or contradictions in the way islanders symbolically represent or express their cultural identities are symptoms of the multiplicity of competing cultures and ideologies in contemporary society.

Personal identities

Once colonised, the mind can never be truly decolonised. Education continues to be in the language of the coloniser ('because it is the only way to progress'), while lip-service is paid to the teaching of Pacific languages. The literature taught in schools and at university level is still predominantly European or American. For example, Shakespeare is still being forced on Fijian and Indian students as they prepare to take their places in the sugarcane fields or the cassava plantations. Many parents, teachers, and others in a position to influence still believe that what is foreign is best. In such a climate, the oral and written literature and the visual and performing arts of the Pacific are either yet to be introduced or taken seriously as worthy of a place in the school curriculum. As might be expected, those who graduate from such institutions know much more about the history, geography, and cultures of Europe, America, Australia, or New Zealand than they do about their own or those of the rest of the Pacific Islands. The trend towards an education more relevant to islanders is developing slowly.

In its early stages, the University of the South Pacific showed great promise as a leader in the restoration of pride in being Pacific, yet more than two decades later, its Literature and Language Department on the Suva campus has yet to teach Fijian, Samoan, or any Pacific language. The majority of the university's largely expatriate (and even local) staff are rarely seen at cultural events, and students who spend time preparing for their cultural presentations often express resentment that their contributions make no difference to their grades. In fact, the ones who benefit most academically are those who choose not to participate in cultural matters, which they view as a hindrance to their studies. 'The Pacific Way' ideology has yet to filter into and permeate the education system—which holds the key to a mental revolution. Unless there are radical changes in education—beginning from kindergarten—unless politicians, teachers, and lecturers are prepared to introduce sweeping changes in school, college, and university curricula so that they are infused with local content and the local languages are used as mediums of instruction, true decolonisation of the mind will remain a dream.[50]

The cultural chasms that exist for Pacific Island students studying at tertiary institutions are also real for islanders who live in urban centers and hold white-collar jobs. They feel Pacific (for example, in their love of laughter and generosity of spirit, emphasis on people rather than things) yet speak English, wear Western clothing, and pay rent or mortgages. Torn between being traditional (which usually means behaving and holding the same values as their rural counterparts) and being realistic (adopting certain European or

American manners, certain kinds of dress and values), they are often unable to reconcile these seemingly conflicting notions of identity. A way out of this impasse is to realise that there is nothing shameful about having two or more identities, or an identity that is a composite of multiple cultural backgrounds. In fact, in a world that is increasingly becoming aware of the validity of multiculturalism, the individual who is competent in two or more languages or cultures has a distinct advantage. The secret is the ability to adjust to changing circumstances, as Rotumans are prone to do.

In Rotuma, a Rotuman male usually answers the question 'Who are you?' by mentioning his name, parents, and village. Rarely is the question of identity asked directly because it is considered rude. Instead, people usually whisper to each other, 'Who is that person there?' Since Rotumans do not customarily take on their father's name as their surname (although many Rotumans now follow the European custom), a person's name does not usually mean anything unless both parents' names are mentioned. Sometimes this is adequate, otherwise mention of the village suffices. This 'consocial'[51] identity reflects an emphasis on the value of kinship and the importance of the extended family. This view of personhood is true of other Pacific islands as well. As Lieber said of Kapingamarangi, 'The person is not an individual in [the] Western sense of the term'. Instead, the person is 'a locus of shared *biographies:* personal histories of people's relationships with other people and with things'.[52]

Outside one's island of birth, identity becomes variable and more susceptible to manipulation. For example, if asked the same question 'Who are you?' by a Fijian, the same Rotuman is likely to say that he is Rotuman; if asked the same question in Hawai'i by a stranger, he may say he is Fijian, since constitutionally Rotuma is part of Fiji. If asked the same question in England, he will usually claim the Pacific Islands as his place of origin. If the questioner is another Polynesian staying in England, he will respond by saying that he is from Fiji, or Rotuma, depending on whether or not the questioner seems to know the geography. If he wants to establish some affinity with Polynesia, he might claim to be Polynesian. If the questioner is Melanesian, he is likely to say he is from the Pacific. The motivation for the variations in defining identity is to try and be inclusive, particularly if the forging of a common background is desirable. No Rotuman I know wants to be identified as a Fijian if the association will not bring credit. Thus identity for Rotumans, and for other Pacific Islanders, is 'situationally variable' and is a 'continual reconstruction—process rather than structure'.[53]

The process of negotiating a shared identity, however, is problematic in relation to whites, whose physical appearance and values (apart from being regarded as members of the colonising group) make islanders only too aware of cultural difference. Instead of a better appreciation of Euro-American values, the effect is usually the opposite, as evidenced by the number of educated islanders in colleges and universities who are among

Young girls in Rotuma perform a Rotuman version of Cook Islands dancing, mak *Rarotonga, in 1992, wearing natural leaves and flowers as well as manufactured fabric. The wrap-around cotton garment (*haʻfali *in Rotuma,* lavalava *in Samoa) is seen throughout the Pacific, especially Polynesia. (Alan Buckley)*

the most assertive about an ethnic or cultural identity rooted in the past. Although these islanders may work in professions that have more in common with the dominant cultures, they deliberately and consciously cultivate symbols that express their cultural roots. In these situations, these symbols of cultural identity are signifiers of difference and resistance to certain values of the dominant cultures.

For political purposes, members of the dominant cultures may be useful and desirable to islanders. For example, *haole* (whites) who support the struggle for Hawaiian sovereignty are welcomed by Hawaiian political activists. White Australians or New Zealanders at the East-West Center are included in its Pan-Pacific club. Geography and the need to increase numbers play a more important part in the inclusion of 'white' Pacific Islanders from the dominant cultures. In this context, both the indigenous islanders and the 'white islanders' stand to gain from the union. In their desire to resist being swamped by the large numbers from East and West, this alliance is politically expedient and necessary. Howard aptly described this process: 'As once-distinct peoples increasingly come into contact with one another, as their lots are cast together within (culturally) arbitrary political units, the possibilities for alliance and disengagement are multiple and shifting'.[54]

When asked about their identities outside their islands but still within the Pacific, educated Pacific Islanders usually respond by naming the island of their birth. Yet should these individuals return to their islands or villages, they may feel just as alienated as the New Zealand–educated protagonist in Wendt's *Sons for the Return Home*.[55] However, there are islanders who are able to switch from a pakeha (white) way of behaving to a localised Pacific one. Among them are educated islanders who are willing to return to their home islands regularly, and to invest money, time, and energy in maintaining their links with migrant communities from their island wherever they find themselves. These dual or multiple identities, consciously and deliberately cultivated, are best suited to life in the contemporary Pacific. Keri Hulme, a New Zealand writer of Maori and Lancashire English ancestry, sees this as a joy and advantage because she can be on both sides of the fence, as well as having 'more than one set of ears . . . more than one set of eyes'.[56] Wendt explores a variant of the same idea in the character Galupo in *Leaves of the Banyan Tree*.[57]

Galupo returns to Sapepe to find a village perched precariously between the old and the new ways of life. Tauilopepe—the most powerful chief in the village of Sapepe, reared on the belief that the European values of thrift, hard work, and money are the keys to success—had propelled his village towards a path of modernisation. Through manipulation and exploitation, Tauilopepe's selfish ambitions are being realised. But the cost in terms of community cohesion and human dignity has been enormous. Galupo arrives and commits himself to saving this community from self-destruction. Unlike the protagonist in *Sons*, who flies back to New Zealand rather than face the challenges at home, or Faleasa Osovae, the old chief in *Pōuliuli* who fails to reconcile the opposing forces in his village, in *Leaves* Galupo succeeds in reconciling the world of 'lions and *aitu*' with the world of the *papalagi* (whites). His secret: he is well versed in the ways of the Samoan and in those of the *papalagi*, and confident about his own identity and his place in history. Further, the community see him as their ally, a benevolent leader committed to the restoration of justice.

Unfortunately, few Pacific Islanders today have such a clear and confident vision of who they are and their place in modern society, or are as committed as Galupo to political action that will unite their people and restore their pride. Although they pay lip-service to a Pacific identity, they have only a vague idea of how such an identity translates into concrete actions. Everyday behaviour and responses to questions of identity are therefore misleading—they claim to be islanders and deny their colonial heritage. If Galupo is to be the model for the new Pacific Islander, then European or American culture and what it has to offer—its methods, perspectives, and technology—has to be harnessed creatively to suit changing circumstances even as the individual remains firmly grounded in a cultural centre and is not afraid to criticise and resist institutions or ideologies that perpetuate oppression. Only then will islanders have a chance of succeeding in their attempts to confront the legacies and challenges imposed by the dominant cultures.

National identities

The creation of national unity is difficult, particularly when colonialism's implicit policy was one of divide and rule. In the coral atolls or smaller volcanic islands, national unity is generally easier to achieve, although the tendency is to put kin-group and faction interests first and national interests second. For the larger islands of the Solomons and Papua New Guinea, where geographical and linguistic barriers are legion, the forging of a national unity is a major preoccupation. Fiji faces the same problem: it has a large Indian population with a cultural identity extremely different from that of the Fijians. Divisions also exist within both the Fijian and the Indian communities. For these newly independent nations, the quest for national unity often involves the selection of cultural symbols of the more dominant political group. A small Western-educated elite usually defines these symbols, which may or may not be effective or acceptable to the majority. Whether the symbols chosen are slit-gongs, pigs' teeth, and decorative leaves as in Vanuatu,[58] the bird of paradise of Papua New Guinea, or the flag of the Federated States of Micronesia, the intention is the same—to create a feeling of identification and pride in one's nation. At the best of times, such symbols are accepted as inevitable by the local population; at other times, rumblings of resentment rise to the surface.

Contemporary architectural designs for important national buildings constitute one of the most obvious ways in which Pacific nations try to assert their distinct identities. The rebuilding of Maori meetinghouses complete with Maori designs in New Zealand and the parliament buildings in Samoa and Papua New Guinea are good examples of national architecture that uses modern tools to construct a distinctly local design. The result is magnificent buildings that derive their strength and beauty by drawing on the best in the foreign and the local cultures. However, as national symbols, these buildings are sometimes criticised for favouring a particular political group at the expense of others. For example, although the building of Parliament House in Papua New Guinea has been met with criticism, from without and within,[59] it still stands as an excellent example of what can be achieved when a nation (or individual or region) is not afraid to fuse the best from modern and local cultures. These symbolic structures represent an ideal in the minds of those in power and serve to evoke, confirm, or build a national identity, if not in the course of everyday political or social life, then in the imagination.

For island peoples who are still struggling for sovereignty, symbols that emphasise an ethnic identity serve a dual purpose: they unite even as they create divisions within. After the 1987 coups in Fiji, there were rushed attempts to establish a distinctly Fijian presence in the civil service and commerce. The most powerful symbol of this assertion of Fijian rights is the new parliament building modelled on a Fijian *bure* that will replace the British-style government buildings erected by the colonial government. Whereas formerly the colonial government building projected a neutral position in regard to Fijian–Indian power relations, the new building reinforces an unmistakably Fijian bias. Other examples of symbolism designed to affirm a cultural identity rooted in ethnicity include the wearing of gourd helmets by Hawaiians in front of the Federal Court Building in 1976,[60] the revival of the tattoo in Tahiti,[61] the use of the vernacular language to address a predominantly English-speaking audience, and the practice of certain rituals (such as the Maori *tangihangi*) that serve as a focus for the assertion of indigenous practices in the face of pakeha hegemony.[62] By clearly signifying difference, individuals and nations are making cultural and political statements that will further their pursuit of supremacy or the right to self-determination in their own land.

Perhaps the most potent symbol in the quest for self-determination is the revival of indigenous languages. In New Zealand, Maori has now been elevated to the legal status of English and is taught in a number of schools. 'Language nests' where pre-school children can be immersed in a Maori-speaking environment are also beginning to effect changes at the national level.[63] The Hawaiian language has made significant inroads into the education system, and in February 1992 the State Board of Education approved 'a policy allowing public school students to be taught almost entirely in the Hawaiian language through high school'.[64] A range of courses taught by the Center for Hawaiian Studies at the University of Hawai'i ensures that Hawaiian history, culture, mythology, and language are taught to Hawaiians wanting to learn about their cultural heritage.

Through film, issues of national identity and concern to Pacific Islanders are raised and disseminated. Merata Mita's *Patu,* Albert Wendt's book-made-into-film *Flying Fox in a Freedom Tree,* and Puhipau and Joan Lauder's documentary *Act of War* present a Pacific perspective on history and Pacific politics that eclipses the romantic images on celluloid that pervade South Seas cinema from the 1890s to the 1990s. In their struggle for self-determination, islanders are now realising that film is potentially their most powerful weapon; the documentary film is likely to be the most exploited medium for political purposes in the twenty-first century.

Meanwhile, a national identity is most clearly expressed in imaginative literature. Maori writers such as Witi Ihimaera, Patricia Grace, Keri Hulme and, most recently, Alan Duff continue to present a Maori world-view of events and situations that bring to the fore the values of Maori society, the racial prejudices of the pakeha, the tensions inherent in Maori society, and the effects of colonialism on the land and the Maori race.[65] Contemporary writing in Papua New Guinea tends to focus on issues of identity and desirable aspects of life in post-independence Papua New Guinea.[66] Many stories explore the consequences of living in urban centres and having to deal with the legacy of colonialism and the post-independence experience. Among these writers, Russel Soaba's novels *Wanpis*[67] and *Maiba*[68] and Nora Brash's plays[69] appear to best capture the realities of contemporary life in Papua New Guinea. A few collections of poetry and short stories from the Solomon Islands and Vanuatu have also been published. Worthy of note are Grace Mera Molisa's collection of poems entitled *Black Stone*[70] and Jully Makini Sipolo's *Civilized Girl*,[71] both of which focus on female issues of identity, the oppression of women by men, and culture. Like writings from the rest of the Pacific, these stories and poems invariably are set in the writer's country of birth and deal with national issues. These writings act as 'counter-histories' to those written by members of the dominant cultures.

In Micronesia, the corpus of published material is relatively small. In these islands, a coordinated effort to encourage or facilitate the publishing of creative literature is just beginning. Communication of local sentiment still remains largely in the more ephemeral realms of oratory, dance, or dramatic performance. Hezel reported, 'In Yap church history was danced; in Truk it was sung in a number of hymns, each composed by a separate island group; and in Pohnpei it was dramatized in a series of humorous tableaux. . . . Each of the island groups had its history, presented in an art form that best suited its genius'.[72] Here, as in most other parts of the Pacific, a sophisticated and rich sense of history—as embodied in performance as well as oral historical narratives, past and present—serves as an effective retort to outsiders' constructions of local histories.

With regard to national representations at arts festivals or promotional visits to overseas countries, the usual tendency is to project images of a static culture. For example, the emphasis of arts festivals is primarily on the revival of art forms of earlier times, to look back at the past rather than look ahead to the future. Vigorous attempts to revive canoe-building skills in preparation for the 1992 Festival of Arts constitute one such example. Again, these symbolic representations of culture tend to minimise the element of change, partly because of a cyclical view of history, but also because of the need to assert cultural roots that have changed but little and to symbolise cultural autonomy, real or imagined.

In the matter of religion, a contradiction emerges: the majority of islanders have no intention of resurrecting the old gods of their ancestors. Instead, Christianity and its practice are regarded as traditional. Most important ceremonies therefore include Christian prayers and hymns in the native languages. At a 1991 tourism conference held at the Sheraton Waikiki in Honolulu, for example, Tongans living in Honolulu sang an ensemble of

The Hawaiian voyaging canoe Hokuleʻa *en route to Rarotonga in 1984.
The canoe's voyages to Tahiti and Aotearoa have fostered renewed
contacts and awareness of the common culture throughout Polynesia.
(Hawaiʻi Maritime Center)*

Christian hymns as their contribution to the evening's cultural programme.
When a visiting intellectual learned from a fellow Tongan that Christian
hymns were planned, she responded: 'That's good. Keep the culture alive!'[73]
This statement was interpreted literally by the fellow Tongan, though the
respondent, who shared this 'joke' with me, was being ironic. This instance
illustrates that not all Pacific Islanders hold identical views on what are
appropriate representations of culture or tradition; it also highlights the
co-optation and indigenisation of Christianity by Pacific Islanders.

In multicultural societies such as Fiji or Papua New Guinea, national
unity is projected through images that highlight diversity or multiculturalism.
Sometimes there are attempts to create productions that combine elements drawn from various ethnic components, as has been the practice
with Papua New Guinea's *Raun Raun* theatre. In this kind of community
theatre—a similar project has been developed in the Solomon Islands—local
people are involved at the grassroots level, and cultural expression is
therefore less tied to the interests and needs of the ruling elite or foreigners, particularly if it is for home consumption. For export, negative images
are often left out in an attempt to attract tourists and investment. Most
nations have a tendency to project favourable stereotyped images, creating
discrepancies between these romantic images and the modernisation of the
national character. In the contemporary Pacific, this search for images that

will capture the complexity of contemporary modern island life and also unite diverse groups as well as promote a sense of national identity is a constant challenge.

Regional identities

Whether individuals who work at the three hundred or so regional organisations in the Pacific see themselves first and foremost as regionals is debatable.[74] At the University of the South Pacific, students have a tendency to eat, play, dance, and sing with other students from their own islands. They are not unaware of a shared identity with other islanders—through the common experiences of colonialism, smallness, and a love of laughter and merrymaking. Now that the Pacific Cultural Programme (formerly known as Pacific Week) has been carved up into separate weeks for each of the islands, heightened awareness of differences from each other is likely as each island group attempts to make its programme bigger and better than the others. The most important aspect of this programme is the opportunity for students who have come from relatively insulated backgrounds to experience the cultures of their Pacific neighbours and to become better informed. When these students leave for their home countries to take up positions in the professions or in government, they will take with them firsthand experiences of having lived and interacted with other Pacific Islanders.

Some of the friendships established by university students during their undergraduate days last forever. Islanders who work in regional institutions such as the South Pacific Commission, the Forum Secretariat, the Pacific Conference of Churches, or the University of the South Pacific tend to see themselves as 'pan-Pacific' or international persons,[75] with a commitment to the Pacific region, although they may still strongly identify themselves as belonging to a specific ethnic or cultural group.[76] These individuals are usually the products of multicultural experiences. Educated overseas and used to a more liberal and stimulating atmosphere, they are attracted to regional institutions where there is more room for differences in opinion and more tolerance of different values. The pressure to conform to societal expectations once they are out of their home environment is reduced, and they are freer to pursue individual interests. However, immigration restrictions and neo-colonial attitudes sometimes act like water on fire, dousing commitment to a regional ideal and chasing many of these islanders away to metropolitan countries.

The South Pacific Games (which include the French territories and Micronesia) are another context in which a feeling of regionalism is promoted, even though athletes compete for their island nations. Like the Festival of Pacific Arts, it allows a rare opportunity for islanders to meet, share, and compete in a friendly atmosphere. For the host country, it provides an avenue for fostering co-operation among diverse and competing cultural groups. This opportunity was not lost on Papua New Guinea, the host of the 1991 games. A spectacular display of its diverse and rich cultural heritage was enacted to portray a united country in the face of widespread fears that law and order (as in the Bougainville case) were breaking down. Such large-scale celebrations or competitions help to promote national as well as regional identities.

In recent years, the islands in the North Pacific that were known as Micronesia are beginning to identify themselves with their South Pacific neighbours. For example, when the University of the South Pacific was established, its member countries were confined to Melanesia (except Papua New Guinea), Micronesia (Kiribati, Nauru), and Polynesia (excluding the French territories and Hawai'i), but now the Federated States of Micronesia and the Republic of the Marshall Islands are contributors to its financial management. A handful of students from these islands are now studying at the university, participating in its Pacific programme, and sharing their cultures with a student population that was previously ignorant of them. However, south of the equator there is still a vacuum of information about the North Pacific and a need for the rest of the Pacific to foster closer ties with these islands.

Because membership of the South Pacific Forum is confined to independent or self-governing nations, the French territories, Hawai'i, American Samoa, the Northern Mariana Islands, Guam, Palau, and Easter Island (which is a territory of Chile) are excluded, an indication that these islands are not closely aligned with the rest of the Pacific. In fact, Australia and New Zealand are more involved, as evidenced by their membership in the Forum. In non-independent or self-governing islands, the question of a national identity is of more pressing concern than regionalism. Political activists in these territories—or state in the case of Hawai'i—are now fighting for independence and their right to self-determination. Once self-determination at the national level is achieved, these islands are likely to be more closely integrated with the rest of the Pacific region. A clearer articulation of a cultural identity rooted in the past, with affinities to the rest of the Pacific islands, will follow.

The emergence of ideologies such as *fa'a Samoa* or *Maoritanga* are partly the result of reactions against white colonial values that threaten to marginalise core values in island societies. These include concern for kin and the land, generosity, hospitality, feasting, merrymaking, and reciprocity. For islanders to be able to maintain their cultural identities and participate in white colonial society, however, a new synthesis is necessary, and elements from the dominant cultures are sometimes incorporated into new cultural constructions of identity. Many Pacific women have embraced Western feminism as an important part of their search for an identity that is free of both colonialism and male oppression. For example, Maori women are becoming increasingly assertive about female identity; their involvement in contemporary protest movements implies a rejection of the 'authenticity of the male elders so intrinsic to Maori culture, where to be young and female is traditionally a liability'.[77] The same trend is also noticeable in Hawai'i, Fiji, and Guam.[78] This new resistance to male oppression is best exemplified in the previously quoted poem by Grace Molisa of Vanuatu (page 370).[79]

On the other hand, in places such as Tonga and Samoa, there appears to be a strong anti-feminist movement among women intellectuals. Regardless of the different positions women take in relation to feminism, they are likely to play an increasingly powerful role in forging regional organisations based on gender, circumventing the barriers of race, nation, and patriarchy.[80]

Similarly, innovation and creativity are evident in the work of many contemporary Pacific artists, challenging Western constructions of the 'primitive' in art.[81] Refusing to adhere to the constraints of purity, tradition, and authenticity, artists such as Aloi Pilioko of Wallis Island (needlework tapestries using brightly coloured wool), Tanya Whiteside of Fiji (Pacific-inspired motifs on fabric), and Iosua Toafa of Western Samoa (blockmaking and painting) are producing works that depict Pacific motifs and themes in original styles using modern materials and media. Even more innovative in style are the works of Papua New Guinea artists such as Akis, Jakupa, and Kauage. What Narokobi says of recent developments in artistic expression in Papua New Guinea is applicable to the work of many young contemporary Pacific artists, particularly in New Zealand, who use modern tools or technology. Their creations are 'symbolic of a society in change, in transformation'.[82]

In literature, a complex but distinctly Pacific sensibility that encompasses a regional consciousness is manifest in Epeli Hau'ofa's *Tales of the Tikongs* and *Kisses in the Nederends*.[83] His works, as well as the writings of Albert Wendt, present a Pacific world that is full of manipulation, contradiction, political intrigue, and, in Hau'ofa's case, comic laughter to combat this mish-mash of madness and confusion. For example, in 'The Wages of Sin' Ti Pilo Simini, 'a weedy little man who smokes continuously', wakes up in the middle of the night, gropes in the dark, and finds a page from a book which he rips, lights, and smokes. Then he dreams of 'Moses, the lawgiver of Israel' and 'his trusted friend Joshua' who accuse him of sacrilege. They force a stick of dynamite in Ti's mouth, light the fuse, and disappear. The dynamite explodes, and Ti wakes up screaming. At dawn he discovers his sin: he had smoked a page from the Bible, the one containing the Ten Commandments! In his attempt to seek redemption he commits one sin after another, until he learns the secret of forgiveness: he had to commit two sins simultaneously, 'one the equal and opposite of the other'.[84] This incident highlights two things about Pacific identities: first, the pervading presence of Christianity and the sharing of common Christian values throughout the Pacific; second, that islanders have always been and still are active agents in their struggles to maintain their dignity, even as cultural bombs are going off all around them.

A final example from Hauʻofa: In 'The Glorious Pacific Way', Ole Pasifikiwei—collector of oral traditions—discovers that there is money to be had for the work he is doing. He learns how to play by the rules of the game and after six years has received a total of $14 million. Further, his name has become famous in influential circles in cities such as Paris, The Hague, New York, Tokyo, and Moscow, 'as well as in such regional laundry centers as Bangkok, Kuala Lumpur, Manila, Suva, and Noumea'. He commits himself totally to development through foreign aid, 'relishing the twists and turns of international funding games'.[85] Here we see an individual who is content to be a 'first-rate, expert beggar', a condition that afflicts many individuals and nations in the Pacific. Ole's dictum for happy living is the advice offered by Bagarap, a veteran of this game: 'They set the rules and we go along trying to bend them for our benefit'. Under the constraints of an imposed and oppressive system, Pacific Islanders in contemporary society are faced with the challenge of negotiating their identities to achieve their wishes for equality and self-determination, for themselves and their children's children.

Conclusion

In general terms, the *ao maksul ta* (time of darkness) was a period of *contested* identities, marked by a great deal of indigenous exploration and trade. Then came the *ao taf ta* (time of light), when missionisation *transformed* cultural identities of Pacific Islanders by converting them to a new religious order while suppressing certain cultural practices. However, as islanders embraced Christianity, they infused it with their own cultural symbols and ways of worshipping that reflect their cultural heritage. Then came World War Two, decolonisation, and independence movements. In their quest for a cultural identity at the personal, national, and regional levels, islanders sought ways to reconcile indigenous culture, Christianity, and Euro-American values of materialism and progress. A wide range of possible fusions ensued, creating different identities from which to choose and multiple ways of symbolising each particular one.[86] In the contemporary phase, which Rotumans refer to as *ao foʻou ta* (new time), cultural identities are *negotiable*.

In islands where political autonomy has been won, anticolonial feelings have been tempered by more pressing internal matters such as the forging of national unity or the search for a collective identity among diverse cultural groups. In these independent or self-governing nations, key cultural symbols that the majority of the population can relate to have become 'icons of collective identity'.[87] For New Caledonia, Hawaiʻi, and New Zealand, where the indigenous peoples are a minority, the search for collective symbols of identity at the national or regional levels that will motivate the majority (including non-islanders) to political action has yet to bear fruit. Meanwhile, the coconut trees along Waikīkī best symbolise the destructive effects of colonialism on these cultures.

According to legend, the Pacific coconut tree was a special gift from an eel, a token of sacrificial love for Sina, that ubiquitous female in Pacific lore who epitomizes beauty and symbolises the land. The eel died, but it left Sina and her descendants a gift that was binding and enduring. Brown on the outside and white on the inside, the coconut became a symbol of islanders whose values are those of whites. Such an analogy is too simplistic: identity for Pacific Islanders has never been a clear 'black and white' issue, as evident in the words *contested, transformed,* and *negotiable.* Who we are is always in process, constituted within, yet continually being modified or affected by external factors such as other people's prejudices, negative or positive. In this sense, the Rotuman *tähroro* is a more apt symbol of identity in the contemporary Pacific.

To make *tähroro,* a green coconut is husked and its juice sucked through a hole at the top. Thin strips of coconut flesh from other nuts are then inserted through the hole, and salt water added. The hole in the nut is then corked (with a rolled-up strip of brown banana leaf) and the coconut allowed to stand for several weeks until the salt water acts to reduce the white flesh of the coconut to a fermented sauce that can be used to enhance the flavour of all kinds of foods. This transformation from white flesh to an amorphous, fused concoction symbolises the diversity of elements that constitute Pacific identities. Such a fusion of different elements is not 'inauthentic' or an 'invention' of tradition, but necessary for the creation of identities that enhance dignity and pride in Pacific cultures and yet are capable of confronting the challenges introduced by Euro-American cultures. Brown on the outside, a myriad of colors inside—this is the Rotuman *tähroro,* a symbol not just of Rotuman identity but also of the fluid nature of present Pacific identities.

To produce a good *tähroro*—one that does not have a bad smell—is an art. The secret is in the quality of the ingredients and the careful handling of the coconut during the fermentation process as the various elements fuse and act on each other. Similarly, the present search for cultural identities rooted in the past but relevant in the present has to be carefully conducted, if self-determination for individuals, nations, and the Pacific region is to be a reality. The challenge is in the art of selection and negotiation.

* * *

I GRATEFULLY ACKNOWLEDGE comments on early drafts of this chapter by Alan Howard, Jan Rensel, Niko Besnier, Francis Hezel, Haunani-Kay Trask,

Geoffrey White, Terry Teaiwa, Tom Farber, Len Mason, Jane Moulin, and the students of my Pacific Literature course at the University of Hawai'i (spring 1992).

Notes

1 See Epeli Hau'ofa, 'Technology and Culture in the Pacific: Alignment or Conflict of Interest', paper presented at plenary session of Symposium on Technology and Culture Change, 17th Pacific Science Congress, Honolulu, May–June 1991.
2 Donna Awatere, *Maori Sovereignty*, Broadsheet Publications, Auckland, 1984, 62.
3 Albert Wendt, *Pouliuli*, Longman Paul, Auckland, 1977, 145.
4 See also Paul Sharrad, 'Imagining the Pacific', *Meanjin* 49 (4, 1990): 597–606.
5 Rubellite Kawena Johnson, *Kumulipo: Hawaiian Hymn of Creation*, volume 1, Topgallant, Honolulu, 1981.
6 Francis X. Hezel, personal communication, 11 March 1992.
7 For Samoa, see Bradd Shore, *Sala'ilua: A Samoan Mystery*, Columbia University Press, New York, 1982; for the Marshall Islands, see Leonard Mason, 'Economic Organization of the Marshall Islands: Economic Survey of Micronesia', *U.S. Commercial Company Report*, no. 9, 1975.
8 Roger Keesing, 'Creating the Past: Custom and Identity in the Contemporary Pacific', *The Contemporary Pacific* 1 (1989): 22.
9 Lord Amherst of Hackney and B. Thompson, eds, *The Discovery of the Solomon Islands*, Hakluyt Society, London, 1901; see also Geoffrey White, *Identity through History: Living Stories in a Solomon Islands Society*, Cambridge University Press, 1991.
10 Albert Wendt, 'Introduction', in *Lali: A Pacific Anthology*, ed. Albert Wendt, Longman Paul, Auckland, 1980, *xiv*.
11 Leonard Mason, 'Introduction', in *The Art of Micronesia*, University of Hawai'i Art Gallery, Honolulu, 1986, 13.
12 Donald Sloan, *Polynesian Paradise: An Elaborated Travel Journal Based on Ethnological Facts*, Robert Hale, London, 1941, 107.
13 T. Henry, *Ancient Tahiti*, Bulletin 48, B. P. Bishop Museum, Honolulu, 1928, 4–5.
14 Hiram Bingham, *A Residence of Twenty-one Years in the Sandwich Islands*, New York, 1847, 28–29.
15 Geoffrey White, personal communication, 24 April 1992.
16 Francis X. Hezel, *The First Taint of Civilization: A History of the Caroline and Marshall Islands in Pre-Colonial Days, 1521–1855*, Pacific Islands Monograph Series no. 1, University of Hawai'i Press, Honolulu, 1983, 146.
17 Hezel 1983, 148.
18 Roger Oppenheim, *Maori Death Customs*, A. H. & A. W. Reed, Wellington, 1973, 19.
19 Malama Meleiseā, 'Ideology in Pacific Studies: A Personal View', in *Class and Culture in the South Pacific*, ed. Antony Hooper et al, Centre for Pacific Studies, University of Auckland and Institute of Pacific Studies, University of the South Pacific, Auckland and Suva, 1987, 144.

20 Albert Wendt, 'Towards a New Oceania', *Mana Review* 1 (1 January 1976): 56.

21 Wendt 1976, 56.

22 Haunani-Kay Trask, personal communication, April 1992.

23 See Vilsoni Hereniko, *Polynesian Clowns and Satirical Comedies*, PhD dissertation, University of the South Pacific, Suva, 1990.

24 Sloan 1941, 78.

25 Richard Henry Dana, *Two Years before the Mast*, Bantam Books, New York, 1959, 117.

26 R. Lovett, ed., *James Chalmers: His Autobiography and Letters*, London, 1902, 95.

27 Penguin Books, Auckland, 1979.

28 Wendt 1979, 400.

29 Tunumafono Apelu Aiavao, 'Who Is Playing Naked Now? Religion and Samoan Culture', *Pacific Perspective* 12 (2, n.d.): 8–10.

30 See Vilsoni Hereniko and David Hanlon, 'An Interview with Albert Wendt', *The Contemporary Pacific* 5 (1993): 112–131; see also John Garrett, *To Live among the Stars*, World Council of Churches in association with Institute of Pacific Studies, Geneva and Suva, 1982.

31 See Geoffrey M. White and Lamont Lindstrom, eds, *The Pacific Theater: Island Representations of World War II*, Pacific Islands Monograph Series no. 8, University of Hawai'i Press, 1989.

32 Lamont Lindstrom and Geoffrey M. White, 'War Stories', in White and Lindstrom 1989, 8.

33 B. J. Kernot, cited in Karen Sinclair, 'Tangi: Funeral Rituals and the Construction of Maori Identity', in *Cultural Identity and Ethnicity in the Pacific*, ed. Jocelyn Linnekin and Lin Poyer, University of Hawai'i Press, Honolulu, 1990, 223.

34 See Bernard Smith, *European Vision and the South Pacific*, Oxford University Press, Melbourne, 1989.

35 Wendt 1976, 58.

36 See also Paul Theroux, *The Happy Isles of Oceania: Paddling the Pacific* (G. P. Putnam's Sons, New York, 1992) for new stereotypes that are reminiscent of the literature of imperialism.

37 See Subramani, *South Pacific Literature: From Myth to Fabulation*, University of the South Pacific, Suva, 1985.

38 Leo Hannet, 'The Ungrateful Daughter', in *Five New Guinea Plays*, ed. Ulli Beier, Jacaranda Press, Port Moresby, 1971.

39 Norman Simms, *Writers from the South Pacific: A Bio-Bibliographical Critical Encyclopedia*, Three Continents Press, Washington, DC, 1991.

40 Albert Leomala 'Cross', in *Some Modern Poetry from the New Hebrides*, ed. Albert Wendt, Mana Publications, Suva, 1975, 19. Only the first and last stanzas are quoted here.

41 Vincent Eri, *The Crocodile*, 2nd edn, Penguin Books, Ringwood, VIC, in association with Robert Brown and Associates, Port Moresby, 1973, 178.

42 Makiuti Tongia, 'Missionary', in *Korero*, Mana Publications, Suva, 1977, 6.

43 Vanessa Griffen, 'The Concert', in *Roots*, rev. edn, Fiji Extension Services Centre, University of the South Pacific, Suva, 1981, 18–22.

44 Griffen, 22.

45 Konai Thaman, 'Reality', in *You, the Choice of My Parents*, Mana Publications, Suva, 1974, 17.

46 Albert Maori Kiki, *Ten Thousand Years in a Lifetime*, Longman Cheshire, Melbourne, 1968, 163.

47 Keesing 1989, 35.

48 This is not the argument of Allan Hanson, 'The Making of the Maori: Culture Invention and Its Logic', *American Anthropologist* 91 (1989): 890–902; or of Jocelyn Linnekin, 'Defining Tradition: Variations on the Hawaiian Identity', *American Ethnologist* 10 (1983): 241–252. For other sources on the invention of culture in the Pacific, see Roger Keesing and Robert Tonkinson, eds, *Reinventing Traditional Culture: The Politics of* Kastom *in Island Melanesia, Mankind* 13 (special issue, 1982); Peter France, *The Charter of the Land: Custom and Colonization in Fiji*, Oxford University Press, Melbourne, 1969; and Margaret Jolly, 'Specters of Inauthenticity', *The Contemporary Pacific* 4 (1992): 49–72.

49 The appearance of Keesing's article (1989) sparked considerable heat among Pacific Islanders studying at the University of Hawai'i in 1990; see also the following responses in *The Contemporary Pacific* 3 (1991): Haunani-Kay Trask, 'Natives and Anthropologists: The Colonial Struggle', 159–167; Roger M. Keesing, 'Reply to Trask', 168–171; and Jocelyn Linnekin, 'Text Bites and the R-Word: The Politics of Representing Scholarship', 172–177. See also Jolly, 1992.

50 See Ngugi Wa Thiongo, *Decolonising the Mind: The Politics of Language in African Literature*, James Curry, London, 1986.

51 See Michael Lieber, 'Lamarckian Definitions of Identity on Kapingamarangi and Pohnpei', in Linnekin and Poyer 1990, 71.

52 Lieber, 72.

53 Alan Howard, 'Cultural Paradigms, History, and the Search for Identity in Oceania', in Linnekin and Poyer 1990, 267.

54 Howard 1990, 270.

55 Albert Wendt, *Sons for the Return Home*, Longman Paul, Auckland, 1973.

56 Andrew Peek, 'An Interview with Keri Hulme', *New Literatures Review*, no. 20 (winter south 1990): 3–4 (New Literatures Research Centre, University of Wollongong).

57 Longman Paul, Auckland, 1979.

58 Joan Larcom, 'Custom by Decree: Legitimation Crisis in Vanuatu', in Linnekin and Poyer, 1990, 176.

59 See Pamela C. Rosi, 'Papua New Guinea's New Parliament House: A Contested National Symbol', *The Contemporary Pacific* 3 (1991): 289–324.

60 Haunani-Kay Trask, 'Fighting the Battle of Double Colonization: The View of a Hawaiian Feminist', *Renaissance in the Pacific* 4 (8–9–10, 1989): 61–67.

61 Karen Stevenson, '"Heiva": Continuity and Change of a Tahitian Celebration', *The Contemporary Pacific* 2 (1990): 255–278.

62 See Oppenheim 1973; Sinclair 1990, 219–236.

63 Richard Benton, 'Maori and Pacific Island Languages in New Zealand Education', *Renaissance in the Pacific* 4 (8–9–10, 1989): 7–12.

64 *Ka Leo O Hawai'i: The Voice of Hawaii*, University of Hawai'i at Mānoa, 10 February 1992, 1.

65 See Karen Sinclair, 'Maori Literature: Protest and Affirmation', *Pacific Studies* 15 (4, 1992): 283–309.

66 See Steven Edmund Winduo, 'Papua New Guinean Writing Today: The Growth of a Literary Culture', *Mānoa* 2 (1990): 37–41.

67 Russel Soaba, *Wanpis*, Institute of Papua New Guinea Studies, Port Moresby, 1978.

68 Russel Soaba, *Maiba*, Three Continents Press, Washington, DC, 1979.

69 For example, see Nora Vagi Brash, 'Which Way Big Man?' in *Through Melanesian Eyes: An Anthology of Papua New Guinea Writing*, ed. G. Powell, Macmillan, Sydney, 1987, 170–185; and 'Pick the Bone Dry', *Ondobondo: A Papua New Guinea Literary Magazine* 7 (1985–86): 20–30.

70 Grace Mera Molisa, *Black Stone*, South Pacific Creative Arts Society, Suva, 1983.

71 Jully Makini Sipolo, *Civilized Girl*, South Pacific Creative Arts Society, Suva, 1981.

72 Francis X. Hezel, 'New Directions in Pacific History: A Practitioner's Critical View', *Pacific Studies* 11 (3, 1988): 103.

73 I was present at this performance. Permission has not been sought to use this response, so the speaker will remain anonymous.

74 Ron Crocombe, *The South Pacific: An Introduction*, Institute of Pacific Studies, Suva, 1989, 171.

75 Ron Crocombe, 'The Pan-Pacific Person: Staffing the Regional Organisations', *Pacific Perspective* 12 (2, n.d.): 51.

76 For example, see interview of Esekia Solofa, 'Solofa: Playing a Role in Education', *Pacific Islands Monthly*, February 1992, 17–20.

77 See Michele D. Dominy, 'Maori Sovereignty: A Feminist Invention of Tradition', in Linnekin and Poyer 1990, 237–257.

78 See Laura Marie Torres Souder-Jaffery, *Daughters of the Island: Contemporary Chamorro Women Organizers on Guam*, Micronesian Area Research Center, University of Guam, Mangilão, 1987.

79 Molisa, 24.

80 See Dominy 1990.

81 See Patricia Hereniko, *Pacific Artists*, Institute of Pacific Studies in association with Fiji Extension Services Centre, University of the South Pacific, Suva, 1986; Sidney Mead and Bernie Kernot, eds, *Art and Artists of Oceania*, Dunmore Press and Ethnographic Arts Publications, Palmerston North, New Zealand, and Mill Valley, CA, 1983; Adrienne L. Kaeppler, 'Art and Aesthetics', in *Developments in Polynesian Ethnology*, ed. Alan Howard and Robert Borofsky, University of Hawai'i Press, Honolulu, 1989, 211–240; Sally Price, *Primitive Art in Civilized Places*, University of Chicago Press, 1989.

82 Bernard M. Narokobi, 'Transformations in Art and Society', *Look! Look! Gen! Look Again! Contemporary Art from Papua New Guinea*, ed. Susan Cochrane Simons and Hugh Stevenson, Percy Tucker Regional Gallery, Townsville, 1990, 17.

83 Epeli Hau'ofa, *Tales of the Tikongs*, Longman Paul, Auckland, 1983; and *Kisses in the Nederends*, Penguin Books, Auckland, 1987.

84 Hau'ofa 1983, 35–42.

85 Hau'ofa 1983, 83–93.

86 Howard 1990, 275.

87 Linnekin 1990, 158.

18

The passage out

Brij V. Lal

The world's a ship on its passage out, and not a voyage complete.
Herman Melville

For most peoples of the Pacific Islands, as the essays in this volume have shown, the twentieth century has been a time of rapid, often bewildering change. They saw the consolidation of social, economic, and political trends that originated in the nineteenth century, and the advent of new forces that, for better or for worse, have forever altered their destiny. So profound has been the pace of change that, as the twentieth century draws to a close, only one thing is certain above all else: the islands of the Pacific Ocean, small, scattered, vulnerable, buffeted from all sides, are islands in the physical sense alone.

The essays in this book have clearly delineated the main agents and contours of the social, political, and economic developments that have impinged on the lives of the Pacific Island peoples, and the cultural and political contexts in which they have taken place. They do not require further summary or elaboration. What follows are some overarching comments that draw on, but are not confined to, the themes raised in the preceding pages. My main concern is to raise some broad issues that illustrate the nature and meaning of colonialism and its legacy for the Pacific Islands as they stand on the threshold of a new millennium. In the process, I have found it necessary to revisit some assumptions that have long influenced the way students of the Pacific Islands have viewed their past.

By the late nineteenth century, when the foundations of the modern Pacific had been laid, except for some parts of Melanesia, the era of itinerant contact between most of the major islands and the outside world had long been over.[1] The islands, settled for thousands of years by people whom the world now knows as Melanesians, Polynesians, and Micronesians, had been charted by European explorers from the sixteenth century onwards, and their existence added to the growing corpus of Western geographical knowledge. By then, too, the islands, especially in Polynesia, had become deeply embedded in the European romantic imagination as a place of warmth and beauty, free from the corrupting constraints of civilisation, the home of the 'noble savage'. Subsequent closer and more intensive contact diluted, but did not always obliterate, this initial Western enthusiasm.[2]

That contact came with European trading, beginning in the early years of the nineteenth century, in sandalwood, coconut oil, copra, pork, bêche-de-mer, tortoiseshell, and similar items. The gradual incorporation of the isolated, subsistence economies of the islands into the emerging nexus of a global economy apart, this trading also introduced new tools, ideas, and ways of doing things, that amounted, in the words of Dorothy Shineberg, to a kind of 'technological revolution' in the islands.[3] More was to come. From the 1850s a new trend became evident: the arrival of 'the large-scale, heavily-capitalised, vertically integrated company as the regulator of economic activity'.[4] The fortunes of these companies varied greatly due to particular circumstances and the vicissitudes of the international market prices of basic commodities, but their names are legion in the nineteenth century economic history of the islands: J. C. Godeffroy und Sohn, Deutsche Handels- und Plantagen-Gesellschaft der Sudsee Inseln zu Hamburg, Jaluit Company, the New Guinea Company, the Colonial Sugar Refining Company, Lever Brothers Pacific Plantations, Société le Nickel, Burns, Philp. They or their successors would continue to dominate the export sectors of many Pacific Island economies well into the twentieth century.[5]

Other changes of a perhaps more profound nature came with the spread of Christianity in the islands. The new *lotu* had entered the Pacific through the evangelists and artisans of the London Missionary Society at Tahiti in 1797, hoping for prompt evangelisation and convinced that 'the sharing of the message of salvation with all nations [was] a necessary prelude to the final coming of Christ and the end of the present age.'[6] In the beginning that task of conversion was understandably tortuous and incomplete for both theological and practical reasons, generating controversy and frustration as missionaries of different Christian denominations became embroiled in local conflicts and the ambitions of rival chiefs. Nevertheless, by the middle of the nineteenth century, Christian missions were established on most Polynesian islands, and had made forays into the culturally and geographically more difficult terrain of Melanesia.

More often than not, the message of Christ was brought to the Pacific Islanders not by white missionaries but by other islanders, among the most notable of whom were Cook Islander Ta'unga and Tongan Joeli Bulu.[7] By the twentieth century, the process of conversion was nearly complete in all the major islands. While *dakuwaqa, degei, moroa*, and other such local gods might still receive the supplication of a few covert followers in times of acute personal stress or family crisis, pre-Christian Pacific Island religions have effectively been banished to the dim underworld of supernatural spirits, sometimes at the instigation of colonial governments, which found them threatening to the moral order they were trying to create.[8] Attempts to resurrect them—like that of the Fijian rugby team to the 1991 World Cup—are met with strong disapproval and even derision. Routinely, modern Pacific Islanders refer to their pre-Christian past as 'heathenish', and draw a distinction, as they do in Samoa, between *pōuliuli* (the time of darkness) and *mālamalama* (the time of enlightenment).[9]

The role of Christianity in the making of the history of the twentieth-century Pacific cannot be over-exaggerated. Although the nineteenth century is often seen as the great missionary era in the Pacific Islands, with mass conversions and martyrdoms and the like, the twentieth century has seen more missionaries in the islands than ever before, with more islanders converting to the new faith, if in less spectacular fashion. Sometimes, Christian missions played a direct role in facilitating the colonial aims of their national governments, as for example in the French colonisation of New Caledonia, or the eventual American colonisation of Hawai'i.

Elsewhere, their role was indirect in suppressing indigenous customs, rituals, and ceremonies that threatened the colonial order or were offensive to Christian notions of morality and decency. Sir William McGregor, Lieutenant-Governor of British New Guinea, wrote: 'The missions contribute powerful aids towards the settlement of the country. All missionaries of British citizenship and some of those that are not constantly inculcate the sentiment and duty of loyalty to the Queen and of obedience to the Government'.[10] Charles Abel, a missionary from the London Missionary Society, in Kwato in Papua between 1890 and 1930, was equally forthright. Speaking about the purpose of mission education, he said: 'Our first idea of secular education is to place the Word of God in the hands of the Papuan and enable him by mental training to grasp its meaning and to use it in personal study. But latterly beyond this we educate him to take his place as a British subject, under British rule, living in touch with British civilization.'[11]

It would be misleading to give the impression that the missions were merely organs of the colonial state, for the history of the Pacific Islands is littered with numerous instances of intense debate between the two regarding the fate of the people among whom they worked or whom they ruled.[12] In some areas the missions made important contributions with lasting effects, particularly in the fields of health and education. Not surprisingly, the leading literary educators, political leaders, and administrators in the Pacific Islands today are either mission educated or active ordained ministers. Some of them dominate the political landscape, as, for example, in Vanuatu. There, the churches, as the only institution with the capacity to train people beyond the primary level, were the main avenues for social mobility for aspiring leaders. The leadership of the Vanua'aku Pati, and indeed the Cabinet of the independent government, was dominated by Presbyterian and Anglican ministers.[13] The churches saw their role as the 'conscience of the nation', fostering 'high moral value and standards throughout the nation's life'.[14] In a number of Pacific islands, Christianity is recognised as the official state religion; in some of them (such as Kosrae and Tonga) a strict observance of the sabbath is rigidly enforced.

The increased European presence in the islands coincided with, and perhaps even helped accelerate, the great struggles for power and political supremacy among rival chiefs in such places as Hawai'i, Tahiti, Tonga, Samoa, and Fiji.[15] The failure or inability of the indigenous political systems to effectively resist the combined resident consular pressure for greater political concessions and settler demand for more land and cheap labour, contributed to the acceleration of European penetration of the islands. The process was so rapid and extensive that by 1900 only one Pacific island group, Tonga, was able to retain a semblance of its traditional political sovereignty—but as a British protectorate.[16]

All the others had come under varying forms and degrees of European control. The French occupied Tahiti and the Marquesas in 1842, Wallis and Futuna informally in 1843 and formally in 1877–1888, New Caledonia and its dependencies in 1853, and the New Hebrides as a joint naval commission with Great Britain in 1877 and as a condominium in 1906. The Germans, latecomers in the game of colonial rivalry, moved into Micronesia and New Guinea in the mid-1880s, and into Samoa in 1900, though, of course, German companies had long been active there and elsewhere in the Pacific. The British, the dominant colonial power in the South Pacific in the nineteenth and twentieth centuries, annexed New Zealand in 1840 and acquired Fiji as a Crown Colony in 1874. From Fiji, it extended its political influence to groups such as Tokelau in 1889, the Solomons in 1893, the Gilbert and Ellice Islands in 1892, and Niue in 1900 through the agency of the Western Pacific High Commission.[17] In the twentieth century, new 'colonial' masters entered the scene, New Zealand in Western Samoa and the Cook Islands, Japan in Micronesia, and Australia in New Guinea after World War One, as League of Nations mandate powers. Australia had already taken over the administration of British New Guinea (Papua) in 1906. After World War Two, the United Nations conferred on the United States the responsibility to administer the Trust Territory of the Pacific Islands in Micronesia.[18]

Some islands were governed successively by different colonial powers. The Micronesians, for example, came under the rule of the Spanish, the Germans, the Japanese, and the Americans. The Western Samoans were ruled by the Germans from 1900 to 1914, then by New Zealand until they gained independence in 1962, while the island of Tutuila had come under the Americans at the time the group was partitioned in 1899. Parts of Papua New Guinea were ruled by the Germans, the British, the Australians, the

Dutch, and, later, the Indonesians. New Hebrideans, as already mentioned, were jointly governed by the French and the British. Some islands were arbitrarily partitioned to suit imperial interests. The Germans handed over Choiseul and Santa Isabel to the British in 1900 for concessions to German colonial interests in Africa. Bougainville, culturally and ethnically associated with the Solomon Islands, was attached to Australian New Guinea in 1914, sowing the seeds for secession attempts in later years. Samoa was divided between the Germans and the Americans. The Gilberts, although Micronesian, were ruled by the British jointly with Tuvalu, a Polynesian group. And so it went.

The national boundaries that the colonial powers created, with scant regard to the existing cultural and political realities of the island peoples, persisted well into the twentieth century. Some of them are likely to persist well into the future. There is little chance of the unification of the two Samoas, for example. Some colonially defined boundaries were amicably terminated at the time of independence, the best example being that of Tuvalu and Kiribati.[19] Other attempts ended in failure, as happened in the case of the Santo rebellion in Vanuatu at independence and the Rotuman rebellion in Fiji soon after the coups of 1987. Elsewhere, as in Papua New Guinea and Melanesia generally, secessionist tendencies, drawing sustenance from their pre-colonial independence, cultural distinctiveness, and fragmentation (and fear of exploitation and domination at the hands of their numerically more powerful compatriots), continue to fester.[20] The fate of the 'nation state' in the islands, itself a colonial creation, cannot be taken for granted, especially in the culturally diverse islands of Melanesia.

The consensus of both popular and scholarly contemporary opinion suggests that colonialism, and Western impact generally, was generally not as destructive a phenomenon in the Pacific Islands as it was in many other parts of the world. In part, this results from the general aversion most students of Pacific Islands history have to the long-standing 'fatal impact' theory of culture contact in the Pacific Islands, perhaps best publicised by Alan Moorehead in his 1967 book of that name.[21] Moorehead detailed the trail of devastation and destruction of aboriginal cultures in Tahiti and Australia that accompanied the arrival of Europeans. Subsequently, his work was invested with larger meaning, pushed beyond the specific places he had written about, and liberally extended by scholars and others to describe effects of culture contact throughout the islands. The impression created was of Pacific Island peoples as helpless victims of outside manipulation, of their being 'implicitly or explicitly inferior, passive, and unable to cope with the white man's all-powerful way of life.'[22] This view is no longer fashionable in modern Pacific historiography. Islander agency is an idea that informs much of the recent Pacific historical literature.[23]

It is appropriate to reject the cruder versions of the fatal-impact theory for reasons too obvious to enumerate here. The pre-colonial Pacific Islanders were 'adaptable, resourceful, and resilient', K. R. Howe has written. 'A history of culture contact can no longer be interpreted in terms of European initiatives; the course of events was very much influenced by the nature of the Islanders' own social and political arrangements'.[24] Caution of the type that Howe offers is salubrious, but exuberant celebration of islander agency can—and has—put students in danger of reaching misleading conclusions from specific case studies and exulting in premature optimism. Already, some historians are offering cautions. 'The new historiography is in danger of promoting a new orthodoxy', writes Mālama Meleiseā, 'if it tries to diminish the tragic consequences of land grabbing, king-making, and gunboat diplomacy by Europeans in destroying the political capacities of Islanders to respond on equal terms'.[25] Stewart Firth made a similar point several years ago: 'Eager to show the local diversity of the Pacific, the discipline has lacked world perspective'. Criticism of the control of island economies by foreigners, the subordination of the islands' political sovereignty to suit the strategic interests of metropolitan powers and other such factors 'have been generally liberal and benign, as if to say: the Islanders were at the centre of the picture, they must have triumphed'. To depict the Pacific Islanders as 'exploited victims of the Europeans has become close to a sin in the new Pacific historiography. In fact, the islanders did not triumph. The island economies are still today owned by foreigners. Political independence, where it has been achieved, is limited'.[26]

There are several ways out of this impasse created by the two conflicting views of the effects of culture contact and colonial rule in the islands. To start with, some clear distinctions have to be made, for example, between the pre-colonial and colonial periods in the islands' history. Similarly, a distinction has to be made between those islands where contact with the outside world was demonstrably destructive and those where its impact was marginal. Certain parts of the highlands of New Guinea, for example, came into contact with the outside world only in the 1930s, and then only very marginally. Some other islands with a much longer history of contact with the West, such as the Loyalty Islands, also escaped harmful consequences of encounters with the outside world. The Loyalties' modern historian, K. R. Howe, found 'no evidence to suggest that the indigenous society experienced any social, political and economic upheaval, leading to bewilderment and demoralisation, as a consequence of European presence'.[27] Similar claims could be made for some other islands as well, such as Tuvalu, where 'the difficulties and upheavals often associated with European activity in the Pacific were either absent or muted'.[28]

On the other hand, in many places in the Pacific the consequence of contact with the outside world was tragic. Severe depopulation caused by the introduction of new diseases such as dysentery, smallpox, and influenza, or generalised cultural violence accompanied culture contact. In some places, such as the Marquesas, the decline was disastrous.[29] An epidemic of measles in Fiji in 1875 reduced the indigenous population by 40 000 to 110 000 in 1879. On the island of Pohnpei, a similar calamity killed 50 per cent of the population in 1854,[30] while in the New Hebrides, especially on the islands of Aneityum and Eromanga, the indigenous populations 'were almost wiped out'.[31] Recent demographic research in Hawai'i suggests the pre-contact population of the islands to have been much higher (800 000) than the 200 000–300 000 figure universally accepted.[32] We may, sometimes with good reason, dispute the strict accuracy of these figures or seek different explanations for the magnitude of the decline, but the fact of an externally induced decline is beyond doubt.

The story of the varying impact of culture contact and colonial rule on land alienation in the Pacific is similar. In some places, very little occurred. In Fiji, for instance, Sir Arthur Gordon's policies placed 83 per cent of all land in the country in inalienable indigenous Fijian ownership. In Vanuatu and the Solomon Islands, too, only relatively small percentages—20 per cent and 17 per cent respectively—were alienated and passed into fee simple titles, though the European claims were much more extensive and some of the best low-lying coastal areas passed into outsiders' hands. Elsewhere, however, the story is different. In New Caledonia, for example, some 5400 square kilometres, or 81 per cent of the total land area, were alienated from the indigenous people.[33] In New Zealand today, less than 12 000 of the total 270 000 square kilometres that make up New Zealand remain in the legal category of communally owned Maori Land.[34] In Australia, the total land area in Aboriginal hands today amounts to 1 005 292 square kilometres, or 13.1 per cent of the total land area of Australia.[35] And the impact of the Great Mahele for the Hawaiian people is well known; as Lawrence Fuchs wrote, 'no single event so drastically changed the social system of Hawaii as the Great Mahele'.[36]

This leads to a further distinction, all too obvious on reflection, but not sufficiently recognised either by scholars or by indigenous nationalists whose grand generalisations tend to place all the indigenous peoples of the Pacific in the same pot. This is the difference in the situation of indigenous people in societies of massive European (colonial) settlement, such as Australia, New Zealand, New Caledonia, and Hawai'i, and the rest of the decolonised Pacific islands. In the polities where massive settlement occurred, the indigenous people have been comprehensively colonised. They have lost much of their land, their cultural base has been destabilised, and, for the most part, they have been shunted to the political and economic margins of their own societies. Their quest for a measure of sovereignty and independence shows just how desperate their struggle is. The battle lines are drawn in politically charged, stark terms, between the oppressed, colonised 'natives' and the oppressive, colonising outsiders (*haole*, pakeha).[37]

In post-colonial Pacific Island states, on the other hand, the distinctions between the exploiters and the exploited, between 'haves' and 'have-nots', between friends and enemies, are not so simple, nor so easily made. Increasingly in these societies, issues of inequality and oppression centre rather more around the class interests of the indigenous elites and decision makers and cut across ethnic and racial lines. Indigenous consultants and intellectuals, Epeli Hauʻofa has written, 'are becoming more effective for the cause of capitalist development than their non-islander counterparts'.[38] They are also the most powerful opponents of their compatriots who seek cultural sustenance in the pre-Christian, pre-Western past of their societies.

Even in Pacific Island societies where colonialism is usually thought to have had a mild impact or benign influence, recent revisionist research is pointing to some new, unsettling conclusions. Three examples will suffice. One is Fiji, where Sir Arthur Gordon's paternalistic system of indirect rule is widely credited with preserving the 'Fijian way of life' from the corrosive influences of the modern world. That is true to some extent, but it is equally true, as Peter France has shown, that Gordon's conception of Fijian life, and its subsequent institutionalisation, was based on a series of mistakes and misrepresentations of what constituted the basic social patterns and practices of Fijian life.[39] Gordon imposed a set of uniform laws regarding the system of indigenous land ownership on a society where evidence by the Fijians themselves showed the existence of great fluidity and variety. His policies empowered those sections or regions of Fijian society that served as his allies and punished those that resisted his designs.[40] Others more recently have shown the existence of great disparity between the rhetoric of benevolent protectionism and the practice of expediency in the administration of Fijian society, leading one scholar to conclude that colonial rule in Fiji was 'one ruled from the top down by a single, defining, ruling class that insisted on one government and one god'.[41]

A similar revisionist exercise has recently been undertaken in Samoa regarding the policies and motivations of Wilhelm Solf, the first governor of German Samoa. Solf has received almost universal praise from scholars: as a 'man of quite unusual talent, clear thinking, sensitive to the nuances of Samoan attitude and opinion . . . [for having a] natural respect for the intrinsic value of exotic cultures and a readiness to deal with the Samoans on their own terms . . . [who believed] his real metier in Samoa to be governing the Samoans and protecting Samoan culture from the depredation of boorish European settlers'.[42] A Samoan scholar, Mālama Meleiseā, however, has offered a different perspective: 'From the Samoan point of view Solf was no benefactor. . . . [His policies aimed to] destroy Samoan political institutions and to replace them with modern, rationalised (in the sociological sense given to this term by Max Weber) institutions which would consolidate German authority and the expansion of German commercial interests'.[43]

Sir Hubert Murray's administration of Papua between 1906 and 1940 has been subjected to a similar reassessment by historians. Murray's biographer portrayed the lieutenant-governor as an enlightened man with progressive views, in the intellectual vanguard of his generation, an 'educated, widely-read and thoughtful man of action who, for most of his life, felt at odds with society'.[44] Murray, he suggested, belonged to the same great gallery of enlightened colonial administrators as Gordon in Fiji and Lord Lugard in Nigeria. In recent years, however, Murray's record has come under critical scrutiny by a host of scholars though, to be fair to the governor, they have underplayed the political and economic constraints on his work. They have found the governor's policies excessively paternalistic, retrogressive, racist, and ill considered in terms of preparing the Papuans for eventual political autonomy.[45] The net effect of Murray's policies, wrote Edward Wolfers, was 'to make the village the centre of political attention; and to erect new geographical and political boundaries around it; both at the expense of pre-existing kin-, marriage- and exchange-based ties that many individuals in almost every community had with members of other communities'.[46] With these assessments, the first salvos in the revisionist phase in the historiography of colonial administrations in the Pacific Islands have been fired.

With few exceptions, such as in Micronesia under the Japanese,[47] the colonial state did not carry out systematic economic development in the islands. This is often seen as a plus in favour of the colonising power insofar as it did not result in any massive disruption of the indigenous way of life. It is true that Gordon's policy of indirect rule sheltered the indigenous Fijians from the full force of plantation life and let them develop at their own pace in their subsistence environment (which fostered stagnation); but by resorting to Indian indentured immigration to solve his labour problems, Gordon also introduced an element that was to have a profound effect on Fijians in subsequent years. Benevolence did not always underpin colonial policy and practice. If the colonisers did not exploit the islands more thoroughly, it was not out of altruistic motives but rather because of the enduring realities in the islands, their isolation, difficult conditions, absence of exploitable resources, or marginal strategic significance in the larger game of imperial rivalry. The New Guinea Company failed not for lack of trying but because of the ignorance, incompetence, and excessive ambition of its directors.[48] The Gilbert and Ellice Islands, impoverished as they were, were not exploited because they had no exploitable resources—apart from labourers. Quite the reverse occurred at Ocean Island (Banaba), which was a part of the Gilbert and Ellice Islands Colony under the same colonial power.

Where resources could be exploited with advantage to the colonial power, however, they were. Expatriate companies mined phosphate in Ocean Island, Nauru, Angaur in Belau, and Makatea in French Polynesia; nickel in New Caledonia; gold in Fiji and Papua New Guinea; copper in Bougainville; and harvested cash crops such as copra in a number of places. The profit motive superseded concern for the welfare of the indigenous people, who were often progressively marginalised in their own societies, or permanently dislocated. An obvious, and tragic, example is the situation of the people of Ocean Island, who 'steadily resisted the encroachment of the [phosphate] mining industry onto their lands and their lifestyle',[49] but were defeated in the end by the combined pressure of the British Colonial Office and the Pacific Phosphate Company. The company mined some 20 million tonnes of phosphate under a 999-year lease, while the demoralised indigenous inhabitants of the island were relocated to the island of Rabi in Fiji. Ironically, one of the leading lights of the company was none other than Sir Arthur Gordon. The systematic dislocation and marginalisation of the Kanaks on the main island of New Caledonia to make way for settler-planter and mining interests, and the use of immigrant labour to keep the indigenous people in a minority, is too well known to require retelling.[50]

Colonialism is ultimately about controlling and subjugating one group of people for the benefit of another. It is about an unequal, essentially exploitative relationship and, in the modern world, is marked with racial connotations. In certain important respects, colonialism was no different in the Pacific Islands than it was elsewhere. Confronted with the bizarre, the different, and the incomprehensible, the colonial administrators promulgated the minutest of regulations to impose Western notions of order on, and impart meaning to, the bewildering world they encountered. Their ultimate aim was the subversion of the indigenous cultural and moral order. Sorcery, magic, pagan beliefs, worship of ancestral spirits, human sacrifice, and similar activities, were all outlawed, their continued practice by islanders punishable by fine or imprisonment or both. In Australian New Guinea, 'Native Regulations' promulgated in 1923 outlawed sorcery, adultery, threats, assault, abuse, insults, obscene language, the spreading of false reports, and, from 1936 on, homosexuality. Punishment for any of these 'crimes' could be a fine of up to £3 or imprisonment for up to six months.[51] Some of the clothing laws were ironic too. While the missionaries attempted to clothe the islanders, the Papuan administration discouraged them. Papuans were not allowed to wear shirts, lest this give the idea that they were rising above their station and following the ways of the white men.

Similarly restrictive laws were effective in Fiji, where the colonial officials sometimes went to lengths that today would be unthinkable. An example concerns the drinking of *yaqona*, a mildly narcotic drink that was a central part of Fijian ceremonial life. A regulation in 1927 forbade males under eighteen and females under twenty-five or those suckling children from drinking *yaqona*. The punishment for boys under fourteen was 5–10 strokes of the cane on the breech; women had to make plaited mats, native cloth, fishing nets, or pottery at their own homes for fourteen days for the first offence and for a month for any subsequent offence. Anyone, including adult males, caught drinking *yaqona* 'indiscriminately' or 'immoderately' or between the prohibited hours of 11 PM and 6 AM could be fined £1 or face imprisonment for up to two months! How many individuals were convicted and punished for breaches of these regulations is not known, but the intent of the colonial state is unmistakably clear.[52]

Throughout the period of colonial rule, many Pacific Islanders actively resisted the various demands of the colonial order.[53] Some resisted silently, refusing to pay their taxes or continuing their traditional cultural practices in the face of official opposition. The Fijians of interior Viti Levu in Fiji, for example, refused to cut their hair short, the wearing of long hair being seen, in colonial eyes, as evidence of 'heathenish' life. Others expressed their views through organisations. Their movements were not always well organised or directed, and their goals were not always articulated with a clarity the Europeans could understand as 'rational', but resistance and dissent did exist in several forms, depending on the circumstances. Outright violent rebellions against the brutality of the colonial regime, such as the Sokehs uprising of 1910 on the island of Pohnpei, or the murder of District Officer William Bell in the Solomons in 1927 represented one extreme.[54] Strikes by workers against European companies, such as those against the Colonial Sugar Refining Company in Fiji in 1921, 1943, and 1960, and against an expatriate company in 1959, or the Rabaul strike in Papua New Guinea in 1927 were another form.[55] Others set up alternative companies or cooperatives to circumvent or challenge European commercial dominance in the islands, such as Apolosi Nawai's Viti Company or the *Tonga Ma Tonga Kautaha*.[56] Or more overtly political movements sought greater autonomy, such as the Mau movement in Western Samoa in the 1920s and 1930s, or Maasina Rule in the Solomons around the time of World War Two.[57]

Maintaining strict separation between the races was an essential component of the colonisers' desire to control the colonised, at least in the British Pacific colonies. The institution and practice of colonial rule was premised on the ideology of inequality. The colonisers, the bringers of 'civilisation' and owners of superior technology, were, by their definition, naturally superior to the people they ruled. How else could they justify their presence in the islands? The colonisers' emphasised their sense of difference and separateness from the world they ruled in a variety of ways. One was residential segregation in urban areas. Elaborate rules were designed to ensure that people of different races did not live in the same neighbourhoods, in some places through legislation, in others through administrative practice. Separate schools and public facilities were established for Europeans, a practice that did not disappear, in Fiji at least, until well after World War Two. Towns were 'administered by expatriates, for expatriates, and according to expatriate models'.[58] Restrictions were placed on the amount of time 'natives' could spend in areas of European residence. In Papua New Guinea, after 1923, noise, shouting, beating of drums, singing, and dancing had to cease after 9 PM, and street games were illegal.[59] In Fiji, even high chiefs and Indo-Fijians acquainted with modern ways had to seek special liquor permits, while Europeans were exempt from this requirement. No non-European could serve on a jury until well after World War Two. Political and trade union activity was closely monitored. In Papua New Guinea, for example, it was illegal until the 1960s for workers to organise among themselves to secure better pay and terms of employment.[60] Sports were racially segregated, and interracial marriages unheard of. In New Guinea, the penalty for even attempted rape of a white woman was capital punishment.[61]

Legal mechanism, however, was only one means of controlling the colonised. Missions wittingly or unwittingly helped in the task of pacification, though in several instances the purposes of mission and colonial power were in conflict. Education also played an important role in the cultural and intellectual pacification of the islanders. Here, as elsewhere, a clear and mutually reinforcing correlation between knowledge and power existed. In most Pacific islands, the governments lacked the resources to develop adequate educational facilities for the ordinary people, devoting their resources to educating 'the responsible race'. But other considerations entered such decisions. Fear of an educated colonised elite and the threat it posed to the colonial order was one. Another was the widespread belief in the innate inferiority of the non-white colonised peoples. As Hubert Murray wrote: 'I do not think that we should attempt to give the Papuan anything in the nature of a higher education, nor do I think that we should ever dream of conferring upon him any political rights. He is inferior to the European, and, if we wish to avoid trouble, we should never forget this, and should never look upon him as a social or political equal'. Instead, he hoped for a 'pacified Papua, a skilled and industrious native population'.[62] Murray was not alone in that view. Writing in the 1960s, Harry Maude noted that 'the seemingly innocuous study of the history of dependent territories was regarded as politically dangerous . . . Feed and clothe, cosset and pamper your dependent subjects if you will, but do not (if you wish them to remain dependent) assist them to recapture a "pride in their own country and ancestral heritage" '.[63]

To this end, the colonial governments directed their meagre efforts, intent on creating disciplined, obedient subjects well versed in the culture of the colonised. An Empire Day circular sent to Fiji and other British possessions in the Pacific in 1927 told head teachers 'to promote in your pupils' minds a deeper sense of patriotism, a stricter self-discipline, a hardier endurance, a deeper respect for others and a strict obedience to lawful authority'.[64] In 1931, Admiral Lord Jellicoe of the British Fleet said in his Empire Day message, 'We have a vast responsibility; the greatest Empire the world has ever known has been handed down to us by our forefathers. It is an Empire which stands for all that is good in the modern world. Let us be worthy of our destiny'. To become worthy, the colonised were required to acquire a rudimentary knowledge of English and to learn to accept their subordinate place in the compartmentalised world of colonial society.

A similar sentiment was propagated by the Japanese in Micronesia, where a two-tiered school curriculum was introduced, the higher one for the Japanese and the other, more vocationally oriented one, for the local people.[65] For the Japanese, the emphasis was on the inculcation of the values of citizenship, science, physical training, and arts, while for the Micronesians, the emphasis was on 'new behavioral regularities of complete obedience and respect for authority'. As David Ramurai recalled, 'The basic aim of the Japanese school system was the indoctrination of the natives with Japanese ideas and was characterised by the emphasis on the Japanese language and ethics. It was designed to make Micronesians understand the Japanese and to obey their orders'.

In Hawai'i during the territorial period, the situation was similar. School-teachers were required to develop good character in their pupils, this being defined 'in terms of white middle class American respectability'.[66] The *Hawaii Educational Review* in 1914 proudly proclaimed that 'the schools of Hawaii stand foremost among the agencies at work in the Americanization and uplift of this important part of the United States'. The legacies of the colonial system of education remain. One island-born writer summed up the impact of colonial education as a process that radically transformed the 'configuration of the interior landscape of our mind and imagination. That is why the decolonization of the mind is almost impossible for the mind is shaped by multiple layers of experience. Colonialism is a vital stratum embedded in it'.[67]

The advent of colonial rule in the Pacific altered the history of the islands in other ways, in some cases permanently, as with the initiation of the labour trade. Labour migration started with the arrival of the first European traders in the islands, such as whalers, sandalwood, bêche-de-mer, and copra traders. However, not until the establishment of plantations in the islands after the middle of the nineteenth century did large-scale recruitment of Pacific Islanders begin. Some half million workers were engaged before 1914 and another three hundred thousand since.[68] Many of them were recruited for service on plantations or for other work within their islands. In the New Hebrides, 37 871 people engaged in local contracts between 1908 and 1941; in the Solomon Islands, 54 110 between 1913 and 1940; in Papua, 212 546 between 1909 and 1950; and in New Guinea, 309 499 between 1920 and 1950. Others were recruited to serve on plantations outside their islands. The principal destinations were Queensland, where some 62 565 Pacific Islanders were employed between 1863 and 1904, and Fiji, which indentured 27 027 Pacific Islanders between 1863 and 1914. Samoa received 19 694 indentured labourers from 1967 to 1934, of whom 12 700 were Pacific Islanders.

The majority of the labourers who were indentured for overseas service came from the Solomon Islands and especially the New Hebrides, though there were also smaller numbers recruited from the Gilberts and the Loyalty Islands. The Pacific Island labour trade is significant for a number of reasons. First, it has left a legacy of immigrant Pacific Island communities scattered across the Pacific—in Samoa, Fiji, New Caledonia, and Queensland. For the most part, the descendants of these islanders have been assimilated into the ways and mores of their host societies, more of necessity than by choice. However, the bulk of the recruits returned to their home islands. The returned migrants, with broadened social and cultural horizons, better knowledge of the white people's world, and prized material goods, became leaders of their home communities and 'figured prominently in the process of social and cultural change which soon followed'.[69] Some became leaders in local administrative bodies, while others became involved in attempts to convert their pagan compatriots to Christianity. Naturally enough, the regions that sent workers abroad benefited more on their return, but also suffered greater social and cultural disruptions than those that had not.

The story of Pacific labour migration was an important building block in the edifice of modern Pacific Island historiography. The conventional wisdom on this topic, and much else in Pacific history, was that labour recruiting was stained with the blood of islanders who were violently wrenched from their communities by unscrupulous, unsupervised recruiters, herded onto ships like cattle, and shipped off to far away places in the most sordid of conditions. Popularly characterised as blackbirding, the Pacific labour trade was just another name for slavery.[70] However, new studies of the trade have demonstrated that, except in the early years of recruiting, the labour trade was less violence ridden and European dominated than the more sensational accounts of the time suggested.[71] These new studies have demonstrated islander agency and explained why the islanders themselves had good reason to enlist. They emphasise the role of indigenous intermediaries, and the social and economic factors that contributed to the pressure on the islanders to migrate. More recently, Clive Moore has deepened the thrust of the earlier works by demonstrating a close correlation between, among other things, labour-recruiting patterns and traditional residential mobility and population movement in the islands, arguing that islanders 'perceived the recruiting trade as part of a cosmological life-cycle, not in European terms'.[72] The contribution of the revisionist research in labour history to the development of a more culturally sensitive islander-oriented Pacific Island history cannot be over-emphasised.

Pacific Islanders, however, were not the only ones recruited for plantation work in the Pacific. Indentured labourers were also recruited from Asia, either as the sole source of labour or to supplement other dwindling sources. The major destinations of Asian indentured workers were Hawai'i and Fiji.[73] By 1899, Hawai'i had imported 56 720 Chinese indentured workers and 68 279 Japanese, and between 1907 and 1929 another 102 069 came from the Philippines. Fiji imported 60 965 Indian indentured workers between 1879 and 1916, when other sources of labour, including Pacific islands, proved unreliable, expensive, and unable to meet the projected rapid pace of economic development in that colony. The competing demands of Queensland, Fiji, and Samoa (not to mention New Guinea) placed an impossible strain on the Melanesian labour reserve. Smaller numbers of Asian indentured workers were sent to other places as well; 6984 Chinese to Samoa and 1100 to Tahiti, 33 000 Indonesians and 14 000 other Asians to New Caledonia.

The labour communities that resulted have been the subject of several excellent case studies, but these do not yet constitute an integrated corpus of scholarly literature with common themes and approaches comparable to that of the Pacific Islands labour trade. Still, the impact of these communities on their host countries has been immense. In some cases (Hawai'i and Fiji), the descendants of the original indentured migrants constitute a significant proportion of the total population and make a preponderant contribution to the economy. Their success has invited the wrath of the indigenous communities, which, for various social and cultural reasons, have been less successful. Consequences include renewed debate about the rights of 'immigrant' and 'indigenous' communities, and various efforts to redistribute power and wealth under the umbrella of positive discrimination strategies. This issue is likely to remain for a long time.

In the first half of the twentieth century, perhaps the most dramatic events to have a decisive impact on the lives of the Pacific peoples were the two world wars. The Pacific Islands were not a battleground in World War One, but islands under German administration—Samoa, New Guinea, Micronesia—were transferred to new colonial rulers. During World War Two, many islanders were caught in the vortex as fierce battles erupted in their lands. In such places as Guadalcanal, Rabaul, and Guam the devastation wrought by the war was massive. The fighting left behind a legacy of savagery, violence, and destruction such as the indigenous people had not seen before. In New Guinea alone, 150 000 Japanese, half of the number there, died in the jungles, while a further 26 000 died of illness in Bougainville, 16 000 were killed in battle, and 23 000 surrendered at the end of the war.[74] No one bothered to ask how many indigenous people died in a war that was not of their making but was fought on their land. The war lives on in their memories, as a marker of time, an important rite of passage.[75]

The war brought new things to the islands, in quantities never before imagined. In the New Hebrides,[76] on the island of Santo, the Americans constructed a major aviation and supply base that included three bomber airfields, two fighter airstrips, patrol torpedo boats and maintenance and repair shops, a large navy yard, six wharves, a comprehensive telephone system, fifty kilometres of roads, tennis courts, sports grounds, offices, and workshops. In addition were the entertainment centres: 54 cinemas screened different shows every night, including such titles as 'Sex Takes a Holiday' and 'Withering Tights', and such luminaries as Bob Hope, Bing Crosby, Larry Adler, and Poogie entertained the troops. More than one hundred thousand men were permanently stationed on Santo and more than half a million passed through it during the war. The presence of such an unprecedentedly large amount of cargo on their small island posed problems of comprehension to a people used to a simple subsistence life-style. Unsurprisingly, the post-war period saw the emergence or acceleration of a number of so-called cargo cult movements, which held that with appropriate supplication, the indigenous people, too, could obtain the cargo that the whites possessed in such abundant quantities.

The war had many profound effects for all the Pacific Islands. It heralded improved modern communication in the form of regular air transport, improved roads, new bridges and wharves, airports, telephones, and cable service in the major islands. It alerted the colonial powers to the need for more coordinated efforts to improve the lot of the Pacific Islanders, and led eventually to the creation of the South Pacific Commission in 1947. The war marked the beginning of the end of colonialism in the world, except for the Micronesian islands, which passed from the Japanese to the Americans; Irian Jaya, which passed from the Dutch to the Indonesians; and the French territories in the South Pacific. After the war, with Asia and Africa leading the way to independence, the question often was not if but when the Pacific Islands would be decolonised. Or, as Harold Brookfield wrote, 'Henceforth the opposition was rather between gradualism and speed, than between exploitation and a more humanitarian view of the "white man's burden"'.[77]

In global terms, independence came late to the Pacific Islands. As Barrie Macdonald has written, this was due not so much to foot-dragging on the part of the colonial powers, especially Great Britain, as to the slow pace set by the island leaders themselves, for reasons that he discusses (chapter 8). France and the United States are obvious exceptions, for reasons discussed by Paul de Deckker and Robert Kiste (chapters 10 and 11). With increasing clamour for decolonisation from the United Nations General Assembly's Committee on Colonialism, Samoa led the way in 1962, followed by the Cook Islands in 1965, Nauru in 1968, Fiji and Tonga in 1970, Niue in 1974, Papua New Guinea in 1975, Tuvalu and the Solomon Islands in 1978, Kiribati in 1979, and Vanuatu in 1980.[78]

Except in Vanuatu, where some Francophone elements obstructed the path to independence and attempted secession, independence was achieved peacefully through constitutional negotiation with the colonial power. Except for Kiribati and Tuvalu, which agreed to political separation at the time of independence, and the former Trust Territory of the Pacific Islands, which split up into several political units (the Republic of the Marshall Islands, Belau, the Federated States of Micronesia) all the other island nations accepted the legitimacy of their colonially created political boundaries. Some of these have been threatened, most notably in Melanesia, by various secessionist movements that want to recapture their pre-colonial social and political autonomy. They have thus far been contained, either because of internal contradictions in the different movements or through promises and programmes of greater decentralisation of state power, though the results are not encouraging.[79] A centralised bureaucracy, bequeathed by the colonial state, is simply too well entrenched and anxious to protect its prerogatives to want to share power with the periphery. Secessionist movements will continue to arise from time to time.

Independence was generally greeted with a deep sense of pride and satisfaction and with great expectations for the future, especially in islands with a relatively homogeneous political culture. Post-colonial development plans proclaimed the determination of the governments in power to abolish poverty, increase self-reliance, and promote balanced social and economic development.[80] Papua New Guinea went further than most by promulgating 'National Goals and Directive Principles' in its constitution. Among other goals, these principles required the country's leaders to promote integrated human development to free their compatriots from oppression and domination; provide equal opportunity for all to participate in and benefit from the development of the country; preserve national sovereignty and economic self-reliance; develop natural resources and preserve the natural environment for the collective benefit of the nation; and find ways to 'achieve development primarily through the use of Papua New Guinean forms of social, political and economic organisation'.[81]

These are noble ideals which echo in the national goals of other independent Pacific Island states. It would be overly cynical not to record some progress. Except for Fiji, with its recent history of military coups, and Papua New Guinea with its unending saga of urban violence, not to mention the Bougainville secession attempt, many Pacific islands have managed to escape the deep social and political tensions that have destabilised many post-colonial states around the world. Again with the exception of Fiji, political power in the islands still flows not from the barrel of the gun but from the ballot box, if imperfectly; the rule of law is observed and the constitution remains the supreme law of the land. There is room for some satisfaction, but not complacency, when problems facing the independent states of the Pacific are enormous, in some cases almost insurmountable. The list is unending. There are the usual problems of great disparity between the rhetoric of the egalitarian ideology preached by the leaders and the realities of their practice. Leaders talk of sharing and caring, but as Ron Crocombe said, 'sharing and caring works in such a way that those at the lucky end in order of birth get the bigger shares and much more care. Nepotism, the favouring of relatives, subordinates, and associates of the powerful, traditionally an accepted principle, has become a major problem in the central Pacific aristocracies today, where it reduces the confidence and motivation of the ordinary people'.[82] The problem is endemic not only in the central Pacific but throughout the region.

A related problem is the tension between the forces of tradition and those of change in the islands. The traditional elite and other privileged groups, naturally enough, want to have it both ways: to preserve their customs while enjoying all the fruits of capitalism.[83] Their desire to protect tradition and culture in the face of the dreary, universalising forces of the modern world is entirely understandable, but problematic. Leaving aside the thorny question of what constitutes traditional culture,[84] these very same leaders promulgate policies whose ultimate effect will be to undermine the basis of traditional culture. Promoting Western education and competitive examinations, which reward individual initiative and talent rather than social status; encouraging the capitalist market economy with World Bank assistance and multinational corporations; privatising important local enterprises for short-term economic gain: all these measures will do little to preserve traditional culture under chiefly rule. What is required is a massive rethinking of the nature and purposes of development, but this, for reasons to be discussed, is not likely to happen soon. The record of the past two decades is not encouraging.

The dilemma was eloquently summed up by the late Fijian anthropologist, Rusiate Nayacakalou. Writing about the Fijian people in the 1960s, he said that 'one of the greatest obstacles facing the Fijian people today is the failure to recognise that there is a contradiction; they must now make a momentous choice between preserving and changing their way of life. . . . The belief that they can do both simultaneously is a monstrous nonsense with which they have been saddled for so many years now that its eradication may be very difficult to achieve'.[85] His prophetic words are even more relevant in post-coup Fiji today than they were thirty years ago. Anthropologist Raymond Firth agrees: 'What is quite certain is that we cannot keep a cultural heritage of a purely traditional kind, with its values intact, and at the same time expect to get full advantage of what we want from a modern developing economic system and its wealth of consumer goods and services. A question of priorities has to be faced'.[86] As O. H. K. Spate said in his inimitable way, 'You can hold back the hands of the clock but it doesn't do the clock any good'.[87]

Signs are everywhere that traditional values and institutions in the Pacific Islands are under great pressure from the market economy, urbanisation, new and rapid forms of communication, and Western education. The suicide epidemic in Micronesia, Francis Hezel has argued, is related directly to the emergence of a modern 'youth culture' and the declining importance of the bonds of family that have long represented 'the core of Micronesian thinking and practice'.[88] The neglect of the aged in Pacific societies is yet another consequence of these changes. In a moving article, anthropologist Leonard Mason shows how the power and authority of the aged in Micronesia has shifted to the younger generation schooled in Western ways, and how the migration of the young and the middle-aged to urban areas in search of employment has left the old alone and vulnerable in the villages.

The old 'must, of necessity, continue to depend on a subsistence way of life but without the security once guaranteed them by a fully functioning system of family and community cooperation and obligation'.[89] Such problems (and others such as urban violence, homelessness, poverty) are not unique to Micronesia but are prevalent throughout the islands and, for that matter, in much of the Third World.

What, then, of the future of the islands as they stand on the threshold of a new era? President Ieremia Tabai of Kiribati told a Papua New Guinea audience in 1986 that he wanted development of the kind that enabled his people 'to live a viable and dignified way of life. . . . Development is not dependence on others; development is earning and living within one's means and above all, development is the ability to make a free decision, a free choice, in pursuit of one's interest'.[90] Most island leaders would happily endorse this view, but the realities, alas, are different. The isolation of the smaller islands in the central Pacific, their generally limited resource base and consequent dependence on the vagaries of the global market for their primary products, and the powerful strategic and economic interests of the larger powers encircling the Pacific, make true independence a dream. Continued dependence, on the other hand, is the more likely reality, though perhaps less so for such places as Fiji and Papua New Guinea.

On this, virtually every serious (and sympathetic) observer of the islands is agreed. 'That the Pacific islands will ever again be truly self-reliant is an impossibility. . . . Because they are in an economy that will not allow them to be', Epeli Hau'ofa has said.[91] Barrie Macdonald has been equally candid: 'It is thus questionable whether on strategic issues any more than economic ones the small states of Oceania have any real choices. Their development, political stability, and security all depend on the largesse of and relationships with the Western Alliance. Their political attitudes, like their constitutions, systems of education and their social and economic aspirations, derive from this colonial relationship and those same powers'.[92] Geographer R. Gerard Ward made a similar assessment: 'Distance from markets, small size and archipelagic nature impose severe constraints and limit the influence Pacific Island states can have on their trade, aid or political partners. Island governments may find that they can do little to alter the outcomes of the internal trends in agriculture which are now evident or the external economic and political contexts in which markets must be found for their agricultural products'.[93]

To these already considerable difficulties might be added the changes in the values, expectations, and aspirations of the people that have taken place in most Pacific Island societies over the last two decades. It is becoming increasingly clear that the rural subsistence sector is not an attractive alternative to the younger generation, no longer the path to power, prestige, and wealth. They try to escape, often with the encouragement of their parents, to urban centres and even overseas, to better their prospects. As Richard

Bedford stated, for most rural Melanesians (and other Pacific Islanders generally), 'the ideal life-style to be sought after is that of their leaders—urban, materialistic, consumer oriented'.[94] This trend is likely to continue in the foreseeable future.

Pacific Island leaders and intellectuals have responded to the predicaments facing them in a variety of conflicting ways. In Fiji, for example, the Fijian leaders have rejected the notion of parliamentary democracy and Western constitutionalism as a 'foreign flower' unsuited to Fijian soil, and have tried to stem the tide of modern change by creating a feudalistic, chief-dominated structure instead.[95] They are attempting to re-create the structures of nineteenth-century Fijian society on the shifting sands of the late twentieth century, with what results only time will tell. Some smaller islands of Polynesia and Micronesia have entered into various forms of constitutional arrangement with their former colonial powers that provide them with a semblance of sovereignty in an effectively dependent relationship.[96] Others, especially indigenous intellectuals in settler societies, reject the ethos of the modern world and seek cultural and intellectual sustenance in the pre-colonial past of their societies. One Hawaiian scholar says: 'The Hawaiian stands firmly in the present, with his back to the future, and his eyes fixed upon the past, seeking historical answers for present-day dilemmas. Such an orientation is to the Hawaiian an eminently practical one, for the future is always unknown whereas the past is rich in glory and knowledge'.[97]

Perhaps there is an unproblematic, uncontested Hawaiian past that holds the key to how the indigenous Hawaiian people can cope with the problems of the future. But that is not the case everywhere, especially in the diverse islands of Melanesia, where often no single culture or tradition encompasses an entire island. 'Those of us who like to live in yesterday's world and turn the clock back are defeated foes', said Sir Peter Kenilorea of the Solomon Islands.[98] Isireli Lasaqa of Fiji noted the impossibility of returning to the past and the need to cautiously embrace change: 'The islanders cannot shut themselves off from outside influences and thus attempt to control their lives. However, they must realize that their homeland is a part of a constantly changing world, and that change will itself alter a changed situation'.[99] Sione Lātūkefu of Tonga is more scathing of those Pacific Island leaders and intellectuals who seek solutions to today's problems in the past: 'There is in the Pacific today a tendency among a vocal few to denounce the present and advocate a return to the cultures of our forefathers, claiming that we can find in them all the answers to our present day problems'. That is dangerous romanticism. 'To try to pretend that the needs of the twentieth century, of the atomic and jet age, in a world which is fast shrinking every day, could be met by these customs and traditions is absurd, to say the least. Those who advocate it are either confused, if they are sincere, or downright dishonest, deliberately exploiting mass emotion to achieve their own social, economic or political ends'.[100]

These harsh words capture something of the complexity of the problems facing the islands today and the corresponding difficulty of finding solutions. Ultimately, though, solutions will have to be found by the peoples of the Pacific Islands themselves. As they navigate their course in the uncharted, treacherous waters ahead, they will do well to bear in mind the words of the Samoan historian Mālama Meleiseā: 'It is time for us to get past pre-formulated solutions and a mentality that would blame everything onto imperialism and the colonial inheritance. It is so much easier to blame the world system for all our problems'. It is more difficult to engage in critical self-examination. It is painful to chart a course in the face of extremely limited and limiting available alternatives. 'It is harder to look critically at the way in which we ourselves have made choices prior to, during, and since the colonial period. It is harder still to ask why we made these choices and ask whether we might still have other options'.[101]

These are agonizing questions for sensitive Pacific Island leaders or intellectuals caught between two worlds and trying to bridge the gap between the past and the present without in the process losing the essence of their being. But these questions will have to be asked and answered now, in the face of the inescapable, enduring reality: the past is another country, and the islands of the Pacific are islands in the physical sense alone.

Notes

1 The best single summary of the pre-colonial Pacific is in K. R. Howe, *Where the Waves Fall: A New South Sea Islands History from First Settlement to Colonial Rule*, Allen & Unwin, Sydney, and University of Hawai'i Press, Honolulu, 1984.

2 See, for example, Bernard Smith, *European Vision and the South Pacific, 1768–1850: A Study in the History of Art and Ideas*, Oxford, 1969; and Gavan Daws, *A Dream of Islands: Voyages of Self-Discovery in the South Seas*, Norton, New York, 1980.

3 Dorothy Shineberg, *They Came for Sandalwood: A Study of the Sandalwood Trade in the Southwest Pacific, 1830–1865*, Melbourne University Press, 1967. See also H. E. Maude, *Of Islands and Men: Studies in Pacific History*, Oxford University Press, Melbourne, 1968, chs 5 and 6.

4 Doug Munro and Stewart Firth, 'Company Strategies—Colonial Policies', in *Labour in the South Pacific*, ed. Clive Moore, Jacqueline Leckie, and Doug Munro, James Cook University of North Queensland, Townsville, 1990, 4.

5 See, for example, Michael C. Howard, 'Transnational Corporations: The Influence of the Capitalist World Economy', in *Foreign Forces in Pacific Politics*, ed. Ron Crocombe and Ahmed Ali, Institute of Pacific Studies, Suva, 1983, 264–289.

6 John Garrett, *To Live Among the Stars: Christian Origins in Oceania*, Institute of Pacific Studies, Suva, 1982, 10. See also his *A Way in the Sea: Aspects of Pacific Christian History*, Spectrum Publications, Melbourne, 1982; and Niel Gunson, *Messengers of Grace: Evangelical Missionaries in the South Seas, 1797–1860*, Oxford University Press, Melbourne, 1978.

7 See *Polynesian Missions in Melanesia*, ed. Ron and Marjorie Crocombe, Institute of Pacific Studies, Suva, 1982; *The Works of Ta'unga: Records of a Polynesian Traveller in the South Seas, 1833–1896*, ed. Ron and Marjorie Crocombe, Australian National University Press, Canberra, 1968.

8 See, for example, Martha Kaplan, '*Luve Ni Wai* as the British Saw It: Constructions of Custom and Disorder in Colonial Fiji', *Ethnohistory* 36 (4, 1989): 349–371.

9 Mālama Meleiseā, 'Ideology in Pacific Studies', in *Class and Culture in the South Pacific*, ed. Anthony Hooper, et al, Institute of Pacific Studies, Suva, 1987, 144. See also Vilsoni Hereniko (chapter 17, this volume).

10 J. D. Legge, *Australian Colonial Policy*, Angus & Robertson, Sydney, 1956, 81.

11 Quoted in Peter Smith, *Education and Colonial Control in Papua New Guinea: A Documentary History*, Longman Cheshire, Melbourne, 1987, 13.

12 See, for example, David Hilliard, 'Colonialism and Christianity: The Melanesian Mission in the Solomons', *Journal of Pacific History* 9 (1974): 93–116.

13 See James Jupp, 'Custom, Tradition, and Reform in Vanuatu Politics', in *Evolving Political Cultures in the Pacific Islands*, ed. J. K. Loveland, Brigham Young University, La'ie, 1982, 143–158.

14 'The Church and Party Politics in the New Hebrides: A Statement by the Presbyterian Church of the New Hebrides', *Pacific Perspective* 5 (2, 1976): 36–38.

15 The literature on this subject is vast, but W. P. Morrell's *Britain in the Pacific Islands*, Clarendon Press, Oxford, 1960, remains an important factual source of information.

16 See Penelope A. Lavaka, 'The Limits of Advice: Britain and the Kingdom of Tonga, 1900–1970', PhD dissertation, Australian National University, 1981.

17 See Deryck Scarr, *Fragments of Empire: A History of the Western Pacific High Commission, 1877–1914*, Australian National University Press, Canberra, 1967.

18 See Mark Peattie, *Nan'yō: The Rise and Fall of the Japanese in Micronesia, 1885–1945*, University of Hawai'i Press, Honolulu, 1988; and Roger Gale, *The Americanization of Micronesia: A Study of the Consolidation of US Rule in the Pacific*, University Press of America, Washington, DC, 1979). See also Mary Boyd, 'The Record in Western Samoa to 1945', in *New Zealand's Record in the Pacific Islands in the Twentieth Century*, ed. Angus Ross, Longman Paul, Auckland, 1969, 115–188.

19 See Barrie Macdonald, 'Secession in the Defence of Identity: The Making of Tuvalu', *Pacific Viewpoint* 16 (1, 1975): 26–44.

20 The literature here is vast, but see Hugh Laracy, 'Bougainville Secessionism', *Journal de la Société des Océanistes* 92–93 (1991): 53–59; Jill Nash and Eugene Ogan, 'The Red and the Black: Bougainvillean Perceptions of Other Papua New Guineans', *Pacific Studies* 13 (2, 1990): 1–17; and Jim Griffin, Hank Nelson, and Stewart Firth, *Papua New Guinea: A Political History*, Heinemann Educational Australia, Melbourne, 1979.

21 Alan Moorehead, *The Fatal Impact: An Account of the Invasion of the South Pacific, 1767–1840*, Penguin, Harmondsworth, 1968.

22 Howe, 350.

23 Howe, 350. See his 'The Fate of the "Savage" in Pacific Historiography', *New Zealand Journal of History* 11 (1977): 137–154.

24 Howe, 352.

25 Mālama Meleiseā, Review Forum, *Pacific Studies* 9 (1, 1985): 149.

26 In John A. Moses, ed., *Historical Disciplines and Culture in Australasia*, University of Queensland Press, St Lucia, 1979, 128.

27 K. R. Howe, *The Loyalty Islands: A History of Culture Contacts, 1840–1900*, Australian National University Press, Canberra, 1977.

28 See Doug Munro, 'The Lagoon Islands: A History of Tuvalu, 1820–1908', PhD dissertation, Macquarie University, Sydney, 1982, iii.

29 See Greg Dening, *Islands and Beaches: Discourse on a Silent Land, Marquesas, 1774–1880*, University of Hawai'i Press, Honolulu, 1980. On Pacific Islands demography generally, see Norma MacArthur, *Island Populations of the Pacific*, Australian National University, Canberra, 1967.

30 David Hanlon, *Upon A Stone Altar: A History of the Island of Pohnpei to 1890*, Pacific Islands Monograph Series no. 5, University of Hawai'i Press, Honolulu, 1988, 204.

31 Jupp, 145.

32 See David Stannard, *Before the Horror: The Population of Hawai'i on the Eve of Western Contact*, Social Science Research Institute, University of Hawai'i, Honolulu, 1989.

33 See Peter Larmour, 'Alienated Land and Independence in Melanesia', *Pacific Studies* 8 (1, 1984): 10.

34 See R. T. Mahuta, 'The Issue of Land in New Zealand', paper presented at conference, Resources, Development and Politics in the South Pacific, Australian National University, 7–9 November 1990.

35 J. C. Altman, 'Land Rights and Land Use in Aboriginal Australia, with a Specific Focus on the Northern Territory', paper presented at conference, Resources, Development and Politics in the South Pacific, Australian National University, Canberra, 7–9 November 1990.

36 Lawrence Fuchs, *Hawaii Pono*, Harcourt, Brace & World, New York, 1961, 14. See also Lilikalā Dorton, 'Land and the Promise of Capitalism', PhD dissertation, University of Hawai'i, Honolulu, 1986.

37 See Haunani-Kay Trask, 'Hawai'i: Colonization and Decolonization', in Hooper et al, 154–174; and exchange between her and Roger Keesing in *The Contemporary Pacific: A Journal of Island Affairs* 3 (1991): 159–171.

38 Epeli Hau'ofa, 'The New South Pacific: Integration and Independence', in Hooper et al, 17.

39 Peter France, *The Charter of the Land: Custom and Colonisation in Fiji*, Oxford University Press, Melbourne, 1969.

40 See Simione Durutalo, 'Buccaneers and Chiefly Historians', *Journal of Pacific Studies* 11 (1985): 117–156.

41 Martha Kaplan, '*Luve ni Wai* as the British Saw It: Constructions of Custom and Disorder in Colonial Fiji', *Ethnohistory* 63 (4, 1989): 358. See also Nicholas Thomas, 'Sanitation and Seeing: The Creation of State Power in Early Colonial Fiji', *Comparative Studies in Society and History* 32 (1, 1990): 149–170; and 'Atu Bain, 'A Protective Labour Policy? An Alternative Interpretation of Early Colonial Labour Policy in Fiji', *Journal of Pacific History* 23 (2, 1988): 119–136.

42 Quotes from Mālama Meleiseā, *The Making of Modern Samoa: Traditional*

Authority and Colonial Administration in the Modern History of Western Samoa, Institute of Pacific Studies, Suva, 1987, 49.

43 Meleiseā 1987, 50.

44 Francis West, *Hubert Murray: The Australian Pro-Consul*, Oxford University Press, Melbourne, 1968, 263.

45 For a historiographical survey of Murray, see Roger Thompson, 'Hubert Murray and the Historians', *Pacific Studies*, 10 (1, 1986): 79–96.

46 Edward P. Wolfers, *Race Relations and Colonial Rule in Papua New Guinea*, Australia and New Zealand Book Company, Sydney, 1975, 5.

47 See David Purcell, 'The Economics of Exploitation: The Japanese in the Mariana, Caroline and Marshall Islands, 1915–1940', *Journal of Pacific History* 11 (3, 1976): 189–211.

48 See Stewart Firth, *New Guinea Under the Germans*, Melbourne University Press, 1982.

49 Barrie Macdonald, *Cinderellas of the Empire: Towards a History of Kiribati and Tuvalu*, Australian National University Press, Canberra, 1982, 94. The standard history of the phosphate industry is Maslyn Williams and Barrie Macdonald, *The Phosphateers: A History of the British Phosphate Commissioners and the Christmas Island Phosphate Commission*, Melbourne University Press, 1985.

50 But see John Connell, *New Caledonia or Kanaky? The Political History of a French Colony*, National Centre for Development Studies, Australian National University, Canberra, 1987; and Alan Ward, 'New Caledonia: The Politics of Land', in *Melanesia: Beyond Diversity*, ed. R. J. May and Hank Nelson, Australian National University, Canberra, 1982, 531–548.

51 Wolfers, 95.

52 Colony of Fiji, *Regulations of the Native Regulation Board*, Government Printer, Suva, 1936.

53 For some excellent case studies on this subject, see Peter Hempenstall and Noel Rutherford, *Protest and Dissent in the Colonial Pacific*, Institute of Pacific Studies, Suva, 1984.

54 See Peter Hempenstall, *Pacific Islanders under German Rule: A Study in the Meaning of Colonial Resistance*, Australian National University, Canberra, 1978; and Roger Keesing and Peter Corris, *Lightning Meets the West Wind: The Malaita Massacre*, Oxford University Press, Melbourne, 1980.

55 See Bill Gammage, 'The Rabaul Strike, 1929', *Journal of Pacific History* 10 (3, 1975): 3–29; and Brij V. Lal, *Broken Waves: A History of the Fiji Islands in the Twentieth Century*, Pacific Islands Monograph Series no. 11, University of Hawai'i Press, Honolulu, 1992.

56 A. D. Couper, 'Protest Movements and Proto-Cooperatives in the Pacific Islands', *Journal of the Polynesian Society* 77 (3, 1968): 263–274.

57 See Michael Field, *Mau: Samoa's Struggle for Freedom*, Polynesian Press, Auckland, 1991; and Hugh Laracy, *The Maasina Rule Movement, Solomon Islands, 1944–1952*, Institute of Pacific Studies, Suva, 1983.

58 R. G. Ward, 'Urbanisation in the Pacific: Facts and Policies', quoted by John Connell, 'Urbanization and Inequality in Melanesia', in May and Nelson, 463. See also M. E. P. Bellam, 'The Colonial City: Honiara, A Pacific Island Case Study', *Pacific Viewpoint* 11 (1, 1976): 66–96.

59 Wolfers 97.

60 Connell 1982, 468.

61 See Amirah Inglis, *Not a White Woman Safe: Sexual Anxiety and Politics in Port Moresby, 1920–1934*, Australian National University Press, Canberra, 1974.

62 D. J. Dickson, 'Murray and Education Policy in Papua, 1906–1941', in *Papua New Guinea Education*, ed. E. Barrington Thomas, Oxford University Press, Melbourne, 1976, 23.

63 H. E. Maude, book review, *Journal of Pacific History* 1 (1966): 244.

64 This and the following quote are from Lal 1992, 104–105.

65 The quotes on the experience of the Micronesians under the Japanese come from Donald R. Shuster, 'Major Patterns of Social Change Instituted in Micronesia during Japanese Colonial Rule, 1914–1940', University of Hawai'i, Department of Educational Foundations, April 1978 (typescript, 84 pages). See also Peattie.

66 For this quote and the next, see B. K. Hyams, 'School Teachers as Agents of Cultural Imperialism in Territorial Hawaii', *Journal of Pacific History* 20 (3–4, 1985): 202–219.

67 Satendra Nandan, 'Higher Education in the South Pacific: Diversity and the Humanities', in *A South Pacific Critique*, ed. David Jones et al, Centre for the Study of Higher Education, University of Melbourne, 1991, 133–148.

68 Labour recruitment statistics mentioned here are culled from Moore, Leckie, and Munro 1990, *xxxix–li*.

69 Peter Corris, *Passage, Port and Plantation: A History of Solomon Island Labour Migration, 1870–1914*, Melbourne University Press, 1973, 138.

70 See, for example, E. W. Docker, *The Blackbirders: The Recruiting of South Seas Labour for Queensland, 1863–1907*, Sydney, 1970; and T. Dunabin, *Slavers of the South Seas*, Sydney, 1935. See also O. W. Parnarby, *Britain the Labour Trade in the Southwest Pacific*, Duke University Press, Durham, NC, 1964.

71 See Corris; and Deryck Scarr's 'Recruits and Recruiters: A Portrait of the Pacific Islands Labour Trade', *Journal of Pacific History* 2 (1967): 5–24. For an excellent summary of the main issues and trends in Pacific labour historiography, see Doug Munro, 'The Pacific Islands Labor Trade: Approaches, Methodologies, Debates', paper presented to Inter-University Seminar on Working Class History, Atlanta, GA, 7 October 1991.

72 Clive Moore, *Kanaka: A History of Melanesian Mackay*, Institute of Papua New Guinea Studies, Port Moresby, 1985, 48.

73 Again, statistics in this paragraph are derived from Moore, Leckie, and Munro, 1990, *xxxix–li*.

74 Griffin, Nelson, and Firth, 81.

75 See Geoffrey M. White and Lamont Lindstrom, eds, *The Pacific Theater: Island Representations of World War II*, Pacific Islands Monograph Series no. 8, University of Hawai'i Press, 1989; and Geoffrey M. White et al, eds, *The Big Death: Solomon Islanders Remember World War II*, Institute of Pacific Studies, Suva, 1988.

76 Information here is from Jeremy MacClancy, *To Kill A Bird With Two Stones: A Short History of Vanuatu*, Vanuatu Cultural Centre Publication no. 1, Vila, n.d., 105–110.

77 Brookfield, *Colonialism, Development and Independence: The Case of the Melanesian Islands in the South Pacific*, Cambridge University Press, 1972, 96.

78 See, among others, J. W. Davidson, 'The Decolonization of Oceania', *Journal of Pacific History* 6 (1971): 133–150; and Peter Larmour, 'The Decolonization of the Pacific', in *Foreign Forces in Pacific Politics*, ed. Ron Crocombe et al, Institute of Pacific Studies, Suva, 1983, 1–23.

79 See studies in *Decentralisation in the South Pacific*, ed. Ropate Qalo and Peter Larmour, Institute of Pacific Studies, Suva, 1985.

80 See, among many other sources, *The Pacific Way: Social Issues in National Development*, ed. Sione Tupouniua, Ron Crocombe, and Claire Slatter, Institute of Pacific Studies, Suva, 1975.

81 From the Papua New Guinea Constitution, in *Pacific Constitutions: Independent States of Melanesia and Micronesia*, Institute of Pacific Studies, Suva, 1983.

82 Ron Crocombe, 'The Pacific in the 21st Century', in *The Ethics of Development: The Pacific in the 21st Century*, ed. Susan Stratigos and Philip J. Hughes, University of Papua New Guinea Press, Port Moresby, 1987, 14. See also Asesela Ravuvu, *Development or Dependency: The Pattern of Change in a Fijian Village*, Institute of Pacific Studies, Suva, 1988.

83 See, for example, Asesela Ravuvu, 'Fiji: Contradictory Ideologies of Development', in Hooper et al, 230–241.

84 But see Robert Tonkinson, 'Vanuatu Values: A Changing Symbiosis', *Pacific Studies* 5 (2, 1982): 45.

85 Rusiate Nayacakalou, *Leadership in Fiji*, Oxford University Press, Melbourne, 1975, 135.

86 Raymond Firth, 'Development and the Cultural Heritage', in Topouniua, Crocombe and Slatter, 190.

87 *Bulletin*, 20 September 1988 (Sydney, weekly).

88 Francis X. Hezel, 'Suicide in Micronesia', *The Contemporary Pacific: A Journal of Island Affairs* 1 (1989): 54.

89 Leonard Mason, 'Growing Old in Changing Micronesia', *Pacific Studies* 6 (1, 1982): 1.

90 'The Ethics of Development: A Kiribati View', in Stratigos and Hughes, 49.

91 Hau'ofa, 10.

92 Barrie Macdonald, 'Decolonization and Beyond: The Framework for Post-Colonial Relationships in Oceania', *Journal of Pacific History* 21 (3–4, 1986): 124.

93 R. G. Ward, 'Reflections on Pacific Island Agriculture in the Late 20th Century', *Journal of Pacific History* 21 (3–4, 1986): 226.

94 Quoted by John Connell, 'Modernity and Its Discontents: Migration and Change in the South Pacific', in *Migration and Development in the South Pacific*, ed. John Connell, National Centre for Development Studies, Australian National University, Canberra, 1990, 3.

95 See Asesela Ravuvu, *The Facade of Democracy: Fijian Struggles for Political Control, 1830–1987*, Reader Publishing House, Suva, 1991.

96 See Stewart Firth, 'Sovereignty and Independence in the Contemporary Pacific', *The Contemporary Pacific: A Journal of Island Affairs* 1 (1989): 75–98.

97 Lilikalā Kame'eleihiwa quoted in Haunani-Kay Trask, 'Natives and Anthropologists: The Colonial Struggle', *The Contemporary Pacific* 3 (1991): 164.

98 'Cultural Values versus the Acquistiveness of Man: A View from the Solomon Islands', *Pacific Perspective* 5 (2, 1976): 8.

99 Lasaqa, 'Geography and Geographers in the Changing Pacific: An Islander's View', in *The Pacific in Transition: Geographical Perspectives on Adaptation and Change*, ed. Harold Brookfield, Australian National University Press, Canberra, 1973, 311.

100 Lātūkefu, 'Tradition and Modernization in the Pacific Islands', *Pacific Perspective* 5 (2, 1976): 19.

101 Mālama Meleiseā, 'Ideology in Pacific Studies: A Personal View', in Hooper et al, 152.

Index

Tokyo
JAPAN
CHINA
Wake
International Dateline
NORTHERN
MARIANA
ISLANDS
Saipan
GUAM
MARSHALL ISLANDS
Ratak Chain
Ralik Chain
Majuro
Kwajalein
Manila
Yap
Chuuk
Pohnpei
Kosrae
BELAU
FEDERATED STATES OF MICRONESIA
Sunday
Saturday
Gilbert Islands
K I R I
equator
NAURU
Banaba
New Ireland
Bougainville
SOLOMON
ISLANDS
IRIAN
JAYA
PAPUA
NEW GUINEA
New Britain
TUVALU
Santa Cruz
Islands
Guadalcanal
Wallis
&
Futu
VANUATU
FIJI
Vanua Levu
Lau
Group
Viti Levu
Coral Sea
Loyalty Islands
NEW
CALEDONIA
AUSTRALIA
Brisbane
Norfolk
Sydney
Auckland
Tasman Sea
NEW ZEALAND
Tasmania
130°E
145°E
160°E
175°E